Investment Treaty Arbitration

Investment Treaty Arbitration

PROBLEMS AND EXERCISES

Kaj Hobér

Uppsala University, Sweden

with

Joel Dahlquist Cullborg

Uppsala University, Sweden

 Edward Elgar
PUBLISHING

Cheltenham, UK • Northampton, MA, USA

Published by
Edward Elgar Publishing Limited
The Lypiatts
15 Lansdown Road
Cheltenham
Glos GL50 2JA
UK

Edward Elgar Publishing, Inc.
William Pratt House
9 Dewey Court
Northampton
Massachusetts 01060
USA

A catalogue record for this book
is available from the British Library

Library of Congress Control Number: 2018931775

ISBN 978 1 78643 361 9 (cased)
ISBN 978 1 78643 984 0 (paperback)
ISBN 978 1 78643 362 6 (eBook)

Typeset by Servis Filmsetting Ltd, Stockport, Cheshire.
Printed by CPI Group (UK) Ltd, Croydon CR0 4YY

Contents

Extended contents

Preface

This publication is intended as a teaching tool at university courses in investment treaty arbitration. As such, it can be used in many different settings. It should be pointed out that although most of the material is based on real cases, some parts have been edited with respect to formatting and scope. The excerpts should therefore not be relied upon for any other purpose than teaching.

The material draws heavily on my experience from the Master Programme in Investment Treaty Arbitration at Uppsala University. I would like to thank the many students who have attended the Programme. In particular, I owe thanks to Yunus Emre Akbaba, Oisin Challoner, Elina Iakovleva, Paata Simsive, Theresa Tseung, Shuanghui Wu, and our amanuensis Kristians Goldsteins, for assisting me with the preparation of this book. A special thanks is also owed to Cornel Marian, a frequent teacher at the Programme.

Table of cases

1

Introduction

1.1　Problem-based learning

The present publication is not a textbook. Nor is it a casebook. It is a teaching tool to be used in courses on investment treaty arbitration based on the problem-based learning method. This method essentially means that all teaching is based on problems – real or hypothetical – focusing on how to analyse, understand and solve them.

From a lawyer's perspective it is not difficult to understand the philosophy underlying this method, nor its superiority. The task of lawyers in practice is to solve problems. The best method for preparing and training to solve problems – is to solve problems.

The material is built on the problem-based learning method which has been employed, albeit in a slightly revised form, since the early 1990s at my home university. The teaching methodology underlying the material is a revised version of the problem-based learning method, adapted to the practice and theory of law, particularly to international law as applied in investment treaty disputes. I call this approach 'structured problem-based learning'. Save for a few introductory lectures, all teaching is based on problems. Another critical element of this method is that all teaching is focused on skills, rather than knowledge. The ultimate objective is thus not to give the students knowledge, but rather to teach them the skills how to use the knowledge. In other words, the objective is to teach the students how to apply and interpret the law in respect of a set of facts. An important consequence of this teaching method is that written tests are all so-called open book exams. This means that the students are allowed to bring all the course materials to the test. They are then expected to use the course materials to analyse and discuss the problems that they are given at the exam.

Another consequence of the focus on skills is that the teaching is not about finding the right answer, or solution, to a problem. It is about teaching the students different approaches to analysing, discussing and understanding a particular problem.

A further important ingredient of our structured problem-based learning method is the fact that the teaching is based on progression in the learning process. Put differently, the teaching and learning are done gradually, step by step. The three sections of the book cover, in chronological order, international arbitration in general, substantive protection of foreign investment under international law and procedural aspects of investment treaty arbitration. All three sections ensure progression in the learning. I usually mention the following metaphor to the students to explain the underlying idea:

> If you are going to learn how to build a brick wall, it is not necessary first to read a treatise on the theory of building brick walls. You read the first chapter on how to build the first layer. Then you build the first layer. You then read the second chapter on how to build the second layer. Then you build the second layer. Etc., etc.

In this way, by the end of each section of the book, the students will have acquired the necessary *skills* as to how to use the *knowledge* that they will also have acquired during their studies within the section in question.

For the structured problem-based learning method to work, active student participation is absolutely necessary. One way to achieve this is to divide the students into smaller so-called study groups of four to six students in each group. All teaching is done in the form of seminars with the full group. The preparatory work for each seminar is done in the study groups. Each study group must be prepared to discuss, analyse and report with respect to the problem which is to be discussed at each seminar. In addition, each study group will have responsibility for a specific sub-issue of the problem. At the seminar in question, the study groups will essentially lead the discussion, with the teacher taking a rather passive role, intervening only when the discussion threatens to go off in a completely wrong direction.

In addition to the preparatory work done in the study groups, each student will usually have done some reading and thinking on her/his own before meeting with her or his study group. Ideally, therefore, when the problem is discussed at the seminar, it will be the third time that the student is confronted with the problem in question.

1.2 How to use the book

Each seminar is referred to as an exercise. The problem chosen for a particular seminar is chosen to ensure progression in the learning process. The seminars thus build on each other, and should, therefore ideally be held in the order in which they appear in the book. As explained above, typically each study group would have primary responsibility for one problem/sub-problem at each seminar and should thus lead the discussion with respect to that issue. All study groups must, however, prepare for the seminar such that they can analyse and discuss all the problems.

In addition to the more traditional seminar, there are several so-called mini-mock arbitrations. The idea here is to use the mini-mock arbitrations as a teaching tool with respect to a specific issue. It is thus not about advocacy. Each mini-mock arbitration focuses on one specific issue, or aspect of a problem. The study groups are given different roles for the mini-mock arbitration. One group will act as claimant; another group as respondent; a third group will be the decision maker, i.e., court, arbitral tribunal or arbitration institution depending on the situation which is the focus of the of the mini-mock arbitration in question. The fourth group is called the observer group. Its role is to comment on the arguments advanced by the parties and on the decision rendered by the decision maker. When the observer group has made its comments, all groups will discuss the problem that has been chosen for the mini-mock arbitration. The group which has been given the role of decision maker also has the task of organising and chairing the mini-mock arbitration. This includes ensuring that the parties have sufficient time to present their respective cases and to provide rebuttal arguments, as well as ensuring that sufficient time is available for the observer group and for general discussion. The mini-mock arbitrations do not require that the students submit anything in writing.

Each mini-mock arbitration seminar usually takes between two to three hours; a regular seminar usually two hours.

As mentioned above, this publication is not a textbook. True to the underlying philosophy of problem-based learning, the students must thus themselves seek and find the information they need to analyse and discuss the problems. The following publications could be used by the students: Dolzer and Schreuer, *Principles of International Investment Law* (2nd. ed. 2012), Hobér, *International Commercial Arbitration in Sweden* (2011), Hobér, Selected Writings on Investment Treaty Arbitration (2013) and Nadakavukaren Schefer, *International Investment Law – Text, Cases and Materials* (2nd. ed.

2016). Other publications with similar coverage can of course be used. In addition, the students will have electronic access to relevant treaties, conventions, arbitration rules and national legislation.

1.3 Interpreting and understanding arbitral awards

Most of the problems identified and discussed in this book are illustrated by arbitral awards. It is therefore necessary to have a basic understanding of how to deal with, and treat, arbitral awards in an educational and scholarly setting.

Relying on arbitral awards raises two fundamental and significant issues, *viz*: (i) the availability of arbitral awards; and (ii) the status and value of arbitral awards as a source of law, or rather as a basis for legal analysis.

The availability of arbitral awards, or rather the lack thereof, has always been the traditional ball-and-chain of education and research concerning international arbitration, in particular international commercial arbitration. This is a consequence of the fact that one of the reasons why parties typically choose arbitration to resolve disputes is the private and confidential nature of arbitration. Unless the parties agree otherwise, the proceedings before the arbitrators are private and the resulting award is usually treated as confidential and therefore not published. As a consequence of this, few awards were traditionally published, or otherwise made public. This state of affairs made it difficult systematically to analyse and discuss arbitral practice in a comprehensive way.

During the last two decades, the situation has changed significantly, both with respect to international commercial arbitration and investment treaty arbitration.

Many of the leading arbitration institutions – the International Court of Arbitration (ICC), the London Court of International Arbitration (LCIA), and the Stockholm Chamber of Commerce (SCC) and others – are publishing awards rendered under their auspices, with or without the consent of the parties. Another way to obtain copies of arbitral awards is through challenge proceedings or enforcement proceedings in national courts. In many jurisdictions, such proceedings mean that the arbitral award in question becomes a document in the public domain since it must, as a rule, be submitted to the court hearing the case in question.

As far as interstate arbitration is concerned, the situation has always been different. A significant number of awards, resulting from interstate arbitration have been, and continue to be, published in, for example, Reports of International Arbitral Awards, published by the United Nations and in International Legal Materials.

With respect to investment treaty arbitration, the situation is also different nowadays. The virtual explosion of this kind of arbitration during the last 15–20 years has resulted in a large number of awards. Today almost all of them are published, sooner or later, or reach the public domain otherwise. Most, if not all, ICSID awards are published, as well as other decisions taken by tribunals operating under the ICSID Rules. Also, awards rendered under the auspices of other institutions and rules usually find their way to publications and websites.

Today we can safely say that the availability of arbitral awards, or rather the previously existing lack thereof, does not constitute a problem for education and research in this area.

Even though it is debated, and debatable, whether arbitral awards constitute a source of law *stricto sensu*, it is obviously central to review and analyse what arbitral tribunals in fact do. In so doing, it is necessary to address the question of what importance should be given to arbitral awards. In particular, it is important to ask oneself the question whether all awards should be given the same weight when analysing arbitral practice. The short answer is no.

It must be remembered that international arbitral awards are rendered within a legal framework, which is decentralised and non-hierarchic, where there is no principle of binding precedent, *stare decisis*. Therefore, it should not be surprising that arbitral awards sometimes go in different directions and that there is a certain degree of inconsistency. Every arbitral award is not good law and should not be treated as such. It is not prudent to focus on one or two awards and extrapolate from them. While arbitral awards seem to be getting longer and longer, they are not necessarily getting clearer and clearer.

When evaluating and analysing arbitral awards, there are several important aspects to take into account.

At the outset, it is important to determine why and for what purpose the reader is analysing and interpreting the award(s) in question. One objective could be to try to find out what the arbitrators in a specific case actually had in mind. What did they intend to express in the award? If this is the objective, it might be necessary to look at other sources of information than the text of the award, as well as at writings published by the arbitrators sitting in the case in question, Sometimes it may be necessary to interview the arbitrators, if possible, about the case. Another objective could be to analyse the award with a view to determining whether a specific award, or a group of awards, forms part of a pattern which might serve as confirmation of a consensus, or widespread acceptance, with respect to a specific issue. If this is the objective, it is necessary to focus also on other awards which could be relevant to ascertaining whether such a pattern exists.

Very often, it would seem that what is in fact done represents a combination of the two aforementioned objectives. Whatever the ultimate objective is, it is submitted that the following factors must be analysed and evaluated:

(a) The date of the award

Generally speaking, older cases should be treated with more caution than recent cases. It is important to determine if an award has been 'overruled' and replaced by subsequent awards and/or whether the facts and circumstances have been overtaken by subsequent events and developments. On the other hand, the fact that an award is old does not *per se* detract from its value as a bearer of an important principle of law. The important thing is to analyse the award on the basis of the facts and circumstances of the individual case.

(b) Background and training of arbitrators

Another relevant factor is the experience and prominence of the arbitrators. An award which has been rendered by arbitrators who have particular knowledge and experience from the issues resolved in the award would typically have greater weight than an award rendered by arbitrators who have no such experience and knowledge. It may also be relevant to take account of the legal education and training of the arbitrators. The fact that arbitrators may come from different legal cultures should not be underestimated. This may find its reflection in drafting techniques and the judicial styles used in the award. While this will probably not affect the outcome of a case, it might be relevant to understanding the approach taken by the tribunal and the reasoning in the award. As far as investment treaty arbitration is concerned, it could also be relevant for a proper understanding of the award whether the arbitrators have training in and experience of public international law.

(c)   Dissenting opinions

Another factor which should be taken into account is the existence of dissenting opinions. It would seem that a unanimous award should be given greater weight than an award with one or several dissenting opinions. In this context, it might be of importance to review and analyse any comments and statements made by the dissenting arbitrator about his dissenting opinion.

(d)   Acceptance of the award

The extent to which an award has been accepted by the parties and by subsequent tribunals as well as by scholars and commentators in writings on the award is also something that must be taken into account when analysing the award. An award which stands out as a peculiarity is typically less important than an award which has been complied with by the parties and which has been universally approved by commentators.

(e)   The operative part of the award

It is always necessary to identify and analyse the prayers for relief raised by the parties, since an arbitral tribunal cannot give a party something that it has not asked for. The prayers for relief must then be compared to the operative part of the award, i.e., the actual decision rendered by the tribunal. This is an important element in defining the *res judicata* effect of the award. Depending on how the award has been drafted, it may sometimes be necessary to review the briefs submitted by the parties to find out exactly what prayers for relief have been raised by the parties, and thus to ascertain what the tribunal has actually ruled on.

(f)   *Ratio decidendi* and *obiter dicta*

It is also important to analyse and understand the factual and legal arguments relied on by the parties in support of their prayers for relief and how they have been treated by the tribunal. In particular, it is important to analyse the reasons of the tribunal with a view to finding out what is *obiter dicta* and what constitutes the true reasons, *ratio decidendi*, underlying the conclusions of the tribunal, in particular the operative part of the award. This may also be crucial for determining the *res judicata* effect of the award. Again, it may be necessary to review the briefs of the parties and supporting documentation and evidence properly to understand the arguments presented by them. In this context, it should be mentioned again that the legal background and training of the arbitrator may play a role. In some legal systems, it is only the operative part of an award which has *res judicata* effect, whereas in others the reasons or parts thereof also have *res judicata* effect. The different approaches may have an effect on how the reasons in the award are drafted.

(g)   Possible compromises

A final point to keep in mind is the fact that the reasoning in awards is often the result of compromise. Arbitrators are sometimes willing to compromise with respect to the outcome and the reasoning in an award with a view to avoiding a dissenting opinion. This may result in the reasons been less coherent and convincing than a reader would have wished. Many, if not most, arbitrators take the view that their role is to decide the case before them, rather than to contribute to the development of law and scholarly analysis. Opinions differ whether this is good or bad, but it is a fact of life, which must be taken into account when analysing arbitral awards.

These seven factors call for a critical and differentiated approach to arbitral awards as a basis for research, analysis and educational activities. If this is done, arbitral awards constitute an indispensable source for the study of international arbitration.

2

Investment treaty arbitration – an overview

2.1 Background

Since the early twentieth century, the property of foreigners has enjoyed protection under international law from unacceptable measures of the host State. While the scope and contents of the rules and principles of international law in this respect were unclear, these rules and principles of international law were collectively referred to as the international minimum standard. This field of international law has always been, and continues to be, controversial.

Today the debate and development of international investment law are to a very large extent based on investment protection treaties, in particular on so-called bilateral investment protection treaties (BITs). The first BIT was entered into in 1959 between the Federal Republic of Germany and Pakistan. Today there are approximately 3,000 BITs. The vast majority of BITs have clauses providing for so-called investor-state arbitration, also referred to as investment treaty arbitration. The BITs thereby entitle investors to commence arbitration against the host State, even though the investor is not a party to the treaty. In this way BITs create an international forum for investors, not otherwise available under customary international law.

In addition to the BITs, there are a number of multilateral investment protection treaties, for example, the Energy Charter Treaty (ECT) and the North American Free Trade Agreement (NAFTA). They also have arbitration clauses providing for investor-state arbitration.

During the last 15–20 years there has been a virtual explosion of investment arbitrations. Most arbitration clauses in investment protection treaties offer the investor a choice between different arbitration regimes. The most frequently used arbitration regime is the ICSID Convention and the ICSID Arbitration Rules, based on the 1965 Washington Convention on the

Settlement of Investment Disputes between States and Nationals of Other States, establishing the International Centre for Settlement of Investment Disputes (ICSID). Other options include the UNCITRAL Arbitration Rules, the Arbitration Rules of the Stockholm Chamber of Commerce and the ICC Rules of Arbitration.

The heart and soul of every investment protection treaty is protection against expropriation, which represents the most severe form of governmental interference with the property and property rights of foreign investors. Under international law, it is generally accepted, however, that the host State has the right to expropriate foreign property, but only under certain conditions. One of these conditions is that the investor be paid compensation for the expropriated property. In most investment treaty arbitrations, the investor will be asking for compensation, because he is of the view that an expropriation has taken place.

Most investment protection treaties have provisions entitling the investor to compensation in cases of an expropriation. In many investment treaty arbitrations the amount of the compensation is one of the disputed issues; it is usually an intricate task to quantify the losses in such cases.

In addition to protection against expropriation, most investment protection treaties also provide for other standards of protection, most notably 'fair and equitable treatment'. Today fair and equitable treatment is the most frequently relied upon standard of protection. While protection against expropriation is at the centre of all investment protection treaties, the fair and equitable treatment standard is from a practical point of view the more relevant standard. The majority of successful claims in investment treaty arbitrations are based on fair and equitable standards.

Other standards of protection often found in investment protection treaties include full protection and security, national treatment, prohibition against arbitrary and discriminatory measures, as well as most-favoured nation treatment.

Many investment protection treaties also have so-called umbrella clauses. In such clauses, typically, the host State guarantees the observation of obligations it has assumed in relation to the investor, for example, in a contract which the State has entered into with the investor. It is a controversial issue if, and under which circumstances, such clauses transform a claim based on a contract between the investor and host State; i.e., a contractual claim, into a claim under the treaty in question, a so-called treaty claim.

While investment protection treaties cover more or less the same issues and have similar clauses, it is important to keep in mind that the clauses are seldom identical. When there is a dispute, relevant clauses must be interpreted. This is done on the basis of the Vienna Convention on the Law of Treaties. The basic rule of interpretation is that a treaty must be interpreted in good faith in accordance with the ordinary meaning to be given to the terms of the treaty in their context and in the light of the object and purpose of the treaty. Investment protection treaties are thus interpreted like any other treaty, with due account taken of the object and purpose of such treaties. This is, generally speaking, a different interpretative exercise than the one done when faced with a contract under municipal law.

Another important aspect of investment treaty arbitration is the extent to which the host State is responsible for the acts and omissions of its organs. As a rule of thumb, the State is responsible for all its organs, including territorial units, provinces and municipalities. A threshold question in disputes is often to ascertain whether certain conduct is attributable to the State. Such issues are addressed by the so-called rules of attribution in customary international law. Rules of attribution are set out in the Articles of State Responsibility, prepared by the International Law Commission.

Recognition and enforcement of ICSID awards are handled within the framework of the self-contained system based on the ICSID Convention. Other investment awards are recognized and enforced pursuant to the provisions of the 1958 New York Convention On the Recognition and Enforcement of Foreign Arbitral Awards, or other similar arrangements.

In this context, it should be noted that neither the ICSID Convention, nor the New York Convention, deals with questions of State immunity. In fact, there is no generally applicable international convention on State immunity in force. Issues concerning State immunity which arise at the enforcement stage, or otherwise in investment treaty arbitration, are therefore dealt with on the basis of municipal law.

2.2 Criticism of investment treaty arbitration

By and large investment arbitration has been a success, in the sense that it has been used to a large extent; at any given point in time nowadays there are literally hundreds of investment arbitrations pending – albeit in different stages of progress – at the leading arbitration centres of the world. Investment arbitration is now an everyday occurrence, whereas in the past it was regarded as an extraordinary measure.

This success of investment treaty arbitration is explained by the fact that this form of arbitration is very attractive for the foreign investor, certainly if compared with the alternative of going to local courts in the host State. Investment arbitration is also in the interest of host States, since the possibility to go to arbitration against the host State tends to encourage businessmen to make foreign investments. Most host States are typically interested in attracting foreign investment.

Despite the success of investment arbitration, critical voices have been raised. They have mostly come from some States and NGOs. These critical voices have led some commentators to question the future of investment arbitration.

For example, investment treaty arbitration has recently been questioned within the European Union. When the Lisbon Treaty entered into force in December 2009, the power to conclude BITs was transferred from EU Member States to the EU itself. Since then, the EU Commission has largely taken over the task of negotiating new treaties with third states. There are a number of such treaties, in various stages of negotiation. They have in common a reformed variant of arbitration clause. Rather than the current system of separate arbitration tribunals, the Commission seems to prefer a more court-like structure with permanent rosters of arbitrators and the possibility to appeal awards on matters of law. This new approach has formed the basis for the EU's negotiations on large bilateral investment and trade treaties with third countries such as the United States, Canada and Singapore. Although the fate of these treaties is far from certain at the time this book is published, they demonstrate an intention to move away from investment arbitration as it has been traditionally understood.

Furthermore, investment protection treaties concluded between EU Member States have also been subject to criticism from the EU Commission, which views these treaties as conflicting with the internal order of EU law and has asked the Member States to get rid of them entirely.

The combination of the Commission's approach to both extra-EU and intra-EU treaties might bring about radical changes to the system of investment treaty arbitration as far as EU Member States are concerned. If and when that happens, the map of investment arbitration will undoubtedly be redrawn, but investment arbitrations will not, it is submitted, disappear.

More generally, it has also been suggested that host States usually are on the losing side in investment disputes and that the system as such systematically favours investors. Some States, particularly in Latin America, have been unhappy with their roles as respondents in arbitrations. They have therefore taken measures to distance themselves from investment arbitrations, or at least limit their exposure to investment arbitration; this has led some States to denunciate the ICSID Convention pursuant to its Article 71 and/or to terminate BITs. The number of States having taken such measures is, however, small. In addition, both the ICSID Convention and most BITs provide for transitional periods, or have so-called sunset provisions, meaning that the treaty will continue in force for a specified number of years following termination.

As far as decided cases are concerned, the fact is that there is no evidence of any bias in favour of investors. On the contrary, host States have in general done very well, in the sense that they have probably won more cases than they have lost. Investors sometimes fail to meet the jurisdictional requirements of BITs. In addition, they often fail to convince arbitral tribunals that the investment has been expropriated, or that they have been subject to unfair and inequitable treatment. For investors it is clearly of critical importance to have access to the dispute settlement mechanisms provided in BITs and multilateral treaties. In fact, this is perhaps the most important aspects of BITs, i.e., that they provide for a neutral forum for the resolution of disputes, mostly in the form of international arbitration. As mentioned above, foreign investments have always enjoyed protection under customary international law. Prior to the BIT era, however, the foreign investor did not have access to a neutral forum. The traditional method then was to use diplomatic channels, typically by asking the home State to exercise diplomatic protection, its *ius protectionis*. In this respect it is probably fair to assume that most host States also welcome the arbitration mechanism in most BITs. This way they can escape the economic and political pressures often exercised by powerful home States of foreign investors within the framework of diplomatic protection. On balance, it would seem therefore that the system of investment arbitration has served host States, as well as investors, well.

Another aspect with respect to which critical voices have been raised is that of sovereignty. The argument is that BITs impose restrictions on, and indeed undermine, the sovereignty of the host State by preventing it from implementing its policies in various areas such as, for example, health and environment. It is of course correct that a BIT constitutes a limitation on the sovereignty of the host State, in the sense that it is bound by the undertakings in the BIT, as it is by the undertakings in any other treaty. That is indeed the whole purpose of the BIT and in fact of most treaties. This consequence is not unique to investment treaties. One of the hallmarks of sovereignty is that a State must be sovereign enough to agree to certain limitations of its sovereignty. The advocates of this argument fear that arbitral tribunals will interfere with the formulation and implementation of government policies. As the saying goes, however: 'the proof of the pudding is in the eating'. Even though environmental and health regulations have been tried by several arbitral tribunals in investment treaty arbitrations, it is submitted that there are no examples of where they have unduly interfered with governmental measures. On the whole, it would seem that arbitral tribunals have taken a very balanced approach to such questions.

2.3 The future of investment treaty arbitration

The number of BITs has been growing for the last decade and continues to grow. Presumably, therefore, host States take the view that some benefits follow from investment protection treaties, be they bilateral or multilateral. From a legal point of view, BITs do provide a clear and reliable framework for protecting foreign investments. Among economists views are divided as to the extent to which BITs actually have any effect at all on the volume of foreign investments.

Several commentators have questioned whether there is any empirical data supporting the assumption – and the hope – that investment protection treaties do indeed increase the volume of foreign investment. For the purposes of this discussion, that kind of criticism is really irrelevant. Most States apparently take the view that they benefit from BITs, which is why they continue to negotiate and sign them, albeit with updated provisions.

Not only the EU has reacted to the earlier practice of investment arbitration. If one views the history of investment treaty practice in terms of different 'generations' of treaties, the latest such generation is marked by much more informed State practice. Currently, a relatively large number of States are updating their 'model treaties' and are negotiating new treaties, as well as modifying existing treaties, that are more detailed than the previous generations of treaties. These new treaties are both bilateral and multilateral; an emerging trend is to include investment chapters in large-scale trade treaties such as the Trans-Pacific Partnership (TPP).

As alluded to above, however, the fate of some of the more ambitious treaties is unclear when this book is published, since the investment treaty universe is not shielded from the trend towards nationalism and protectionism currently sweeping many parts of the world. It is submitted, however, that despite its shortcomings, investment arbitration – in one form or another – is likely to remain the most efficient and reliable dispute settlement mechanism for disputes between foreign investors and their host States. States will adapt and amend investment arbitration, as need be. At the end of the day, there is simply no better, realistic alternative.

Part I

International arbitration

3

The arbitration agreement

EXERCISE 1 – THE ARBITRATION AGREEMENT I – SEMINAR

DISCUSSION QUESTIONS

Problem 1
Review and analyse the House of Lord's decision in the attached *Fiona Trust*. What is the 'fresh start' envisioned by the Lords?

Problem 2
Discuss pros and cons with the presumption established in *Fiona Trust*.

Problem 3
Review and analyse the Swedish Supreme Court decision in the *Bulbank* case, in particular the differences between the decisions of the Svea Court of Appeal and the Supreme Court.

Problem 4
Discuss pros and cons of including a confidentiality provision in the arbitration agreement.

CASE

Opinions of the Lords of Appeal for judgment in the cause

Premium Nafta Products Ltd (20th Defendant) and others (respondents)
v
Fili Shipping Co Ltd (14th Claimant) and others (appellants)

Wednesday 17 October 2007

Lord Hoffmann

My Lords,
1. This appeal concerns the scope and effect of arbitration clauses in eight charterparties in Shelltime 4 form made between eight companies forming part of the Sovcomflot group of companies (which is owned by the Russian state) and eight charterers. It is alleged by the owners that the charters were procured by the bribery of senior officers of the Sovcomflot group by a Mr

Nikitin, who controlled or was associated with the charterer companies. It is unnecessary to set out the details of these allegations because it is not disputed that the owners have an arguable case. They have purported to rescind the charters on this ground and the question is whether the issue of whether they were entitled to do so should be determined by arbitration or by a court. The owners have commenced court proceedings for a declaration that the charters have been validly rescinded and the charterers have applied for a stay under section 9 of the Arbitration Act 1996. Morison J [2007] 1 All ER (Comm) 81 refused a stay but the Court of Appeal (Tuckey, Arden and Longmore LJJ) [2007] Bus LR 686 allowed the appeal and granted it.

2. The case has been argued on the basis that there are two issues: first, whether, as a matter of construction, the arbitration clause is apt to cover the question of whether the contract was procured by bribery and secondly, whether it is possible for a party to be bound by submission to arbitration when he alleges that, but for the bribery, he would never have entered into the contract containing the arbitration clause. It seems to me, however, that for the reasons I shall explain, these questions are very closely connected.

3. I start by setting out the arbitration clause in the Shelltime 4 form:

> 41.
> (a) This charter shall be construed and the relations between the parties determined in accordance with the laws of England.
> (b) Any dispute arising under this charter shall be decided by the English courts to whose jurisdiction the parties hereby agree.
> (c) Notwithstanding the foregoing, but without prejudice to any party's right to arrest or maintain the arrest of any maritime property, either party may, by giving written notice of election to the other party, elect to have any such dispute referred . . ..to arbitration in London, one arbitrator to be nominated by Owners and the other by Charterers, and in case the arbitrators shall not agree to the decision of an umpire, whose decision shall be final and binding upon both parties. Arbitration shall take place in London in accordance with the London Maritime Association of Arbitrators, in accordance with the provisions of the Arbitration Act 1950, or any statutory modification or re-enactment thereof for the time being in force.
>
> > (i)   A party shall lose its right to make such an election only if: (a) it receives from the other party a written notice of dispute which –
> >
> > > (1)   states expressly that a dispute has arisen out of this charter;
> > > (2)   specifies the nature of the dispute; and
> > > (3)   refers expressly to this clause 41(c) And

(b) it fails to give notice of election to have the dispute referred to arbitration not later than 30 days from the date of receipt of such notice of dispute . . ..

4. It will be observed that clause 41(b) is a jurisdiction clause in respect of 'any dispute arising under this charter' which is then incorporated by reference (by the words 'any such dispute') in the arbitration clause in 41(c). So the first question is whether clause 41(b) refers the question of whether the charters were procured by bribery to the jurisdiction of the English court. If it does, then a party may elect under clause 41(c) to have that question referred to arbitration. But I shall for the sake of convenience discuss the clause as if it was a simple arbitration clause. The owners say that for two reasons it does not apply. The first is that, as a matter of construction, the question is not a dispute arising under the charter. The second is that the jurisdiction and arbitration clause is liable to be rescinded and therefore not binding upon them.

5. Both of these defences raise the same fundamental question about the attitude of the courts to arbitration. Arbitration is consensual. It depends upon the intention of the parties as expressed in their agreement. Only the agreement can tell you what kind of disputes they intended to submit to arbitration. But the meaning which parties intended to express by the words which they used will be affected by the commercial background and the reader's understanding of the purpose for which the agreement was made. Businessmen in particular are assumed to have entered into agreements to achieve some rational commercial purpose and an understanding of this purpose will influence the way in which one interprets their language.

6. In approaching the question of construction, it is therefore necessary to inquire into the purpose of the arbitration clause. As to this, I think there can be no doubt. The parties have entered into a relationship, an agreement or what is alleged to be an agreement or what appears on its face to be an agreement, which may give rise to disputes. They want those disputes decided by a tribunal which they have chosen, commonly on the grounds of such matters as its neutrality, expertise and privacy, the availability of legal services at the seat of the arbitration and the unobtrusive efficiency of its supervisory law. Particularly in the case of international contracts, they want a quick and efficient adjudication and do not want to take the risks of delay and, in too many cases, partiality, in proceedings before a national jurisdiction.

7. If one accepts that this is the purpose of an arbitration clause, its construction must be influenced by whether the parties, as rational businessmen,

were likely to have intended that only some of the questions arising out of their relationship were to be submitted to arbitration and others were to be decided by national courts. Could they have intended that the question of whether the contract was repudiated should be decided by arbitration but the question of whether it was induced by misrepresentation should be decided by a court? If, as appears to be generally accepted, there is no rational basis upon which businessmen would be likely to wish to have questions of the validity or enforceability of the contract decided by one tribunal and questions about its performance decided by another, one would need to find very clear language before deciding that they must have had such an intention.

8. A proper approach to construction therefore requires the court to give effect, so far as the language used by the parties will permit, to the commercial purpose of the arbitration clause. But the same policy of giving effect to the commercial purpose also drives the approach of the courts (and the legislature) to the second question raised in this appeal, namely, whether there is any conceptual reason why parties who have agreed to submit the question of the validity of the contract to arbitration should not be allowed to do so.

9. There was for some time a view that arbitrators could never have jurisdiction to decide whether a contract was valid. If the contract was invalid, so was the arbitration clause. In *Overseas Union Insurance Ltd v AA Mutual International Insurance Co Ltd* [1988] 2 Lloyd's Rep 63, 66 Evans J said that this rule 'owes as much to logic as it does to authority'. But the logic of the proposition was denied by the Court of Appeal in *Harbour Assurance Co (UK) Ltd v Kansa General International Insurance Co Ltd* [1993] QB 701 and the question was put beyond doubt by section 7 of the Arbitration Act 1996: 'Unless otherwise agreed by the parties, an arbitration agreement which forms or was intended to form part of another agreement (whether or not in writing) shall not be regarded as invalid, non-existent or ineffective because that other agreement is invalid, or did not come into existence or has become ineffective, and it shall for that purpose be treated as a distinct agreement.'

10. This section shows a recognition by Parliament that, for the reasons I have given in discussing the approach to construction, businessmen frequently do want the question of whether their contract was valid, or came into existence, or has become ineffective, submitted to arbitration and that the law should not place conceptual obstacles in their way.

11. With that background, I turn to the question of construction. Your Lordships were referred to a number of cases in which various forms of words in arbitration clauses have been considered. Some of them draw a distinc-

tion between disputes 'arising under' and 'arising out of' the agreement. In *Heyman v Darwins Ltd* [1942] AC 356, 399 Lord Porter said that the former had a narrower meaning than the latter but in *Union of India v E B Aaby's Rederi A/S* [1975] AC 797 Viscount Dilhorne, at p. 814, and Lord Salmon, at p. 817, said that they could not see the difference between them. Nevertheless, in *Overseas Union Insurance Ltd v AA Mutual International Insurance Co Ltd* [1988] 2 Lloyd's Rep 63, 67, Evans J said that there was a broad distinction between clauses which referred 'only those disputes which may arise regarding the rights and obligations which are created by the contract itself' and those which 'show an intention to refer some wider class or classes of disputes'. The former may be said to arise 'under' the contract while the latter would arise 'in relation to' or 'in connection with' the contract. In *Fillite (Runcorn) Ltd v Aqua-Lift* (1989) 26 Con LR 66, 76 Slade LJ said that the phrase 'under a contract' was not wide enough to include disputes which did not concern obligations created by or incorporated in the contract. Nourse LJ gave a judgment to the same effect. The court does not seem to have been referred to *Mackender v Feldia AG* [1967] 2 QB 590, in which a court which included Lord Denning MR and Diplock LJ decided that a clause in an insurance policy submitting disputes 'arising thereunder' to a foreign jurisdiction was wide enough to cover the question of whether the contract could be avoided for non-disclosure.

12. I do not propose to analyse these and other such cases any further because in my opinion the distinctions which they make reflect no credit upon English commercial law. It may be a great disappointment to the judges who explained so carefully the effects of the various linguistic nuances if they could learn that the draftsman of so widely used a standard form as Shelltime 4 obviously regarded the expressions 'arising under this charter' in clause 41(b) and 'arisen out of this charter' in clause 41(c)(1)(a)(i) as mutually interchangeable. So I applaud the opinion expressed by Longmore LJ in the Court of Appeal (at para 17) that the time has come to draw a line under the authorities to date and make a fresh start. I think that a fresh start is justified by the developments which have occurred in this branch of the law in recent years and in particular by the adoption of the principle of separability by Parliament in section 7 of the 1996 Act. That section was obviously intended to enable the courts to give effect to the reasonable commercial expectations of the parties about the questions which they intended to be decided by arbitration. But section 7 will not achieve its purpose if the courts adopt an approach to construction which is likely in many cases to defeat those expectations. The approach to construction therefore needs to be re-examined.

13. In my opinion the construction of an arbitration clause should start from the assumption that the parties, as rational businessmen, are likely to

have intended any dispute arising out of the relationship into which they have entered or purported to enter to be decided by the same tribunal. The clause should be construed in accordance with this presumption unless the language makes it clear that certain questions were intended to be excluded from the arbitrator's jurisdiction. As Longmore LJ remarked, at paragraph 17: 'if any businessman did want to exclude disputes about the validity of a contract, it would be comparatively easy to say so'.

14. This appears to be the approach adopted in Germany: see the Bundesgerichtshof's Decision of 27 February 1970 (1990) Arbitration International, vol 6, No 1, p 79: 'There is every reason to presume that reasonable parties will wish to have the relationships created by their contract and the claims arising therefrom, irrespective of whether their contract is effective or not, decided by the same tribunal and not by two different tribunals.'

15. If one adopts this approach, the language of clause 41 of Shelltime 4 contains nothing to exclude disputes about the validity of the contract, whether on the grounds that it was procured by fraud, bribery, misrepresentation or anything else. In my opinion it therefore applies to the present dispute.

16. The next question is whether, in view of the allegation of bribery, the clause is binding upon the owners. They say that if they are right about the bribery, they were entitled to rescind the whole contract, including the arbitration clause. The arbitrator therefore has no jurisdiction and the dispute should be decided by the court.

17. The principle of separability enacted in section 7 means that the invalidity or rescission of the main contract does not necessarily entail the invalidity or rescission of the arbitration agreement. The arbitration agreement must be treated as a 'distinct agreement' and can be void or voidable only on grounds which relate directly to the arbitration agreement. Of course there may be cases in which the ground upon which the main agreement is invalid is identical with the ground upon which the arbitration agreement is invalid. For example, if the main agreement and the arbitration agreement are contained in the same document and one of the parties claims that he never agreed to anything in the document and that his signature was forged, that will be an attack on the validity of the arbitration agreement. But the ground of attack is not that the main agreement was invalid. It is that the signature to the arbitration agreement, as a 'distinct agreement', was forged. Similarly, if a party alleges that someone who purported to sign as agent on his behalf had no authority whatever to conclude any agreement on his behalf, that is an attack on both the main agreement and the arbitration agreement.

18. On the other hand, if (as in this case) the allegation is that the agent exceeded his authority by entering into a main agreement in terms which were not authorised or for improper reasons, that is not necessarily an attack on the arbitration agreement. It would have to be shown that whatever the terms of the main agreement or the reasons for which the agent concluded it, he would have had no authority to enter into an arbitration agreement. Even if the allegation is that there was no concluded agreement (for example, that terms of the main agreement remained to be agreed) that is not necessarily an attack on the arbitration agreement. If the arbitration clause has been agreed, the parties will be presumed to have intended the question of whether there was a concluded main agreement to be decided by arbitration.

19. In the present case, it is alleged that the main agreement was in uncommercial terms which, together with other surrounding circumstances, give rise to the inference that an agent acting for the owners was bribed to consent to it. But that does not show that he was bribed to enter into the arbitration agreement. It would have been remarkable for him to enter into any charter without an arbitration agreement, whatever its other terms had been. Mr Butcher QC, who appeared for the owners, said that but for the bribery, the owners would not have entered into any charter with the charterers and therefore would not have entered into an arbitration agreement. But that is in my opinion exactly the kind of argument which section 7 was intended to prevent. It amounts to saying that because the main agreement and the arbitration agreement were bound up with each other, the invalidity of the main agreement should result in the invalidity of the arbitration agreement. The one should fall with the other because they would never have been separately concluded. But section 7 in my opinion means that they must be treated as having been separately concluded and the arbitration agreement can be invalidated only on a ground which relates to the arbitration agreement and is not merely a consequence of the invalidity of the main agreement.

20. Mr Butcher submitted that the approach to construction and separability adopted by the Court of Appeal infringed the owners' right of access to a court for the resolution of their civil disputes, contrary to article 6 of the European Convention on Human Rights. I do not think there is anything in this point. The European Convention was not intended to destroy arbitration. Arbitration is based upon agreement and the parties can by agreement waive the right to a court. If it appears upon a fair construction of the charter that they have agreed to the arbitration of a particular dispute, there is no infringement of their Convention right.

21. For these reasons, which are substantially the same as those given by Longmore LJ in the Court of Appeal, I would hold that the charterers are entitled to a stay of the proceedings to rescind the charters and dismiss the appeal.

Lord Hope of Craighead

My Lords,

22. I have had the advantage of reading in draft the speech of my noble and learned friend Lord Hoffmann. I entirely agree with it, and for the reasons he gives I too would dismiss the appeal. I wish to add only a few brief comments.

23. There are, as my noble and learned friend has said, two issues in this appeal. The first is an issue of construction: whether the appellants' claims that the charterparties have been validly rescinded are disputes which arise under, or out of, the charterparties within the meaning of clause 41. The second is an issue of separability: whether, assuming that the appellants have an arguable case that the charterparties have been validly rescinded, they also have an arguable case that the arbitration agreements in clause 41 have been rescinded as well. The appellants submit that they were entitled to rescind the charterparties, including the arbitration agreements, because the charterparties were induced by bribery. The allegations of bribery are directed to the terms on which the charters were entered into by the Sovcomflot group of companies as owners with Mr Nikitin's chartering companies. They are said to have been uncommercial and unbelievably generous. The bribes are said to impeach not only the charters themselves but also the arbitration clause. The argument is essentially one of causation. It is that the charters would not have been entered into in the absence of these bribes or other benefits, and that but for the agreement to enter into them there would have been no agreement to go to arbitration. Had it not been for the bribes provided by Mr Nikitin to their director-general, Mr Skarga, Sovcomflot would not have done business with Mr Nikitin's companies at all.

24. On the first issue, the appellants say that it is highly unlikely that the parties, in agreeing to an arbitration provision, intended it to cover disputes as to whether the contract itself was induced by bribery, as to which it must be assumed one party would be entirely ignorant. The clear trend of recent authorities, they say, is to give a narrow meaning to the words used in the arbitration agreement to identify the disputes that are referred by it. They must be taken to have informed any decision to use the clause which is set out in the Shelltime 4 standard forms. I think that there are two answers to this argument. One is to be found in the wording of clause 41 itself. The

other is to be found by considering whether its consequences make sense in the international commercial context within which these standard forms are designed to operate.

25. As for the wording, contracts negotiated between parties in the international market are commonly based upon standard forms the terms of which are well known. Because they have a well-understood meaning, they enable contracts to be entered into quickly and efficiently. The Shelltime 4 standard form is a good example of this practice. It has been in frequent use since at least 1984, and it is still in use. But it must be appreciated that the various clauses in these forms serve various functions. In some a high degree of precision is necessary. Terms which define the parties' mutual obligations in relation to price and performance lie at the heart of every business transaction. They fall into that category. In others, where the overall purpose is clear, the parties are unlikely to linger over the words which are used to express it.

26. Clause 41 falls into the latter category. No contract of this kind is complete without a clause which identifies the law to be applied and the methods to be used for the determination of disputes. Its purpose is to avoid the expense and delay of having to argue about these matters later. It is the kind of clause to which ordinary businessmen readily give their agreement so long as its general meaning is clear. They are unlikely to trouble themselves too much about its precise language or to wish to explore the way it has been interpreted in the numerous authorities, not all of which speak with one voice. Of course, the court must do what it can to provide charterers and shipowners with legal certainty at the negotiation stage as to what they are agreeing to. But there is no conflict between that proposition and the guidance which Longmore LJ gave in paragraphs 17–19 of the Court of Appeal's judgment about the interpretation of jurisdiction and arbitration clauses in international commercial contracts. The proposition that any jurisdiction or arbitration clause in an international commercial contract should be liberally construed promotes legal certainty. It serves to underline the golden rule that if the parties wish to have issues as to the validity of their contract decided by one tribunal and issues as to its meaning or performance decided by another, they must say so expressly. Otherwise they will be taken to have agreed on a single tribunal for the resolution of all such disputes.

27. The overall purpose of clause 41 is identified in the two opening paragraphs. These are the choice of law and jurisdiction clauses. There is no sign here – leaving aside the question of arbitration for a moment – that the parties intended that the disputes which were to be determined in accordance

with the laws of England and be decided by the English courts were not to include disputes about the charter's validity. The simplicity of the wording is a plain indication to the contrary. The arbitration clause which follows is to be read in that context. It indicates to the reader that he need not trouble himself with fussy distinctions as to what the words 'arising under' and 'arising out of' may mean. Taken overall, the wording indicates that arbitration may be chosen as a one-stop method of adjudication for the determination of all disputes. Disputes about validity, after all, are no less appropriate for determination by an arbitrator than any other kind of dispute that may arise. So I do not think that there is anything in the appellants' point that it must be assumed that when the charters were entered into one party was entirely ignorant that they were induced by bribery. The purpose of the clause is to provide for the determination of disputes of all kinds, whether or not they were foreseen at the time when the contract was entered into.

28. Then there are consequences that would follow, if the appellants are right. It is not just that the parties would be deprived of the benefit of having all their disputes decided in one forum. The jurisdiction clause does not say where disputes about the validity of the contract are to be determined, if this is not to be in the forum which is expressly mentioned. The default position is that such claims would have to be brought in the jurisdiction where their opponents were incorporated, wherever and however unreliable that might be, while claims for breach of contract have to be brought in England. But why, it may be asked, would any sensible businessmen have wished to agree to this? As Bingham LJ said in *Ashville Investments Ltd v Elmer Contractors Ltd* [1989] QB 488, 517, one should be slow to attribute to reasonable parties an intention that there should in any foreseeable eventuality be two sets of proceedings. If the parties have confidence in their chosen jurisdiction for one purpose, why should they not have confidence in it for the other? Why, having chosen their jurisdiction for one purpose, should they leave the question which court is to have jurisdiction for the other purpose unspoken, with all the risks that this may give rise to? For them, everything is to be gained by avoiding litigation in two different jurisdictions. The same approach applies to the arbitration clause.

29. The Court of Appeal said that the time had come for a fresh start to be made, at any rate for cases arising in an international commercial context. It has indeed been clear for many years that the trend of recent authority has risked isolating the approach that English law takes to the wording of such clauses from that which is taken internationally. It makes sense in the context of international commerce for decisions about their effect to be informed by what has been decided elsewhere.

30. The Bundesgerichtshof's Decision of 27 February 1970 to which Lord Hoffmann has referred makes two points that are relevant to this issue. The first is that haphazard interpretations should be avoided and a rule of construction established which presumes, in cases of doubt, that reasonable parties will wish to have the claims arising from their contract decided by the same tribunal irrespective of whether their contract is effective or not. The second is that experience shows that as soon as a dispute of any kind arises from a contract, objections are very often also raised against its validity. As the Bundesgerichtshof said, entrusting the assessment of the facts of the case to different tribunals according to the approach that is taken to the issues between them is unlikely to occur to the contracting parties.

31. In *AT & T Technologies Inc v Communications Workers of America,* 475 US 643 (1986), 650, the United States Supreme Court said that, in the absence of any express provision excluding a particular grievance from arbitration, only the most forceful evidence of a purpose to exclude the claim from arbitration could prevail. In *Threlkeld & Co Inc v Metallgesellschaft Ltd* (London), 923 F 2d 245 (2d Cir 1991), the court observed that federal arbitration policy required that any doubts concerning the scope of arbitral issues should be resolved in favour of arbitration and that arbitration clauses should be construed as broadly as possible. In *Comandate Marine Corp v Pan Australia Shipping Pty Ltd* [2006] FCAFC 192, para 165 the Federal Court of Australia said that a liberal approach to the words chosen by the parties was underpinned by the sensible commercial presumption that the parties did not intend the inconvenience of having possible disputes from their transaction being heard in two places, particularly when they were operating in a truly international market. This approach to the issue of construction is now firmly embedded as part of the law of international commerce. I agree with the Court of Appeal that it must now be accepted as part of our law too.

32. It is in the light of these observations that the issue of severability should be viewed also. Section 7 of the Arbitration Act 1996 reproduces in English law the principle that was laid down by section 4 of the United States Arbitration Act 1925. That section provides that, on being satisfied that the making of the agreement for arbitration or the failure to comply therewith is not in issue, the court shall make an order directing the parties to proceed to arbitration. Section 7 uses slightly different language, but it is to the same effect. The validity, existence or effectiveness of the arbitration agreement is not dependent upon the effectiveness, existence or validity of the underlying substantive contract unless the parties have agreed to this. The purpose of these provisions, as the United States Supreme Court observed in *Prima Paint Corpn v Flood & Conklin Mfg Co,* 388 US 395 (1967), 404, is that the

arbitration procedure, when selected by the parties to a contract, should be speedy and not subject to delay and obstruction in the courts. The statutory language, it said, did not permit the court to consider claims of fraud in the inducement of the contract generally. It could consider only issues relating to the making and performance of the agreement to arbitrate. Dicey, Morris and Collins, The Conflict of Laws, 14th ed (2006), vol 1, para 12-099, acknowledge that there are excellent reasons of policy to support this approach.

33. The appellants' case is that, as there was no real consent to the charter-parties because they were induced by bribery, there was no real consent to the arbitration clauses. They submit that a line does not have to be drawn between matters which might impeach the arbitration clause and those which affect the main contract. What is needed is an analysis of whether the matters that affect the main contract are also matters which affect the validity of the arbitration clause. As the respondents point out, this is a causation argument. The appellants say that no substantive distinction can be drawn between various situations where the complaint is made that there was no real consent to the transaction. It would be contrary to the policy of the law, which is to deter bribery, that acts of the person who is alleged to have been bribed should deprive the innocent party of access to a court for determination of the issue whether the contract was induced by bribery.

34. But, as Longmore LJ said in paragraph 21 of the Court of Appeal's judgment, this case is different from a dispute as to whether there was ever a contract at all. As everyone knows, an arbitral award possesses no binding force except that which is derived from the joint mandate of the contracting parties. Everything depends on their contract, and if there was no contract to go to arbitration at all an arbitrator's award can have no validity. So, where the arbitration agreement is set out in the same document as the main contract, the issue whether there was an agreement at all may indeed affect all parts of it. Issues as to whether the entire agreement was procured by impersonation or by forgery, for example, are unlikely to be severable from the arbitration clause.

35. That is not this case, however. The appellants' argument was not that there was no contract at all, but that they were entitled to rescind the contract including the arbitration agreement because the contract was induced by bribery. Allegations of that kind, if sound, may affect the validity of the main agreement. But they do not undermine the validity of the arbitration agreement as a distinct agreement. The doctrine of separability requires direct impeachment of the arbitration agreement before it can be set aside. This is an exacting test. The argument must be based on facts which are specific to the arbitration agreement. Allegations that are parasitical to a challenge to

the validity to the main agreement will not do. That being the situation in this case, the agreement to go to arbitration must be given effect.

Lord Scott of Foscote

My Lords,
36. I have had the advantage of reading in advance the opinion of my noble and learned friend Lord Hoffmann and find myself in complete agreement with the conclusion he has reached and his reasons for that conclusion. I cannot improve upon those reasons and shall not try to do so. I, too, would dismiss this appeal.

Lord Walker of Gestingthorpe

My Lords,
37. I have had the privilege of reading in draft the opinion of my noble and learned friend Lord Hoffmann. I am in full agreement with it. It gives full effect to the legislative purpose of section 7 of the Arbitration Act 1996. It marks a fresh start, leaving behind some fine verbal distinctions (on the language of particular arbitration clauses) which few commercial men would regard as significant. For these reasons I too would dismiss this appeal.

Lord Brown of Eaton-Under-Heywood

My Lords,
38. For the reasons given in the speeches prepared by my noble and learned friends, Lord Hoffmann and Lord Hope of Craighead, with which I am in full agreement, I too would dismiss this appeal.

 CASE

Judgment of the Swedish Supreme Court

Case No. T 1881-99, given in Stockholm on 27 October 2000 T 1881-99

Bulgarian Foreign Trade Bank Ltd (Appellant)
v
A.I. Trade Finance Inc (Counterparty)

The Supreme Court confirms the judgment of the Court of Appeal.
Bulgarian Foreign Trade Bank Ltd is ordered to compensate A.I. Trade Finance

Inc. for its litigation costs before the Supreme Court in the amount of SEK two-hundred-sixty-eight-thousand two-hundred-twenty-eight (268,228), out of which SEK 245,000 comprises of costs for legal counsel, plus interest according to Section 6 of the Swedish Act on Interest from the date of the Supreme Court's judgment until the day of payment.

Motions before the Supreme Court

Bulgarian Foreign Trade Bank Ltd (Bulbank) has moved that the Supreme Court shall grant Bulbank's claim, discharge it from the order to compensate A.I. Trade Finance Inc. (AIT) for its litigation costs before the District Court and the Court of Appeal, and shall order AIT to compensate it for its litigation costs before the District Court and the Court of Appeal.

On 6 September 1999, the Supreme Court granted Bulbank leave to appeal in so far as relates to the issue of whether the arbitration clause could be terminated for breach of contract or not, but did not grant it with respect to the other grounds referenced by Bulbank.

AIT has disputed any amendments to the judgment of the Court of Appeal.

The parties have claimed compensation for the litigation costs before the Supreme Court.

Grounds

The background to the dispute is that AIT requested arbitration against Bulbank based on an arbitration clause in a loan agreement between Bulbank and an Austrian creditor. In the arbitration proceedings, Bulbank objected that the arbitration clause was not binding upon Bulbank in relation to AIT. The arbitral tribunal rendered a separate decision on the matter, in which it found it had jurisdiction to try the case and that the proceedings should proceed to the merits of the case.

Some time after the arbitral tribunal's decision, it was published in Mealy's International Arbitration Report, a publication published in the USA. The decision had been submitted to the publication by representatives of AIT.

When Bulbank became aware of the publication, Bulbank notified AIT and the arbitral tribunal in writing and, referencing the publication, declared its immediate termination of the arbitration clause, and further motioned that the arbitral tribunal should declare the arbitration clause invalid on the same grounds.

In a separate decision, the arbitral tribunal dismissed the aforementioned claim, and subsequently rendered an arbitral award on the merits. Bulbank has subsequently challenged the arbitral award and motioned that the arbitral award shall be annulled or, in the alternative, be set aside.

The issue in the present case is whether Bulbank's case can be granted on the grounds that it had terminated the arbitration clause for breach of contract and that as a result no valid arbitration clause was at hand when the arbitral award was rendered.

AIT has claimed that public courts lack jurisdiction to try the relevant issue since the arbitral tribunal already has, upon Bulbank's motion thereto, tried the issue.

According to AIT, the test was based on the merits, and since no procedural error has been committed or even claimed, the issue cannot be tried within the scope of challenge proceedings.

An essential ground for challenge proceedings is that no valid arbitration clause was at hand. The fact that the arbitral tribunal in such a case has tried the issue does not entail a procedural impediment to the issue subsequently being tried by public courts. That the lack of a valid arbitration clause is claimed to not to have been at hand initially, but rather the result of a termination during ongoing arbitration proceedings bears no relevance to this conclusion.

The agreement comprising the arbitration clause provides that the agreement shall be governed by the laws of Austria. There is, however, no particular provision on the laws applicable to the arbitration clause. In these circumstances, the question of the validity of the arbitration clause shall be tried under the laws of the country where the arbitration proceedings took place, i.e., the laws of Sweden. The parties have not claimed otherwise. As provided by the arbitration clause, the Arbitration Rules of the United Nations Commission for Europe (the ECE-rules) are also applicable.

AIT has claimed that Bulbank has introduced new grounds before the Supreme Court and claimed that these shall be dismissed. What has been the contention is that Bulbank has claimed that the separate decision contained financially sensitive information and that the publication was made in bad faith and caused damage to Bulbank. The Supreme Court notes that Bulbank already before the District Court claimed that a material breach of contract was at hand, that what has been referenced by Bulbank appears to mainly comprise opinions included in the closing statements based on grounds referenced already before the District Court and that, undisputedly, corresponding statements have been made before the Court of Appeal and finds that what has been referenced by Bulbank cannot be considered to mean that Bulbank has referenced new grounds before the Supreme Court.

One condition required in order for Bulbank to be successful in this case is that AIT was, as a result of the agreement, bound by a confidentiality undertaking. It is uncontested as between the parties that the arbitration clause does not contain any such undertaking. Further, there is no confidentiality undertaking in the Swedish Arbitration Act of 1929, which is applicable. It could further be noted that there is no provision thereon in the new Swedish Arbitration Act replacing the Act of 1929.

As grounds for AIT being bound by a confidentiality undertaking, Bulbank has referenced Article 29 of the ECE-rules, which provides that 'The proceedings shall be held in camera unless both parties request that they shall be held in public.' This provision must, according to Bulbank, be interpreted as a confidentiality undertaking applicable to the entire arbitration proceedings including separate decisions, albeit that the literal wording could be deemed to cover only the oral proceedings. However, from the literal wording no other conclusion can be drawn, even when read in conjunction with the remainder of the ECE-rules, than that oral proceedings shall be held in camera unless the parties agree that they shall be held in public. There is no explicit provision in the ECE-rules on the parties' possible obligation to hold information in confidence and no other circumstance has been presented in the case that would give cause to interpret the provisions as including a confidentiality undertaking of the extent claimed by Bulbank.

Bulbank has further claimed that the parties through the arbitration clause are bound by a confidentiality undertaking with respect to arbitration proceedings and that the undertaking is based on general principles and the very nature of arbitration proceedings.

Information given out with respect to arbitration proceedings can relate to various things, mainly the fact that arbitration proceedings are taking place (or have taken place) between certain named parties in a particular matter, the contents of a rendered arbitration award or a decision rendered during the proceedings and circumstances of various nature that have come to light during the proceedings. Bulbank has not differentiated between various circumstances but has claimed that a general confidentiality undertaking applies, irrespective of the nature of the information.

When considering the issue of whether a confidentiality undertaking of the nature Bulbank claims applies, there is, in principle, no ground for differentiating between information of different nature. In this context, it should be noted that Section 6 of the Swedish Act on the Protection of Trade Secrets (SFS 1990:409) provides that anyone who willfully or negligently reveals a trade secret of a trader, which the revealing person has received in confidence when trading with the trader, is liable for the damages caused by his actions. If these conditions are met with respect to circumstances related to arbitration proceedings, there is an obligation under law to not reveal the information that is sanctioned by the liability to pay damages (cf. NJA II 1990 p. 590). This fact is ignored below.

A general starting point for deciding the confidentiality issue is that arbitration proceedings are based on an agreement. (Arbitration proceedings prescribed by law are ignored herein.) It follows from this that arbitration proceedings are of a private nature, which is not changed by the fact that certain aspects thereof are regulated by law. The purpose of the legislation is mainly to grant the institution of arbitration some stability and quality and is further required to grant legal effect to arbitral awards, with respect to, amongst other things, procedural impediments and enforceability (see NJA II 1929 p. 6 f. and Government Bill 1998/99:35 p. 41 f.). That arbitration proceedings are governed by legislation can consequently not affect the issue of a party's possible obligation to hold information in confidence. It is also irrelevant for resolving this issue that it is the Swedish Arbitration Act of 1929, and not of 1999, that has been applicable to the dispute.

From the private nature of arbitration proceedings follows that third parties do not have the right to be present at the proceedings or access written documents of the file. Further, there is probably an almost unanimous view that arbitrators directly, as a result of the assignment with which they have been entrusted, shall treat the arbitration proceedings as confidential; this applies also when the arbitrator has been appointed by a public court. A party's counsel has a similar obligation as to its client, also as a result of the assignment as such. From these circumstances no conclusion can be drawn, however, with respect to the question of whether a party is bound by a confidentiality undertaking sanctioned by law, for which a whole set of different circumstances are relevant.

One of the advantages of having a dispute by arbitration rather than by public courts and that causes companies to choose arbitration is the confidentiality connected to arbitration proceedings. Often, this is expressed by the wording that arbitration proceedings are protected from the public eye. A large portion of the jurisprudence referenced by Bulbank refers to this aspect. This advantage, however, does not necessarily assume that the parties are bound by a confidentiality undertaking. The actual meaning thereof, as compared with trials before public courts, is obviously that the proceedings are not public, i.e., the general public does not have the right to be present at oral hearings and does not have the right to access written documents in the file (see, for example, Government Bill 1998/99:35 p. 40 f.). It is not contradictory to this that the parties concurrently should be allowed to provide information to third parties about the arbitration proceedings.

In most cases, both parties to arbitration proceedings would prefer that third parties do not know the existence of the dispute, and what occurs during the proceedings. However, this is not always the case. For example, a party in a position inferior to a strong counterparty, which it considers to act in bad faith, might want to put pressure on the counterparty by making the dispute public. A party might also for other reasons wish, or even be obliged, to inform a third party about arbitration proceedings and decisions rendered therein.

That a party to arbitration proceedings generally wishes that information about the dispute is not disclosed and assumes that the counterparty is of the same opinion, as well as that parties most commonly actually would not disclose information, is, however, something completely different than a legal obligation to not disclose information at the risk of sanctions – most likely damages – in case of breach of that obligation.

In the present case, reasons referenced against a confidentiality undertaking are that arbitration proceedings can be made public by, relying on the provisions set out in the arbitration legislation, turning to public courts for, amongst other things, the appointment of arbitrator, obtaining security measures, recording evidence or challenge proceedings. This argument, however, is not convincing. In case there are grounds for a confidentiality undertaking, it could apply without impeding the possibility to turn to court as permitted by law, i.e., an obligation to not disclose information on the arbitration proceedings in bad faith. Such is the situation when parties have agreed specifically on a confidentiality undertaking.

It is clear that parties that resolve a dispute through negotiations or arrange for it to be resolved through other means than arbitration are not bound by any confidentiality undertaking without specifically agreeing thereto. Thus, the question is what could form the basis for the undertaking when the dispute is resolved by arbitration. Above, it has been established that it cannot be the legislation as such or the contents of the provisions therein. Nor has the privacy of the proceedings or the obligation of other involved parties to not disclose information been considered sufficient grounds for establishing a confidentiality undertaking binding the parties. What then remains is the question of whether a general opinion has been formed to the effect that each of the parties to a dispute are bound by a confidentiality undertaking as towards each other, based on the nature of arbitration proceedings. Of interest in this context are the opinions expressed in the preparatory works and in jurisprudence.

From the investigations presented in the present case, no opinion that a general confidentiality undertaking binding on the parties exists has been established. The generally held opinion among counsels and arbitrators appears to be that no confidentiality undertaking exists without a specific agreement thereon.

The fact that such a radical obligation as a confidentiality undertaking has not been prescribed by legislation, at least in the new Swedish Arbitration Act, is a strong indicator that no such obligation can be deemed to exist. The Arbitration Report states in its separate report Dispute resolution in commercial relations (Sw. Näringslivets tvistlösning) (SOU 1995:65 p. 186) that the confidential nature of arbitration proceedings is based on rather weak legal grounds and that a party wishing to disclose information about a dispute is free to do so.

On the other hand, there is some support in jurisprudence for a confidentiality undertaking. In Jarvin, Sekretess i svenska och internationella skiljeförfaranden in Juridisk Tidskrift 1996–97 p. 149 ff. it is stated that such an obligation exists, but it appears rather unclear what this would entail more precisely in a Swedish legal environment. In Cars, Lagen om skiljeförfarande (1999) p. 103, it is held that it must be assumed that a confidentiality undertaking applies, unless otherwise agreed between the parties, and that this means that the parties may not disclose information about the proceedings to third parties. The rationale for this is that one reason for parties to choose arbitration over trial before public courts commonly is that the proceedings are not public, a rationale that above has been held insufficient. Also in Heuman, Skiljemannarätt (1999), it is held that parties are bound by a confidentiality undertaking, at least to some extent (p. 30 ff.). It is held therein, amongst other things, that it is generally assumed that arbitration proceedings are not public, and that consequently parties entering into an arbitration clause should be deemed to have agreed that the proceedings shall be confidential (p. 32 f.).

Thus, there is no coherent and well-founded view in jurisprudence and in the preparatory works as to whether a confidentiality undertaking binds the parties. With respect to foreign law, the investigations made available to the Supreme Court do not permit any other firm conclusion than that in different countries, different principles apply in this matter. Under English law, it appears that the common view is that the parties are bound by a confidentiality undertaking (see, e.g., *Ali Shipping Corp. v Shipyard Trogir* [1998] 2 All ER 136). A judgment of 1986 by a French appellate court (G. Aïta c. A. Ojjeh, restated in Revue de l'Arbitrage 1986, No 4, p. 583) appears based on a confidentiality undertaking resulting from the nature of arbitration proceedings. In a famous case from 1995 (*Esso Australia Resources Ltd v Plowman*, 183 CLR 10), the High Court of Australia held the opposite view. Already from the above, it has been established that there is no united view in other countries that can help enlighten the contents of Swedish law.

In view of the foregoing, the Supreme Court holds that a party to arbitration proceedings cannot be deemed bound by a confidentiality undertaking, unless the parties have agreed thereon specifically.

Consequently, AIT has not committed breach of contract by having the decision rendered by the arbitrators during the arbitration proceedings published. Thus, Bulbank had no grounds for terminating the arbitration clause and Bulbank's claim to have the arbitral award annulled or set aside shall be dismissed.

EXERCISE 2 – THE ARBITRATION AGREEMENT II – SEMINAR

DISCUSSION QUESTIONS

Problem 1
Is it possible for a bank to be bound by an arbitration agreement in the manner referred to by Plenty of Oil?

Problem 2
Is the arbitration clause sufficiently clear to constitute a valid agreement to arbitrate or could it be successfully challenged in court?

Problem 3
In case there is a valid arbitration agreement, is Emieux bound to accept to arbitrate with Plenty of Oil?

Problem 4
In case Emieux should be bound to arbitrate with Plenty of Oil, should the arbitration be conducted under the Rules of the Arbitration Institute of the Stockholm Chamber of Commerce?

Emieux International is a company incorporated under the laws of Finland. In early 1998 it enters into an agreement with Let's do Business AB, situated in Stockholm, by which Emieux purchases 100 per cent of the stock of Let's do Business AB's subsidiary Berghem Industries. The purchase price is divided into four partial payments of USD 57,000 and a final payment of USD 50,000. The partial payments are to be effected over a period of three years from the closing date. The first payment is to be effected the same year. According to the agreement, the partial payments and the final payments are both subject to adjustments for warranty claims.

For its liability to pay the first partial payment, Emieux provides an irrevocable guarantee issued by the Bank of North Pole in the amount of USD 57,000.

On 25 January 1999, the Norwegian company Plenty of Oil acquires Let's do Business' rights and obligations under the agreement. On 25 February 1999, Emieux raises warranty claims against Plenty of Oil in the amount of USD 50,000. Subsequently, it withholds a corresponding amount of its payments due under the agreement.

Plenty of Oil objects to the claims of Emieux and requests that the withheld payment should be effected. Negotiations between the parties are initiated but no agreement is reached. Emieux refuses to accept any settlement proposals from Plenty of Oil by which the total purchase price is not reduced by the withheld USD 50,000. Plenty of Oil on the other hand is convinced that

Emieux's position is a clear breach of contract but is willing to negotiate in order to save what they believed to be a fruitful business relationship for the future. However, as negotiations break down this scenario appears less and less likely and Plenty of Oil therefore decides to pursue the matter further to ensure they receive full payment under the agreement.

The agreement contains the following arbitration clause.

9. Dispute Resolution
Arbitration Court in Stockholm, unless the parties have settled the dispute through friendly negotiations.

Plenty of Oil initiates arbitration under the Swedish Arbitration Act by filing a request for arbitration on 15 July 1999 against Emieux and the Bank of North Pole. The request arrives at the respective main offices of the two respondents on 17 July 1999. In its request Plenty of Oil claims that the arbitral tribunal shall establish Emieux's failure to fulfil the second payment. Through the irrevocable guarantee, Plenty of Oil argues, the Bank of North Pole has assumed Emieux's liabilities under the agreement and is therefore bound by the agreement, including the agreement to arbitrate.

The management of Emieux is very surprised when the request for arbitration arrives. The President turns to the General Counsel and asks him to 'make sure that those idiots at Plenty of Oil understand that this is nonsense'.

EXERCISE 3 – THE ARBITRATION AGREEMENT III – MINI MOCK ARBITRATION

Lokomotiv International (Lokomotiv), a Russian corporation, has been contracted by the Russian Federation to develop the railway system in northern Siberia. In 2009 Lokomotiv entered into an agreement with the German company Eisenbahn GmbG (Eisenbahn), by which Lokomotiv bought 100 engines from Eisenbahn to be delivered over a period of ten years, starting with ten engines in 2010. The total purchase price was US$10 billion to be paid with US$1 billion in January each year of the ten-year period.

The first partial payment was provided in January 2010 and in March the same year the first five engines were delivered, the remaining five engines of the 2010 delivery to be effected in October.

When the first engines were put into service in Siberia it turned out that they did not function properly. There were problems both with starting the engines and reaching the guaranteed speed. Lokomotiv alleged that the engines were not able to endure the cold in Siberia, a matter that was particularly addressed and guaranteed in the contract, while Eisenbahn is of the view, after having examined the engines, that they are in perfect condition, fit for use in an even colder climate than in Siberia. Eisenbahn argues that the malfunction is due to Lokomotiv's inability to handle the engines properly.

Lokomotiv terminates the contract and requests that Eisenbahn pay back the US$1 billion already provided. It also requests damages, the amount of which is to be specified later. Eisenbahn rejects the termination, saying that Lokomotiv has not presented any grounds whatsoever which would give Lokomotiv the right to terminate the contract.

The President of Lokomotiv is, however, determined to release Lokomotiv from the contract with Eisenbahn and get the money back. He orders Lokomotiv's legal department to initiate arbitration against Eisenbahn.

A request for arbitration is filed with the Arbitration Institute of the Stockholm Chamber of Commerce (SCC Institute) under the following arbitration clause.

> Article 33
> All disputes and differences which may arise out of this contract shall be settled by friendly negotiations. If a settlement is not reached in such way the dispute shall

be settled by arbitration court in Stockholm. The award shall be final and binding upon the parties.

In its reply to the request for arbitration Eisenbahn objected to the jurisdiction of the SCC Institute, arguing that:

(a) Under the arbitration clause any dispute between the parties shall, in the first place, be settled by friendly negotiations. No such negotiations have taken place.

(b) The arbitration clause does not provide for arbitration under the SCC Institute Rules. It is clearly a clause contemplating ad hoc arbitration.

 **GROUP**

Group 1

Present Lokomotiv's best counter-arguments to (a) and (b).

Group 2

How should the *SCC Institute* decide on the objections in (a) and (b)?

Group 3

How should the *Tribunal* decide (a) and (b) if the case is not dismissed by the SCC Institute and the objections to jurisdiction are renewed before the Tribunal where it becomes clear *that*:

(i) Eisenbahn has made several attempts to initiate friendly negotiations without Lokomotiv giving any reaction whatsoever to such attempts;

(ii) The Russian language version – which is equally applicable – of the arbitration clause instead of 'by arbitration court in Stockholm' says 'by arbitrators in Stockholm'?

Group 4

You are the observer group. Have the best arguments been presented? Are the decisions by the SCC Institute and the Tribunal correct?

EXERCISE 4: THE ARBITRATION AGREEMENT IV – SEMINAR

 DISCUSSION QUESTIONS

Problem 1
Review and analyse the United States Supreme Court's decisions in *Mitsubishi Motors Corp v Soler Chrysler-Plymouth* and *Scherk v Alberto-Culver Co.* Argue that questions of antitrust/competition law should be arbitrable.

Problem 2
Review and analyse the United States Supreme Court's decisions in *Mitsubishi Motors Corp v Soler Chrysler-Plymouth* and *Scherk v Alberto-Culver Co.* Argue that questions of antitrust/competition law should not be arbitrable.

Problem 3
Review and analyse the ICC Interim Award in Case Nr. 6097 (1989). Argue that questions of patent law should be arbitrable. Use examples from different jurisdictions.

Problem 4
Review and analyse the ICC Interim Award in Case Nr. 6097 (1989). Argue that questions of patent law should not be arbitrable. Use examples from different jurisdictions.

 CASE

Mitsubishi v Soler Chrysler-Plymouth 473 US 614 (1985)

US Supreme Court: *Mitsubishi Motors Corp v Soler Chrysler-Plymouth, Inc.* No. 83-1569

Certiorari to the United States Court of Appeals for the First Circuit

Syllabus

Petitioner-cross-respondent (hereafter petitioner), a Japanese corporation that manufactures automobiles, is the product of a joint venture between Chrysler International, SA (CISA), a Swiss corporation, and another Japanese corporation, aimed at distributing through Chrysler dealers outside the continental United States automobiles manufactured by petitioner. Respondent-cross-petitioner (hereafter respondent), a Puerto Rico corporation, entered into distribution and sales agreements with CISA. The sales agreement (to which petitioner was also a party) contained a clause providing for arbitration by the Japan Commercial Arbitration Association of all disputes arising out of certain articles of the agreement or for the breach thereof. Thereafter, when attempts to work out disputes arising from a slackening of the sale of new automobiles failed, petitioner withheld shipment of automobiles to respondent, which disclaimed responsibility for them. Petitioner then brought an action in Federal District Court under the Federal Arbitration Act and the Convention on the Recognition and Enforcement of Foreign Arbitral Awards, seeking an order to compel arbitration of the disputes in accordance with the arbitration clause. Respondent filed an answer and counterclaims, asserting, inter alia, causes of action under the Sherman Act and other statutes. The District Court ordered arbitration of most of the issues raised in the complaint and counterclaims, including the federal antitrust issues. Despite the doctrine of *American Safety Equipment Corp v J P & Co*, 391 F2d 821 (CA2), uniformly followed by the Courts of Appeals, that rights conferred by the antitrust laws are inappropriate for enforcement by arbitration, the District Court, relying on *Scherk v Alberto-Culver Co*, 417 US 506, held that the international character of the undertaking in question required enforcement of the arbitration clause even as to the antitrust claims. The Court of Appeals reversed in so far as the District Court ordered submission of the antitrust claims to arbitration.

Held

1. There is no merit to respondent's contention that, because it falls within the class for whose benefit the statutes specified in the counter-claims were passed, but the arbitration clause at issue does not mention these statutes or statutes in general, the clause cannot be properly read to contemplate arbitration of these statutory claims. There is no warrant in the Arbitration Act for implying in every contract within its ken a presumption against arbitration of statutory claims. Nor is there any reason to depart from the federal policy favoring arbitration where a party bound by an arbitration agreement raises claims founded on statutory rights.

2. Respondent's antitrust claims are arbitrable pursuant to the Arbitration Act. Concerns of international comity, respect for the capacities of foreign and transnational tribunals, and sensitivity to the need of the international commercial system for predictability in the resolution of disputes, all require enforcement of the arbitration clause in question even assuming that a contrary result would be forthcoming in a domestic context. *See Scherk v Alberto-Culver Co, supra.* The strong presumption in favor of freely negotiated contractual choice-of-forum provisions is reinforced here by the federal policy in favor of arbitral dispute resolution, a policy that applies with special force in the field of international commerce. The mere appearance of an antitrust dispute does not alone warrant invalidation of the selected forum on the undemonstrated assumption that the arbitration clause is tainted. So too, the potential complexity of antitrust matters does not suffice to ward off

arbitration; nor does an arbitration panel pose too great a danger of innate hostility to the constraints on business conduct that antitrust law imposes. And the importance of the private damages remedy in enforcing the regime of antitrust laws does not compel the conclusion that such remedy may not be sought outside an American court.

Blackmun, J, delivered the opinion of the Court, in which Burger, C J, and White, Rehnquist, and O'Connor, J J, joined. Stevens, J, filed a dissenting opinion, in which Brennan, J, joined, and in which Marshall, J, joined except as to Part II, *post*, Powell, J, took no part in the decision of the cases.

Justice Blackmun delivered the opinion of the Court.

The principal question presented by these cases is the arbitrability, pursuant to the Federal Arbitration Act, 9 U.S.C. § 1 et seq., and the Convention on the Recognition and Enforcement of Foreign Arbitral Awards (Convention), [1970] 21 U.S.T. 2517, T.I.A.S. No. 6997, of claims arising under the Sherman Act, 15 U.S.C. § 1 et seq., and encompassed within a valid arbitration clause in an agreement embodying an international commercial transaction.

I

Petitioner-cross-respondent Mitsubishi Motors Corporation (Mitsubishi) is a Japanese corporation which manufactures automobiles and has its principal place of business in Tokyo, Japan. Mitsubishi is the product of a joint venture between, on the one hand, Chrysler International, SA (CISA), a Swiss corporation registered in Geneva and wholly owned by Chrysler Corporation, and, on the other, Mitsubishi Heavy Industries, Inc., a Japanese corporation. The aim of the joint venture was the distribution through Chrysler dealers outside the continental United States of vehicles manufactured by Mitsubishi and bearing Chrysler and Mitsubishi trademarks. Respondent-cross-petitioner Soler Chrysler-Plymouth, Inc. (Soler), is a Puerto Rico corporation with its principal place of business in Pueblo Viejo, Guaynabo, Puerto Rico.

On October 31, 1979, Soler entered into a distributor agreement with CISA which provided for the sale by Soler of Mitsubishi-manufactured vehicles within a designated area, including metropolitan San Juan. App. 18. On the same date, CISA, Soler, and Mitsubishi entered into a Sales Procedure Agreement (sales agreement) which, referring to the distributor agreement, provided for the direct sale of Mitsubishi products to Soler and governed the terms and conditions of such sales, ibid. at 42. Paragraph VI of the Sales Agreement, labelled 'Arbitration of Certain Matters', provides:

> All disputes, controversies or differences which may arise between [Mitsubishi] and [Soler] out of or in relation to Articles I-B through V of this Agreement or for the breach thereof, shall be finally settled by arbitration in Japan in accordance with the rules and regulations of the Japan Commercial Arbitration Association (at 52–53).

Initially, Soler did a brisk business in Mitsubishi-manufactured vehicles. As a result of its strong performance, its minimum sales volume, specified by Mitsubishi and CISA, and agreed to by Soler, for the 1981 model year was substantially increased, ibid. at 179. In early 1981, however, the new-car market slackened. Soler ran into serious difficulties in meeting the expected sales volume, and by the spring of 1981, it felt itself compelled to request that Mitsubishi delay or cancel shipment of several orders. 1 Record 181, 183. About the same time, Soler attempted to arrange for the transshipment of a quantity of its vehicles for sale in the continental United States and Latin America. Mitsubishi and CISA, however, refused permission for any such diversion, citing a variety of reasons, and no vehicles were transshipped. Attempts to work out these difficulties failed. Mitsubishi eventually withheld shipment of 966 vehicles, apparently representing orders placed for May, June, and July, 1981, production, responsibility for which Soler disclaimed in February, 1982. App. 131.

The following month, Mitsubishi brought an action against Soler in the United States District Court for the District of Puerto Rico under the Federal Arbitration Act and the Convention. Mitsubishi sought an order, pursuant to 9 U.S.C. §§ 4 and 201, to compel arbitration in accord with Article VI of the Sales Agreement. App. 15. Shortly after filing the complaint, Mitsubishi filed a request for arbitration before the Japan Commercial Arbitration Association. Ibid. at 70.

Soler denied the allegations and counterclaimed against both Mitsubishi and CISA. It alleged numerous breaches by Mitsubishi of the Sales Agreement, raised a pair of defamation claims, and asserted causes of action under the Sherman Act, 15 U.S.C. § 1 *et seq.;* the federal Automobile Dealers' Day in Court Act, 70 Stat. 1125, 15 U.S.C. § 1221 *et seq.;* the Puerto Rico competition statute, PR Laws Ann., Tit. 10, § 257 *et seq.* (1976); and the Puerto Rico Dealers' Contracts Act, PR Laws Ann., Tit. 10, § 278 *et seq.* (1976 and Supp.1983). In the counterclaim premised on the Sherman Act, Soler alleged that Mitsubishi and CISA had conspired to divide markets in restraint of trade. To effectuate the plan, according to Soler, Mitsubishi had refused to permit Soler to resell to buyers in North, Central, or South America vehicles it had obligated itself to purchase from Mitsubishi; had refused to ship ordered vehicles or the parts, such as heaters and defoggers, that would be necessary to permit Soler to make its vehicles suitable for resale outside Puerto Rico; and had coercively attempted to replace Soler and its other Puerto Rico distributors with a wholly owned subsidiary which would serve as the exclusive Mitsubishi distributor in Puerto Rico. App. 91–6.

After a hearing, the District Court ordered Mitsubishi and Soler to arbitrate each of the issues raised in the complaint and in all the counterclaims save two and a portion of a third. With regard to the federal antitrust issues, it recognised that the Courts of Appeals, following *American Safety Equipment Corp v J P Maguire & Co.*, 391 F 2d 821 (CA2 1968), uniformly had held that the rights conferred by the antitrust laws were 'of a character inappropriate for enforcement by arbitration'. App. to Pet. for Cert. in No. 83-1569, p. B9, quoting *Wilko v Swan*, 201 F 2d 439, 444 (CA2 1953), rev'd, 346 US 427 (1953). The District Court held, however, that the international character of the Mitsubishi-Soler undertaking required enforcement of the agreement to arbitrate even as to the antitrust claims. It relied on *Scherk v Alberto-Culver Co*, 417 US 506, 515–20 (1974), in which this Court ordered arbitration, pursuant to a provision embodied in an international agreement, of a claim arising under the Securities Exchange Act of 1934 notwithstanding its assumption, arguendo, that *Wilko, supra,* which held nonarbitrable claims arising under the Securities Act of 1933, also would bar arbitration of a 1934 Act claim arising in a domestic context.

The United States Court of Appeals for the First Circuit affirmed in part and reversed in part. 723 F 2d 155 (1983). It first rejected Soler's argument that Puerto Rico law precluded enforcement of an agreement obligating a local dealer to arbitrate controversies outside Puerto Rico. It also rejected Soler's suggestion that it could not have intended to arbitrate statutory claims not mentioned in the arbitration agreement. Assessing arbitrability 'on an allegation-by-allegation basis', ibid. at 159, the Court then read the arbitration clause to encompass virtually all the claims arising under the various statutes, including all those arising under the Sherman Act.

Finally, after endorsing the doctrine of *American Safety*, precluding arbitration of antitrust claims, the Court of Appeals concluded that neither this Court's decision in *Scherk* nor the Convention required abandonment of that doctrine in the face of an international transaction 723 F 2d at 164–8. Accordingly, it reversed the judgment of the District Court in so far as it had ordered submission of 'Soler's antitrust claims' to arbitration. Affirming the remainder of the judgment, the Court directed the District Court to consider in the first instance how the parallel judicial and arbitral proceedings should go forward. We granted certiorari primarily to consider whether an American court should enforce an agreement to resolve antitrust claims by arbitration when that agreement arises from an international transaction. 469 US 916 (1984).

II

At the outset, we address the contention raised in Soler's cross-petition that the arbitration clause at issue may not be read to encompass the statutory counterclaims stated in its answer to the complaint. In making this argument, Soler does not question the Court of Appeals' application of Article VI of the Sales Agreement to the disputes involved here as a matter of standard contract interpretation. Instead, it argues that, as a matter of law, a court may not construe an arbitration agreement to encompass claims arising out of statutes designed to protect a class to which the party resisting arbitration belongs 'unless [that party] has expressly agreed' to arbitrate those claims, *see* Pet. for Cert. in No. 83-1733, pp. 8, i, by which Soler presumably means that the arbitration clause must specifically mention the statute giving rise to the claims that a party to the clause seeks to arbitrate. *See* 723 F.2d at 159. Soler reasons that, because it falls within the class for whose benefit the federal and local antitrust laws and dealers' Acts were passed, but the arbitration clause at issue does not mention these statutes or statutes in general, the clause cannot be read to contemplate arbitration of these statutory claims.

We do not agree, for we find no warrant in the Arbitration Act for implying in every contract within its ken a presumption against arbitration of statutory claims. The Act's centerpiece provision makes a written agreement to arbitrate 'in any maritime transaction or a contract evidencing a transaction involving commerce . . . valid, irrevocable, and enforceable, save upon such grounds as exist at law or in equity for the revocation of any contract'. 9 USC § 2. The 'liberal federal policy favoring arbitration agreements,' *Moses H. Cone Memorial Hospital v. Mercury Construction Corp*, 460 US 1, 24 (1983), manifested by this provision and the Act as a whole, is at bottom a policy guaranteeing the enforcement of private contractual arrangements: the Act simply 'creates a body of federal substantive law establishing and regulating the duty to honor an agreement to arbitrate', ibid. at 460 US 25, n. 32. As this Court recently observed, '[t]he preeminent concern of Congress in passing the Act was to enforce private agreements into which parties had entered', a concern which 'requires that we rigorously enforce agreements to arbitrate'. *Dean Witter Reynolds Inc v Byrd*, 470 US 213, 221 (1985).

Accordingly, the first task of a court asked to compel arbitration of a dispute is to determine whether the parties agreed to arbitrate that dispute. The court is to make this determination by applying the 'federal substantive law of arbitrability, applicable to any arbitration agreement within the coverage of the Act'. *Moses H Cone Memorial Hospital* at 460 US 24. *See Prima Paint Corp v Flood & Conklin Mfg Co*, 388 US 395, 400–404 (1967); *Southland Corp v Keating*, 465 US 1, 12 (1984). And that body of law counsels:

> that questions of arbitrability must be addressed with a healthy regard for the federal policy favoring arbitration . . .The Arbitration Act establishes that, as a matter of federal law, any doubts concerning the scope of arbitrable issues should be resolved in favor of arbitration, whether the problem at hand is the construction of the contract language itself or an allegation of waiver, delay, or a like defense to arbitrability.

Moses H Cone Memorial Hospital, 460 US 24–5. See, e.g., *Steelworkers v Warrior & Gulf Navigation Co*, 363 US 574, 582–3 (1960). Thus, as with any other contract, the parties' intentions control, but those intentions are generously construed as to issues of arbitrability.

There is no reason to depart from these guidelines where a party bound by an arbitration agreement raises claims founded on statutory rights. Some time ago, this Court expressed 'hope for [the Act's] usefulness both in controversies based on statutes or on standards otherwise created', *Wilko v Swan*, 346 US 427, 432 (1953) (footnote omitted); *see Merrill Lynch, Pierce, Fenner & Smith, Inc v Ware*, 414 US 117, 135, n. 15 (1973), and we are well past the time when judicial suspicion of the desirability of arbitration and of the competence of arbitral tribunals inhibited the development of arbitration as an alternative means of dispute resolution. Just last Term in *Southland Corp, supra*, where we held that § 2 of the Act declared a national policy applicable equally in state as well as federal courts, we construed an arbitration clause to encompass the disputes at issue without pausing at the source in a state statute of the rights asserted by the parties resisting arbitration. 465 US at 15, and n. 7. Of course, courts should remain attuned to well-supported claims that the agreement to arbitrate resulted from the sort of fraud or overwhelming economic power that would provide grounds 'for the revocation of any contract'. 9 USC § 2; *see Southland Corp*, 465 US 16, n. 11; *The Bremen v Zapata Off-Shore Co*, 407 US 1, 15 (1972). But, absent such compelling considerations, the Act itself provides no basis for disfavoring agreements to arbitrate statutory claims by skewing the otherwise hospitable inquiry into arbitrability.

That is not to say that all controversies implicating statutory rights are suitable for arbitration. There is no reason to distort the process of contract interpretation, however, in order to ferret out the inappropriate. Just as it is the congressional policy manifested in the Federal Arbitration Act that requires courts liberally to construe the scope of arbitration agreements covered by that Act, it is the congressional intention expressed in some other statute on which the courts must rely to identify any category of claims as to which agreements to arbitrate will be held unenforceable.

See Wilko v Swan, 346 US 434–5; *Southland Corp*, 465 US 16, n. 11; *Dean Witter Reynolds Inc*, 470 US 224–5 (concurring opinion). For that reason, Soler's concern for statutorily protected classes provides no reason to color the lens through which the arbitration clause is read. By agreeing to arbitrate a statutory claim, a party does not forgo the substantive rights afforded by the statute; it only submits to their resolution in an arbitral, rather than a judicial, forum. It trades the procedures and opportunity for review of the courtroom for the simplicity, informality, and expedition of arbitration. We must assume that, if Congress intended the substantive protection afforded by a given statute to include protection against waiver of the right to a judicial forum, that intention will be deducible from text or legislative history. *See Wilko v Swan, supra*. Having made the bargain to arbitrate, the party should be held to it unless Congress itself has evinced an intention to preclude a waiver of judicial remedies for the statutory rights at issue. Nothing, in the meantime, prevents a party from excluding statutory claims from the scope of an agreement to arbitrate. *See Prima Paint Corp*, 388 US 406.

In sum, the Court of Appeals correctly conducted a two-step inquiry, first determining whether the parties' agreement to arbitrate reached the statutory issues, and then, upon finding it did, considering whether legal constraints external to the parties' agreement foreclosed the arbitration of those claims. We endorse its rejection of Soler's proposed rule of arbitration clause construction.

III

We now turn to consider whether Soler's antitrust claims are nonarbitrable even though it has agreed to arbitrate them. In holding that they are not, the Court of Appeals followed the decision of the Second Circuit in *American Safety Equipment Corp v J P Maguire & Co*, 391 F 2d 821 (1968). Notwithstanding the absence of any explicit support for such an exception in either the Sherman Act or the Federal Arbitration Act, the Second Circuit there reasoned that 'the pervasive public interest in enforcement of the antitrust laws, and the nature of the claims that arise in such cases, combine to make . . . antitrust claims . . . inappropriate for arbitration', ibid. at 827–8. We find it unnecessary to assess the legitimacy of the *American Safety* doctrine as applied to agreements to arbitrate arising from domestic transactions. As in *Scherk v Alberto-Culver Co,* 417 US 506 (1974), we conclude that concerns of international comity, respect for the capacities of foreign and transnational tribunals, and sensitivity to the need of the international commercial system for predictability in the resolution of disputes require that we enforce the parties' agreement, even assuming that a contrary result would be forthcoming in a domestic context.

Even before *Scherk,* this Court had recognised the utility of forum-selection clauses in international transactions. In *The Bremen, supra,* an American oil company, seeking to evade a contractual choice of an English forum and, by implication, English law, filed a suit in admiralty in a United States District Court against the German corporation which had contracted to tow its rig to a location in the Adriatic Sea. Notwithstanding the possibility that the English court would enforce provisions in the towage contract exculpating the German party which an American court would refuse to enforce, this Court gave effect to the choice-of-forum clause. It observed:

> The expansion of American business and industry will hardly be encouraged if, notwithstanding solemn contracts, we insist on a parochial concept that all disputes must be resolved under our laws and in our courts . . .. We cannot have trade and commerce in world markets and international waters exclusively on our terms, governed by our laws, and resolved in our courts, 407 US 9.

Recognizing that 'agreeing in advance on a forum acceptable to both parties is an indispensable element in international trade, commerce, and contracting', ibid. at 407 US 13–14, the decision in *The Bremen* clearly eschewed a provincial solicitude for the jurisdiction of domestic forums.

Identical considerations governed the Court's decision in *Scherk,* which categorised:

> [a]n agreement to arbitrate before a specified tribunal [as], in effect, a specialized kind of forum-selection clause that posits not only the situs of suit but also the procedure to be used in resolving the dispute, 417 US 519.

In *Scherk,* the American company Alberto-Culver purchased several interrelated business enterprises, organised under the laws of Germany and Liechtenstein, as well as the rights held by those enterprises in certain trademarks, from a German citizen who, at the time of trial, resided in Switzerland. Although the contract of sale contained a clause providing for arbitration before the International Chamber of Commerce in Paris of 'any controversy or claim [arising] out of this agreement or the breach thereof', Alberto-Culver subsequently brought suit against Scherk in a Federal District Court in Illinois, alleging that Scherk had violated § 10(b) of the Securities Exchange Act of 1934 by fraudulently misrepresenting the status of the trademarks as unencumbered. The District Court denied a motion to stay the proceedings before it and enjoined the parties from going forward before the Arbitral Tribunal in Paris. The Court of Appeals for the Seventh Circuit affirmed, relying on this Court's holding in *Wilko v Swan*, 346 US 427 (1953), that agreements to arbitrate disputes arising under the Securities Act of 1933 are nonarbitrable. This Court reversed, enforcing the arbitration agreement even while assuming for purposes of the decision that the controversy would be nonarbitrable under the holding of *Wilko* had it arisen out of a domestic transaction. Again, the Court emphasised:

> A contractual provision specifying in advance the forum in which disputes shall be litigated and the law to be applied is . . . an almost indispensable precondition to achievement of the orderliness and predictability essential to any international business transaction . . ..
>
>   A parochial refusal by the courts of one country to enforce an international arbitration agreement would not only frustrate these purposes, but would invite unseemly and mutually destructive jockeying by the parties to secure tactical litigation advantages . . . [It would] damage the fabric of international commerce and trade, and imperil the willingness and ability of businessmen to enter into international commercial agreements, 417 US 516–17.

Accordingly, the Court held Alberto-Culver to its bargain, sending it to the international Arbitral Tribunal before which it had agreed to seek its remedies.

The Bremen and *Scherk* establish a strong presumption in favor of enforcement of freely negotiated contractual choice-of-forum provisions. Here, as in *Scherk,* that presumption is reinforced by the emphatic federal policy in favor of arbitral dispute resolution. And at least since this Nation's accession in 1970 to the Convention, *see* [1970] 21 UST 2517, TIAS 6997, and the implementation of the Convention in the same year by amendment of the Federal Arbitration Act, that federal policy applies with special force in the field of international commerce. Thus, we must weigh the concerns of *American Safety* against a strong belief in the efficacy of arbitral procedures for the resolution of international commercial disputes and an equal commitment to the enforcement of freely negotiated choice-of-forum clauses.

At the outset, we confess to some skepticism of certain aspects of the *American Safety* doctrine. As distilled by the First Circuit, 723 F 2d at

162, the doctrine comprises four ingredients. First, private parties play a pivotal role in aiding governmental enforcement of the antitrust laws by means of the private action for treble damages. Second, 'the strong possibility that contracts which generate antitrust disputes may be contracts of adhesion militates against automatic forum determination by contract'.

Third, antitrust issues, prone to complication, require sophisticated legal and economic analysis, and thus are 'ill-adapted to strengths of the arbitral process, i.e., expedition, minimal requirements of written rationale, simplicity, resort to basic concepts of common sense and simple equity'.

Finally, just as 'issues of war and peace are too important to be vested in the generals, ... decisions as to antitrust regulation of business are too important to be lodged in arbitrators chosen from the business community – particularly those from a foreign community that has had no experience with or exposure to our law and values'.

See *American Safety*, 391 F.2d at 826–827.

Initially, we find the second concern unjustified. The mere appearance of an antitrust dispute does not alone warrant invalidation of the selected forum on the undemonstrated assumption that the arbitration clause is tainted. A party resisting arbitration of course may attack directly the validity of the agreement to arbitrate. See *Prima Paint Corp v Flood & Conklin Mfg Co*, 388 US 395 (1967). Moreover, the party may attempt to make a showing that would warrant setting aside the forum-selection clause – that the agreement was '[a]ffected by fraud, undue influence, or overweening bargaining power'; that 'enforcement would be unreasonable and unjust'; or that proceedings 'in the contractual forum will be so gravely difficult and inconvenient that [the resisting party] will for all practical purposes be deprived of his day in court'.

The Bremen, 407 US at 407 US 12, 15, 18. But absent such a showing – and none was attempted here – there is no basis for assuming the forum inadequate or its selection unfair.

Next, potential complexity should not suffice to ward off arbitration. We might well have some doubt that even the courts following *American Safety* subscribe fully to the view that antitrust matters are inherently insusceptible to resolution by arbitration, as these same courts have agreed that an undertaking to arbitrate antitrust claims entered into *after* the dispute arises is acceptable. See, e.g., *Coenen v R W Pressprich & Co*, 453 F 2d 1209, 1215 (CA2), *cert. denied*, 406 US 949 (1972); *Cobb v Lewis*, 488 F 2d 41, 48 (CA5

1974). *See also* in the present cases, 723 F 2d at 168, n. 12 (leaving question open). And the vertical restraints which most frequently give birth to antitrust claims covered by an arbitration agreement will not often occasion the monstrous proceedings that have given antitrust litigation an image of intractability. In any event, adaptability and access to expertise are hallmarks of arbitration. The anticipated subject matter of the dispute may be taken into account when the arbitrators are appointed, and arbitral rules typically provide for the participation of experts either employed by the parties or appointed by the tribunal. Moreover, it is often a judgment that streamlined proceedings and expeditious results will best serve their needs that causes parties to agree to arbitrate their disputes; it is typically a desire to keep the effort and expense required to resolve a dispute within manageable bounds that prompts them mutually to forgo access to judicial remedies. In sum, the factor of potential complexity alone does not persuade us that an Arbitral Tribunal could not properly handle an antitrust matter.

For similar reasons, we also reject the proposition that an arbitration panel will pose too great a danger of innate hostility to the constraints on business conduct that antitrust law imposes. International arbitrators frequently are drawn from the legal as well as the business community; where the dispute has an important legal component, the parties and the arbitral body with whose assistance they have agreed to settle their dispute can be expected to select arbitrators accordingly. We decline to indulge the presumption that the parties and arbitral body conducting a proceeding will be unable or unwilling to retain competent, conscientious, and impartial arbitrators.

We are left, then, with the core of the *American Safety* doctrine – the fundamental importance to American democratic capitalism of the regime of the antitrust laws. See, e.g., *United States v Topco Associates, Inc,* 405 US 596, 610 (1972); *Northern Pacific R Co v United States,* 356 US 1, 4 (1958). Without doubt, the private cause of action plays a central role in enforcing this regime. See, e.g., *Hawaii v Standard Oil Co,* 405 US 251, 262 (1972). As the Court of Appeals pointed out:

> A claim under the antitrust laws is not merely a private matter. The Sherman Act is designed to promote the national interest in a competitive economy; thus, the plaintiff asserting his rights under the Act has been likened to a private attorney-general who protects the public's interest 723 F.2d at 168, quoting *American Safety,* 391 F 2d at 826.

The treble damages provision wielded by the private litigant is a chief tool in the antitrust enforcement scheme, posing a crucial deterrent to potential violators. See, e.g., *Perma Life Mufflers, Inc v International Parts Corp,* 392 US 134, 138–139 (1968).

The importance of the private damages remedy, however, does not compel the conclusion that it may not be sought outside an American court. Notwithstanding its important incidental policing function, the treble damages cause of action conferred on private parties by § 4 of the Clayton Act, 15 U.S.C. § 15, and pursued by Soler here by way of its third counterclaim, seeks primarily to enable an injured competitor to gain compensation for that injury.

> Section 4 . . . is in essence a remedial provision. It provides treble damages to '[a] ny person who shall be injured in his business or property by reason of anything forbidden in the antitrust laws. . . .' Of course, treble damages also play an important role in penalizing wrongdoers and deterring wrongdoing, as we also have frequently observed. . . .It nevertheless is true that the treble damages provision, which makes awards available only to injured parties, and measures the awards by a multiple of the injury actually proved, is designed primarily as a remedy *Brunswick Corp v Pueblo Bowl-O-Mat, Inc,* 429 US 477, 485–6 (1977).

After examining the respective legislative histories, the Court in *Brunswick* recognized that, when first enacted in 1890 as § 7 of the Sherman Act, 26 Stat. 210, the treble damages provision 'was conceived of primarily as a remedy for *[t]he people of the United States as individuals,*' 429 US at 486, n. 10, quoting 21 Cong. Rec. 1767–1768 (1890) (remarks of Sen George); when reenacted in 1914 as § 4 of the Clayton Act, 38 Stat. 731, it was still, 'conceived primarily as "open[ing] the door of justice to every man, whenever he may be injured by those who violate the antitrust laws, and giv[ing] the injured party ample damages for the wrong suffered."' 429 U.S. at 486, n. 10, quoting 51 Cong.Rec. 9073 (1914) (remarks of Rep. Webb). And, of course, the antitrust cause of action remains at all times under the control of the individual litigant: no citizen is under an obligation to bring an antitrust suit, *see Illinois Brick Co. v. Illinois,* 431 US 720, 746 (1977), and the private antitrust plaintiff needs no executive or judicial approval before settling one. It follows that, at least where the international cast of a transaction would otherwise add an element of uncertainty to dispute resolution, the prospective litigant may provide in advance for a mutually agreeable procedure whereby he would seek his antitrust recovery as well as settle other controversies.

There is no reason to assume at the outset of the dispute that international arbitration will not provide an adequate mechanism. To be sure, the international

Arbitral Tribunal owes no prior allegiance to the legal norms of particular states; hence, it has no direct obligation to vindicate their statutory dictates. The tribunal, however, is bound to effectuate the intentions of the parties. Where the parties have agreed that the arbitral body is to decide a defined set of claims which includes, as in these cases, those arising from the application of American antitrust law, the tribunal therefore should be bound to decide that dispute in accord with the national law giving rise to the claim. *Cf. Wilko v Swan*, 346 US at 433–434. And so long as the prospective litigant effectively may vindicate its statutory cause of action in the arbitral forum, the statute will continue to serve both its remedial and deterrent function.

Having permitted the arbitration to go forward, the national courts of the United States will have the opportunity at the award-enforcement stage to ensure that the legitimate interest in the enforcement of the antitrust laws has been addressed. The Convention reserves to each signatory country the right to refuse enforcement of an award where the 'recognition or enforcement of the award would be contrary to the public policy of that country.' Art. V(2)(b), 21 U.S.T. at 2520; *see Scherk*, 417 US at 417 US 519, n. 14. While the efficacy of the arbitral process requires that substantive review at the award-enforcement stage remain minimal, it would not require intrusive inquiry to ascertain that the tribunal took cognizance of the antitrust claims and actually decided them.

As international trade has expanded in recent decades, so too has the use of international arbitration to resolve disputes arising in the course of that trade. The controversies that international arbitral institutions are called upon to resolve have increased in diversity as well as in complexity. Yet the potential of these tribunals for efficient disposition of legal disagreements arising from commercial relations has not yet been tested. If they are to take a central place in the international legal order, national courts will need to 'shake off the old judicial hostility to arbitration,' *Kulukundis Shipping Co v Amtorg Trading Corp.*, 126 F 2d 978, 985 (CA2 1942), and also their customary and under-standable unwillingness to cede jurisdiction of a claim arising under domes-tic law to a foreign or transnational tribunal. To this extent, at least, it will be necessary for national courts to subordinate domestic notions of arbitrability to the international policy favoring commercial arbitration. *See Scherk, supra.*

Accordingly, we 'require this representative of the American business com-munity to honor its bargain,' *Alberto-Culver Co v Scherk*, 484 F 2d 611, 620 (CA7 1973) (Stevens, J., dissenting), by holding this agreement to arbitrate 'enforce[able] . . . in accord with the explicit provisions of the Arbitration Act.' *Scherk*, 417 US at 520.

The judgment of the Court of Appeals is affirmed in part and reversed in part, and the cases are remanded for further proceedings consistent with this opinion.

It is so ordered.

Justice Powell took no part in the decision of these cases.

* Together with No. 83-1733, *Soler Chrysler-Plymouth, Inc v Mitsubishi Motors Corp*, also on certiorari to the same court.
The reasons advanced included concerns that such diversion would interfere with the Japanese trade policy of voluntarily limiting imports to the United States, App. 143, 177–8; that the Soler-ordered vehicles would be unsuitable for use in certain proposed destinations because of their manufacture, with use in Puerto Rico in mind, without heaters and defoggers, *id.* at 182; that the vehicles would be unsuitable for use in Latin America because of the unavailability there of the unleaded, high-octane fuel they required, *id.* at 177, 181–182; that adequate warranty service could not be ensured, *id.* at 176, 182; and that diversion to the mainland would violate contractual obligations between CISA and Mitsubishi, *id.* at 144, 183.

The complaint alleged that Soler had failed to pay for 966 ordered vehicles; that it had failed to pay contractual 'distress unit penalties,' intended to reimburse Mitsubishi for storage costs and interest charges incurred because of Soler's failure to take shipment of ordered vehicles; that Soler's failure to fulfill warranty obligations threatened Mitsubishi's reputation and goodwill; that Soler had failed to obtain required financing; and that the Distributor and Sales Agreements had expired by their terms or, alternatively, that Soler had surrendered its rights under the Sales Agreement. *Id.* at 11–14.

Section 4 provides in pertinent part:

> A party aggrieved by the alleged failure, neglect, or refusal of another to arbitrate under a written agreement for arbitration may petition any United States district court which, save for such agreement, would have jurisdiction under title 28, in a civil action or in admiralty of the subject matter of a suit arising out of the controversy between the parties, for an order directing that such arbitration proceed in the manner provided for in such agreement. . . .The court shall hear the parties, and upon being satisfied that the making of the agreement for arbitration or the failure to comply therewith is not in issue, the court shall make an order directing the parties to proceed to arbitration in accordance with the terms of the agreement.

Section 201 provides: 'The Convention on the Recognition and Enforcement of Foreign Arbitral Awards of June 10, 1958, shall be enforced in United States courts in accordance with this chapter.'

Article II of the Convention, in turn, provides:

> 1. Each Contracting State shall recognize an agreement in writing under which the parties undertake to submit to arbitration all or any differences which have arisen or which may arise between them in respect of a defined legal relationship, whether contractual or not, concerning a subject matter capable of settlement by arbitration.
>
> . . .
>
> 3. The court of a Contracting State, when seized of an action in a matter in respect of which the parties have made an agreement within the meaning of this article, shall, at the request of one of the parties, refer the parties to arbitration, unless it finds that the said agreement is null and void, inoperative or incapable of being performed.

21 U.S.T. at 2519. Title 9 U.S.C. § 203 confers jurisdiction on the district courts of the United States over an action falling under the Convention.

Mitsubishi also sought an order against threatened litigation. App. 15–16.

The alleged breaches included wrongful refusal to ship ordered vehicles and necessary parts, failure to make payment for warranty work and authorized rebates, and bad faith in establishing minimum-sales volumes. *Id.* at 97–101.

The fourth counterclaim alleged that Mitsubishi had made statements that defamed Soler's good name and business reputation to a company with which Soler was then negotiating the sale of its plant and distributorship. *Id.* at 96. The sixth counterclaim alleged that Mitsubishi had made a willfully false and malicious statement in an affidavit submitted in support of its application for a temporary restraining order, and that Mitsubishi had wrongfully advised Soler's customers and the public in its market area that they should no longer do business with Soler. *Id.* at 98–99.

The District Court found that the arbitration clause did not cover the fourth and sixth counterclaims, which sought damages for defamation, or the allegations in the seventh counterclaim concerning discriminatory treatment and the establishment of minimum sales volumes. App. to Pet. for Cert. in No. 83-1569, pp. B10–B11. Accordingly, it retained jurisdiction over those portions of the litigation. In addition, because no arbitration agreement between Soler and CISA existed, the court retained jurisdiction, in so far as they sought relief from CISA, over the first, second, third, and ninth counterclaims, which raised claims under the Puerto Rico Dealers' Contracts Act, the federal Automobile Dealers' Day in Court Act, the Sherman Act, and the Puerto Rico competition statute, respectively. *Id.* at B12. These aspects of the District Court's ruling were not appealed, and are not before this Court.

Soler relied on P.R.Laws Ann., Tit. 10, § 278b-2 (Supp.1983), which purports to render null and void '[a]ny stipulation that obligates a dealer to adjust, arbitrate or litigate any controversy that comes up regarding his dealer's contract outside of Puerto Rico, or under foreign law or rule of law.'

See Walborg Corp v Superior Court, 104 P.R.R. 258 (1975). The Court of Appeals held this provision preempted by 9 U.S.C. § 2, which declares arbitration agreements valid and enforceable 'save upon such grounds as exist at law or in equity for the revocation of any contract.' 723 F.2d at 158. *See Southland Corp v Keating,* 465 US 1 (1984). *See also Ledee v Ceramiche Ragno,* 684 F 2d 184 (CA1 1982). Soler does not challenge this holding in its cross-petition here.

As the Court of Appeals saw it,

> [t]he question . . . is not whether the arbitration clause mentions antitrust or any other particular cause of action, but whether the factual allegations underlying Soler's counterclaims – and Mitsubishi's bona fide defenses to those counterclaims – are within the scope of the arbitration clause, whatever the legal labels attached to those allegations 723 F.2d at 159.

Because Soler's counterclaim under the Puerto Rico Dealers' Contracts Act focused on Mitsubishi's alleged failure to comply with the provisions of the Sales Agreement governing delivery of automobiles, and those provisions were found in that portion of Article I of the Agreement subject to arbitration, the Court of Appeals placed this first counterclaim within the arbitration clause. *Id.* at 159–160.

The court read the Sherman Act counterclaim to raise issues of wrongful termination of Soler's distributorship, wrongful failure to ship ordered parts and vehicles, and wrongful refusal to permit transshipment of stock to the United States and Latin America. Because the existence of just cause for termination turned on Mitsubishi's allegations that Soler had breached the Sales Agreement by, for example, failing to pay for ordered vehicles, the wrongful termination claim implicated at least three provisions within the arbitration clause: Article I-D(1), which rendered a dealer's orders 'firm'; Article I-E, which provided for 'distress unit penalties' where the dealer prevented timely shipment; and Article I-F, specifying payment obligations and procedures. The court therefore held the arbitration clause to cover this dispute. Because the nonshipment claim implicated Soler's obligation under Article I-F to proffer acceptable credit, the court found this dispute covered as well. And because the transshipment claim prompted Mitsubishi defenses concerning the suitability of vehicles manufactured to Soler's specifications for use in different locales and Soler's inability to provide warranty service to transshipped products, it implicated Soler's obligation under Article IV, another covered provision, to make use of Mitsubishi's trademarks in a manner that would not dilute Mitsubishi's reputation and goodwill or damage its name and reputation. The court therefore found the arbitration agreement also to include this dispute, noting that such trademark concerns 'are relevant to the legality of territorially based restricted distribution arrangements of the sort at issue here' 723 F.2d at 160–161, citing *Continental TV, Inc v GTE Sylvania Inc,* 433 US 36 (1977).

The Court of Appeals read the federal Automobile Dealers' Day in Court Act claim to raise issues as to Mitsubishi's good faith in establishing minimum sales volumes and Mitsubishi's alleged attempt to coerce Soler into accepting replacement by a Mitsubishi subsidiary. It agreed with the District Court's conclusion, in which Mitsubishi acquiesced, that the arbitration clause did not reach the first issue; it found the second, arising from Soler's payment problems, to restate claims already found to be covered. 723 F.2d at 161.

Finally, the Court of Appeals found the antitrust claims under Puerto Rico law entirely to reiterate claims elsewhere stated; accordingly, it held them arbitrable to the same extent as their counterparts. *Ibid.*

Soler suggests that the court thereby declared antitrust claims arising under Puerto Rico law nonarbitrable as well. We read the Court of Appeals' opinion to have held only the federal antitrust claims nonarbitrable. *See id.* at 157 ('principal issue on this appeal is whether arbitration of federal antitrust claims may be compelled under the Federal Arbitration Act'); *id.* at 161 ('major question in this appeal is whether the antitrust issues raised by Soler's third counterclaim [grounded on Sherman Act] are subject to arbitration'). In any event, any contention that the local antitrust claims are nonarbitrable would be foreclosed by this Court's decision in *Southland Corp v Keating,* 465 US at 10, where we held that the Federal Arbitration Act, 'withdrew the power of the states to require a judicial forum for the resolution of claims which the contracting parties agreed to resolve by arbitration'.

In this Court, Soler suggests for the first time that Congress intended that claims under the federal Automobile Dealers' Day in Court Act be non-arbitrable. Brief for Respondent and Cross-Petitioner 21, n. 12. Because Soler did not raise this question in the Court of Appeals or present it in its cross-petition, we do not address it here.

Following entry of the District Court's judgment, both it and the Court of Appeals denied motions by Soler for a stay pending appeal. The parties accordingly commenced preparation for the arbitration in Japan. Upon remand from the Court of Appeals, however, Soler withdrew the antitrust claims from the arbitration tribunal and sought a stay of arbitration pending the completion of the judicial proceedings on the ground that the antitrust claims permeated the claims that remained before that tribunal. The District Court denied the motion, instead staying its own proceedings pending the arbitration in Japan. The arbitration recommenced, but apparently came to a halt once again in September, 1984, upon the filing by Soler of a petition for reorganization under Chapter 11 of the Bankruptcy Code, 11 U.S.C. § 1101 *et seq.*

We therefore have no reason to review the Court of Appeals' construction of the scope of the arbitration clause in the light of the allegations of Soler's counterclaims. *See Southland Corp v Keating,* 465 US at 15, n. 7.

Soler does suggest that, because the title of the clause referred only to 'certain matters', App. 52, and the clause itself specifically referred only to 'Articles I-B through V,' *ibid.,* it should be read narrowly to exclude the statutory claims. Soler ignores the inclusion within those 'certain matters' of '[a]ll disputes, controversies or differences which may arise between [Mitsubishi] and [Soler] out of or in relation to [the specified provisions] or for the breach thereof.'

Contrary to Soler's suggestion, the exclusion of some areas of possible dispute from the scope of an arbitration clause does not serve to restrict the reach of an otherwise broad clause in the areas in which it was intended to operate. Thus, in so far as the allegations underlying the statutory claims touch matters covered by the enumerated articles, the Court of Appeals properly resolved any doubts in favor of arbitrability. *See* 723 F.2d at 159.

The Court previously has explained that the Act was designed to overcome an anachronistic judicial hostility to agreements to arbitrate, which American courts had borrowed from English common law. *See Dean Witter Reynolds Inc v Byrd,* 470 U. S. 213, 470 U. S. 219–221, and n. 6 (1985); *Scherk v. Alberto-Culver Co.,* 417 US 506, 510, and n. 4 (1974).

The claims whose arbitrability was at issue in *Southland Corp* arose under the disclosure requirements of the California Franchise Investment Law, Cal. Corp. Code Ann. § 31000 *et seq.* (West 1977). While the dissent in *Southland Corp* disputed the applicability of the Act to proceedings in the state courts, it did not object to the Court's reading of the arbitration clause under examination. Act of July 31, 1970, Pub.L. 91-368, 84 Stat. 692, codified at 9 U.S.C. §§ 201–208.

See, e.g., Japan Commercial Arbitration Association Rule 26, reprinted in App. 218-219; L. Craig, W. Park, & J. Paulsson, International Chamber of Commerce Arbitration §§ 25.03, 26.04 (1984); Art. 27, Arbitration Rules of United Nations Commission on International Trade Law (UNCITRAL) (1976), reprinted in 2 Yearbook Commercial Arbitration 167 (1977).

See Craig, Park, & Paulsson, *supra,* § 12.03, p. 28; Sanders, Commentary on UNCITRAL Arbitration Rules § 15.1, in 2 Yearbook Commercial Arbitration, *supra,* at 203.

We are advised by Mitsubishi and *amicus* International Chamber of Commerce, without contradiction by Soler, that the arbitration panel selected to hear the parties' claims here is composed of three Japanese lawyers, one a former law school dean, another a former judge, and the third a practicing attorney with American legal training who has written on Japanese antitrust law. Brief for Petitioner in No. 83-1569, p. 26; Brief for International Chamber of Commerce as *Amicus Curiae* 16, n. 28.

The Court of Appeals was concerned that international arbitrators would lack 'experience with or exposure to our law and values.' 723 F 2d at 162. The obstacles confronted by the arbitration panel in this case, however, should be no greater than those confronted by any judicial or arbitral tribunal required to determine foreign law. See, e.g., Fed.Rule Civ.Proc. 44.1. Moreover, while our attachment to the antitrust laws may be stronger than most, many other countries, including Japan, have similar bodies of competition law. See, e.g., 1 Law of Transnational Business Transactions, ch. 9 (Banks, Antitrust Aspects of International Business Operations), § 9.03[7] (V. Nanda ed.1984); H. Iyori and A. Uesugi, *The Antimonopoly Laws of Japan* (1983).

In addition to the clause providing for arbitration before the Japan Commercial Arbitration Association, the Sales Agreement includes a choice-of-law clause which reads: 'This Agreement is made in, and will be governed by and construed in all respects according to the laws of the Swiss Confederation as if entirely performed therein.'

App. 56. The United States raises the possibility that the arbitral panel will read this provision not simply to govern interpretation of the contract terms, but wholly to displace American law even where it otherwise would apply. Brief for United States as *Amicus Curiae* 20. The International Chamber of Commerce opines that it is

> [c]onceivabl[e], although we believe it unlikely, [that] the arbitrators could consider Soler's affirmative claim of anticompetitive conduct by CISA and Mitsubishi to fall within the purview of this choice-of-law provision, with the result that it would be decided under Swiss law rather than the U.S. Sherman Act.

Brief for International Chamber of Commerce as *Amicus Curiae* 25. At oral argument, however, counsel for Mitsubishi conceded that American law applied to the antitrust claims, and represented that the claims had been submitted to the arbitration panel in Japan on that basis. Tr. of Oral. Arg. 18. The record confirms that, before the decision of the Court of Appeals, the arbitral panel had taken these claims under submission. *See* District Court Order of May 25, 1984, pp. 2–3.

We therefore have no occasion to speculate on this matter at this stage in the proceedings, when Mitsubishi seeks to enforce the agreement to arbitrate, not to enforce an award. Nor need we consider now the effect of an Arbitral Tribunal's failure to take cognizance of the statutory cause of action on the claimant's capacity to reinitiate suit in federal court. We merely note that, in the event the choice-of-forum and choice-of-law clauses operated in tandem as a prospective waiver of a party's right to pursue statutory remedies for antitrust violations, we would have little hesitation in condemning the agreement as against public policy. See, e.g., *Redel's Inc v General Electric Co*, 498 F2d 95, 98–99 (CA5 1974); *Gaines v Carrollton Tobacco Board of Trade, Inc*, 386 F 2d 757, 759 (CA6 1967); *Fox Midwest Theatres v Means*, 221 F 2d 173, 180 (CA8 1955). *Cf. Lawlor v National Screen Service Corp*, 349 US 322, 329 (1955). *See generally* 15 S. Williston, Contracts § 1750A (3d ed.1972).

See n.19, *supra*. We note, for example, that the rules of the Japan Commercial Arbitration Association provide for the taking of a 'summary record' of each hearing, Rule 28.1; for the stenographic recording of the proceedings where the tribunal so orders or a party requests one, Rule 28.2; and for a statement of reasons for the award unless the parties agree otherwise, Rule 36.1(4). *See* App. 219 and 221.

Needless to say, we intimate no views on the merits of Soler's antitrust claims.

We do not quarrel with the Court of Appeals' conclusion that Art. II(1) of the Convention, which requires the recognition of agreements to arbitrate that involve 'subject matter capable of settlement by arbitration,' contemplates exceptions to arbitrability grounded in domestic law. *See* 723 F.2d at 164–166; G. Gaja, *International Commercial Arbitration: New York Convention I.B.2* (1984); A. van den Berg, *The New York Convention of 1958: Towards a Uniform Judicial Interpretation* 152–4 (1981); Contini, 'International Commercial Arbitration: The United Nations Convention on the Recognition and Enforcement of Foreign Arbitral Awards', 8 Am. J. Comp. L. 283, 296 (1959). *But see* Van den Berg, *supra*, at 154, and n. 98 (collecting contrary authorities); Gaja, *supra*, at I.D., n. 43 (same). And it appears that, before acceding to the Convention, the Senate was advised by a State Department memorandum that the Convention provided for such exceptions. *See* S.Exec.Doc. E, 90th Cong., 2d Sess., 19 (1968).

In acceding to the Convention, the Senate restricted its applicability to commercial matters, in accord with Art. I(3). *See* 21 U.S.T. at 2519, 2560. Yet in implementing the Convention by amendment to the Federal Arbitration Act, Congress did not specify any matters it intended to exclude from its scope. *See* Act of July 31, 1970, Pub.L. 91-368, 84 Stat. 692, codified at 9 U.S.C. §§ 201-208. In *Scherk*, this Court recited Art. II(1), including the language relied upon by the Court of Appeals, but paid heed to the Convention delegates'

> frequent[ly voiced] concern that courts of signatory countries in which an
> agreement to arbitrate is sought to be enforced should not be permitted to
> decline enforcement of such agreements on the basis of parochial views of their
> desirability or in a manner that would diminish the mutually binding nature of the
> agreements.

417 US at 520, n. 15, citing G. Haight, Convention on the Recognition and Enforcement of Foreign Arbitral Awards: Summary Analysis of Record of United Nations Conference, May/June 1958, pp. 24–28 (1958).

There, moreover, the Court dealt, *arguendo*, with an exception to arbitrability grounded in express congressional language; here, in contrast, we face a judicially implied exception. The utility of the Convention in promoting the process of international commercial arbitration depends upon the willingness of national courts to let go of matters they normally would think of as their own. Doubtless, Congress may specify categories of claims it wishes to reserve for decision by our own courts without contravening this Nation's obligations under the Convention. But we decline to subvert the spirit of the United States' accession to the Convention by recognizing subject matter exceptions where Congress has not expressly directed the courts to do so.

Justice Stevens, with whom Justice Brennan joins, and with whom Justice Marshall joins except as to Part II, dissenting.

One element of this rather complex litigation is a claim asserted by an American dealer in Plymouth automobiles that two major automobile companies are parties to an international cartel that has restrained competition in the American market. Pursuant to an agreement that is alleged to have violated § 1 of the Sherman Act, 15 U.S.C. § 1, those companies allegedly prevented the dealer from transshipping some 966 surplus vehicles from Puerto Rico to other dealers in the American market. App. 92.

Petitioner denies the truth of the dealer's allegations and takes the position that the validity of the antitrust claim must be resolved by an arbitration tribunal in Tokyo, Japan. Largely because the auto manufacturers' defense to the antitrust allegation is based on provisions in the dealer's franchise agreement, the Court of Appeals concluded that the arbitration clause in that agreement encompassed the antitrust claim. 723 F.2d 155, 159 (CA1 1983). It held, however, as a matter of law, that arbitration of such a claim may not be compelled under either the Federal Arbitration Act or the Convention on the Recognition and Enforcement of Foreign Arbitral Awards. *Id.* at 161–168.

This Court agrees with the Court of Appeals' interpretation of the scope of the arbitration clause, but disagrees with its conclusion that the clause is unenforceable in so far as it purports to cover an antitrust claim against a Japanese company. This Court's holding rests almost exclusively on the federal policy favoring arbitration of commercial disputes and vague notions of international comity arising from the fact that the automobiles involved here were manufactured in Japan. Because I am convinced that the Court of Appeals' construction of the arbitration clause is erroneous, and because I strongly disagree with this Court's interpretation of the relevant federal statutes, I respectfully dissent. In my opinion, (1) a fair construction of the language in the arbitration clause in the parties' contract does not encompass a claim that auto manufacturers entered into a conspiracy in violation of the antitrust laws; (2) an arbitration clause should not normally be construed to cover a statutory remedy that it does not expressly identify; (3) Congress did not intend § 2 of the Federal Arbitration Act to apply to antitrust claims; and (4) Congress did not intend the Convention on the Recognition and Enforcement of Foreign Arbitral Awards to apply to disputes that are not covered by the Federal Arbitration Act.

I

On October 31, 1979, respondent, Soler Chrysler-Plymouth, Inc. (Soler), entered into a 'distributor agreement' to govern the sale of Plymouth passenger cars to be manufactured by petitioner, Mitsubishi Motors Corporation of Tokyo, Japan (Mitsubishi). Mitsubishi, however, was not a party to that agreement. Rather, the 'purchase rights' were granted to Soler by a wholly owned subsidiary of Chrysler Corporation that is referred to as 'Chrysler' in the agreement. The distributor agreement does not contain an arbitration clause. Nor does the record contain any other agreement providing for the arbitration of disputes between Soler and Chrysler.

Paragraph 26 of the distributor agreement authorizes Chrysler to have Soler's orders filled by any company affiliated with Chrysler, that company thereby becoming the 'supplier' of the products covered by the agreement with Chrysler. Relying on paragraph 26 of their distributor-agreement, Soler, Chrysler, and Mitsubishi entered into a separate Sales Procedure Agreement designating Mitsubishi as the supplier of the products covered by the distributor agreement. The arbitration clause the Court construes today is found in that agreement. As a matter of ordinary contract interpretation, there are at least two reasons why that clause does not apply to Soler's antitrust claim against Chrysler and Mitsubishi.

First, the clause only applies to two-party disputes between Soler and Mitsubishi. The antitrust violation alleged in Soler's counterclaim is a three-party dispute. Soler has joined both Chrysler and its associated company, Mitsubishi, as counterdefendants. The pleading expressly alleges that both of those companies are 'engaged in an unlawful combination and conspiracy to restrain and divide markets in interstate and foreign commerce, in violation of the Sherman Antitrust Act and the Clayton Act.'

App. 91. It is further alleged that Chrysler authorized and participated in several overt acts directed at Soler. At this stage of the case, we must, of course, assume the truth of those allegations. Only by stretching the language of the arbitration clause far beyond its ordinary meaning could one possibly conclude that it encompasses this three-party dispute.

Second, the clause only applies to disputes 'which may arise between MMC and BUYER out of or in relation to Articles I-B through V of this Agreement or for the breach thereof. . . .' *Id.* at 52. Thus, disputes relating to only five out of a total of 15 Articles in the Sales Procedure Agreement are arbitrable. Those five Articles cover: (1) the terms and conditions of direct sales (matters such as the scheduling of orders, deliveries, and payment); (2) technical and engineering changes; (3) compliance by Mitsubishi with customs laws and regulations, and Soler's obligation to inform Mitsubishi of relevant local laws; (4) trademarks and patent rights; and (5) Mitsubishi's right to cease production of any products. It is immediately obvious that Soler's antitrust claim did not arise out of Articles I-B through V, and it is not a claim 'for the breach thereof.' The question is whether it is a dispute 'in relation to' those Articles.

Because Mitsubishi relies on those Articles of the contract to explain some of the activities that Soler challenges in its antitrust claim, the Court of Appeals concluded that the relationship between the dispute and those Articles brought the arbitration clause into play. I find that construction of the clause wholly unpersuasive. The words 'in relation to' appear between the references to claims that arise under the contract and claims for breach of the contract; I believe all three of the species of arbitrable claims must be predicated on contractual rights defined in Articles I-B through V.

The federal policy favoring arbitration cannot sustain the weight that the Court assigns to it. A clause requiring arbitration of all claims 'relating to' a contract surely could not encompass a claim that the arbitration clause was itself part of a contract in restraint of trade. *Cf. Paramount Famous Lasky Corp v United States,* 282 US 30 (1930); *see also United States v Paramount Pictures, Inc,* 334 US 131, 176 (1948). Nor in my judgment should it be read to encompass a claim that relies, not on a failure to perform the contract, but on an independent violation of federal law. The matters asserted by way of defense do not control the character, or the source, of the claim that Soler has asserted. Accordingly, simply as a matter of ordinary contract interpretation, I would hold that Soler's antitrust claim is not arbitrable.

II

Section 2 of the Federal Arbitration Act describes three kinds of arbitrable agreements. Two – those including maritime transactions and those covering the submission of an existing dispute to arbitration – are not involved in this case. The language of § 2 relating to the Soler-Mitsubishi arbitration clause reads as follows:

> A written provision in . . . a contract evidencing a transaction involving commerce to settle by arbitration a controversy thereafter arising out of such contract . . . or the refusal to perform the whole or any part thereof, . . . shall be valid, irrevocable, and enforceable, save upon such grounds as exist at law or in equity for the revocation of any contract.

The plain language of this statute encompasses Soler's claims that arise out of its contract with Mitsubishi, but does not encompass a claim arising under federal law, or indeed one that arises under its distributor agreement with Chrysler. Nothing in the text of the 1925 Act, nor its legislative history, suggests that Congress intended to authorize the arbitration of any statutory claims.

Until today, all of our cases enforcing agreements to arbitrate under the Arbitration Act have involved contract claims. In one, the party claiming a breach of contractual warranties also claimed that the breach amounted to fraud actionable under § 10(b) of the Securities Exchange Act of 1934, *Scherk v Alberto-Culver Co.*, 417 US 506 (1974).

But this is the first time the Court has considered the question whether a standard arbitration clause referring to claims arising out of or relating to a contract should be construed to cover statutory claims that have only an indirect relationship to the contract. In my opinion, neither the Congress that enacted the Arbitration Act in 1925 nor the many parties who have agreed to such standard clauses could have anticipated the Court's answer to that question.

On several occasions, we have drawn a distinction between statutory rights and contractual rights and refused to hold that an arbitration barred the assertion of a statutory right. Thus, in *Alexander v Gardner-Denver Co*, 415 US 36 (1974), we held that the arbitration of a claim of employment discrimination would not bar an employee's statutory right to damages under Title VII of the Civil Rights Act of 1964, 42 U.S.C. §§ 2000e – 2000e-17, notwithstanding the strong federal policy favoring the arbitration of labor disputes. In that case, the Court explained at some length why it would be unreasonable to assume that Congress intended to give arbitrators the final authority to implement the federal statutory policy:

> [W]e have long recognized that 'the choice of forums inevitably affects the scope of the substantive right to be vindicated.' *US Bulk Carriers v Arguelles*, 400

US 351, 359–360 (1971) (Harlan, J, concurring). Respondent's deferral rule is necessarily premised on the assumption that arbitral processes are commensurate with judicial processes and that Congress impliedly intended federal courts to defer to arbitral decisions on Title VII issues. We deem this supposition unlikely.

Arbitral procedures, while well suited to the resolution of contractual disputes, make arbitration a comparatively inappropriate forum for the final resolution of rights created by Title VII. This conclusion rests first on the special role of the arbitrator, whose task is to effectuate the intent of the parties, rather than the requirements of enacted legislation. . ..But other facts may still render arbitral processes comparatively inferior to judicial processes in the protection of Title VII rights. Among these is the fact that the specialized competence of arbitrators pertains primarily to the law of the shop, not the law of the land. *United Steelworkers of America v. Warrior & Gulf Navigation Co.,* 363 US 574, 581–583 (1960). Parties usually choose an arbitrator because they trust his knowledge and judgment concerning the demands and norms of industrial relations. On the other hand, the resolution of statutory or constitutional issues is a primary responsibility of courts, and judicial construction has proved especially necessary with respect to Title VII, whose broad language frequently can be given meaning only by reference to public law concepts 415 US at 56–57 (footnote omitted).

In addition, the Court noted that the informal procedures which make arbitration so desirable in the context of contractual disputes are inadequate to develop a record for appellate review of statutory questions. Such review is essential on matters of statutory interpretation in order to assure consistent application of important public rights.

In *Barrentine v Arkansas-Best Freight System, Inc,* 450 US 728 (1981), we reached a similar conclusion with respect to the arbitrability of an employee's claim based on the Fair Labor Standards Act, 29 U.S.C. §§ 201–219. We again noted that an arbitrator, unlike a federal judge, has no institutional obligation to enforce federal legislative policy:

Because the arbitrator is required to effectuate the intent of the parties, rather than to enforce the statute, he may issue a ruling that is inimical to the public policies underlying the FLSA, thus depriving an employee of protected statutory rights.

Finally, not only are arbitral procedures less protective of individual statutory rights than are judicial procedures, *see Gardner-Denver, supra,* at 415 US 57–58, but arbitrators very often are powerless to grant the aggrieved employees as broad a range of relief. Under the FLSA, courts can award actual and liquidated damages, reasonable attorney's fees, and costs. 29 U.S.C. § 216(b). An arbitrator, by contrast, can award only that compensation authorized by the wage provision of the collective bargaining agreement. . ...It is most unlikely that he will be authorized to award liquidated damages, costs, or attorney's fees. 450 US at 744-745 (footnote omitted).

The Court has applied the same logic in holding that federal claims asserted under the Ku Klux Act of 1871, 42 U.S.C. § 1983, and claims arising under § 12(2) of the Securities Act of 1933, 15 U.S.C. § 771(2), may not be finally resolved by an arbitrator, *McDonald v City of West Branch*, 466 US 284 (1984); *Wilko v Swan*, 346 US 427 (1953).

The Court's opinions in *Alexander, Barrentine, McDonald*, and *Wilko* all explain why it makes good sense to draw a distinction between statutory claims and contract claims. In view of the Court's repeated recognition of the distinction between federal statutory rights and contractual rights, together with the undisputed historical fact that arbitration has functioned almost entirely in either the area of labor disputes or in 'ordinary disputes between merchants as to questions of fact,' it is reasonable to assume that most lawyers and executives would not expect the language in the standard arbitration clause to cover federal statutory claims. Thus, in my opinion, both a fair respect for the importance of the interests that Congress has identified as worthy of federal statutory protection, and a fair appraisal of the most likely understanding of the parties who sign agreements containing standard arbitration clauses, support a presumption that such clauses do not apply to federal statutory claims.

III

The Court has repeatedly held that a decision by Congress to create a special statutory remedy renders a private agreement to arbitrate a federal statutory claim unenforceable. Thus, as I have already noted, the express statutory remedy provided in the Ku Klux Act of 1871, the express statutory remedy in the Securities Act of 1933, the express statutory remedy in the Fair Labor Standards Act, and the express statutory remedy in Title VII of the Civil Rights Act of 1964, each provided the Court with convincing evidence that Congress did not intend the protections afforded by the statute to be administered by a private arbitrator. The reasons that motivated those decisions apply with special force to the federal policy that is protected by the antitrust laws.

To make this point, it is appropriate to recall some of our past appraisals of the importance of this federal policy, and then to identify some of the specific remedies Congress has designed to implement it. It was Chief Justice Hughes who characterized the Sherman Antitrust Act as 'a charter of freedom' that may fairly be compared to a constitutional provision. *See Appalachian Coals, Inc v United States,* 288 US 344, 359–60 (1933). In *United States v Philadelphia National Bank,* 374 U.321, 371 (1963), the Court referred to the extraordinary 'magnitude' of the value choices made by Congress in enacting the Sherman Act. More recently, the Court described the weighty public interests underlying the basic philosophy of the statute:

> Antitrust laws in general, and the Sherman Act in particular, are the Magna Carta of free enterprise. They are as important to the preservation of economic freedom and our free enterprise system as the Bill of Rights is to the protection of our fundamental personal freedoms. And the freedom guaranteed each and every business, no matter how small, is the freedom to compete – to assert with vigor, imagination, devotion, and ingenuity whatever economic muscle it can muster. Implicit in such freedom is the notion that it cannot be foreclosed with respect to one sector of the economy because certain private citizens or groups believe that such foreclosure might promote greater competition in a more important sector of the economy *United States v Topco Associates, Inc,* 405 US 596, 610 (1972).

The Sherman and Clayton Acts reflect Congress' appraisal of the value of economic freedom; they guarantee the vitality of the entrepreneurial spirit. Questions arising under these Acts are among the most important in public law.

The unique public interest in the enforcement of the antitrust laws is repeatedly reflected in the special remedial scheme enacted by Congress. Since its enactment in 1890, the Sherman Act has provided for public enforcement through criminal as well as civil sanctions. The preeminent federal interest in effective enforcement once justified a provision for special three-judge district courts to hear antitrust claims on an expedited basis, as well as for direct appeal to this Court bypassing the courts of appeals. *See, e.g., United States v National Assn. of Securities Dealers, Inc.,* 422 US 694 (1975).

The special interest in encouraging private enforcement of the Sherman Act has been reflected in the statutory scheme ever since 1890. Section 7 of the original Act, used the broadest possible language to describe the class of litigants who may invoke its protection. 'The Act is comprehensive in its terms and coverage, protecting all who are made victims of the forbidden practices by whomever they may be perpetrated.'

Mandeville Island Farms, Inc v American Crystal Sugar Co., 334 US 219, 236 (1948); *See also Associated General Contractors of California, Inc v Carpenters,* 459 US 519, 529 (1983).

The provision for mandatory treble damages – unique in federal law when the statute was enacted – provides a special incentive to the private enforcement of the statute, as well as an especially powerful deterrent to violators. What we have described as 'the public interest in vigilant enforcement of the antitrust laws through the instrumentality of the private treble damage action,' *Lawlor v National Screen Service Corp*, 349 US 322, 329 (1955), is buttressed by the statutory mandate that the injured party also recover costs, 'including a reasonable attorney's fee.' 15 U.S.C. § 15(a). The interest in wide and effective enforcement has thus, for almost a century, been vindicated by enlisting the assistance of 'private Attorneys General'; we have always attached special importance to their role because '[e]very violation of the antitrust laws is a blow to the free enterprise system envisaged by Congress.' *Hawaii v Standard Oil Co*, 405 US 251, 262 (1972).

There are, in addition, several unusual features of the antitrust enforcement scheme that unequivocally require rejection of any thought that Congress would tolerate private arbitration of antitrust claims in lieu of the statutory remedies that it fashioned. As we explained in *Blumenstock Brothers Advertising Agency v Curtis Publishing Co*, 252 US 436, 440 (1920), an antitrust treble damages case 'can only be brought in a District Court of the United States.' The determination that these cases are 'too important to be decided otherwise than by competent tribunals' surely cannot allow private arbitrators to assume a jurisdiction that is denied to courts of the sovereign States.

The extraordinary importance of the private antitrust remedy has been emphasized in other statutes enacted by Congress. Thus, in 1913, Congress passed a special Act guaranteeing public access to depositions in Government civil proceedings to enforce the Sherman Act. 37 Stat. 731, 15 U.S.C. § 30. The purpose of that Act plainly was to enable victims of antitrust violations to make evidentiary use of information developed in a public enforcement proceeding. This purpose was further implemented in the following year by the enactment of § 5 of the Clayton Act providing that a final judgment or decree in a Government case may constitute *prima facie* proof of a violation in a subsequent treble damages case. 38 Stat. 731, 15 U.S.C. § 16(a). These special remedial provisions attest to the importance that Congress has attached to the private remedy.

In view of the history of antitrust enforcement in the United States, it is not surprising that all of the federal courts that have considered the question have uniformly and unhesitatingly concluded that agreements to arbitrate federal antitrust issues are not enforceable. In a landmark opinion for the Court of Appeals for the Second Circuit, Judge Feinberg wrote:

> A claim under the antitrust laws is not merely a private matter. The Sherman
> Act is designed to promote the national interest in a competitive economy;
> thus, the plaintiff asserting his rights under the Act has been likened to a private
> attorney-general who protects the public's interest. . . .Antitrust violations can
> affect hundreds of thousands – perhaps millions – of people, and inflict staggering
> economic damage. . . .We do not believe that Congress intended such claims to
> be resolved elsewhere than in the courts. We do not suggest that all antitrust
> litigations attain these swollen proportions; the courts, no less than the public,
> are thankful that they do not. But in fashioning a rule to govern the arbitrability of
> antitrust claims, we must consider the rule's potential effect. For the same reason,
> it is also proper to ask whether contracts of adhesion between alleged monopolists
> and their customers should determine the forum for trying antitrust violations.

American Safety Equipment Corp v J P Maguire & Co, 391 F 2d 821, 826–827
(1968) (footnote omitted). This view has been followed in later cases from
that Circuit and by the First, Fifth, Seventh, Eighth, and Ninth Circuits. It is
clearly a correct statement of the law.

This Court would be well advised to endorse the collective wisdom of the
distinguished judges of the Courts of Appeals who have unanimously concluded that the statutory remedies fashioned by Congress for the enforcement of the antitrust laws render an agreement to arbitrate antitrust disputes
unenforceable. Arbitration awards are only reviewable for manifest disregard
of the law, 9 U.S.C. §§ 10, 207, and the rudimentary procedures which make
arbitration so desirable in the context of a private dispute often mean that the
record is so inadequate that the arbitrator's decision is virtually unreviewable.
Despotic decisionmaking of this kind is fine for parties who are willing to
agree in advance to settle for a best approximation of the correct result in
order to resolve quickly and inexpensively any contractual dispute that may
arise in an ongoing commercial relationship. Such informality, however, is
simply unacceptable when every error may have devastating consequences
for important businesses in our national economy, and may undermine their
ability to compete in world markets. Instead of 'muffling a grievance in the
cloakroom of arbitration,' the public interest in free competitive markets
would be better served by having the issues resolved 'in the light of impartial
public court adjudication.' *See Merrill Lynch, Pierce, Fenner & Smith, Inc v
Ware,* 414 US 117, 136 (1973).

IV

The Court assumes for the purposes of its decision that the antitrust issues
would not be arbitrable if this were a purely domestic dispute, *ante* at 473 US

629, but holds that the international character of the controversy makes it arbitrable. The holding rests on vague concerns for the international implications of its decision and a misguided application of *Scherk v Alberto-Culver Co,* 417 US 506 (1974).

International obligations of the United States Before relying on its own notions of what international comity requires, it is surprising that the Court does not determine the specific commitments that the United States has made to enforce private agreements to arbitrate disputes arising under public law. As the Court acknowledges, the only treaty relevant here is the Convention on the Recognition and Enforcement of Foreign Arbitral Awards. [1970] 21 U.S.T. 2517, T.I.A.S. No. 6997. The Convention was adopted in 1958 at a multilateral conference sponsored by the United Nations. This Nation did not sign the proposed convention at that time; displaying its characteristic caution before entering into international compacts, the United States did not accede to it until 12 years later.

As the Court acknowledged in *Scherk v Alberto-Culver Co,* 417 US 520, n. 15, the principal purpose of the Convention:

> was to encourage the recognition and enforcement of commercial arbitration agreements in international contracts and to unify the standards by which agreements to arbitrate are observed and arbitral awards are enforced in the signatory countries.

However, the United States, as *amicus curiae,* advises the Court that the Convention 'clearly contemplates' that signatory nations will enforce domestic laws prohibiting the arbitration of certain subject matters. Brief for United States as *Amicus Curiae* 28. This interpretation of the Convention was adopted by the Court of Appeals, 723 F.2d at 162–166, and the Court declines to reject it, *ante* at 473 US 639–640, n. 21. The construction is beyond doubt.

Article II(3) of the Convention provides that the court of a Contracting State, 'when seized of an action in a matter in respect of which the parties have made an agreement within the meaning of this article, shall, at the request of one of the parties, refer the parties to arbitration.'

This obligation does not arise, however, (i) if the agreement 'is null and void, inoperative or incapable of being performed,' Art. II(3), or (ii) if the dispute does not concern 'a subject matter capable of settlement by arbitration,' Art. II(1). The former qualification principally applies to matters of fraud, mistake, and duress in the inducement, or problems of procedural fairness and feasibility. 723 F.2d at 164. The latter clause plainly suggests the possibility that some subject matters are not capable of arbitration under the domestic laws of the signatory nations, and that agreements to arbitrate such disputes need not be enforced.

This construction is confirmed by the provisions of the Convention which provide for the enforcement of international arbitration awards. Article III provides that each 'Contracting State shall recognize arbitral awards as binding and enforce them.' However, if an arbitration award is 'contrary to the public policy of [a] country' called upon to enforce it, or if it concerns a subject matter which is 'not capable of settlement by arbitration under the law of that country,' the Convention does not require that it be enforced. Arts. V(2) (a) and (b). Thus, reading Articles II and V together, the Convention provides that agreements to arbitrate disputes which are nonarbitrable under domestic law need not be honored, nor awards rendered under them enforced.

This construction is also supported by the legislative history of the Senate's advice and consent to the Convention. In presenting the Convention for the Senate's consideration, the President offered the following interpretation of Article II(1):

> The requirement that the agreement apply to a matter capable of settlement by arbitration is necessary in order to take proper account of laws in force in many countries which prohibit the submission of certain questions to arbitration. In some States of the United States, for example, disputes affecting the title to real property are not arbitrable.

S.Exec.Doc. E at 19. The Senate's consent to the Convention presumably was made in light of this interpretation, and thus it is to be afforded considerable weight. *Sumitomo Shoji America, Inc v Avagliano*, 457 US 176, 184–185 (1982).

International comity   It is clear then that the international obligations of the United States permit us to honor Congress' commitment to the exclusive resolution of antitrust disputes in the federal courts. The Court today refuses to do so, offering only vague concerns for comity among nations. The courts of other nations, on the other hand, have applied the exception provided in the Convention, and refused to enforce agreements to arbitrate specific subject matters of concern to them.

It may be that the subject matter exception to the Convention ought to be reserved – as a matter of domestic law – for matters of the greatest public interest which involve concerns that are shared by other nations. The Sherman Act's commitment to free competitive markets is among our most important civil policies. *Supra* at 473 US 650–657. This commitment, shared by other nations which are signatory to the Convention, is hardly the sort of parochial concern that we should decline to enforce in the interest of international comity. Indeed, the branch of Government entrusted with the conduct of political relations with foreign governments has informed us that the 'United States' determination that federal antitrust claims are nonarbitrable under the Convention . . . is not likely to result in either surprise or recrimination on the part of other signatories to the Convention.' Brief for United States as *Amicus Curiae* 30.

Lacking any support for the proposition that the enforcement of our domestic laws in this context will result in international recriminations, the Court seeks refuge in an obtuse application of its own precedent, *Scherk v Alberto-Culver Co*, 417 US 506 (1974), in order to defend the contrary result. The *Scherk* case was an action for damages brought by an American purchaser of three European businesses in which it was claimed that the seller's fraudulent representations concerning the status of certain European trademarks constituted a violation of § 10(b) of the Securities Exchange.

Act of 1934, 15 U.S.C. § 78j(b). The Court held that the parties' agreement to arbitrate any dispute arising out of the purchase agreement was enforceable under the Federal Arbitration Act. The legal issue was whether the Court's earlier holding in *Wilko v Swan*, 346 US 427 (1953) – 'that an agreement to arbitrate could not preclude a buyer of a security from seeking a judicial remedy under the Securities Act of 1933,' *see* 417 US at 510 – was 'controlling authority.' Ibid.

The Court carefully identified two important differences between the *Wilko* case and the *Scherk* case. First, the statute involved in *Wilko* contained an express private remedy that had 'no statutory counterpart' in the statute involved in *Scherk, see* 417 US at 513. Although the Court noted that this difference provided a 'colorable argument' for reaching a different result, the Court did not rely on it. *Id.* at 513–14.

Instead, it based its decision on the second distinction – that the outcome in *Wilko* was governed entirely by American law, whereas, in *Scherk,* foreign rules of law would control and, if the arbitration clause were not enforced, a host of international conflict-of-laws problems would arise. The Court explained:

Alberto-Culver's contract to purchase the business entities belonging to Scherk was a truly international agreement. Alberto-Culver is an American corporation with its principal place of business and the vast bulk of its activity in this country, while Scherk is a citizen of Germany whose companies were organized under the laws of Germany and Liechtenstein. The negotiations leading to the signing of the contract in Austria and to the closing in Switzerland took place in the United States, England, and Germany, and involved consultations with legal and trademark experts from each of those countries and from Liechtenstein. Finally, and most significantly, the subject matter of the contract concerned the sale of business enterprises organized under the laws of and primarily situated in European countries, whose activities were largely, if not entirely, directed to European markets.

Such a contract involves considerations and policies significantly different from those found controlling in *Wilko*. In *Wilko*, quite apart from the arbitration provision, there was no question but that the laws of the United States generally, and the federal securities laws in particular, would govern disputes arising out of the stock purchase agreement. The parties, the negotiations, and the subject matter of the contract were all situated in this country, and no credible claim could have been entertained that any international conflict-of-laws problems would arise. In this case, by contrast, in the absence of the arbitration provision, considerable uncertainty existed at the time of the agreement, and still exists, concerning the law applicable to the resolution of disputes arising out of the contract. 417 US at 515–16 (footnote omitted).

Thus, in its opinion in *Scherk*, the Court distinguished *Wilko* because, in that case, 'no credible claim could have been entertained that any international conflict-of-laws problems would arise.' 417 US 516. That distinction fits this case precisely, since I consider it perfectly clear that the rules of American antitrust law must govern the claim of an American automobile dealer that he has been injured by an international conspiracy to restrain trade in the American automobile market.

The critical importance of the foreign law issues in *Scherk* was apparent to me even before the case reached this Court. *See* n. 12, *supra*. For that reason, it is especially distressing to find that the Court is unable to perceive why the reasoning in *Scherk* is wholly inapplicable to Soler's antitrust claims against Chrysler and Mitsubishi. The merits of those claims are controlled entirely by American law. It is true that the automobiles are manufactured in Japan and that Mitsubishi is a Japanese corporation, but the same antitrust questions would be presented if Mitsubishi were owned by two American companies instead of by one American and one Japanese partner. When Mitsubishi enters the American market and plans to engage in business in that market over a period of years, it must recognize its obligation to comply with American law and to be subject to the remedial provisions of American statutes.

The federal claim that was asserted in *Scherk,* unlike Soler's antitrust claim, had not been expressly authorized by Congress. Indeed, until this Court's recent decision in *Landreth Timber Co v Landreth,* 471 US 681 (1985), the federal cause of action asserted in *Scherk* would not have been entertained in a number of Federal Circuits, because it did not involve the kind of securities transaction that Congress intended to regulate when it enacted the Securities Exchange Act of 1934. The fraud claimed in *Scherk* was virtually identical to the breach of warranty claim; arbitration of such claims arising out of an agreement between parties of equal bargaining strength does not conflict with any significant federal policy.

In contrast, Soler's claim not only implicates our fundamental antitrust policies, *supra* at 473 US 650–657, but also should be evaluated in the light of an explicit congressional finding concerning the disparity in bargaining power between automobile manufacturers and their franchised dealers. In 1956, when Congress enacted special legislation to protect dealers from bad-faith franchise terminations, it recited its intent 'to balance the power now heavily weighted in favor of automobile manufacturers.' 70 Stat. 1125. The special federal interest in protecting automobile dealers from overreaching by car manufacturers, as well as the policies underlying the Sherman Act, underscore the folly of the Court's decision today.

V

The Court's repeated incantation of the high ideals of 'international arbitration' creates the impression that this case involves the fate of an institution designed to implement a formula for world peace. But just as it is improper to subordinate the public interest in enforcement of antitrust policy to the private interest in resolving commercial disputes, so is it equally unwise to allow a vision of world unity to distort the importance of the selection of the proper forum for resolving this dispute. Like any other mechanism for resolving controversies, international arbitration will only succeed if it is realistically limited to tasks it is capable of performing well – the prompt and inexpensive resolution of essentially contractual disputes between commercial partners. As for matters involving the political passions and the fundamental interests of nations, even the multilateral convention adopted under the auspices of the United Nations recognizes that private international arbitration is incapable of achieving satisfactory results.

In my opinion, the elected representatives of the American people would not have us dispatch an American citizen to a foreign land in search of an uncertain remedy for the violation of a public right that is protected by the Sherman Act. This is especially so when there has been no genuine bargaining over the terms of the submission, and the arbitration remedy provided has not even the most elementary guarantees of fair process. Consideration of a fully developed record by a jury, instructed in the law by a federal judge, and subject to appellate review, is a surer guide to the competitive character of a commercial practice than the practically unreviewable judgment of a private arbitrator.

Unlike the Congress that enacted the Sherman Act in 1890, the Court today does not seem to appreciate the value of economic freedom. I respectfully dissent.

 CASE

Scherk v Alberto-Culver Co, (1974), No. 73-781 US Supreme Court

Respondent, an American manufacturer based in Illinois, in order to expand its overseas operations, purchased from petitioner, a German citizen, three enterprises owned by him and organised under the laws of Germany and Liechtenstein, together with all trademark rights of these enterprises. The sales contract, which was negotiated in the United States, England, and Germany, signed in Austria, and closed in Switzerland, contained express warranties by petitioner that the trademarks were unencumbered and a clause providing that 'any controversy or claim [that] shall arise out of this agreement or the breach thereof' would be referred to arbitration before the International Chamber of Commerce in Paris, France, and that Illinois laws would govern the agreement and its interpretation and performance. Subsequently, after allegedly discovering that the trademarks were subject to substantial encumbrances, respondent offered to rescind the contract, but when petitioner refused, respondent brought suit in District Court for damages and other relief, contending that petitioner's fraudulent representations concerning the trademark rights violated 10 (b) of the Securities Exchange Act of 1934 and Rule 10b-5 promulgated thereunder. Petitioner moved to dismiss the action or alternatively to stay the action pending arbitration, but the District Court denied the motion to dismiss and, as sought by respondent, preliminarily enjoined petitioner from proceeding with arbitration, holding, in reliance on *Wilko v Swan*, 346 US 427, that the arbitration clause was unenforceable. The Court of Appeals affirmed. Held: The arbitration clause is to be respected and enforced by federal courts in accord with the explicit provisions of the United States Arbitration Act that an arbitration agreement, such as is here involved, 'shall be valid, irrevocable, and enforceable, save upon such grounds as exist at law or in equity for the revocation of any contract.' 9 U.S.C. 1, 2. *Wilko v Swan, supra*, distinguished. pp. 510–520.

(a) Since uncertainty will almost inevitably exist with respect to any contract, such as the one in question here, with substantial contacts in two or more countries, each with its own substantive laws and conflict-of-laws rules, a contractual provision specifying in advance the forum for litigating disputes and the law to be applied is an almost indispensable precondition to achieving the orderliness and predictability essential to any international business transaction. Such a provision obviates the danger that a contract dispute might be submitted to a forum hostile to the interests of one of the parties or unfamiliar with the problem area involved. pp. 515–17.

(b) In the context of an international contract, the advantages that a security buyer might possess in having a wide choice of American courts and venue in which to litigate his claims of violations of the securities laws, become chimerical, since an opposing party may by speedy resort to a foreign court block or hinder access to the American court of the buyer's choice. pp. 517–18.

(c) An agreement to arbitrate before a specified tribunal is, in effect, a specialized kind of forum-selection clause that posits not only the situs of suit but also the procedure to be used in resolving the dispute, and the invalidation of the arbitration clause in this case would not only allow respondent to repudiate its solemn promise but would, as well, reflect a 'parochial concept that all disputes must be resolved under our laws and in our courts.' *The Bremen v Zapata Off-Shore Co*, 407 US 1, 9 P. 519. 484 F.2d 611, reversed and remanded.

Stewart, J, delivered the opinion of the Court, in which Burger, C J, and Blackmun, Powell, and Rehnquist, J J, joined. Douglas, J, filed a dissenting opinion, in which Brennan, White, and Marshall, J J., joined, post, p. 521.

Robert F Hanley argued the cause for petitioner. With him on the briefs was Lynne E McNown.

Francis J Higgins argued the cause for respondent. With him on the brief was A Charles Lawrence.

Gerald Aksen argued the cause for the American Arbitration Assn. as *amicus curiae* urging reversal. With him on the brief were Whitney North

Seymour, Sol Neil Corbin, Rita E Hauser, Howard M Holtzmann, Andreas F Lowenfeld, John R Stevenson, and Rosemary S Page.

Mr Justice Stewart delivered the opinion of the Court.

Alberto-Culver Co., the respondent, is an American company incorporated in Delaware with its principal office in Illinois. It manufactures and distributes toiletries and hair products in this country and abroad. During the 1960's Alberto-Culver decided to expand its overseas operations, and as part of this program it approached the petitioner Fritz Scherk, a German citizen residing at the time of trial in Switzerland. Scherk was the owner of three interrelated business entities, organised under the laws of Germany and Liechtenstein, that were engaged in the manufacture of toiletries and the licensing of trademarks for such toiletries. An initial contact with Scherk was made by a representative of Alberto-Culver in Germany in June 1967, and negotiations followed at further meetings in both Europe and the United States during 1967 and 1968. In February 1969 a contract was signed in Vienna, Austria, which provided for the transfer of the ownership of Scherk's enterprises to Alberto-Culver, along with all rights held by these enterprises to trademarks in cosmetic goods. The contract contained a number of express warranties whereby Scherk guaranteed the sole and unencumbered ownership of these trademarks. In addition, the contract contained an arbitration clause providing that 'any controversy or claim [that] shall arise out of this agreement or the breach thereof' would be referred to arbitration before the International Chamber of Commerce in Paris, France, and that '[t]he laws of the State of Illinois, USA shall apply to and govern this agreement, its interpretation and performance.'

The closing of the transaction took place in Geneva, Switzerland, in June 1969. Nearly one year later Alberto-Culver allegedly discovered that the trademark rights purchased under the contract were subject to substantial encumbrances that threatened to give others superior rights to the trademarks and to restrict or preclude Alberto-Culver's use of them. Alberto-Culver thereupon tendered back to Scherk the property that had been transferred to it and offered to rescind the contract. Upon Scherk's refusal, Alberto-Culver commenced this action for damages and other relief in a Federal District Court in Illinois, contending that Scherk's fraudulent representations concerning the status of the trademark rights constituted violations of 10 (b) of the Securities Exchange Act of 1934, 48 Stat. 891, 15 U.S.C. 78j (b), and Rule 10b-5 promulgated thereunder, 17 CFR 240.-10b-5.

In response, Scherk filed a motion to dismiss the action for want of personal and subject-matter jurisdiction as well as on the basis of *forum non conveniens*, or, alternatively, to stay the action pending arbitration in Paris pursuant to the agreement of the parties. Alberto-Culver, in turn, opposed this motion and sought a preliminary injunction restraining the prosecution of arbitration proceedings. On December 2, 1971, the District Court denied Scherk's motion to dismiss, and, on January 14, 1972, it granted a preliminary order enjoining Scherk from proceeding with arbitration. In taking these actions the court relied entirely on this Court's decision *in Wilko v Swan*, 346 US 427, which held that an agreement to arbitrate could not preclude a buyer of a security from seeking a judicial remedy under the Securities Act of 1933, in view of the language of 14 of that Act, barring '[a]ny condition, stipulation, or provision binding any person acquiring any security to waive compliance with any provision of this subchapter . . . .' 48 Stat. 84, 15 U.S.C. 77n. The Court of Appeals for the Seventh Circuit, with one judge dissenting, affirmed, upon what it considered the controlling authority of the Wilko decision. 484 F.2d 611. Because of the importance of the question presented we granted Scherk's petition for a writ of certiorari. 414 US 1156.

I

The United States Arbitration Act, now 9 U.S.C. 1 et seq., reversing centuries of judicial hostility to arbitration agreements, was designed to allow parties to avoid 'the costliness and delays of litigation,' and to place arbitration agreements 'upon the same footing as other contracts . . . .' H. R. Rep. No. 96, 68th Cong., 1st Sess., 1, 2 (1924); see also S. Rep. No. 536, 68th Cong., 1st Sess. (1924). Accordingly, the Act provides that an arbitration agreement such as is here involved 'shall be valid, irrevocable, and enforceable, save upon such grounds as exist at law or in equity for the revocation of any contract.' 9 U.S.C. 2. 5 The Act also provides in 3 for a stay of proceedings in a case where a court is satisfied that the issue before it is arbitrable under the agreement, and 4 of the Act directs a federal court to order parties to proceed to arbitration if there has been a 'failure, neglect, or refusal' of any party to honor an agreement to arbitrate.

In *Wilko v Swan, supra*, this Court acknowledged that the Act reflects a legislative recognition of the 'desirability of arbitration as an alternative to the complications of litigation.' 346 US, at 431 , but nonetheless declined to apply the Act's provisions. That case involved an agreement between Anthony Wilko and Hayden, Stone & Co., a large brokerage firm, under which Wilko agreed to purchase on margin a number of shares of a corporation's common stock. Wilko alleged that his purchase of the stock was induced by false representations on the part of the defendant concerning the value of the shares, and he brought suit for damages under 12(2) of the Securities Act of 1933, 15

U.S.C. 77l. The defendant responded that Wilko had agreed to submit all controversies arising out of the purchase to arbitration, and that this agreement, contained in a written margin contract between the parties, should be given full effect under the Arbitration Act.

The Court found that '[t]wo policies, not easily reconcilable, are involved in this case.' 346 US, at 438 . On the one hand, the Arbitration Act stressed 'the need for avoiding the delay and expense of litigation,' id., at 431, and directed that such agreements be 'valid, irrevocable, and enforceable' in federal courts. On the other hand, the Securities Act of 1933 was '[d]esigned to protect investors' and to require 'issuers, underwriters, and dealers to make full and fair disclosure of the character of securities sold in interstate and foreign commerce and to prevent fraud in their sale,' by creating 'a special right to recover for misrepresentation . . ..' 346 US at 431 (footnote omitted). In particular, the Court noted that 14 of the Securities Act, 15 U.S.C. 77n, provides: 'Any condition, stipulation, or provision binding any person acquiring any security to waive compliance with any provision of this subchapter or of the rules and regulations of the Commission shall be void.'

The Court ruled that an agreement to arbitrate 'is a "stipulation," and [that] the right to select the judicial forum is the kind of "provision" that cannot be waived under 14 of the Securities Act.' 346 US at 434–435. Thus, Wilko's advance agreement to arbitrate any disputes subsequently arising out of his contract to purchase the securities was unenforceable under the terms of 14 of the Securities Act of 1933.

Alberto-Culver, relying on this precedent, contends that the District Court and Court of Appeals were correct in holding that its agreement to arbitrate disputes arising under the contract with Scherk is similarly unenforceable in view of its contentions that Scherk's conduct constituted violations of the Securities Exchange Act of 1934 and rules promulgated thereunder. For the reasons that follow, we reject this contention and hold that the provisions of the Arbitration Act cannot be ignored in this case.

At the outset, a colorable argument could be made that even the semantic reasoning of the Wilko opinion does not control the case before us. Wilko concerned a suit brought under 12 (2) of the Securities Act of 1933, which provides a defrauded purchaser with the 'special right' of a private remedy for civil liability, 346 US at 431. There is no statutory counterpart of 12(2) in the Securities Exchange Act of 1934, and neither 10(b) of that Act nor Rule 10b-5 speaks of a private remedy to redress violations of the kind alleged here. While federal case law has established that 10(b) and

Rule 10b-5 create an implied private cause of action, see L. Loss, Securities Regulation 3869-3873 (1969) and cases cited therein; cf. *J I Case Co v Borak*, 377 US 426, the Act itself does not establish the 'special right' that the Court in *Wilko* found significant. Furthermore, while both the Securities Act of 1933 and the Securities Exchange Act of 1934 contain sections barring waiver of compliance with any 'provision' of the respective Acts, certain of the 'provisions' of the 1933 Act that the Court held could not be waived by Wilko's agreement to arbitrate find no counterpart in the 1934 Act. In particular, the Court in *Wilko* noted that the jurisdictional provision of the 1933 Act, 15 U.S.C. 77v, allowed a plaintiff to bring suit 'in any court of competent jurisdiction – federal or state – and removal from a state court is prohibited.' 346 US at 431. The analogous provision of the 1934 Act, by contrast, provides for suit only in the federal district courts that have 'exclusive jurisdiction,' 15 U.S.C. 78aa, thus significantly restricting the plaintiff's choice of forum.

Accepting the premise, however, that the operative portions of the language of the 1933 Act relied upon in *Wilko* are contained in the Securities Exchange Act of 1934, the respondent's reliance on *Wilko* in this case ignores the significant and, we find, crucial differences between the agreement involved in *Wilko* and the one signed by the parties here. Alberto-Culver's contract to purchase the business entities belonging to Scherk was a truly international agreement. Alberto-Culver is an American corporation with its principal place of business and the vast bulk of its activity in this country, while Scherk is a citizen of Germany whose companies were organised under the laws of Germany and Liechtenstein. The negotiations leading to the signing of the contract in Austria and to the closing in Switzerland took place in the United States, England, and Germany, and involved consultations with legal and trademark experts from each of those countries and from Liechtenstein. Finally, and most significantly, the subject matter of the contract concerned the sale of business enterprises organised under the laws of and primarily situated in European countries, whose activities were largely, if not entirely, directed to European markets.

Such a contract involves considerations and policies significantly different from those found controlling in Wilko. In Wilko, quite apart from the arbitration provision, there was no question but that the laws of the United States generally, and the federal securities laws in particular, would govern disputes arising out of the stock-purchase agreement. The parties, the negotiations, and the subject matter of the contract were all situated in this country, and no credible claim could have been entertained that any international conflict-of-laws problems would arise. In this case, by contrast, in the absence of the arbitration provision considerable uncertainty existed at the time of the agreement, and still exists, concerning the law applicable to the resolution of disputes arising out of the contract.

Such uncertainty will almost inevitably exist with respect to any contract touching two or more countries, each with its own substantive laws and conflict-of-laws rules. A contractual provision specifying in advance the forum in which disputes shall be litigated and the law to be applied is, therefore, an almost indispensable precondition to achievement of the orderliness and predictability essential to any international business transaction. Furthermore, such a provision obviates the danger that a dispute under the agreement might be submitted to a forum hostile to the interests of one of the parties or unfamiliar with the problem area involved.

A parochial refusal by the courts of one country to enforce an international arbitration agreement would not only frustrate these purposes, but would invite unseemly and mutually destructive jockeying by the parties to secure tactical litigation advantages. In the present case, for example, it is not inconceivable that if Scherk had anticipated that Alberto-Culver would be able in this country to enjoin resort to arbitration he might have sought an order in France or some other country enjoining Alberto-Culver from proceeding with its litigation in the United States. Whatever recognition the courts of this country might ultimately have granted to the order of the foreign court, the dicey atmosphere of such a legal no-man's-land would surely damage the fabric of international commerce and trade, and imperil the willingness and ability of businessmen to enter into international commercial agreements.

The exception to the clear provisions of the Arbitration Act carved out by Wilko is simply inapposite to a case such as the one before us. In Wilko the Court reasoned that '[w]hen the security buyer, prior to any violation of the Securities Act, waives his right to sue in courts, he gives up more than would a participant in other business transactions. The security buyer has a wider choice of courts and venue. He thus surrenders one of the advantages the Act gives him . . . .' 346 US at 435. In the context of an international contract, however, these advantages become chimerical since, as indicated above, an opposing party may by speedy resort to a foreign court block or hinder access to the American court of the purchaser's choice.

Two Terms ago in *The Bremen v Zapata Off-Shore Co*, 407 US 1 , we rejected the doctrine that a forum-selection clause of a contract, although voluntarily adopted by the parties, will not be respected in a suit brought in the United States 'unless the selected state would provide a more convenient forum than the state in which suit is brought.' Id., at 7. Rather, we concluded that a 'forum clause should control absent a strong showing that it should be set aside.' Id., at 15. We noted that:

> much uncertainty and possibly great inconvenience to both parties could arise if a suit could be maintained in any jurisdiction in which an accident might occur or if jurisdiction were left to any place [where personal or in rem jurisdiction might be established]. The elimination of all such uncertainties by agreeing in advance on a forum acceptable to both parties is an indispensable element in international trade, commerce, and contracting. ibid., at 13–14.

An agreement to arbitrate before a specified tribunal is, in effect, a specialised kind of forum-selection clause that posits not only the situs of suit but also the procedure to be used in resolving the dispute. The invalidation of such an agreement in the case before us would not only allow the respondent to repudiate its solemn promise but would, as well, reflect a 'parochial concept that all disputes must be resolved under our laws and in our courts. . ..We cannot have trade and commerce in world markets and international waters exclusively on our terms, governed by our laws, and resolved in our courts.' Id., at 9.

For all these reasons we hold that the agreement of the parties in this case to arbitrate any dispute arising out of their international commercial transaction is to be respected and enforced by the federal courts in accord with the explicit provisions of the Arbitration Act.

Accordingly, the judgment of the Court of Appeals is reversed and the case is remanded to that court with directions to remand to the District Court for further proceedings consistent with this opinion.

It is so ordered.

 CASE

ICC Interim Award in Case Nr. 6097 (1989)

Original: German

Arbitrability of related claims concerning alleged patent infringement and breach of license agreement/ Interaction of Japanese law governing contract and West German law applicable to patent issues/ Application of Japanese legal principle favouring arbitration, resulting in broad interpretation of parties' arbitration clause/ Ability of parties to define scope of Arbitral

Tribunal's jurisdiction/ Patent infringement claims held arbitrable inter parties/Inapplicability of arbitrators' decision to third parties' rights; inability of arbitrators to declare patent invalid *erga omnes* under German law/ Patent holder's rights to enter into agreements concerning exploitation of the patent.

[The dispute between claimant (a Japanese company) and defendant (a company incorporated in the FRG) arose in connection with two licensing contracts for the exploitation of industrial patents owned by defendant. The arbitration clause relating to these contracts provided that:

> All disputes, controversies or differences which may arise between the parties hereto, out of or in relation to or in connection with this Agreement, or for the breach thereof, shall be finally settled by arbitration pursuant to the Rules of Conciliation and Arbitration of the International Chamber of Commerce in Paris. The award of the Court of Arbitration shall be final and binding.

In the Terms of Reference, the parties affirmed that the arbitrators had been nominated and confirmed according to the ICC Rules. They also affirmed that they had drafted a valid arbitration clause and selected Zurich as the seat of arbitration and the site of any hearings. Furthermore, they agreed that their contract should be interpreted according to Japanese law, and that the laws in force in the Federal Republic of Germany should be applied with respect to the alleged infringement of industrial property rights and any resulting legal and contractual consequences. They also agreed that the arbitral procedure would be governed by the Swiss Concordat.]

The Arbitral Tribunal also has jurisdiction to rule on claims based on the infringement of patents since these are grounded in facts alleged by claimant and already set out above. As already mentioned, the parties did not restrict the jurisdiction of the Arbitral Tribunal to certain limited questions of law, but rather submitted for decision their respective positions as to certain facts underlying their dispute, as listed in the arbitration clause. Thus, as regards a factual situation alleged by claimant which presents itself as a dispute arising directly or indirectly from the contract, the intent of the parties is that such a case be considered in its entirety by the Arbitral Tribunal. The question of determining the precise legal grounds on which claims arising from such a situation can be based does not affect the jurisdiction of the Arbitral Tribunal. It would be contrary to the meaning and purpose of these arbitral proceedings to divide jurisdiction according to the different legal aspects of a single alleged factual situation and to declare that the Arbitral Tribunal would only have jurisdiction over claims based on breach of contract while national courts would have jurisdiction over claims grounded in law (such as those alleging patent infringement).

Such a bifurcation of jurisdiction would, in particular, contradict the common intent expressed by both parties in the arbitration clause. In listing the disputes to be submitted to the Arbitral Tribunal, the parties indicated that they wished it to consider a very wide range of claims. They even went so far as to call upon the Arbitral Tribunal to settle not only actual disputes but also 'controversies' and other 'differences', even if these are only indirectly related to the contract. The arbitration clause thus has a very broad scope. This being so, any causal link between the dispute or the difference alleged and the 1981 and 1986 contracts is a sufficient basis for the Arbitral Tribunal's jurisdiction. This very broad provision has its origin in a principle of Japanese law, which favours arbitration over recourse to the national courts in the settlement of disputes (see Raidl, *Vertragsrecht und Vertragswirklichkeit in Japan*, Zeitschrift für Rechtsvergleichung 1977, 180, 1985 s). Takeyoshi Kawashima expresses this concept in the following words: 'when problems arise, it is far better to discuss the problem in good faith, to calm over-heated spirits and to seek a harmonious solution' (. . .) 'the parties prefer to reach an amicable settlement, a solution that is also recognized in Japanese law and frequently made use of.' (Vertragliches Rechtsbewusstsein in Japan, *Schriftenreihe Grundprobleme des Privatrechts*, a Japanese publication in German, published by Gottfried Baumgärtel, (ed.) Carl Heymanns, 1985, pp 119–22). On the Law and legal principles in Japan, Rahn writes (GRUR Int. 1979, 491, 497):

> Thus, even if they scrupulously comply with legal formalities, the Japanese currently have a tendency to leave the Jaw aside and to settle their private problems personally. Even in business, legal relations are often merged into broader personal relations. (. . .) The merging of business contracts with private relationships makes it possible for the parties not to be tied by rigid rules and to adapt flexibly to changes in circumstances.

In his expert opinion, relied upon by claimant, X reaches the conclusion that, given the presence of an arbitration clause, a division of legal claims between national courts and arbitral tribunals based on a distinction between those allegations flowing from a licensing agreement and those claims related to possible patent infringement

> would only lead to the devaluation and rejection of the social function of arbitral proceedings and would be contrary to the fundamental purpose of the law, which is to promote, wherever possible, the settlement of disputes by means of a procedure based on an agreement between the parties concerned. The law clearly states that even if a

party invokes such a division of jurisdiction, the arbitrators are authorised to proceed with the arbitration and to render an award (Code of Civil Procedure, art. 797).

By adding to these considerations the principle of good faith and fair dealing which appears in § 1 sub-para 2 of the Japanese Civil Code and exhibits a close resemblance to German law (see Masamichi Okuda, *Civil Law and Civil Case Law in Japan since the Introduction of European Legal Principles in the 19th Century, Schriftenreihe Grundprobleme des Privatrechts*, above, pp 1 *et seq.*), it follows that in the present case, keeping in mind the Japanese legal principle described above, the parties have given the Arbitral Tribunal broad jurisdiction, as the very wording of the arbitration clause clearly shows. The parties have thus agreed that the Arbitral Tribunal is equally competent to rule on claims based on alleged patent infringements brought by the claimant on the basis of the same facts, and which, in the claimant's eyes, also amount to a breach of contract. This is a dispute arising out of or, at very least, linked, to the contract ('in connection with the Agreements'). The intent of the parties to resolve disputes concerning alleged infringement of the patents through arbitration is apparent in the obligation undertaken by defendant in the 1981 Contract cited above, in which it agreed to use the claimant's patents only within a framework defined by the claimant and not to involve itself in areas beyond those covered by the license agreements. Such a provision can be explained by claimant's commitments vis-à-vis other licenses, and non-compliance with this clause gives rise to a typical dispute between contract partners. However, given that a violation of the subject matter and territorial restrictions on the right to exploit a patent may be construed as a patent infringement as well as a breach of contract, according to accepted patent law principles (as provided in the German law 1981 on patents, § 15 sub-para 2, 2nd sentence), it should be accepted that the Arbitral Tribunal has jurisdiction to rule on the validity of purported infringements of patents that are based on the factual situation alleged by the claimant.

The contractual claims which are the subject matter of the present arbitral proceedings, namely those arising from an alleged breach of contract and those based on alleged infringements of claimant's patents, are objectively capable of submission to arbitration within the meaning of article 5 of the Swiss Concordat on arbitral jurisdiction. The parties are thus as free to rely on such claims as they would be if a suit based on them had been filed in a national court.

This question should be considered in light of the substantive law applicable to the arbitration clause (*Rüede/ Hadenfeldt, Schweizerisches Schiedsgerichtsrecht*, 1980, § II, 3 a; Pfaff, *Grenzbewegungen der Schiedsfühigkeit – Patentnichtigkeit im Schiedsverfahren, Festschrift für Nagel*, 1987, pp 278 *et seq.*, 281). Pursuant to the parties' agreement, Japanese law is applicable to contractual issues and West German law to patent issues. With regard to the disputes covered by the arbitration clause, neither of the two applicable national law restricts the parties' power to submit such matters to arbitration, nor does either grant sole jurisdiction over such disputes to national courts of law.

Claims based on alleged patent infringements are no exception to this rule. Under German law, the parties are free to decide how such disputes should be resolved, including the possibility of settling such claims by means of a private arrangement, as long as such arrangement does not violate competition law. The validity of arbitral jurisdiction over patent infringement cases is generally accepted under German l aw (see e.g., BGHZ 3, 193 – *Tauchpumpe*; Chrocziel, 'Gewerbliche Schutzrechte als Gegenstand eines Schiedsverfahrens' in *Festschrift für Albert Preu*, pp 177–90; Schweyer, 'Patentnichtigkeit und Patentverletzung und deren Beurteilung durch internationale private Schiedsgerichte nach dem Recht des Schweiz, Deutschlands, Italiens und Frankreichs' in *Rechtswissenschafteliche Forschung und Entwicklung*, published by von Lehmann, vol. 15, 1981, p. 114; Benkard, PatG/GebrMG, 8 ed, § 14 Rn. 133; Reimer, PatG/GebrMG, 33 ed, § 5 1, no. 96, 104).

Within the framework of its interpretation of the arbitration clause presented, the Arbitral Tribunal decides, that in light of the Japanese legal principle described above, it has also been empowered by the parties to consider the claims concerning the legal validity of the patents referred to by claimant that the defendant has put forward within the context of its defence. For the sake of legal certainty, the parties agreed to authorise the Arbitral Tribunal to also settle this issue in this interim award. They had the right to grant such jurisdiction to the Arbitral Tribunal under article 11 of the ICC Rules of Arbitration and articles 1 para. 2 and 24 para.1 of the Swiss Concordat on arbitral jurisdiction.

Given the preponderance of the legal principle discussed above and the general rejection of contentious means of dispute resolution in Japan (See Raidl, Kawashima and Rahn, previously cited) as well as the opinion of Y [Japanese expert] on the arbitration clause, the Arbitral Tribunal is led to the conclusion that this clause should be interpreted broadly, in accordance with the Japanese legal principle. According to Y (above mentioned opinion), all disputes arising in connection with the contract should be resolved in the arbitral award, as the arbitrators are free 'to apply a wide range of logical principles'. The Arbitral Tribunal infers from Y's analysis, and in light of the above-mentioned doctrine, that the arbitration clause also encompasses the defendant's defences, which are directly related to the licensing agreement, and claimant's allegations that arise 'in connection with the agreement'. It goes without saying that the Arbitral Tribunal must take into account all of defendant's allegations in so far as it has jurisdiction to rule on claimant's claims. But here we are faced with a special case, since defendant argues that at the time of registration, the technical training on which patent XOO1 was based could not validly be protected because of its insufficient novelty, and that claimant cannot therefore assert any claim for that patent's infringement. Under German law, which is applicable to this question, a patent must be recognised as valid unless it has been declared null and void by the Federal Patent Court or the Federal Supreme Court. In the absence of such a declaration, no party can assert the invalidity of a patent. Even a court called upon to resolve claims arising from such a patent must assume its validity. Given this West German legal doctrine, the defence advanced by the defendant would not be considered in a lawsuit on patent infringement before an ordinary West German court; in such a case the court would advise the defendant to bring a separate action seeking to declare the patent invalid.

Nevertheless, the situation in this case is different. In light of the Japanese legal principle discussed above, which is decisive for the interpretation of the arbitration clause, the parties sought to confer broad jurisdiction upon the Arbitral Tribunal. Their common intent was, as stated in the clause, that the arbitral award should be 'final and binding' (see also art. 24. 1 of the ICC Rules of Arbitration). By using these words they meant not only that the decision should be formally definitive, but also and above all, keeping in mind the Japanese legal principle, that all disputes in connection with the 1981 and 1986 contracts should be resolved in the arbitral proceeding, to the exclusion of any litigation. This interpretation implies that the parties intended to exclude the possibility that the Arbitral Tribunal would have to stay its proceedings to allow the defendant to bring an action to declare the patent invalid before the Federal Patent Court in Munich. Such parallel proceedings before arbitral and judicial tribunals would be contrary to both the intent of the parties, as expressed in the arbitration clause, and the Japanese legal principle favouring arbitration, since experience tells us that they would delay the outcome of the arbitral proceedings by five years or more. It would be unacceptable to leave the parties in a state of uncertainty with regard to the outcome of the dispute for that long and such a delay would prejudice their legal rights. Such a result would be in obvious contradiction with the meaning and the purpose of these arbitral proceedings and arbitration generally. (. . .)

That is why the Arbitral Tribunal is convinced that the parties, in light of circumstances and of the Japanese conception of arbitration clauses and arbitral proceedings, have clearly given it complete jurisdiction to rule on defendant's objections to the legal validity of claimant's patents. In order to eliminate any remaining doubt, it should be specified that this power to decide does not affect the formal validity of the patent registered in West Germany by means of a sovereign governmental act, and that it will carry no consequences vis-à-vis third parties.

By allocating it this jurisdiction, the parties wanted to give the Arbitral Tribunal, in accordance with the meaning and purpose of arbitral proceedings, the possibility to settle this dispute *inter partes* in a simple, quick and definitive way.

This agreement between the parties can also be submitted to arbitration within the meaning of article 5 of the Swiss Concordat on arbitral proceedings, since claimant, as owner of the patents, is free to make use of its material rights to the patents and thus to enter into agreements in this regard, including those involving a commercial exchange. Confirmation of the protectability of the material covered by the patents, in so far as this is being questioned by defendant, is a necessary first step in the process in light of the abovementioned considerations, in so far as the legal underpinnings of claimant's allegations must be determined before a decision on their merits can be made. The existence of the rights on which claimant has based its allegations should thus be confirmed by the Arbitral Tribunal, either on its own motion or in response to defendant's reasoned request. It is true that in the case of patents one must keep on mind the principle noted above, by which only a national court having jurisdiction over the matter can invalidate a patent *erga omnes*. Nonetheless, this principle cannot be relied on to allow a defendant in arbitral proceedings to challenge the underlying validity of the patent asserted by a claimant, without having to bring an action seeking to declare the patent invalid before a competent national court. That is why in some countries, such as Switzerland and the United States, arbitrators are allowed to rule, even explicitly, on the possible invalidity of a patent. But the Arbitral Tribunal in this case does not claim such jurisdiction for itself.

As we have noted, it is well established under German substantive law (cf. Pfaff; Schweyer, pp 116–37 *et seq.*; Schlosser, no. 318; Chrocziel above, p. 191) that it is not possible for the parties to empower an Arbitral Tribunal to invalidate a patent. However, a growing number of leading scholars have challenged this restrictive principle in the literature, arguing that it can no longer be supported and that it is therefore unacceptable for an Arbitral Tribunal to rule on the validity, as between the parties to an arbitration, of a patent invoked by a claimant (Pfaff, pp.186 *et seq*; Schlosser, no 319; also

Festschrift für Bühlow, pp 192–3 and *Festschrift für Fasching,* p 432 and sources cited therein; Chrocziel). The Arbitral Tribunal in this case shares this view, but as already made clear, it in no way claims such jurisdiction; it merely believes itself to be entitled to confirm whether the claimant can substantiate the allegations based on its patents despite defendant's objections, or whether defendant can prove that the material covered by the patents in question was not in fact patentable (for a similar argument, see Stauder, 'Gerichtliche Zuständigkeit für Klagen aus ausländischen Patenten', in *Gewerblicher Rechtsschutz –Urheberrecht –Wirtschaftsrecht, Mitarbeiterschrift für Eugen Ulmer,* Cologne, pp 197, 509 *et seq.,* 514 and sources cited therein). The Arbitral Tribunal believes that the parties have entrusted it with the task of examining this issue by using their right to enter into an agreement as to the extent of the protection provided by a patent. In West Germany, The Federal Supreme Court has recognised (cf. BGH GRUR 1962, 294 – *Hafendrehkran*; cf. also BGH GRUR 1979, 309 *et seq.* – *Auspuffkanal für Schaltgase* – with note by Eisenführ pp 312–13 – Benkard, § 81 p. 333, and sources cited therein) that the rights flowing from a patent can be the subject of a commercial transaction and thus of a contract. In a dispute concerning the infringement or invalidity of a patent, the owner of the patent at issue may wholly or partially waive its rights against the other party; it may also undertake to make this waiver or restriction known to the Patent Office; transfer the right to exploit the patent to the other party either in exchange for payment or free of charge; commit itself not to exercise all or part of its rights; sell the patent in whole or in part; assign its total or partial rights to the patent's exploitation to a third party, or give it as security. The patent holder is thus free to transfer his material rights under a patent to the same degree as those to any other property. Under German law, only decisions concerning the formal validity of a patent are subject to the jurisdiction of a specific national court. Consequently, the right to contractually transfer (a commercial transaction is also a contract) legal rights under a patent can be used by the parties to an arbitration, in that they may decide to assign this contractual power to the Arbitral Tribunal. In principle, therefore, there is no legal obstacle that bars an Arbitral Tribunal, thus empowered by the parties, to rule, as a preliminary matter, on the material validity of a patent.

Consequently, the Arbitral Tribunal is of the opinion that, pursuant to the agreement by which it has been given jurisdiction, it can arbitrate the issue raised by defendant's challenge to the material validity of intellectual property rights invoked by claimant, and issue a ruling on this question that is binding *inter partes.*

EXERCISE 5 – THE ARBITRATION AGREEMENT V – SEMINAR

The Ruritanian company Gold and Minerals Ltd (G&M) is active primarily in the domestic mining sector in Ruritania. It is currently negotiating a sales contract to sell mining equipment to FZG International (FZG), a large group of companies in the energy sector. FZG is incorporated in Farawaystan, is partially State-owned and allegedly controlled by the President of Farawaystan and/or members of his family.

The parties have never done business before, but G&M is looking to expand internationally and might be interested in a long-term relationship with FZG, since Farawaystan might be an interesting future market for G&M.

The contract is almost finalised and drafted in English. Under the contract, G&M undertakes to deliver equipment to FZG continually during the life span of a ten-year-long mining project in Farawaystan. FZG undertakes to pay $750,000 annually during the ten years, subject to certain stipulated requirements that the delivered equipment has to meet.

A couple of issues remain to be agreed upon, including the arbitration clause and the applicable law.

Groups 1 and 2
You represent G&M. Draft an arbitration clause to be inserted into the contract.

Groups 3 and 4
You represent FZG. Draft an arbitration clause to be inserted into the contract.

Each group shall draft its clause independently and send it to the other participants on the day before the seminar, as well as bring it to the seminar. During the seminar the four draft clauses will be the basis for the discussion.

4

The arbitrators

 DISCUSSION QUESTIONS

Problem 1

In his Acceptance and Confirmation Form, arbitrator Mr Senior of law firm Senior & Associates LLP disclosed the following:

> The law firm has/have had matters for [respondent] and its subsidiaries and has/have had matters against [respondent] and its subsidiaries. These matters are not handled/ have not been handled by undersigned but by other persons at the firm.

Mr Senior was based in Paris, however the matters referred to in the disclosure had been handled by colleagues in Dubai, Hong Kong and San Francisco. Following the disclosure by Mr Senior, his appointment as arbitrator was challenged by the claimant. In an ensuing comment, Mr Senior held *inter alia* that the circumstance that Senior & Associates had acted both for and against the respondent and its subsidiaries demonstrated a balance in relation to the respondent.

Make a reasoned (oral) decision on the challenge, followed by a general discussion.

Problem 2

The Korean company Y&Y, represented by Mr Beta, a partner with the firm Epsilon law, initiated arbitration in 2010 against a US corporation. Y&Y appointed Ms Delta as its arbitrator. In her confirmation of acceptance, Ms Delta made the following disclosure:

(a) She had been a partner with Epsilon law until 2000, where Mr Beta was one of her assistants and also assisted Ms Delta in an arbitration case referred to her by the founder of one of the law firms currently representing the respondent.

(b) Ms Delta was involved in a court case during the period of 1998–2005 concerning a challenge of an arbitral award. Mr Beta assisted her in this challenge and has since 2005 been counsel in matters relating to the case.

After having been so requested by the respondent, Ms Delta submitted further information regarding her working relationship with Mr Beta. The respondent subsequently challenged Ms Delta. In its submission, claimant points to the case mentioned in (b) above, the fact that Ms Delta has acted as co-counsel with Mr Beta for more than eight years, the fact that Mr Beta continues to work on the same case, that Ms Delta was instructed to assist with an oral hearing as late as in 2009 in relation to the case, and that Ms Delta provides ongoing advice to Mr Beta. The claimant argues that the relationship appears to be more akin to that of a professional mentor that provides advice, counsel and professional guidance to a colleague she has known for more than 15 years.

Make a reasoned (oral) decision on the challenge, followed by a general discussion.

Problem 3

Shortly after receiving the final award in a case against its former joint-venture partner in Russia, the Dutch party ABC learned that the arbitrator appointed by the respondent in the now concluded case, Ms Busy, also had been appointed by the respondent in a number of other arbitrations. Further research and disclosure by the arbitrator revealed that Ms Busy over the past four years had been appointed by the respondent in five different proceedings. Furthermore, the law firm representing the respondent in the case against ABC had appointed Ms Busy in eight different proceedings over the past five years. In addition, Ms Busy had appeared as chairperson in two cases in which the same law firm had been involved in the past two years. ABC concluded that it had enough ground to challenge the award.

Make a reasoned (oral) decision on the challenge, followed by a general discussion.

Problem 4

In an investor-state arbitration, the respondent State challenges both the arbitrator appointed by the investor and the chairman appointed by agreement between the two party-appointed arbitrators.

When the tribunal is in place, but before the parties have exchanged briefs, the State alleges, inter alia, that both challenged arbitrators have 'preconceived opinions'. In the arbitration, the investor has alleged that the State's judiciary mistreated the investor in a manner that amounts to denial of justice under international law, which is expected to become a key question in the arbitration.

The arbitrator appointed by the investor, Mr X, has previously sat on another tribunal, in an arbitration between different parties and based on a different treaty. In that case, the concept of denial of justice was at the centre of the award, which was rendered by a majority including Mr X. In addition, Mr X has spoken at a large arbitration conference about the concept of denial of justice. The State argues that at both these instances, Mr X has demonstrated a very broad view of the concept, which shows that he cannot be impartial in this case.

The chairperson, Ms Z, has written the leading commentary on the concept of denial of justice in international law, published by a large academic publishing company. In the book, the State argues, Ms Z extensively discussed denial of justice in a way that systematically 'conforms to the interests of an investor, but not to a state'. Ms. Z has also defended her analyses in other cases, as both sole arbitrator and legal expert. Viewed together, the State feels that these factors make it clear that Ms Z cannot be open-minded and that the state has 'no chance' of convincing Ms Z of its view.

Make a reasoned (oral) decision on the challenge, followed by a general discussion.

EXERCISE 7 – THE ARBITRATORS II – MINI MOCK ARBITRATION

 CASE

Case 1

Claimant

The company AB (CAB), Sweden.

Respondent

The Association A/S (AAS), Denmark

Claimant CAB is represented in this SCC arbitration by advokat Smart, partner with the law firm Sharp & Associates in Malmö.

Each party has appointed a co-arbitrator, and the two co-arbitrators have since, in accordance with the parties' agreement, jointly appointed a chairperson advokat Solid.

Advokat Solid is a partner with Svensson Law AB in Stockholm. After the appointment, advokat Solid discloses to the parties that claimant's counsel is a former colleague of his at Svensson law AB. However, in the opinion of the chairperson, this does not prevent him from confirming his impartiality and independence in the present arbitration.

The employment of advokat Smart at Svensson Law ended three years and two months before the appointment of advokat Solid as chairperson in the present arbitration.

Respondent AAS challenges advokat Solid, arguing that the fact that advokat Solid has been a colleague to advokat Smart for eight years raises reasonable doubts as regards advokat Solid's impartiality and independence. Respondent relies on Swedish case law in support of its challenge, and stresses the importance of applying objective criteria for the assessment of impartiality.

Claimant CAB objects to the challenge. Claimant notes that a disclosed circumstance should not automatically be deemed to constitute a conflict. Furthermore, claimant refers to IBA Guidelines in support of its request to dismiss the challenge.

The arbitrator sees no grounds for the challenge and decides to stay in the case, leaving it up to the SCC to decide the challenge.

GROUP

Group 1

Discuss the case and comment specifically on the appropriate time frame that should pass before an arbitrator may be able to accept an appointment in a case where a former colleague is acting as counsel.

Group 2

You are the SCC. Decide the challenge.

Group 3

You represent the respondent. Argue that the challenge shall be sustained, and advokat Solid removed from the case.

Group 4

You represent the claimant. Argue that the challenge shall be dismissed.

 CASE

Case 2

Claimant

Going for Victory Ltd (GVL), United States

Respondent

Smith & Jones AB (S&J), Sweden

In late 2010, claimant GVL initiated SCC arbitration against S&J under a share purchase agreement (the SPA).

Earlier the same year, another party of the SPA had also filed a request for arbitration against S&J. The week before GVL's filing, this case had been referred to a tribunal under the UNCITRAL Rules.

In the now second case under the SPA, Claimant GVL appoints advokat Happy as co-arbitrator.

At the same time, advokat Happy is sitting as an arbitrator also in the first case under the SPA, having been so appointed by the claimant in that case.

Respondent S&J challenges the arbitrator appointed by the claimant, holding that it would be improper to appoint the same arbitrator in two proceedings. First, as the disputes are related the arbitrator may form opinions in one case that unduly affects him in the adjudication of the other case. Second, respondent claims that claimants in both cases are so closely affiliated that that this will in effect constitute a risk for breach of confidentiality between the two separate proceedings, to the potential detriment of respondent.

Claimant GVL opposes the challenge. According to claimant, the mere fact that the issues in the respective disputes are identical, but for the identity of the claimants, does not create any justifiable doubts as to the impartiality or independence of the arbitrator.

The arbitrator does not provide any comments.

 GROUP

Group 1
You are the appointing authority. Decide the challenge.

Group 2
You represent the claimant. Argue that the challenge shall be dismissed

Group 3
Discuss the case and comment specifically on the appropriate time frame that should pass before an arbitrator may be able to accept an appointment in a case where a former colleague is acting as counsel.

Group 4
You represent the respondent. Argue that the challenge shall be sustained, and that advokat Happy shall be released from the case.

5
Applicable law

 DISCUSSION QUESTIONS

Problem 1
To what extent must arbitrators apply so-called mandatory rules of:

(a) *lex contractus* and;
(b) other national jurisdictions?

Problem 2
To what extent must arbitrators take account of the public policy of:

(a) *lex contractus*, and;
(b) other national jurisdictions and/or of international public policy?

Problem 3
Review the *BP Petroleum v Libya* award. What law did the arbitrator apply? Was it the right law?

Problem 4
Explain the difference, if any, between public international law, international development law and the general principles of law. Is there a role for the application of (public) international law in international commercial arbitration?

 CASE

BP v Libyan Arab Republic

Part I
Constitution of the Tribunal

The respondent on 7 December 1971 passed a law (the 'BP Nationalisation Law') providing that the activities of the claimant in Oil Concession 65 were nationalised. Concession 65 comprises an area of over 8,000 sq kms in the heart of the Sarir desert. The claimant, by a letter to the respondent dated 11 December 1971, addressed to the Minister of Petroleum, Tripoli, which was delivered on the same day, protested against the action taken by the respondent and took steps to institute arbitration proceedings pursuant to clause 28 of the Concession Agreement of 1966, as amended, between the respondent and the claimant (the 'BP Concession'). The said clause 28 provides as follows:

1. If at any time during or after the currency of this Concession any difference or dispute shall arise between the Government and the Company concerning the interpretation or performance hereof, or anything herein contained or in connection herewith, or the rights and liabilities of either of such parties hereunder and if such parties should fail to settle such difference or dispute by agreement, the same shall, failing any agreement to settle it any, other way, be referred to two Arbitrators, one of whom shall be appointed by each such party, and an Umpire who shall be appointed by the Arbitrators immediately after they are themselves appointed.

   In the event of the Arbitrators failing to agree upon an Umpire within 60 days from the date of the appointment of the second Arbitrator, either of such parties may request the President or, if the President is a national of Libya or of the Country where the Company was incorporated, the Vice-President, of the International Court of Justice to appoint the Umpire.

2. The institution of Arbitration proceedings shall take place upon the receipt by one of such parties of a written request for Arbitration from the other which request shall specify the matter in respect of which Arbitration is required and name the Arbitrator appointed by the party requiring Arbitration.

3. The party receiving the request shall within 90 days of such receipt appoint its Arbitrator and notify this appointment to the other of such parties failing which such other party may request the President, or in the case referred to in paragraph 1 above, the Vice-President, of the International Court of Justice to appoint a Sole Arbitrator and the decision of a Sole Arbitrator so appointed shall be binding upon both such parties.

4. If the Arbitrators appointed by such parties fail to agree upon a decision within six months of the institution of Arbitration proceedings or any such Arbitrator becomes unable or unwilling to perform his functions at any time within such period, the Umpire shall then enter upon the Arbitration. The decision of the Arbitrators, or in case of a difference of opinion between them the decision of the Umpire, shall be final. If the Umpire or the Sole Arbitrator, as the case may be, is unable or unwilling to enter upon or complete the Arbitration, then, unless such parties otherwise agree, a substitute will be appointed at the request of either such party by the President, or, in the case referred to in paragraph 1 above, the Vice-President, of the International Court of Justice.

5. The Umpire however appointed or the Sole Arbitrator shall not be either a national of Libya or of the country in which the Company or any Company which directly or indirectly controls it was incorporated nor shall he be or have been in

the employ of either of such parties or of the Government of Libya or of any such Country as aforesaid. The Arbitrators or, in the event they fail to agree within 60 days from the date of appointment of the second Arbitrator, then the Umpire, or, in the event a Sole Arbitrator is appointed, then the Sole Arbitrator, shall determine the applicability of this Clause and the procedure to be followed in the Arbitration.

In giving a decision the Arbitrators, the Umpire or the Sole Arbitrator, as the case may be, shall specify an adequate period of time during which the party to the difference or dispute against whom the decision is given shall conform to the decision, and such party shall not be in default if that party has conformed to the decision prior to the expiry of that period.

6. The place of Arbitration shall be such as may be agreed by such parties and in default of agreement between them within 120 days from the date of institution of Arbitration proceedings as specified in paragraph 2 above, shall be determined by the Arbitrators or, in the event the Arbitrators fail to agree within 60 days from the date of appointment of the second Arbitrator, then by the Umpire or, in the event a Sole Arbitrator is appointed, then by the Sole Arbitrator.

7. This Concession shall be governed by and interpreted in accordance with the principles of law of Libya common to the principles of international law and in the absence of such common principles then by and in accordance with the general principles of law, including such of those principles as may have been applied by international tribunals.

8. The costs of the Arbitration shall be borne by such parties in such proportion and manner as may be provided in the decision.

The full text of the claimant's letter of 11 December 1971 is set out below; it appears from it that, in conformity with paragraph 2 of clause 28 quoted above, the letter did specify the matter in respect of which arbitration was required, and the claimant therein did name an arbitrator appointed by it:

We refer to the action taken by the Government of the Libyan Arab Republic on December 7th 1971 by the issue of the Law which, inter alia, provides for the nationalisation of the activities of the BP Exploration Company (Libya) Ltd in Petroleum Concession Number 65' and for the vesting of 'all the funds, rights, assets and shares related to said activities' in the Arab Gulf Company for Exploration which is to be formed under this Law.

It is evident that this action purports to deprive the Company of the rights which it possesses under and in relation to Concession Number 65 dated 18th December 1957.

This action amounts to an attempt at total and unilateral repudiation by the Government of the Libyan Arab Republic of the company's rights and accordingly to a grave breach thereof. In addition the arbitrary and discriminary action of the Government in this respect also constitutes a violation of established principles of international law.

The company does not accept this purported repudiation or breach of its rights and accordingly, a difference and dispute has arisen between the Government and the company within the terms of clause 28 of the Concession.

Since the manner and form of the Government's action do not leave open any other form of settlement of this difference and dispute, the company now requests, in accordance with clause 28(2) of the Concession, that this difference and dispute be referred to arbitration and hereby informs the Government that it has appointed as its arbitrator Professor Sir Humphrey Waldock, QC. Further, the company hereby requests the Government to nominate its arbitrator in accordance with clause 28(3).

Meanwhile the company desires to make it clear that as the rights of the company are capable of alteration only by mutual consent and not by unilateral action the rights of the company continue to be those under and in relation to its Concession.

The company, therefore, advises you that it will take such steps as it may consider necessary or desirable to assert or protect all its rights.

No reply having been received by the claimant, it addressed a letter of reminder to the respondent on 11 February 1972. By a further letter dated 13 March 1972, the claimant drew the attention of the respondent to the fact that the period of 90 days for the nomination of its arbitrator, stipulated in paragraph 3 of the said clause 28, had expired and informed the respondent of the claimant's intention to request the President of the International Court of Justice to appoint a sole arbitrator. The claimant attached a Memorandum to the letter in which it was stated that it 'presently calculates its claim for damages against [the respondent] to be in the amount of £220 million as at 7th December, 1971', and in addition the claimant would claim interest thereon between such date and the date of settlement. The letter described the Memorandum as being an expression of the claimant's 'present thoughts regarding the basis on which it will present its claim for damages in the arbitration'.

On 15 March 1972, the claimant applied to the President of the International Court of Justice for the appointment of a sole arbitrator pursuant to the provisions of paragraph 3 of the aforesaid clause 28. Citing the BP Nationalisation Law, the claimant stated that, 'this premature repudiation of the Agreement, 40 years before the expiry of its term, is a fundamental breach of the Concession occasioning a claim by the Company for reparation, and giving rise to a dispute within the meaning of Clause 28'.

The President of the International Court of Justice, Sir Muhammad Zafrullah Khan, on 28 April 1972 appointed Judge Gunnar Lagergren, President of the Court of Appeal for Western Sweden, Sole Arbitrator to hear and determine the dispute. He is qualified under paragraph 5 of clause 28 to receive such appointment. Thus the Tribunal was duly constituted.

Part II

Proceedings of the Tribunal

The Sole Arbitrator, on 8 May 1972, invited both parties to attend a first meeting of the Tribunal in Gothenburg. By letters of 8 June 1972, similarly sent to both parties, the meeting was fixed to take place on 4 July 1972. In the case of the respondent, the latter communication was addressed to, the Minister of Petroleum and delivered against acknowledgment of receipt to the Chargé d'affaires of the Embassy of the Libyan Arab Republic in Copenhagen, and the letter of 8 May 1972 in addition was delivered against acknowledgment of receipt to the Minister of Petroleum at Tripoli. No reply was received from the respondent, and at the meeting of the Tribunal on 4 July 1972, the Sole Arbitrator decided that the arbitration would proceed in spite of the respondent's default but that copies of all correspondence and documents in the case would be communicated to the respondent, and this has been done throughout the subsequent proceedings.

The Sole Arbitrator announced the appointment of Dr J Gillis Wetter as Secretary and Professor Jan Sandström as Deputy Secretary to the Tribunal.

The Tribunal determined that it would have power to provide for such secretarial and other assistance as it would deem necessary and further, with the consent of the claimant, decided that the language of the arbitration would be English, that the Tribunal should have power to appoint one or more experts, if necessary, and that the name of the Tribunal would be The BP/Libya Concession Tribunal.

The Tribunal, with the consent of the claimant, made various directions as to financial matters, including a decision that the parties should be jointly and severally liable for making deposits as required by the Sole Arbitrator, but such deposits should, as between the parties, be borne in equal shares.

With respect to the further course of the proceedings, upon motion of the claimant for an order to divide the proceedings into a first and a second stage, the Tribunal decided that the claimant within six weeks should submit a memorial setting forth its views as to the seat of the Tribunal and presenting argument in support of its request for a first, preliminary award.

The claimant, on 8 August 1972, submitted a Memorial as directed by the Tribunal at the meeting on 4 July 1972.

In the Memorial of 8 August 1972, the claimant requested that Copenhagen be fixed as the place of arbitration and that the arbitration proceedings be divided into two stages, viz., broadly speaking, a first stage to be concerned with the merits of the case, and a second stage to be concerned with the assessment of damages.

In support of the latter request, the claimant argued that the amount of damages flowing from the alleged breach by the respondent of the concession agreement was of the order of £240 million. The establishment of such a claim would call both for a consideration of the rules relating to the assessment of damages and the application of those rules to the facts of the present case. This would require examination of highly technical matters in great detail, and the sheer size of the damages claimed would call for the submission and scrutiny of a very large volume of material. Expert testimony must be produced. The process of assessing damages therefore was bound to be lengthy, and the claimant believed that it would assist the course of relations between the parties if a decision on the merits of the case were not delayed until the necessarily extended question of assessing the damages was answered. The arbitration process thus could serve an additional function in the resolution of the differences between the parties.

Two copies of the Memorial of 8 August 1972 were sent with a letter dated 14 August 1972 to the Minister of Petroleum at Tripoli and delivered against acknowledgment of receipt with an invitation to submit the respondent's comments within four weeks of receipt.

No reply having been received from the respondent, the Tribunal, by letters of 19 September 1972, invited both parties to attend a meeting in Gothenburg on 4 October 1972. The letter to the respondent was addressed and delivered against acknowledgment of receipt to the Minister of Petroleum at Tripoli.

The respondent failed to appear at the meeting of the Tribunal on 4 October 1972 which was thus held in the presence of the claimant alone.

The Tribunal, having heard the claimant, made the following order:

1. The place of arbitration shall be Copenhagen, Denmark.
2. The arbitration proceedings shall be divided into two parts, the first dealing with the merits of the claim and the second with the assessment of possible damages.
3. The claimant, on or before 31 December 1972, shall file with the Tribunal ten copies of a Memorial.
4. The Memorial shall contain:

    (i)   a full statement of the claimant's main claim, divided, as the case may be, into alternatives and stating the grounds upon which the claim is based;

    (ii) the claimant's request for an interim award in respect of the merits of the claim, divided, as the case may be, into alternative submissions and containing a full statement of the relevant facts and law. The Memorial ought to be accompanied by the written evidence upon which the claimant wants to rely. The Memorial shall not deal with questions relating to the assessment of possible damages;

    (iii) the claimant's submissions on the status of Mr Nelson Bunker Hunt in relation to the present proceedings.

5. The respondent shall, upon the receipt of a copy of the claimant's Memorial and within a period to be fixed by the Tribunal at a later stage, inform the Tribunal whether it desires to file a Counter-Memorial in reply thereto and, if so, how long a period is required by it to do so.

Upon application of the claimant by letter and cable dated 22 December 1972, the Tribunal on 9 January 1973 ruled that the time limit for the submission of the claimant's Memorial stipulated in paragraph 3 of the order cited above should be extended until 31 March 1973.

On 28 March 1973, the claimant submitted to the Tribunal 12 copies of the claimant's Memorial, divided into two printed volumes (Part One, stating the facts and reproducing in 34 Annexes certain documents adduced in evidence, and Part Two, devoted to an exposition of the claimant's argument and containing also an opinion of Professor Mohamed A Omar).

Two copies of the Memorial of the claimant were sent by the Tribunal with a covering letter dated 2 April 1973 to the Minister of Petroleum at Tripoli and were delivered against acknowledgment of receipt at the Embassy of the Libyan Arab Republic at Copenhagen. The letter stated, with reference to paragraph 5 of the minutes of the meeting of the Tribunal on 4 October 1972, cited above, that the respondent was invited to inform the Tribunal on or before 15 May 1973 whether it proposed to file a Counter-Memorial in reply to the claimant's Memorial and, if so how long a period of time it would require for the preparation and submission thereof.

No reply has been received to the letter of 2 April 1973.

By letter of 21 May 1973 to both parties, the Tribunal recorded the fact that no reply had been received from the respondent within the prescribed time limit and advised the parties that the Tribunal was preparing questions to the claimant. By letter of 6 July 1973, the Tribunal directed 16 questions to the claimant with the request that written answers be submitted by 1 August 1973, and such replies, dated 30 July 1973, were duly received. By letters dated 6 August 1973, both parties were invited to attend a meeting in Copenhagen on 20 September 1973. The respondent failed to appear at the meeting of the Tribunal, which was held on such date in the premises of Østre Landsret (the Court of Appeal for Eastern Denmark) in the presence of the claimant alone. In the course of it, the Tribunal sought and received from the claimant orally certain clarifications respecting the matters dealt with in the Tribunal's questions of 6 July 1973 and otherwise. At the conclusion of the meeting, the case was declared closed for purposes of the present, first stage of the proceedings.

Part III

The jurisdiction of the Tribunal; the procedural law of the arbitration; the effect of the respondent's default

1. The jurisdiction of the Tribunal

The jurisdiction of the Tribunal derives from clause 28 which is cited in Part I above and which provides, in particular, that, the Tribunal shall determine the applicability of the said clause and the procedure to be followed in the arbitration. In conformity with paragraph 6 of clause 28, the Tribunal, as mentioned earlier, has fixed Copenhagen as the place of arbitration.

The Tribunal holds the said clause 28 to be applicable to the present arbitration proceedings, and to vest the Tribunal with the required jurisdiction.

2. The procedural law of the arbitration

The procedural law of the arbitration will be decided at the outset. The first issue which falls to be considered in that context is whether the proceedings, on account of the fact that one party is a sovereign State, are governed by international law or by some other body of law not being a particular municipal legal system.

In the *Aramco* case of 1955, between Saudi Arabia and the Arabian American Oil Co (Aramco), the arbitral tribunal discussed this question of principle at some length and arrived at the following conclusion:

Considering the jurisdictional immunity of foreign States, recognised by international law in a spirit of respect for the essential dignity of sovereign power; the Tribunal is unable to hold that arbitral proceedings to which a sovereign State is a party could be subject to the law of another State. Any interference by the latter State would constitute an infringement of the prerogatives of the State which is a party to the arbitration. This would render illusory the award given in such circumstances. For these reasons, the Tribunal finds that the law of Geneva cannot be applied to the present arbitration.

It follows that the arbitration, as such, can only be governed by International Law, since the parties have clearly expressed their common intention that it should not be governed by the law of Saudi Arabia, and since there is no ground for the application of the American law of the other party. This is not only because the seat of the Tribunal is not in the United States, but also because of the principle of complete equality of the Parties in the proceedings before the arbitrators. (Cited from the privately printed edition of the Award, p. 47, *cf.* 27 *International Law Reports* (1963) p. 117, at pp. 155–6.)

The Tribunal cannot share the view that the application of municipal procedural law to an international arbitration like the present one would infringe upon such prerogatives as a State party to the proceedings may have by virtue of its sovereign status. Within the limits of international law, the judicial or executive authorities in each jurisdiction do, as a matter both of fact and of law, impose limitations on the sovereign immunity of other States within such jurisdictions. Clearly, in some legal systems the degree of control exercised by the courts over arbitral proceedings is greater than in others, and at times extensive. By providing for arbitration as an exclusive mechanism for resolving contractual disputes, the parties to an agreement; even if one of them is a State, must, however, be presumed to have intended to create an effective remedy. The effectiveness of an arbitral award that lacks nationality – which it may if the law of the arbitration is international law – generally is smaller than that of an award founded on the procedural law of a specific legal system and partaking of its nationality. Moreover, even where the arbitrators do, as the Tribunal does in this instance, have full authority to determine the procedural law of the arbitration, the attachment to a developed legal system is both convenient and constructive.

The Tribunal has fixed Copenhagen as its seat. For the reasons stated in the foregoing and having particular regard to the wide scope of freedom and independence enjoyed by arbitration tribunals under Danish law, the Tribunal considers that the procedural law of the arbitration is Danish law. The Tribunal is not competent to establish conclusively the nationality of its award, for this can only be decided by the courts of Denmark and of other jurisdictions in which enforcement of the award may be sought. However, the Tribunal deems this award to be Danish, and the proceedings have been conducted in a manner designed to be consistent with this view and intent.

This holding of the Tribunal is supported by practice, in arbitrations between States and aliens. Thus, both Judge Python in the *Alsing* case (*Alsing Trading Co v Greece*, 1954)[1] and Judge Cavin in the *Sapphire* case (*Sapphire International Petroleum Ltd v The National Iranian Oil Co*, 1963)[2] held that the relevant procedural law was the law of the seat of the arbitration. Judge Python, acting as umpire, who rendered his award prior to the adoption of the agreement on arbitration procedure among certain Swiss cantons called the 'Concordat sur l'arbitrage' of 27 March 1969, referred to the fact that, according to the terms of Article 2 of the Geneva Protocol Relating to Arbitration Clauses of 24 September 1923, the arbitration procedure, including the constitution of the arbitration tribunal, is governed by the will of the parties and by the law of the State in whose territory the arbitration takes place. According to the latter rule, the Code of Civil Procedure of the Canton of Vaud would apply, as the arbitrator sat at Lausanne. However, in accordance with the Protocol, the territorial law applied only in a subsidiary fashion, in the absence of provision made by the parties or the arbitrators appointed by them. Accordingly Judge Python held that the rules of procedure agreed upon by the parties were the only valid ones in the case, as indeed in international arbitrations under the Protocol even the mandatory provisions of the internal law must give way to the will of the parties. As for the procedure applicable to the inquiry and to the decision, the umpire, exercising the power conferred upon him by the parties and, in view of the fact that the case fell within his exclusive competence, and that he was a Swiss Federal judge exercising his powers in Switzerland, decided to apply the Swiss Federal law of civil procedure to all questions not governed by the rules agreed by the parties. (See the

---

1   23 I.L.R. 633.
2   35 I.L.R. 136.

unprinted Award, pp. 34–35; *cf.* Schwebel, 'The Alsing Case', 8 *International and Comparative Law Quarterly* (1959), p. 320, at p. 328.)

Judge Gavin considered it unavoidable that a specific procedural law should apply to the proceedings but that the parties were free to elect domicile for the arbitration. If they had agreed to confer upon the arbitrator the right to choose the seat of the tribunal, they had impliedly submitted themselves to the procedural law of the State decided by the arbitrator to be the seat. Judge Gavin implicitly assumed that the law of the seat of the arbitration would then apply, and he went on to state that even if the will of the parties were disregarded, the rule was that an arbitration is subject to the judicial sovereignty of the State where the proceedings take place:

> En l'espèce, par leur convention les parties ont laissé l'arbitre libre de déterminer le siège de l'arbitrage, faute d'accord entre elles. Acceptant ainsi d'avance le siège tel qu'il a été fixé par l'arbitre, qui a choisi par délégation de la volonté des parties, les contractants ont pris l'engagement de se soumettre à la loi de procédure qui résulte de ce choix. . . Si même cette interprétation de la volonté des parties était rejetée, la règle est qu'à défaut d'accord des parties, l'arbitrage est soumis à la souveraineté judiciaire du siège de l'arbitrage, au lieu où se déroule l'instance.

(Quoted from the unprinted Award, pp. 69–70; *cf.* 35 *International Law Reports* (1967), p. 156, at p. 169.)

It may be mentioned in this context that the Tribunal has satisfied itself as to the conformity with Danish law of a decision made by the Tribunal at an earlier stage in the proceedings, viz., the Order of 4 July 1972 cited in Part II above, to the effect that the arbitration proceedings be divided into two stages, the first dealing with the merits of the claim and the second with the assessment of possible damages. The Danish statute on procedure (*retsplejeloven*) provides that the court at its discretion may render interim or partial judgments. It may also render declaratory judgments. The competence of an arbitral tribunal to render interim, partial or declaratory awards cannot under Danish law be less than that of a court of law.

3. *The effect of the respondent's default*

The respondent has failed to reply to all communications of the Tribunal and has clearly elected not to appear as a party in the proceedings before the Tribunal.

Under the clause from which the Tribunal derives its jurisdiction, and under the law applicable to the arbitration, the Tribunal is empowered to render this award despite the respondent's non-appearance. The Tribunal has been duly constituted. The respondent has been notified of every meeting of the Tribunal and has received copies of all documents submitted by the claimant to the Tribunal, and of all communications by the Tribunal to the claimant.

In the circumstances the Award is similar to a default judgment, and it is necessary to comment on the procedural law aspects of an arbitration having such a character.

The arbitration statute of Denmark of 24 May 1972, and the body of customary law which supplements it give an arbitral tribunal a measure of freedom to conduct the proceedings which is greater than that of the ordinary Danish courts. A Danish arbitral tribunal is not obliged to apply Danish procedural law to its actions, but such law clearly can be of guidance. (See on these principles particularly Hjejle, *Frivillig Voldgift*, 1937, pp. 119–129; *Betaenkning vedrdrende lovgivning om voldgift*, 1966, p. 13.)

With respect to court proceedings in which the defendant fails to appear, Danish law, as stated by Professor Hurwitz, represents a compromise between the extremes to be found among various jurisdictions:

The various procedural codes provide different solutions in this respect, extending from complete preclusion to systems attempting to protect the non-appearing defendant by requiring a wide measure of proof on the part of the plaintiff of the truth of his claims, cf. H Munch–Petersen II, pp. 213 ff. with references. The [Danish] Procedural Code, in conformity with Norwegian and German law, has adopted an intermediary solution.

(Hurwitz, *Tvistemål*, 1959, p. 197.)

Briefly, the general principle of Danish procedural law on the point is:

> In other words, the principle of Section 341 of the Procedural Code is that the court will base its judgment on the plaintiff's allegations of fact but will decide independently what legal consequences follow from those allegations. (Hurwitz, ibid.)

The leading authority on Danish arbitral law, Dr Bernt Hjejle, has expressed the applicable principle in the following manner:

> However, in contradistinction to ordinary court procedure, the arbitrator in my opinion must be allowed greater flexibility in that he should hardly be confined

> to the claimant's statement of the facts but might check it and, if he finds it to be
> at variance with the actual circumstances, base his award on the latter. Unlike a
> court of law, the arbitrator is not bound by a statutory provision – which, in turn,
> to a certain extent has to be seen in its historical context – but is absolutely free as
> regards his appraisal and consequently also with respect to estimating how far he is
> willing, without more, to base his decision on the claimant's statement of facts or
> subject the latter to a critical investigation. (Hjejle, p. 135.)

The committee which prepared the Danish arbitration statute of 24 May 1972 concurred in the opinion of Dr Hjejle, and stated:

> It is the opinion of the Committee that the power, recognised in this country, of
> the arbitrators in each instance to decide in their discretion what the consequences
> should be of the non-appearance of a party, constitutes a satisfactory solution and
> that no statutory provisions are needed. (*Betaenkning*, p. 28.)

The jurisdiction of the Tribunal, as defined in clause 28, and the law applicable to the proceedings necessarily confine its task to a consideration of the claims and submissions formulated by the claimant, and the award therefore, rules exclusively on them.

The facts deemed relevant and taken as established by the Tribunal have been gathered from evidence produced by the claimant alone. With respect to certain facts the Tribunal has sought and received from the claimant the submission of additional documentary evidence and explanations. The Tribunal deeply regrets the absence of further elucidation on the part of the respondent.

With respect to the analysis of facts and their legal implications the Tribunal has had the benefit of argument presented by the claimant alone. However, the Tribunal has felt both entitled and compelled to undertake an independent examination of the legal issues deemed relevant by it, and to engage in considerable legal research going beyond the confines of the materials relied upon by the claimant. The conclusions in the award therefore are based on a broader consideration of the issues than that permitted by the format of the claimant's argument in support of its claims. Thus, the Tribunal to the greatest extent possible has endeavoured to eliminate any inherent adverse effects for the respondent of its decision not to appear as a party in the proceedings.

Part IV

The facts

1. *The nationalisation*

On the basis of a contractual relationship with the respondent, which will be explained and analysed in detail in Section 2 of this Part IV, the claimant over a period of 12 years made substantial investments in Libya and operated a major enterprise in that country for the extraction, processing, and export of petroleum. The claimant indirectly is and has at all times been wholly owned by the British Petroleum Company Ltd, an English public company, between 48 and 49 per cent of whose ordinary share capital is held by the British Government. The claimant was incorporated in England on 28 January 1938 and its head office is at Britannic House, Moor Lane, London E.C.2. All the statutory and other records are maintained at that address. The board consists of nine persons all of whom are British subjects resident in England. The whole of the administration, management and control of the claimant's affairs is exercised by the board in London. Activities overseas are carried on through local representatives appointed and supervised by and subject to the directions of the board in London.

On 7 December 1971, the respondent passed the BP Nationalisation Law which nationalised the operations of the claimant in Concession 65. The BP Nationalisation Law claimed to restore to the State and then to transfer to a new company, the Arabian Gulf Exploration Company, ownership of all properties, rights, assets and shares relating to the above-mentioned operations.

The BP Nationalisation Law provided that the State should pay compensation to the claimant. The amount of compensation was to be determined by a committee to be established by the Minister of Petroleum. The decision of the committee was to be documented and final, to admit of no appeal by any means, and to be communicated to the Minister of Petroleum who was to notify the claimant of it within 30 days of its issue.

In the claimant's submission, the BP Nationalisation Law was a measure of a unique character in that no similar step was taken against any other concessionaire of the Government or against other concessions owned by the claimant. The claimant states that to the best of its knowledge it believes that some 133 concessions had been granted to American, British, German, Italian and French companies prior to 7 December 1971; that in 1971 there were some 91 concessions in existence and that then and as of the date of the claimant's submissions there were concessionaires operating in Libya who were of American, British, German, Italian and French nationality. Although the claimant gave notice of surrender of four of its remaining six concessions on 18 December 1971, it continues to hold Concessions 80 and 81.

In the aspects unrelated to compensation, the BP Nationalisation Law was rapidly implemented. The claimant's operations in Concession 65 were brought to a complete halt: its staff were immediately excluded from its premises and from its production and transportation facilities. These were then taken over by the Arabian Gulf Exploration Company.

As regards compensation, no action was taken until 13 February 1972. Then, according to reports in the Libyan press on 14 February 1972, a three-man committee was appointed. According to Article 7 of the BP Nationalisation Law, this committee should have reported within three months from 14 February 1972, that is, by 14 May 1972, and the report should have been notified to the claimant by the Minister of Petroleum within 30 days of that date, i.e., by 14 June 1972. The claimant has received no such notification. On 28 September 1972 a cable was received which read:

> Before preparing its final report the Committee wishes to learn the company's viewpoint and remarks on the accounts prepared in respect of the compensation that may be due to or from your company. The Chairman and members of the Committee will be in Tripoli on Thursday 5th October 1972 at the company's Tripoli office to meet with your representatives on the same day. For Compensation Committee.

No representative of the claimant attended such meeting but a letter was sent to the Minister of Petroleum, referring to the cable and saying: 'As you know BP is willing to attempt to resolve the dispute which exists between it and your Government by negotiation.'

Some indication of the circumstances in which the BP Nationalisation Law was adopted is called for at this point. On 29 and 30 November 1971, the Government of Iran occupied three islands in the Gulf, Abu Musa and the Greater and the Lesser Tumb. The Iranian claim to these islands was contested by the Rulers of Sharjah and of Ras-al-Khaimah. At the moment of the occupation of the islands both were still nominally under British protection, although the treaties of protection were due to end on 30 November 1971. The British Government did not react to the occupation of the islands and was accordingly blamed in the Arab world for the loss of islands which were regarded as Arab.

On 5 December 1971, President Qadhafi of Libya sent a cable to the Ruler of Ras-al-Khaimah saying that:

> In our opinion Britain is primarily responsible for Iran's occupation of the islands and we hold it responsible for the consequences of this action, through which it has demonstrated its malice towards the Arabs and its failure to fulfil its pledges.

On 9 December 1971, in the course of a discussion in the Security Council of the United Nations on the question of the islands, the Libyan Representative, Mr Maghribi, made, inter alia, the following comments on the nationalisation of the claimant's interest in Concession 65:

> We have witnessed that a big Power can do anything it wishes, anything it deems in accordance with its chauvinistic interests, in violation of the Charter of the United Nations. The small States have always been left powerless against such actions and behaviour. Furthermore, we have seen that any State in agreement with a big Power can take similar liberties without respect for the Charter or international law. The Iranian military aggression in occupying the three Arab islands of Abu Musa and the Greater and Lesser Tumb, in connivance with Great Britain, is a clear manifestation of this.
>
> The Government of Great Britain has violated the provisions of the very treaties it had itself imposed upon the Sheikhdoms of the Arabian Gulf decades ago. The treaties imposed occupation and colonialism. However, they also provided for the protection of the territorial integrity of those Sheikhdoms and their islands. For many decades Great Britain has exploited all the provisions of those treaties to its own advantage and until now it has readily exploited the natural wealth of the Sheikhdoms. On the one occasion that Great Britain was called upon to apply the protection provision, it failed miserably and intentionally, reflecting the true nature by which the world has known it for centuries: 'divide and rule', trickery, treachery and butchery.
>
> A glance through past centuries gives proof of this. Indeed, hardly any major conflict or turmoil the modern world has known has not been the creation of Britain or its like-minded States, either directly or indirectly. And in the present instance of the Iranian aggression and occupation of the Arab islands Britain has been faithful to its nature and tradition. Has not Great Britain done the same in Palestine, although on a larger scale?
>
> Great Britain violated the treaties that it had itself imposed on the Sheikhdoms of the Arabian Gulf. It violated the principles of the Charter of the United Nations.
>
> My Government, an Arab Government, replied in the only way understood by the

imperialists – by nationalizing the oil interests of Great Britain in the Libyan Arab Republic and withdrawing our deposits from British banks. The British Petroleum Company, owned in essence by the British imperialist Government, has exploited the natural wealth of my country for many years. Our step violates no principle of the Charter or international law; it is in accordance with those principles and also with the General Assembly resolutions concerning the natural resources of States.

(UN Security Council, Provisional Verbatim Record of the 1610th Meeting, S/PV 1610, p. 93.)

The reaction of the British Government during December, 1971 to the actions of the respondent may be summarised as follows.

On 8 December 1971, the Minister of State for Foreign and Commonwealth Affairs said in reply to a question in the House of Commons:

Obviously, I shall wish to protest in the strongest terms when I know precisely what to protest about. I have to ascertain the facts first. The important thing is to get the facts and then to decide on action in relation to them. At present we have only hearsay evidence but, in so far as any question of nationalisation or expropriation is concerned, we have never said that it is our view that countries are not entitled to nationalise of course they can nationalise–but we do expect prompt and adequate compensation when that occurs. This will be a matter which we shall certainly want to have in the forefront of our minds.

(House of Commons, Official Report, Parliamentary Debates (Hansard), Vol 827, No 27, Wednesday, 8 December 1971, Columns 1299–1302.)

On 21 December 1971, the Minister of State for Foreign and Commonwealth Affairs made the following statement:

. . .the taking of the property of [the Claimant] is not a legitimate act of nationalisation because it is discriminatory against the company and for purposes which are not admissible in international law. We are of course supporting the company in its efforts to obtain redress.

(House of Commons, Official Report, Parliamentary Debates (Hansard), Vol 828, No 36, Tuesday, 21 December 1971, Written Answers to Questions, Column 312.)

On 23 December 1971, a note of protest was handed to the Ambassador of the Libyan Arab Republic in London, reading as follows:

> Her Britannic Majesty's Government present their compliments to the Government of the Libyan Arab Republic and have the honour to refer to the request, made to the Libyan Ambassador on 8 December 1971 by the Minister of State at the Foreign and Commonwealth Office and subsequently to the Libyan Government by Her Britannic Majesty's Embassy in Tripoli, for an explanation of the action of the Libyan Government in nationalising the assets of British Petroleum's production operation in Libya.
>
> Her Britannic Majesty's Government note with regret that the Libyan Government have not yet provided the explanation requested. In the absence of any such explanation and in the light of the public statements of the Libyan Government, Her Majesty's Government are bound to conclude that the measures in question amount to a breach of international law and are invalid.
>
> An act of nationalisation is not legitimate in international law unless it satisfies the following requirements:
>
> (i) it must be for a public purpose related to the internal needs of the taking State; and
>
> (ii) it must be followed by the payment of prompt, adequate and effective compensation.
>
> Nationalisation measures which are arbitrary or discriminatory or which are motivated by considerations of a political nature unrelated to the internal well-being of the taking State are, by a reference to those principles, illegal and invalid.
>
> Her Majesty's Government must, therefore, call upon the Libyan Government to act in accordance with the established rules of international law and make reparation to British Petroleum Exploration (Libya) Limited, either by restoring the company to its original position in accordance with the Concession No. 65 or by payment of full damages for the wrong done to the company.

The respondent did not furnish any reply to the note of the British Government.

The reaction of the claimant to the nationalisation has been described above in Part I with respect to the institution and conduct of the present arbitration proceedings. Certain further steps taken by the claimant, and evidenced in letters sent to the Minister of Petroleum, may be mentioned in this context.

On 30 December 1971, by a letter, addressed to the Minister of Petroleum,

Tripoli, the claimant informed him that in the ordinary course of events the claimant would have paid to the respondent on that date in respect of Concession 65 the sum of £2,882,955 by way of royalty on crude oil produced and tax and supplemental payment on crude oil exported by the claimant during the fourth quarter of 1971. The claimant stated that in the circumstances it was withholding this payment, but that it was lodging the sum 'in a special account. . . where the monies will be held pending the outcome of the arbitral proceedings and against such sums as are due from the Government to the company by way of damages'.

By a letter dated 17 January 1972, addressed to the Minister of Petroleum, Tripoli, the claimant placed on record the fact that the introduction and implementation within Libya of the BP Nationalisation Law in violation of the claimant's rights under Concession 65 had compelled the claimant to discontinue its operations under the concession, to withdraw its staff and to surrender to the Libyan authorities its offices, installations, equipment, oil stocks and other assets in Libya. The claimant also pointed out that these steps were taken under duress and could not prejudice the claimant's legal position and in particular could not prevent the vesting in the claimant of title to its share of oil extracted from the area of Concession 65.

By a letter dated 28 January 1972, addressed to the Minister of Petroleum, the claimant informed him, in terms similar to its letter of 30 December 1972, that on 30 July 1972, £2,882,955 would, in the normal course of events, have fallen due for payment to the respondent on 30 January 1972, but that this sum would be lodged in a special account in a London bank pending the outcome of the arbitral proceedings.

Similar letters relating to payments of £3,001,133 and £10,290,136 otherwise due on 29 February and 30 April 1972 were addressed by the claimant to the Minister of Petroleum on 28 February and 28 April 1972, respectively.

The letter of 28 April 1972 stated that the amount in question was withheld by the claimant without being lodged in a bank account.

All sums above referred to, amounting in the aggregate to £19,057,179 are presently withheld by the claimant without being deposited in a special bank account.

2. *The contractual relationship between the claimant and the respondent*

(a) Outline of contractual developments The Libyan Petroleum Law of 1955, as amended, established a framework within which exploration and production of petroleum in Libya might take place. In particular, it set up a Petroleum Commission (the 'Commission') which was to be responsible for the implementation of the provisions of the Law. The Commission was empowered in Article 9 to grant concessions 'in the form set out in the Second Schedule to the Law and not otherwise, provided that they may contain such minor non-discriminatory variations as may be required to meet the circumstances of any particular case'.

On December 1957 the Commission granted a Deed of Concession, designated as Concession 65, to Mr Nelson Bunker Hunt, a citizen of the United States of America, of Dallas, Texas, USA (the 'Hunt Concession'). It was substantially in the form set out in the Second Schedule of the Libyan Petroleum Law of 1955.

By clause 1 of the Deed of Concession, Mr Hunt was granted the exclusive right for 50 years to search for and extract petroleum within a designated area, and to take away and dispose of the same. The area was marked out on an annexed map and originally covered 32,944 sq.kms. However, pursuant to Article 10 of the Libyan Petroleum Law of 1955 and clause 2 of the Deed of Concession, the area was progressively reduced by surrender to 8,234 sq kms as at 7 December 1971.

Clause 25 provided that, save in circumstances which do not apply in the present case, the concession could only be assigned with the consent of the Commission and subject to such conditions as the latter might deem appropriate.

Following discussions in early 1960, the claimant and Mr. Hunt entered into an agreement on 24 June 1960 consisting of a Memorandum and attachments in which it was agreed, inter alia, that Mr Hunt would assign to the Claimant an undivided one-half interest in Concession 65. By a letter to the Commission dated 12 July 1960, Mr Hunt asked for formal approval of the assignment to the claimant of an undivided one-half interest in Concession 65. The claimant wrote in similar terms to the Commission in a letter of the same date. The first letter was accompanied by a draft Deed of Assignment. After consultation with the Commission, an amended draft thereof was presented to the Commission with a letter dated 17 August 1960 together with a programme for carrying out the terms of the concession.

On 9 September 1960 the Commission resolved to agree to the assignment and informed the claimant of its decision by a letter dated 11 September 1960. Its resolution was approved by the Minister of National Economy on 28 September 1960 and a copy of its decision was sent to the claimant on 2 October 1960.

On 10 November 1960, the arrangements between Mr Hunt and the claimant were formally settled by the signing of a Deed of Assignment in the same terms as the draft presented to the Commission with the letter of 17 August 1960 by which Mr Hunt assigned to the claimant an undivided one-half interest and title in Concession 65. In consideration of this assignment, the claimant agreed to undertake a work programme in which it would advance all the costs. This programme was to include seismic surveys, the commencement of drilling operations before 17 December 1960, the drilling of six exploratory wells and the construction of production facilities, pipelines, etc. The claimant undertook to purchase all or any part of Mr Hunt's share of the production when required by Mr Hunt to do so. In addition, it was provided that the claimant should be entitled to three-eighths of Mr Hunt's share of the oil production delivered f.o.b. Libyan sea-board until the claimant had received a quantity of crude oil equal in value to 125 per cent of all costs and expenses advanced by the claimant for Mr Hunt's account for exploration, development or any other work performed in connection with Concession 65.

Between 21 May 1955, i.e., the date of the coming into force of the Libyan Petroleum Law of 1955, and 20 January 1966, a number of amendments were made by the respondent to the Libyan Petroleum Law of 1955. The legislative measures containing these amendments were the following: two Royal Decrees of 21 May 1955; Royal Decree signed 3 July 1961; Royal Decree signed 9 November 1961; Royal Decree signed 26 April 1962; Royal Decree signed 16 July 1963; and Royal Decree signed 20 November 1965.

The changes introduced by these amendments into the Libyan Petroleum Law of 1955 and its Schedules did not by themselves affect existing concessions. However, the Royal Decree of 20 November 1965 contemplated that certain provisions of these amending decrees might by agreement be incorporated into and given effect as part of existing concessions.

On 14 December 1965 the claimant gave the respondent an undertaking of the kind referred to in Article XII of the Royal Decree of 20 November 1965 and on 20 January 1966 concluded an agreement with the respondent as contemplated in that article. This agreement amended, inter alia, Concession 65. Mr Hunt on the same date executed an amendment to Concession 65 in a form identical with the agreement made between the claimant and the respondent.

A number of legislative decrees and decisions concerning the petroleum industry were made after the Royal Decree of 20 November 1965 but these scarcely touched and affected Concession 65. A major amendment to the Libyan Petroleum Law of 1955 came into effect on 8 December 1968 with the passing of Petroleum Regulation No 8. This closely followed the OPEC Proforma Regulation for the Conservation of Petroleum Resources and empowered the Ministry of Petroleum to limit exploration and production and required the concessionaire to provide the Ministry with certain data relating to exploration, drilling and production. The claimant and Mr Hunt were the only concessionaires not to have their production cut back under this Regulation prior to 7 December 1971. In October, 1970 all the oil companies operating in Libya agreed to increase posted prices with effect from 1 September 1970 and to a general increase in tax from 50–55 per cent. Finally, on 18 October 1970 a Law Organising Petroleum Affairs was issued which was concerned with governmental organisation.

(b) Certain contractual aspects The contractual arrangements among the respondent, the claimant and Mr Hunt, which have been described in broad outline under subsection (a) of Section 2 above, call for specific analysis and consideration in certain respects.

The subject matter of the transaction between the claimant and Mr Hunt was 'Concession 65'. By the Deed of Assignment of 10 November 1960, Mr Hunt assigned to the claimant 'an undivided one-half (1/2) interest and title in and to the Concession. . .'

The agreement of 24 June 1960, of which the operating agreement forms an integral part, is not by its terms subject to a designated legal system.

As required under paragraph 2 of clause 25 of the Deed of Concession, the assignment received the approval of the Commission. The Commission did not have occasion to consider either the form of letter agreement attached to the Memorandum executed on 24 June 1960, nor the form of operating agreement (with three exhibits) likewise so attached.

The Libyan Petroleum Law of 1955 provided in its Article 1 (which has not since been amended) as follows:

1. All petroleum in Libya in its natural state in strata is the property of the Libyan State.
2. No person shall explore or prospect for, mine or produce petroleum in any part of Libya, unless authorised by a permit or concession issued under this Law.

The Hunt Concession granted the holder the exclusive right for a period of 50 years within a defined area, inter alia, to search for and extract petroleum, to take it away by pipeline or otherwise and to use, process, store, export and dispose of the same. For such purpose, the holder had the right within the concession area to erect and maintain any constructions, installations and works required for its activities and, outside the concession area, to erect and operate transport, harbour and terminal facilities.

The assignment clause in the Deed of Concession (Clause 25) did forsesee an assignment thereof 'in whole or in part'.

As between the parties to the assignment, the operating agreement established certain basic principles, two of the most important of which were, *firstly*, the designation of the claimant as operator with exclusive rights to conduct, direct and have full control over all operations in the concession area (Section 6), and, *secondly*, joint ownership (as to 50 per cent each) of all equipment and material, and all oil and gas produced in the concession area (Section 2, and specific provisions in Section 10(a) on extracted petroleum, and in Section 21 on facilities, materials and equipment). In so far as the Hunt Concession and the parties' activities thereunder gave rise to ownership of or other rights of property in related physical installations in Libya, or petroleum extracted from the concession area, neither party could exercise and dispose of such property rights save in accordance with the terms and conditions of the agreement of 24 June 1960. The principal object of joint ownership, Concession 65, as granted by and defined in the Deed of Concession, remained an integral, undivided whole.

It may be mentioned in this context that on 20 September 1973 the claimant submitted a letter from Mr Nelson Bunker Hunt, dated 12 September 1973, in which he declares that he has no objection to the present arbitration proceedings, including in particular the requested Declaration No. 5.

As mentioned under subsection (a) of Section 2 above, the Libyan Royal Decree of 20 November 1965 stipulated that certain amendments to existing concessions might be incorporated therein by agreement, and the claimant by a separate undertaking submitted on 14 December 1965 consented to such modifications with respect to its interests both under Concession 65 and under certain other concession agreements. An agreement was concluded between the respondent (acting through the Minister of Petroleum Affairs in the name of the Government of Libya) and the claimant, dated 20 January 1966 and entitled 'Agreement for Amendment of Petroleum Concession No. 34, 36, 37, 63, 64, 80, 81, 65'. This agreement was executed on a standardised form and mainly incorporated certain fiscal provisions which were more onerous to the concessionaire than the conditions previously applicable. It included as clause 28 the arbitration clause quoted in Part I above and, as clause 16, the following provision:

1. The Government of Libya will take all the steps necessary to ensure that the company enjoys all the rights conferred by this Concession. The contractual rights expressly created by this concession shall not be altered except by mutual consent of the parties.
2. This Concession shall throughout the period of its validity be construed in accordance with the Petroleum Law and the Regulations in force on the date of execution of the agreement of amendment by which this paragraph 2 was incorporated into this concession agreement. Any amendment to or repeal of such Regulations shall not affect the contractual rights of the company without its consent.

Part V

The claims

As stated in Part I above, the Tribunal at the request of the claimant has decided to divide the proceedings into two stages. The present stage concerns what the claimant refers to as the merits of the claim. The claimant is asking the Tribunal to render a declaratory award dealing with certain specific questions, viz., to make the following declarations:

(1) The Libyan Nationalisation Law of 7 December 1971 and the subsequent implementation thereof were each a breach of the obligations of the Libyan Government owed to the claimant under the Concession Agreement and so remain;
(2) The said breaches were and are ineffective to terminate the Concession Agreement, which remains in law valid and subsisting;
(3) The claimant is entitled to elect, at any time so long as the respondent's breach continues, to treat the Concession Agreement as at an end;

(4) The claimant is entitled to be restored to the full enjoyment of its rights under the Concession Agreement;

(5) The claimant is the owner of its share of any crude oil extracted from the area of the Concession Agreement after as well as before 7 December 1971 and of all installations and other physical assets, and the Libyan Government has no right to any such oil, installations or physical assets, which it can enjoy or transfer to any third party;

(6) Performance of the claimant's obligations under the Concession Agreement is suspended for so long as the Libyan Government remains in breach thereof; and

(7) The claimant is entitled to damages in respect of the interference by the Libyan Government with the claimant's enjoyment of its rights under the Concession Agreement. If the claimant does not exercise its rights under Declaration (3) above, then it is entitled to damages accruing up to the date of the final award herein. If the claimant does exercise the rights under Declaration (3) above, it is entitled to all damages arising from the wrongful act of the Libyan Government.

(8) The claimant further respectfully requests the Sole Arbitrator to reserve for a subsequent stage of the proceedings the assessment of the damages due under Declaration (7) above.

The claimant also asks the Tribunal to give directions in principle as to costs.

Part VI

The issues

The declarations which the claimant asks the Tribunal to make raise certain principal issues. This part will identify these issues and state the claimant's submissions regarding them.

1. Nature of the concession

The first issue is the nature of the BP Concession. The claimant submits that 'Concession No. 65 is a contractual instrument concluded pursuant to legislation which contemplated a contractual relationship.' It also maintains that the BP Concession constitutes a direct contractual link between the claimant and the respondent. The claimant places particular reliance on clause 16 of the BP Concession which, inter alia, provides: 'The contractual rights expressly created by this concession shall not be altered except by mutual consent of the parties.'

The claimant, in July 1973, submitted to the Tribunal an opinion of Professor Mohamed A Omar of Cairo University in which it is stated that concession contracts under Libyan law are considered to belong to the category of administrative contracts. The following principles are said to apply to such agreements:

> The Government have the right to change unilaterally the clauses of the concession and have also the right to terminate the concession. But these two rights are not absolute: the change of the clauses of the concession or its termination must be in pursuance of a true public interest. The judges have the right to review the change or termination to see whether they are based on good reasons or not. If the change or termination are not lawful, the concessionaire is entitled to obtain complete damages covering not only his actual losses but also all the profits he would have realised had the change or termination not taken place.

2. Applicable law

The second issue is what law applies to the relationship between the claimant and the respondent. It will be recalled that paragraph 7 of clause 28 of the BP Concession contains an express provision on the law governing the concession. The claimant argues that Libyan law has been excluded as the sole governing law and that the law governing the BP Concession is public international law. Alternatively, the BP Concession itself constitutes the sole source of law controlling the relationship between the parties. Orally, the claimant submits that it does not place emphasis on the word 'sole'. In the further alternative the claimant submits that the legal position of the parties falls to be decided by reference to 'the general principles of law'.

3. Breach of contract

The third issue is whether the nationalisation by the respondent constituted a breach of the contractual relationship allegedly existing between the claimant and the respondent. The claimant submits that the action of the respondent was a fundamental breach or repudiation of the concession agreement and that there was no legal justification for it.

4. The effect of the breach of contract

The fourth issue is the legal effects of the nationalisation by the respondent which in the claimant's submission constitutes a breach of contract. The basic proposition upon which the claimant relies in this respect is that where an agreement has been fundamentally violated by one party, the breach does not of itself put an end to the agreement. Some further act on the part of the innocent party is required. The party in breach does not have the power to put an end to the relationship by his own wrongful act. The claimant argues that, as it has not exercised its undoubted right to treat the BP Concession as at an end, it continues in full force and effect. The claimant submits, however, that it is not bound to fulfil its own obligations while the respondent remains in breach.

The claimant argues further that the primary remedy to which it is entitled by virtue of the continuing validity of the BP Concession is restoration of the position as it was prior to the BP Nationalisation Law. The claimant also submits that it follows from the continuity of the claimant's rights under the BP Concession to its share of oil extracted from the concession area that it remains the owner and that the respondent has no power (either itself or through its agents) to transfer to third parties any valid title to such oil.

In particular any dealing with such oil by the Libyan Government, the Libyan National Oil Company or the Arab Gulf Exploration Company is a dealing with oil which does not belong to any of them. Such a dealing is unlawful and cannot serve as a basis for a claim to title to such oil anywhere in the world by anyone other than the claimant.

The claimant submits that the tribunal is competent to make a declaration in these terms as between the parties, because the requested declaration is limited to a statement regarding the legal position existing under and in connection with the BP Concession.

Lastly, the claimant submits for the purposes of the present stage of the proceedings that so long as the BP Concession remains in force, the claimant is entitled to damages for actual loss caused to it by the respondent's breaches of contract up to the date of the Tribunal's final Award. If and when the claimant exercises its right to treat the BP Concession as terminated, it will be entitled not only to damages flowing from the specific breaches of contract (*damnum emergens*) but also damages for loss of the benefit of the contract as a whole (*lucrum cessans*).

Part VII

Opinion of the Tribunal

1. Introduction

The Tribunal will now analyse the issues which arise in the arbitration at its present stage.

It is necessary as an initial step to treat in conjunction certain fundamental questions which are inherent in the two first issues defined in Part VI above, and which relate to the nature of the BP Concession and the law applicable to it.

In contradistinction to all national courts, the ad hoc international arbitral tribunal created under an agreement between a State and an alien, such as the present Tribunal, at least initially has no *lex fori* which, in the form of conflicts of law rules or otherwise, provides it with the framework of an established legal system under which it is constituted and to which it may have ultimate resort. With respect to the law of the arbitration, the attachment to a designated national jurisdiction is restricted to what, broadly speaking, constitute procedural matters and does not extend to the legal issues of substance. It is erroneous to assume, as has been done doctrinally, on the basis of the territorial sovereignty of the State where the physical seat of an international arbitral tribunal is located, that the *lex arbitri* necessarily governs the applicable conflicts of law rules. (See in this connection the award of 1964 in Case No. 1250 of the International Chamber of Commerce, in which Professor Henry Batiffol presided as chairman.) Even less does it necessarily constitute the proper law of the contract. Instead, if the parties to the agreement have not provided otherwise, such an arbitral tribunal is at liberty to choose the conflicts of law rules that it deems applicable, having regard to all the circumstances of the case. (*Cf.* Article VII of the European Convention on International Commercial Arbitration of 1961, *U.N. Economic Commission for Europe*, E/ECE/423; E/ECE/Trade 48.)

The Tribunal deems Danish conflicts of law rules – which not only are those of the *lex arbitri* but by virtue of not containing any relevant restrictive rules provide a wide leeway for the free exercise of party autonomy – to be applicable in the present case. This in the circumstances seems to be the most natural solution.

The contract containing the arbitration clause from which the Tribunal derives its jurisdiction is an elaborate document carefully drafted and conceived of by the parties as a legal instrument binding upon them. Therefore primary reference must be made to that instrument itself in determining the law which governs the agreement.

As stated earlier, the Tribunal deems Danish conflicts of law rules to be applicable. Having regard to them, the Tribunal accepts the distinct provisions of paragraph 7 of clause 28 of the BP Concession as conclusive with respect to the issue of which legal system governs the agreement, including the remedies available in the event of breach.

The paragraph is analysed in detail in Section 3 below.

2. Nature of the concession

It follows from the analysis of the contractual arrangements among the respondent, the claimant and Mr Hunt made in subsection (b) of Section 2 of Part IV above that the BP Concession constitutes a direct contractual link between the respondent and the claimant with respect to the interests of the claimant under Concession 65. Hence the Tribunal, with respect to the first issue arising in this case, accepts the claimant's submissions set forth in Section 1 of Part VI above.

3. Applicable law

Paragraph 7 of Clause 28 of the BP Concession, quoted in Part I above, stipulates which law is to govern the agreement. While the provision generates practical difficulties in its implementation, it offers guidance in a negative sense by excluding the relevance of any single municipal legal system as such. To the extent possible, the Tribunal will apply the clause according to its clear and apparent meaning. Natural as this would be in any event, such an interpretation is the more compelling as the contractual document is of a standardised type prescribed by the respondent. The governing law clause moreover was the final product of successive changes made in the Libyan petroleum legislation in the decade between 1955 and 1965 by which the relevance of Libyan law was progressively reduced.

In paragraph 7 of Clause 28, reference is made to the principles of law of Libya common to the principles of international law, and only if such common principles do not exist with respect to a particular matter, to the general principles of law. The claimant argues, in the first of three alternative submissions, that international law alone is applicable.

This argument has two aspects.

(a) After indicating that a relevant distinction exists between 'principles' and 'rules' – a line of reasoning which is not further pursued in this connection – the claimant states:

> . . .the acceptance of a principle must be supported by both Libyan and
> international law if it is to govern the Concession. Therefore if the conduct
> of a party to the Concession cannot be justified by the principles of both
> Libyan law and international law, it is not justifiable under the Concession.
> It is justifiable only if the principles of both systems of law – Libyan and
> international – support it. Thus conduct which is a breach of the principles of
> international law must necessarily be a breach of the Concession, even if not in
> breach of the principles of Libyan law.

This reasoning is clearly incomplete since it entirely leaves out of the picture the direction which follows from paragraph 7 of clause 28. That – conduct, etc. in the last analysis should be tested by reference to the general principles of law. It is not correct to say that 'a principle must be supported by both Libyan law and international law [in order to be] justifiable under the Concession' and that conduct 'is justifiable only if principles of both systems of law – Libyan and international – support it'. The principle may still be acceptable, and the conduct justifiable, if supported by the general principles of law. To take a few examples, one system may prescribe that payments shall be made in one currency and the other system that payment shall be made in a different currency. Clearly, in such a case, under paragraph 7 of clause 28 the general principles of law must provide the answer to the question what currency is to be used. One system imposes automatic, obligatory limitation after the lapse of a given period, but the other does not, again the general principles of law will be resorted to for the purpose of determining whether a claim is barred by the lapse of time. Similarly, if one system contains the principle that any default by a debtor entitles a creditor to accelerate payment of principal and interest with immediate effect, but the other system does not offer the creditor such a remedy, the general principles of law will govern the issue respecting – the availability of that remedy. And so the situation must be also in regard to breach of contract. If a particular action by a party amounts to breach of contract under one system but not under the other, the issue is one which can only be decided by reference to the general principles of law. Thus, the first part of the claimant's argument must be rejected. It is not sufficient for the claimant to show that the conduct of the respondent is a breach of international law as a basis for maintaining a claim based on breach of contract. In the event that international law and Libyan law conflict on that issue, the question is to be resolved by the application of the general principles of law.

(b) Secondly, the claimant argues that since the parties have expressly excluded the direct and sole application of Libyan law, but have made reference to the general principles of law, and since 'a' system must govern, 'the only system that is left is public international law'.

The Tribunal cannot accept the submission that public international law applies, for paragraph 7 of clause 28 does not so stipulate. Nor does the BP Concession itself constitute the sole source of law controlling the relationship between the parties. The governing system of law is what that clause expressly provides, *viz.* in the absence of principles common to the law of Libya and international law, the general principles of law, including such of those principles as may have been applied by international tribunals.

4. Breach of contract

No elaborate reasons are required to resolve the third issue in this case. The BP Nationalisation Law and the actions taken thereunder by the respondent, do constitute a fundamental breach of the BP Concession as they amount to a total repudiation of the agreement and the obligations of the respondent thereunder, and, on the basis of rules of applicable systems of law too elementary and voluminous to require or permit citation, the Tribunal so holds. Further, the taking by the respondent of the property, rights and interests of the claimant clearly violates public international law as it was made for purely extraneous political reasons and was arbitrary and discriminatory in character. Nearly two years have now passed since the nationalisation, and the fact that no offer of compensation has been made indicates that the taking was also confiscatory. [. . .]

EXERCISE 9– APPLICABLE LAW I – MINI MOCK ARBITRATION

A is a limited liability company registered in country X and is majority-owned and controlled by the government of X.

B is a limited liability company registered in country Y. It is majority-owned and controlled by the government of Y.

Both A and B have representative offices and subsidiaries with active business operations in the other country.

Both X and Y are parties to the United Nations Convention on Contracts for the International Sale of Goods (the CISG). Neither of the countries is a party to the Convention on the Law Applicable to International Sales of Goods (the Hague Convention).

In 1995, X and Y entered into an Intergovernmental Protocol. The Protocol was signed by the respective heads of state at a ceremony in the capital of Y. The protocol *inter alia* envisaged that the state-owned entities of the countries, i.e., A and B, were to enter into contracts for the sale and delivery of gas from X to Y.

In 1999, A and B concluded a 25-year contract for the sale and delivery of gas from A to B. The contract had been negotiated since 1995, at meetings in both X and Y, and was signed during a state visit in the capital of Y. Three weeks before the contract was signed the parties had signed a non-binding term sheet in the capital of X.

According to the contract, the gas is to be delivered at the border between X and Y. The contract includes a provision whereby each party is entitled to request renegotiation of the contract price in case of significant changes on the gas market. The contract further stipulates that if the parties cannot reach agreement on a revised price, each of the parties may refer the matter to arbitration.

In 2012, B requested renegotiation of the contract price with reference to changed circumstances in the market. When renegotiations failed, the matter was referred to arbitration. The seat of arbitration is Stockholm. B has requested that the tribunal determine a new price formula, as specified by B. A has requested that the tribunal dismiss B's claims.

In the arbitration, the parties disagree on the law applicable to the contract. The contract includes the following clause.

The arbitrators shall decide the dispute by majority vote, taking into account the provisions of this contract, as well as the legal rules applied in accordance with the conflict of laws rules of the country in which the arbitration takes place.

 **GROUP**

Group 1
Present arguments in favour of the application of the law of country X.

Group 2
You are the observer group. Have the best arguments been put forward? Could other arguments have been presented? Did the Tribunal make the right decision?

Group 3
Present arguments in favour of the application of the law of country Y.

Group 4
You are the Tribunal. You must determine which law to apply.

6

The procedure before the arbitrators

 EXERCISE 10 – THE PROCEDURE BEFORE THE ARBITRATORS I – SEMINAR

In discussing your answers, each group must discuss the ICC Rules, the SCC Rules as well as the UNCITRAL Rules.

 DISCUSSION QUESTIONS

Problem 1
Does the principle of *iura novit curia* apply in international commercial arbitration? Should it apply? Discuss the pros and cons.

Problem 2
To what extent do parties have the right to change and/or amend their claims during the arbitration? What is the role – if any – of the principle of *audi alterum partem in* this connection? Can parties file counterclaims during the arbitration?

Problem 3
Explain how evidence is presented in an arbitration. Do the arbitrators have the right to call for evidence, written and oral? Who has the burden of proof in international arbitration? How is this issue decided?

Problem 4
To what extent and how can parties obtain interim relief in international arbitration, including through so-called 'emergency arbitration'? Is there a need to change national legislation and/or arbitration rules in this respect? Discuss pros and cons.

EXERCISE 11 – THE PROCEDURE BEFORE THE ARBITRATORS II – SEMINAR

Kaareelian Kulta Olut has become a very popular beer in Finland and the north-western part of Russia. It is produced by the Saiman Brewing Company in Finland. To meet increasing demand from beer lovers in Finland and Russia it has decided to increase its production capacity. On October 14 2014 it signs a contract with Pensacola Lighthouse Breweries, which is a Belgian company specialising in producing and manufacturing equipment for producing highly potent beer. Under the contract Pensacola Lighthouse Breweries undertakes to deliver equipment and technology for the Kaareelian Kulta Olut Turbo, a beer which Saiman Brewing company plans to market as the King of Beers. Upon signing the contract the management of Saiman discloses to the stock markets in Finland and Russia that the new beer will soon reach the consumers and that it will dramatically increase revenues of the company. Following this announcement the value of the shares skyrockets to an all-time high.

It turns out, however, that the equipment delivered by Pensacola does not quite meet Saiman's expectations. The beer produced tastes like water – a far cry from the potent beer promised by Pensacola – which leads to numerous complaints from consumers and to a dramatic fall of the Saiman shares in Helsinki and Moscow. In addition, the equipment delivered by Pensacola explodes one night and causes extensive damage to Saiman's production facility and to adjacent buildings belonging to another company. As a result of this explosion Saiman is forced to build a new production facility and to build new offices for the company whose buildings were damaged.

Under the contract between Pensacola and Saiman the last payment for the delivery and installation of the equipment was to be made by Saiman six months after commencement of production, which would have been on December 1 2015. Saiman decides to not make this payment, which amounts to $10 million, and instead retain it as compensation for its sustained losses.

The outstanding payment severely hurts Pensacola's business and Pensacola therefore decides to initiate arbitration against Saiman. The contract contains the following arbitration clause.

> Any and all disputes between the parties shall be settled exclusively through arbitration [according to X]. [The seat of arbitration shall be Y]. The parties shall agree upon the number of arbitrators, who must have expertise in the field of international commercial law.

 **GROUP**

Group 1

Assume that X is the ICC Rules and that Y is Paris. Draft a document that will initiate the arbitration.

Group 2

Assume that the wording within square brackets X and Y is not included in the clause. Draft a document that will initiate the arbitration.

Group 3

Assume that X is the UNCITRAL Rules and that Y is Stockholm. Draft a document that will initiate the arbitration.

Group 4

Assume that X is the LCIA Rules and that Y is London. Draft a document that will initiate the arbitration.

Each group shall draft its request of arbitration independently and send it to the other participants on the day before the seminar, as well as bring it to the seminar. During the seminar the four draft requests will be the basis for the discussion.

EXERCISE 12 – THE PROCEDURE BEFORE THE ARBITRATORS III – SEMINAR

This exercise is based on the fact pattern from Exercise 11, with the following modifications.

Pensacola initiates arbitration under the following clause:

> Disputes arising out of this Contract and the legal relationship between the parties to this Contract are to be finally settled by arbitration in London.

In the written submissions filed during the proceedings Saiman takes the position that it is under no obligation to pay the outstanding amount, since the equipment delivered by Pensacola did not meet the quality standards under the contract.

Three days before the main hearing Saiman files a counterclaim with the arbitral tribunal. The counterclaim amounts to USD 15 million, 10 million of which corresponds to the cost that Saiman has incurred to build its new production facility and the new offices for the company whose buildings were damaged. The remaining 5 million is compensation for the dramatic fall of the Saiman shares on the stock exchanges in Helsinki and Moscow.

 DISCUSSION QUESTIONS

Problem 1
How should the Tribunal handle Saiman's counterclaim?

At the main hearing Saiman files an additional counterclaim, this time amounting to USD 5 million. This counterclaim is based on a contract which was entered into one month after the contract concerning the equipment was signed. The second contract concerns deliveries from Saiman to Pensacola of 500,000 litres of the Djingis Khan Special, a beer which Saiman has produced for the Russian market, especially Siberia. Pensacola was interested in marketing this brand in Europe and therefore wanted to try it first. In the event the management of Pensacola has consumed every litre of the Djingis Khan Special, but not paid for it. This contract stipulates that all disputes are to be resolved by the District Court of Helsinki.

Problem 2
How should the Tribunal handle this second counterclaim filed by Saiman? With respect to both new claims filed by Saiman: should the Tribunal treat them differently if they had been presented as set-off claims?

On the first day of the main hearing Pensacola introduces its leading engineer, Ms Stella Artois, as a witness. She is to testify to the fact that the equipment delivered by Pensacola was of top quality. Saiman protests and argues that it is too late to rely on new witnesses. Pensacola then explains that shortly after signing the contract concerning Djingis Khan beer, Ms Artois mysteriously disappeared and was nowhere to be found, despite numerous attempts by Pensacola's management to find her. She is a key person with respect to beer production technology, a fact which must have been obvious to Saiman. It was not until the night before the commencement of the main hearing that she re-appeared, explaining that she had been 'abducted' to Siberia and put under the constant 'influence of Djingis Khan'.

Problem 3
How should the Tribunal handle Pensacola's request to hear Ms Stella Artois as a witness?

Problem 4
Assume that Saiman does *not* file a counterclaim. Instead it institutes criminal proceedings in Helsinki against the management of Pensacola for wilfully having produced the faulty equipment. Shortly thereafter Saiman requests the arbitral tribunal to stay the proceedings awaiting the outcome of the criminal case. How should the Tribunal handle this request?

7

The arbitral award

DISCUSSION QUESTIONS

Probem 1

An arbitral award is rendered in State X. When the winning claimant attempts to enforce the award in State Y, the losing respondent finds evidence indicating that the arbitrator appointed by the claimant had several *ex parte* meetings with claimant's counsel before and during the arbitration. The evidence also indicates that the arbitrator in question might have received a separate additional fee, in addition to the one provided to all tribunal members, and that the separate fee was paid by a subsidiary to the claimant.

The losing respondent comes to you and wishes to 'avoid paying a nickel'. Present the best argument for your client.

The Arbitration Act in both State X and State Y closely follow the UNCITRAL Model Law. Both States are signatories to the New York Convention.

Problem 2

What is the rationale for allowing parties to enter into so-called exclusion agreements (allowed under, for example, Swiss and Swedish arbitration law)? Is it compatible with the aims behind the New York Convention?

Problem 3

Argue that the award outlined below should be set aside.

Problem 4

Argue that the award outlined below should stand.

An arbitral award is rendered in Stockholm, ordering Farawayi energy company TNG to pay \$173 million to Ruretanian oil company FNG in damages for breaching a cooperation agreement relating to the exploitation of an oil field in Farawaystan. Before the hearing, the Tribunal had included a decision in a procedural order stating that it would review and decide the dispute based solely on circumstances and facts referenced in a 'joint summary of grounds' (the summary) submitted by the parties. In the first draft of the summary, before the hearing, the parties had attempted to include the following reservation:

> This summary does not exclude or replace any legal grounds, arguments or circumstances contained in the parties' previous submissions. This summary is provided pursuant to the Tribunal's order and for its convenience.

The Tribunal did not accept this reservation and the chairman replied to the parties:

> The Tribunal notes that the joint summary contains a reservation in that the parties refer to their previous pleadings declaring that what is contained in the joint summary does not fully reflect the legal grounds relied on. The Tribunal requires to be perfectly clear on what grounds are relied at this stage. Each of the parties is therefore ordered to submit a specified account of such legal grounds and legal theories on which they rely and which are not set out in the joint summary. It is specifically pointed out that general references to previous pleadings will not suffice.

During the hearing, which took place in Paris, the parties jointly submitted a final version of the summary. After the hearing the Tribunal sent a new message to the parties, which included among other things this paragraph:

> In considering the issues in this case the Tribunal will base its decision on the assumption that the parties rely on the legal grounds as they have been set out in the final version of the summary. The Tribunal will assume that this reflects the final positions of the parties in this respect. It follows that the references to prior pleadings will not be considered. For the sake of clarity the Tribunal wishes to point out that ensuring absolute clarity on the legal grounds is a fundamental duty of the Tribunal and that this duty applies irrespective of the position taken in that regard by the parties. As counsel will be fully aware failure by the Tribunal to ensure this may lead to a ground for challenging the award. Hence, in accordance with the Tribunal's overriding duty to deliver a valid award, references in the final statement of the legal grounds/arguments to what may have been said in other pleadings will not be considered unless this has been covered in the final formulation thereof.

The final version of the summary was included in the award, which was rendered five months after the hearing.

When TNG received the award, it was unpleasantly surprised. A key part of the award centred on the level of oil reserves in the field. During the Paris hearing FNG had alleged that TNG fraudulently had given incorrect information about the level of the oil reserves and thereby breached the contract, which the Tribunal agreed with. In the summary, however, not a word was mentioned about the level of oil reserves; among the grounds recapitulated in the summary was the level of *oil flow rates* but not the level of *oil reserves.*

TNG now feels that the Tribunal went beyond its mandate by basing its award on something that was not included in the summary. Throughout the award the Tribunal maintained the distinction between oil flow rates and oil reserves – which are two very different things – so it is clear that the Tribunal understood the difference.

EXERCISE 14 – THE ARBITRAL AWARD II – SEMINAR

DISCUSSION QUESTIONS

Problem 1
Explain the reasons relied on by the British Columbia Court of Appeal in *Quintette Coal v Nippon Steel*. Do they make sense? Should international awards and domestic awards be treated differently?

Problem 2
Present the best arguments why the award should be set aside.

Problem 3
In international commercial arbitration:

(a) Are price review disputes arbitrable?
(b) To what extent can arbitrators fill gaps in contracts?

Problem 4
To what extent are arbitrators allowed to review the merits of a dispute within the framework of challenge proceedings?

CASE

In the matter of the International Commercial Arbitration Act, SBC 1986 (c. 14) and between Quintette Coal Ltd, petitioner (appellant) and Nippon Steel Corp, and others, respondents (respondents)

Reasons for judgment of The Honourable Mr Justice Hutcheon

I agree with the conclusion reached by Mr Justice Gibbs in his reasons for judgment that the decision of the arbitration board was not a matter beyond the scope of the submission to arbitration and that the appeal must be dismissed. However, I arrive at those results by a different route which I shall attempt to explain. Briefly stated, I am of the view that the decision, in so far as it staged the reduction of the fixed component of the Base Price, was one justified under clause 9 of the Metallurgical Coal-Sale – Purchase Agreement.

With the facts fully set out in the reasons of Mr Justice Gibbs and of Chief Justice Esson reported at (1990) 47 BCLR(2d) 201 I can go directly to a discussion of the issue.

The crux of the objection taken to the decision by Quintette Coal Ltd was that the arbitrators went beyond the scope of the submission to arbitration by staging a reduction of the fixed component over the four-year period. The precise changes in the fixed component are set out in this extract I have taken from Appendix A to the award.

	Awarded Fixed Component
1987.2	26.50
1988.2	23.50
1989.2	20.50
1990.2	18.50
1990.3	8.00
1990.4	7.00
1991.1	6.00

According to Quintette the fixed component at 1987.2 [April 1, 1987] was the only dispute raised by the submission about the fixed component: under the terms of the agreement the fixed component was settled once every four years subject only to an adjustment under clause 9. That result, it is said, is required by the language of the agreement and in particular by these two clauses:

> 7. Price Review
> The Base Price shall be reviewed during the four months prior to March 31, 1987, March 31, 1991 and March 31, 1995 at the request of either seller or buyer. The review shall be made taking into consideration the then prevailing market price of metallurgical coal being supplied and sold to buyer from major Canadian suppliers under long-term contracts and also the quality differential, if any, in comparison with those coals.
> 9. Inequity Review
> If any significant change in the metallurgical coal market takes place at any time during the term of the contract either party shall have the right to request a price review. The parties shall discuss the matter in good faith to reach a fair and reasonable adjustment.

The make-up of the Base Price is set forth in clause 5.

I quote the relevant parts:

> 5. Base Price and Price Adjustment
> 5.1 The Base Price as at April 1, 1980 shall be $75.00 per Ton.
> 5.2 The Base Price shall be subject to adjustment commencing April 1, 1980 in accordance with the following formula and principles:
>
> $$Px = P1 \times L\, x/Lr + Pm \times Mx/Mr - Pd \times Dx/Dr + Pf$$

Where:

5.2.1 "Px" is the adjusted Base Price to be applied from July 1, 1990 and every three months thereafter in respect of the Diesel Fuel component (Pd), the Labour component (P1) and the Materials and Supplies component (Pm).

5.2.11 "Pf" is the fixed component of the Base Price not subject to escalation and is $35.00:

5.3 The Labour, Materials and Supplies and Diesel Fuel components will be adjusted every three months on July 1, October 1, January 1 and April 1 as provided in paragraphs 5.2.4 and 5.2.7 and 5.2.10.

I can agree that clause 7 is not a model of clarity. Indeed one of the first tasks of the arbitrators was to decide, as they did, that clause 7 was a matter for arbitration. Quintette had taken the position that the price review was not arbitrable.

But the striking thing about this dispute is that, according to the material supplied to us on the appeal, both parties had the same understanding of the meaning of clause 7. Both understood clause 7 to mean that the parties would emerge from a review of the price or from the arbitration with the amount of the fixed component set at April 1, 1987 for the delivery of all coal up to the next review in 1991, subject, of course, to clause 9. That is a rational approach to clause 7. At the very least, that common approach to clause 7 is a strong indication that a dispute about staging the reduction of the fixed component through the four years and the decision by the arbitrators resolving that dispute (1) were not contemplated by the terms of the submission to arbitration and (2) were beyond the scope of the submission. Those are the two tests for judicial review provided by s.34(2)(a)(iv) of the International Commercial Arbitration Act.

For the purpose of this appeal the relevant submission to arbitration is to be found in the Notice of Request for Arbitration of November 1987 in this question: '1(b) What Base Price should be set pursuant to clauses 7 or 9 of the Agreement, or both, for coal contracted to be delivered between March 31, 1987 and March 31, 1991?'

Before this notice was delivered, clause 9 had been invoked in 1985, 1986 and 1987. In each case the fixed component had been reduced by agreement from $35 set out in clause 5.2.11 to 326,50. In writing the award, the chairman, The Honourable N T Nemetz, relied upon that experience under clause 9 as establishing 'a pattern of price setting that in effect amounts to staging the price reduction'.

The reference by the award to the experience of the parties under clause 9 and an earlier reference in the award to the requirement under clause 9 for the parties 'to discuss the matter in good faith to reach a fair and reasonable adjustment' lead me to the conclusion I have reached that the approach taken by the board of arbitration in staging the reduction of the fixed component is supportable under clause 9.

I recognise that the chairman stated: 'it is not necessary for me to make an order pursuant to clause 9'. The jurisdiction, however, to do what the arbitrators did was available to them in clause 9, a clause invoked by the claimant in the submission to arbitration. That being so, I cannot agree that the decision was beyond the scope of that submission.

I agree with Mr Justice Gibbs in his discussion on the issue of judicial intervention under the International Commercial Arbitration Act. By way of addition, I would paraphrase a passage in *Parsons & Whittemore Overseas Co Inc* 508 F 2d 969 (1974) at p.976 that Quintette must overcome a powerful presumption that the arbitral board acted within its powers. Applying that presumption, I find that the decision in this case was within the scope of the submission to arbitration.

I would dismiss the appeal.

 CASE

In the matter of the International Commercial Arbitration Act, S.B.C 1986 (c 14) and between Quintette Coal Ltd, petitioner (appellant) and Nippon Steel Corp, and others respondents (respondents)

Reasons for judgment of The Honourable Mr Justice Gibbs

In a judgment reported at (1990) 47 BCLR (2d) 201 Esson, C J S C dismissed proceedings brought by the appellant Quintett Coal Ltd ('Quintette') to set aside the award of an arbitration board setting the price to be paid by the respondent Japanese companies for coal deliveries made by Quintette between March 31, 1987 and March 31, 1991. This is an appeal from that judgment.

In clause 15 of their contract of July 31, 1981, entitled 'Metallurgical Coal-Sale-Purchase Agreement', the parties agreed upon arbitration to resolve disputes:

> All unresolved disputes, controversies or differences between the parties arising out of or in connection with or resulting from this Agreement, or the breach

hereof, any failure of the parties to reach agreement with respect to matters provided for herein and all matters of dispute relating to the sale of Coal by Seller to Buyer shall be finally determined by arbitration. . ..

The parties also agreed, in clause 19.4, that the law of British Columbia would apply: 'This Agreement shall be construed and relations between the parties determined in accordance with the law of British Columbia, Canada.'

It is common ground that the statute law of British Columbia which has direct application is the International Commercial Arbitration Act, S B C 1986, Ch 3, in that the arbitration was an international commercial arbitration as defined in s 1. The Act severely circumscribes the jurisdiction of the court to interfere with arbitrations to which it applies. The first limitation is in s 5 which confines the court to intervention only where authorised by the statute:

> 5. In matters governed by this Act,
> (a) no court shall intervene except where so provided in this Act, and
> (b) no arbitral proceedings of an arbitral tribunal or an order, ruling or arbitral award made by an arbitral tribunal shall be questioned, reviewed or restrained by a proceeding under the Judicial Review Procedure Act or otherwise except to the extent provided in this Act.

The second limitation is in s 34 which specifies the narrow grounds upon which the court is empowered to set aside an 'arbitral award'. The ground relied upon by Quintette in this appeal is found in s 34(2)(a)(iv):

> (2) An arbitral award may be set aside by the Supreme Court only if—
> (a) the party making the application furnishes proof that
> . . .
> (iv) the arbitral award deals with a dispute not contemplated by or not falling within the terms of the submission to arbitration, or it contains decisions on matters beyond the scope of the submission to arbitration, provided that, if the decisions on matters submitted to arbitration can be separated from those not so submitted, only that part of the arbitral award which contains decisions on matters not submitted to arbitration may be set aside.

Specifically the ground is that the arbitral award 'contains decisions on matters beyond the scope of the submission to arbitration'. That is apparent from Quintette's factum (the Notice of Appeal does not Specify grounds). The factum states:

ERROR IN JUDGMENT

41. The learned Chief Justice erred in failing to hold there was a ground for setting aside the Award to the extent it contained a decision on a matter beyond the scope of the submission to arbitration, namely. . .

In order to ascertain the 'scope of the submission' it is necessary to have recourse to three sources. The first is the Notice of Request for Arbitration sent by the Japanese companies to Quintette on November 16, 1987. Of the three issues spelled out in the Notice only the second is relevant to the appeal. It is expressed as follows in the Notice:

1. The claimant requests that the following issues be finally determined by arbitration pursuant to clause 15 of the Agreement:

(b) What Base Price should be set pursuant to clauses 7 or 9 of the Agreement, or both, for coal contracted to be delivered between March 31, 1987 and March 31, 1991?

The second source is clause 7 of the contract between the parties. Although the notice also refers to clause 9, which is one of the pricing provisions, clause 7 was the focus of the argument on the appeal and, evidently, before the Chief Justice. It provides:

The Base Price shall be reviewed during the four months prior to March 31, 1987, March 31, 1991 and March 31, 1995 at the request of either seller or buyer. The review shall be made taking into consideration the then prevailing market price of metallurgical coal being supplied and sold to buyer from major Canadian suppliers under long term contracts and also the quality differential, if any, in comparison with those coals.

Base Price is defined in clause 5 of the contract. It has three variable components, Labour, Material and Supplies, and Diesel Fuel, which are to be adjusted every three months according to specified indices. It also has a fixed component stated to be 'not subject to escalation'. The contract set the fixed component at $35.00 per ton but it is not contended that it had to remain at that level throughout the life of the contract. The words 'not subject to escalation' merely removed the fixed price from the automatic three: month adjustments of the variable components.

The third source for the scope of the submission is the pleadings exchanged between the parties. Section 23.(1) of the Act requires the exchange of statements by the claimant and the respondent. In his statement the claimant (the Japanese companies) is obliged to 'state the facts supporting his claim, the points at issue and the relief or remedy sought'.

23. (1) Within the period of time agreed upon by the parties or determined by the arbitral tribunal, the claimant shall state the facts supporting his claim, the points at issue and the relief or remedy sought, and the respondent shall state his defence in respect of these particulars, unless the parties have otherwise agreed as to the required elements of those statements.

By way of 'relief or remedy sought' the Japanese companies put forward several pricing alternatives. The last of the alternatives is: 'such other formula or method of adjustment as may be appropriate'.

In the result, after some 142 days of hearings over a two-year period, on May 28, 1990 the arbitration board delivered its award in the form of a schedule of prices for the period March 31, 1987 to March 31, 1991:

The first line of the schedule (for the calendar year quarter 1987.2) equates to April 1, 1987, and it also coincides, as does each line thereafter, with the

Quintette coal and nippon steel

(1) Calendar Year Quarters	(2) Awarded Fixed Component	(3) Escalated Component	(4) Total Price Awarded	(5) Price Actually Received
1987.2	26.50	68.80	95.30	95.30
1987.3	26.50	68.42	94.92	94.92
1987.4	26.50	69.41	95.91	95.91
1988.1	26.50	70.18	96.68	96.68
1988.2	23.50	71.97	95.47	98.47
1988.3	23.50	72.00	95.50	98.50
1988.4	23.50	73.22	96.72	99.72
1988.1	23.50	72.56	96.06	99.06
1989.2	20.50	73.19	93.69	99.69
1989.3	20.50	74.36	94.86	100.86
1989.4	20.50	75.03	95.53	101.53
1990.1	20.50	75.93	96.43	102.43
1990.2	18.50	76.40	94.90	102.90
1990.3	8.00	*	**	
1990.4	7.00	*	**	
1990.1	6.00	*	**	

* The formula for determining the escalated component for periods 1990.3, 1990.4 and 1991.1 shall continue as set out in clause 5 of the contract.
** The sum of the awarded fixed component plus the escalated component for the periods 1990.3, 1990.4 and 1991.1.

quarterly adjustment of the variable components of the Base Price pursuant to clause 5 of the contract. The award was delivered on May 28, 1990, midway between calendar year quarter 1990.2 and 1990.3. In substance, therefore, what had occurred before 1990.3 was history and what was anticipated to occur after 1990.2 must necessarily have been based upon projections, except the variable components which would automatically be determined from time to time in accordance with clause 5.

It was Quintette's position before Chief Justice Essen, and before this court, that the arbitration board had no jurisdiction beyond determining the dollar values for calendar year quarter 1987.2, and that everything after that was outside the mandate of the board. The Chief Justice described the Quintette submission in these words at p. 207:

> Quintette's contention is that the jurisdiction of the board was confined to fixing a base price 'as of April 1, 1987' and that, in fixing a series of base prices for the 15 quarters after 30th June 1987, it did something which it was not asked to do and had no power to do what flows from that, in the submission of Quintette, is that the only part of the award which is valid is the first line of App A.

Although Quintette challenges all of the award below the first line, the real focus is upon the downward adjustments in the fixed price component over the four-year period. Presumably the escalated component adjustments would have occurred in any event through application of the indices agreed upon in Clause 5. In respect of the fixed price component, Quintette contends that, when set as at April 1, 1987, upon a proper construction of clause 7 of the contract, it must remain at that level for the ensuing four years. That is to say, that it cannot again be adjusted until April 1, 1991. The threshold question which must be answered however before embarking upon an assessment of the merits of the Quintette contention is whether, in the words of s 34(2)(a)(iv) of the Act, 'the arbitral award . . .contains decisions on matters beyond the scope of the submission to arbitration'. If it does not the court has no jurisdiction to set the award aside even if it could be shown that the arbitration board erred when interpreting the contract.

At p. 204 of his Judgment Chief Justice Essen drew attention to the relationship between the domestic law of arbitration and the law which applies to international arbitrations and he referred to 'a world-wide trend toward restricting judicial control over international commercial arbitration awards'. Perhaps the strongest expression of that trend is to be found in the majority judgment of the Supreme Court of the United States in *Mitsubishi Motors*

Corporation v Solar Chrysler-Plymouth, Inc (1985), 473 US 614. At p. 629, Blackmun, J said:

> we conclude that concerns of international comity, respect for the capacities of foreign and transnational tribunals, and sensitivity to the need of the international commercial system for predictability in the resolution of disputes require that we enforce the parties' agreement, even assuming that a contrary result would be forthcoming in the domestic context.

And at pp 638 and 639 he said:

> As international trade has expanded in recent decades, so too has the use of international arbitration to resolve disputes arising in the course of that trade. The controversies that international arbitral institutions are called upon to resolve have increased in diversity as well as in complexity. Yet the potential of these tribunals for efficient disposition of legal disagreements arising from commercial relations has not yet been tested. If they are to take a central place in the international legal order, national courts will need to 'shake off the old judicial hostility to arbitration.' *Kulukundis Shipping Co v Amtorg Trading Corp* 126 F2d 978, 985 (CA2 1942), and also their customary and understandable unwillingness to cede jurisdiction of a claim arising under domestic law to a foreign or transnational tribunal. To this extent, at least, it will be necessary for national courts to subordinate domestic notions of arbitrability to the international policy favouring commercial arbitration. See Scherk, supra.

In 1988, in *CBI NZ Ltd v Badger Chiyoda* (1989), 2 NZR 669, the New Zealand Court of Appeal was called upon to determine whether the award of an international commercial arbitration carried out under the International Chamber of Commerce rules, which exclude any form of appeal, was immune from review by the New Zealand courts. The several lengthy judgments refer to international conventions and statutes, including the British Columbia statute, and review judicial pronouncements about the approach to be followed by domestic courts, including the remarks of Blackmun, J in *Mitsubishi*, supra. At p 687 Richardson, J, appearing to reflect the views of the other members of the court, speaks of the trend Chief Justice Esson referred to:

> As to that, the trend in international commercial arbitrations is clearly towards giving greater emphasis to party autonomy and contracting judicial control over the legal content of the reference and the award.

The respondents cited two other United States cases, both at the Court of Appeals level, which found in favour of restraint upon domestic judicial review of international commercial arbitration awards: *Parsons & Whittemore Overseas Co Inc v Societe Generale de L'Industrie du Papier (RAKTA)* (1974), 508 F2d 969 (US Court of Appeals, Second Circuit), and *Management & Technical Consultants SA v Parsons-Jurden; International Corp* (1987), 820 F2d 1531 (US Court of Appeals, Ninth Circuit).

Chief Justice Esson concluded that the views expressed in *CBI NZ Ltd*, and the cases therein referred to represented the 'consensus' referred to in the preamble to the British Columbia Act. At p 206 he said:

> While the *CBI NZ Ltd* decision is not directly applicable to the issue in this case, I have quoted at length from the judgment of Richardson J for its extensive analysis of authorities from various jurisdictions, all holding that courts should exercise restraint in reviewing arbitration awards in the international arena. The views expressed by those courts, in my view, are substantially the same as the 'consensus' referred to in the preamble to our International Act, and thus reflect the purpose of that Act.

This is the preamble clause which speaks of a 'consensus':

> AND WHEREAS the United Nations Commission on International Trade Law has adopted the UNCITRAL Model Arbitration Law which reflects a consensus of views on the conduct of, and degree and nature of judicial intervention in, international commercial arbitrations

We are advised that this is the first case under the British Columbia Act in which a party to an international commercial arbitration seeks to set the award aside. It is important to parties to future such arbitrations and to the integrity of the process itself that the court express its views on the degree of deference to be accorded the decision of the arbitrators. The reasons advanced in the cases discussed above for restraint in the exercise of judicial review are highly persuasive. The 'concerns of international comity, respect for the capacities of foreign and transnational tribunals, and sensitivity to the need of the international commercial system for predictability in the resolution of disputes' spoken of by Blackmun, J are as compelling in this jurisdiction as they are in the United States or elsewhere. It is meet therefore, as a matter of policy, to adopt a standard which seeks to preserve the autonomy of the forum selected by the parties and to minimise judicial intervention when reviewing international commercial arbitral awards in British Columbia. That is the standard to be followed in this case.

The disposition of the appeal turns upon whether what the arbitrators did amounted to a decision on 'matters beyond the scope of the submission to arbitration'. The matter within the scope of the submission was, as expressed in the Notice of Request for Arbitration, 'What Base Price should be set. . . for coal contracted to be delivered between March 31, 1987 and March 31, 1991.' The arbitrators answered the question. As an alternative remedy they were asked to set the price by 'such other formula or method of adjustment as may be appropriate'. They did so by setting prices at quarterly intervals. They were called upon to construe clauses 7 and 9 of the contract within their context and they did so. Even applying the domestic test (*Shalansky et al v Board of Governors of Regina Pasqua Hospital* (1983), 145 DLR (3d) 413 (SCC)) their interpretation is one which the words of the contract can reasonably bear. The conditions precedent to intervention by the court spelled out in s 34(2)(a)(iv) of the Act have not been met. The language of the statute forecloses the court from intervention.

Chief Justic Esson disposed of the application in these words:

> At p. 1 of his award the chairman stated: This tribunal was established under the provisions of clause 15 of the agreement to determine the unresolved price of coal for the period April 1, 1987 to March 31, 1991.
>
> That, I am satisfied correctly states the agreed scope of the submission to arbitration. There is no merit in the suggestion that the board's jurisdiction was limited to fixing a base price as of the beginning of the period.
>
> At one stage, I was concerned by the question whether it was open to the board to alter the fixed component within the four-year period rather than leaving it at a fixed level until the next four-year review, as is arguably contemplated by some of the language of clause 5 of the contract. But even if the board was wrong in its conclusion on that point, that would constitute mere error in interpreting the contract and would not, under the International Act, provide a ground for setting it aside. I will add that, despite my original doubts, I am now persuaded, essentially for the reasons stated by the learned chairman in his award, that the board did not err in its interpretation.

Quintette has not shown the Chief Justice to have been in error. On the contrary, and with respect, his decision is correct in law and in accord with the standard to be followed in this kind of case.

I would dismiss the appeal.

EXERCISE 15 – THE ARBITRAL AWARD III – MINI MOCK ARBITRATION

This mini mock arbitration is devoted to several aspects of the *Eco Swiss v Benetton* case decided by the European Court of Justice (ECJ).

GROUP

Group 1
You are the observer group. You are to review the arguments and analyses presented by the other groups. Have they presented the best arguments? Has the Court taken the right decision?

Group 2
You are counsel to respondent. Your task is to present as many convincing arguments as possible as to why the decision must be upheld.

Group 3
You are counsel to a party who is seeking to have the decision of the ECJ set aside in a new action which is pending before the ECJ (we thus assume that such an action is possible). Your task is to present as many convincing arguments as possible which should lead to the setting aside of the ECJ's previous decision in the *Eco Swiss v Benetton* case. Your basic assumption should be that the case, if it is allowed to stand, will have very negative consequences for international commercial arbitration. (This second case before the ECJ is of course hypothetical. There are no formal grounds on the basis of which the *Eco Swiss* decision could be set aside.)

Group 4
You are the ECJ. Your task is to render a decision based on the arguments presented by Groups 2 and 3.

CASE

Eco Swiss China Time Ltd v Benetton International NV (Case 126/97) ECJ

Judgment of the court

1 June 1999, (Competition Application by an Arbitration Tribunal, of its own motion, of Article 81 EC (ex Article 85) – Power of national courts to annul arbitration awards) in Case C-126/97, Reference to the Court under Article 234 EC (ex Article 177) by the HogeRaad der Nederlanden (Netherlands) for a preliminary ruling in the proceedings pending before that court between Eco Swiss China Time Ltd and Benetton International NV on the interpretation of Article 81 EC (ex Article 85),

1. By order of 21 March 1997, received at the Court on 27 March 1997, the Hoge Raad der Nederlanden (Supreme Court of the Netherlands)

referred to the Court for a preliminary ruling under Article 234 EC (ex Article 177) five questions on the interpretation of Article 81 EC (ex Article 85).

2.Those questions have been raised in proceedings brought by Benetton International NV ('Benetton') for stay of enforcement of an arbitration award ordering it to pay damages to Eco Swiss China Time Ltd ('Eco Swiss') for breach of a licensing agreement concluded with the latter, on the ground that the award in question was contrary to public policy within the meaning of Article 1065(1)(e) of the Wetboek van Burgerlijke Rechtsvordering (here-inafter referred to as 'the Code of Civil Procedure') by virtue of the nullity of the licensing agreement under Article 81 EC (ex Article 85).

The national legislation

3. Article 1050(1) of the Code of Civil Procedure provides: 'No appeal shall lie from an arbitration award to a higher arbitration tribunal unless otherwise agreed by the parties.'

4. Article 1054(1) of the Code states: 'In making their awards, arbitration tribunals shall apply rules of law.'

5. Article 1059 of the Code provides:

> 1. An arbitration award, whether complete or partial, shall not acquire the force of *res judicata* unless it is a final award. It shall acquire that force from the date on which it is made.
> 2. However, where, in accordance with the agreement between the parties, an appeal may be made to a higher arbitration tribunal against a complete or partial final award, that award shall acquire the force of *res judicata* as from the date on which the time-limit for appealing expires or, if an appeal is lodged, from the date on which the decision is given in the appeal proceedings, if and in so far as that decision upholds the award appealed against.

6. As regards judicial review of arbitration awards, Article 1064 of the Code of Civil Procedure provides:

> 1. An action contesting:
>
>   (a)   a final arbitration award, whether complete or partial, against which no appeal may be made to a higher arbitration tribunal or
>   (b)   a final arbitration award, whether complete or partial, made on appeal to

a higher arbitration tribunal may be brought only by way of an application for annulment or a *request-civiel* in accordance with the provisions of this section.

2. An application for annulment shall be made to the Rechtbank, at the registry of which the original of the award must be lodged pursuant to Article1058(1).

3. A party may lodge an application for annulment as soon as the award has acquired the force of *res judicata*. The right to bring an action shall expire three months after the date of lodgement of the award at the registry of the Rechtbank. However, where the award, endorsed with an order for its enforcement, is served on the other party to the proceedings, that party may, notwithstanding the expiry of the period of three months referred to in the previous sentence, lodge an application for annulment within three months from the date of such service.

4. An application may be lodged for annulment of an interim arbitration award only together with the application for annulment of the complete or partial final arbitration award. . ..

7. Article 1065 of the Code provides:

1. Annulment may be ordered only on one or more of the following grounds:
   (a) there is no valid arbitration agreement;
   (b) the arbitration tribunal has been constituted in breach of the applicable rules;
   (c) the arbitration tribunal has failed to comply with its terms of reference;
   (d) the award has not been signed or does not state the reasons on which it is based, contrary to the provisions of Article 1057;
   (e) the award or the manner in which it has been made is contrary to public policy or accepted principles of morality.

...

4. An award may not be annulled on the ground referred to in paragraph 1(c) above if the party pleading that ground took part in the proceedings without raising it in those proceedings despite having been aware that the arbitration tribunal was failing to comply with its terms of reference.

8. Finally, Article 1066(1) and (2) of the Code of Civil Procedure provides that an application for annulment does not operate to stay enforcement of the award, but the court seised of such an application may, if a stay is justified and at the request of either party, order a stay of enforcement pending a definitive decision on the application for annulment. An application for a stay must be based on the existence of a reasonable prospect that the arbitration award will be annulled.

The main proceedings

9. On 1 July 1986 Benetton, a company established in Amsterdam, concluded a licensing agreement for a period of eight years with Eco Swiss, established in Kowloon (Hong Kong), and Bulova Watch Company Inc ('Bulova'), established in Wood Side (New York). Under that agreement, Benetton granted Eco Swiss the right to manufacture watches and clocks bearing the words 'Benetton by Bulova', which could then be sold by Eco Swiss and Bulova.

10. Article 26.A of the licensing agreement provides that all disputes or differences arising between the parties are to be settled by arbitration in conformity with the rules of the Nederlands Arbitrage Instituut (Netherlands Institute of Arbitrators) and that the arbitrators appointed are to apply Netherlands law.

11. By letter of 24 June 1991, Benetton gave notice of termination of the agreement with effect from 24 September 1991, three years before the end of the period originally provided for. Arbitration proceedings were instituted between Benetton, Eco Swiss and Bulova in relation to the termination of the agreement.

12. In their award of 4 February 1993, entitled 'Partial Final Award' (hereinafter 'the PFA'), lodged at the registry of the Rechtbank (District Court) te 's-Gravenhageon the same date, the arbitrators directed inter alia that Benetton should compensate Eco Swiss and Bulova for the damage which they had suffered as a result of Benetton's termination of the licensing agreement.

13. When the parties failed to come to agreement on the quantum of damages to be paid by Benetton to Eco Swiss and Bulova, the arbitrators on 23 June 1995 made an award entitled 'Final Arbitral Award' (hereinafter 'the FAA'), which was lodged at the registry of the Rechtbank on 26 June 1995, ordering Benetton to pay US$23,750,000 to Eco Swiss and US$2,800,000 to Bulova by way of compensation for the damage suffered by them. By order of the President of the Rechtbank of 17 July 1995, leave was given to enforce the FAA.

14. On 14 July 1995, Benetton applied to the Rechtbank for annulment of the PFA and the FAA on the ground, inter alia, that those arbitration awards were contrary to public policy by virtue of the nullity of the licensing agreement under Article 81EC (ex Article 85), although during the arbitration proceedings neither the parties nor the arbitrators had raised the point that the licensing agreement might be contrary to that provision.

15. The Rechtbank dismissed that application by decision of 2 October 1996, whereupon Benetton appealed to the Gerechtshof (Regional Court of Appeal) Gravenhage, before which the case is pending.

16. By application lodged at the registry of the Rechtbank on 24 July 1995 Benetton also requested that court to stay enforcement of the FAA and, in the alternative, to order Eco Swiss to provide security.

17. By order of 19 September 1995 the Rechtbank allowed only the alternative claim.

18. Benetton lodged an appeal against that decision. By order of 28 March 1996 the Gerechtshof essentially allowed the primary claim.

19. The Gerechtshof took the view that Article 81 EC (ex Article 85) is a provision of public policy within the meaning of Article 1065(1)(e) of the Code of Civil Procedure, infringement of which may result in annulment of an arbitration award.

20. However, the Gerechtshof considered that, in the proceedings before it for stay of enforcement, it was unable to examine whether a partial final award such as the PFA was in conformity with Article 1065(1)(e) of the Code of Civil Procedure, since Benetton had not lodged an application for annulment within three months after the lodging of that award at the registry of the Rechtbank, as required by Article 1064(3) of the Code of Civil Procedure.

21. Nevertheless, the Gerechtshof took the view that it was able to examine the FAA in relation to Article 1065(1)(e), particularly as regards the effect of Article 81(1)and (2) EC (ex Article 85(1) and (2)) on the assessment of damage, since to award compensation for damage flowing from the wrongful termination of the licensing agreement would amount to enforcing that agreement, whereas it was, at least in part, void under Article 81(1) and (2) EC (ex Article 85(1) and (2)). The agreement in question enabled the parties to operate a market-sharing arrangement, since Eco Swiss could no longer sell watches and clocks in Italy and Bulova could no longer do so in the other countries which were then Member States of the Community. As Benetton and Eco Swiss acknowledge, the licensing agreement was not notified to the Commission and is not covered by a block exemption.

22. The Gerechtshof considered that, in the procedure for annulment, the FAA could be held to be contrary to public policy, and therefore decided to grant the application for a stay in so far as it related to the FAA.

23. Eco Swiss brought proceedings in cassation before the Hoge Raad against the decision of the Gerechtshof and Benetton lodged a cross-appeal.

24. The Hoge Raad observes that an arbitration award is contrary to public policy within the meaning of Article 1065(1)(e) of the Code of Civil Procedure only if its terms or enforcement conflict with a mandatory rule so fundamental that no restrictions of a procedural nature should prevent its application. It states that, in Netherlands law, the mere fact that, because of the terms or enforcement of an arbitration award, a prohibition laid down in competition law is not applied is not generally regarded as being contrary to public policy.

25. However, referring to the judgment in Joined Cases C-430/93 and C-431/93 *Van Schijndel and Van Veen v SPF* [1995] ECR I-4705, the Hoge Raad wonders whether the position is the same where, as in the case now before it, the provision in question is a rule of Community law. The Hoge Raad infers from that judgment that Article 81 EC (ex Article 85) is not to be regarded as a mandatory rule which is so fundamental that no restrictions of a procedural nature should prevent it from being observed.

26. Moreover, since it is not disputed that the question whether the licensing agreement might be void under Article 81 EC (ex Article 85) was not raised in the course of the arbitration proceedings, the Hoge Raad considers that the arbitrators would have gone beyond the ambit of the dispute if they had inquired into and ruled on that question. In such a case, their award would have been open to annulment pursuant to Article 1065(1)(c) of the Code of Civil Procedure, because they would have failed to comply with their terms of reference. Furthermore, according to the Hoge Raad, the parties themselves could not have raised the question of the possible nullity of the licensing agreement for the first time in the context of the proceedings for annulment.

27. The Hoge Raad states that such rules of procedure are justified by the general interest in having an effectively functioning arbitration procedure and that they are no less favourable to application of rules of Community law than to application of rules of national law.

28. However, the Hoge Raad is uncertain whether the principles laid down by the Court in *Van Schijndel and Van Veen*, cited above, also apply to arbitrators, particularly since, according to the judgment in Case 102/81 *Nordsee v Reederei Mond* [1982] ECR 1095, an Arbitration Tribunal constituted pursuant to an agreement under private law, without State intervention, is not to be regarded as a court or tribunal for the purposes of Article

234 EC (ex Article 177) and cannot therefore make references for a preliminary ruling under that article.

29. The Hoge Raad explains that, under Netherlands' procedural law, where arbitrators have settled part of a dispute by an interim award which is in the nature of a final award, that award has the force of *res judicata* and, if annulment of that interim award has not been sought in proper time, the possibility of applying for annulment of a subsequent arbitration award proceeding upon the interim award is restricted by the principle of *res judicata*. However, the Hoge Raad is uncertain whether Community law precludes the Gerechtshof from applying such a procedural rule where, as in the present case, the subsequent arbitration award, the annulment of which has been applied for in proper time, proceeds upon an earlier arbitration award.

30. In those circumstances, the Hoge Raad der Nederlanden decided to stay proceedings and to refer the following questions to the Court for a preliminary ruling:

> (1) To what extent is the ruling of the Court of Justice in Joined Cases C-430/93 and C-431/93 *Van Schijndel and Van Veen v SPF* [1995]ECR I-4705 applicable by analogy if, in a dispute concerning a private law agreement brought before arbitrators and not before the national courts, the parties make no reference to Article 85 of the EC Treaty and, according to the rules of national procedural law applicable to them, the arbitrators are not at liberty to apply those provisions of their own motion?
>
> (2) If the court considers that an arbitration award is in fact contrary to Article 85 of the EC Treaty, must it, on that ground and notwithstanding the rules of Netherlands procedural law set out in paragraphs 4.2 and 4.4 above [according to which a party may claim annulment of an arbitration award only on a limited number of grounds, one ground being that an award is contrary to public policy, which generally does not cover the mere fact that through the terms or enforcement of an arbitration award no effect is given to a prohibition laid down by competition law], allow a claim for annulment of that award if the claim otherwise complies with statutory requirements?
>
> (3) Notwithstanding the rules of Netherlands procedural law set out in paragraph 4.5 above [according to which arbitrators must not go outside the ambit of disputes and must keep to their terms of reference], is the court also required to allow such a claim if the question of the applicability of Article 85 of the EC Treaty remained outside the ambit of the dispute in the arbitration proceedings and the arbitrators therefore made no determination in that regard?
>
> (4) Does Community law require the rules of Netherlands procedural law set out in paragraph 5.3 above [according to which an interim arbitration award that is in

the nature of a final award acquires the force of *res judicata* and is open to appeal only within a period of three months following lodgement of the award at the registry of the Rechtbank] to be disapplied if this is necessary in order to examine, in proceedings for annulment of a subsequent arbitration award, whether an agreement which an interim arbitration award having the force of *res judicata* has held to be valid may nevertheless be void because it conflicts with Article 85 of the EC Treaty?

(5) Or, in a case such as that described in Question 4, is it necessary to refrain from applying the rule that, in so far as an interim arbitration award is in the nature of a final award, annulment of that award may not be sought simultaneously with that of the subsequent arbitration award?

The second question

31. By its second question, which is best examined first, the referring court is asking essentially whether a national court to which application is made for annulment of an arbitration award must grant such an application where, in its view, that award is in fact contrary to Article 81 EC (ex Article 85) although, under domestic procedural rules, it may grant such an application only on a limited number of grounds, one of them being inconsistency with public policy, which, according to the applicable national law, is not generally to be invoked on the sole ground that, because of the terms or the enforcement of an arbitration award, effect will not be given to a prohibition laid down by domestic competition law.

32. It is to be noted, first of all, that, where questions of Community law are raised in an arbitration resorted to by agreement, the ordinary courts may have to examine those questions, in particular during review of the arbitration award, which may be more or less extensive depending on the circumstances and which they are obliged to carry out in the event of an appeal, for setting aside, for leave to enforce an award or upon any other form of action or review available under the relevant national legislation (*Nordsee*, cited above, para 14).

33. In paragraph 15 of the judgment in *Nordsee*, the Court went on to explain that it is for those national courts and tribunals to ascertain whether it is necessary for them to make a reference to the Court under Article 234 EC (ex Article 177) in order to obtain an interpretation or assessment of the validity of provisions of Community law which they may need to apply when reviewing an arbitration award.

34. In this regard, the Court had held, in paragraphs 10–12 of that judgment, that an Arbitration Tribunal constituted pursuant to an agreement between

the parties is not a 'court or tribunal of a Member State' within the meaning of Article 234 EC (ex Article 177) since the parties are under no obligation, in law or in fact, to refer their disputes to arbitration and the public authorities of the Member State concerned are not involved in the decision to opt for arbitration nor required to intervene of their own accord in the proceedings before the arbitrator.

35. Next, it is in the interest of efficient arbitration proceedings that review of arbitration awards should be limited in scope and that annulment of or refusal to recognise an award should be possible only in exceptional circumstances.

36. However, according to Article 3(g) of the EC Treaty (now, after amendment, Article 3(1)(g) EC), Article 81 EC (ex Article 85) constitutes a fundamental provision which is essential for the accomplishment of the tasks entrusted to the Community and, in particular, for the functioning of the internal market. The importance of such a provision led the framers of the Treaty to provide expressly, in Article 81(2) EC (ex Article 85(2)), that any agreements or decisions prohibited pursuant to that article are to be automatically void.

37. It follows that where its domestic rules of procedure require a national court to grant an application for annulment of an arbitration award where such an application is founded on failure to observe national rules of public policy, it must also grant such an application where it is founded on failure to comply with the prohibition laid down in Article 81(1) EC (ex Article 85(1)).

38. That conclusion is not affected by the fact that the New York Convention of 10 June 1958 on the Recognition and Enforcement of Foreign Arbitral Awards, which has been ratified by all the Member States, provides that recognition and enforcement of an arbitration award may be refused only on certain specific grounds, namely where the award does not fall within the terms of the submission to arbitration or goes beyond its scope, where the award is not binding on the parties or where recognition or enforcement of the award would be contrary to the public policy of the country where such recognition and enforcement are sought (Art V(1)(c) and (e) and II(b) of the New York Convention).

39. For the reasons stated in paragraph 36 above, the provisions of Article 81 EC (ex Article 85) may be regarded as a matter of public policy within the meaning of the New York Convention.

40. Lastly, it should be recalled that, as explained in paragraph 34 above, arbitrators, unlike national courts and tribunals, are not in a position to request this Court to give a preliminary ruling on questions of interpretation of Community law. However, it is manifestly in the interest of the Community legal order that, in order to forestall differences of interpretation, every Community provision should be given a uniform interpretation, irrespective of the circumstances in which it is to be applied (Case C-88/91 *Federconsorzi* [1992] ECR I-4035, para 7). It follows that, in the circumstances of the present case, unlike *Van Schijndel and Van Veen*, Community law requires that questions concerning the interpretation of the prohibition laid down in Article 81(1) EC (ex Article 85(1)) should be open to examination by national courts when asked to determine the validity of an arbitration award and that it should be possible for those questions to be referred, if necessary, to the Court of Justice for a preliminary ruling.

41. The answer to be given to the second question must therefore be that a national court to which application is made for annulment of an arbitration award must grant that application if it considers that the award in question is in fact contrary to Article 81 EC (ex Article 85), where its domestic rules of procedure require it to grant an application for annulment founded on failure to observe national rules of public policy.

The first and third questions

42. In view of the reply given to the second question, there is no need to answer the first and third questions.

The fourth and fifth questions

43. By its fourth and fifth questions, which can be examined together, the referring court is asking essentially whether Community law requires a national court to refrain from applying domestic rules of procedure according to which an interim arbitration award which is in the nature of a final award and in respect of which no application for annulment has been made within the prescribed time-limit acquires the force of *res judicata* and may no longer be called in question by a subsequent arbitration award, even if this is necessary in order to examine, in proceedings for annulment of the subsequent award, whether an agreement which the interim award held to be valid in law is nevertheless void under Article 81 EC(ex Article 85).

44. According to the relevant domestic rules of procedure, application for annulment of an interim arbitration award which is in the nature of a final

award may be made within a period of three months following the lodging of that award at the registry of the court having jurisdiction in the matter.

45. Such a period, which does not seem excessively short compared with those prescribed in the legal systems of the other Member States, does not render excessively difficult or virtually impossible the exercise of rights conferred by Community law.

46. Moreover, domestic procedural rules which, upon the expiry of that period, restrict the possibility of applying for annulment of a subsequent arbitration award proceeding upon an interim arbitration award which is in the nature of a final award, because it has become *res judicata*, are justified by the basic principles of the national judicial system, such as the principle of legal certainty and acceptance of *res judicata*, which is an expression of that principle.

47. In those circumstances, Community law does not require a national court to refrain from applying such rules, even if this is necessary in order to examine, in proceedings for annulment of a subsequent arbitration award, whether an agreement which the interim award held to be valid in law is nevertheless void under Article 81 EC (ex Article 85).

48. The answer to be given to the fourth and fifth questions must therefore be that Community law does not require a national court to refrain from applying domestic rules of procedure according to which an interim arbitration award which is in the nature of a final award and in respect of which no application for annulment has been made within the prescribed time-limit acquires the force of *res judicata* and may no longer be called in question by a subsequent arbitration award, even if this is necessary in order to examine, in proceedings for annulment of a subsequent arbitration award, whether an agreement which the interim award held to be valid in law is nevertheless void under Article 81 EC (ex Article 85).

Costs

49. The costs incurred by the Netherlands, French, Italian and United Kingdom Governments and by the Commission, which have submitted observations to the Court, are not recoverable. Since these proceedings are, for the parties to the main proceedings, a step in the action pending before the national court, the decision on costs is a matter for that court.

On those grounds, The Court, in answer to the questions referred to it by the Hoge Raad der Nederlanden by order of 21 March 1997, hereby rules:

1. A national court to which application is made for annulment of an arbitration award must grant that application if it considers that the award in question is in fact contrary to Article 81 EC (ex Article 85), where its domestic rules of procedure require it to grant an application for annulment founded on failure to observe national rules of public policy.

2. Community law does not require a national court to refrain from applying domestic rules of procedure according to which an interim arbitration award which is in the nature of a final award and in respect of which no application for annulment has been made within the prescribed time-limit acquires the force of *res judicata* and may no longer be called in question by a subsequent arbitration award, even if this is necessary in order to examine, in proceedings for annulment of a subsequent arbitration award, whether an agreement which the interim award held to be valid in law is nevertheless void under Article 81 EC (ex Article 85).

Delivered in open court in Luxembourg on 1 June 1999.

8

Recognition and enforcement of the arbitral award

EXERCISE 16 – RECOGNITION AND ENFORCEMENT OF THE ARBITRAL AWARD I – SEMINAR

DISCUSSION QUESTIONS

Problem 1 (The *Aeroflot* Case)
Was the decision by the United States Court of Appeals, Second circuit, correct? If the transactions between MGM/Russo and Aeroflot had violated the US embargo on Iran, could/should enforcement of the award have been refused in the US based on the New York Convention?

Problem 2 (The *Aeroflot* Case)
The choice of law clause in the contract between MGM/Russo and Aeroflot stipulated that the contract was governed by Russian law and the law of the state of New York. In the arbitral award the arbitrators applied conflict of laws rules to identify the applicable substantive law. The conflicts rules used by the arbitrators resulted in the application of the substantive law of the state of New York. On these facts, is it possible to refuse enforcement of the arbitral award under the New York Convention?

Problem 3 (The *Swiss* Case)
Was the decision of the Federal Supreme Court correct with respect to Article V(I)(e) of the New York Convention? What is really the meaning of 'final and binding' in the New York Convention? What is the *ratio legis* of this provision?

Problem 4 (The *Swiss* Case)
Was the decision of the Federal Supreme Court correct with respect to public policy? Give examples of and discuss violations of 'procedural public policy'. Let us assume that the contract was governed by Swiss law and that the sole arbitrator completely misunderstood – and consequently misapplied – Swiss law. Would the award violate Swiss public policy?

CASE

US No. 478, MGM Productions Group, Inc (US) v Aeroflot Russian Airlines (Russian Federation), United States Court of Appeals, Second Circuit, 03-7561, 9 February 2004.

This summary was originally published in ICCA's Yearbook Commercial Arbitration, Volume XXIX (2004) pp 1215–17 (US no. 478) (Kluwer, 2004)

Facts

The facts of this case are also reported in Yearbook XXVIII (2003) at pp. 1271–3 (US no. 442). In June 1992, Russo International Ventures, Inc and Russo International Management, Inc (collectively, Russo), US corporations owned by Mr Craig Saroudi, entered into a Consultation Agreement with Aeroflot Russian Airlines (Aeroflot) to provide consulting services for the leasing of commercial aircraft to Iran Air against commissions. The agreement contained a clause for arbitration of disputes at the Arbitration Institute of the Stockholm Chamber of Commerce under the laws of New York State and Russia.

Between January 1993 and August 1996, Russo provided consulting services and Aeroflot made payments totalling US$1,822,207.42. A dispute subsequently arose between the parties concerning Russo's right to certain commissions and, on 27 October 1998, Russo commenced arbitration in Stockholm as provided for in the consultation agreement. Aeroflot maintained in the arbitration that the agreement was null and void as it had been executed in violation of US Executive Orders prohibiting imports from and certain transactions with Iran and their implementing regulations (the US embargo on Iran).

On 29 November 2002, the arbitrators issued an award which upheld the consultation agreement and directed Aeroflot to pay Russo US$13,155,000 plus interest and costs for Aeroflot's breach of the agreement. The arbitrators held that the transactions in which Russo was engaged under the agreement were not related to goods or services originated in Iran or owned or controlled by the Iranian Government and, consequently, did not violate the US embargo.

On 9 January 2003, Russo transferred its interest in the award to MGM Productions Group, Inc (MGM), a company owned by Mr Saroudi. On 23

January 2003, MGM sought enforcement of the Swedish award before the United States District Court for the Southern District of New York. On 14 May 2003, the district court granted enforcement, denying Aeroflot's argument that enforcement would violate public policy as the award compensated Russo for Aeroflot's breach of an agreement which violated the US embargo on Iran. The district court also dismissed Aeroflot's request for a stay of the proceedings pending a setting aside action before the Svea Court of Appeals in Sweden. This decision is reported in Yearbook XXVIII (2003) pp. 1271–8 (US no. 442).

The United States Court of Appeals for the Second Circuit, per Amalya L Kearse, Guido Calabresi and Robert A Katzmann, CJJ, affirmed the lower court's decision by a summary opinion. The Court stated briefly that '[w]e accord great deference to the arbitrator's factual findings and contractual construction', and noted that the arbitrators found that the agreement provided only for transactions between Russo and Aeroflot and thus did not violate the US embargo on Iran. The Court further reasoned that, even if it were to review the arbitrators' findings, 'it would be doubtful' the agreement at issue violated the embargo.

Excerpt

[1] [MGM], a California corporation, is the assignee of a 29 November 2002 award (award) of over US$13 million plus interest and costs, obtained by [Russo], a New York corporation, against [Aeroflot], in an arbitration held in Stockholm, Sweden, pursuant to a 1992 agreement (agreement) between Russo and Aeroflot. The award compensated Russo for Aeroflot's breach of the agreement, under which Russo provided consulting services to Aeroflot in connection with the Russian airline's leasing of airplanes and other equipment to Iran Air.

[2] MGM filed suit in federal district court, seeking confirmation of the arbitral award, pursuant to the [1958 New York Convention]. Aeroflot opposed page '1216' confirmation, arguing that the award fell under the 'public policy exception' in Article V(2)(b) of the New York Convention, because it compensated Russo for Aeroflot's non-performance of an agreement whose provisions allegedly violated the Iranian Transactions Regulations (ITRs), 31 CFR Sect. 560.101 et seq., adopted by the Office of Foreign Assets Control of the Department of the Treasury pursuant to Executive Orders issued by the President of the United States under the International Emergency Economic Powers Act, 50 USC Sects. 1701–1706. The district court confirmed the award, and we affirm.

[3] The arbitrators considered Aeroflot's argument that the agreement violated the ITRs promulgated in 1995, and found that since the agreement provided only for transactions between Russo and Aeroflot, it did not contravene the regulations. We accord great deference to the arbitrators' factual findings and contractual construction. See *Europcar Italia, SpA v Maiellano Tours, Inc*, 156 F 3d 310, 316 (2d Cir 1998) ('An arbitration award cannot be avoided solely on the ground that the arbitrator may have made an error of law or fact.'). Even if, in these circumstances, we did not, it would be, at most, doubtful that the agreement violated the 1995 ITRs. And, as such, the agreement cannot be said to violate fundamental public policy. See *Parsons & Whittemore Overseas Co v Société Générale de L'Industrie du Papier (RAKTA)*, 508 F 2d 969, 973–974 (2d Cir. 1974).

[4] Aeroflot also argues that performance of the agreement after 20 August 1997, the date that amended ITRs went into effect, would have been illegal, and that MGM should not be compensated for breach of the agreement when its performance by MGM's predecessor in interest would have violated US public policy. We need not reach this question, however, since Aeroflot breached the agreement before the 1997 ITRs went into effect. We cannot know, therefore, whether the parties would subsequently have amended their agreement to avoid potential violations of the regulations, were it not for Aeroflot's breach. Under these circumstances, Aeroflot cannot now sustain an argument that enforcement of the agreement would violate US public policy.

[5] We have considered all of the appellant's arguments, and found them to be without merit. Accordingly, we affirm the judgment of the district court.

 CASE

Switzerland No. 38, A SA (Switzerland) v B Co Ltd (British Virgin Islands), C SA (Ecuador), Tribunal Fédéral [Federal Supreme Court], 8 December 2003.

This summary was originally published in ICCA's Yearbook Commercial Arbitration, Volume XXIX (2004) pp. 834-842 (Switzerland no. 38) (Kluwer, 2004).

Facts

By a contract of 6 October 1999, A SA (the seller) sold B Co Ltd 20,000 tons of granulated fertilizer to be delivered to C SA in Ecuador. The contract contained a clause for arbitration of disputes under the rules of the International Chamber of Commerce (ICC) in London. A dispute arose between the parties and B Co Ltd and C SA (collectively, the buyers) commenced ICC arbitration against the seller. By an award on jurisdiction of 18 May 2001, the sole arbitrator denied the seller's objection and held that he had jurisdiction to hear the dispute. The seller sought to have this award set aside by the Court of Appeal in Paris; on 11 October 2001, the Paris court denied the request and directed the seller to pay the costs of the court proceedings. On 2 May 2002, the sole arbitrator rendered a partial award directing the seller to pay the buyers UK£12,838.53 and interest thereon starting 18 May 2001 for costs of the award on jurisdiction and UK£9,927.85 and interest thereon starting 9 December 2001 for costs and fees relating to the 18 May–22 November 2001 period. The sole arbitrator also directed the seller to reimburse US$24,000 and interest thereon starting 4 April 2001 to the buyers, being the advance payment made by the buyers towards the costs of the ICC arbitration.

On 24 September 2002, the buyers requested the *Office des Poursuites* [bailiff] of Geneva to notify an order to pay under the partial arbitral award of 2 May 2002 to the seller (proceedings A). The buyers subsequently sought and obtained from the *Office des Poursuites* the notification of a second order to pay FFr25,795.61, being the sum awarded by the Paris Court of Appeal in costs and fees (proceedings B). The seller initiated proceedings opposing both orders.

On 23 December 2002, the sole arbitrator rendered a final award in favour of the buyers, directing the seller to pay US$636,023.20 and US$48,000 for the costs of the arbitration. On 26 February 2003, the seller sought the setting aside of the final award before the High Court of Justice, Queen's Bench Division. This proceeding was pending at the time the present decision was rendered.

In the meantime, on 22 January 2003, the buyers requested the Court of First Instance of the Canton Geneva to enforce the partial arbitral award of 2 May 2002 and the order of the Paris Court of Appeal of 11 October 2001 denying the seller's request to set aside the award on jurisdiction. On 17 March 2003, the court granted enforcement of the partial award and the order of the Paris Court of Appeal. On 19 June 2003, the Court of Appeal of the Canton Geneva affirmed.

The seller brought a public law appeal (*recours de droit public*) to the Federal Supreme Court. By the present decision, the Supreme Court affirmed the lower court's decision. The Court first noted that the buyers submitted a photocopy of the arbitral clause to the court of first instance and only submitted the original arbitration agreement in the proceedings before the Court of Appeal. The Supreme Court reasoned that, although the procedural law of the Canton Geneva does not allow the submission of new documents in appellate proceedings, the authenticity of the arbitral clause in the case at issue was undisputed and the court of first instance had a copy of the clause in its file when it reached its decision to enforce the award. Hence, the Supreme Court agreed with the Geneva Court of Appeal that refusing the submission of the arbitral clause in the appellate proceedings would have been an act of excessive formalism, which is prohibited by cantonal law, in the present case. The Court then examined the seller's objection that the award was not binding on the parties and concluded that the seller did not furnish any proof in support of its page '835' objection other than merely arguing that English law allows appeals against arbitral awards and that such appeals forbid *ipso jure* that the award enters into force. The Supreme Court also dismissed the seller's allegation that the award violated public policy because the sole arbitrator by his partial award of 2 May 2002 directed the seller to pay the costs of the arbitral proceedings relating to the objection on lack of jurisdiction and to reimburse the arbitration fees paid in advance by the buyers. The seller alleged that by so doing the sole arbitrator prejudiced the final award on the merits; hence, 'all procedural acts following the partial award [were] a sham' and due process and the seller's right to be heard were violated. The Court deemed this argument unconvincing. It reasoned that the costs relating to the award on jurisdiction manifestly did not affect the arbitrator's decision on the merits of the dispute, and that the order to reimburse the advance payment for the costs of the arbitration made by the buyers only concerned the seller's share of the costs of the arbitration.

Excerpt

(. ...)

[1] Pursuant to Article 194 LDIP, the recognition and enforcement of foreign arbitral awards is governed by [the 1958 New York Convention]. Since the Convention is an international treaty, cantonal court decisions applying it may be reviewed in a public law appeal for violation of an international treaty (Art 84(1)(c)) if any other form of recourse is excluded (Art. 84(2) OJ; ATF 126 III page '836' 534 consid. 1a and decisions cited therein).

[2] Pursuant to Art. 90(1)(b) OJ, the seller must indicate which provision of the treaty was allegedly violated by the attacked decision and in what manner (ATF 126 III 534 consid. 1b and decisions cited therein).

[3] When seized of a [public law] appeal pursuant to Art. 84(1)(c) OJ, the Supreme Court freely ascertains, in the context of the grounds for appeal, whether an international treaty has been violated (ATF 108 Ib 85 consid. 2a). However, when the attacked decision emanates from a judicial authority the Court can only review that decision for arbitrariness as far as the examination of the facts is concerned. New submissions are therefore not allowed (ATF 129 I 110 consid 1.1). The Supreme Court shall freely examine, in conformity with these principles, whether the decision at issue, which was rendered by the higher jurisdiction of the Canton Geneva, violates the provisions of the New York Convention invoked by the seller. However, it shall only review the factual findings of the cantonal court, if contested by the seller, for arbitrariness.

I. Submission of original arbitral clause in appellate proceedings (Art IV(1)(b))

[4] According to Article IV(1)(b) together with Article II of the New York Convention, the party relying on a foreign arbitral award can only obtain its recognition and enforcement if it supplies the original arbitration clause or agreement binding the parties or a duly certified copy thereof. In the present case, the buyers submitted to the Court of First Instance a photocopy of the arbitral clause; hence, they did not comply with the letter of the above provision. In the appellate proceedings, however, the buyers submitted the original contract of 6 October 1999 containing the arbitral clause at issue. The buyers thus supplied the document required by the above-mentioned provision.

[5] The issue whether the original arbitral clause could be submitted in the appellate proceedings, while only a copy of the contract containing the arbitral page '837' clause was supplied in the first instance proceedings is a question of cantonal procedure. The Court of Appeal recognised that Geneva procedural law does not allow new documents to be supplied in appellate proceedings. The Court of Appeal considered, however, that it would be acting with excessive formalism if it refused the submission of the above-mentioned document, since its authenticity was undisputed and a copy thereof was supplied in the first instance proceedings.

[6] The application of cantonal law is limited by the prohibition of excessive formalism. The seller does not argue that the constitutional law prohibiting excessive formalism was incorrectly applied in the case at issue, so that this question shall not be examined (Art 90(1)(b) OJ). Since the cantonal court had the original contract containing the arbitral clause in its file at the

moment of rendering a decision, its decision granting enforcement does not violate Article IV(1)(b) of the New York Convention.

II. 'Binding' (Art V(1)(e))

[7] Pursuant to Article V(1)(e) of the New York Convention, enforcement of an arbitral award shall be refused where the party against whom it is invoked furnishes proof that the award has not yet become binding on the parties, or has been set aside or suspended by a competent authority of the country in which, or under the law of which, that award was made. Enforcement shall thus be refused where the award can still be impugned by an ordinary means of recourse before a State court, where the award has been declared null and void or has been annulled in the country of rendition or where suspensive effect has been granted to a request for setting aside the award by a competent authority (for more details, see, among others, Paolo Michele Patocchi/ Cesare Jermini, in *Commentaire bâlois*, no. 116 et seq. to Art 194 LDIP).

[8] The burden to prove one of the grounds for refusal under the above-mentioned provision is on the party resisting enforcement (ATF 110 Ib 191 consid. 2c p. 195 and decisions cited therein; Andreas Bucher, *Die neue internationale Schiedsgerichtsbarkeit in der Schweiz*, p 156 no. 437). Hence, in the present case, the resisting party shall to this aim furnish proof of the foreign law (ATF 108 Ib 85 consid. 3 p. 88; Patocchi/Jermini, op. cit., no. 114 to Art. 194 PILA). In order to obtain enforcement of the award, the award need not have page '838' executory force in the country of rendition; it suffices that it can be enforced in the State where enforcement is sought, as the New York Convention aimed at avoiding 'double exequatur' (ATF 108 Ib 85 consid. 4e p 91 and references therein; Frédéric-Edouard Klein, '*The New York Convention pour la reconnaissance et l'exécution des sentences arbitrales étrangères*', in: RSJ 57/1961, p. 248 no. 15; Andreas Bucher, p 160 no. 451).

[9] In the present case, the cantonal court noted that the effect of the partial award of 2 May 2002 was not suspended by the arbitrator. The court further noted that the recourse against the final award of 23 December 2002 did not dispute the binding nature of the partial award which preceded it. The court added that the seller did not prove that the recourse [against the final award] was granted suspensive effect. In support of its objection, the seller merely argues that English law allows appeals against arbitral awards and that such appeals forbid *ipso jure* that the award enters into force. The seller, however, does not furnish even the merest of proofs in support of its thesis. In particular, it does not prove that the recourse to the English State court

is an ordinary means of recourse, nor, if this is not the case, that the English court seised with this recourse granted it a suspensive effect.

[10] Hence, the ground based on the violation of Article V(1)(*e*) of the New York Convention must be denied.

III. Public policy (Art V(2)(b))

[11] The seller also alleges a violation of Article V(2)(*b*) of the New York Convention, that is, a violation of Swiss public policy, because the sole arbitrator by his partial award of 2 May 2002 directed the seller to pay part of the costs of the proceedings on the merits and to reimburse the fees paid in advance by the buyers, before rendering a final award. [The seller alleges that] such behaviour prejudiced the decision on the merits, made all procedural acts following the partial award a sham and was at odds with the 'most elementary principles of (the) legal system, inter alia, the right to be heard'.

[12] According to Article V(2)(*b*) of the New York Convention, recognition and enforcement of an arbitral award may also be refused if the competent authority in the country where recognition and enforcement is sought finds that the recognition or enforcement of the award would be contrary to the public policy of that country.

[13] Public policy, being an objection, must be interpreted restrictively, especially in the context of the recognition and enforcement of foreign decisions, p '839' where its scope is narrower than in the context of direct application of foreign law (attenuated effect of public policy: ATF 116 II 625 consid. 4a p 630 and references therein). There is a violation of public policy where the recognition or enforcement of a foreign decision is intolerably at odds with the Swiss concept of justice. A foreign decision can be incompatible with the Swiss legal system not only because of its substantive contents, but also because of the procedure that led to it. In this respect, Swiss public policy requires compliance with the fundamental principles of procedure, as deduced from the Constitution, such as the right to a fair process and the right to be heard (ATF 126 III 101 consid. 3b pp 107–108; 122 III 344 consid. 4a pp 348–349 and references therein). These principles also apply to the recognition and enforcement of foreign arbitral awards (ATF 101 Ia 521 consid. 4a and references therein).

[14] In the present case, the seller complains that the cantonal court affirmed the decision [of the court of first instance] enforcing the partial award regardless of the seller's right to be heard. [It alleges that] the sole arbitrator ignored

this right by deciding on costs and fees in the partial award; by so doing, he prejudiced the decision on the merits.

[15] This argument is unconvincing. We note first that the ICC Rules of Arbitration explicitly provides for interim and partial awards (Art 2 at (iii)). The seller does not prove at all that Article 31 of the same Rules forbids a decision on costs and fees in this type of awards. In any case, [the awarding of] costs and fees relating to the proceedings concerning the objection of lack of jurisdiction manifestly has no impact on the solution of the merits of the dispute referred to the sole arbitrator. Further, [the seller alleges that] the fact that the sole arbitrator directed the seller to reimburse the advance payment made by the buyers to the International Court of Arbitration of the ICC, being half of the advance payment of costs, that is, US$24,000, indicates the arbitrator's intention to render a final award in favour of the buyers. In reality, this order to pay US$24,000 as advance payment of the costs only concerned the share of the costs of the arbitration which was to be paid by the seller, a share which the seller did not pay and which was advanced by the buyers in order to allow the arbitration to proceed.

[16] In so far as the arbitrator directed in the course of the proceedings that the seller reimburse the advance payment made by the buyers, rather than the totality of the costs of the arbitration, that is, US$48,000, the partial award of 2 May 2002 cannot reasonably be deemed to prejudice the outcome of the arbitration and the decision reached in the final award of 23 December 2002. Consequently, the procedural acts following the second partial arbitral award of 2 May 2002 are fully valid, in particular for the seller, which therefore cannot argue that its right to be heard was violated.

[17] Consequently, the Court of Appeal did not disregard public policy in the sense of Article V(2)(b) of the New York Convention. The seller's argument on this point is therefore unfounded.

IV. Arbitrary application of Art 80 LP

[18] The seller in the last place argues that the attacked decision is an arbitrary application of Article 80 LP. In the case at issue, the buyers had [the *Office des Poursuites*] notify two payment orders: an order in proceedings A for the sums which were awarded to the buyers in the partial arbitral award of 2 May 2000 and an order in proceedings B for the sums awarded by the Court of Appeal of Paris in its order of 11 October 2001. The buyers further requested, by a joint request, that both oppositions filed against each of the above-mentioned payment orders be finally lifted. This ground therefore

concerns lifting (*mainlevée*), which is regulated by the Cantons since federal law does not contain specific provisions thereon (Art 25(2)(a) LP; ATF 123 III 271 consid. 4b p. 272 and references therein).

[19] The Court of Appeal found that the buyers filed different conclusions in their joint request for a final *mainlevée* with respect to each of the two proceedings commenced against the seller. It added that the seller did not allege that the buyers' conclusions were imprecisely formulated. Before the Supreme Court, the seller does not indicate which provision of Geneva procedural law was violated or interpreted arbitrarily.

[20] In so far as sufficiently articulated with respect to the requirements of Article 90(1)(b) OJ (ATF 129 I 113 consid. 2.1, p 120 and decisions cited therein), this ground is unfounded. Considering the buyers' conclusions, the seller could be aware of the subject matter of the *mainlevée* decision and easily understand that this decision concerned the amount listed in the first payment order for the partial arbitral award of 2 May 2002 and, as to the second payment order, for the order of 11 October 2001 of the Court of Appeal of Paris.

V. Conclusion

[21] The seller, as the losing party, shall pay the costs of this proceedings (Art 156(1) OJ) and reimburse the buyers' costs (Art 159(1) OJ).

[22] For the above reasons, the Supreme Court dismisses the appeal and directs the seller to pay CHFr4,000 for costs and to reimburse CHFr5,000 for costs to the buyers.

(...)

EXERCISE 17 – RECOGNITION AND ENFORCEMENT OF THE ARBITRAL AWARD II – MINI MOCK ARBITRATION

The Cyprus based oil exploration and production company Midnight Oil entered into a production sharing agreement with the government of Farawaystan. Under the agreement Midnight Oil was granted the right to explore a potentially very large oil and gas field in a remote area of Farawaystan. The agreement provided for arbitration pursuant to the UNCITRAL Arbitration Rules. The Stockholm Chamber of Commerce was named the appointing authority and as such had to appoint all three arbitrators. The place of arbitration was to be chosen by the arbitrators. The production sharing agreement was governed by Swiss law.

Eventually Midnight Oil initiated arbitration alleging that the government of Farawaystan had violated the production sharing agreement by not granting land use rights and by revoking Midnight Oil's exploration license as well as previously granted drilling permits. Midnight Oil asked the Tribunal to order the government of Farawaystan to pay compensation for all damage inflicted on it.

Farawaystan refused to participate in the arbitration, which was held in Farawaystan pursuant to the decision of the Tribunal, alleging that since it is a sovereign State it has no obligation to do so, in particular when the acts complained of are sovereign in nature (granting and revoking permits) and that as a sovereign it has an absolute right to appoint its own arbitrator.

An award was eventually rendered in favour of Midnight Oil. The government of Farawaystan files an application with a local court to have the award set aside. The government relies on two arguments *viz.*, (i) it has been denied due process since it was not given the opportunity to appoint an arbitrator and since it did not participate in the arbitration and (ii) the award violates public policy since the matters decided by the Tribunal (granting and revoking permits) were governed by mandatory provisions of the law of Farawaystan and could therefore not be governed by Swiss law.

Farawaystan has ratified the New York Convention and has recently adopted a law on international commercial arbitration, which closely follows the UNCITRAL Model Law.

While annulment proceedings in Farawaystan are pending, Midnight Oil seeks to have the award enforced in London. One week before the final hearing in London the local court in Farawaystan declares the award null and void and consequently sets it aside.

GROUP

Group 1

You are the London Court. Your task is to decide the case on the basis of the arguments presented by Groups 3 and 4 and by applying the New York Convention.

Group 2

You are counsel to Midnight Oil in the proceedings in London. You must convince the Court that the award must be enforced on the basis of the New York Convention.

Group 3

You represent the government of Farawaystan in London. Your task is to convince the Court that the award cannot be enforced under the New York Convention.

Group 4

You are the observer group. Have the best arguments been presented?

Part II

International investment law

9

Treaty interpretation

 EXERCISE 18 – TREATY INTERPRETATION I – SEMINAR

Read and review the jurisdictional awards in *RosInvestCo UK Ltd v The Russian Federation* and *Renta 4 et al v The Russian Federation* (including the separate opinion by Charles N Brower).

? DISCUSSION QUESTIONS

Problem 1
Study the different approaches to treaty interpretation based on the Vienna Convention on the Law of Treaties that are demonstrated by the cases. Explain the different approaches:

(a) to treaty interpretation in general;
(b) to Article 31(1) specifically.

Problem 2
Study the different approaches to treaty interpretation based on the Vienna Convention on the Law of Treaties that are demonstrated by the cases. Explain the different approaches:

(a) to the use of *travaux préparatoires* in treaty interpretation;
(b) to the use of Article 32.

Problem 3
Based on the facts in *RosInvestCo*, present the best arguments for claimant's case, i.e., that the claims are covered by the treaty's dispute resolution clause.

Problem 4
Based on the facts in *Renta 4*, present the best arguments for the respondent's case, i.e., that the claims are *not* covered by the treaty's dispute resolution clause.

CASE

RosInvestCo UK Ltd (claimant) v The Russian Federation (respondent) Arbitration Institute of the Stockholm Chamber of Commerce, Case no: Arbitration V 079 / 2005 Award on Jurisdiction

[...]

3. The Tribunal

70. The Tribunal has carefully examined the memorials and exhibits submitted, as well as the presentations at the hearing by each of the parties on this issue. It is not necessary to recall these arguments in detail here, but the Tribunal has taken them fully into account in reaching the following findings and conclusions.

71. In the present context, to avoid misunderstanding, one has to distinguish two different questions:

(1) Is there a binding consent to arbitration with the effect that a prospective party to the arbitration proceedings does not need the agreement of the other prospective party to start arbitration proceedings?
(2) If there is such a consent, what is its scope, in other words, which issues can be submitted to such arbitration proceedings?

The second question will be discussed later in this Award with regard both to Article 8 and to Article 3. It is only the first of these questions which will be discussed here. And since claimant argues that the UK-Soviet BIT provides a consent both under Article 8 and under Article 3, this first question has to be examined with regard to both of these provisions.

3.1 Consent under Article 8 UK-Soviet BIT

72. The Tribunal does not see great difficulty in interpreting Article 8 in this context. That provision, irrespective of its material scope, which will be discussed later in this Award, contains express and unambiguous language in its second paragraph: first, by using the word '*shall*', which makes clear that it is mandatory; and second, by adding the words '*if either party to the dispute wishes*', which clearly indicates that the initiation of the arbitration proceedings depend solely on the unilateral decision by either party and that the other party does not have to agree again in order to permit the arbitration

to start. This interpretation is confirmed by the third paragraph of Article 8 which authorises the investor to choose between various arbitration rules; that provision would not make sense if the investor had first to obtain once again the agreement of the host State to start the arbitration proceedings. Finally, the Tribunal notes that the wording of Article 8, again irrespective of its scope, uses language which is found often in BITs, of both the UK and the Soviet Union, and of many other States, and which has generally been interpreted as a binding consent to arbitration.

3.2 Consent by Article 3 UK-Soviet BIT in connection with Article 8 Denmark-Russia BIT

73. The question whether the MFN clauses in Article 3 UK-Soviet BIT can attract the application of arbitration clauses in other BITs will be discussed later in this Award. Here, the only question to be examined is whether, if Article 8 of the Denmark-Russia BIT can be resorted to, it provides a binding consent to arbitration authorising the investor to start arbitration proceedings without the need to obtain afresh the agreement of the host State.

74. Taking into account the analysis above of Article 8 of the UK-Soviet BIT, the Tribunal concludes that there can also be no doubt that Article 8 of the Denmark-Russia BIT provides such a binding consent to arbitration. The language in its second paragraph, under which 'the investor shall be entitled to submit the case either to', and which then once again offers several options for the applicable arbitration rules, leaves no room for any interpretation other than that the investor can initiate the arbitration, without the need for further agreement by the host State.

3.3 Conclusion

75. In view of the above considerations, the Tribunal concludes that respondent has submitted in a binding way to arbitration and that respondent's renewed prior consent was not needed when claimant initiated this arbitral procedure. This is without prejudice to the question whether this Tribunal also has jurisdiction over the claims, which will be discussed hereafter in this award.

Subject-matter jurisdiction – *ratione materie*

[...]

3. The Tribunal

101. The Tribunal has carefully examined the memorials and exhibits submitted, as well as the presentations at the hearing by each of the parties on this issue. It is not necessary to recall these arguments in detail here, but the Tribunal has taken them fully into account in reaching the following findings and conclusions.

102. The Tribunal, having already found that respondent has indeed consented to arbitration, both in Article 8 of the UK-Soviet BIT and Article 8 of the Denmark-Russia BIT, now turns in this section to the scope of the submission to arbitration and in particular whether the submission also covers a jurisdiction of the Tribunal to decide on whether an expropriation occurred and, if so, its legality.

103. To avoid misunderstanding, it may be recalled here again that the examination of the Tribunal in the present section only deals with its jurisdiction over this issue, and that, should jurisdiction be found to exist, the examination of whether the respondent's actions have indeed to be considered as an expropriation will be joined to the merits phase of this arbitration.

104. Since claimant bases its contention that the Tribunal does have jurisdiction alternatively on Article 8 and on Article 3, and both have been extensively discussed by the parties, the Tribunal will take up each issue separately.

3.1 Jurisdiction based on Article 8 UK-Soviet BIT

105. The text of Article 8 is quoted above in section E of this award. Nevertheless, that part of its wording which is relevant in the present context may be recalled:

> Article 8
> Disputes between an investor and the host contracting party
> (1) This Article shall apply to any legal disputes between an investor of one Contracting Party and the other Contracting Party in relation to an investment of the former either concerning the amount or payment of compensation under Articles 4 or 5 of this Agreement, or concerning any other matter consequential upon an act of expropriation in accordance with Article 5 of this Agreement, or concerning the consequences of the non-implementation, or of the incorrect implementation, of Article 6 of this Agreement.
> (2) Any such disputes which have not been amicably settled shall, after a period

of three months from written notification of a claim, be submitted to international arbitration if either party to the dispute so wishes.

(3) Where the dispute is referred to international arbitration, the investor concerned in the dispute shall have the right to refer the dispute either to:

(a) the Institute of Arbitration of the Chamber of Commerce of Stockholm; . . ..

106. The Russian text of Article 8(1) is translated unofficially by the respondent in its First Memorial on Jurisdictional Issues as follows (R II, para. 21, fn. 15). The translation was acknowledged by the claimant at least with respect to all relevant parts (C II, para. 58, fn. 55; para. 65). It was, however, emphasised by the parties that the inclusion in the Common Bundle (CB) of an unofficial translation prepared by one party does not constitute acceptance by the other party of the accuracy of that translation.

> The provisions of this Article shall apply to any disputes of a legal character between an investor of one Contracting Party and the other Contracting Party in relation to issues of the investor's investment concerning either the amount and the procedure for the payment of compensation provided for in Articles 4 or 5 of this Agreement, or any other matters being the result of an act of expropriation in accordance with Article 5 of this Agreement, or regarding the consequences of the non-implementation, or of the incorrect implementation, of undertakings under Article 6 of this Agreement.

107. In the view of the Tribunal the slight variations in the translation by the respondent do not contain anything of relevance for the issue to be examined in the present section of this award. The Tribunal will therefore focus on the official English text as quoted above.

108. Paragraph (1) of the provision, after its introductory wording ending with the words 'either concerning', continues with what has been called, by the parties and the Tribunal, three *jurisdictional clauses*, namely:

> 1. the amount or payment of compensation under Articles 4 or 5 of this Agreement,
> 2. or concerning any other matter consequential upon an act of expropriation in accordance with Article 5 of this Agreement,
> 3. or concerning the consequences of the non-implementation, or of the incorrect implementation, of Article 6 of this Agreement.

109. While the third jurisdictional clause is obviously not relevant in the present context, the parties have widely debated whether the first or second jurisdictional clauses provide jurisdiction for this Tribunal.

110. In interpreting these Articles, the Tribunal is primarily guided by the provisions of Article 31.1. of the Vienna Convention on the Law of Treaties (VCLT) according to which a 'Treaty shall be interpreted in good faith in accordance with the ordinary meaning to be given to the terms of the treaty in their context and in the light of the object and purpose.' To start with the *first jurisdictional clause*, rather than referring generally to Articles 4 and 5, it expressly contains a qualification by the words 'concerning the amount or payment of compensation under'. In order to give an ordinary meaning to that qualification, it can only be understood as a limitation of the jurisdiction conferred by that clause. Though no documents from the negotiation of the BIT have been produced, the parties including the claimant agree that the rather complicated wording in Article 8 presented a compromise between the UK's intention to have a wide arbitration clause and the Soviet intention to have a limited one. If that is so, it is hard to arrive at an interpretation all the same that the clause is so wide as to include all aspects of an expropriation.

111. If one further considers the wording of Article 5 to which this first jurisdictional clause refers, it can be seen that that provision first determines that, in principle, an investment shall not be expropriated, and then adds exceptions to that principle by the word 'except'. Of the exceptions mentioned thereafter, payment of compensation is "only" the third. And the following sentence in Article 5 then gives a number of concrete requirements regarding the compensation.

112. In view of this order in Article 5, the Tribunal cannot see how the reference in the first jurisdictional clause expressly to *the amount or payment of compensation under Articles 4 or 5* only can nevertheless be interpreted as a reference also to the earlier sections of Article 5 which deal with expropriation in general and the first two exceptions mentioned in that provision.

113. This limiting interpretation is confirmed by a comparison with arbitration clauses in BITs concluded by the UK, the Soviet Union, Russia and other States in which a general reference to expropriation or the article dealing with expropriation makes it clear that every aspect of expropriation is under the jurisdiction of the arbitral tribunal. An example from the Russian practice is Article 8 of the Denmark-Russia BIT quoted in Section E above. An example from the practice of the UK is Article 9(2) of the 1988 UK Model BIT (CB-9 = R-34). These examples may suffice to illustrate the obvious, namely how easily it can be and is in practice indicated in clear and unambiguous terms that every aspect of expropriation shall be under the jurisdiction of an arbitral tribunal.

114. Therefore, the Tribunal concludes that the wording of the first jurisdictional clause does not include jurisdiction over the questions whether an expropriation occurred and was legal.

115. The Tribunal now turns to the *second jurisdictional clause* in Article 8. Again, one must first recall the wording by which that clause expressly qualifies the jurisdiction, namely 'or concerning any other matter consequential upon an act of expropriation in accordance with Article 5 of this Agreement'. In a potential analogy with the issue of Kompetenz-Kompetenz, it may be argued that, in order to exercise its undoubted competence to decide a disputed issue consequential on an expropriation, a tribunal must (implicitly) be endowed with the power to determine whether the issue is 'consequential upon an act of expropriation', and that from that it is only a short step to saying that it has therefore the power to determine whether there was an expropriation or not. However, at least in the present context of the wording of Article 8(1), such an interpretation would deprive the wording 'or concerning any other matter consequential upon' in the above-mentioned qualification of any substantive meaning and turn this jurisdictional clause into an arbitration clause with a general reference to Article 5. For similar reasons as discussed above regarding the first jurisdictional clause, this qualification can only be understood to the effect that not all aspects of Article 5 and particularly of expropriation are included, but that jurisdiction is only granted over the specific aspects mentioned in the clause. In particular, the words any other matter are not placed on their own, but are combined with the words 'consequential upon an act of expropriation in accordance with Article 5 of this Agreement'. This can only be interpreted to mean that not all other matters are included but only those falling under this further qualification.

116. Now, regarding that qualification, the Tribunal considers that the ordinary meaning in the sense of Article 31 VCLT of the word 'consequential' cannot be interpreted to include, in addition to the consequences of an expropriation according to Article 5, also the preconditions laid down in Article 5, i.e., that an act of expropriation occurred and within the conditions specified for a lawful expropriation.

117. If these preconditions were to be considered as also included, the qualification would be meaningless – as would the qualification stated in the first jurisdictional clause – because not only the issues mentioned in these qualifications, but all other aspects of expropriation would be included.

118. Therefore the Tribunal concludes that the second jurisdictional clause does equally not confer jurisdiction on this Tribunal over the occurrence or the validity of an expropriation.

119. Since the Tribunal has come to the above conclusions on the basis of the ordinary meaning of Article 8 in the context of the object and purpose of the BIT in accordance with paragraph (1) of Article 31 VCLT, there is no need to go into the additional criteria for interpretation mentioned in the further paragraphs of that Article. In this context, the Tribunal notes that none of the various agreements, instruments, practice or rules of international law to which paragraph (2) or (3) of Article 31 refer can be found to be of relevance for the interpretation of Article 8. All of these subsections (a) and (b) of Article 31(2) and (a) to (c) of Article 31(3) require some relation or connection to the treaty to be interpreted, a requirement not fulfilled by earlier or later BITs or other agreements or other practice either of the UK or the Soviet Union or Russia.

120. Even less applicable are the supplementary means of interpretation identified in Article 32 VCLT. It needs no further explanation that the meaning of Article 8 found above is neither *ambiguous or obscure nor manifestly absurd or unreasonable.*

121. The above considerations, in the view of the Tribunal, also do not permit in particular the *dynamic interpretation* which claimant has proposed to be applied in this regard. In this regard, the Tribunal refers to its separate section above containing a more general analysis of the principles of interpretation. At least in the present context it cannot be justified under Articles 31 and 32 VCLT that later developments can be found to change the ordinary and unambiguous meaning of a treaty provision like Article 8 of the BIT. Since the present context is that of a bilateral treaty, the Tribunal does not have to take up the questions whether other considerations may justify such an interpretation in the context of a long-term multilateral convention or human rights.

122. The Tribunal has taken note of the references the parties have submitted to other treaties and decisions of arbitral tribunals regarding dispute settlement clauses in other treaties. Indeed, there are clauses which contain limiting language similar to that of Article 8 such as Article 10 of the Belgium/Luxemburg-Soviet BIT quoted above in section E, as well as clauses which provide a wider language such as Article 7 of the France-Soviet BIT ('concerning the effects of a measure taken' and 'particularly but not exclusively concerning') also quoted above. However, the Tribunal feels there is no need

to enter into a discussion of these or other treaties or decisions concerning them, because the combined wording of the three jurisdictional clauses in Article 8 is unique and not identical to that in any of such other treaties and thus must be interpreted by itself as has been done above.

123. As a final conclusion, therefore, the Tribunal determines that it has no jurisdiction as to the occurrence and validity of an expropriation on the basis of Article 8. In addition to this negative conclusion, there is no need for the Tribunal to determine in detail at this stage by a positive conclusion what extent of jurisdiction is indeed covered by Article 8, because the Tribunal will now have to examine whether it has jurisdiction on the aspects not covered by Article 8 by application of the MFN-clause in Article 3.

(Co-Arbitrator Sir Franklin Berman wishes to add the following declaration:

> I am in full agreement with my colleagues that Article 8 of the BIT does not suffice to confer jurisdiction on the Tribunal to pronounce on the claims advanced by the claimant in this arbitration. I note only that Article 8 is quite plainly, and on its very face, a difficult compromise between opening positions on the part of the two Contracting States which must have been far apart from one another (as indeed the parties have argued at length before us). In a circumstance of that kind – which one encounters from time to time in treaty practice – it will seldom if ever be justified for the interpreter to arrive at a conclusion that corresponds to all intents and purposes with the position of either the one Contracting State or that of the other. In other words, I would not want our common conclusion that Article 8 does not confer jurisdiction in this case to be taken in any way as an expression of opinion on how that article or other similar treaty clauses relates to other claims that might be brought forward in other cases based on an allegation of expropriation.)

3.2 Jurisdiction based on the MFN-clauses in Article 3 UK-Soviet BIT in connection with the Denmark-Russia BIT

124. The parties have extensively engaged on the question whether the MFN-provisions in Article 3(1) and (2) of the UK-Soviet BIT are effective to import the wide wording of Article 8 of the Denmark-Russia BIT so as to submit expropriations to arbitration under the UK-Soviet BIT. The provisions in question are quoted above in section E of this Award. But, for the present context, the relevant wording may be recalled here. The Denmark-Russia BIT provides:

> Article 8
> Disputes between an investor of one contracting party and the other contracting party:

(1) Any dispute which may arise between an investor of one Contracting Party and the other Contracting Party in connection with an investment on the territory of that other Contracting Party shall be subject to negotiations [sic] [betwee the] parties in dispute.

(2) If the dispute cannot be settled in such a way within a period of six months from the date of written notification of the claim, the investor shall be entitled to submit the case either to:

(a) a sole arbitrator or an ad hoc arbitral tribunal established under the Arbitration Rules of the United Nations Commission on International Trade Law (UNCITRAL), or

(b) the Institute of Arbitration of the Chamber of Commerce in Stockholm.

125. There is no dispute between the parties, and the Tribunal agrees, that that provision, by its wording: 'Any dispute . . . in connection with an investment' confers jurisdiction on the arbitral tribunal on issues such as those at stake in the present context, i.e., whether an act of the host state was an expropriation and was legal under the BIT.

126. It may also be recalled that the relevant paragraphs of Article 3 of the UK- Soviet BIT provide:

Article 3
Treatment of Investments
(1) Neither Contracting Party shall in its territory subject investments or returns of investors of the other Contracting Party to treatment less favourable than that which it accords to investments or returns of investors of any third State.
(2) Neither Contracting Party shall in its territory subject investors of the other Contracting Party, as regards their management, maintenance, use, enjoyment or disposal of their investments, to treatment less favourable than that which it accords to investors of any third State.

127. As can be seen, the first paragraph deals with investments and the second with the investors. The two paragraphs provide MFN protection by quite different wordings and thus with a different scope. Therefore the Tribunal will consider them separately hereafter.

128. Paragraph (1) of Article 3 grants MFN protection for investments to the effect that they shall not be subject *to treatment less favourable than that which it accords to investments . . . of any third State.* Can the term *treatment* include the protection by an arbitration clause? The Tribunal feels that, for the purposes of this award, it does not have to answer that question in gen-

eral, but only regarding the sub-question whether it includes an arbitration clause covering expropriation. In that latter regard, it is difficult to doubt that, first, an expropriation is indeed a 'treatment' of the investment by the host State. However, secondly, while the protection by an arbitration clause covering expropriation is a highly relevant aspect of that 'treatment', if compared with the alternative that the expropriation of an investment can only be challenged before the national courts of the host State, it does not directly affect the 'investment', but rather the procedural rights of the 'investor' for whom paragraph (2) of Article 3 provides a separate rule.

129. Therefore, without entering into the much more general question whether MFN-clauses can be used to transfer arbitration clauses from one treaty to another, the Tribunal concludes that, for the specific wording of Article 3(1) of the UK-Soviet BIT, and for the specific purpose of arbitration with regard to expropriation, the wide wording of Article 8 of the Denmark-Russia BIT is not applicable.

130. In view of the above conclusion regarding paragraph (1) of Article 3, the Tribunal now has to consider whether it has jurisdiction based on Paragraph (2) of Article 3. As seen above, the provision grants MFN-protection for '*investors*' by a wording which is quite different to paragraph (1), namely regarding 'their management, maintenance, use, enjoyment or disposal of their investments'. Again limiting its considerations to the possible application of the MFN-clause to arbitration regarding expropriation, the terms '*use*' and '*enjoyment*' in paragraph (2) lead the Tribunal to different conclusions from those reached with regard to paragraph (1). For it is difficult to doubt that an expropriation interferes with the investor's use and enjoyment of the investment, and that the submission to arbitration forms a highly relevant part of the corresponding protection for the investor by granting him, in case of interference with his '*use*' and '*enjoyment*', procedural options of obvious and great significance compared to the sole option of challenging such interference before the domestic courts of the host State.

131. Does that conclusion have to be changed in view of the further conclusion reached above that Article 8 of the UK-Soviet BIT expressly limits the jurisdiction of the Tribunal and does not give jurisdiction in respect of other aspects of expropriation? In the Tribunal's view, that is not so. While indeed the application of the MFN clause of Article 3 widens the scope of Article 8 and thus is in conflict to its limitation, this is a normal result of the application of MFN clauses, the very character and intention of which is that protection not accepted in one treaty is widened by transferring the protection accorded in another treaty.

132. If this effect is generally accepted in the context of substantive protection, the Tribunal sees no reason not to accept it in the context of procedural clauses such as arbitration clauses. Quite the contrary, it could be argued that, if it applies to substantive protection, then it should apply even more to 'only' procedural protection. However, the Tribunal feels that this latter argument cannot be considered as decisive, but that rather, as argued further above, an arbitration clause, at least in the context of expropriation, is of the same protective value as any substantive protection afforded by applicable provisions such as Article 5 of the BIT.

133. In view of these considerations, the Tribunal concludes that, on the basis of the MFN Clause in Article 3(2) of the UK-Soviet BIT taken together with Article 8 of the Denmark-Russia BIT, it has jurisdiction beyond that granted by Article 8 of the UK-Soviet BIT and which extends to the issues whether respondent's actions have to be considered as expropriations and were valid.

134. The above interpretations by the Tribunal of the MFN-clauses in Article 3(1) and (2) are confirmed by a consideration of Article 7 of the same BIT. Though quoted above in section E, its relevant parts may be recalled here:

> Article 7
> Exceptions
> The provisions of Articles 3 and 4 of this Agreement shall not be construed so as to oblige one Contracting Party to extend to the investors of the other the benefit of any treatment, preference or privilege resulting from;
>
> (a) any existing or future customs union, organisation for mutual economic assistance or similar international agreement, whether multilateral or bilateral, to which either of the Contracting Parties is or may become a party, or
> (b) any international agreement or arrangement relating wholly or mainly to taxation or any domestic legislation relating wholly or mainly to taxation.

135. As can be seen, Article 7 contains certain exceptions, in particular regarding the application of Article 3 which, as we know, contains the MFN clauses. Article 7 expressly excludes the transfer of MFN-protection from other treaties with regard to the fields mentioned in its subsections (a) and (b). While it can be argued that the multilateral commitments mentioned in (a) are of quite different character and are obvious exceptions in order to avoid that the States concluding the BIT receive the benefits of such multilateral arrangements without joining them, the exception in (b) regarding taxation does not contain such an obvious background. It presents a clear

decision of the two States when concluding the BIT that the MFN clauses shall not apply to such taxation issues. It shows that the two States considered the question, which issues should not benefit from the MFN protection. Now, it needs no further explanation that, just as taxation is a highly important matter for an investor, so is the submission to arbitration which 'protects' the investor, should a dispute arise with the host State, from having to depend on the national courts of the same host State. In view of the careful drafting of Article 8 and the limiting language therein, it can certainly not be presumed that the parties 'forgot' arbitration when drafting and agreeing on Article 7. Had the parties intended that the MFN clauses should also not apply to arbitration, it would indeed have been easy to add a subsection (c) to that effect in Article 7. The fact that this was not done, in the view of the Tribunal, is further confirmation that the MFN clauses in Article 3 are also applicable to submissions to arbitration in other treaties.

136. The Tribunal has taken note of the references the parties have submitted to other treaties and decisions of arbitral tribunals regarding MFN-clauses and arbitration submissions in other treaties. In particular, the Tribunal has taken note of the decisions in the following cases:

- *Telenor v Hungary*, ICSID Award of 13 September 2006 (CB-48 = C-21)
- *Suez and Vivendi v Argentina*, ICSID decision on Jurisdiction of 3 August 2006 (CB-47 = C-15)
- *National Grid v Argentina*, UNCITRAL/BIT arbitration, Decision on Jurisdiction of 20 June 2006 (CB-52 = C-41)
- *Suez and InterAguas v Argentina*, ICSID decision on Jurisdiction of 16 May 2006 (CB-53 = C-42)
- *Berschader v The Russian Federation*, SCC Award of 21 April 2006 (CB-37 = R-33). In this context see also the dissenting opinion of Weiler regarding the MFN-clause (CB-55 = C-49)
- *Gas Natural SDG v Argentina*, ICSID decision on Jurisdiction of 17 June 2005 (CB-51 = C-40)
- *Plama v Bulgaria*, ICSID decision on Jurisdiction of 8 February 2005, ICSID Review – Foreign Investment Law Journal Vol.20 No.1 issue 2005 (CB-35 = R-6)
- *Siemens v Argentina*, ICSID decision on Jurisdiction of 3 August 2004 (CB-45 = C-9)
- *MTD Equity v Chile*, ICSID Award of 25 May 2004 (CB-54 = C-48)
- *Salini v Jordan*, ICSID decision on Jurisdiction of 23 July 2001 (CB-44 = C-5)
- *Maffezini v Spain*, ICSID decision on Jurisdiction of 25 January 2000 (CB-50 = C-39)

137. After having examined them, the Tribunal feels there is no need to enter into a detailed discussion of these decisions. The Tribunal agrees with the parties that different conclusions can indeed be drawn from them depending on how one evaluates their various wordings both of the arbitration clauses and the MFN-clauses and their similarities in allowing generalisations. However, since it is the primary function of this Tribunal to decide the case before it rather than developing further the general discussion on the applicability of MFN clauses to dispute-settlement-provisions, the Tribunal notes that the combined wording in Article 3 and 7 of the UK-Soviet BIT is not identical to that in any of such other treaties considered in these other decisions. Therefore, they must be interpreted by themselves as was done above and, in the view of this Tribunal, these other decisions do not mandate a change of the interpretation found above.

138. The same is true for the extensive UNCTAD Report (2007) on Bilateral Investment Treaties 1995–2006 – Trends in Investment Rulemaking which respondent submitted just before the hearing (CB-75) and which both parties have referred to during the hearing. Its section on The MFN-Standard in Relation to Dispute Resolution (pp.39 seq.) is indeed interesting as a piece of research which demonstrates the great variety of solutions to be found in BITs. But the research, though different readers may draw different conclusions regarding what can be considered the modern 'trend', certainly does not provide any basis to interpret a specific MFN-clause in a BIT in one way rather than another. Therefore this Report provides no reason to change the interpretation this Tribunal has given above to Article 3.

139. Thus, at the end of its analysis of the relevant factors, the Tribunal concludes, on the basis of the MFN clause in Article 3(2) of the UK-Soviet BIT in conjunction with Article 8 of the Denmark-Russia BIT, that it has jurisdiction extending beyond that granted by Article 8 of the UK-Soviet BIT and covering the issues whether Respondent's actions have to be considered as expropriations and were valid.

 CASE

Award on preliminary objections

Renta 4 SVSA, Ahorro Corporación Emergentes FI, Ahorro Corporación Eurofondo FI, Rovime Inversiones Sicav SA, Quasardevalorssicav SA, Orgordevaloressicav SA, GBI 9000 SICAV S A (claimants) and The Russian Federation (respondent)

20 March 2009

[. . .]

2. Jurisdiction

17. The oral arguments were dominated by a debate concerning the scope of Article 10 of the Spanish BIT. This debate concerns two fundamental issues. The first is the inherent ambit of the article. The second is the possibility of extending that ambit by reference to the Treaty's promise of treatment equivalent to that accorded to most-favoured nationals (MFN). These two matters were given more attention in the course of the hearing than all others combined. They will therefore be considered first. The Tribunal will then turn to three issues of standing.

18. Russia had also argued in its written pleadings that specific consent was required for any individual case to be arbitrated under Article 10 due to its non-mandatory nature: '[B]oth parties must agree to refer arbitrable disputes to arbitration before the proceedings can be commenced.' This contention viewed the words 'may be referred' in Article 10(2) as insufficient consent to arbitration. It was withdrawn by letter dated 20 October 2008.

2.1 Does Article 10 allow arbitration of this claim?

19. Article 10 of the Spanish BIT (quoted in para 5 above) covers investor-State disputes 'relating to the amount or method of payment of the compensation due under Article 6 of this Agreement'. Article 6 reads as follows:

> Nationalization and Expropriation
> Any nationalization, expropriation or any other measure having similar consequences taken by the authorities of either party against investments made within its territory by investors of the other party, shall be taken only on the grounds of public use and in accordance with the legislation in force in the territory. Such measures should on no account be discriminatory. The party adopting such measures shall pay the investor or his beneficiary adequate compensation, without undue delay and in freely convertible currency.

20. Russia argues that Article 10 plainly does not encompass all conceivable disputes under the Spanish BIT and that the claimants' request for arbitration was therefore misguided when it relied on Articles 4–6. Article 4 proscribes 'unjustified or discriminatory measures affecting investments'. Article 5 warrants fair and equitable treatment as well as MFN benefits. International

investor-state arbitration is expressly accessible under the Treaty only with respect to claims under Article 6. Even such claims are subject to the further limitation that they must relate to disputes about the amount or the method of payment of the compensation due. Russia considers that there is continuing disagreement as to whether any of the criticised measures were expropriatory in the first place. That controversy must therefore (in Russia's contention) be resolved in some other proper forum before matters of quantum may go to international arbitration under Article 10. The present claims therefore perforce fall outside the scope of Article 10.

21. It is important to survey the layers of limitation Russia places on Article 10. Russia seeks not just to restrict arbitration to disputes concerning 'compensation'. That might leave the door open to disputes whether there should be any compensation at all. Russia considers that the words 'amount or method of payment' allow nothing but a narrow debate about quantum or timing and currency. Even that might leave a door open to say that 'amount' includes 'no amount' (e.g., because the asset has nil value or because no expropriation has occurred). Yet Russia contends that it has a further rampart: the dispute must concern amounts already established as 'due' under Article 6. The measures of nationalisation and expropriation dealt with in that article are subject to familiar requirements of lawfulness and non-discrimination. Those requirements may naturally lead to debate. Russia asserts that such matters may be heard in one of two types of fora. There may be litigation in Russian courts. Spain might act on behalf of its nationals under the Spanish BIT. But Article 10 does not allow investor-state arbitration of disputes as to compliance with Article 6.

22. *Vladimir and Moïse Berschader v Russian Federation* (2006) involved a claim by Belgian nationals under the 1989 BIT entered into by the Belgium/Luxembourg Economic Union and the Soviet Union. It is relied upon by Russia in the present case because the arbitrators in *Berschader* faced a virtually identical conjunction of treaty provisions. Article 5 of that BIT defined the elements of permissible expropriation and nationalisation. Those elements included compensation reflecting 'the real value' of the investment to be paid promptly in convertible currency. Article 10 gave investors the right to arbitrate disputes 'concerning the amount or mode of compensation to be paid under Article 5'. (Nothing apparently turns on the choice between the English words 'method' or 'mode' in the translations.) *Berschader* considered that this limitation excluded 'disputes concerning whether or not an act of expropriation actually occurred under Article 5' (para 153).

23. The impact of *Berschader's* consideration of this point is attenuated by the fact that its conclusion was superfluous. The arbitrators gave primary

attention to what they deemed to be an unprecedented feature of the case: whether 'the sole claimants are foreign shareholders in a foreign incorporated company seeking to rely on the terms of a BIT without having made any direct investment on their own part' (para 135). They devoted 26 paragraphs of the award to this issue. Their conclusion was that there was no jurisdiction with respect to the claimants' indirect investment. The door had therefore already been shut on the claimants by the time the arbitrators next turned to consider the phrase 'amount or mode of compensation'. Their conclusion in this regard may be considered *obiter*. It is explained in seven short paragraphs. It cannot be adopted by the present arbitrators because it does not do justice to the extensive and refined debate which has emerged in the present case. There is no way of knowing from their award how the *Berschader* arbitrators would have reacted to the points raised here. (*Berschader* was decided by a majority but the dissenting arbitrator did not take issue with these seven paragraphs.)

24. *Berschader* basically repeats that 'the ordinary meaning' of the limitation 'is quite clear[ly]' to the effect that only disputes 'concerning the amount or mode of compensation' may be subject to arbitration. This is no more than a restatement of the problem. It is necessary to determine whether these words exclude disputes over entitlement to compensation (with the effect of limiting jurisdiction to mere quantification or mode of payment). The quoted words do not exclude that a claimant may react to a respondent's refusal to accept that any 'amount' is due by bringing into play the substantive predicate of arbitral jurisdiction: an expropriation carried out in such a fashion as to create an entitlement to compensation pursuant to Article 6.

25. *Berschader's* only conceptual treatment of this issue is contained in para 153. The arbitrators there state that they were 'satisfied' that Article 10 excluded 'disputes concerning whether or not an act of expropriation actually occurred under Article 5'. This is a simple affirmation. It does not appear to be supported by analysis. The rationale is set down in two sentences. They are founded on an explicit assumption:

> From the ordinary meaning of Article 10.1, it can only be assumed that the Contracting Parties intended that a dispute concerning whether or not an act of expropriation actually occurred was to be submitted to dispute resolution procedures provided for under the applicable contract or alternatively to the domestic courts of the Contracting Party in which the investment is made. It is only a dispute which arises regarding the amount or mode of compensation to be paid subsequent to an act of expropriation already having been established, either

by acknowledgement of the responsible Contracting Party or by a court or arbitral tribunal, which may be subject to arbitration under the Treaty.

26. The words 'it can only be assumed' will not do for present purposes. The 'assumption' is certainly not inevitable. Words may have an 'ordinary meaning' as units of language. It does not follow that their import is self-evident when viewed in context.

27. Russia invites the arbitrators to conclude that Article 10(1) lexically excludes the claimants' reading. The words 'compensation due' are said to modify 'amount' or 'method' (T:56). That grammatical inference is less than convincing. The plainest proposition to be derived from Article 10(1) is that it allows arbitration with respect to debates about the amount or method of such compensation as may be due under Article 6. The difficulty begins precisely once one asks: Who determines whether compensation is indeed 'due' under Article 6?

28. Consideration of this question leads the Tribunal to conclude that the word 'due' in fact disfavours Russia. The reference to disputes relating to 'compensation due under Article 6' is found in Article 10 itself. The logical progression seems straightforward. Article 6 establishes that there shall be no expropriation unless it is lawful by reference to criteria set out in that Article. Article 10 gives an investor the right to seek arbitration with respect to '[a]ny dispute . . . relating to the amount or method of payment of the compensation due under Article 6'. The claimants allege expropriation. Russia denies any obligation under this head. There is therefore a dispute as to whether compensation is 'due'. The force of this simple proposition is buttressed by the open texture of the introductory words: *any disputes . . . relating to.*

29. Russia argues that there is no dispute as to quantification. It does not assert that the value of the putative investment is zero. For jurisdictional purposes it need not deny that the assets have whatever value the claimants seek to ascribe to them. The claimants are in Russia's view really seeking to debate whether expropriation occurred. Russia submits that Article 10 does not allow them to do so.

30. The flaw in Russia's argument is that there is more than one basis on which a respondent State could say 'zero'. One might indeed be a divergence as to quantification. Another could be a denial of any obligation on account of alleged expropriation. The first raises no problem. Russia would accept (purely hypothetically) that the Tribunal could decide whether the value of

allegedly expropriated assets was zero or some higher number as a matter of proper valuation. But the second is different. Russia denies that the Tribunal is empowered to decide that the basic predicate to its jurisdiction has arisen: an event of such a nature as to require the compensation unquestionably to be assessed by the arbitrators.

31. An investor seeking an award of compensation under Article 10 may thus face more than one conceptual building block. It may face a disagreement as to quantification. But it may also (or only) face a challenge as to whether an obligation has arisen under Article 6. Such an obligation is the evident predicate to any amount being 'due' and thus the object of the type of debate allowed under Article 10. The existence of the basic predicate of a remedy under Article 10 cannot be deemed outside the purview of a tribunal constituted under that very Article. Russia correctly observes that 'international courts and tribunals must decline jurisdiction over prerequisite cognate issues that are outside the bounds of the parties' consent' (in footnote 22 of Russia's Memorial on Preliminary Objections). But this principle does not apply here. It is precisely Article 10 that defines the bounds of the State-parties' consent. The present Tribunal is both empowered and obligated to construe the scope of authority thereby created.

32. The arbitrators have considered whether their conclusion contradicts the familiar canon of interpretation which holds that all expressions in an agreement should if possible be given meaning. It is not always evident how isolated the relevant expression must be. Article 10 contains some 200 words arranged within four paragraphs. Its purported overall effect is to create international arbitral jurisdiction. It is constructive; its *raison d'être* is not to limit a pre-existing jurisdiction. The search to give meaning to the eight (or 11) words that follow 'relating to' in Article 10(1) simply cannot be allowed to deprive the remaining text of its essential positive meaning.

33. There is more. Article 10(1) does not inevitably identify a narrower mandate than would have been the result of a simpler text referring curtly to 'disputes concerning Article 6'. Consider the case of an expropriation which has led to payment in an amount established by a municipal administrative or judicial body. There is no issue of legality or discrimination. The investor wishes to challenge the amount of compensation. The State retorts that the adequacy of compensation was established in accordance with law and should not be questioned internationally. An international tribunal may be reluctant to exercise jurisdiction to second-guess a procedure presenting prima facie regularity. Such a scenario is a central concern of investors who

are averse to allowing the host State to act as judge and party in measuring the monetary extent of its own liability. The wording of Article 10(1) would give comfort in these circumstances: 'any dispute . . . relating to the amount' of 'compensation due' would be internationalised. These words would certainly not be perceived as superfluous. A similar example is plainly conceivable with respect to 'method' (currency and timing).

34. Both sides sought to derive support from the judgment rendered by the English High Court in *The Czech Republic v European Media Ventures SA* (2007). The BIT in that case limited jurisdiction to disputes 'concerning compensation due' by virtue of 'dispossession'. An UNCITRAL Arbitral Tribunal had found jurisdiction to hear a claim for indirect expropriation. The High Court rejected a challenge to that jurisdictional finding. The claimants rely on the judgment because it interprets the arbitration clause to extend to 'entitlement as well as quantification'. Russia counters *a contrario* that the arbitration clause did not contain the words 'amount or method of payment' which it says further limits the concept of compensation.

35. What the High Court would have decided if these additional words had been found in the BIT relevant in the *European Media Venture* case must remain a matter of conjecture. Yet it should be noted that the presence of the word 'due' did not dissuade the High Court from finding that the arbitrators had jurisdiction to determine entitlement. Indeed the word 'due' was relied upon as establishing a linkage between the provisions concerning dispossession and arbitration in the BIT in question. That linkage brought within the purview of arbitral authority a range of matters concerning the application of the dispossession provision itself (as notably explained in the judgment in para 45). It was not necessary that entitlement be pre-established under the provision relating to dispossession to which the arbitration clause referred.

36. Counsel for Russia were asked on the first day of the hearing whether the simple denial that an expropriation had taken place would have the result of 'an insurmountable loss of jurisdiction without qualification'. They confirmed that this was indeed Russia's position and proposed the following illustration:

> The Spanish investor buys a farm. And Russia comes in and they take the farm, and they don't tell the investor why, but they say, 'You're not due any compensation; you have no right to this', period, end of story, and they don't even say 'well, can this panel then have jurisdiction?' The answer is no, because you don't know whether that taking was lawful or not. You don't know if it was taken because claimants never had property rights. You don't know whether they didn't pay

their taxes. You don't know whether there was a regulatory matter that they were growing marijuana. You just don't know. And that's an area that the State may have the right to come after the host country, but not an individual investor to come in, as with every single taxing matter, every single taking. This treaty is to go to the issue where there is a dispute over the amount of compensation due under the treaty. And if there's a situation where there is not simply the fight on the amount of compensation due, then you have, respectfully, no jurisdiction in this case. (T:26-27.)

37. They later added that: 'if there 's a dispute as to whether there was an expropriation, then you have no jurisdiction'. (T:31.)

38. They confirmed that this meant that even if there had been a decree of expropriation a subsequent denial that the event had been properly characterised would prevent a claim under Article 10 (T:32).

39. On the second day of the hearing counsel for Russia seemed to retreat. They stated that arbitrators acting under Article 10 of the Treaty could 'proceed' in the presence of a 'final court order' acknowledging that there has been a compensable event as defined in Article 6. They were asked whether this was so 'no matter what we're told by the Russian Federation with respect to it'. They then assented (T:320). One can hardly resist the impression that this wavering posture reflects the difficulty of maintaining Russia's rather extreme stance. The Tribunal does not believe that the text allows a curtailment of the international tribunal's authority to decide whether compensation is 'due'. That perforce entrains the power to determine whether there has been a compensable event in the first place.

40. Indeed counsel for Russia also observed straightforwardly that 'Article 10 limits you to some aspects of Article 6' (T:82). The arbitrators do not rush to attribute decisive effect to one utterance among many. But they are struck by the tension between this plainly sensible remark and Russia's insistence that the Tribunal must treat Article 6 as a locked and inviolable strongbox to which the present arbitrators have no key. This cannot be so. Article 6 defines the precondition of compensation being 'due' for the purposes of Article 10. It is an 'aspect' of Article 6 which cannot be beyond the arbitrators' reach.

41. The claimants also submitted that the wording of Article 10 allows the Tribunal to deal with only certain aspects of Article 6. Their analysis proceeds as follows. 'Nationalisation or expropriation' is compliant with the BIT (according to Art 6) if four requirements are met: (1) existence of grounds of public use; (2) conformity with legislation in force in the territory; (3)

absence of discrimination; (4) payment of 'adequate compensation without undue delay and in freely convertible currency' (see para 19 above). The first three of these requirements constitute criteria of international lawfulness. A State party which satisfies each of them ensures that the measure of compensation can be only that set out under the fourth element of Article 6. But a failure of compliance with those three criteria would open the door to a measure of compensation which is not so restricted. This leads the claimants to say that the reference in Article 10 to 'the amount or method of the compensation due under Article 6' serves the specific function of excluding the Tribunal's authority to decide whether an expropriation is internationally unlawful – e.g., to adjudicate upon any of the first three criteria in Article 6. Article 10 would thus leave only the possibility of determining the monetary concomitant of internationally lawful expropriation.

42. This analysis was advanced by the claimants in conjunction with an important specific concession to the effect that Article 10 of the BIT 'precludes jurisdiction over disputes arising from . . . three of four conditions imposed on the contracting parties by Article 6 when they expropriate property' (T: 183).

43. Russia maintains that this analysis undercuts the claimants' own position. It explains that the last sentence of Article 6 defines an agreed standard of compensation. Standards of international law pertaining to unlawful expropriation would be inapplicable even if Article 10 allowed a full inquiry into compliance with all requirements of Article 6. Hence (so Russia argues) the claimants' position impermissibly renders superfluous the phrase 'the amount or method of the compensation due under Article 6' in Article 10.

44. The Tribunal finds this argument to be hyper-technical and unpersuasive. Russia views the claimants' position as more intricate than it is. There can be no expectation (let alone certainty) that an international tribunal would – in the absence of the restrictive words of Article 10 – read the last sentence of Article 6 to exclude international norms as to the measure of compensation. It seems equally clear that the restrictive language has potential weight as regards the issue whether international norms relating to unlawful expropriation are excluded (and by the same token whether the Tribunal may adjudicate upon the first three criteria in Art 6).

45. It is convenient to articulate succinctly the Tribunal's conclusions so far:

(i)   The arbitrators are not asked to determine whether Russia has acted discriminatorily or without the justification of public purpose. Nor would they be entitled to do so given the claimants' concession (see para 42 above). It is unnecessary to consider issues that might have arisen if this concession had not been made. (A familiar feature of this area of international law is precisely the proposition that the lawfulness or otherwise of a measure of dispossession may affect the amount of compensation.)

(ii) The arbitrators are therefore not entitled to determine generally whether Russia's actions contravened its 'legislation' on nationalisation and expropriation. They may however assess whether Russia's actions breached international law by depriving the claimants of adequate compensation for the dispossession of which they complain.

46. The textual analysis above is sufficient to decide the issue at hand. There is strictly speaking no need to consider whether extraneous considerations confirm the conclusion. Nevertheless the Tribunal believes it appropriate to explain why it finds that both evidence of the purported intentions of the parties and inferences as to the object and purpose of the Spanish BIT validate the arbitrators' conclusion.

47. *Berschader* asserts that 'support' for its contrary conclusion is to be found in other BITs signed by the Soviet Union at the time of the Belgian/Luxembourg BIT. It expresses the view that these other treaties reflect a policy of limiting the arbitral option open to investors under BITs to 'disputes concerning the amount or method of compensation to be paid on foot [sic] of an expropriatory act' (para 155). This of course does no more than restate the issue. Moreover the award notes that two BITs (those concluded in 1989 with France and Canada) allowed arbitration with respect to the 'consequences' of host State measures. The very exemplar cited for the policy of limitation (the BIT signed in 1989 by the UK and the USSR) refers to 'the amount or payment of compensation' and therefore appears to put into question the very predicate of any payment at all.

48. It is true that *Ros1nvestCo v Russia* (2007) did not accept that the UK BIT's formulation conferred jurisdiction to rule whether expropriation had occurred. But that award does not consider whether the word 'payment' may lead to consideration of the reality of its predicate: expropriation. This may be because it was not argued. Nor does the formulation in that treaty include the word 'due'. It is also noteworthy that the Tribunal at any rate found that it had jurisdiction on another ground (MFN). Lastly, one cannot overlook the following unusual declaration by one of the arbitrators in paragraph 123 of the award:

I would not want our common conclusion that Article 8 does not confer jurisdiction in this case to be taken in any way as an expression of opinion on how that article or other similar treaty clauses relate to other claims that might be brought forward in other cases based on an allegation of expropriation.

49. Russia made eight jurisdictional objections in *Sedelmayer v Russia* (1998). The claim there was brought under the USSR-FRG BIT. One of Russia's objections was to the effect that there had been no expropriation. Russia argued that the claimant's activities had been declared to be illegal by two court orders. Thereafter property was 'returned' to the Russian State under a lawful order. This contention was submitted to the Arbitral Tribunal for decision. The treaty limited the scope of investor-State arbitration to disputes relating either to 'the amount of compensation or the method of its payment' or to 'freedom of transfer' of funds invested or repatriated. Yet no point was apparently made that (as Russia has put it in the present case; see para 37 above) 'if there's a dispute as to whether there was an expropriation, then you have no jurisdiction'. The failure to take this point in *Sedelmayer* is by no means decisive here. Yet it is natural to reflect that the alleged non-arbitrability of expropriation appears to have been less than striking and fundamental. This observation is even more clearly supported by the fact that BITs signed by the Soviet Union present significant textual variations in this respect. It is difficult to say that the USSR had a single objective of public policy in negotiating the scope of its consent to international adjudication as expressed in BITs.

50. Indeed a paper on BITs published in 1991 by a member of the USSR's negotiating team (Mr R Nagapetyants) referred to the 'special practical significance' for foreign investors of the 'opportunity to appeal' to international arbitration in cases of expropriatory measures. The author did not mention the proposition now being advanced by Russia to the effect that the existence of a compensable expropriation is beyond international jurisdiction. Such a restriction would have had vast 'practical significance'. The failure to mention it would have been inexplicable if such had indeed been the author's understanding of the USSR's approach. (Russia complains that Mr Nagapetyants' statement is taken out of context inasmuch as his paper elsewhere mentions the restrictive language in Article 10. The arbitrators do not see it that way. The recitation of the terms of Article 10 simply restate the problem. The comments about the 'special practical significance' of international arbitration shed light on Treaty objectives.)

51. The premise that one may consider the intentions of one of the parties to a BIT is questionable in the first place. The preceding paragraphs confirm

that even if one did so in this case the result would be inconclusive. The alleged policy of the Soviet Union did not find a consistent expression in the various BITs concluded at the relevant time. Nor is it persuasive to suggest that socialist doctrines upheld for many decades should lead to a presumption against the acceptance of international determinations of whether State measures are expropriatory. A series of BITs were signed by the USSR in the years of *perestroika* shortly before the dissolution of the Union. They may with at least equal logic be viewed as a rupture with past dogma and the acceptance of an international regime intended to reassure investors.

52. It was one thing for the BIT not to give access to international arbitration with respect to the other terms of Article 6. It is understandable that a State might agree to international arbitration with respect to its duty to pay compensation for expropriation but not with respect to allegations that its measures were wrongful under international law due to discrimination or lack of public purpose. Investors would surely prefer assurance that expropriations be non-discriminatory and for a public purpose. Yet they might tolerate such violations as long as they were confident that takings would be followed by compensation. This has been the central desideratum of investor protection for two centuries of international arbitration. As counsel to the claimants put it: 'the threat of one's property being taken without compensation is existential' (T:215). It cannot seriously be thought that investors would be attracted by a regime that gave them access to international arbitration of the issue of the quantum of compensation but not of whether any compensation is due at all.

53. It moreover appears equally relevant (or irrelevant) to give weight to the objectives or understanding of the other party to the BIT. The Tribunal has not had access to any official Spanish comment directly on point. The Spanish BIT and the Belgium/Luxembourg BIT are virtually identical with respect to this matter. Evidence is available of Belgium's understanding. The Belgian Ministers of Foreign Affairs and Foreign Trade explained to their Parliament in an official *Exposé des motifs* of 28 February 1990 that the treaty they were recommending for ratification allowed arbitration 'in all areas covered by Article 5'. *Berschader* notes this fact and recognises that the Ministerial statement envisaged that the issue to be arbitrated could therefore also include whether or not there had been an expropriation. The Tribunal explicitly rejected the statement on the footing that the language of the BIT is 'quite clear' and 'could not possibly' lend itself to the interpretation given by the two Ministers. This is the very last word on the subject to be found in *Berschader*. It leads the reader back to the starting point: a simple assertion that the words are clear. *Berschader's* treatment of this matter is essentially to

endorse an assumption. That simply cannot be decisive either way. As the same arbitrators put it with respect to a different issue:

> When, as in the Genin case, an arbitral award provides no reasons for the course o faction [sic] chosen by the tribunal, such an award has very little relevance as a persuasive source of law (para 134).

54. It is instructive to consider the relevant terms of the Belgian Ministers' statement:

> There was a difference of views between the Belgian and Soviet delegations concerning both field of application and procedure, the Soviets refusing to accept the idea of a State submitting to international arbitration at the beginning of the negotiations.
>
> Eventually, the Soviet delegation accepted 'ad hoc' arbitration before the SCC in all matters covered by article 5.
>
> It should be underlined that the concept of nationalization in this article extends to 'all other measures having similar effects', hereby rendering Article 10's field of application extremely broad.

The middle paragraph is of course debatable. Article 10 of the Belgian BIT would not (if the claimants' concession noted in para 41(i) above is correct) allow SCC arbitration with respect to disputes as to whether an expropriation is for public purpose or whether it is discriminatory. But as seen above (in para 52) these are undoubtedly secondary considerations as compared to the principle that expropriation must in any event be compensated (see para 52 above). In this respect the two Ministers' explanation emphasises both the importance of international arbitration (which the USSR negotiators had initially resisted) and their perception that the scope of Article 10 was 'extremely broad' with respect to nationalisations and all other measures having similar effect. It would be unimaginable in this light that the Ministers had understood that the respondent State could avoid Article 10 by claiming that it did not allow arbitrators to determine whether there had been a compensable event at all.

55. Article 31 of the Vienna Convention is frequently debated in the context of BITs. It provides that treaties are to be interpreted 'in good faith in accordance with the ordinary meaning to be given to the terms of the treaty in their context and in the light of its object and purpose'. Article 31 must be considered with caution and discipline lest it become a palimpsest constantly altered by the projections of subjective suppositions. It does not for example compel the result that all textual doubts should be resolved in favour of

the investor. The long-term promotion of investment is likely to be better ensured by a well-balanced regime rather than by one which goes so far that it provokes a swing of the pendulum in the other direction.

56. Yet some considerations of purpose have a solid foundation. It must be accepted that investment is not promoted by purely formal or illusory standards of protection. It must more specifically be accepted that a fundamental advantage perceived by investors in many if not most BITs is that of the internationalisation of the host State's commitments. It follows that it is impermissible to read Article 10 of the BIT as a vanishingly narrow internationalisation of either Russia's or Spain's commitment. Yet that would be the consequence if Russia – taken at the international level as a State composed of all of its organs including national courts – could determine unilaterally and conclusively whether the very predicate of the Tribunal's jurisdiction were operative or not. That predicate is the existence of an obligation to make compensation. If there is no obligation to make compensation the arbitration clause would never operate. The dispute would not be internationalised if the respondent State could simply declare whether there is an obligation to compensate. Either signatory State could thus by its fiat (including that of its courts given the State's responsibility for their acts under international law) ensure that there would never be an arbitration under Article 10. This would be an illusion which the Tribunal cannot accept as consonant with Article 31 of the Vienna Convention if ever that article is to be given full weight.

57. The Tribunal in *SGS v Philippines* (2004) wrote:

> The BIT is a treaty for the promotion and reciprocal protection of investments. According to the preamble it is intended 'to create and maintain favourable conditions for investments by investors of one Contracting Party in the territory of the other'. It is legitimate to resolve uncertainties in its interpretation so as to favour the protection of covered investments.

This paragraph was cited with approval by the English Court of Appeal in *Ecuador v Occidental* (2007). To 'favour the protection of covered investments' is not equivalent to a presumption that the investor is right (cf. para 55 above).

58. Russia contends that two relevant fora may be available to determine whether compensation is due: the Russia courts or State-to-State arbitration. Yet each of these avenues is problematic. Remedies by means of diplomatic protection are from the investors' perspective notoriously unreliable

in practice. It is moreover implausible that States would want to provide for interstate arbitration of controversies as to whether an expropriation had occurred at the same time as they carve out the possibility of separate investor-state arbitration with respect to the amount and method of compensation. Such pointless and unprecedented complications would be absurd. The notion of actions before the courts of the host country are problematic in principle. Courts are on the international level equivalent to other organs of the State. This means that the predicate of obtaining any amount of compensation according to any method would be hostage to the host State's self-determination as to whether it is due at all.

59. The present Tribunal does not deny that such a provision could be given effect if such was the clear import of the Treaty. Article 6 might have explained how entitlement is to be determined. Article 10 might have stipulated that the proposition that compensation is 'due' may be established only by an authority identified in Article 6. But there is nothing of the kind. The present Tribunal is more inclined to give weight to the Belgian Foreign Ministers' unequivocal explanation (see para 54 above) of their understanding of an identical text – not so much as an expression of intent as the reflection of a proper reading to the effect that an international tribunal could decide whether there was a duty to compensate for an expropriatory measure. The claimants have provided the text of an opinion by the Spanish Council of State in 1991 concluding that the Spanish BIT called for 'special arbitration' with respect to 'disputes arising from expropriation' and noting that this constituted a departure from the 'general' Spanish regime. The absence of any reference to the limitation of arbitral jurisdiction now argued by Russia would be curious if the Spanish understanding had been to similar effect.

60. Article 10 of Russia's Federal Law No. 160-F2 provides: 'Foreign investments in the USSR shall not be subject to nationalisation except for instances when it is effectuated in accordance with legislative acts of the USSR and republics.' Counsel for Russia relied on the following gloss added in a published commentary: 'By its very nature nationalisation is always a measure which cannot be taken other than by the adoption of some sort of legislative act' (T:308). The commentary surely goes further than the law. Nevertheless it is the proposition advanced by Russia and falls to be assessed as such.

61. Russia's posture is not easily reconciled with its argument as to the restricted scope of the Spanish BIT. Article 6 of the Treaty establishes protections not only in the event of nationalisation; it also covers 'any other measures having similar consequences'. Such a broadly-defined category of governmental measures is not limited to legislation. Indeed it would be peculiar to find a legislative

act proclaiming itself to have consequences 'similar' to those of other texts. National lawmakers do not generally draft in simile. But anyone familiar with practice and commentary in the field of investment treaties is well aware of the frequent use of the broad criterion of similarity. Its purpose is precisely to establish an international norm that transcends the peculiarities of national classifications of governmental acts. It gives rise to a strong inference that the reality of the compensable event was understood to be within the purview of international control. Whether the claimants here are claiming explicit dispossession (nationalisation or expropriation) or a 'measure having similar consequence' is immaterial in this respect. The point is that Article 6 of the Treaty naturally suggests susceptibility to international control under Article 10.

62. The claimants explicitly allege expropriation and not indirect or regulatory acts equivalent to expropriation. They affirm that there is therefore no need when examining this particular jurisdictional objection for a debate as to whether the State's actions gave rise to a compensable taking. Whether this allegation succeeds is a matter for the merits. In the arbitrators' view it suffices at this stage and with respect to this aspect of the jurisdictional debate to say that the Tribunal has jurisdiction to determine the compensation which is due on the *pro tem* assumption that there has been an expropriation.

63. Russia argues that the claimants' position is 'ideological' rather than 'legal' in that they insist that all forms of dispossession are perforce expropriations. The effect would be to disavow (for example) the widely accepted notion that dispossession in the exercise of police powers need not trigger a duty of compensation as it would in the case of expropriation. The Tribunal does not accept this characterisation of the claimants' case. The fact that an international tribunal may consider whether compensation is 'due' does not prejudice the ultimate determination of such issues. It is as simple as that. The debate may become complex in due course. It concerns the merits of the case. In sum: the Tribunal has jurisdiction under the BIT to hear the contention that there has been a compensable expropriation.

64. The claimants have an alternative defence to the challenge. They argue that measures taken by Russia constitute an obvious and direct expropriation with respect to which Russia has effectively acknowledged that compensation is due. In the claimants' view these measures therefore inherently pass the Article 6 threshold and 'require[e] no exercise of judgment on the part of this Tribunal . . .' (T:139).

65. The claimants cite the OECD Working Paper on International Investment 2004/4 to the effect that: 'International law is clear that a seizure

of legal title of property constitutes a compensable expropriation' (p 3). They add the following proposition as formulated by G C Christie in an oft-cited article:

> [T]here are certain types of State interference which, from the outset, will be considered expropriation even though not labelled as such. Among these are the appointment of a receiver to liquidate the business or other property. "What Constitutes a Taking of Property under International Law?" 38 *Brit. YB Int. Law* 307 (1962).

Against the background of these principles the claimants make their argument succinctly thus:

> Beginning with the seizure and sale of [Yuganskneftegasin 2004], every asset of Yukos was seized by order of Russian courts and other agencies of the Russian state, and then sold to third parties, principally the state-owned oil company, Rosnefl, and to other State-owned enterprises. This process resulted in the complete liquidation of Yukos, as a legal entity.
>
> Respondent has not challenged any of these facts. They are now part of the common ground in this case. As Christie observed, there are certain types of state interference which, from the outset, would be considered expropriation, even though not labelled as such. And among these are the appointment of the receiver to liquidate the business or other property.
>
> In addition – and this is what I think is somewhat surprising about what's happened here – in addition to explicitly taking all assets of Yukos and liquidating the company, Russia, in fact, has compensated Yukos for this taking, and it has done this by applying the proceeds of each sale to the satisfaction of Yukos' tax assessments and other debts. (T: 147–148.)

66. Russia rejects the characterisation and significance attributed by the claimants to the relevant governmental measures. The debate is entangled within the vaster web of circumstances of Yukos's demise. The arbitrators are reluctant to make conclusive factual findings without the benefit of insights likely to emerge in the course of the merits phase of the arbitration. They have in mind the claimants' explanation: 'We have not put in at this stage all of the evidence that might be put in concerning the nature of the seizure of the assets. There's a lot of documentation that could come in concerning the way in which the assets were received' (T:167). Naturally such evidence might be countered by what Russia will present.

67. What suffices for now is this. The claimants have established that the Tribunal has jurisdiction to decide whether compensation is 'due' to them

under international law by reason of the conduct of which they complain (and if so in which amount).

2.2 Does Article 5 expand this Tribunal's jurisdiction on the foundation of a more favourable treaty?

68. The promise of most favoured nation (MFN) treatment is found in Article 5(2) of the Spanish BIT. It is necessary to read all of Article 5. It is entitled 'Treatment of investments' and provides as follows:

1. Each party shall guarantee fair and equitable treatment within its territory for the investments made by investors of the other party.
2. The treatment referred to in paragraph 1 above shall be no less favourable than that accorded by either party in respect of investments made within its territory by investors of any third State.
3. Such treatment shall not, however, include privileges which may be granted by either party to investors of a third State, by virtue of its participation in:

   - a free trade area;
   - a customs union;
   - a common market;
   - an organization of mutual economic assistance or other agreement concluded prior to the signing of this agreement and containing conditions comparable to those accorded by the party to the participants in said organisation.

   The treatment granted under this article shall not include tax exemptions or other comparable privileges granted by either Party to the investors of a third State by virtue of a double taxation agreement or any other agreement concerning matters of taxation.
4. In addition to the provisions of paragraph 2 above, each party shall, in accordance with its national legislation, accord investments made by investors of the other party treatment no less favourable than that granted to its own investors.

69. The claimants argue that Article 5(2) would entitle them to bring their case before this Arbitral Tribunal even if Article 10 did not. They observe that Russia is a party to BITs with third States containing liberal arbitration clauses. They invoke notably Article 8(1) of the Denmark-Russia BIT. Its definition of the scope of disputes susceptible of being brought before an SCC Institute tribunal is unquestionably broader than that of Article 10 of the Spanish BIT. Article 8(1) does not limit arbitration to disputes 'relating

to the amount or method of payment of the compensation due under Article 6'. It refers to:

> Any dispute which may arise between an investor of one Contracting Party and the other Contracting Party in connection with an investment on the territory of that other Contracting Party. . ..

70. Russia objects preliminarily that the claimants forfeited the possibility of invoking the Danish BIT because they did not do so in their Request for Arbitration. Article 2 of the SCC Arbitration Rules requires that the request include 'a copy or description' of the relevant arbitration agreement. Article 25 allows the amendment of claims only if it is 'comprised by the arbitration agreement'. Russia therefore argues that it was impermissible for the claimants to invoke a new or expanded jurisdictional foundation as late as the Counter-Memorial on Preliminary Objections. Russia adds that unawareness of a MFN-based jurisdictional assertion could lead to the constitution of a tribunal without proper consideration of issues of conflict of interest by reason of the identity of the third country in question. Moreover an extension of jurisdiction 'in the midst of an arbitration' would prejudice the respondent's 'right to challenge unfounded assertions of jurisdiction'.

71. The Tribunal observes that the Request for Arbitration included a copy of the Spanish BIT. The claimants sought relief 'in accordance with the terms of the treaty'. They are entitled to seek to establish that those terms incorporate benefits accorded by Russia by virtue of the promise of MFN treatment. The Tribunal is unwilling to infer that the SCC requirement would implicitly extend to a duty to 'include or describe' the Danish BIT. The claimants are not in fact seeking arbitration under the Danish BIT at all; they are drawing the full consequences (as they see them) of the terms of the Spanish BIT.

72. These observations are sufficient to defeat this formal objection. It may be added that Russia's complaint of prejudice is unpersuasive in light of the fact that the claimants gave notice in the Request for Arbitration of their 'intention to rely as necessary on the MFN clause' in the Spanish BIT (notably in footnote 1 on p 14 of the Request for Arbitration). The request also claimed breaches of Articles 4 and 5 of that BIT. It is common ground that Article 10 cannot encompass claims of breaches of the material provisions of those two articles. It should therefore have been passably clear that the claimants were envisaging a jurisdictional foundation which could have been derived only from the MFN provision. Russia did not press for clarification.

73. The Tribunal's conclusion with respect to this objection is consonant with *RosInvest Co*. That case was conducted under the 1999 SCC Arbitration

Rules. They were not materially different from the 2007 SCC Rules relevant here.

74. Russia also argues preliminarily that the Danish BIT is automatically excluded from application here because it states in Article 11(3): 'The provisions of this Agreement shall not apply to taxation.' The present claimants could therefore not have proceeded even if they were Danish investors because they complain precisely of tax measures taken with respect to Yukos. This argument was not pursued with great insistence. Nor should it have been. The claimants allege that Russia imposed a bogus reassessment of taxes in order to effect a spoliation of Yukos assets. To think that ten words appearing in a miscellany of incidental provisions near the end of the Danish BIT would provide a loophole to escape the central undertakings of investor protection would be absurd. Complaints about types and levels of taxation are one thing. Complaints about abuse of the power to tax are something else. A 'decree' to the effect that 'all tax inspectors are henceforth instructed to collect everything they can get their hands on from Danish investors' would not be insulated because of Article 11(3) of the BIT. Abuse and pretext are at the heart of the claimants' allegations. Whether they are true is a matter for the merits.

75. Russia's final preliminary argument is that the claimant's invocation of MFN treatment in respect of jurisdiction breaches a prior arbitration agreement (namely Art 10 of the Treaty). This contention appears to presume that the arbitration provisions of the Spanish BIT excluded the possibility of invoking an expanded scope of consent by virtue of third-country BITs. And so the argument seems to proceed on the footing that claims under the Spanish BIT cannot conceivably be brought to SCC arbitration outside the constraints set down in Article 10.

76. That premise is unsustainable. Consider the effect of a stipulation in Article 5 (however oddly placed) that 'any investor complaints about fair and equitable treatment may be brought to SCC arbitration'. There is no reason why such a claim would fail on jurisdictional grounds merely because Article 10 itself does not encompass matters of fair and equitable treatment. The stipulation is made by the same respondent State; the beneficiary is the same presumptively qualified investor. There is no logical leap from this hypothesis to the jurisdictional foundation asserted by the claimants here. Their argument is that Article 5(2) in effect contains an inchoate stipulation having the very same effect of broadening the possibility of recourse to investor-state arbitration. (Notionally: 'any investor may bring the same types of complaint to the SCC as the host State has agreed may be brought by investors

of a third State'.) Article 5 was thus precisely so enlivened the moment the Danish BIT came into effect. Spanish investors too could accordingly seek SCC arbitration of claims within the broad ambit of the subsequent Treaty. Whether access to arbitration may in principle fall within the scope of the MFN undertaking is a different issue (see paras 86–102 below). Whether such an effect flows from a proper reading of the terms of Article 5 is yet another (see paras 103–119 below). But there is no substance to the thesis that Article 10 is an inherently exclusive portal to investor-state arbitration under the Treaty. Otherwise the debate as to whether MFN treatment may ever include matters of dispute resolution would be over before it began; in all cases the original arbitration provisions would self-evidently not be those sought to be invoked by reference to MFN.

77. The stage is now set to consider the substance of the MFN debate. Some first principles need to be recalled. The treaty that contains the MFN promise is conventionally referred to as the 'basic treaty'. The treaty invoked as evidence of more favourable treatment may be referred to as the 'comparator treaty'. The party asserting a MFN entitlement is a stranger to the comparator treaty and is therefore in no position to make any claim under it. The claim can arise only under the basic treaty. Article 9(1) of the International Law Commission's 1978 Draft Articles on MFN Clauses defines the mechanism thus: 'the beneficiary State acquires, for itself or for the benefit of persons or things in a determined relationship with it', a right to the more favourable treatment accorded to third States or their nationals. The third-party treaty is incorporated by reference into the basic treaty without any additional act of transformation.

78. These basic points should be kept in mind as the substantive discussion begins with the broadest of Russia's objections: that the claimants simply have no warrant to invoke the Danish BIT. If this were true there is no reason to examine whether it (as the comparator treaty) contains any element of MFN as contrasted with the Spanish BIT.

79. Russia relies in this respect on the *Anglo-Iranian* case. Iran's unilateral declaration of acceptance of ICJ jurisdiction had been expressly limited to disputes under future treaties. The UK nevertheless sought to invoke two longstanding treaties it had entered into with Iran that contained MFN clauses (but no ICJ jurisdiction clause). The alleged more favoured nation again happened to be Denmark; it had a treaty with Iran that allowed access to the ICJ for complaints of breach. The ICJ rejected the UK's claim as an impermissible attempt to rely on instruments – i.e., 'basic treaties' – which were not extant at the date of Iran's acceptance of compulsory ICJ jurisdic-

tion. The UK could not rely on its old treaties for the purposes of establishing ICJ jurisdiction. There was therefore no basis on which the ICJ could either rule on the scope of the MFN clauses or on the material terms of the Danish treaty. Russia relies on this holding to support its argument that Article 10 of the Spanish BIT simply does not allow an inquiry into Article 5(2) and its promise of MFN treatment.

80. The Tribunal is unpersuaded. The starting point of its analysis is to observe that Russia cannot deny the Tribunal's authority to decide whether it has jurisdiction to deal with a claim under Article 5(2) of the Spanish BIT. A constant attribute of international tribunals (one of the 'universally recognised norms and principles of international law' referred to in Article 10(3) of the Treaty) is that they have the authority to rule on questions pertaining to their own jurisdiction. Abundant citations could be given. It seems sufficient to recall the ICJ's reference in *Nottebohm* (1953) to:

> a rule consistently accepted by general international law in the matter of international arbitration. Since the *Alabama* case, it has been generally recognised, following the earlier precedents, that, in the absence of any agreement to the contrary, an international tribunal has the right to decide as to its own jurisdiction and has the power to interpret for this purpose the instruments which govern that jurisdiction. (1953 *ICJ Reports* 119; this passage was explicitly recalled in para 46 of the ICJ's 1991 judgment in the Case Concerning the Arbitral Award of 31 July 1989 (*Guinea- Bissau v Senegal*)).

Such authority is specifically established in Article 2 of the Swedish Arbitration Act which applies to these proceedings. The Tribunal needs no further warrant to consider and dispose of jurisdictional arguments. It may well be that its jurisdictional rulings are susceptible to challenge before another authority. This alters nothing. It would mean only that the other authority has the capacity to review the scope of arbitral jurisdiction and not that the present Tribunal lacked the power to make the initial determination.

81. The consequence should be manifest when one considers the mighty debate about the scope of jurisdiction created by Article 10 (see s 2.1 above). Russia argues that the arbitrators may decide only some controversies arising with respect to Article 6. This is a debate about the terms of Article 10. It is a debate which Russia unreservedly asks the Tribunal to decide in its favour. Russia makes no issue of the fact that Article 10 does not stipulate that a dispute about its own terms may be decided by the arbitrators. Nor could Russia seriously make such an argument; it is foreclosed by Article 2 of the Arbitration Act.

82. No difference in principle arises when the debate focuses on the jurisdictional consequences of Article 5 of the Spanish BIT. There is no rule that the entirety of arbitration agreements must be contained in a single article of an instrument. There is no rule that elements of arbitral jurisdiction may not be defined in an article (like Article 5) which also contains substantive provisions. These are trivial observations. The important question is whether there has been consent to arbitrate the claims raised in this case. The claimants say that the scope of jurisdiction in the Spanish BIT is derived from both Article 5 and Article 10. This contention is denied by Russia. It may be true or false. But the Tribunal has the right to decide (subject to such review as may be available). There was no need for Article 10 to stipulate that controversies with respect to jurisdictional implications of particular provisions of the BIT may be decided by the Tribunal – whether those provisions appear in Article 10 or elsewhere. In the end the matter is thus quite simple.

83. To be clear: the claimants are not seeking to establish that Russia breached an obligation under the basic treaty (the Spanish BIT) by failing *explicitly* to grant to Spanish investors the same access to international arbitration as the access the claimants say is enjoyed by Danish investors. The question is instead simply whether Article 5(2) of the Spanish BIT evidences Russia's consent that this Tribunal's jurisdiction should have an ambit beyond that of Article 10.

84. The *Anglo-Iranian* case turned on a fundamentally different point. The ICJ of course also has power to decide its own jurisdiction (Art 38(6) of the ICJ Statute). It was asked to rule on the consequences of treaties that predated Iran's consent to ICJ jurisdiction. That consent was limited to disputes arising out of future treaties entered into by Iran. They were the 'basic treaties' (see para 77 above). It followed that the UK could not invoke the antecedent treaties before the ICJ. Invocation of a 'comparator treaty' could not alter that basic jurisdictional fact. The ICJ held: 'A third-party treaty, independent of and isolated from the basic treaty, cannot produce any legal effect as between the UK and Iran: it is *res inter alios acta*'. (1952 *ICJ Reports* 109.) The ICJ had no warrant to consider the basic treaties because they were antecedent to consent. Had they been subsequent the UK may have prevailed. It would have come down to the content of the comparator treaty. Access to ICJ jurisdiction granted to Denmark might have been imported into the UK treaties; that is the equivalent of the present question; what the ICJ would have thought of it will never be known.

85. The claimants argue that Article 5(2) of the Spanish BIT contains no restriction as to the date when more favoured nation treatment may be estab-

lished. They are right. Article 5(2) does not in fact prevent the right to MFN treatment from arising out of undertakings to third nations which are given in the future. That is typically how MFN promises are enlivened. It is therefore open to the claimants to invoke the Danish BIT. *Anglo-Iranian* is simply inapposite.

86. What remains is of course to determine what the claimants are able to derive from the Danish BIT. And so the analysis moves to the more specific issue of the possibility of expanding investor-state arbitration via MFN provisions. It is a familiar topic. Yet it comes in a great variety of guises. The answers may change as the questions become more refined. May one conclude that qualifying 'investments' under the Spanish BIT are given less favourable treatment than such investments enjoy under the Danish BIT if the latter are given greater access to international arbitration? Is such access an element of the types of treatment that may be compared for purposes of assessing compliance with the MFN standard? These questions are at the heart of a current debate on this aspect of investor-state arbitrations. Yet they are not decisive in this case. It is to the contrary indispensable to understand that in light of the wording of the Spanish BIT either of them may be answered affirmatively without defeating Russia's objection.

87. The Tribunal approaches this matter against a normative background which merits a brief overview.

88. The International Court of Justice in the *Rights of US Nationals in Morocco* (1952) considered the effects of MFN clauses contained in a treaty of 1836 with respect to the 'footing' of 'commerce' with the US and to the entitlement of US nationals to 'whatever indulgence, in trade or otherwise' were granted to nationals of certain other States. The UK subsequently became entitled under an 1861 treaty to insist that its nationals must be brought before consular jurisdictions to the exclusion of local courts. The ICJ was satisfied that the MFN provisions in the basic treaty created an entitlement to the same advantage for US nationals. It was not necessary that there be explicit mention of jurisdictional advantages. (1952 *ICJ Reports* 190.) This was however the statement of a premise rather than a conclusion. The decisive issue in the case was different: whether the entitlement to MFN treatment expired with the renunciation of the UK treaty (as well as that of a treaty involving Spain). The ICJ answered affirmatively.

89. The 1956 case of the *Ambatielos Claim* (23 ILR 306) is seminal. It examined the *ejusdem generis* principle: 'the most-favoured nation clause can only attract matter belonging to the same category of subject as that to which the

clause itself relates'. The field of application of the relevant treaty containing a MFN clause was defined as 'all matters relating to commerce and navigation'. Greece sought to derive a jurisdictional extension by virtue of MFN rights. The UK countered that scope of jurisdiction was not among the matters that could be considered common objects of the treaties under comparison. The commissioners rejected the UK's argument:

> It is true that 'the administration of justice', when viewed in isolation, is a subject matter other than 'commerce and navigation', but this is not necessarily so when it is viewed in connection with the protection of the rights of traders. Protection of the rights of traders naturally finds a place among the matters dealt with by Treaties of commerce and navigation.
>
> Therefore it cannot be said that the administration of justice, in so far as it is concerned with the protection of these rights, must necessarily be excluded from the field of application of the most-favoured-nation clause, when the latter includes 'all matters relating to commerce and navigation'. The question can only be determined in accordance with the intention of the Contracting Parties as deduced from a reasonable interpretation of the Treaty.

90. It is undoubtedly fair to compare BITs for the purpose of assessing compliance with promises of MFN treatment given their congruent objective: the promotion and protection of investments. Yet such a general statement is insufficient to decide any particular case. It is a matter of the wording of the relevant instruments. This is one of the reasons awards under BITs are of variable relevance and value in subsequent cases.

91. There are other reasons why alleged precedents may be of limited normative applicability. Quotations of incidental comments are not entitled to be considered as precedents at all; they are not part of the *ratio decidendi* and thus are not part of the reasoning by which the arbitrators fulfil their mandate to decide. That is where they exercise personal responsibility. *Obiter dicta* are commentary. They may be persuasive but are *a priori* of less weight.

92. Speculations as to policy desiderata thought to favour one reading or another of an instrument should be considered with care. An example is the occasional reflection that access to different types of dispute resolution mechanism should not be held to be part of 'treatment' for MFN purposes because it would lead to forum shopping. That proposition may have adherents but may equally well be rejected. The use of the expression 'forum shopping' in a derogatory sense is but the assertion of an opinion. It does not deal with the countervailing consideration to the effect that dispute resolution mechanisms accepted by a State in various international instruments are all

legitimate in the eyes of that State. Some may be inherently more efficient. Others may be more reliable in a particular context. Having options may be thought to be more 'favoured' for MFN purposes than not having them. It is not convincing for a State to argue in general terms that it accepted a particular 'system of arbitration' with respect to nationals of one country but did not so consent with respect to nationals of another. The extension of commitments is in the very nature of MFN clauses. Drafters wishing to do so would have little difficulty in defining restrictions that would go further than the general *esjudem generis* constraint. Some BITs exhaustively enumerate acceptable MFN extensions. Others explicitly exclude dispute resolution from the reach of MFN provisions. Absent such stipulations it is the task of international tribunals to determine whether arbitration clauses in comparator treaties in fact comport more favoured treatment.

93. To choose one of the contending policy theses as the reason to read a BIT in a particular way may be presumptuous. The stakes are high and the policy decisions appertain to the State-parties to the treaties. Speculations relied upon as the basis of purposive readings of a text run the risk of encroachment upon fundamental policy determinations. The same is true when 'confirmation' of hypothetical intentions is said to be found in considerations external to the text. The duty of the Tribunal is to discover and not to create meaning.

94. A considerable number of awards under BITs have dealt with the jurisdictional implications of MFN. Many of them have been invoked in the present arbitration. They are of uneven persuasiveness and relevance. The present Tribunal would find it jejune to declare that there is a dominant view; it is futile to make a head-count of populations of such diversity. What can be said with confidence is that a *jurisprudence constante* of general applicability is not yet firmly established. It remains necessary to proceed BIT by BIT.

95. Two contrasting awards are nevertheless of particular interest: *Berschader* and *RoslnvestCo*. Each involved a BIT to which Russia is a party. *Berschader* refused to extend the scope of investor-state arbitration in the USSR/ Belgium-Luxembourg BIT notwithstanding an MFN clause which guaranteed MFN 'in all matters covered by this Agreement'. The majority of the arbitrators relied on the jurisdictional decision in *Plama v Bulgaria* (2005). They were persuaded by the view expressed in that decision (at para 223) that there should be a presumption that a MFN provision 'does not incorporate by reference dispute settlement provisions in whole or in part set forth in another treaty'. This was *dictum* since *Plama* upheld jurisdiction under alternative grounds. (*Berschader* so acknowledged in para 171.) *Plama* also suggested elliptically that the expression 'with respect to all matters'

is insufficient to overcome this presumption. Yet the only authority cited in support of this significant hardening of the presumption was *Siemens v Argentina* (2004). But that decision upheld *an extension of arbitral authority on the basis of an MFN undertaking which did not refer to 'all matters'*. The *Berschader* majority thus seems to have relied on a dictum which in turn had relied on another *dictum*.

96. The contrary reasoning of *Ambatielos* (set out in para 89 above) strikes the present Tribunal as more persuasive. *Ambatielos* had been preceded by an attempt to bring the matter before the ICJ. That court held (1953 *ICJ Reports* 10) that (i) it had no jurisdiction to deal with the merits of the claim but (ii) directed the UK to submit to the jurisdiction of an arbitration commission. That gave rise to the award quoted above. The court's judgment (rendered by a 10:4 majority) said nothing about the scope and applicability of the MFN clauses relied upon by Greece. The four dissenting judges opined on the other hand that a clause referring to 'matters of commerce and navigation . . . cannot be extended' to cover aspects of 'the administration of justice'. This brief conclusion appears to be pure affirmation. It was of course known to the commissioners whose reasoned conclusion was to opposite effect. Moreover all BITs were unknown in 1953. What the four dissenters would have thought of the relationship between 'favoured treatment' of foreign investment and access to neutral arbitration cannot be divined.

97. The reasoned view of the commissioners who finally decided *Ambatielos* have found echoes (half a century later) in a number of modern investor-State cases. Thus the unanimous arbitrators in *RoslnvestCo* adopted a similar position in the following passages:

> For it is difficult to doubt that an expropriation interferes with the investor's use and enjoyment of the investment, and that the submission to arbitration forms a highly relevant part of the corresponding protection for the investor by granting him, in case of interference with this 'use' and 'enjoyment', procedural options of obvious and great significance compared to the sole option of challenging such interference before the domestic courts of the host state. . ..
>
> While indeed the application of the MFN clause . . . widens the scope of Article 8 and thus is in conflict to its limitation, this is a normal result of the application of MFN clauses, the very character and intention of which is that protection not accepted in one treaty is widened by transferring the protection accorded in another treaty.
>
> If this effect is generally accepted in the context of substantive protection, the Tribunal sees no reason not to accept it in the context of procedural clauses such as arbitration clauses. Quite the contrary, it could be argued that, if it applies

to substantive protection, then it should apply even more to 'only' procedural protection. However, the Tribunal feels that this latter argument cannot be considered as decisive, but that rather, as argued further above, an arbitration clause, at least in the context of expropriation, is of the same protective value as any substantive protection afforded by applicable provisions such as Article 5 of the BIT. (paras 130–132.)

98. This reasoning is similar to that of paras 19–20 of the dissenting opinion in *Berschader*. It contrasts with that of *Plama* (of which the *RosInvestCo* arbitrators indicated they had taken note; see para 136). *Plama* reasoned that it may be 'argued with equal force' that the fact that the identified exceptions to MFN treatment made in the relevant basic treaty related to 'privileges' demonstrated that the MFN treatment involved 'substantive protection to the exclusion of the procedural provisions relating to dispute settlement' (para 191). Yet this assertion of 'equal force' depends on the premise – stated but not substantiated – that there is a significant distinction between procedural and substantive protection.

99. It may be that some international lawyers reflexively adopt the dichotomy of primary/secondary obligations made familiar by the International Law Commission. This might explain the temptation to consider 'treatment' a matter of primary or substantive rules and thus distinct from 'secondary' rules – such as remedies – in the event of alleged breach. Perhaps this idea merges into that of a substance/procedure distinction. Yet there is nothing *normative* about the primary/secondary dichotomy; it has simply been the classification by which the ILC determined its field of work on State responsibility:

> The law relating to the content and the duration of substantive State obligations is as determined by the primary rules. The law of State responsibility as articulated in the Draft Articles provides the framework – those rules, denominated 'secondary', which indicate the consequences of a breach of an applicable primary obligation. (James Crawford, *The International Law Commission's Articles on State Responsibility* 16 (2002).)

100. There is no authority for the proposition that MFN is limited to 'primary' obligations. The established proper criterion is rather *ejusdem generis*. That criterion resounds through the quotations in the preceding paragraphs – from *Ambatielos* onward. Nor can it be doubted that access to international arbitration has been a fundamental and constant desideratum for investment protection and therefore a weighty factor in considering the object and purpose of BITs. The arbitrators are aware of the concern that 'it would be

invidious for international tribunals to be finding (in the absence of specific evidence) that host State adjudication of treaty rights was necessarily inferior to international arbitration'. This is how Messrs McLachlan, Shore and Weiniger put it in their monograph *International Investment Arbitration* (at p 257). It is however possible that the invidiousness rather lies in this way of articulating the issue. Investors who desire access to a neutral international forum are not 'necessarily' denigrating national justice. They do no more than make clear that their comfort is greater knowing that the international alternative is open to them. This is a rational concern. Nor is there anything illegitimate about the desideratum of an option to seise a neutral forum. History is replete with examples of investment disputes which have overwhelmed the capacity   of national institutions – in countries of all stages of development – for dispassionate judgment.

101. Under *Ambatielos* both of the questions noted under paragraph 86 above therefore in principle could be answered in the affirmative. Rights and obligations may be classified as substantive or jurisdictional or procedural. Such classifications are not watertight and in any event primarily of pedagogical use. There is no textual basis or legal rule to say that 'treatment' does not encompass the host State's acceptance of international arbitration. Whether MFN treatment is stated in the relevant BIT to relate to investors rather than investments is in principle of no moment. Investors will not claim access to international arbitration by way of MFN treatment in the abstract. They will assert a breach and harm in connection with a qualifying investment under the relevant BIT. The investor's gateway to MFN treatment is the status of protected investor and ownership of a qualifying investment in terms of the BIT as the 'basic treaty'. This is the position the claimants here seek to establish under the Spanish BIT. There is nothing unsound about the general proposition they seek to vindicate.

102. Yet the general proposition is not a laser beam pointing to an answer (see para 90 above). To move from broad purposive considerations to a specific determination of what has been agreed requires coming to grips with the singular features of the case at hand. Russia has invoked a specific textual impediment to expanding the scope of arbitral jurisdiction. That decisive argument now moves centre-stage.

103. The MFN promise affects only matters within the scope of Article 5(2) of the Spanish BIT which in turn covers only 'treatment referred to in paragraph 1 above'. The treatment in question is 'fair and equitable treatment' (FET). FET is a substantive standard of treatment. Russia insists that access to international arbitration is not an inherent part of FET. This is confirmed

by the existence of BITs guaranteeing FET without any recourse to international arbitration whatever. A promise to match the level of FET extended to third-party nationals therefore cannot in Russia's submission widen the scope of arbitral jurisdiction.

104. One immediately perceives that the present case is unlike *Berschader* in that the latter involved a promise of MFN 'in all matters covered by this Agreement' (see para 95 above). That is simply not the case with the Spanish BIT. (Nor did the UK BIT under consideration in *RoslnvestCo* have such breadth. Given the dissimilarities between the UK BIT and the Spanish BIT it is unnecessary for the present Tribunal to comment on how *RoslnvestCo* nevertheless concluded that the MFN clause in that case expanded arbitral jurisdiction.)

105. This then becomes the crux of the matter: the Spanish BIT does not contain an MFN clause entitling investors to avail themselves in generic terms of more favourable conditions found 'in all matters covered' by other treaties. Instead it establishes the right to enjoy a no less favourable level of FET. The obvious questions arise immediately: is access to international arbitration a necessary part of FET? May it be said that a BIT which does not give access to international arbitration provides for less FET than one that does? Negative answers to these questions would be fatal to the claimants' attempt to enlarge arbitral jurisdiction.

106. Notwithstanding the existence of a BIT it may be the case that an investor has no other avenue for the enforcement of its rights except through the national courts of the host State. There is no legal authority known to the present Tribunal in support of the proposition that this state of affairs would violate an FET undertaking in the treaty. Instances of denial of justice by such courts may assuredly trigger the State's international responsibility. Yet that possibility does not mean that access to international arbitration per se implies a higher level of FET. The neutrality of an international tribunal may legitimately be said to enhance investor protection. Access to it may be more *favourable* than lack of access. But that does not mean that failure to give access to such a tribunal is *unfair* or *inequitable*. The implications of a contrary inference would be extraordinary. (For one thing it would plainly justify the objection of Messrs McLachlan *et al* quoted in para 100 above.)

107. The claimants argue that FET is an invariable standard and that it would be nonsense to speak of more or less favourable FET treatment. The purpose of this argument was to suggest that the word 'treatment' in Article 5(2) should not be qualified by the adjectives 'fair and equitable' found

in Article 5(1) (reproduced in para 68 above). The implication would be that the MFN clause in Article 5(2) should be construed broadly so that the claimants could invoke all types of advantage stipulated in other BITs. The importance of this point hardly needs to be emphasised. It was much debated in the hearings.

108. The proposition that FET should have a universal meaning has an undeniable cogency if one considers FET as part and parcel of a general minimum standard of international law. That standard may evolve over time. It is nevertheless a single standard. The notion of a 'variable general standard' would be oxymoronic. Yet international legal standards may also be created by treaties that bind only the parties to that particular instrument. It is true that the use in individual treaties of heterogeneous ad hoc definitions of expressions which are also used elsewhere to denote a general principle may give birth to confusion and therefore be undesirable. But nothing can prevent its occurrence if States so decide. Indeed it has happened.

109. One well-known example is the 'interpretation' proclaimed in 2001 by the three NAFTA State-parties to the effect that FET (for NAFTA purposes) does not require 'treatment in addition to or beyond that, which is required by the customary international law minimum standard of treatment of aliens'. This initiative of the three governments was sharply criticised by Sir Robert Jennings in an opinion delivered in *Methanex v United States* in which he challenged 'the impropriety of the three governments making such an intervention well into the process of the arbitration, not only after the benefit of seeing the written pleadings of the parties but also virtually prompted by them'. What matters here is not whether the three governments were right to act as they did. What is significant is rather that a former President of the ICJ perceived that the three governments were agreeing to *amend* general principles. Such was indeed also the opinion of the Arbitral Tribunal whose interim award apparently triggered the 'interpretation' (see *Pope & Talbot v Canada* at paras 47–59 (2002)). Other examples could be given. One instance arising in the BIT context is that of *MTD v Chile* (2004). An MFN clause contained in the Chile-Malaysian BIT was expanded by reference to two other BITs concluded by Chile which contained more detailed treaty language on 'fair and equitable' treatment. The basic treaty was thus enlarged to encompass obligations (i) to grant permits subsequent to approval of an investment and (ii) to fulfil contractual obligations.

110. Of particular relevance for present purposes is the fact that Russia itself has elsewhere explicitly stipulated that FET may be more or less favourable. Thus Article 3(1) of its Danish BIT provides:

> Each Contracting Party shall accord investments made by investors of the other Contracting Party in its territory fair and equitable treatment no less favourable than that which it accords to investments of its own investors or to investments of investors of any third state, whichever treatment is more favourable.

This text unmistakably contemplates variable levels of FET. Investors would therefore find it meaningful to be assured that they may invoke the most favourable level of FET. Other equally clear instances may be imagined apart from the example of treaty practice. A State may unilaterally take a formal position that FET has a particular meaning with respect to nationals of a particular country. An investor entitled to MFN treatment would be in a position to insist that that State could not legitimately treat it in a less favourable manner.

111. The Tribunal finally turns to some lexical difficulties. Article 5 (reproduced in para 68 above) uses the word 'treatment' at least once in each of its four subparagraphs. Moreover the pronoun 'that' in subparagraph 2 replaces 'treatment'. The result is not ideal in terms of understanding the quite different senses which the word may carry in its various iterations. It is best to consider the uses as they occur. This involves rather arid yet indispensable parsing.

112. Subparagraph 1 speaks of 'fair and equitable treatment'. Subparagraph 2 begins by referring to the 'treatment referred to in paragraph 1 above'. So far so good. The difficulty begins with the pronoun *that* which appears next in subparagraph 2. If Article 5 contained only two subparagraphs there would be no problem; one would conclude that the pronoun simply avoids a third iteration of 'fair and equitable treatment'. But then comes subparagraph 3. It begins: 'Such treatment shall not, however, include privileges' of certain types: advantages created e.g., by membership in a free trade area or a customs union. The fact that an import duty may be set at x or y per cent is naturally not a matter of FET. This strongly suggests that the pronoun 'such' in subparagraph 3 cannot be read to stand for 'fair and equitable treatment' but rather for 'treatment' simpliciter.

113. The exception made for negotiated tax advantages in the final section of subparagraph 3 is to similar effect. It may indeed be described as even more troubling since it refers to 'treatment under this article'. One might infer that every time the word 'treatment' appears *throughout Article 5* it is intended to have the same meaning. Tax advantages are like customs tariffs in that they are not ordinarily matters of FET.

114. The claimants say this proves that 'treatment' is generic and not limited to FET. The focus of subparagraph 2 is of course the hypothetical treatment

accorded to a third-party national under a 'comparator treaty'. If this is broad treatment (the claimants reason) it gives them access to investor-state arbitration.

115. Now that the lexical ground has been traversed the problem may be restated in simpler terms. One logical sequence is the following. Subparagraph 1 explicitly concerns FET. Subparagraph 2 equally unmistakeably refers back to FET. Subparagraph 2's promise of MFN therefore does not encompass access to investor-state arbitration.

116. Yet if MFN treatment is restricted to FET subparagraph 3 was unnecessary. One should if possible avoid the conclusion that treaty provisions are superfluous. Therefore the MFN clause should be understood in a broad sense. It captures investor-state arbitration. Thus subparagraph 2 seems to envisage MFN treatment which is simultaneously restricted and broad.

117. Something has to give. The choice is between an explicit stipulation and a revelation by grammatical deconstruction. The Tribunal naturally prefers the former. Why then would the drafters have included subparagraph 3 unless they understood the pronoun 'such' to stand for broader treatment? The arbitrators believe the answer lies ready to hand. The drafters were conscious of the ramifications of the MFN promise. They were determined to ensure that it would not encroach on their freedom to extend special privileges in the context of regional integration or other arrangements envisaged in subparagraph 3. Such exceptions to MFN clauses are commonplace in BIT practice. This may have led to a reflexive insertion of the clause in the Spanish BIT. A searching exegetical endeavour would have revealed that this was unnecessary in this particular instance. The drafters may not have realised this. Or they may not have wished to rely on others – including trade representatives or tribunals – to reach the same recondite conclusion. Either way the attribution to subparagraph 3 of sophisticated implications simply cannot dislodge the qualifying adjectives 'fair and equitable' in subparagraph 1. Even less can it undermine the unambiguous reference in subparagraph 2 to 'treatment referred to in paragraph 1 above'.

118. The final subparagraph 4 presents its own difficulty. It contains a promise of 'treatment no less favourable than that' granted to nationals. Here there are no qualifying adjectives. Nor is there a cross-reference having that effect. Arguably this is therefore 'treatment' writ large. So imagine that Russia were to offer international arbitration to its own citizens making claims against the State. The claimants too would then be entitled to international arbitration by virtue of this subparagraph. Such a provision is as far as the Tribunal knows unheard of in international treaty practice. It would be odd indeed if *national*

treatment were in this respect sharply more favourable than MFN. One might therefore wonder if the drafters of the Spanish BIT truly applied their minds to the issue of arbitration when drafting Article 5. The doubt may be justified. Yet it hardly advantages the claimants. The Treaty must be taken as it is written.

119. The conclusion must be that the specific MFN promise contained in Article 5(2) of the Spanish BIT cannot be read to enlarge the competence of the present Tribunal. This conclusion (and the analysis in paras 105–118 upon which it is built) is that of a majority of the Tribunal. The separate opinion appended hereto is viewed with full respect by the majority. They agree that 'more favourable' may in principle include accessibility to international fora. Ultimately however their view is that the terms of the Spanish BIT restrict MFN treatment to the realm of FET as understood in international law. This in the majority view relates to normative standards and does not extend to either (i) the availability of international as opposed to national fora or (ii) 'more' rather than 'less' arbitration (as the separate opinion puts it).

120. The claimants have also invoked Russia's BITs with other countries. The Tribunal's conclusion makes it superfluous to analyse them, since the impediment to expansion of arbitral jurisdiction via the MFN avenue lies in the Spanish BIT itself and cannot be overcome by the texts of such other instruments.

[. . .]

4. Decision

155. The Tribunal hereby decides that:

(i)   it has subject matter jurisdiction under Article 10 of the Spanish BIT to decide whether compensation is due by virtue of claims of expropriation raised in this arbitration;

(ii)   it has no subject matter jurisdiction under Article 5 of the Spanish BIT;

(iii)   its jurisdiction is limited to the claims of the following four entities:

> Rovime Inversions SICAV SA
> Quasar de Valors SICAV SA
> Orgor de ValoresSICAV SA
> OBI 9000 SICAV SA

(iv)   the claims of the four corporate entities identified in subparagraph (iii) are admissible within the scope of subparagraph (i).

156. Costs are reserved.

CASE

Arbitration Institute of the Stockholm Chamber of Commerce

In anarbitration between Renta 4 SVSA; Ahorro Corporacion Emergentes FI; Ahorro Corporacion Eurofondo FI; Rovime Inversiones Sicav SA; Quasar De Valors Sicav SA; Orgor De Valores Sicav SA; Gbi 9000 Sicav SA (claimants) and The Russian Federation (respondent)

Separate opinion of Charles N Brower

Introduction

1. I begin by confirming what is stated in paragraph 154 of the Award on Preliminary Objections (the Award) to which this separate opinion is appended. The fact that the award does result from such 'extensive and collegial deliberations' with co-arbitrators whose integrity and intellect I respect most highly renders me particularly hesitant to air the views set forth below. Yet, I choose to articulate my partially differing views for two reasons. First, I believe that by doing so I may contribute usefully to the public debate over the issues addressed by this Tribunal in this case, a debate reflected in past awards of other tribunals and doubtless to be continued in ongoing and future arbitrations. Second, given what we have been informed may be the practical impact of the award,[1] it may not be amiss to anticipate the possibility of judicial proceedings in due course in which the correctness of the award is put in issue, in which case I entertain the fond hope that the views I express may further illuminate certain issues for the benefit of any such forum.

2. I agree entirely with subparagraph (i) of paragraph 155 of the award. Hence I am in agreement with what has been said in paragraphs 19–67 of the Award, while adding only my own emphasis to the statements in its paragraph 45 to the effect that it is solely the claimants' own insistence that we may not address the issue of whether the alleged expropriation of which they

---

1 At the hearing leading to the award claimants' counsel noted that:

> owners of about $10 billion in losses reside in countries that have bilateral investment treaties with Russia, and the large majority of those live in countries that have bilateral investment treaties with Russia that are similar to the UK treaty [involved in *RosInvest Co v Russia*, referred to in the Award at paragraphs 48, 73, 95, 97, 98 and 104] and the Spanish treaty (T:378).

Hence, counsel stated, '[t]his is a very important case. This is about more than the few million dollars that are at stake for the claimants in this case' (T:377).

complain was lawful or unlawful that has precluded us from addressing such issue, and that the award therefore expresses no opinion as to whether, in the absence of that insistence, we would have had jurisdiction under the Spanish treaty to address that issue.

3. I am in disagreement with, and hence dissent from, subparagraph (ii) of paragraph 155 of the award. While I do embrace some of the award's conclusions leading up to its rejection of jurisdiction based on Article 5(2), namely those establishing that claimants' raising of the MFN issue was timely, that it is not precluded by Article 11(3) of the Danish treaty with Russia nor is it negated by Article 10 of the Spanish treaty, and that dispute settlement mechanisms may be encompassed by the term 'treatment', I disagree with the majority's analysis in so far as it denies claimants access through the MFN clause of the Spanish treaty to the broader consent to international arbitration respondent gave under Article 8(1) of the Danish treaty. Thus I would have ruled that this Tribunal has jurisdiction not only to consider claimants' claim of expropriation, with all of its ramifications, under Article 6 of the Spanish treaty, but also to hear claims arising under Articles 4 (protection against arbitrary or discriminatory measures) and 5(1) (fair and equitable treatment) of that treaty.

4. Finally, I also am in disagreement with, and hence dissent from, subparagraph (iii) of paragraph 155 of the Award in so far as it excludes from this arbitration the claimants Emergentes, Eurofondo and Renta 4 SVSA, who, in my view, either should be admitted as qualified claimants or given an opportunity to undertake whatever formalities may be required for their claims to be presented to this Tribunal. That is to say, while I concur with paragraphs 135–153 of the award, holding that ADRs qualify as 'investments' under the Spanish treaty, that ownership is proven and that there is no problem as regards admissibility, I reject paragraphs 121–134 of the Award, which find Emergentes, Eurofondo and Renta 4 SVSA not to be qualified investors under the Spanish treaty.

Article 5(2) of the Spanish Treaty

5. In my view the majority in this case is mistaken in its view that Article 5(2) of the Spanish treaty grants most-favoured-nation treatment only in respect of fair and equitable treatment, and does not permit claimants to incorporate respondent's broader consent to arbitration under Article 8(1) of the Danish treaty with Russia, which accords the right to SCC arbitration in respect of any dispute under that treaty, for the benefit of investors covered under the Spanish treaty.

6. At the outset, while the award deals with *Plama* (in paras 95 and 98) and rightly ascribes to it no weight for present purposes, I think it nonetheless important to emphasise, as part of what the award in paragraph 87 calls 'normative background', the wrongheadedness of *Plama*'s analytical diktat to the effect that:

> an MFN provision in a basic treaty does not incorporate by reference dispute settlement provisions in whole or in part set forth in another treaty, unless the MFN provision in the basic treaty leaves no doubt that the contracting parties intended to incorporate them.[2]

7. The principle basis on which the *Plama* tribunal reached its conclusion, and on which also the tribunals in *Telenor, Berschader* and *Wintershall* relied, i.e., that a State's acceptance of jurisdiction must be 'clear and unambiguous', however, is a principle that, whatever validity it may have had in an earlier era, is patently incompatible with Articles 31 and 32 of the Vienna Convention

---

2 *Plama v Bulgaria,* ICSID Case No. ARB/03/24, Decision on Jurisdiction of 8 Feb. 2005, para 223. The same point was expressed repeatedly by the *Plama* Tribunal in terms of the MFN provision needing to be 'clear and unambiguous' in that respect:

> ... [A]n agreement of the parties to arbitrate ... should be clear and unambiguous (para. 198). ... [T]he parties' clear and unambiguous intention ... (para. 199). ... [T]he reference [in the MFN clause] must be such that the parties' intention to import the arbitration provision of the other agreement [BIT] is clear and unambiguous (para. 200). ... [C]learly and unambiguously ... (para. 200). ... [T]he intention to incorporate [into the primary BIT] dispute settlement provisions [from the BIT sought to be accessed] must be clearly and unambiguously expressed (para. 204). ... [U]nless the States have explicitly agreed thereto ... (para. 212). ... [A]n arbitration clause must be clear and unambiguous and the reference to an arbitration clause [via an MEN clause] must be such as to make the clause part of the contract (treaty) (para 218 – the parenthesised reference to 'treaty' is in the original).

Following *Plama v Bulgaria,* see also *Telenor Mobile Communications AS v The Republic of Hungary,* ICSID Case No. ARB/04/15, Award of 13 Sept. 2006, para 90 (stating that '[t]his Tribunal wholeheartedly endorses the analysis and statement of principle furnished by the *Plama* tribunal'); *Vladimir Berschader and Moïse Berschader v The Russian Federation,* SCC Case No. 080/2004, Award of 21 April 2006, para 181, stating that:

> the present Tribunal will apply the principle that an MFN provision in a BIT will only incorporate by reference an arbitration clause from another BIT where the terms of the original BIT clearly and unambiguously so provide or where it can otherwise be clearly inferred that this was the intention of the contracting parties

Wintershall Aktiengesellschaft v Argentine Republic, ICSID Case No. ARB/04/14, Award of 8 Dec. 2008, para 167, observing that:

> ordinarily and without more, the prospect of an investor selecting at will from an assorted variety of options provided in other treaties negotiated with other parties under different circumstances, dislodges the dispute resolution provision in the basic treaty itself — *unless of course the MFN Clause in the basic treaty clearly and unambiguously indicates that it should be so interpreted* (emphasis in the original).

I note, however, that the award in *Wintershall AG v Argentina* was rendered after the close of the oral hearings in the present case, without the Parties having had an opportunity to comment upon this decision. Therefore, it is, in the present context, cited solely for purposes of completeness.

on the Law of Treaties. Thus, the International Court of Justice and numerous arbitral tribunals have repeatedly stated that instruments containing a State's consent to submit to the jurisdiction of an international court or tribunal are to be interpreted like any other international legal instrument, that is neither restrictively nor liberally, but according to the standards set down in the Vienna Convention.

8. Thus, after a meticulous review of the jurisprudence of both the Permanent Court of International Justice as well as the International Court of Justice, Judge Rosalyn Higgins, in her separate opinion in the *Oil Platforms* case, concluded that:

> [i]t is clear from the jurisprudence of the Permanent Court and of the International Court that there is no rule that requires a restrictive interpretation of compromissory clauses. But equally, there is no evidence that the various exercises of jurisdiction by the two Courts really indicate a jurisdictional presumption in favour of the plaintiff. ... The Court has no judicial policy of being either liberal or strict in deciding the scope of compromissory clauses: they are judicial decisions like any other.[3]

9. The same approach to interpreting jurisdictional instruments also dominates the practice of arbitral tribunals. Thus, as Professor Berthold Goldman and his colleagues famously said more than a quarter of a century ago in the jurisdictional decision in the first *Amco Asia* ICSID arbitration, which has been followed by a number of other tribunals:

> [L]ike any other conventions, a convention to arbitrate is not to be construed restrictively, nor, as a matter of fact, broadly or liberally. It is to be construed in a way which leads to find out and to respect the common will of the parties: such a method of interpretation is but the application of the fundamental principle pacta sunt servanda, a principle common, indeed, to all systems of internal law and to international law.[4]

10. In view of this broad consensus on the interpretative methodology to be applied to questions regarding the jurisdiction of international dispute

3 *Oil Platforms (Islamic Republic of Iran v United States of America)*, Preliminary Objections, Judgment of 12 Dec. 1996, Separate Opinion by Judge Higgins, I.C.J. Reports 1996, p 857, para 35.
4 *Amco Asia Corporation and Others v The Republic of Indonesia*, ICSID Case No. ARB/81/1, Award on Jurisdiction of 25 Sept. 1983, para 14(i), 23 I.L.M. 351, 359 (1984) (emphasis in the original); see also, e.g., *Ethyl Corporation v The Government of Canada*, Award on Jurisdiction of 24 June 1998, para 55; *Mondev International Ltd v United States of America*, ICSID Case No. ARB(AF)/99/2, Award of 11 Oct. 2002, para 43; *Suez, Sociedad General de Aguas de Barcelona, SA and Interaguas Servicios Integrates del Agua, SA v The Argentine Republic*, ICSID Case No. ARB/03/17, Decision on Jurisdiction of 16 May 2006, para 64.

settlement bodies, the principle basis of the decisions in *Plama, Telenor, Berschader* and *Wintershall* is, with respect, wrong and cannot be followed. In consequence, I see no reason why an issue of the incorporation of broader consent to arbitration under the host State's third-country investment treaties should be treated differently from the consistently accepted application of MFN clauses to substantive standards of treatment, or the (rather) consistently accepted application of MFN clauses to the shortening of waiting periods.[5] While, on the one hand, there is no reason to differentiate between admissibility-related aspects of accessing investor-state arbitration and matters of jurisdiction, there equally is little merit in distinguishing between matters of substantive investment protection and the enforcement of these rights through investor-state dispute settlement.[6]

11. Against this 'normative background', my dissent from the majority's reasoning relates to the construction of Article 5(2) of the Spanish treaty. While in the majority's view that provision constitutes an MFN clause which, due to its reference to paragraph 1 of Article 5, encompasses only matters forming part of fair and equitable treatment, I consider this construction not to be in conformity with the interpretative rules set out in the Vienna Convention on the Law of Treaties and hence mistaken. I am further of the view that, even if the majority's construction of Article 5(2) were correct, the result reached should not differ from that which follows from the construction I give to Article 5(2); namely, the respondent's broader consent to arbitration under the Danish treaty is an aspect of fair and equitable treatment, hence Article 5(2) enlarges the jurisdiction of this Tribunal to encompass claims made under Articles 4, 5(1) and 6 of the Spanish treaty.

12. The award spells out, in paragraphs 102–120, the conundrum presented by the unofficial English translation of the Spanish treaty as regards the reference that Article 5(2) makes to '[t]he treatment referred to in paragraph 1'. The award, in this context, acknowledges (in its para 111) what it calls 'some lexical difficulties'. They are easily recapitulated thusly: if it is con-

---

5 It may be noted that, so far, only the tribunal in *Wintershall v Argentina*, paras 108–197, has declined to rule that waiting periods can be shortened based on an MFN clause. Unlike earlier tribunals it qualified the requirement to pursue local remedies for 18 months before turning to international arbitration as a jurisdictional condition to the host State's consent to arbitration, rather than as an admissibility-related question, and declined to shorten waiting periods based on an MFN clause.

6 *Cf.* in this respect *Gas Natural SDG, SA v The Argentine Republic*, ICSID Case No. ARB/03/10, Decision on Jurisdiction of 17 June 2005, para 29; *Suez InterAguas v Argentina*, Decision on Jurisdiction, May 16, 2006, para 57; *AWG Group Ltd v The Argentine Republic*, UNCITRAL, Decision on Jurisdiction of 3 Aug 2006, para 59; *Suez, Sociedad General de Aguas de Barcelona, SA and Vivendi Universal, SA v The Argentine Republic*, ICSID Case No. ARB/03/19, Decision on Jurisdiction of 3 Aug 2006, para 59 (all pointing out that differentiating between substance and procedure has no merit).

cluded that the reference in Article 5(2) to '[t]he treatment referred to in paragraph 1 above' is only to 'fair and equitable treatment' rather than 'treatment' more broadly, how can this be reconciled with the fact that (1) Article 5(3) excludes from '[s]uch treatment . . . privileges' accorded to third-state investors pursuant to a 'free trade area', a 'customs union', a 'common market', or certain 'mutual economic assistance' arrangements, while providing also that '[t]he treatment under this article shall not include tax exemptions or other comparable privileges' granted to third-state investors 'by virtue of a double taxation [or similar] agreement', all of which privileges and exemptions extend well beyond any concept of 'fair and equitable treatment' and have nothing whatsoever to do with it; and (2) Article 5(4) provides that, '[i]n addition to the provisions of paragraph 2 above' [note the reference is not to paragraph 1], each of the treaty parties will grant national treatment, a concept likewise entirely separate and apart from the notion of 'fair and equitable treatment', and which grants treatment extending well beyond it. In the end, the award resolves these 'lexical difficulties' by declaring (in its para 117): 'Something has to give. The choice is between an explicit stipulation and a revelation by grammatical deconstruction. The Tribunal naturally prefers the former.' It then proceeds to speculate on why the treaty's drafters acted as they did, suggesting their actions may have been 'reflexive', and that had they engaged in a 'searching exegetical endeavour' they might have realised that some of Article 5's language was 'unnecessary in this particular instance'.

13. I believe that Articles 31 and 32 of the Vienna Convention on the Law of Treaties preclude the existence of such a 'choice' as that which the majority has posited. It is rather like Alexander the Great severing the Gordian Knot, instead of untying it, as the ancient King of Phrygia had prescribed, and as I understand the Vienna Convention requires. The result of interpretation may be 'unambiguous', but it nonetheless must result from a process that includes the very 'grammatical deconstruction' rejected by the majority. Under Article 31 of the Vienna Convention one looks not just to the 'ordinary meaning' of a word or words; words must be viewed 'in light of [the treaty's] object and purpose', and in their 'context', which under Article 31(2) of the Convention includes the entire text of the treaty. If the meaning of a term remains unclear following application of Article 31 of the Convention, or is ambiguous, or is 'manifestly absurd or unreasonable', a tribunal then must look to supplementary means of interpretation as prescribed in Article 32. The majority here has not followed the prescribed route.

14. Furthermore, in placing such heavy emphasis on the 'lexical' implications of the reference in Article 5(2), the award bases its analysis and reasoning

exclusively on the English translation of a treaty which, according to its terms, was executed only in the Spanish and Russian languages, each being equally authentic. Conclusions derived from a non-authentic version of an international treaty, however, must be treated with utmost caution. This is all the more so considering that Article 33 of the Vienna Convention provides both a special rule of interpretation where two authentic texts may vary and a rule for when a non-authentic translation can be considered as an authentic text. The Tribunal, however, has discussed neither the Spanish nor the Russian version of the treaty provision in question, nor has it indicated that the English translation could be considered as authentic pursuant to Article 33(2) of the Vienna Convention.[7]

15. As a matter of textual analysis, I would have found that the reference in Article 5(2) to that article's paragraph (1) should, in context, be read as referring to 'treatment', not to 'fair and equitable treatment'. In support of this conclusion, I note that the Spanish heading of Article 5, which is part of the 'context', is *Tratamiento*, or simply 'Treatment'. Moreover, the Spanish text of Article 5(1) and (2) is more consistent than the non-authentic English version with the interpretation I favour. They state:

1. Cada Parte garantizará en su territorio un tratamiento justo y equitativo a las inversiones realizadas por inversores de la otra Parte.
2. El tratamiento mencionada en el punto anterior no será menos favorable que el otorgado por cada Parte a las inversiones realizadas en su territorio por inversores de un tercer Estado.

The combination of the heading and the text support the conclusion that the term 'treatment' in Article 5(2) refers to all treatment (*'tratamiento'*) under the treaty, not just 'fair and equitable treatment', considering that Article 5 itself deals with MFN treatment and national treatment in addition to fair and equitable treatment.

16. The Russian version of the Spanish treaty lends further support to the broad understanding of Article 5(2) as a general most-favoured-nation clause. Thus, the heading of Article 5 reads as *'Rezhim kapitalovlozhenii'* which, translated literally, means 'Investment regime', in the sense of overall conditions relating to investment. This suggests that every subparagraph in Article 5 concerns a quality or characteristic of the investment regime the contracting parties must accord to investors covered under the Spanish

---

7 In fairness it must be noted, however, that neither party has put forward arguments relating to the Russian version of the treaty and references to the Spanish text were limited.

treaty, i.e., a regime that is fair and equitable and no less favourable than that granted to domestic or third-country investors. This is consonant with the Russian version of Article 5(2), which provides that;

> [t]he regime mentioned in point 1 of this article shall be no less favourable than the regime granted by each party in relation to investments carried out on that party's territory by investors of any third state.

This makes rather clear that the investor is not limited to such 'fair and equitable' regime as Russia may grant to third-country investors, but can avail itself of any other regime under which third-country investors operate.

17. Apart from the parsing of the article's text, i.e., the 'lexical difficulties', I find comfort in this regard in other sources, ones on which the award has relied in part in concluding that is has jurisdiction of claimants' claims under Article 10. For example, the legislative history concerning the ratification of the Spanish treaty suggests that Spain understood the provision in Article 5(2) on most-favoured-nation treatment in a broad sense as encompassing all treatment accorded to foreign investors. Thus, the Spanish Council of State observed in an opinion concerning the question of whether the approval of the Cortes Generales was necessary prior to the ratification of the treaty that:

> [i]f, in addition, we take into account the most favoured nation clause contained in article 5.2, guaranteeing to USSR investors in all events the same benefits as that granted by Spain to any investment of a third-party nation, it is clear . . . that this text requires preliminary authorization from the Cortes Generales for the declaration of consent of the state to be bound thereunder[8]

18. As regards the understanding of the USSR, a comparable legislative history is missing. However, in the paper on BITs published in 1991 by a member of the USSR's negotiating team (Mr R Nagapetyants), to which the Tribunal has referred in paragraph 50, the author stated in regard to most-favoured-nation clauses in Soviet BITs:

> By according most-favoured treatment, the host country established the terms of business for the partner country's investors equal to those under which the investors of any third country operate. This means that if any agreement concerning the protection of investment that was signed at a later date provides more benefits and advantages, then they automatically are extended to all investors

---

8 Council of State Opinion No. 55-810/RS, 14 March 1991, Exhibit C-55 – emphasis added.

from countries with which investment agreements were previously signed on most-favoured terms.[9]

19. Even were the award correct in its conclusion that Article 5(2) refers exclusively to 'fair and equitable treatment', the question remains whether the respondent's broader consent to international arbitration given under Article 8 of the Danish treaty must be extended to the claimants as part of the 'more favourable' fair and equitable treatment available under that treaty. Succinctly, the issue here is whether the Danish treaty's provision of broader arbitration possibilities represents an aspect of 'fair and equitable treatment' that is more favourable than the Spanish treaty's restriction of such dispute settlement mechanisms to issues of 'compensation due' for an expropriation under its Article 10.

20. Here the majority, once again in my view, goes astray when it rejects such a possibility. Notably, the majority does not reject the notion that dispute settlement mechanisms can be included in the broader concept of 'treatment' of foreign investors and investments. Instead, it expresses concern that 'it would be invidious for international tribunals to be finding (in the absence of specific evidence) that host State adjudication of treaty rights was necessarily inferior to international arbitration' (para 100, quoting McLachlan, Shore and Weiniger, *International Investment Arbitration*, at p 257; similarly para 106). That, I submit, is not the issue. It is not a question of whether the broader access to international arbitration accorded under the Danish treaty is more favourable than domestic adjudication in Russia. Instead, the question is solely whether the scope of international arbitration available under Article 8 of the Danish treaty is 'more favourable' than that under Article 10 of the Spanish treaty. I dare say that it is undeniable that 'more' arbitration, i.e., that additional causes of action may be pleaded and decided by an international arbitral tribunal, is 'more favourable' than a more limited scope of arbitration. To state the question is to answer it.

21. In any case, strictly speaking, it is not relevant, in my view, to attempt evaluation of whether one dispute settlement mechanism objectively is 'more favourable' than another. What is relevant is that Danish and Spanish

---

9 R Nagapetyants, *Agreements Concerning the Promotion and Mutual Protection of Investment*, Foreign Trade 1991, No. 5, at 11, Exhibit C-49. It may be noted, however, that such statements made by government officials in a non-official quality are not attributable to the State. In consequence, they do not constitute context in the sense of Article 31 of the Vienna Convention on the Law of Treaties and may not be relied on as *travaux preparatoires* under Article 32 of the Convention. However, they may be useful as an indicator of the ordinary sense of the wording used in an international instrument and reflect the general understanding of certain provisions of those involved at the time an international treaty was negotiated and concluded.

investors in Russia are afforded 'different' dispute settlement options. The purpose and rationale of MFN clauses is, as the International Court of Justice has so clearly stated in *Rights of Nationals of the United States of America in Morocco* to 'establish and to maintain at all times fundamental equality without discrimination among all of the countries concerned'.[10] From this perspective, the mere existence of differences in the available dispute settlement mechanisms is sufficient to trigger an MFN clause and thereby to extend the treatment afforded by the Danish treaty to those benefitting from the MFN clause in the Spanish treaty.

22. The focus, then, again assuming that the majority is correct in understanding Article 5(2) as incorporating only more favourable fair and equitable treatment, must be on whether international arbitration is an aspect of fair and equitable treatment. My view is that it is. Yet, the question here is not whether the standard of fair and equitable treatment requires access to international arbitration, or, as the award puts it in paragraph 105, whether 'access to international arbitration [is] a necessary part of FET'. That is an entirely separate subject and irrelevant to determining the scope of more favourable fair and equitable treatment actually accorded to a third party. Rather the issue is whether the Danish treaty's grant of across-the-board treaty dispute arbitration is a form of fair and equitable treatment granted to those third-party investors.

23. That consent to arbitrate investment treaty disputes is a form of fair and equitable treatment that a State may grant to investors also becomes evident if we consider that the prohibition against denial of justice not only forms part of customary international law, but also is an integral part of the fair and equitable treatment standard itself.[11] Thus, a State that does not provide foreign investor dispute settlement procedures at all necessarily will deny that investor any fair and equitable treatment when a dispute arises. The means by which the State in questions offers dispute settlement, in order to avoid a denial of justice, is largely in its discretion. It can do so by setting up a domestic court system, but it may equally provide dispute settlement by consenting to arbitration.

---

10 *Rights of Nationals of the United States of America in Morocco (France v United States of America)*, Judgment of 27 Aug 1952, I.C.J. Reports 1952, p 192.

11 See Stephan W Schill, *Fair and Equitable Treatment under Investment Treaties as an Embodiment of the Rule of Law*, IILJ Working Paper 2006/6 (Global Administrative Law Series), pp 18–19, 26–7, available at http://iilj.org/publications/documents/2006-6-GAL-Schill-web.pdf (visited 16 March 2009); see generally on the development of the modern definition of denial of justice, including the jurisprudence in investor-state arbitration relating to fair and equitable treatment, Jan Paulsson, *Denial of Justice in International Law*, pp 57 *et seq.* (CUP 2007).

24. For these reason, I conclude that Article 5(2) of the Spanish treaty, on any interpretation, grants claimants the benefits of the respondent's broader consent to SCC arbitration provided in Article 8 of the Danish treaty, both as a jurisdictional alternative to Article 10 of the Spanish treaty in respect of claimants' claim of uncompensated expropriation pursuant to Article 6 and as a basis for the Tribunal hearing their claims under Articles 4 and 5(1).

Article 1(1) (B) of the Spanish Treaty (exclusion of Emergentes, Eurofundo and Renta 4 S.V.S.A.)

25. Finally, in my view the majority is equally mistaken in declining jurisdiction over the claimants Emergentes, Eurofondo and Renta 4 SVSA on the basis that they are not protected investors under Article 1(1) of the Spanish treaty because they are not, in the case of Emergentes and Eurofondo, corporate bodies with independent legal personality under Spanish law, or, in the case of Renta 4 SVSA, because it does not own the ADRs in question. In my view, however, all three entities either should have been admitted as qualified claimants or should have been given an opportunity to undertake whatever formalities may be required for their claims to be presented to this Tribunal.

26. As regards Emergentes and Eurofondo, the award correctly notes (in its para 127) that:

> No rational basis has been proposed to explain why either of the State-parties to the Spanish BIT should have desired to promote and protect the investments of physical persons and corporate bodies but not those of entities that are able to mobilise capital but lack legal personality.

Well said! The ensuing sentence – 'Yet the words of the Treaty are what they are' – however, hardly answers the question.

27. The majority cites the letter of 25 April 2008 of claimants' Spanish counsel stating that 'it is clear that [both claimants] are not a corporate body ("persona jurídica")', while at the same time making it;

> also clear that they are capable of acquiring rights and obligations of a contractual nature . . . were authorised to operate by the Spanish stock market regulator . . . and are registered entities, as required . . . [and that when involved in legal proceedings] the Funds' claims are asserted on their behalf by their management companies, following the same pattern established by [the Spanish] civil system to have

represented by a court the interest of minors or of other entities that can own rights and obligation, but cannot act directly at Court.

The record shows that these two funds fall into the Spanish legal category of an 'entity' which may invest abroad and is the owner of its investments, but whose assets will be held by a depositary and which must be represented in judicial proceedings by a management company. This tripartite foreign investment system under Spanish law was in place at the time the Spanish treaty was concluded (T:277). The majority proceeds on the basis that since these two funds are not themselves '*personas jurídicas*', i.e., they are not 'juridical persons' having themselves the power to sue though existing as legal entities, that is the end of the story. It beggars imagination, however, to conclude that the investment fund cannot appear before us because it is not itself, technically speaking, a '*persona jurídica*'; and that the '*persona jurídica*' who is entitled under Spanish law to represent it in judicial proceedings is not able to represent it here because it has not itself made the investment.

28. The award arrives at its result based on a mistaken approach to interpretation of the term 'corporate body', or, as the authentic Spanish version of the treaty states '*persona jurídica*'. Instead of interpreting this term from the perspective of international law, the award equates it with the same term under domestic Spanish law. Thus, in the majority's view the fact that Emergentes and Eurofondo, as investment funds, are not 'corporate bodies'/'*personas jurídicas*' in the sense of the Spanish Civil Code, disqualifies them as 'corporate bodies'/ '*personas jurídicas*' under Article 1(1)(b) of the Spanish treaty. This interpretative approach violates the principle of the primacy of international law over domestic law and the principle that international treaties must be interpreted autonomously, i.e., not in accordance with the domestic legal orders of the contracting State parties involved.

29. Thus, from the point of view of an autonomous interpretation of the term 'corporate body'/ '*persona jurídica*' we need not concern ourselves with the lack of legal personality of investment funds under Spanish legislation. Instead, the term 'corporate body'/ '*persona jurídica*' under the treaty encompasses any legal entity (other than a physical person) provided that it has been established, in the case at hand, in accordance with Spanish legislation, is domiciled in Spain, and is not precluded by Spanish legislation from investing in the Yukos ADRs in question. An investment fund that has been created in accordance with Spanish legislation and is designed to engage in investment activities, both domestic and foreign, qualifies as a 'corporate body' in the sense of Article 1(1)(b) of the BIT

independent of its legal personality (or lack thereof) under domestic law. All these criteria are fulfilled as regards the claimants Emergentes and Eurofondo.

30. The majority further comforts itself, in part, with the conclusion (in its para 130) that this interpretation of Article 1(1)(b) 'would parallel the possible disqualification of minors or other incompetent persons under Article 1(a)', which deals with natural persons. Here, as when confronting the 'lexical difficulties' of Article 5, the majority follows this with the declaration that '[w]hy this was desirable leads to further speculation. The exercise is futile; it is what was agreed'. That minors are excluded as covered investors, however, is nowhere to be found in Article 1(1)(a). Instead, this provision merely requires that an individual have the nationality of either party and be entitled to invest in the territory of the other party. This entitlement in the Spanish version is designated by the use of the words *facultada, de acuerdo con la legislación vigente en esa misma Parte, para realizar inversiones en el territorio de la otra Parte*. The term 'facultada' does not concern, however, as the majority mistakenly assumes, the legal capacity of an individual, but rather that individual's entitlement to invest abroad, an entitlement that could be limited by domestic legislation restricting investments in third countries.[12] This mistaken conclusion regarding the potential disqualification of minors as investors seems to have affected the majority's view that corporate bodies must have legal personality under domestic law. Yet, such requirement equally is nowhere to be found in Article 1(1)(b) of the treaty which merely states:

> Cualquier persona jurídica constituida con arreglo a la legislación de una Parte, domiciliada en su territorio y facultada, de acuerdo con la legislación vigente en esa misma Parte, para realizar inversiones en el territorio de la otra Parte.

31. With respect to claimant Renta 4 SVSA, which is the depositary for the Yukos ADRs of Renta 4 Europa Este FIM, an entity apparently of the same type as Eurofundo and Emergentes, the majority comes to an equally unacceptable conclusion: just as the funds themselves cannot come before the Tribunal because they do not have the right under Spanish law to represent themselves, so the custodian of Renta 4 SVSA's Yukos ADRs has no

---

12 This conclusion is also supported by the Russian text of the treaty. The word in the Russian text corresponding to 'facultada' ('allowed' in the English text before us) is, transliterated, '*pravopolnomochnoye*'. While Russian-English dictionaries translate this as 'competence', Russian-Russian dictionaries define the term as 'having a legal right' to do something. This richer definition of the word corresponding to '*facultada*' ('allowed') is consonant with the two roots comprising the word: '*pravo*' (meaning 'law') and '*polnomochiye*' (meaning 'authority' or 'power').

standing because it is not itself the investor. This decision by the majority results literally in a 'Catch 22' situation and makes no more sense of the situation than did the dismissal of Eurofondo and Emergentes. While Renta 4 SVSA may not be the entity owning the Yukos ADRs in question, it is clear that it is bringing this action for the real party in interest, which is Renta 4 Europa Este FIM. Since the ADRs are, as the Award correctly finds, protected investments, one should either have accepted Renta 4 SVSA's standing as acting for the funds owning the ADRs, or have allowed whatever amendment might be necessary to remedy any lack of standing on behalf of the real party in interest, i.e., Renta 4 Europe Este FIM.

32. I would at least have granted the three claimants in question a period of time within which to cure the situation by prevailing on their respective management companies to enter the fray, based on my conclusion that a proper interpretation of Article 1(1)(b) should allow the management companies to act here in the interests of the funds.

EXERCISE 19 – TREATY INTERPRETATION II – MINI MOCK ARBITRATION

The Dutch company Amdam BV has made a significant investment in the Republic of Senegal. After some years, certain events occur which in the view of the Dutch company amount to expropriation of its investment. It therefore commences an arbitration against the Republic of Senegal based on the 1979 BIT between the Netherlands and Senegal.

The Republic raises a jurisdictional objection to the effect that whatever consent to arbitration it may have given applies only to natural persons, not legal entities.

 GROUP

Group 1
You represent Senegal. Based on the rules of interpretation in the Vienna Convention and on the BIT, you are to present the best arguments in support of Senegal's position.

Group 2
You represent the Dutch company. Present the best arguments in favour of its position, i.e., that Senegal's consent also covers legal entities. Your arguments are to be based on the Vienna Convention and the BIT.

Group 3
You are the observer group.

Group 4
You are the Arbitral Tribunal. You must rule on this issue.

 TREATY

Netherlands and Senegal

Agreement concerning the encouragement and protection of investments. Signed at Dakar on 3 August 1979 Authentic text: French. Registered by the Netherlands on 30 January 1982.

Agreement between the Kingdom of the Netherlands and the Republic of Senegal concerning the encouragement and protection of in vestments

The Government of the Kingdom of the Netherlands and the Government of the Republic of Senegal, desiring to intensify economic co-operation between the two States; considering the agreement on economic and technical co-operation between the Kingdom of the Netherlands and the Republic of Senegal concluded at Dakar on 12 June 1965; desirous of creating conditions favourable to capital investment by nationals and companies of one of the two States in the territory of the other State; and recognising that the encouragement of such investment may stimulate economic initiative and increase the prosperity of the two nations, Have agreed as follows:

Article 1

1. The term 'capital investments' shall comprise every kind of asset, including all kinds of rights and interests.

2. The term 'proceeds' shall mean the amounts realised from profit or interest on capital investment.

3. The term 'nationals' shall comprise with regard to either Contracting Party natural persons having the nationality of that Contracting Party in accordance with its law.

4. The term 'companies' shall refer with regard to either Contracting Party:
(a) Without prejudice to the provisions of subparagraph (b) below, to legal persons constituted in accordance with the law of that Contracting Party;
(b) To legal persons controlled, directly or indirectly, by nationals of that Contracting Party but constituted in accordance with the law of the other Contracting Party.

Article 2

Each Contracting Party, in accordance with its legislation, shall encourage and allow in its territory capital investments of nationals and companies of the other Contracting Party.

Article 3

Neither Contracting Party shall subject nationals and companies of the other Contracting Party, in respect of their capital investments in the territory of the above-mentioned party, the professional and economic activity in which they engage in connection with those investments or the administration, management, maintenance, enjoyment and use of those investments, to conditions less favourable than those to which its own nationals and companies, or those of third States, are subjected.

Article 4

1. Capital investments made by nationals and companies of one Contracting Party shall enjoy full protection and security in the territory of the other Contracting Party.

2. Nationals and companies of one Contracting Party may not be directly or indirectly dispossessed of their capital investments in the territory of the other Contracting Party except for reasons of public interest, by non-discriminatory legal proceedings and against fair compensation. The compensation shall correspond to the real value of the investment in question and shall be established and paid without undue delay; it shall be effectively available and freely transferable in the currency of the country of the national or company concerned or in any other convertible currency. The legality of the above measures and the amount of compensation shall be verifiable by ordinary judicial proceedings without prejudice to the provisions of Articles 10 and 11 of this Agreement.

3. If nationals and companies of one Contracting Party incur, as a result of war or other armed conflict, revolution or uprising in the territory of the other Contracting Party, losses of capital investments located there, they shall receive from the latter Contracting Party, as regards restitution, indemnity, compensation or other damages, a treatment no less favourable than that accorded to nationals and companies of that Party. In respect of the transfer of such payments, the Contracting Parties shall mutually guarantee to grant to the rights of nationals and companies of the other Contracting Party a treatment no less favourable than that accorded to similar rights of nationals and companies of a third State.

Article 5

The provisions of Articles 3 and 4 of this Agreement shall also apply to the proceeds from capital investments.

Article 6

In respect for the principle of freedom of transfer and in accordance with its legislation, each Contracting Party shall authorise nationals and companies of the other Contracting Party to transfer to the country of the other Contracting Party, without restrictions or undue delays, invested capital, dividends and proceeds of any kind from invested capital, as well as the proceeds from the liquidation or sale of their assets. The transfer shall be effected in the currency provided at the time when the investment was constituted; if the investment was in kind, the transfer shall be made in a convertible currency established by mutual agreement.

Article 7

The Contracting Party in whose territory an investment approved by it has been made, for which a financial guarantee against non-commercial risks has been granted by the other Contracting Party or by one of its nationals, shall recognise the subrogation of the guarantor in the rights of the investor, which are transferred by virtue of the guarantor's obligation to make a payment to the investor in respect of damages.

Article 8

If the legislation of one of the Contracting Parties or international obligations currently existing or to be established in the future between the Contracting Parties, in conjunction with this Agreement, establish a regulation to the effect that capital investments made by nationals or companies of the other Contracting Party shall receive a treatment more favourable than the one provided for in this Agreement, the Agreement shall not affect the regulation in question. Each Contracting Party shall abide by any other commitments assumed by it concerning capital investments made in its territory by nationals or companies of the other Contracting Party.

Article 9

Without prejudice to any special tax privilege granted by one of the Contracting Parties under an international agreement on the avoidance of double taxation, by virtue of its participation in a customs union, an economic union or similar institutions, or on the basis of reciprocity, that Contracting Party shall, in respect of the levying of taxes, duties and charges as well as the granting of tax deductions and exemptions, accord to nationals of the other Contracting Party engaged in economic activities in its territory a treatment no less favourable than that accorded to its own nationals or to nationals of third States, if the latter treatment is more favourable.

Article 10

The Contracting Party in the territory of which a national of the other Contracting Party makes or intends to make an investment shall assent to any request on the part of such national to submit, for arbitration or conciliation, any dispute that may arise in connection with that investment, to the centre established by the Washington Convention of 18 March 1965 on the settlement of investment disputes between States and nationals of other States.

Article 11

1. Disputes concerning the interpretation or application of this Agreement shall, if possible, be settled by the Governments of the two Contracting Parties.

2. If a dispute cannot be settled in this manner, it shall be submitted to an Arbitral Tribunal at the request of one of the two Contracting Parties.

3. The Arbitral Tribunal shall be established ad hoc; each Contracting Party shall appoint one member and the two members shall agree to select as chairman the national of a third State, who shall be appointed by the Governments of the two Contracting Parties. The members shall be appointed within a period of two months, and the Chairman within a period of three months, after one of the Contracting Parties has notified the other that it wishes to submit the dispute to an Arbitral Tribunal.

4. If the time-limits provided for in paragraph 3 of this article are not observed, and in the absence of any other arrangement, each Contracting Party may request the President of the International Court of Justice to make the necessary appointments. If the President is a national of one of the two Contracting Parties or is disqualified for another reason, the Vice-President shall make the appointments. If the Vice-President is also a national of one of the two Contracting Parties or is also disqualified, the next-ranking member of the Court who is not a national of one of the Contracting Parties shall make the appointments.

5. The Arbitral Tribunal shall take its decisions by majority vote. Its decisions shall be binding. Each Contracting Party shall pay the costs arising from the activity of its own arbitrator as well as the cost of its representation in the proceedings before the Arbitral Tribunal; the costs of the Chairman and the other costs shall be borne equally by the two Contracting Parties. The Arbitral Tribunal may establish another arrangement concerning expenses. For the rest, the Arbitral Tribunal shall determine its own procedure.

6. The Tribunal shall decide on the basis of respect for the law.

7. If the parties consent, the Tribunal shall settle the case *ex aequo et bono*.

Article 12

1. Each of the Contracting Parties shall notify the other of the completion of the constitutional procedures required for the application of this Agreement, which shall enter into force on the date of the last notification. This Agreement shall remain in force for ten years and shall be extended for an unlimited period unless denounced in writing by one of the two Contracting Parties one year before it expires. On the expiry of a period of ten years, this Agreement may be denounced at any time, but it shall remain in force for one year after its denunciation.

2. In the case of the Kingdom of the Netherlands, this Agreement shall apply to the territory of the Kingdom in Europe and to the Netherlands Antilles.

3. In view of the time-limits mentioned in paragraph 1 of this article, the Government of the Kingdom of the Netherlands may separately terminate the application of this Agreement in respect of the Netherlands Antilles.

4. In respect of capital investments made before the date of expiry of this Agreement, Articles 1 to 11 shall continue to be applicable for an additional period of ten years after the expiry of this Agreement.

Article 13

On the date of entry into force of this Agreement, the provisions of this Agreement shall supersede Articles 3, 4, 5, 5 *bis*, 5 *ter* and 10 concerning investments in the Agreement on economic and technical co-operation between the Government of the Kingdom of the Netherlands and the Government of the Republic of Senegal concluded at Dakar on 12 June 1965.

In witness whereof the undersigned representatives, duly authorised thereto, have signed the present Agreement. Done at Dakar on 3 August 1979 in duplicate in the French language.

10
Investors

 DISCUSSION QUESTIONS

Problem 1

Review the *Tokios Tokelės v Ukraine* Decision on Jurisdiction. Discuss who is right: the majority or the dissenting arbitrator?

Problem 2

In the *Plama v Bulgaria* Decision on Jurisdiction, the Tribunal addressed the issue of denial of benefits. Explain the reasoning of the Tribunal. Does it make sense? In which situations would Article 17(1) be applicable? Would the application of this article have changed the outcome of *Tokios Tokelės*?

Problem 3

What is meant by treaty shopping by way of nationality planning? Is it/should it be allowed in investment treaty arbitrations? Discuss pros and cons.

Problem 4

Mr X, a Turkish citizen, owns shares in two Turkish power plants. In 2013 the power plants are expropriated by the Turkish Government. At the time when the expropriation takes place Mr X has lived for five years in France, having been granted political asylum there. Mr X came to France after having spent 18 months under house arrest in Istanbul because of his political activities. He was arrested in Istanbul on a visit to relatives, but had then been living in London for several years. Mr X initiates an arbitration the ECT against Turkey. The first objection made by Turkey is that Mr X is not an 'investor' under the ECT. Analyse and discuss.

 CASE

Tokios Tokelės (claimant) v Ukraine (respondent) Case No. ARB/02/18 International Centre for Settlement of Investment Disputes, Washington, DC

Decision on jurisdiction

I. The dispute

1. The claimant, Tokios Tokelės, is a business enterprise established under the laws of Lithuania. It was founded as a cooperative in 1989, and, since

1991, has been registered as a 'closed joint-stock company'. The claimant is engaged primarily in the business of advertising, publishing and printing in Lithuania and outside its borders.

2. In 1994, Tokios Tokelės created Taki spravy, a wholly owned subsidiary established under the laws of Ukraine. Taki spravy is in the business of advertising, publishing, and printing, and related activities in Ukraine and outside its borders. The claimant made an initial investment of US$170,000 in Taki spravy in 1994, consisting of office furniture, printing equipment, and the construction of and repairs to office facilities. Since that time, the claimant has reinvested the profits of Taki spravy in the subsidiary, purchasing additional printing equipment, computer equipment, bank shares, and automobiles. The claimant asserts that it has invested a total of more than US$6.5 million in its Ukrainian subsidiary in the period 1994–2002.

3. The claimant, Tokios Tokelės, alleges that governmental authorities in Ukraine engaged in a series of actions with respect to Taki spravy that breach the obligations of the bilateral investment treaty between Ukraine and Lithuania ('Ukraine-Lithuania BIT' or 'Treaty').[1] The claimant contends that, beginning in February 2002, the respondent engaged in a series of unreasonable and unjustified actions against Taki spravy that adversely affected the claimant's investment. The claimant alleges that governmental authorities of the respondent: (1) conducted numerous and invasive investigations under the guise of enforcing national tax laws; (2) pursued unsubstantiated actions in domestic courts, including actions to invalidate contracts entered into by Taki spravy; (3) placed the assets of Taki spravy under administrative arrest; (4) unreasonably seized financial and other documents; and (5) falsely accused Taki spravy of engaging in illegal activities. The claimant argues that the governmental authorities took these actions in response to the claimant's publication in January 2002 of a book that favourably portrays a leading Ukrainian opposition politician, Yulia Tymoshenko.

4. The claimant contends that it objected to this treatment by the governmental authorities of the respondent and made multiple unsuccessful efforts to settle the dispute. These efforts included meeting with local tax officials, sending written complaints to tax and law enforcement officials, and sending

---

1 Agreement between the Government of Ukraine and the Government of the Republic of Lithuania for the Promotion and Reciprocal Protection of Investments, Feb. 8, 1994 (entered into force on Feb. 27, 1995) ('Ukraine-Lithuania BIT'). The Treaty was done in the 'Ukrainian, Lithuanian and English languages, both texts being equally authentic. In case of devergency (sic) of interpretation the English text shall prevail.' Ibid. at 11.

a letter of appeal to the President of Ukraine. In each case, the claimant contends, these efforts were unsuccessful and the governmental action complained of by the claimant continued.

II. Procedural history

5. The claimant initiated this proceeding on August 14, 2002, when it filed a request for arbitration (RFA) with the International Centre for Settlement of Investment Disputes (ICSID) along with its wholly owned subsidiary, Taki spravy. The RFA included letters of consent to arbitration from Tokios Tokelės and Taki spravy dated August 7 and August 9, respectively. In the RFA, the claimant alleged that various actions by Ukrainian governmental authorities during 2002 constituted violations of the Ukraine-Lithuania BIT.

6. The requesting parties filed a supplement to their request on September 4, 2002, seeking, among other damages, just and adequate compensation for the losses sustained by Tokios Tokelės and Taki spravy for the requisitioning and destruction of their property by Ukraine's forces or authorities.

7. On October 15, 2002, ICSID notified the requesting parties that the dispute had not been subject to negotiation for a period of six months as required by Article 8 of the Ukraine-Lithuania BIT. On October 17, 2002, the requesting parties withdrew their RFA until such time as it 'may be renewed and resubmitted for consideration to the Centre'. The RFA was reinstated by Tokios Tokelės and Taki spravy on November 22, 2002.

8. On December 6, 2002, ICSID notified the requesting parties that Ukraine and Lithuania had not agreed that Taki spravy, an entity organised under the laws of Ukraine, should be treated as national of Lithuania under Article 25(2)(b) of the Convention on the Settlement of Investment Disputes between States and Nationals of Other States (ICSID Convention or Convention[2]) and Article 1(2)(c) of the Ukraine-Lithuania BIT. In response, Tokios Tokelės removed Taki spravy as a requesting party on December 9, 2002, which ICSID acknowledged in a letter on the same date.

9. On December 9, 2002, Ukraine requested of ICSID the opportunity to present preliminary observations on jurisdiction prior to the registration of the RFA. In Ukraine's view, the content of the RFA might have prompted

---

2 Ukraine and Lithuania became parties to the ICSID Convention on July 7, 2000, and Aug. 5, 1992, respectively. See ICSID, 'List of Contracting States and other Signatories of the Convention (as of November 3, 2003)' available at http://www.worldbank.org/icdis/constate/c-states-en.htm.

the Secretary-General not to register the same because, pursuant to Article 6(1)(b) of the Rules of Procedure for the Institution of Conciliation and Arbitration Proceedings, 'the dispute is manifestly outside the jurisdiction of the Centre'. After receiving the views of both Ukraine and the requesting party, the Secretary-General of ICSID registered the RFA on December 20, 2002.

10. To constitute the Tribunal, the claimant chose the option provided in Article 37(2)(b) of the Convention to constitute the Tribunal, which provides for each party to appoint one arbitrator and the two parties to agree on the third arbitrator to serve as President of the Tribunal. In March 2003, the claimant appointed Mr Daniel Price, a national of the United States, and Ukraine appointed Professor Piero Bernardini, a national of Italy. When the parties were unable to agree on the President of the Tribunal, the claimant requested that the Chairman of the Administrative Council appoint the presiding arbitrator, pursuant to Article 38 of the Convention and Rule 4(1) of the Arbitration Rules. After consultation with the parties, Professor Prosper Weil, a national of France, was appointed to serve as President of the Tribunal. The Tribunal was officially constituted on April 29, 2003 and Ms Martina Polasek was designated to serve as Secretary of the Tribunal.

11. The Tribunal held its first session on June 3, 2003, in Paris, France. At this session, the respondent raised objections to the jurisdiction of the Tribunal and requested that the proceeding be bifurcated so that jurisdiction could be addressed first and separately from the merits of the case. The claimant opposed this request, arguing that the merits of the case are inextricably linked to the jurisdiction of the Tribunal. In addition, the claimant submitted a request for provisional measures, namely, the suspension of parallel court proceedings in Ukraine and investigations being conducted by Ukrainian tax authorities, which the claimant argued could seriously impact its rights. The respondent opposed this request.

12. After receiving written submissions from the parties, on July 1, 2003, the Tribunal granted the claimant's request for provisional measures and the respondent's request to bifurcate the proceedings.

13. In accordance with the Tribunal's order, the respondent filed its memorial on jurisdiction on July 29, 2003, and the claimant filed its counter-memorial on August 25, 2003. The respondent's reply and the claimant's rejoinder were filed on September 9 and September 24, 2003, respectively. On December 10, 2003, the Tribunal held an oral hearing on jurisdiction in Paris, France.

III. Relevant legal provisions

14. In reaching its majority decision on jurisdiction,[3] this Tribunal is guided by Article 25 of the ICSID Convention as well as Articles 1 and 8 of the Ukraine-Lithuania BIT.

15. Article 25 of the ICSID Convention sets forth the objective criteria for ICSID's jurisdiction and provides in relevant part:

> (1) The jurisdiction of the Centre shall extend to any legal dispute arising directly out of an investment, between a Contracting State. . .and a national of another Contracting State, which the parties to the dispute consent in writing to submit to the Centre. When the parties have given their consent, no party may withdraw its consent unilaterally.
> (2) National of another Contracting State means:
> . . .
> (b) any juridical person which had the nationality of a Contracting State other than the State party to the dispute on the date on which the parties consented to submit such dispute to conciliation or arbitration and any juridical person which had the nationality of the Contracting State party to the dispute on that date and which, because of foreign control, the parties have agreed should be treated as a national of another Contracting State for the purposes of this Convention.

16. Article 8 of the Ukraine-Lithuania BIT sets forth the disputes that may be submitted to international arbitration:

> (1) Any dispute between an investor of one Contracting Party and the other Contracting Party in connection with an investment on the territory of that other Contracting Party shall be subject to negotiations between the parties in dispute.
> (2) If any dispute between an investor of one Contracting Party and the other Contracting Party cannot be thus settled within a period of six months, the investor shall be entitled to submit the case to:
>
> > (a) The International Centre for Settlement of Investment Disputes (ICSID). . ..

17. Article 1(1) of the BIT defines 'investment' as 'every kind of asset invested by an investor of one Contracting Party in the territory of the other Contracting Party in accordance with the laws and regulations of the latter. . .'. The definition includes a non-exhaustive list of the forms that an investment may take,

---

3 The dissenting opinion of Professor Weil is attached to this Decision.

such as '(a) movable and immovable property. . .(b) shares [and] stocks. . .(c) claims to money. . .'. Article 1(1) further provides that '[a]ny alteration of the form in which assets are invested shall not affect their character as investment provided that such an alteration is made in accordance with the laws of the Contracting Party in the territory of which the investment has been made. . .'.

18. Article 1(2) defines 'investor' as:

(a) in respect of Ukraine:

- natural person [sic] who are nationals of the Ukraine according to Ukrainian laws;
- any entity established in the territory of the Ukraine in conformity with its laws and regulations;

(b) in respect of Lithuania:

- natural person [sic] who are nationals of the Republic of Lithuania according to Lithuanian laws;
- any entity established in the territory of the Republic of Lithuania in conformity with its laws and regulations;

(c) in respect of either Contracting Party – any entity or organisation established under the law of any third State which is, directly or indirectly, controlled by nationals of that Contracting Party or by entities having their seat in the territory of that Contracting Party; it being understood that control requires a substantial part in the ownership.

19. The jurisdiction of the centre depends first and foremost on the consent of the Contracting Parties, who enjoy broad discretion to choose the disputes that they will submit to ICSID.[4] Tribunals shall exercise jurisdiction over all disputes that fall within the scope of the Contracting Parties' consent as long as the dispute satisfies the objective requirements set forth in Article 25 of the Convention.

20. Based on Article 25 of the Convention and the BIT, this Tribunal has jurisdiction over the present dispute if the following requirements

---

4 See Report of the Executive Directors of the International Bank for Reconstruction and Development on the Convention on the Settlement of Investment Disputes between States and Nationals of Other States, 1 ICSID Reports 28, at para. 23 (stating that '[c]onsent of the parties is the cornerstone of the jurisdiction of the Centre') ('Executive Directors' Report').

are met: (1) the claimant is an investor of one Contracting Party; (2) the claimant has an investment in the territory of the other Contracting Party; (3) the dispute arises directly from the investment; and (4) the parties to the dispute have consented to ICSID jurisdiction over it. We turn now to examine the respondent's arguments that these requirements have not been met.

IV. Analysis of respondent's objections to jurisdiction

First objection: claimant is not a genuine 'Investor' of Lithuania

1. *Arguments of the respondent*   21. The respondent does not dispute that the claimant is a legally established entity under the laws of Lithuania. The respondent argues, however, that the claimant is not a 'genuine entity' of Lithuania first because it is owned and controlled predominantly by Ukrainian nationals. There is no dispute that nationals of Ukraine own 99 per cent of the outstanding shares of Tokios Tokelės and comprise two-thirds of its management.[5] The respondent also argues, but the claimant strongly contests, that Tokios Tokelės has no substantial business activities in Lithuania and maintains its *siège social*, or administrative headquarters, in Ukraine. The respondent contends, therefore, that the claimant is, in terms of economic substance, a Ukrainian investor in Lithuania, not a Lithuanian investor in Ukraine.

22. The respondent argues that to find jurisdiction in this case would be tantamount to allowing Ukrainian nationals to pursue international arbitration against their own government, which the respondent argues would be inconsistent with the object and purpose of the ICSID Convention.[6] To avoid this result, the respondent asks the Tribunal to 'pierce the corporate veil', that is, to disregard the claimant's state of incorporation and determine its nationality according to the nationality of its predominant shareholders and managers, to what the respondent contends is the claimant's lack of substantial business activity in Lithuania, and to the alleged situs of its *siège social* in Ukraine.

---

5 Messrs Sergiy Danylov and Oleksandr Danylov, who are nationals of Ukraine, own 99 per cent of the shares in Tokios Tokelės, and Ms Ludmilla Zhyltsova, a national of Lithuania, owns the remaining 1 per cent. See Request for Arbitration, at Annex 6, 'Statute of the Closed Joint-Stock Company Tokios Tokelės' at para. 3.6. Messrs Danylov and Ms Zhyltsova serve as managers of Tokios Tokelės. See ibid. at Annex 7.

6 'The Convention is designed to facilitate the settlement of investment disputes between States and nationals of other States. It is not meant for disputes between States and their own nationals.' Christoph H Schreuer, *The ICSID Convention: A Commentary* 290 (2001).

23. In support of its request to 'pierce the corporate veil,' the respondent makes three arguments, which we encapsulate as follows:

- The context in which the ICSID Convention and the Ukraine-Lithuania BIT reference and define corporate nationality allows the Tribunal to disregard the Claimant's state of incorporation and determine its corporate nationality based on the nationality of its controlling shareholders, i.e., to pierce the corporate veil;
- The Tribunal should pierce the corporate veil of the claimant in this case because allowing an enterprise that is established in Lithuania but owned and controlled predominantly by Ukrainians to pursue ICSID arbitration against Ukraine is contrary to the object and purpose of the ICSID Convention and the Ukraine-Lithuania BIT, namely, to provide a forum for the settlement of international disputes; and
- The jurisprudence of ICSID arbitration supports the use of a 'control-test' rather than state of incorporation to define the nationality of juridical entities and it also supports piercing the corporate veil in certain circumstances that apply in the present case.

2. Nationality of juridical entities under Article 25 of the ICSID Convention
24. Article 25 of the Convention requires that, in order for the Centre to have jurisdiction, a dispute must be between 'a Contracting State. . . and *a national of another Contracting State. . .*'[7] Article 25(2)(b) defines 'national of another Contracting State', to include 'any juridical person which had the nationality of a Contracting State other than the State party to the dispute. . .'. The Convention does not define the method for determining the nationality of juridical entities, leaving this task to the reasonable discretion of the Contracting Parties.[8]

25. Thus, we begin our analysis of this jurisdictional requirement by underscoring the deference this Tribunal owes to the definition of corporate nationality contained in the agreement between the Contracting Parties, in this case, the Ukraine-Lithuania BIT. As Mr Broches explained, the purpose of Article 25(2)(b) is not to define corporate nationality but to:

> . . .indicate the outer limits within which disputes may be submitted to conciliation or arbitration under the auspices of the Centre with the consent of the parties thereto. Therefore *the parties should be given the widest possible latitude to agree on*

---

7 Emphasis added.
8 See Aron Broches, 'The Convention on the Settlement of Investment Disputes between States and Nationals of Other States,' 136 *Recueil des Cours* 331, 359–60 (1972-II).

the meaning of 'nationality' and any stipulation of nationality made in connection with a conciliation or arbitration clause which is based on a reasonable criterion.[9]

26. In the specific context of BITs, Professor Schreuer notes that the Contracting Parties enjoy broad discretion to define corporate nationality: '[d]efinitions of corporate nationality in national legislation or in treaties providing for ICSID's jurisdiction will be controlling for the determination of whether the nationality requirements of Article 25(2)(b) have been met.'[10] He adds, '[a]ny reasonable determination of the nationality of juridical persons contained in national legislation or in a treaty should be accepted by an ICSID commission or tribunal.'[11]

3. Definition of 'Investor' in Article 1(2) of the BIT   27. As have other tribunals, we interpret the ICSID Convention and the Treaty between the Contracting Parties according to the rules set forth in the Vienna Convention on the Law of Treaties, much of which reflects customary international law.[12] Article 31 of the Vienna Convention provides that '[a] treaty shall be interpreted in good faith in accordance with the ordinary meaning to be given to the terms of the treaty in their context and in light of its object and purpose.'[13]

28. Article 1(2)(b) of the Ukraine-Lithuania BIT defines the term 'investor,' with respect to Lithuania, as 'any *entity established* in the territory of the Republic of Lithuania in conformity with its laws and regulations.'[14] The ordinary meaning of 'entity' is '[a] thing that has a real existence.'[15] The meaning of 'establish' is to '[s]et up on a permanent or secure basis; bring into being, found (a. . .business)'.[16] Thus, according to the ordinary meaning of the terms of the Treaty, the claimant is an 'investor' of Lithuania if it is a thing of real legal existence that was founded on a secure basis in the territory of Lithuania in conformity with its laws and regulations. The Treaty contains no additional requirements for an entity to qualify as an 'investor' of Lithuania.

---

9 Ibid. at 361 (emphasis added); see also C F Amerasinghe, 'Interpretation of Article 25(2)(B) of the ICSID Convention,' in *International Arbitration in the 21st Century: Towards 'judicialization' and uniformity* 223, 232 (R Lillich and C Brower (eds) 1993).

10 Schreuer (n 6) at 286.

11 Ibid.

12 See, e.g., *Mondev Int'l Ltd v United States of America*, Award, Case No. ARB(AF)/99/2 (Oct. 11, 2002) 42 I.L.M. 85 (2003), at para. 43; *Emilio Agustín Maffezini v Kingdom of Spain*, Decision on Jurisdiction, Case No. ARB/97/7 (Jan. 25, 2000), at para. 27; *Waste Management, Inc v United Mexican States*, Award, Case No. ARB(AF)/98/2 (June 2, 2000), 40 I.L.M. 56 (2001), at n. 2.

13 Vienna Convention on the Law of Treaties, Art. 31(1) (May 22, 1969).

14 Emphasis added.

15 *The New Shorter Oxford English Dictionary* 830 (Thumb Index Edition 1993).

16 Ibid. at 852.

29. The claimant was founded as a co-operative in 1989 and was registered by the municipal government of Vilnius, Lithuania on August 9 of that year.[17] In 1991, the founders of Tokios Tokelès agreed to reorganise the co-operative into a closed joint-stock company, which the municipal government of Vilnius, Lithuania registered on May 2, 1991.[18] According to the Certificate of Enterprise, the address of Tokios Tokelès is Vilnius, vul. Seskines, 13-3. On August 11, 2000, the Ministry of the Economy of the Republic of Lithuania re-registered the claimant as an enterprise and re-registered the claimant's governing statute, both of which note the company's location as Sheshkines, 13-3 (or d. 13 kv. 3), Vilnius.[19] The claimant, therefore, is a thing of real legal existence that was founded on a secure basis in the territory of Lithuania. The registration of Tokios Tokelès by the Lithuanian Government indicates that it was founded in conformity with the laws and regulations of that country. According to the ordinary meaning of Article 1(2)(b), therefore, the claimant is an investor of Lithuania.

30. Article 1(2)(c) of the Ukraine-Lithuania BIT, which defines 'investor' with respect to entities not established in Ukraine or Lithuania, provides relevant context for the interpretation of Article 1(2)(a) and (b). Article 1(2)(c) extends the scope of the Treaty to entities incorporated in third countries using other criteria to determine nationality – namely, the nationality of the individuals who control the enterprise and the *siège social* of the entity controlling the enterprise. The respondent argues that the existence of these alternative methods of defining corporate nationality to *extend* the benefits of the BIT in Article 1(2)(c) should also allow these methods to be used to *deny* the benefits of the BIT under Article 1(2)(b). If the Contracting Parties had intended these alternative methods to apply to entities legally established in Ukraine or Lithuania, however, the parties would have included them in Article 1(2)(a) or (b) respectively as they did in Article 1(2)(c). However, the purpose of Article 1(2)(c) is only to extend the definition of 'investor' to entities established under the law of a third State provided certain conditions are met. Under the well-established presumption *expressio unius est exclusio alterius*, the state of incorporation, not the nationality of the controlling shareholders or *siège social*, thus defines 'investors' of Lithuania under Article 1(2)(b) of the BIT.

31. The object and purpose of the Treaty likewise confirm that the control-test should not be used to restrict the scope of 'investors' in Article 1(2)(b).

---

17 Claimant's June 20, 2003 Submission of Documents, Vol. V, Annex 10.
18 Ibid. at Annex 13.
19 Request for Arbitration, at Annexes 5–6.

The preamble expresses the Contracting Parties' intent to 'intensify economic co-operation to the mutual benefit of both States' and 'create and maintain favourable conditions for investment of investors of one State in the territory of the other State'. The Tribunal in *SGS v Philippines* interpreted nearly identical preambular language in the Philippines-Switzerland BIT as indicative of the treaty's broad scope of investment protection.[20] We concur in that interpretation and find that the object and purpose of the Ukraine-Lithuania BIT is to provide broad protection of investors and their investments.

32. The object and purpose of the Treaty are also reflected in the Treaty text. Article 1, which sets forth the scope of the BIT, defines 'investor' as 'any entity' established in Lithuania or Ukraine as well as '*any* entity' established in third countries that is controlled by nationals of or by entities having their seat in Lithuania or Ukraine. Thus, the respondent's request to restrict the scope of covered investors through a control-test would be inconsistent with the object and purpose of the Treaty, which is to provide broad protection of investors and their investments.

33. The respondent also argues that jurisdiction should be denied because, in its view, the claimant does not maintain 'substantial business activity' in Lithuania. The respondent correctly notes that a number of investment treaties allow a party to deny the benefits of the treaty to entities of the other party that are controlled by foreign nationals and that do not engage in substantial business activity in the territory of the other party.

34. For example, the Ukraine-United States BIT states

> [e]ach Party reserves the right to deny to any company the advantages of this treaty *if nationals of any third country* control such company and, in the case of a company of the other party, that company has no substantial business activities in the territory of the other party. . ..[21]

Similarly, the Energy Charter Treaty, to which both Ukraine and Lithuania are parties, allows each party to deny the benefits of the agreement to 'a

---

20 *SGS Société Générale de Surveillance SA v Republic of the Philippines*, Decision on Jurisdiction, Case No. ARB/02/6 (Jan. 29, 2004), at para. 116:

> The BIT is a treaty for the promotion and reciprocal protection of investments. According to the preamble it is intended 'to create and maintain favourable conditions for investments by investors of one Contracting Party in the territory of the other'. It is legitimate to resolve uncertainties in its interpretation so as to favour the protection of covered investments.

21 Treaty between the United States of America and Ukraine Concerning the Encouragement and Reciprocal Protection of Investment, Mar. 4, 1994, at art. 1(2) (entered into force Nov. 16, 1996) (emphasis added).

legal entity if citizens or nationals of a third state own or control such entity and if that entity has no substantial business activities in the Area of the Contracting Party in which it is organised'.[22]

35. In addition, a number of investment treaties of other States enable the parties to deny the benefits of the Treaty to entities of the other party that are controlled by nationals of the denying party and do not have substantial business activity in the other party. For example, the BIT between the United States and Argentina provides that:

> [e]ach party reserves the right to deny to any company of the other party the advantages of this Treaty if (a) nationals of any third country, *or nationals of such party*, control such company and the company has no substantial business activities in the territory of the other party. . ..[23]

36. These investment agreements confirm that State parties are capable of excluding from the scope of the agreement entities of the other party that are controlled by nationals of third countries or by nationals of the host country. The Ukraine-Lithuania BIT, by contrast, includes no such 'denial of benefits' provision with respect to entities controlled by third-country nationals or by nationals of the denying party. We regard the absence of such a provision as a deliberate choice of the Contracting Parties. In our view, it is not for tribunals to impose limits on the scope of BITs not found in the text, much less limits nowhere evident from the negotiating history. An international tribunal of defined jurisdiction should not reach out to exercise a jurisdiction beyond the borders of the definition. But equally an international tribunal should exercise, and indeed is bound to exercise, the measure of jurisdiction with which it is endowed.[24]

37. We note that the claimant has provided the Tribunal with significant information regarding its activities in Lithuania, including financial statements, employment information, and a catalogue of materials produced

---

22 The Energy Charter Treaty, Annex 1 to the Final Act of the European Energy Charter Conference, at art. 17(1), Dec. 16–17, 1994, Lisbon, Portugal, available at http://www.encharter.org/upload/1/TreatyBook-en.pdf (emphasis added).

23 Treaty between the United States of America and the Argentine Republic Concerning the Reciprocal Encouragement and Protection of Investment, Nov. 14, 1991, art. 1(2).

24 See, e.g., *Compañía de Aguas del Aconquija SA and Vivendi Universal (formerly Compagnie Générale des Eaux) v Argentine Republic*, Decision on Annulment, Case No. ARB/97/3 (July 3, 2002). 'In the Committee's view, the Tribunal, faced with such a claim and having validly held that it had jurisdiction, was obliged to consider and to decide it.' Ibid. at para. 112. '[T]he Committee concludes that the Tribunal exceeded its powers in the sense of Article 52(1)(b), in that the Tribunal, having jurisdiction over the Tucumán claims, failed to decide those claims.' Ibid. at para. 115.

during the period of 1991 to 1994.[25] While these activities would appear to constitute 'substantial business activity,' we need not affirmatively decide that they do, as it is not relevant to our determination of jurisdiction.

38. Rather, under the terms of the Ukraine-Lithuania BIT, interpreted according to their ordinary meaning, in their context, and in light of the object and purpose of the Treaty, the only relevant consideration is whether the claimant is established under the laws of Lithuania. We find that it is. Thus, the claimant is an investor of Lithuania under Article 1(2)(b) of the BIT.

39. We reach this conclusion based on the consent of the Contracting Parties, as expressed in the Ukraine-Lithuania BIT. We emphasise here that Contracting Parties are free to define their consent to jurisdiction in terms that are broad or narrow; they may employ a control-test or reserve the right to deny treaty protection to claimants who otherwise would have recourse under the BIT. Once that consent is defined, however, Tribunals should give effect to it, unless doing so would allow the Convention to be used for purposes for which it clearly was not intended.

40. This Tribunal, by respecting the definition of corporate nationality in the Ukraine-Lithuania BIT, fulfils the parties' expectations, increases the predictability of dispute settlement procedures, and enables investors to structure their investments to enjoy the legal protections afforded under the Treaty. We decline to look beyond (or through) the claimant to its shareholders or other juridical entities that may have an interest in the claim. As the Tribunal in *Amco Asia Corp v Indonesia* said in rejecting the respondent's request to attribute to the claimant the nationality of its controlling shareholder, the concept of nationality in the ICSID Convention is:

> . . .a classical one, based on the law under which the juridical person has been incorporated, the place of incorporation and the place of the social seat. An exception is brought to this concept in respect of juridical persons having the nationality, thus defined, of the Contracting State party to the dispute, where said juridical persons are under foreign control. *But no exception to the classical concept is provided for when it comes to the nationality of the foreign controller, even supposing – which is not at all clearly stated in the Convention – that the fact that the controller is the national of one or another foreign State is to be taken into account. . ..*[26]

---

25 Claimant's December 30, 2003 Submission of Documents, Annexes 1–11, Catalogues of Publications of Tokios Tokelès for 1991, 1992, 1993 and 1994.
26 *Amco Asia Corp and Others v Republic of Indonesia*, Decision on Jurisdiction, Case No. ARB/81/1 (Sept. 25, 1983), 1 ICSID Reports 389, 396 (emphasis added) (Amco).

41. Thus, the decision of this Tribunal with respect to the nationality of the claimant is consistent with *Amco Asia* and other ICSID jurisprudence, as will be discussed further below.

4. Consistency of Article 1(2) of the BIT with the ICSID Convention   42. In our view, the definition of corporate nationality in the Ukraine-Lithuania BIT, on its face and as applied to the present case, is consistent with the Convention and supports our analysis under it. Although Article 25(2)(b) of the Convention does not set forth a required method for determining corporate nationality, the generally accepted (albeit implicit) rule is that the nationality of a corporation is determined on the basis of its *siège social* or place of incorporation.[27] Indeed, 'ICSID Tribunals have uniformly adopted the test of incorporation or seat rather than control when determining the nationality of a juridical person.'[28] Moreover, '[t]he overwhelming weight of the authority. . .points towards the traditional criteria of incorporation or seat for the determination of corporate nationality under Art. 25(2)(b)'.[29] As Professor Schreuer notes, '[a] systematic interpretation of Article 25(2)(b) would militate against the use of the control test for a corporation's nationality'.[30]

43. As discussed above, the claimant is an 'investor' of Lithuania under Article 1(2)(b) of the Ukraine-Lithuania BIT based on its state-of-incorporation. Although not required by the text of the Treaty, an assessment of the *siège social* of the claimant leads to the same conclusion. Among the relevant evidence of *siège social*, the claimant's registration certificate (issued by the Ministry of the Economy of Lithuania),[31] its statute of incorporation,[32] and each of the claimant's 'Information Notices of Payment of Foreign Investment' (registered by Ukrainian governmental authorities),[33] all record the claimant's address as Vilnius, Lithuania. Contrary to the assertion of the

---

27 Schreuer (n 6), at 278–9; see also G R Delaume, 'ICSID Arbitration and the Courts,' 77 *Amer. J. Int'l Law* 784, 793–4 (1983); M. Hirsch, *The Arbitration Mechanism of the International Centre for the Settlement of Investment Disputes* 85 (1993).

28 Schreuer (n 6), at 279–80 (citing *Kaiser Bauxite Co v Jamaica*, Decision on Jurisdiction, Case No. ARB/74/3 (July 6, 1975), 1 ICSID Reports 296, 303 (1993); *SOABI v Senegal*, Decision on Jurisdiction, Case No. ARB/82/1 (Aug. 1, 1984), 2 ICSID Reports 175, 180–81; *Amco*, at 396); see also *Autopista Concesionada de Venezuela, CA v Bolivarian Republic of Venezuela*, Decision on Jurisdiction, Case No. ARB/00/5 (Sept. 27, 2001), 16 ICSID Review-FILJ 469 (2001), at para. 108 (Autopista).

29 Schreuer, ibid. at 281.

30 Ibid. at 278.

31 Request for Arbitration, at Annex 5.

32 Ibid. at Annex 6.

33 Ibid. at Annex 13.

respondent, a nationality test of *siège social* leads to the same result as one based on state of incorporation.[34]

44. The second clause of Article 25(2)(b) provides that parties can, by agreement, depart from the general rule that a corporate entity has the nationality of its state of incorporation. It extends jurisdiction to:

> any juridical person which had the nationality of the Contracting State party to the dispute on [the date on which the parties consented to submit the dispute to arbitration] and which, *because of foreign control*, the parties have agreed should be treated as a national of another Contracting State. . ..[35]

This exception to the general rule applies only in the context of an agreement between the parties. The respondent asks the Tribunal to apply this exception in the present case, not to give effect to an agreement between the Contracting Parties, but, rather, to create an additional exception to the general state-of-incorporation or state-of-seat rule – in the absence of an agreement to that effect between the parties.

45. We find no support for the respondent's request in the text of the Convention. The second clause of Article 25(2)(b) limits the use of the control-test to the circumstances it describes, i.e., when Contracting Parties agree to treat a national of the host State as a national of another Contracting Party because of foreign control. In the present case, the claimant is not a national of the host State nor have the parties agreed to treat the claimant as a national of a State other than its State of incorporation.

46. The use of a control-test to define the nationality of a corporation to restrict the jurisdiction of the centre would be inconsistent with the object and purpose of Article 25(2)(b). Indeed, as explained by Mr Broches, the purpose of the control-test in the second portion of Article 25(2)(b) is to expand the jurisdiction of the centre:

> [t]here was a compelling reason for this last provision. It is quite usual for host States to require that foreign investors carry on their business within their territories through a company organised under the laws of the host country.

---

34 This is not a surprising result. See D P O'Connell, *International Law* 1041 (2nd edn 1970) stating:

> [u]nder French law it is not possible for a corporation to have a *siège social* at a place other than that of incorporation. . . The corporation laws of Continental countries provide that the charter of incorporation must designate this central office, and the inference is that it must be in the country of incorporation.

35 Emphasis added.

> If we admit, as the Convention does implicitly, that this makes the company technically a national of the host country, it becomes readily apparent that there is need for an exception to the general principle that the Centre will not have jurisdiction over disputes between a Contracting State and its own nationals. *If no exception were made for foreign-owned but locally incorporated companies, a large and important sector of foreign investment would be outside the scope of the Convention.*[36]

47. ICSID Tribunals likewise have interpreted the second clause of Article 25(2)(b) to expand, not restrict, jurisdiction. In *Wena Hotels Ltd v Egypt*, the respondent argued that Wena, though incorporated in the United Kingdom, should be treated as an Egyptian company because it was owned by an Egyptian national.[37] Egypt relied on Article 8.1 of the UK-Egypt BIT provision, which states:

> [s]uch a company of one Contracting Party in which before such dispute arises a majority of shares are owned by nationals or companies of the other Contracting Party shall in accordance with Article 25(2)(b) of the Convention be treated for the purposes of the Convention as a company of the other Contracting Party.[38]

48. Egypt argued that this provision could be used to deny jurisdiction over disputes

involving companies of the non-disputing Contracting Party that are owned by nationals or companies of the Contracting Party to the dispute. Wena, on the other hand, argued that this provision could be used only to extend jurisdiction over disputes involving companies of the Contracting Party to the dispute that are owned by nationals or companies of the non-disputing Contracting Party. Although the Tribunal found that both interpretations of the BIT provision were plausible, it decided to adopt Wena's interpretation as the more consistent with Article 25(2)(b) of the Convention.

49. As the Wena Tribunal stated, '[t]he literature rather convincingly demonstrates that Article 25(2)(b) of the ICSID Convention – and provisions like Article 8 of the United Kingdom's model bilateral investment treaty – are

---

36 Broches (n 8), at 358–9 (emphasis added).
37 *Wena Hotels Ltd v Arab Republic of Egypt,* Summary Minutes of the Session of the Tribunal held in Paris on May 25, 1999, Case No. ARB/98/4, 41 I.L.M. 881, 886 (2002).
38 Ibid. at 887.

meant to expand ICSID jurisdiction.'[39] The Tribunal in *Autopista v Venezuela* reached a similar result, concluding that the object and purpose of Article 25(2)(b) is not to limit jurisdiction, but to set its 'outer limits'.[40]

50. ICSID jurisprudence also confirms that the second clause of Article 25(2)(b) should not be used to determine the nationality of juridical entities in the absence of an agreement between the parties. In *CMS v Argentina*, the Tribunal states, '[t]he reference that Article 25(2)(b) makes to foreign control in terms of treating a company of the nationality of the Contracting State party as a national of another Contracting State *is precisely meant to facilitate agreement between the parties. . .*'[41] In the present case, there was no agreement between the Contracting Parties to treat the claimant as anything other than a national of its State of incorporation, i.e., Lithuania.

51. The second clause of Article 25(2)(b) does not mandatorily constrict ICSID jurisdiction for disputes arising in the inverse context from the one envisaged by this provision: a dispute between a Contracting Party and an entity of another Contracting Party that is controlled by nationals of the respondent Contracting Party.

52. In summary, the claimant is an 'investor' of Lithuania under Article 1(2)(b) of the BIT because it is an 'entity established in the territory of the Republic of Lithuania in conformity with its laws and regulations'. This method of defining corporate nationality is consistent with modern BIT practice and satisfies the objective requirements of Article 25 of the Convention. We find no basis in the BIT or the Convention to set aside the Contracting Parties' agreed definition of corporate nationality with respect to investors of either party in favour of a test based on the nationality of the controlling shareholders. While some tribunals have taken a distinctive approach,[42] we do not believe that arbitrators should read in to BITs limitations not found in the text nor evident from negotiating history sources.

---

39 Ibid. at 888.
40 *Autopista*, at para. 109 (quoting Broches (n 8)).
41 *CMS Gas Transmission Co v Republic of Argentina*, Decision on Jurisdiction, Case No. ARB/01/8 (July 17, 2003), 42 I.L.M. 788 (2003), at para. 51 (emphasis added) (*CMS*).
42 See, e.g., *SGS Société Générale de Surveillance SA v Islamic Republic of Pakistan*, Decision on Jurisdiction, Case No. ARB/01/13 (Aug. 6, 2003), 42 I.L.M. 1290 (2003). In this case, a Swiss company asserted claims against the Government of Pakistan for breach of contract and for breach of the BIT between the Swiss Confederation and Pakistan. Art 9 of that BIT provides for ICSID arbitration of 'disputes with respect to investments. . .' ibid. at para. 149. The provision does not in any manner restrict the scope of such disputes. Although the Tribunal recognised that BIT claims and contract claims can both be described as 'disputes with respect to investment', it nonetheless decided – without support from the text or evidence of the parties' intent – to exclude contract claims from the scope of 'disputes' that could be submitted to ICSID arbitration, ibid. at paras 161–162.

5. Equitable doctrine of 'veil piercing'   53. Finally, we consider whether the equitable doctrine of 'veil piercing,' to the extent recognised in customary international law, should override the terms of the agreement between the Contracting Parties and cause the Tribunal to deny jurisdiction in this case.[43]

54. The seminal case, in this regard, is *Barcelona Traction*.[44] In that case, the International Court of Justice (ICJ) stated, 'the process of lifting the veil, being an exceptional one admitted by municipal law in respect of an institution of its own making, is equally admissible to play a similar role in international law'.[45] In particular, the Court noted:

> [t]he wealth of practice already accumulated on the subject in municipal law indicates that the veil is lifted, for instance, to *prevent the misuse of the privileges of legal personality*, as in certain cases of fraud or malfeasance, to protect third persons such as a creditor or purchaser, or to *prevent the evasion of legal requirements or of obligations.*[46]

55. The respondent has not made a prima facie case, much less demonstrated, that the claimant has engaged in any of the types of conduct described in *Barcelona Traction* that might support a piercing of the claimant's corporate veil. The respondent has not shown or even suggested that the claimant has used its status as a juridical entity of Lithuania to perpetrate fraud or engage in malfeasance. The respondent has made no claim that the claimant's veil must be pierced and jurisdiction denied in order to protect third persons, nor has the respondent shown that the claimant used its corporate nationality to evade applicable legal requirements or obligations.

56. The ICJ did not attempt to define in *Barcelona Traction* the precise scope of conduct that might prompt a Tribunal to pierce the corporate veil. We are satisfied, however, that none of the claimant's conduct with respect to

---

43 Article 42(1) of the ICSID Convention states:

> [t]he Tribunal shall decide a dispute in accordance with such rules of law as may be agreed by the parties. In the absence of such agreement, the Tribunal shall apply the law of the Contracting State party to the dispute (including its rules on the conflict of laws) *and such rules of international law as may be applicable* (emphasis added).

44 For the sake of clarity, the Tribunal notes that *Barcelona Traction*, which held that incorporation is the only criterion for nationality in cases of diplomatic protection, is inapplicable with respect to agreements between the parties to treat companies of the host State as a national of the other Party under the second clause of Article 25(2)(b). See Broches (n 8), at 360–61.

45 *Barcelona Traction, Light and Power Co Ltd (Belg v Spain)*, 1970 I.C.J. 3 (Feb. 5), at para. 58 (*Barcelona Traction*).

46 Ibid. at para. 56 (emphases added).

its status as an entity of Lithuania constitutes an abuse of legal personality. The claimant made no attempt whatever to conceal its national identity from the respondent. To the contrary, the claimant's status as a juridical entity of Lithuania is well established under the laws of both Lithuania and Ukraine and well known by the respondent. The claimant manifestly did not create Tokios Tokelės for the purpose of gaining access to ICSID arbitration under the BIT against Ukraine, as the enterprise was founded six years before the BIT between Ukraine and Lithuania entered into force. Indeed, there is no evidence in the record that the claimant used its formal legal nationality for any improper purpose.

6. Other considerations regarding corporate nationality   57. Although not necessary elements of our Decision, the section below addresses the relevant ICSID jurisprudence and the views of ICSID scholars raised by the parties that relate to the issue of defining corporate nationality.

a. ICSID JURISPRUDENCE   58. The arbitral awards cited by the respondent do not support a decision by this Tribunal to set aside the definition of nationality agreed to by the Contracting Parties. Among the awards cited, the respondent quotes the following passage from *Banro American Resources Inc v Congo* in support of its request to pierce the corporate veil of the claimant:

> These few examples demonstrate that in general, ICSID Tribunals do not accept the view that their competence is limited by formalities, and rather they rule on their competence based on a review of the circumstances surrounding the case, and, in particular, the actual relationship among the companies involved. This jurisprudence reveals the willingness of ICSID Tribunals to refrain from making decisions on their competence based on formal appearances, and to base their decisions on a realistic assessment of the situation before them.[47]

59. The 'few examples' to which the *Banro* Tribunal refers, however, are cases in which the claimant, as the party that requested arbitration, was not the same entity as the party that consented to arbitration.[48] The *Banro* Tribunal

---

47 Respondent's Memorial, at 2.1.9 (citing *Banro American Resources, Inc and Société Aurifère du Kivu et du Maniema SARL v Democratic Republic of Congo*, Award, Case No. ARB/98/7 (Sept. 1, 2000), at para. 11 (*Banro*)).

48 *Banro*, at para. 10:

> This was the case, in particular, in two situations: when the request was made by a member company of a group of companies while the pertinent instrument expressed the consent of another company of this group; and when, following the transfer of shares, the request came from the transferee company while the consent had been given by the company making the transfer.

suggests that, in these cases, the Tribunals have been willing to consider the nationalities of the consenting party and the claimant when making their determinations of jurisdiction.

60. In *Banro* itself, the claimant's parent, Banro Resources (Canada), transferred shares in its Congolese investment to its subsidiary, Banro American (US). The Tribunal stated that the claimant, Banro American, could not avail itself of the consent expressed by its parent, Banro Resources, because Banro Resources, as a national of a non-Contracting Party, could not have validly consented to ICSID arbitration and, thus, could not transfer any valid consent to its US subsidiary.[49] Although the *Banro* Tribunal indicated that it 'could have addressed the issue of *jus standi* of Banro American in a flexible manner',[50] in the end, the Tribunal did not deny jurisdiction by piercing the claimant's corporate veil. Instead, the *Banro* Tribunal denied jurisdiction to prevent Banro Resources from availing itself of diplomatic protection while its US subsidiary pursued ICSID arbitration, which, if allowed, would contravene the object and purpose of Article 27 the Convention.[51]

61. Thus, the issue before the Tribunal in *Banro* and in the cases discussed briefly therein was not, as it is here, the proper method of defining the nationality of the claimant. In *Banro*, there was no dispute that the claimant was a national of the United States and Banro Resources was a national of Canada, both by virtue of their incorporation in those countries. The issue in Banro was whether the claimant of one nationality could benefit from the consent given by its parent company of another nationality. In the present case, it is undisputed that the claimant made the request for arbitration and expressed consent to ICSID jurisdiction. Accordingly, the decision in *Banro* provides no justification for looking beyond the nationality of the claimant, Tokios Tokelės, to other related parties or to its controlling shareholders.

62. The decision in *Autopista v Venezuela* is similarly unhelpful to the respondent. The respondent's Memorial in the case before this Tribunal cites, in isolation, the following passage: '[a]s a general matter, the arbitral Tribunal accepts that economic criteria often better reflect reality than legal ones.'[52]

---

49 Id. at para. 5.
50 Ibid. at para. 13.
51 Ibid. at paras 13, 24. Article 27 states:

> [n]o Contracting State shall give diplomatic protection, or bring an international claim, in respect of a dispute which one of its nationals and another Contracting State shall have consented to submit or shall have submitted to arbitration under this Convention, unless such other Contracting State shall have failed to abide by and comply with the award rendered in such dispute.

52 Memorial, para. 2.1.9 (citing *Autopista*, para. 119).

Although seemingly helpful, the text of the decision that follows the quoted passage directly undermines the respondent's objection. In particular, the Tribunal states:

> [h]owever, in the present case, such arguments of an economic nature are irrelevant. Indeed, exercising the discretion granted by the Convention, the parties have specifically identified majority shareholding as the criterion to be applied. They have not chosen to subordinate their consent to ICSID arbitration to other criteria.
>
> As a result, the Tribunal must respect the parties' autonomy and may not discard the criterion of direct shareholding, *unless it proves unreasonable.*[53]

63. In the present case, as in *Autopista*, 'arguments of an economic nature are irrelevant' where 'the parties have specifically identified' the country of legal establishment 'as the criterion to be applied' and 'have not chosen to subordinate their consent to ICSID arbitration to any other criteria.' This Tribunal, like the Tribunal in *Autopista*, is obliged to respect the parties' agreement 'unless it proves unreasonable'. Far from unreasonable, reference to the State of incorporation is the most common method of defining the nationality of business entities under modern BITs and traditional international law.[54]

64. The respondent also cites *Loewen v United States of America* to support its position.[55] In that case, the Canadian claimant declared bankruptcy during the arbitration proceedings and, immediately before going out of business, assigned its claim to a newly created Canadian corporation whose sole asset was the claim against the United States.[56] The newly created corporation was wholly owned and controlled by the US enterprise that emerged from the earlier bankruptcy proceeding. Although the claim remained at all times in the possession of a Canadian enterprise, the *Loewen* Tribunal held that the assignment of the claim changed the nationality of the claimant from Canadian to U.S. origin. Accordingly, the Tribunal denied jurisdiction because the claimant's nationality was not continuous from the date of the events giving rise to the claim through the date of the resolution of the claim, as the Tribunal believed was required by customary international law.[57]

---

53 *Autopista*, at paras. 119–120 (emphases added).
54 Schreuer (n 6), at 277.
55 Respondent's Reply, at 2.1.5.
56 *Loewen Group, Inc and Raymond Loewen v United States of America*, Award, Case No. ARB(AF)/98/3 (June 26, 2003), 42 I.L.M. 811 (2003), at paras. 220, 240.
57 Ibid. at para. 225.

65. Although the *Loewen* Tribunal denied that it pierced the claimant's corporate veil,[58] in reality, the Tribunal did exactly that. Indeed, the Tribunal could not have concluded that the nationality of the claimant had changed from Canadian to US origin without piercing the claimant's corporate veil. Although one may debate whether veil piercing was justified in that case, the *Loewen* decision does not clarify the jurisprudence of veil piercing because the Tribunal did not admit to, much less explain its reasons for, piercing the claimant's corporate veil.

66. As *Loewen* provides no additional guidance on the doctrine of veil piercing, we refer instead to the jurisprudence of *Barcelona Traction*. As noted above, we are convinced that the equitable doctrine of veil piercing does not apply to the present case.

b. VIEWS OF ICSID SCHOLARS 67. The respondent also argues that some ICSID scholars encourage the application of the control-test to determine corporate nationality in the first clause of Article 25(2)(b) as well as the second, citing the views of Dr Amerasinghe and Mr Broches as discussed by Professor Schreuer.[59] The respondent, however, misinterprets the views of these scholars.

68. Dr Amerasinghe does argue that Article 25 of the Convention allows Tribunals to be 'extremely flexible' in using various methods to determine the nationality of juridical entities, including the control-test.[60] He advocates this flexible approach, however, in the context of a challenge to jurisdiction where, unlike here, the parties to the dispute have not agreed on a particular method of determining the nationality of juridical entities. In addition, the respondent fails to mention Dr Amerasinghe's corollary rule of interpretation, that is, 'every effort should be made to give the Centre jurisdiction by the application of the flexible approach'.[61]

69. Likewise, Mr Broches states that the text of Article 25(2)(b) 'implicitly assumes that incorporation is a criterion of nationality'.[62] He argues, however, that this provision does not preclude an agreement between parties to define juridical entities by methods other than State of incorporation, including ownership and control.[63] In other words, the Convention permits deviation

---

58 Ibid. at para. 237.
59 Respondent's Reply, at 2.1.10 (citing Schreuer (n 6), at 278–9).
60 C F Amerasinghe, 'The Jurisdiction of the International Centre for the Settlement of Investment Disputes,' 19 *Indian J. Int'l Law* 166, 214 (Apr–June 1979).
61 Ibid. at 214–15.
62 Broches (n 8), at 360.
63 Ibid. at 360–61.

from the general rule for defining the nationality of juridical entities, but only if there is an agreement between the Contracting Parties to do so. Here, there is no such agreement providing for deviation. On the contrary, the agreement under the Ukraine-Lithuania BIT confirms that the standard rule (incorporation) applies.

c. TRADITIONAL APPROACH UNDER INTERNATIONAL LAW   70. As with the Convention, the definition of corporate nationality in the Ukraine-Lithuania BIT is also consistent with the predominant approach in international law. As the ICJ has explained

> [t]he traditional rule attributes the right of diplomatic protection of a corporate entity to the States under the laws of which it is incorporated and in whose territory it has its registered office. The two criteria have been confirmed by long practice and by numerous international instruments.[64]

According to Oppenheim's International Law:

> [i]t is usual to attribute a corporation to the state under the laws of which it has been incorporated and to which it owes its legal existence; to this initial condition is often added the need for the corporation's head office, registered office, or its *siège social* to be in the same state.[65]

Thus, the Ukraine-Lithuania BIT uses the same well-established method for determining corporate nationality as does customary international law.

7. Conclusion of the Tribunal   71. The Tribunal concludes that the claimant is an 'investor' of Lithuania under Article 1(2)(b) of the BIT and a 'national of another Contracting State,' under Article 25 of the Convention.

[...]

 CASE

Dissenting opinion

1. The chairman of an Arbitral Tribunal dissenting from a decision drafted by his two colleagues: this is not a frequent occurrence. If I have decided

---

64 *Barcelona Traction*, at para. 70.
65 *Oppenheim's International Law* 859–60 (Sir Robert Jennings and Sir Arthur Watts (eds), 9th edn 1996) (footnotes omitted).

to dissent, it is because the approach taken by the Tribunal on the issue of principle raised in this case for the first time in ICSID's history is in my view at odds with the object and purpose of the ICSID Convention and might jeopardise the future of the institution. In other words, my dissent does not relate to any particular aspect of this brilliantly drafted Decision, or to any particular assessment of the facts, but rather to what I would call the philosophy of the Decision. I would fail in my duty if I were to conceal my doubts out of friendship for my colleagues.

2. The ICSID system rests on the Convention on the Settlement of Investment Disputes between States and Nationals of other States signed on March 18, 1965 (hereafter: the Convention), which had been formulated by the Executive Directors of the World Bank and to which both Lithuania and Ukraine are parties. The object and purpose of the Convention are set out in the *Report of the Executive Directors on the Convention* as well as in the provisions of the Convention itself.

3. The *Report of the Executive Directors on the Convention* explains that the creation of ICSID was 'designed to facilitate the settlement of disputes between States and foreign investors' with a view to 'stimulating a larger flow of private international capital into those countries which wish to attract it.'[1] The Report explains that, while:

> investment disputes are as a rule settled under the laws of the country in which the investment concerned is made,. . . both States and investors frequently consider that it is in their mutual interest to agree to resort to international methods of settlement.[2]

It states that 'adherence to the Convention by a country would. . . stimulate a larger flow of private international investment into territories, which is the primary purpose of the Convention,'[3] and adds that 'the broad objective of the Convention is to encourage a larger flow of private international investment.'[4] The object of the Convention, so the Report explains, is to 'offer international methods of settlement designed to take account of the special characteristics of the disputes covered, as well as of the parties to whom it would apply.'[5]

---

1 Report of the Executive Directors, para. 9.
2 Ibid., para 10.
3 Ibid., para 12.
4 Ibid., para 13.
5 Ibid., para 11.

4. The Convention, for its part, refers in its preamble to 'the possibility that from time to time disputes may arise in connection with. . . investment between Contracting States and nationals of other Contracting States'. [W]hile such disputes, so the preamble states, 'would usually be subject to national legal processes, international methods of settlement may be appropriate in certain cases'; that is why it has been regarded as appropriate to establish 'facilities for international arbitration. . . to which Contracting States and nationals of other Contracting States may submit such disputes if they so desire'. Accordingly, Article 25(1) of the Convention establishes the jurisdiction of the Centre over disputes 'between a Contracting State. . . and a national of another Contracting State. . .' Over other disputes the Centre has no jurisdiction.

5. From this it appears that the ICSID arbitration mechanism is meant for *international* investment disputes, that is to say, for disputes between States and *foreign* investors. It is because of their *international* character, and with a view to stimulating private *international* investment, that these disputes may be settled, if the parties so desire, by an *international* judicial body. The ICSID mechanism is not meant for investment disputes between States and their own nationals. This is in effect not disputed by the claimant since in its Opening Statement it declared that:

> . . . this Convention has as its express purpose the encouragement of international private investment. We can agree with the Respondent that the ICSID Convention prohibits a host State from being sued by its own nationals with the single exception of the circumstances foreseen by the second clause of Article 25(2)(b).[6]

6. The Decision rests on the assumption that the origin of the capital is not relevant and even less decisive. This assumption is flying in the face of the object and purpose of the ICSID Convention and system as explicitly defined both in the preamble of the Convention and in the *Report of the Executive Directors*.

7. This, however, is not the only key feature of the ICSID mechanism that, in my view, the Decision ignores. Another one is that once this mechanism comes into play it is exclusive of any other remedy. As the *Report of the Executive Directors* states:

> [i]t may be presumed that when a State and an investor agree to have recourse to arbitration, and do not reserve the right to have recourse to other remedies. . ., the

---

6 Opening Statement of Tokios Tokelés, p 5.

intention of the parties is to have recourse to arbitration to the exclusion of any other remedy.[7]

That is why Article 26 of the Convention decides that consent to arbitration under the Convention 'shall, unless otherwise stated, be deemed consent to such arbitration to the exclusion of any other remedy'. In particular, as provided for by Article 27, such consent shall be exclusive of diplomatic protection.

8. It appears, therefore, that because of its specific object and purpose – namely, the protection of international investments – the ICSID Convention imposes strict obligations and limitations on both the Contracting States and the investors who are nationals of other Contracting States. It prohibits the use of diplomatic protection and excludes the jurisdiction of domestic courts, for which it substitutes the recourse to its own, specific international arbitration mechanism. It follows that ICSID Arbitral Tribunals have to be particularly cautious when they determine their jurisdiction. An unwarranted extension of the ICSID arbitral jurisdiction would entail an unwarranted encroachment on both the availability of diplomatic protection and the jurisdiction of domestic courts.

9. The instant case opposes a Lithuanian corporation, Tokios Tokelés, to Ukraine on measures taken by the Ukrainian authorities against its wholly owned subsidiary, the Ukrainian corporation Taki spravy, in alleged violation of the bilateral investment treaty (BIT) between Ukraine and Lithuania. As stated in the Decision, '[t]here is no dispute that nationals of Ukraine own 99 per cent of the outstanding shares of Tokios Tokelés and comprise two-thirds of its management'.[8] Assuming that the dispute brought before the Tribunal meets the condition of 'arising directly out of an investment' laid out in Article 25 of the ICSID Convention, a question thus arises: Does the dispute fall into the category of 'disputes between States and nationals of other States', as required by the very title of the Convention? Does it qualify as a dispute 'between a Contracting State. . . and a national of another Contracting State', as required by Article 25 of the Convention? In the affirmative, the Tribunal has to affirm its jurisdiction. In the negative, it has to deny it.

10. It is, I think, the first time that an ICSID Tribunal has to address the specific problem of a dispute opposing to State A (Ukraine) a corporation which has the nationality of State B (Lithuania) but which is controlled by

---

7 *Report of the Executive Directors*, para 32.
8 Decision, para 21.

citizens of State A (Ukraine) – so much so that the dispute, while formally meeting the condition of being between a Contracting State and a national of another Contracting State, is in actual fact between a Contracting State and a corporation controlled by nationals of that State. In some instances, there may be doubts about whether the corporation is, or is not, to be regarded as being controlled by nationals of the respondent State, and a choice will then have to be made between various possible criteria. In the present case, however, where Tokios Tokelés is indisputably and totally in the hands of, and controlled by, Ukrainian citizens and interests, there is no evading the issue of principle.

11. The Decision rests on the idea that the Ukrainian origin of the capital invested by Tokios Tokelés in Taki spravy and the Ukrainian nationality of Tokios Tokelés' shareholders and managers are irrelevant to the application of both the Convention and the BIT. What is relevant and decisive, according to the Decision, is the fact that the investment has been made by a corporation of Lithuanian nationality, whatever the origin of its capital and the nationality of its managers. The Decision dismisses any 'origin-of-capital requirement', which, so it maintains, 'is plainly absent from the text' of the relevant instruments and 'is inconsistent with the object and purpose of the Treaty which. . . is to provide broad protection to investors and their investments in the territory of either party':[9]

> The origin of the capital is not relevant to the existence of an investment. . . [T]he ICSID Convention does not require an 'investment' to be financed from capital of any particular origin. . . The origin of the capital used to acquire these assets is not relevant to the question of jurisdiction under the Convention.[10]

The Decision goes so far as to state that:

> Even assuming, *arguendo*, that all of the capital used by the Claimant to invest in Ukraine had its ultimate origin in Ukraine, the resulting investment would not be outside the scope of the Convention.[11]

---

9 Ibid., para 77.
10 Ibid., paras 80–81.
11 Ibid., para 80. This is what the claimant has argued all along in its written pleadings. For example:

> Nowhere in the relevant international treaties or national legislation is there exposed or implied the condition that the claimant realise investments from non-Ukrainian sources. . .[T]he respondent incorrectly attempts to impose the *sui generis* condition that the investment sources not originate from Ukraine. . .For an investment to be foreign it is sufficient to be made by a foreign juridical person, regardless of the funds used to realise the investment (Tokios Tokelés' Rejoinder, p 136, paras 248–249; p 139, para 253.)

12. The Decision states that the Tribunal was 'guided by Article 25 of the ICSID Convention as well as Articles 1 and 8 of the Ukraine-Lithuania BIT'.[12] In so far as the relations *inter partes* under the BIT are concerned, so the Decision maintains, the Contracting Parties are 'free to define their consent to jurisdiction in terms that are broad or narrow';[13] and 'it is not for tribunals to impose limits on the scope of BITs not found in the text'.[14] As to the jurisdiction of the ICSID Tribunals, the provisions of the BIT are governing, so the Decision writes, 'as long as the dispute satisfies the objective requirements set forth in Article 25 of the Convention'; therefore, Tribunals should give effect to the consent of the Contracting Parties as expressed in the BIT 'unless doing so would allow the Convention to be used for purposes for which it clearly was not intended'.[15] As a consequence, so the Decision concludes, '[t]ribunals shall exercise jurisdiction over all disputes that fall within the scope of the Contracting Parties' consent as long as the dispute satisfies the objective requirements set forth in Article 25 of the Convention'.[16]

13. The Decision thus accepts, as a matter of principle, that the provisions of the BIT governing the jurisdiction of the ICSID Tribunals can be given effect only within the limits of the jurisdiction defined in the Convention. It refers to that effect to Broches' well-known phrase that the Convention determines the 'outer limits'[17] of the jurisdiction of the ICSID and its Tribunals. In other words, it is within the limits determined by the basic ICSID Convention that the BITs may determine the jurisdiction and powers of the ICSID Tribunal, and it is not for the Contracting Parties in their BIT to extend the jurisdiction of the ICSID Tribunal beyond the limits determined by the basic ICSID Convention. From this it follows that, while the Contracting Parties to the BIT are free to confer to the ICSID Tribunal a jurisdiction narrower than that provided for by the Convention, it is not for them to extend the jurisdiction of the ICSID Tribunal beyond its determination in the Convention.

14. To decide the jurisdictional issue the Decision should, therefore, have checked *first* whether the Tribunal has jurisdiction under Article 25 of the Convention – interpreted, as the Decision recalls, in light of its object and purpose[18] – and *then*, in a second stage, whether it has jurisdiction *also* under the bilateral investment treaty. It is only if the Tribunal had reached the

---

12 Ibid., para 14.
13 Ibid., para 39.
14 Ibid., para 36.
15 Ibid., paras 19 and 39.
16 Ibid., para 19.
17 A. Broches, as quoted in para 25 of the Decision.
18 Decision, para 27.

conclusion that it has jurisdiction under the Convention that it would have had to examine whether it has jurisdiction *also* under the BIT. This, however, is not how the Decision proceeds. It states that, 'we begin our analysis of this jurisdictional requirement by underscoring the deference this Tribunal owes to the definition of corporate nationality contained in the agreement between the Contracting Parties, in this case, the Ukraine-Lithuania BIT.'[19] And this is what it does: it begins with the 'Definition of 'investor' in Article 1(2) of the BIT', and then in a second stage it turns to the 'Consistency of Article 1(2) of the BIT with the ICSID Convention.'[20]

15. I now turn to what, in my view, should have been the first leg of the reasoning, namely, the question whether the basic requirements of Article 25 of the Convention are met. According to paragraph 1 of Article 25 the jurisdiction of the Centre extends to legal disputes 'between a Contracting State. . . and a national of another Contracting State'. While Ukraine is beyond doubt a 'Contracting State', the question arises whether for the purposes of this provision Tokios Tokelés is to be regarded as 'a national of another Contracting State'. Article 25(2)(b) defines this concept as:

> any juridical person which had the nationality of a Contracting State other than the State party to the dispute on the date on which the parties consented to submit such dispute to. . .arbitration, and any juridical person which had the nationality of the Contracting State party to the dispute on that date and which, because of foreign control, the parties have agreed should be treated as a national of another Contracting State for the purposes of this Convention.

Thus, the question boils down to determining whether Tokios Tokelés, even though undisputedly under Ukrainian control, is to be regarded as having 'the nationality of a Contracting State other than the State party to the dispute', i.e., the nationality of Lithuania, or whether, because undisputedly under Ukrainian control, it is to be regarded, for the purposes of the Convention, as having the nationality of Ukraine.

16. The Decision states that '[t]he Convention does not define the method for determining the nationality of juridical entities, leaving this task to the reasonable discretion of the Contracting Parties',[21] and it begins its analysis, as already mentioned, 'by underscoring the deference this Tribunal owes to the definition of corporate nationality contained in the agreement between

---

19 Ibid., para 25.
20 Ibid., paras 27 ff. and 42 ff.
21 Ibid., para 24.

the Contracting Parties'.[22] While it is true that no definition of the nationality of corporations is to be found in the Convention, it cannot be the case that this definition is left to the discretion of the parties, because it is not for the parties to extend the jurisdiction of ICSID beyond what the Convention provides for. It is the Convention which determines the jurisdiction of ICSID, and it is within the limits of the ICSID jurisdiction as determined by the Convention that the parties may in their BIT define the disputes they agree to submit to an ICSID arbitration.

17. The central question before the Tribunal was thus as follows: Does Tokios Tokelés meet the requirement of having, for the purposes of the Convention, the nationality of Lithuania – in which case the Tribunal has to affirm its jurisdiction –, or is it to be regarded for the purposes of the Convention as being an Ukrainian corporation because it is indisputably under Ukrainian control – in which case the Tribunal has no jurisdiction?

18. This question is answered by the Decision in the following way:

> [I]n light of the object and purpose of the [BIT], the only relevant consideration is whether the claimant is established under the laws of Lithuania. We find that it is. Thus, the claimant is an investor of Lithuania under Article 1(2)(b) of the BIT... We decline to look beyond (or through) the claimant to its shareholders or other juridical entities that may have an interest in the claim... [T]he nationality of a corporation is determined on the basis of its *siège social* or place of incorporation... [T]he Claimant is an 'investor' of Lithuania under Article 1(2)(b) of the Ukraine-Lithuania BIT based on its state-of-incorporation.[23]

19. This raises the single most important issue which lies at the heart of my dissent. As observed earlier, the silence of the Convention on the criterion of corporate nationality does not leave the matter to the discretion of the parties. According to Article 31 of the Vienna Convention on the Law of Treaties, which the International Court of Justice has repeatedly described as the expression of customary international law, '[a] treaty shall be interpreted... in accordance with the ordinary meaning to be given to its terms in their context and *in the light of its object and purpose*'.[24] It is indisputable, and indeed undisputed, that the object and purpose of the ICSID Convention and, by the same token, of the procedures therein provided for are not the settlement of investment disputes between a State and its own

---

22 Ibid., para 25.
23 Ibid., paras 38, 40, 42, 43.
24 Italics supplied.

nationals. It is only the *international* investment that the Convention governs, that is to say, an investment implying a transborder flux of capital. This appears from the Convention itself, in particular from its preamble which refers to 'the role of private international investment' and, of course, from its Article 25. This appears also from the passages in the *Report of the Executive Directors* quoted above.[25] As Professor Schreuer writes:

> The basic idea of the Convention, as expressed in its title, is to provide for dispute settlement between States and foreign investors. . . Disputes between a State and its own nationals are settled by that State's domestic courts. . .
>   The Convention is designed to facilitate the settlement of investment disputes between States and nationals of other States. It is not meant for disputes between States and their own nationals. The latter type of dispute is to be settled by domestic procedures, notably before domestic courts.[26]

The ICSID mechanism and remedy are not meant for investments made in a State by its own citizens with domestic capital through the channel of a foreign entity, whether preexistent or created for that purpose. To maintain, as the Decision does, that 'the origin of the capital is not relevant' and that 'the only relevant consideration is whether the claimant is established under the laws of Lithuania'[27] runs counter to the object and purpose of the whole ICSID system.

20. Contrary to what the Decision maintains, when it comes to ascertaining the *international* character of an investment, the origin of the capital *is* relevant, and even decisive. True, the Convention does not provide a precise and clear-cut definition of the concept of *international* investment – no more than it provides a precise and clear-cut definition of the concept of investment –, and it is therefore for each ICSID Tribunal to determine whether the specific facts of the case warrant the conclusion that it is before an international investment. Given the indisputable and undisputed Ukrainian character of the investment the Tribunal does not, in my view, give effect to the letter and spirit, as well as the object and purpose, of the ICSID institution.

21. The Decision stresses that 'none of the claimant's conduct with respect to its status as an entity of Lithuania constitutes an abuse of legal personal-

25 Supra, para 3.
26 Christoph H. Schreuer, The ICSID Convention: A Commentary, Cambridge University Press, 2001, p. 158, para 165, and p. 290, para 496.
27 See supra, paras 11 and 18.

ity'. The claimant, so it observes, 'made no attempt whatever to conceal its national identity from the respondent' and:

> manifestly did not create Tokios Tokelés for the purpose of gaining access to ICSID arbitration under the BIT against Ukraine, as the enterprise was founded six years before the BIT between Ukraine and Lithuania entered into force. Indeed, there is no evidence in the record that the claimant used its formal legal nationality for any improper purpose.[28]

I agree; but this is beside the point, as is beside the point the issue of the 'lifting of the veil' under the *Barcelona Traction* judgment of the ICJ.[29] What *is* decisive in our case is the simple, straightforward, objective fact that the dispute before this ICSID Tribunal is not between the Ukrainian State and a foreign investor but between the Ukrainian State and an Ukrainian investor – and to such a relationship and to such a dispute the ICSID Convention was not meant to apply and does not apply. There is in this conclusion a merely objective, legal appreciation without any criticism of Tokios Tokelés' or Taki spravy's way of organising and handling their relations.

22. In support of the view it takes, the Decision refers to the provision in Article 25(2)(b) of the ICSID Convention according to which the concept of a 'national of a Contracting State' extends to any juridical person 'which, because of foreign control, the parties have agreed should be treated as a national of another Contracting State for the purposes of this Convention'. The Decision maintains that:

> This exception to the general rule [of the *siège social*] applies only in the context of an agreement between the parties. . . [I]t limits the use of the control-test to the circumstances it describes, i.e., when Contracting Parties agree to treat a national of the host State as a national of another Contracting Party because of foreign control. In the present case, the claimant is not a national of the host State nor have the parties agreed to treat the claimant as a national of a State other than its state of incorporation.[30]

The provision in Article 25(2)(b), so the Decision states, was meant 'to expand the jurisdiction of the Centre'; to use the control-test 'to restrict the jurisdiction of the Centre would be inconsistent with the object and purpose of Article 25(2)(b)'.[31]

---

28 Decision, para 56.
29 Decision, para 54.
30 Decision, paras 44–45.
31 Ibid., para 46.

23. I am unable to concur with this reading of Article 25(2)(b). The object and purpose of this provision is, provided the parties so agree, to have the reality of foreign investment prevail for the purposes of the Convention over its legally domestic character when – because the law of the host State so requires or for whatever other reason – this investment was made through the channel of a domestic corporation, whether preexistent or created for that purpose. The object and purpose of this provision is to give effect to the genuinely international character of an apparently national investment and, therefore, as Broches' comment cited in paragraph 46 of the Decision highlights, to prevent a genuinely foreign investment from being deprived of the protection of the ICSID mechanism because of its legally domestic structure. It is this very same rationale of giving effect to the economic reality over and above the legal structure that should have led the Tribunal to decide that an investment made in Ukraine by Ukrainian citizens with Ukrainian capital – albeit through the channel of a Lithuanian corporation – cannot benefit from the protection of the ICSID mechanism and, as a consequence, to deny Tokios Tokelés, for the purposes of the Convention, the character of a 'foreign investor' in Ukraine. Since the object and purpose of this provision – and, for that matter, of the whole ICSID Convention and mechanism – is to protect *foreign* investment, it should not be interpreted so as to allow domestic, national corporations to evade the application of their domestic, national law and the jurisdiction of their domestic, national tribunals.

24. This is not a question of extending the control test at the expense of the rule of the *siège social*. This is simply giving effect to a provision the rationale of which is to grant the protection of the ICSID procedures to *all* genuinely international investments but, by the same token, *only* to genuinely international investments. In so far as business law and issues of business liability are involved, there is no reason for denying effect to the corporate structure chosen by the economic agents. When it comes to mechanisms and procedures involving States and implying, therefore, issues of public international law, economic and political reality is to prevail over legal structure, so much so that the application of the basic principles and rules of public international law should not be frustrated by legal concepts and rules prevailing in the relations between private economic and juridical players. The object and purpose of the ICSID Convention is not – and its effect, therefore, should not be – to afford domestic, national corporations the means of evading the jurisdiction of their domestic, national tribunals.

25. This is borne out by previous ICSID cases which have upheld jurisdiction where the request had been made by a company member of a group of companies while the consent to arbitration had been expressed in an instru-

ment concluded by another company of that group.[32] In the words of the award in *Banro*;

> . . . in general, ICSID tribunals do not accept the view that their competence is limited by formalities, and rather they rule on their competence based on a review of the circumstances surrounding the case, and, in particular, the actual relationships among the companies involved. This jurisprudence reveals the willingness of ICSID tribunals to refrain from making decisions on their competence based on formal appearances, and to base their decision on a realistic assessment of the situation before them. . .
>
> The problem. . . is not a choice between a flexible and realistic attitude or a formalistic and rigid attitude with respect to private law relationships between companies of the same group. The problem before the Tribunal involves considerations of international public policy and is governed by public international law.[33]

As Schreuer observes, the cases

> . . . show that the tribunals take a realistic attitude when identifying the party on the investor's side. They look for the actual foreign investor. . . The operation of ICSID clauses will not be frustrated through a narrow interpretation of the investor's identity.[34]

Once again, this is not a question of alleging, or sanctioning, any misconduct or fraud of either Tokios Tokelés or its subsidiary Taki spravy, or their management. This is only and exclusively a question of giving effect to the object and purpose of the ICSID Convention and, if I may say so, of preserving its integrity.

26. This is, in substance, the approach I think the Tribunal should have adopted and the conclusion it should have reached. To quote again from *Banro*, '[t]he ICSID mechanisms will be all the more efficient and effective if the conditions to their application provided by the relevant texts are better respected'.[35]

27. Needless to say, this does not mean that, in my view, ICSID Tribunals should in each and every case, and as a matter of principle, look behind the legal structure chosen by the parties with a view to discovering some hidden

---

32 See, e.g., *Holiday Inns v Morocco*, in P Lalive, 'The First World Bank Arbitration (*Holiday Inns v Morocco*) – Some Legal Problems', *British Year Book of International Law* (1980), 151; *Amco v Indonesia*, 1 ICSID Reports, pp 400 ff.

33 *Banro American Resources, Inc and Société Aurifère du Kivu et du Maniema, SARL v Democratic Republic of the Congo* (2000), Excerpts in *Foreign Investment Law Journal*, vol 17 (2002), No. 2, pp 380 ff., at p 385, para 11 and p 391, para 24. (Because of lack of consent of the parties only excerpts of the Award have been published: see p 381.)

34 Schreuer, (n 26), p 178, para 216.

35 *Banro*, (n 33), p 391, para 25.

'reality'. This does not mean that, in my view, ICSID Tribunals should in each and every case, and as a matter of principle, set out to identify the 'real' investor in a situation involving multiple players. This does not mean that I would be inclined to ignore or put into question the flexible approach adopted in previous ICSID cases – in particular the *Holiday Inns v Morocco* and *Fedax v Venezuela* cases – to the overall issue of the extent and limits of the jurisdiction of ICSID Tribunals under Article 25 of the ICSID Convention, and more particularly to the key concepts of 'investment' or 'dispute arising directly out of an investment'. No more is at issue in the instant case [than] the sometimes difficult identification of the corporation within a group of corporations which has specifically to be taken into account for the purposes of determining the jurisdiction of ICSID. The situation in the instant case is crystal clear and in effect undisputed: it is a situation where there is simply no question of any foreign – whether Lithuanian or other – investment in Ukraine, and where there is a question only, and indisputably, of an Ukrainian investment in Ukraine. And to such a situation the ICSID Convention and the ICSID procedures are not meant to apply.

28. Paragraph 82 the Decision states that:

> Ukraine, Lithuania and other Contracting Parties chose their methods of defining corporate nationality and the scope of covered investment in BITs with confidence that ICSID arbitrators would give effect to those definitions. That confidence is premised on the ICSID Convention itself, which leaves to the reasonable discretion of the parties the task of defining key terms. We would be loathe to undermine it.

While it may be for private parties within the framework of a private, purely commercial, contractual relationship 'to chose their methods of defining corporate nationality', this does not hold true to the same extent when the application of the ICSID Convention is involved. The restrictions imposed on, and the rights accorded to, the parties by the Convention are based on the nationality of the party other than the 'Contracting State', and it cannot be assumed that the parties are free to dispose at will of these restrictions and rights by playing with the definition of corporate nationality. In particular, Article 26 provides that, unless otherwise stated, consent of the parties to arbitration under the Convention is exclusive of any other remedy, and Article 27 prohibits a Contracting State from giving diplomatic protection, or bringing an international claim, in respect of a dispute which one of its nationals and another Contracting State have consented to submit, or have submitted, to arbitration under the Convention, unless the State party to the dispute fails to honour the award rendered in that dispute.[36] Chapter II of the Convention

---

36 See *Report of the Executive Directors*, paras 32–33.

('Jurisdiction of the Centre'), which, in the words of the *Report of the Executive Directors*, defines 'the limits within which the provisions of the Convention will apply and the facilities of the Centre will be available',[37] is the cornerstone of the system. Even assuming that the definition of these 'limits' – in particular, the definition of the key term 'national of another Contracting Party' – is left to the discretion of the parties, this, as the Decision recognises, holds true only in so far as this discretion is 'reasonable'.[38] There can be no question of leaving unconditionally to the parties the task of determining the scope of application of the Convention along with the rights and duties it places upon both parties. This would frustrate the system by putting its extent in the hands of the parties and at their discretion, thus making the provisions of its Chapter II, and more particularly of its central and crucial Article 25, a purely optional clause. This, in my view, is unacceptable. This, however, is what the Decision does.

29. As mentioned above, the provisions of the BIT have to be applied and interpreted within the limits of the Convention. The BIT cannot bestow jurisdiction on an ICSID Tribunal beyond the jurisdiction bestowed on it by the ICSID Convention. As a consequence, once the conclusion is reached – as in my view it should have been – that the Tribunal has no jurisdiction under Article 25(2)(b) of the Convention, the question whether Article 1(2) of the BIT is to be read as giving it jurisdiction becomes moot. I can, therefore, dispense with discussing paragraphs 27 to 41 of the Decision.

30. To sum up: The ICSID mechanism and remedy are not meant for, and are not to be construed as, allowing – and even less encouraging – nationals of a State party to the ICSID Convention to use a foreign corporation, whether preexistent or created for that purpose, as a means of evading the jurisdiction of their domestic courts and the application of their national law. It is meant to protect – and thus encourage – *international* investment. It is regrettable, so it seems to me, to put the extraordinary success met by ICSID at risk by extending its scope and application beyond the limits so carefully assigned to it by the Convention. This might dissuade Governments either from adher-

---

37 Ibid., para. 22.
38 Decision, paras 24, 25, 26, 82. – Cf. *Autopista Concesionada de Venezuela, CA v Bolivarian Republic of Venezuela*, Decision on Jurisdiction, Case No. ARB/00/5 (Sept. 27, 2001), 16 ICSID Review-FILJ 465 (2001), at para 99:

> [T]o determine whether these objective requirements are met in a given case, one needs to refer to the parties' own understanding or definition. As long as the criteria chosen by the parties to define those requirements are reasonable, i.e., as long as the requirements are not deprived of their objective significance, there is no reason to discard the parties' choice.

ing to the Convention or, if they have already adhered, from providing for ICSID arbitration in their future BITs or investment contracts.

 CASE

International Centre for Settlement of Investment Disputes Washington, DC

In the proceeding between Plama Consortium Ltd (Claimant) and Republic of Bulgaria (Respondent) (ICSID Case No. ARB/03/24)

Decision on jurisdiction

[...]

Article 17 ECT

143. Article 17 ECT is contained in Part III of the ECT, the same part containing the ECT's substantive protections for investors but a different part from Part V containing the provisions for dispute settlement. Article 17 is entitled 'Non-Application of Part III in Certain Circumstances'; and taken from the ECT's English version, Article 17(1) provides:

> Each Contracting Party reserves the right to deny the advantages of this Part [i.e., Part III] to: (1) a legal entity [*Limb i*] if citizens or nationals of a third state own or control such entity and [*Limb ii*] if that entity has no substantial business activities in the Area of the Contracting Party in which it is organised. . ..

The Tribunal attaches significance to the word 'and' linking both limbs of Article 17(1), thereby requiring both to be satisfied. (For ease of reference below, the Tribunal has added in the quotation above the roman numerals in square brackets to indicate these first and second limbs). Article 17(2) ECT contains a similar provision for an 'Investment' in differently specified circumstances. (The full text of Article 17 ECT is set out in para.26 of this Decision, *supra*).

144. By letter dated 18 February 2003 to ICSID's Acting Secretary-General, the respondent exercised its right under Article 17(1) ECT to deny the advantages of Part III to the claimant, purportedly including the right to refer its claim to arbitration under Article 26 ECT, as follows:

> The application of ECT shall be denied to the claimant since Plama Holding Limited [sic] has not provided any evidence that the ultimate owners of its

shares are nationals or citizens of a Contracting State to ECT and that it has any substantial business activities in the Area of the Contracting Party in which it is organised, namely Cyprus. (Exhibit C36).

In a further letter dated 4 March 2003 to the Acting Secretary-General of ICSID, the respondent clarified its position:

> ... the clear and unambiguous wording of Article 17 of the ECT leaves no doubt that each [Contracting Party] has reserved this right with the conclusion of the ECT and that no prior or subsequent reservation is needed for its exercise ...
>
> Consequently, Article 17 of the ECT confers on each [Contracting Party] a direct and unconditional right of denial which may be exercised at any time and in any manner. (Exhibit C37).

145. It will be noted, as was emphasised by the claimant in its submissions, that the language here first used by the respondent apparently assumed (i) the need to 'exercise' the right of denial and (ii) that its effect was prospective from the right's exercise ('shall be denied'), using the future tense to deny advantages to the claimant as if for the future only. In that event the claimant submitted that, even if Article 17(1) applied in the present case, given that the claimant had already submitted its Request for Arbitration earlier on 24 December 2002, it could not deprive this Tribunal of any jurisdiction or even operate as a defence on the merits to any claims pleaded by the claimant arising from still earlier events. It is necessary for the Tribunal to consider Bulgaria's submissions on Article 17(1) separately as regards jurisdiction and merits.

Article 17 as a jurisdictional issue

146. The first question is whether any issue raised under Article 17(1) by Bulgaria can deprive this Tribunal of all jurisdiction to decide the merits of the parties' dispute. As already described in Section III of this Decision (*supra*), the claimant submits that the respondent's reliance on Article 17(1) can only relate to the merits and not to jurisdiction, whereas Bulgaria primarily contends the opposite. The respondent contends that there can be no dispute over its obligations under Part III of the ECT when the claimant has no relevant 'advantages' under Part III legally capable of giving rise to any claim pleaded under Part III. The respondent contends that the denial of such 'advantages' are not limited to those conferred by Part III of the ECT but include also all advantages relating to Part III, including the right to invoke international arbitration under Article 26 of Part V of the

ECT alleging any breach of Part III. In its counsel's words at the September Hearing: *'it's the whole thing'* [D1.160]; and as the Tribunal has already noted, unlike Article 27, Article 26 is a remedy limited to an alleged breach of Part III.

147. In the Tribunal's view, the respondent's jurisdictional case here turns on the effect of Articles 17(1) and 26 ECT, interpreted under Article 31(1) of the Vienna Convention. The express terms of Article 17 refer to a denial of the advantages 'of this Part', thereby referring to the substantive advantages conferred upon an investor by Part III of the ECT. The language is unambiguous; but it is confirmed by the title to Article 17: 'Non-Application of *Part III* in Certain Circumstances' (emphasis supplied). All authentic texts in the other five languages are to the same effect. From these terms, interpreted in good faith in accordance with their ordinary contextual meaning, the denial applies only to advantages under Part III. It would therefore require a gross manipulation of the language to make it refer to Article 26 in Part V of the ECT. Nonetheless, the Tribunal has considered whether any such manipulation is permissible in the light of the ECT's object and purpose.

148. Article 26 provides a procedural remedy for a covered investor's claims; and it is not physically or juridically part of the ECT's substantive advantages enjoyed by that investor under Part III. As a matter of language, it would have been simple to exclude a class of investors completely from the scope of the ECT as a whole, as do certain other bilateral investment treaties; but that is self-evidently not the approach taken in the ECT. This limited exclusion from Part III for a covered investor, dependent on certain specific criteria, requires a procedure to resolve a dispute as to whether that exclusion applies in any particular case; and the object and purpose of the ECT, in the Tribunal's view, clearly requires Article 26 to be unaffected by the operation of Article 17(1). As already noted above, for a covered investor, Article 26 is a very important feature of the ECT.

149. In the Tribunal's view, the contrary approach would clearly not accord with the ECT's object and purpose. Unlike most modern investment treaties, Article 17(1) does not operate as a denial of all benefits to a covered investor under the Treaty but is expressly limited to a denial of the advantages of Part III of the ECT. A Contracting State can only deny these advantages if Article 17(1)'s specific criteria are satisfied; and it cannot validly exercise its right of denial otherwise. A disputed question of its valid exercise may arise, raising issues of Treaty interpretation, other legal issues and issues of fact, particularly as regards the first and second limbs of Article 17(1) ECT. It is notorious that issues as to citizenship, nationality, ownership, control and the scope and

location of business activities can raise wide-ranging, complex and highly controversial disputes, as in the present case. In the absence of Article 26 as a remedy available to the covered investor (as the respondent contends), how are such disputes to be determined between the host State and the covered investor, given that such determination is crucial to both? According to the respondent, there is no remedy available to a covered investor under the ECT at all: it has no advantages under the ECT at all; it has no rights under Article 26 to amicable negotiations or international arbitration; and any attempt to initiate arbitration before ICSID will be met with a demand by the host State that the request for arbitration should not be registered under Article 36(3) of the ICSID Convention (as the respondent contended in its letter dated 4 March 2003, cited above). Towards the covered investor, under the respondent's case, the Contracting State invoking the application of Article 17(1) is the judge in its own cause. That is a license for injustice; and it treats a covered investor as if it were not covered under the ECT at all. It is not tempered, as the respondent's counsel tentatively suggested at the September hearing, by the possibility that the Contracting State might choose, in its discretion, to extend in a friendly but wholly voluntary way any or all of the advantages of Part III during amicable negotiations with the aggrieved investor [D1.151ff].

150. This contrary approach also cannot be reconciled with Article 27 ECT on State-State arbitration. Under Article 27, a Contracting Party can refer to arbitration a dispute with the host State (as another Contracting Party) any dispute concerning the application or interpretation of the ECT, including the host State's exercise of its right of denial to a covered investor under Article 17(1) ECT. The Contracting Party's right to arbitration is unqualified by the host State's invocation of Article 17(1); and it follows that a Contracting Party could pursue a claim against the host State for its improper reliance on Article 17(1) towards a covered investor. In other words, even if (as the respondent contends), the investor cannot invoke Article 26 at all, it would leave intact its home State's right, as a Contracting State, to invoke Article 27 against the host State. It seems an unnecessarily complicated result to resolve that dispute when, on the ordinary meaning of Article 17(1), the covered investor could invoke Article 26 directly against the host State without the assistance of its home State. The Tribunal notes again that for a covered investor, Article 26 is a very important feature of the ECT; and as a remedy exercisable by an investor by itself and in its own right against the host State, it cannot be equated with Article 27. Under the ECT, the covered investor is more than an object of international law (see *supra*, para 139).

151. *Conclusion*: For these reasons, the Tribunal decides that the respond-

ent's case on Article 17(1) cannot support a complaint to the jurisdiction of the Tribunal in this case. It would ordinarily be appropriate to stop here as regards any further consideration of Article 17(1) ECT. However, for understandable reasons, both parties requested the Tribunal to decide upon the application or non-application of Article 17(1) ECT even if it did not relate to the Tribunal's jurisdiction but related to the merits of their dispute. Accordingly, the Tribunal now proceeds further to meet the parties' request.

Article 17 as an issue on the merits

152. The Tribunal addresses this part of the parties' submissions on the assumption (as decided above) that the Tribunal has jurisdiction to decide the claimant's claims against the respondent for one or more alleged breaches of Part III of the ECT. These submissions raise distinct issues of legal interpretation and related factual issues.

153. *Exercise of the right to deny*: The claimant contends first that where a Contracting State wishes to deny the advantages of Part III of the ECT to a legal entity under Article 17(1) ECT, that State must first exercise its right to deny such advantages or take equivalent positive action that it intends to do so; and further that the denial then operates only prospectively from the date of such exercise or other action. Accordingly, the legal entity enjoys in full the advantages of Part III of the ECT up to that date. In its counsel's words at the September Hearing: '... "reserves the right", this means the right exists, but it's not yet exercised, the right to deny exists, but not the denial' [D2.65]; and reference was made to Professor Wälde's expert opinion filed by the respondent in support of its Memorial on Jurisdiction to the effect that Article 17(1) provides an 'option' for the Contracting State, thereby also suggesting the need for that option to be exercised by the state (at para 62).

154. The respondent contends otherwise: first that Article 17(1) ECT requires no action by Bulgaria; and, second, whether or not it did, the denial of benefits would operate retrospectively. It contends that Article 17(1) is a so-called 'denial of benefits' provision found in many modern investment treaties; that the principal feature of such treaties is the implementation, in a pragmatic way, of the home State's right under customary international law to provide diplomatic protection to its nationals through the mechanism of claims espousal against the host State; and that under such law, the host State is not obliged to entertain a claim presented by the home State unless there is a genuine and continuous link between that State and its national from the date of the alleged injury until the award settling the inter-state claim, relying on the ICJ's decision in the *Nottebohm* Case.

155. In the Tribunal's view, the existence of a 'right' is distinct from the exercise of that right. For example, a party may have a contractual right to refer a claim to arbitration; but there can be no arbitration unless and until that right is exercised. In the same way, a Contracting Party has a right under Article 17(1) ECT to deny a covered investor the advantages under Part III; but it is not required to exercise that right; and it may never do so. The language of Article 17(1) is unambiguous; and that meaning is consistent with the different State practices of the ECT's Contracting States under different bilateral investment treaties: certain of them applying a generous approach to legal entities incorporated in a State with no significant business presence there (such as the Netherlands) and certain others applying a more restrictive approach (such as the USA). The ECT is a multilateral treaty with Article 17(1) drafted in permissive terms, not surprisingly, in order to accommodate these different State practices.

156. Moreover, if the respondent were correct, it is surprising that Article 17(1) should be drafted as it is: it would have been much easier to draft suitable wording to make the respondent's meaning plain. For example, the ASEAN Framework Agreement on Services of December 1995 provides in Article VI ('Denial of Benefits'):

> The benefits of this Framework Agreement shall be denied to a service supplier who is a natural person of a non-Member State or a juridical person owned or controlled by persons of a non-Member State constituted under the laws of a Member State, but not engaged in substantive business operations in the territory of Member States(s). (Exhibit C66).

That simple language requires no exercise or other action by a contracting State; and it leaves no room for ambiguity, even though this Treaty is of a different type from the ECT. It requires little effort to imagine other similarly effective language which could have been used for Article 17(1) ECT – but which has not there been used. In these circumstances, it would clearly not be permissible for the Tribunal to re-write Article 17(1) ECT in the respondent's favour.

157. The Tribunal has also considered whether the requirement for the right's exercise is inconsistent with the ECT's object and purpose. The exercise would necessarily be associated with publicity or other notice so as to become reasonably available to investors and their advisers. To this end, a general declaration in a Contracting State's official gazette could suffice; or a statutory provision in a Contracting State's investment or other laws; or even an exchange of letters with a particular investor or class of investors. Given

that in practice an investor must distinguish between Contracting States with different state practices, it is not unreasonable or impractical to interpret Article 17(1) as requiring that a Contracting State must exercise its right before applying it to an investor and be seen to have done so. By itself, Article 17(1) ECT is at best only half a notice; without further reasonable notice of its exercise by the host state, its terms tell the investor little; and for all practical purposes, something more is needed. The Tribunal was referred to Article 1113(2) NAFTA as an example of a term providing for the denial of benefits which provides for a form of prior notification and consultation; and whilst the wording is materially different from Article 17(1) ECT, this term does suggest that the Tribunal's interpretation is not unreasonable as a practical matter.

158. For these reasons, in the Tribunal's view, the interpretation of Article 17(1) ECT under Article 31(1) of the Vienna Convention requires the right of denial to be exercised by the Contracting State. Accordingly, the Tribunal decides in the present case that the respondent was required to exercise its right against the claimant; and that it did so only on 18 February 2003, more than four years after the claimant made its investment in Nova Plama. The real point at issue, therefore, is whether that exercise had retrospective effect to 1998 or only prospective effect from 2003, on the claimant's 'advantages' under Part III ECT.

159. *Retrospective or prospective effect*: The language of Article 17(1) ECT is not by itself clear on this important point. There is some slight guidance from Article 17(1) suggesting a prospective effect, given the use of the present tense to coincide with the right's exercise ('own or control' . . . 'has no substantial activities' . . . 'is organised'); and likewise, Article 17(2) ECT suggests only a prospective effect to a denial of advantages to an Investment (': . . if the denying Contracting Party establishes . . .' etc). However, the Tribunal would not wish to base its decision on such semantic indications only.

160. The Tribunal returns to the object and purpose of the ECT under Article 31 of the Vienna Convention. The parties did not here invoke under Article 31(3) and (4) any subsequent agreement or practice between the ECT's Contracting Parties or under Article 32 any of the ECT's preparatory work. Accordingly, as with many issues of disputed interpretation turning on a relatively few words, it is a short point of almost first impression.

161. The covered investor enjoys the advantages of Part III unless the host State exercises its right under Article 17(1) ECT; and a putative covered investor has legitimate expectations of such advantages until that right's

exercise. A putative investor therefore requires reasonable notice before making any investment in the host State whether or not that host State has exercised its right under Article 17(1) ECT. At that stage, the putative investor can so plan its business affairs to come within or without the criteria there specified, as it chooses. It can also plan not to make any investment at all or to make it elsewhere. After an investment is made in the host State, the 'hostage-factor' is introduced; the covered investor's choices are accordingly more limited; and the investor is correspondingly more vulnerable to the host State's exercise of its right under Article 17(1) ECT. At this time, therefore, the covered investor needs at least the same protection as it enjoyed as a putative investor able to plan its investment. The ECT's express 'purpose' under Article 2 ECT is the establishment of '. . . a legal framework in order to promote *long-term* co-operation in the energy field . . . in accordance with the objectives and principles of the Charter' (emphasis supplied). It is not easy to see how any retrospective effect is consistent with this 'long-term' purpose.

162. In the Tribunal's view, therefore, the object and purpose of the ECT suggest that the right's exercise should not have retrospective effect. A putative investor, properly informed and advised of the potential effect of Article 17(1), could adjust its plans accordingly prior to making its investment. If, however, the right's exercise had retrospective effect, the consequences for the investor would be serious. The investor could not plan in the 'long term' for such an effect (if at all); and indeed such an unexercised right could lure putative investors with legitimate expectations only to have those expectations made retrospectively false at a much later date. Moreover, in the present case, the respondent asserts a retrospective effect from a very late date, even after the claimant's Request for Arbitration and the accrual of the claimant's causes of action under Part III ECT.

163. The respondent has argued that by the very existence of Article 17(1) in the ECT, the investor is put on notice before it makes its investment that it could be denied ECT advantages if it falls within that Article and, therefore, if it did so fall within Article 17(1) it would have no legitimate expectations of such advantages. Such an interpretation of the ECT would deprive the investor of any certainty as to its rights and the host country's obligations when it makes its investment and must be rejected.

164. For the investor, the practical difference between prospective and retrospective effect is sharp. The former accords with the good faith interpretation of the relevant wording of Article 17(1) in the light of the ECT's object and purpose; but the latter does not. Moreover, if (contrary to the Tribunal's

decision), the effect could be retrospective, the Tribunal would have to decide whether, nevertheless, in the present case it was not so exercised, given the terms of the respondent's letter dated 18 February 2003. In the circumstances, however, it is unnecessary to decide this further question.

165. In conclusion, the Tribunal decides that the respondent's exercise of its right under Article 17(1) ECT by its letter dated 18 February 2003 only deprived the claimant of the advantages under Part III of the ECT prospectively from that date onwards. In the present case, it may well be that this particular decision will render moot, or substantially moot, any further need to consider other issues arising from the first and second limbs of Article 17(1) ECT. Nonetheless, as requested by the parties, the Tribunal has sought to address these issues here also.

Burden and standard of proof

166. The claimant asserts that the respondent bears the burden of showing that Article 17(1) applies factually to the present dispute to disqualify its claim on the merits. The respondent contends that, although it might have borne the burden initially in asserting Article 17(1), the burden subsequently shifted to the claimant to show that its ownership and control has never been held by a national of a third state, being an approach consistent with ECT Understanding No 3 (relating to Article 1(6) defining 'Investment' where there is a 'doubt' as to whether an Investor controls an Investment, directly or indirectly). Further, respondent contended that the burden shifted to the claimant when it alone could produce the relevant documentation and testimony required to resolve disputed factual issues over its own ownership and control.

167. In the Tribunal's view, as already indicated above, the burden of proof on the merits is significantly different from the burden applied to a jurisdictional issue. Further, the parties were not agreed on the standard of proof, including the drawing of adverse inferences; and the parties' submissions may disguise a further difference between the legal and evidential burdens of proof. Given these factors, the Tribunal has experienced difficulties in addressing factual issues disputed between the parties, particularly as regards Article 17(1)'s first limb. It is however convenient to begin with its second limb where no such difficulties arise.

Article 17(1)'s second limb: 'no substantial business activities'

168. Under Article 17(1)'s second limb, the factual question is whether the claimant 'has no substantial business activities in the Area of the Contracting

Party in which it is organised', i.e., Cyprus. In its Request for Arbitration, the claimant asserted that it had 'substantial business activities in Nicosia' (see para. 85). In its Rejoinder, the claimant appeared to concede that it did not conduct substantial business activities in Cyprus. In an equivocal footnote number 49 (at p 24), the claimant there stated that it was 'prepared to accept, for present purposes, that it does not conduct substantial business activities in Cyprus. The same is not true of PHL . . .' At the hearing on 21 September 2004, that concession was confirmed by the claimant's counsel without any qualification: 'We do accept that the second limb of Article 17 is satisfied; we accept that PCL [the claimant] has no substantial business activities in Cyprus, the Area of the Contracting Party in which it is organised, for the purposes of the ECT . . .' [D2.8].

169. In the Tribunal's view, the concession was rightly, if belatedly, made by the claimant. It is clear to the Tribunal that the claimant itself has never had any substantial business activities in Cyprus; and contrary to the claimant's pleading, this shortfall cannot be made good with business activities undertaken by an associated but different legal entity, Plama Holding Ltd (PHL), even where PHL owns or controls the claimant. In the Tribunal's view, the second limb of Article 17(1) is satisfied and applies to the present case.

Article 17(1)'s first limb: 'own or control'

170. Under Article 17(1)'s first limb, the question is whether the claimant is a legal entity owned or controlled 'by citizens or nationals of a third state'. A 'third state' being a non-Contracting State under the ECT, it would not include France (as a Contracting State); and if a national of France 'owned' and 'controlled' the claimant at all material times, it would follow that Article 17(1)'s first limb would not be satisfied in the present case. In the Tribunal's view, the word 'or' signifies that ownership and control are alternatives: in other words, only one need be met for the first limb to be satisfied, as the claimant rightly conceded at the September Hearing [D2.37]. Also, in the Tribunal's view, ownership includes indirect and beneficial ownership; and control includes control in fact, including an ability to exercise substantial influence over the legal entity's management, operation and the selection of members of its board of directors or any other managing body. This interpretation appeared to be common ground between the parties: see the respondent's Memorial at paragraphs 49 ff (p 17) and the claimant's submissions at the September Hearing [D2.38]. What was not remotely common ground were the relevant facts.

Mr Vautrin

171. The claimant's present case relies on Mr Jean-Christophe Vautrin as a French national controlling and owning the claimant at all material times; and accordingly the factual question under this first limb can be reformulated more simply: does the evidence submitted support the claimant's assertion that the claimant's shares were and remain beneficially owned by PHL, incorporated in Cyprus; that PHL's shares were and remain beneficially owned by EMU Investments Ltd (EMU), incorporated in the British Virgin Islands; that EMU's bearer shares were and remain beneficially owned by Mr Vautrin; and that consequently the claimant was a legal entity 'owned' by Mr Vautrin as a French national under Article 17(1) ECT and by virtue of such ownership, Mr Vautrin 'controlled' the claimant? The answer to this question is not, however, simple from the materials currently available to the Tribunal.

172. Mr Vautrin provided three written witness statements dated 25 March, 25 June and 26 August 2004; and he testified orally in French before the Tribunal on 20 September 2004, as recorded in English translation in the corrected transcript. At the outset of his oral evidence to the Tribunal, Mr Vautrin made the following declaration: (translation from the French) 'I solemnly declare upon my honour and conscience that I shall speak the truth, the whole truth and nothing but the truth' (in accordance with Rule 35(2) of the ICSID Arbitration Rules); and he also confirmed the truth of his earlier witness statements [D1.5]. At the September Hearing, he was examined by the claimant and cross-examined by the respondent and answered questions from the Tribunal. [D1.5: examination by the claimant; D1.39: cross-examination by the respondent; and D1.82: examination by the Tribunal]. Subject to Article 21(a) of the ICSID Convention, Mr Vautrin thereby took personal responsibility over his testimony.

173. Mr Vautrin testified that he was a French national and that he had never been the national of any other country [D1.6]. He testified that he was a businessman by profession and, a factor which may bear certain relevance in this case, not a lawyer [D1.6 and 49]. He testified that, in the summer of 1998, he decided to participate in his personal capacity in the purchase of Nova Plama [D1.22 and 83], that it was he who had then given instructions to his own lawyer, Mr Nordtømme, to incorporate the claimant and to act for the claimant in the negotiations for Nova Plama's purchase [D1.23 and 25.]. He unequivocally testified that he was the claimant's ultimate owner from 1998 onwards and that the claimant was run according to his instructions also from 1998 onwards [D1.38–39].

174. Mr Vautrin testified that whilst he had never sought to mislead the Bulgarian Government as to who owned or controlled the claimant in the negotiations and purchase of Nova Plama's shares in 1998, he had also not told them that he did [D1.59]. He explained that subsequently he did not wish to disclose publicly his true role out of concern for his personal safety in Bulgaria; and that he only very belatedly agreed to disclose that role in connection with these arbitration proceedings because 'it was explained to me that I had to do so; but I decided to do so as late in time as possible' [D1.67]. That time was the first session of these arbitration proceedings held in Paris on 25 March 2004, where counsel for the claimant disclosed, in the presence of Mr Vautrin (and in accordance with Mr Vautrin's first witness statement made that same day), that Mr Vautrin was the sole person ultimately owning and controlling the claimant; and further that the reference in the plural to 'ultimate owners' in paragraph 84 of the claimant's Request for Arbitration was a mistake by the claimant's previous legal representatives, which (as the record shows) included Mr Nordtømme.

175. As regards the Dolsamex/O'Neill claim to ownership of PCL's shares, Mr Vautrin unequivocally testified in his second witness statement:

> . . . I confirm that neither Mr O'Neill nor any entity owned or represented by him possess any ownership rights relating to PCL or any of the Plama group entities. No rights of any nature have been recognised to these persons by courts in Switzerland or elsewhere. Neither have these persons at any time prior to this sought to exercise any type of management control over PCL or any of the companies in the project (para 53).

176. As regards the Pledge Agreement of 13 November 2002 whereby EMU shares were apparently pledged to a lending institution as pledgee by Allspice Trading Inc and Panorama Industrial Inc (both incorporated in the Seychelles), Mr Vautrin unequivocally testified that no EMU bearer shares had in fact been transferred to these Seychelles companies for the purpose of this pledge (or at all); and in any event that he had owned and still owned the shares in these two Seychelles companies [D1.37]. Accordingly, the claimant submitted that this Pledge Agreement did not evidence any break in Mr Vautrin's continuous ownership and control of the claimant.

177. Bulgaria complains that the claimant's explanations of its ultimate ownership and control by Mr Vautrin are belated, incomplete, unreliable, incredible and even where technically correct, less than the whole truth. The respondent submits that the Tribunal should reject Mr Vautrin's testimony and decide that the claimant has failed to establish that Mr Vautrin owns

and controls the claimant within the meaning of the first limb to Article 17(1) ECT. For reasons set out below, the Tribunal does not here accept this submission; but it is appropriate to record that Mr Vautrin's evidence as to his ultimate ownership and control of the claimant is not only largely unsupported by contemporary documentation but that it is materially inconsistent with parts of that documentation and also contradicted by other statements apparently attributable to Mr Vautrin, particularly in the several legal proceedings by Mr O'Neill and Dolsamex and in the local and international press. It is also appropriate to record that the Tribunal did not hear relevant testimony at the September Hearing from other important witnesses from the claimant, especially Mr Nordtømme (although as he was tendered by the claimant to the respondent as a witness available for cross-examination).

178. In the Tribunal's view, the fact remains that Mr Vautrin testified under cross-examination before the Tribunal at the September Hearing; his own testimony remained unequivocal on the relevant issues; and on the existing materials, the Tribunal would not wish to reject his evidence as false at this stage of the proceedings. If this were a factual issue relevant only to jurisdiction, the Tribunal would therefore be minded to accept Mr Vautrin's testimony at face value under Judge Higgins' approach, notwithstanding any doubts regarding Mr Vautrin's continuous ownership of the claimant from September 1998 to the present day. As the Tribunal has already decided, however, Article 17(1)'s first limb is not a jurisdictional issue; nor is it necessary to decide this issue on the merits for the non-application of Article 17(1) retrospectively from 18 February 2003. Moreover, the Tribunal is concerned that the factual issue of the claimant's ownership may significantly overlap the 'misrepresentation' case advanced by the respondent on the merits, which cannot be decided by the Tribunal at this stage of these proceedings (as explained further below). There is a risk of the Tribunal prejudicing one or other party's position on these future issues; and for the time being, therefore, the less said here the better. If it later proves necessary for the Tribunal to decide on the merits whether Article 17(1)'s first limb was satisfied, it can always do so. For all these reasons, the Tribunal decides that it would be wrong here to decide whether or not Article 17(1)'s first limb was or was not satisfied; and the Tribunal does not do so. It reserves that decision for a later stage of the proceedings.

Summary on the Energy Charter Treaty

179. It is convenient to summarise the Tribunal's several decisions on the ECT: (A) As to the jurisdictional issues: (1) Under Article 26 ECT and the ICSID Convention, the Tribunal has jurisdiction to decide on the merits

the claimant's claims against the respondent for alleged breaches of Part III of the ECT; (2) Article 17(1) ECT has no relevance to the Tribunal's jurisdiction to determine those claims; (3) Accordingly, the Tribunal rejects the respondent's objection to the Tribunal's jurisdiction under the ECT and ICSID Convention; and (B) as to the merits of the respondent's case under Article 17(1) ECT; (4) Article 17(1) requires the Contracting State to exercise its right of denial and such exercise operates with prospective effect only, as it did in this case from the date of the respondent's exercise by letter of 18 February 2003; (5) the second limb of Article 17(1) regarding 'no substantial business activities' is satisfied to the Tribunal's satisfaction; and (6) the Tribunal declines for the time being to decide the first limb of Article 17(1) regarding the claimant's 'ownership' and 'control'.

[. . .]

11

Investment

EXERCISE 21 – SEMINAR

 DISCUSSION QUESTIONS

Problem 1

Explain what is meant by the so-called *Salini*-criteria. Do they make sense – *pros* and *cons*? Why have these criteria been used?

Problem 2

Review the *Pantechniki v Albania* award below. Discuss and explain how the Tribunal went about defining 'investment'. Did the Tribunal get it right?

Problem 3

Based on the facts set out below, present the best arguments why the activities of the claimant *should* be covered by the Energy Charter Treaty.

Problem 4

Based on the facts set out below, present the best arguments why the activities of the claimant *should not* be covered by the Energy Charter Treaty.

The claimant is a limited liability company with its legal address in Terezes iek 1, Riga LV-1012 Latvia. It has been registered for VAT in Latvia since 1998, has made residents' income tax and social security payments since 2000, has operated a multi-currency bank account in Latvia since March 6, 1998 and has rented an office in Latvia since September 2000.

The claimant asserts that it has investments in Finland, Ukraine, the United States and Latvia. The Latvian investment project, initiated on February 1 2006 relates to a real estate acquisition and development project in Riga which, however, has still not been executed.

EYUM-10 is a closed joint stock company registered in Ukraine. Its Certificate of State Registration was issued on December 9, 1994, with its major types of activities stated be 'installation of electric wiring and reinforcement', 'installation of fire and security alarm systems' and 'painting works'. It has an issued share capital of 1,519 040 UAH, divided into 303,808 shares.

EYUM-10 is the legal successor of a State entity called (in translation) Erection Division No 10 of the EYUM Group that had participated in the construction of the Zaporozhskaya AES (hereafter ZAES) nuclear power plant. EYUM-10 became a supplier of services to ZAES. EYUM-10 was reorganised as a closed joint stock company in 1994.

In late 1999 the claimant sought an investment in the nuclear energy industry in Ukraine and decided to buy shares in EYUM-10. The shareholding was dispersed amongst several hundred employees of EYUM-10. As stated in the 'Minutes No 11 of the session of the Management Board' of EYUM-10 dated August 22, 2000, by August 2000 the claimant had acquired 16 per cent of the shares in EYUM-10.

The claimant continued to purchase shares and on January 21, 2002 a share certificate for 200508 shares was issued to the claimant, with a certificate for a further 3657 shares issued on March 4, 2003. The claimant's total shareholding in March 2003 was therefore 204,165 shares or 67.2 per cent of the total share capital.

ZAES is the largest nuclear power plant in Ukraine. It is a separate division of the National Nuclear Power Generating Company 'Energoatom' (hereafter Energoatom), owned by the respondent. At the time of the claimant's purchase of shares in EYUM-10, EYUM-10 had established relationships with ZAES/Energoatom, and the claimant asserts that by that time ZAES/Energoatom was EYUM-10's largest debtor. A letter from ZAES to EYUM-10 dated February 28, 2002 refers to the financial difficulties of ZAES and the nature of its relationship with EYUM-10.

In 2002 and 2003 EYUM-10 commenced court proceedings in the Commercial Court of Zaporozhskaya Oblast in respect of amounts pursuant to 11 contracts between EYUM-10 and Energoatom/ZAES entered into in 1998, 1999 and 2000. EYUM-10 was successful in its claims, that were upheld on appeal and cassation was denied. The respondent accepts that EYUM-10 obtained judgement against ZAES for the total amount of 28,377,868.04 UAH.

EYUM-10 sought execution on the basis of its judgments. Execution was stayed because of bankruptcy proceedings against Energoatom. There were six separate bankruptcy proceedings commenced between March 2002 and December 2003.

There were numerous procedural steps, orders and appeals related to these proceedings.

CASE

Pantechniki v The Republic of Albania Excerpt from ICSID Case No. ARB/07/21

[...]

(i) A qualifying investment?

32. The claimant must demonstrate that it has made an investment in Albania in order to rely on the protections contained in the Treaty.

33. Article 1(1) of the Treaty provides:

> 1. 'Investment' means every kind of asset and in particular, though not exclusively, includes:
>
> (a) movable and immovable property and any other property rights such as mortgages, liens or pledges.
> (b) shares in and stock and debentures of a company and any other form of participation in a company.
> (c) loans, claims to money, or to any performance under contract having a financial value.
> (d) intellectual and industrial property rights, including rights with respect to copyrights, trademarks trade names, patents, technological processes, know-how, and goodwill.
> (e) rights conferred by law or under contract with a Contracting Party, including the right to search for, cultivate, extract or exploit natural resources.

34. The claimant asserts that the BIT falls within the category of treaties that define investments broadly and that its investment was manifest in:

● the supply of services and materials;
● the contribution of equipment and construction management;
● the mobilisation of the appropriate human and capital resources for the purposes of performing the Contracts; and
● the entitlement to compensation deriving from the above.

35. The claimant appears easily to qualify under the explicit terms of Article 1(1) of the Treaty. The difficulty arises under Article 25(1) of the ICSID Convention:

> The jurisdiction of the Centre shall extend to any legal dispute arising directly out of an investment, between a Contracting State . . . and a national of another Contracting State, which the parties to the dispute consent in writing to submit to the Centre.

36. What does 'an investment' mean here? Other ICSID Tribunals have hesitated. A number of Tribunals have struggled with what has become known as the '*Salini* Test' (by reference to the award in *Salini v Morocco*). This appears to be a misnomer. It is not so much a test as a list of characteristics of investments. The *Salini* award identified five elements as 'typical' of investment but made clear that the absence of one could be compensated by a stronger presence of another. The resulting wide margin of appreciation is unfortunate for the reason articulated succinctly by Douglas:

> If the fundamental objective of an investment treaty is to attract foreign capital, then the concept of an investment cannot be one in search of meaning in the pleadings submitted to an investment treaty tribunal that is established years, perhaps decades, after the decision to commit capital to the host State was made.[1]

Douglas proposes a formulation ('Rule 23' in his Diceyan propositional mode) which excludes two of the *Salini* elements as unacceptably subjective: 'a certain duration' and 'contribution to the host state's development'. Recent cases and commentary suggest that Douglas's Rule 23 may well encapsulate an emerging synthesis. It reads: 'The economic materialisation of an investment requires the commitment of resources to the economy of the host state by the claimant entailing the assumption of risk in expectation of a commercial return.' My own analysis is at any rate as follows.

37. Numerous states have concluded BITs which define investments capaciously. Many of these BITs purport to give access to arbitration under the ICSID Convention. The question that has vexed a number of tribunals is whether the ICSID Convention itself contains an autonomous and more restrictive definition which closes the door irrespective of such BITs.

38. Paragraph 25 of the Report to the Executive Director of the World Bank reflects the problem:

> . . .consent alone will not suffice to bring a dispute within [ICSID] jurisdiction. In keeping with the purpose of the Convention, the jurisdiction of the Centre is further limited by reference to the nature of the dispute and the parties thereto.

---

1 *The International Law of Investment Claims* 190 (2009).

39. Does this mean that the word 'investment' as used in Article 25(1) of the Convention requires objective features that cannot be varied by agreement? Textually the answer need not be affirmative. Article 25(1) defines two other types of limitations which suffice to show that 'consent alone will not suffice'. The first is that the dispute must be *legal*. The second is that it must involve a Contracting State and a national of another Contracting State. Both of these limitations are conscious institutional boundaries established by the founders of ICSID. It stands to reason that these constitutive limitations cannot be ignored by those who would intrude into a system not designed for them or for their problems.

40. This observation satisfies the notion that 'consent alone will not suffice'. There appears to be no explicit requirement that the absence of an investment (in some meaning specifically developed for the purposes of the ICSID Convention) should also defeat purported consent.

41. Indeed in the context of BITs the notion of an autonomous investment requirement would be of a different nature than the 'legal dispute' and 'Contracting States' requirement. It would deny Contracting States the right to refer legal disputes to ICSID if they have defined investments too broadly. One may wonder about the purpose of such a denial. If the words of the Convention nevertheless said so that would of course be decisive. But there is no such express limitation. The drafters of the Convention decided not to define 'investments'. Does this mean that the matter is left to the determination of States?

42. For ICSID Arbitral Tribunals to reject an express definition desired by two States party to a treaty seems a step not to be taken without the certainty that the Convention compels it.

43. It comes down to this: does the word 'investment' in Article 25(1) carry some inherent meaning which is so clear that it must be deemed to invalidate more extensive definitions of the word 'investment' in other treaties? *Salini* made a respectable attempt to describe the characteristics of investments. Yet broadly acceptable descriptions cannot be elevated to jurisdictional requirements unless that is their explicit function. They may introduce elements of subjective judgment on the part of Arbitral Tribunals (such as 'sufficient' duration or magnitude or contribution to economic development) which (a) transform arbitrators into policy makers and above all (b) increase unpredictability about the availability of ICSID to settle given disputes.

44. It may be objected that some types of economic transactions simply cannot be called 'investments' no matter what a BIT may say; one cannot

deem a person to be ten feet tall. The typical example given is that of a 'pure' sales contract. There is force in the argument. Yet it may quickly lose traction in the reality of economic life. It is admittedly hard to accept that the free-on-board sale of a single tractor in country A could be considered an 'investment' in country B. But what if there are many tractors and payments are substantially deferred to allow cash-poor buyers time to generate income? Or what if the first tractor is a prototype developed at great expense for the specificities of country B on the evident premise of amortisation? Why should States not be allowed to consider such transactions as investments to be encouraged by the promise of access to ICSID?

45. The monetary magnitude of investments cannot be accepted as a general restriction. It was considered but rejected in the course of preparing the ICSID Convention. Any State might of course adopt a policy of never giving its consent to ICSID arbitration with respect to investments below a certain magnitude. (The expense of ICSID arbitration at any rate constitutes an important practical obstacle to small claims; there need be no fear of crashing floodgates.) But other States may precisely want to benefit from the aggregate investment flows of attracting the small- to middle-sized businesses which have contributed so notably to the development of economies such as those of Germany and Italy. This is *their* policy choice; not that of ICSID arbitrators.

46. In the end the best outcome might be a consensus to the effect that the word 'investment' has an inherent common meaning. This would avoid unintended conflicts among treaties. Such an inconsistency would be striking in the case of BITs which give the investor a choice between arbitrations under the ICSID Convention and other rules. A special paradox could arise under treaties which allow UNCITRAL arbitration only until the States party become members of ICSID. That would mean that investors' protection may suddenly narrow as a result of an uncertain future event. This is not a fanciful hypothesis; the Treaty in this very case envisages such an abandonment of the UNCITRAL option once the States-party have acceded to the ICSID Convention.

47. Douglas's Rule 23 proposes an inherent common meaning. It would perhaps lead to useful and proper distinctions. An example might be the contrast between residences and rental properties. But it is not my task to make general pronouncements about an emerging synthesis intended to resolve all controversies. My only duty is to determine whether in this case there was an investment that satisfied both the Treaty and the ICSID Convention.

48. To conclude: it is conceivable that a particular transaction is so simple and instantaneous that it cannot possibly be called an 'investment' without doing violence to the word. It is not my role to construct a line of demarcation with the presumption that it would be appropriate for all cases. But I have no hesitation in rejecting this jurisdictional objection in the present case. Albania does not come close to being able to deny the presence of an investment. Albania cannot and does not dispute that the claimant committed resources and equipment to carry out the works under the Contracts. Its own officials have accepted that materiel committed to infrastructural development was brought by the claimant to Albania and lost there.

49. The claimant's project manager (Ms Pinelopi Dourou) testified vividly about the shortage of materiel and skilled personnel in Albania at the time. She said that everything from cement to guardrails had to be imported from Greece. She easily countered Albania's attempt to minimise the claimant's work as mere repairs rather than true construction by describing the work required to rehabilitate roads built during the Italian presence in Albania in the 1940s. There is no need to use one's imagination to list the possible risks associated with the contracts; one need only consider what actually happened. The contracts envisaged aggregate remuneration to the claimant of some US$7 million. The expectation of a commercial return is self-evident. The objection is unsustainable.

12

State responsibility and attribution

EXERCISE 22 – SEMINAR

 DISCUSSION QUESTIONS

Problem 1
Review and analyse the *Lauder v Czech Republic* award below. Explain how the Tribunal dealt with the attribution issues. Present arguments why decision of the Tribunal should have been different.

Problem 2
Review and analyse the *CME v Czech Republic* award. Explain how the Tribunal dealt with the attribution issues. Present arguments why the decision of the Tribunal should have been different.

Problem 3
X-Invest is a semi-official, *sui generis*, organisation with the task of promoting investment, including foreign investment, in the State of Xanadu. Its activities include identifying target companies in priority sectors, organising and conducting seminars for potential investors, visiting representatives of potential investors, and explaining the advantages of investing in Xanadu.

Based on information given at seminars and in documentation distributed by X-Invest several foreign investors decide to make significant investments in Xanadu. It turns out, however, that once the investments have been made rules and regulations are introduced and/or changed such that the financial value of the investments is completely destroyed.

X-Invest is run by Mr Sun Tan on a part-time basis. At the same time he is the CEO of the largest hotel and resort company in Xanadu. X-Invest reports on a regular basis to the Ministry of Tourism and Industry of the State of Xanadu. The Minister is the chairman of the board of X-Invest.

Can the activities of X-Invest be attributed to the State of Xanadu?

Problem 4
The government of Farawaystan is in the process of privatising the entire oil and gas sector of the country. A local investment bank – NoInkomBank – has been entrusted with the task of implementing the privatisation program decided by the government. The board of the bank must, based on the law of Farawaystan, be confirmed by the President of the country. The Chairman of the board is the Minister of Finance.

In implementing the privatisation programme NoInkomBank exercises the State's rights as shareholder in corporatised State enterprises, it sells shares held by the government and acts also in other respects as a shareholder based on the Joint Stock companies act of Farawaystan.

Can NoInkomBank's activities be attributed to Farawaystan?

 CASE

Lauder v Czech Republic, excerpt from UNCITRAL arbitration

5.5.2 The prohibition against arbitrary and discriminatory measures

[. . .]

5.5.2.2 *The media council's 1996 and 1998 reports, and Messrs Štipánek 's and Josefík's statements*

244. The Arbitral Tribunal holds that the claimant's allegations of discriminatory and arbitrary measures with respect to the media council statements in its 1996 and 1998 reports that the target of its efforts was CNTS; to Mr Štipánek 's statements that CNTS was promoting flight of Czech capital abroad; and to Mr Josefík admission that it did not even occur to him to consider the interest of foreign investor after Mr Železný's request of 2 March 1999, are clearly unfounded for similar reasons. Therefore, the Arbitral Tribunal will examine these three allegations together.

245. First, the media council alleged statement in its 1996 and 1998 reports that its target effort was CNTS does not constitute a 'measure' under the Treaty. Such a statement did indeed not have any direct effect on the claimant's investment, and it is not alleged that it had such an effect. In the light most favourable to the claimant, it may only have been evidence of the media council's intent to treat CNTS as a target in the context of a measure contemporaneously taken by the media council. Therefore, such a statement in itself cannot amount to an arbitrary and discriminatory measure.

246. Then, the alleged statements of Mr Štipánek that CNTS was promoting flight of Czech capital abroad does not constitute a 'measure' under the Treaty either. Furthermore, a statement by a member of the media council is not attributable as such to the media council, and to the Czech Republic. On the contrary, it must be considered as a personal opinion of said member, which may or may not reflect the media council's opinion on the subject.

Therefore, it cannot amount to an arbitrary and discriminatory measure. It apparently also did not occur to the claimant that this alleged measure would constitute a violation of the Treaty at the time the statement was made, as this allegation of a violation of the Treaty was raised for the first time in the course of the present arbitration proceedings.

247. Finally, the alleged admission by Mr Josefík that it did not even occur to him to consider the interest of foreign investor after Mr Železný's request of 2 March 1999 is also a personal statement, and, as such, does not constitute a 'measure' under the Treaty. In addition, it is not attributable to the Czech Republic. Therefore, it cannot amount to an arbitrary and discriminatory measure. Apparently it did also not occur to the claimant until the August 2, 1999 letter of CNTS and CME (Exhibit C41)!

[. . .]

5.5.4 The obligation to provide full protection and security

305. The claimant alleges that the respondent failed to provide full protection and security to his investment (i) by forcing a change in the Media Law, (ii) by initiating the administrative proceedings against CNTS in 1996, (iii) by subsequent pressures to bring about the restructuring of CNTS, (iv) by issuing the 15 March 1999 letter, (v) by refusing all CNTS's requests to halt CET 21's dismantling of all dealings with the former, and (vi) by authorising a share capital increase in CET 21 with knowledge that it would frustrate the ICC arbitral panel's interim order and would defy an express contrary request from Parliament (Reply Memorial, p 85).

306. The claimant argues that the obligation of full protection and security requires that the State take all steps necessary to protect foreign investments whatever the requirements of domestic law are and regardless of whether the threat to the investment arises from the State's own actions. The State has an obligation of vigilance under which it must take all measures necessary to ensure the full enjoyment of protection and security of the foreign investment (Memorial, p 55; Reply Memorial, p 83–5).

307. The respondent argues the obligation of full protection and security is not an absolute obligation. A State is only obliged to provide protection which is reasonable under the circumstances. Furthermore, the obligation is limited to the activities of the State itself, and does not extend to the activities of a private person or entity. There can also be no legitimate expectation that there will not be any regulatory change (Response, pp 57–9).

308. Article II(2)(a) of the Treaty provides that '[i]nvestment (. . .) shall enjoy full *protection and security*'. There is no further definition of this obligation in the Treaty. The Arbitral Tribunal is of the opinion that the Treaty obliges the parties to exercise such due diligence in the protection of foreign investment as reasonable under the circumstances. However, the Treaty does not oblige the parties to protect foreign investment against any possible loss of value caused by persons whose acts could not be attributed to the State. Such protection would indeed amount to strict liability, which cannot be imposed to a State absent any specific provision in the Treaty (Dolzer and Stevens, *Bilateral Investment Treaties*, p. 61).

309. The Arbitral Tribunal holds that none of the facts alleged by the claimant constituted a violation by the respondent of the obligation to provide full protection and security.

 CASE

CME v Czech Republic, excerpt from Partial Award

A. Background of the dispute

(1) The parties

1. The claimant CME Czech Republic BV is a corporation organised under the laws of the Netherlands. The Respondent, the Czech Republic, is a sovereign governmental entity, represented in these proceedings by its Ministry of Finance.

(2) The UNCITRAL Arbitration Proceedings

2. CME Czech Republic BV (CME) initiated these arbitration proceedings on February 22, 2000 by notice of arbitration against the Czech Republic pursuant to Article 3 of the Arbitration Rules of the United Nations Commission on International Trade Law (UNCITRAL).

(3) The Netherlands-Czech Republic Bilateral Investment Treaty

3. CME brought this arbitration as a result of alleged actions and inactions and omissions by the Czech Republic claimed to be in breach of the Agreement on Encouragement and Reciprocal Protection of Investments between the Kingdom of the Netherlands and the Czech and Slovak Federal Republic, executed on April 29, 1991 (hereinafter: 'the Treaty'). The Treaty

entered into force in the Czech and Slovak Federal Republic on October 1, 1992 and, after the Czech and Slovak Federal Republic ceased to exist on December 31, 1992, the Czech Republic succeeded to the rights and obligations of the Czech and Slovak Federal Republic under the Treaty.

(4) CME's 'investments' under the Treaty

4. CME holds a 99 per cent equity interest in Česká Nezávislá Televizní Společnost, spol. s r.o. ('ČNTS'), a Czech television services company. CME maintains that, among other things, CME's ownership interest in ČNTS and its indirect ownership of ČNTS' assets qualify as 'investments' pursuant to Article 1 (a) of the Treaty. CME and these investments, therefore, are thereby entitled to the protection and benefits of the Treaty.

(5) CME's shareholding

5. CME acquired its 99 per cent ownership interest in ČNTS in steps. It acquired 5.8 per cent shares in 1997 by purchasing the Czech holding company NOVA Consulting, which owned these shares, and by purchasing, in May 1997, 93.2 per cent from CME's affiliated company, CME Media Enterprises BV, which, in turn, in 1996 had acquired 22 per cent of the shares in ČNTS from the Česká Spořitelna a.s. (Czech Savings Bank) and 5.2 per cent from CET 21 Spol. s r.o. (CET 21).

6. Earlier, in 1994, CME Media Enterprises BV had acquired a 66 per cent shareholding in ČNTS from the Central European Development Corporation GmbH ('CEDC'), a German company under the same ultimate control as CME and CME Media Enterprises B.V. of an American corporation in turn controlled by Mr Ronald S Lauder, an American businessman with domicile in the United States of America.

7. CEDC (with a share of 66 per cent), CET 21 (with a share of 21 per cent) and the Czech Savings Bank (with a share of 22 per cent) were co-founders of ČNTS, formed as a joint venture company in 1993 with the object of providing broadcasting services to CET 21.

(6) The broadcasting licence

8. CME's investments (its ownership interest in ČNTS and its indirect owner- ship of ČNTS' assets) are related to a licence for television broadcasting granted by the Czech Media Council, empowered to issue licences by the Czech Republic's Act on the Operation of Radio and Television

Broadcasting, adopted on October 30, 1991, Act No. 468/1991 Coll. (here-inafter, the 'media law'). This licence was granted to CET 21, acting in con-junction inter alia with CEDC, for the purpose of the acquisition and use of the licence for broadcasting throughout the Czech Republic. CME's and its predecessors' investments in this joint venture, inter alia between CEDC and CET 21, are the object of the dispute between the parties.

9. In late 1992 and early 1993, CEDC, on the invitation of CET 21, which was owned by five Czech nationals and advised by Dr Vladimír Železný, a Czech national, participated in negotiations with the Czech Media Council (hereinafter: 'the council') with the goal of the issuance of the broadcasting licence to CET 21 with a participation therein, either directly or indirectly, by CEDC.

10. The council issued the licence to CET 21 on February 9, 1993 to operate the first nationwide private television station in the Czech Republic. The decision granting the licence acknowledged CEDC's 'substantial involve-ment of foreign capital necessary to begin television station activities' and the conditions attached to the licence acknowledged CEDC's partnership with the holder of the licence, CET 21.

(7) The formation of ČNTS

11. Instead of CEDC taking a direct share in CET 21 (as initially contem-plated), and instead of a license being issued jointly to CET 21 and CEDC (also so contemplated), the partners of CET 21 and Dr Železný agreed with CEDC and the media council to establish CEDC's participation in the form of a joint venture, ČNTS. The media council was of the view that such an arrangement would be more acceptable to Czech parliamentary and public opinion than one that accorded foreign capital a direct ownership or licensee interest.

(8) The ČNTS Memorandum of Association

12. The Memorandum of Association (MOA)was made part of the licence conditions, defining the co-operation between CET 21 as the licence holder and ČNTS as the operator of the broadcasting station. CET 21 contributed to ČNTS the right to use the licence 'unconditionally, unequivocally and on an exclusive basis' and obtained its 12 per cent ownership interest in ČNTS in return for this contribution in kind. Dr Železný served as the general direc-tor and chief executive of ČNTS and as a general director of CET 21. ČNTS' MOA was approved by the council on April 20, 1993 and, in February 1994,

ČNTS and CET 21 began broadcasting under the licence through their newly-created medium, the broadcasting station TV NOVA.

(9) ČNTS' broadcasting services

13. ČNTS provided all broadcasting services, including the acquisition and production of programmes and the sale of advertising time to CET 21, which acted only as the licence holder. In that capacity, CET 21 maintained liaison with the media council. It was CET 21 that appeared before the media council, not CME, though Dr Železný's dual directorships of CET 21 and ČNTS did not lend themselves to clear lines of authority.

(10) TV NOVA's success

14. TV NOVA became the Czech Republic's most popular and successful television station with an audience share of more than 50 per cent with US$109 million revenues and US$30 million net income in 1998. CME claims to have invested totally an amount of US$140 million, including the afore-mentioned share purchase transactions for the acquisition of the 99 per cent shareholding in ČNTS, by 1997. The audience share, the revenues and amount of the investment are disputed by the respondent.

(11) The change of media law

15. As of January 1, 1996, the media law was changed. According to the new media law, licence holders were entitled to request the waiver of licence conditions (and media council regulations imposed in pursuance of those conditions) related to non-programming. Most of the licence holders applied for this waiver, including CET 21, with the consequence that the media council lost its strongest tool to monitor and direct the licence holders.

(12) The amendment of the Memorandum of Association

16. As a consequence of certain interactions between the media council and CET 21, including ČNTS, the shareholders of ČNTS in 1996 agreed to change ČNTS' MOA and replaced CET 21's contribution 'Use of the Licence' by 'Use of the know-how of the licence'. The circumstances, reasons and events related to, and the commercial and legal effects deriving from this change are in dispute between the parties. In conjunction with the change of the contribution of the use of the licence, CET 21 and ČNTS entered into a service agreement. That agreement thereafter was the basis for the broadcasting services provided by ČNTS to CET 21 for operating TV NOVA.

(13) The 1999 events

17. In 1999, after communications between the media council and Dr Železný, the character and the legal impact of these communications being in dispute between the parties, CET 21 terminated the service agreement on August 5, 1999 for what it maintains was good cause.

18. The reason given for this termination was the non-delivery of the day-log by ČNTS to CET 21 on August 4, 1999 for the following day. CET 21 thereafter replaced ČNTS as service provider and operator of broadcasting services by other service providers, with the consequence that ČNTS' broadcasting services became idle and, according to CME, ČNTS' business was totally destroyed.

(14) The Prague Civil Court proceedings

19. ČNTS sued CET 21 for having terminated the service agreement without cause. The Prague District Court on May 4, 2000 judged that the termination was void, the Court of Appeal, however, confirmed the validity of the termination, and the Czech Supreme Court decision was still pending when these arbitration proceedings were closed.

(15) CME's allegations

20. CME claims that ČNTS, the most successful Czech private broadcasting station operator with annual net income of roughly US$30 million, has been commercially destroyed by the actions and omissions attributed to the media council, an organ of the Czech Republic.

21. CME claims, inter alia, that an already signed Merger and Acquisition Agreement between CME's interim parent company and the Scandinavian broadcaster and investor SBS was vitiated by these actions and omissions of the Media Council. CME accordingly suffered damage in the amount of US$500 million, which was the value allocated by that agreement and by the joint venture partners to ČNTS in 1999 before the disruption of the legal and commercial status of ČNTS as a consequence of the Media Council's actions and omissions.

22. The Czech Republic strongly disputes this contention and the purported underlying facts, maintaining that, inter alia, the loss of investment (if any) is the consequence of commercial failures and misjudgements of CME and, in any event, that CME's claim is part of a commercial dispute

between ČNTS and Dr Železný, for which the protection of the Treaty is not available.

(16) Investment dispute and breach of Treaty

23. CME contends that the dispute between the parties is a dispute 'between one Contracting Party and an investor of the other Contracting Party concerning an investment of the latter' as defined by Article 8(1) of the Treaty. As such, it is the position of CME that the dispute is subject to arbitration pursuant to Article 8(2) through 8(7) of the Treaty.

24. CME alleges that the Czech Republic has breached each of the following provisions of the Treaty:

> A. 'Each Contracting Party shall ensure fair and equitable treatment to the investments of investors of the other Contracting Party and shall not impair, by unreasonable or discriminatory measures, the operation, management, maintenance, use, enjoyment or disposal thereof by those investors' (Art. 3(1));
> B. '. . . each Contracting Party shall accord to [the investments of investors of the other Contracting Party] full security and protection which in any case shall not be less than that accorded either to investments of its own investors or to in- vestments of investors of any third State, whichever is more favourable to the investor concerned' (Art. 3(2)); and
> C. 'Neither Contracting Party shall take any measures depriving, directly or indirectly, investors of the other Contracting Party of their investments unless the following conditions are complied with:
>
> (a) the measures are taken in the public interest and under due process of law;
> (b) the measures are not discriminatory;
> (c) the measures are accompanied by provision for the payment of just compensation' (Art. 5).

Relief sought

25. In its notice of arbitration, CME 'requested the Tribunal to provide a relief necessary to restore ČNTS' exclusive rights to provide broadcasting services for TV NOVA and thereby restore to CME the economic benefit available under the arrangement initially approved by the Council' (*restitutio in integrum*). During the proceedings, CME changed the relief sought and requested the Tribunal to give the following relief to the claimant. Both parties instructed the Tribunal that, if damages are to be awarded, the Tribunal shall not decide on the quantum at this stage of the proceedings.

(1) Relief sought by CME Czech Republic BV

26. Claimant seeks an award:

1. Deciding respondent has violated the following provisions of the Treaty:

   (a) The obligation of fair and equitable treatment (Art. 3(1));
   (b) The obligation not to impair the operation, management, maintenance, use, enjoyment or disposal of investments by unreasonable or discriminatory measures (Art. 3(1));
   (c) The obligation of full security and protection (Art. 3(2)); and
   (d) The obligation to treat investments at least in conformity with the rules of international law (Art. 3(5)); and
   (e) The obligation not to deprive claimant of its investment by direct or indirect measures (Art. 5); and

2. Declaring that respondent is obliged to remedy the injury that claimant suffered as a result of respondent's violations of the Treaty by payment of the fair market value of claimant's investment in an amount to be determined at a second phase of this arbitration;
3. Declaring the respondent is liable for the costs that claimant has incurred in these proceedings to date, including the costs of legal representation and assistance.

27. Claimant confirms that it has withdrawn its request for the remedy of *restitutio in integrum*.

28. The respondent sought the following relief:

(2) Relief sought by the Czech Republic

29. The Czech Republic seeks an award that:

(1) CME's claim be dismissed as an abuse of process.
(2) And/or CME's claim be dismissed on grounds that the Czech Republic did not violate the following provisions of the Treaty as alleged (or at all):

   (a) The obligation of fair and equitable treatment of investments (Art. 3(1)).
   (b) The obligation not to impair investments by unreasonable or discriminatory measures (Art. 3(1)).
   (c) The obligation to accord full security and protection to investments (Art. 3(2)).

(d)   The obligation to treat investments in accordance with the standard of international law (Art. 3(5)).

(e)   The obligation to not deprive investors directly or indirectly of
their investments (Art. 5).

(3)   And/or CME's claim be dismissed and/or CME is not entitled to damages, on grounds that alleged injury to CME's investment was not the
direct and foreseeable result of any violation of the Treaty.

(4)   And CME pay the costs of the proceedings and reimburse the reasonable legal and other costs of the Czech Republic.

[...]

(5) Causation of damage by council's actions and omissions

575. The collapse of CME's investment was caused by the media council's
coercion against CME, in requiring in 1996 the amendment of the legal
structure as the basis of its investment and by aggravating the media council's interference with the legal relationship between CET 21 and ČNTS by
issuing an official regulator's letter which eliminated the exclusivity of the
service agreement, an exclusivity that was the cornerstone of CME's legal
protection for its investment. The destruction of CME's investment after
the termination of the service agreement on August 5, 1999 was the consequence of the media council's actions and inactions. The legal disputes,
proceedings and actions between CET 21, ČNTS and CME thereafter do
not affect the qualification of these actions and omissions as breach of the
Treaty.

576. The key question of these arbitration proceedings, whether the
council by coercion forced CME to give up its legal 'safety net' in 1996,
is to a large extent answered by the council's own interpretation of the
sequence of events. In contrast to the respondent's submission in these
arbitration proceedings (according to which CME 1996 voluntarily
agreed on the change of ČNTS' MOA and on the implementation of the
service agreement), the media council's own description of the events
is probative. In the Report of the Council for the Czech Parliament of
September 1999, the council made it abundantly clear that the council
was successfully requiring CME to change the MOA by threatening it
with administrative proceedings. In respect to the exclusivity of the use of
the licence, which was a cornerstone for the protection of the claimant's
investment in the Czech Republic, the council reported to the Parliament
as follows:

Each party has its own version of the heart of the issue based on a different interpretation of concluded agreements. CME insists on exclusivity and claims that CET 21 is obliged to broadcast exclusivity through ČNTS whereas CET 21 denies exclusivity and claims its right to conclude service agreements with any companies it pleases. As in the past, the council's position in this matter is close to the opinion that an exclusive relationship between the licence-holder and a service company is not desirable as it gives an opportunity to manipulate with the licence. However, in this dispute the council will not provide interpretation of relevant provisions of agreements concluded between the two parties of the dispute as it is not its authority from the nature of matters. The council can only state that results of past administrative proceedings, when the council made the licence-holder to remedy certain legal faults in the Memorandum of Association and to adhere to laws, are currently showing in this matter.

577. This is a very modest description of the regulator's pressure put on CME/ČNTS in order to change the legal basis for the co-operation between CET 21 and ČNTS, now describing this as 'the remedy of certain legal fault' in the MOA which, in 1993, the council (at that time composed of other council members) had jointly developed and implemented in order to attract the investment and support of the foreign investor CEDC.

578. Also, the oral report of the chairman of the council, Mr Josefík, at the meeting of the Standing Committee for Mass Media of the Parliament of September 30, 1999, as reported by the minutes of the meeting, explained the background for the council's reversal of its legal position in respect to the 1993 split structure, taking the ex-post-view that the 1993 structure was the illegal transfer of the licence to ČNTS:

The arrangement between the service organisation and the operator was quite unclear from the very beginning, and the Council was criticised for insufficient control of whether, for example, the licence was being transferred from the licensed entity to the ČNTS company. In May 1994 the Council was recalled precisely because, in the opinion of the House of Representatives, it had accepted a situation in which the provisions of the Act on Broadcasting were constantly violated in the case of the operation of nationwide broadcasting by a subject that was not authorised to perform such activity. Therefore it tolerated the illegal transfer of the licence to ČNTS.

Then came a period in which the Council, in its new composition, made a very intensive effort to achieve clear relationships between the service organisation and the operating company which would be in compliance with the Act on Broadcasting. After an unsuccessful attempt to delete an activity entered in the Commercial Register for the ČNTS company, the council initiated an administrative proceeding concerning violation of the Act on Broadcasting by this company's unauthorised broadcasting . . . [in the following Mr Josefík dealt with the new Media Law of 1996. . . . however, it then proceeded with administrative proceedings concerning unauthorised broadcasting and terminated them only when the operator, CET 21, proved that the broadcasts were in compliance with the law. These changes were also reflected in the Memorandum of Association and the modification of relationships between CET and ČNTS.

579. The respondent's position in these arbitration proceedings, according to which the original 1993 split structure did not violate the media law, that (only) its implementation was unlawful and (further) that, in 1996, CME/ČNTS voluntarily agreed to change the MOA is unsustainable, in the light of the media council's and its chairman's own reports to the Parliament. The media council required CME to give up its legal protection for its investment and aggravated its so doing by interfering in conjunction with Dr Železný into the contractual relationship between CET 21 and ČNTS in 1999. These acts caused the complete destruction of CME's investment in the Czech Republic, ČNTS holding now idle assets without a business operation after Dr Železný and his company CET 21 established new service providers for TV NOVA.

580. The respondent further argued that no harm would have come to CME's investment without the actions of Dr Železný; hence, the media council and the Czech State are absolved of responsibility for the fate of CME's investment. This argument fails under the accepted standards of international law. As the United Nations International Law Commission in its Commentary on State responsibility recognises, a State may be held responsible for injury to an alien investor where it is not the sole cause of the injury; the State is not absolved because of the participation of other tortfeasors in the infliction of the injury (Articles on the Responsibility of States for Internationally Wrongful Acts, adopted on second reading by the United Nations International Law Commission, 9 August 2001, Article 31, 'Reparation', Commentary, paras 9–10, 12–13).

581. This approach is consistent with the way in which the liability of joint tortfeasors is generally dealt with in international law and State practice:

> It is the very general rule that if a tortfeasor's behaviour is held to be a cause of the victim's harm, the tortfeasor is liable to pay for all of the harm so caused, notwithstanding that there was a concurrent cause of that harm and that another is responsible for that cause . . ..In other words, the liability of a tortfeasor is not affected vis-à-vis the victim by the consideration that another is concurrently liable

(J.A. Weir, 'Complex Liabilities', in A Tunc (ed.), *International Encyclopedia of Comparative Law* (Tubingen, Mohr, 1983), vol XI p 41).

582. The media council's actions in 1996 interfered with CME's investment by depriving ČNTS's broadcasting operations of their exclusive use of the broadcasting licence, which was contributed by CET 21 to ČNTS as a corporate contribution. This interference with ČNTS' business and the media council's actions and omissions in 1999 must be characterised similar to actions in tort. The Tribunal therefore is of the view that the above described principles apply in this case. CME as aggrieved claimant may sue the respondent in this arbitration and it may sue Dr Železný in separate proceedings, if judicial protection is available under Czech or other national laws. In this arbitration the claimant's claim is not reduced by the claimant's and/or ČNTS's possible claims to be pursued against Dr Železný in other courts or arbitration proceedings, although the claimant may collect from the respondent and any other potential tortfeasor only the full amount of its damage. This question is not dealt with in this partial award, it could be decided when deciding on the quantum of the claimant's claim or by national courts when dealing with the enforcement of an award or judgment, which adjudicates the recovery for the same damage.

583. The UN International Law Commission observed that sometimes several factors combine to cause damage. The Commission in its Commentary referred to various cases, in which the injury was effectively caused by a combination of factors, only one of which was to be ascribed to the responsible State. International practice and the decisions of international tribunals do not support the reduction or attenuation of reparation of concurrent causes, except in cases of contributory fault. The UN International Law Commission referred in particular to the *Corfu Channel* case, according to which the United Kingdom recovered the full amount of its claim against Albania based on the latter's wrongful failure to warn of mines at the Albanian Coast, even though Albania had not itself laid the mines (see Corfu Channel, Assessment of the Amount of Compensation, *ICJ Reports* 1949, p 244 at p 350). 'Such a result should follow a fortiori in cases, where the concurrent cause is not the act of another State (which might be held separately responsible) but of private individuals', (UN International Law Commission as cited). The UN International Law Commission further stated:

It is true that cases can occur where an identifiable element of injury can properly be a/located to one of several concurrently operating causes alone. But unless some part of the injury can be shown to be severable in causal terms from that attributed to the responsible State, the latter is he/d responsible for all of the consequences, not being too remote, of its wrongful conduct.

584. Various terms are used for such allocation of injury under international law.

> The allocation of injury or loss to a wrongful act is, in principle, a legal and not only a historical or causal process. Various terms are used to describe the link which must exist between the wrongful act and the injury in order for the obligation of reparation to arise. For example, reference may be made to losses 'attributable [to the wrongful act] as a proximate cause', or to damage which is 'too indirect, remote, and uncertain to be appraised'.
>   In some cases, the criterion of 'directness' may be used, in others 'foreseeability' or 'proximity'. But other factors may also be relevant: for example, whether State organs deliberately caused the harm in question or whether the harm caused was within the ambit of the rule which was breached, having regard to the purpose of that rule (see U.N. international Law Commission with further extensive citations).

585. Pursuant to these standards, the allocation of injury or loss suffered by CME to the media council's acts and omissions is appropriate. The media council, when coercing ČNTS in 1996 to amend its MOA and to implement the service agreement must have understood the foreseeable consequences of its actions, depriving CME of the legal 'safety net' for its investment in the Czech Republic. Also in 1999 the media council must have foreseen the consequences of supporting Dr Železný, in dismantling the exclusiveness of ČNTS' services for CET 21 by the council's regulatory letter of May 15, 1999, which supported Dr Železný's actions 'to harm ČNTS'.

(6) The respondent breached the Treaty

By the media council's actions and failures to act, the respondent has violated its obligations towards the claimant and its predecessors under the Treaty.

586. The respondent's violation of the Treaty relates only to the media council's actions and omissions, although the Czech Parliament had substantial influence on the media council. For example 'In May 1994, the council was recalled precisely because, in the opinion of the House of Representatives, it had accepted a situation, in which the provisions of the Act on Broadcasting were constantly violated in the case of the operation of nationwide broadcasting by a subject that was not authorised to perform such activity' (minutes of the 6th meeting of the Standing Committee for Mass Media of September 30, 1999, p 9 of the translation). Thereafter, the council 'in its new composition'

reviewed the situation and took certain steps to reverse the relationship between the service company and the operating company.

587. Further, the council was obligated to render regular reports to the Permanent Commission for the Media of the Lower House of the Parliament and further, was obligated to give special reports on certain issues such as 'the situation of the television station NOVA' as requested by the Permanent Commission in its resolution of September 30, 1999.

588. Moreover, the Czech Parliament, by implementing the new Media Law in force as of January 1, 1996, strongly affected broadcasting licences already granted by the media council, in particular by allowing the licence-holder to request the waiver of licence conditions. This amendment of the Media Law had substantial influence on the 1993 split structure as developed by the media council for CET 21/ČNTS and other broadcasters to secure the proper co-operation of the licence-holder and the service provider. By this amendment of the Media Law, the media council lost its tool to monitor and supervise this co-operation. It remained a broadcasting regulator responsible for the fulfilment of the legal requirements and duties under the Media Law, whereas the service provider, providing the broadcasting operation, as a consequence of the new Media Law, escaped the council's survey and control.

589. It transpires from the documents submitted to the Arbitral Tribunal in these proceedings that the media council clearly understood and deplored this development. However it is also clear that the Czech Parliament has the authority to organise national broadcasting in any way it feels suitable, subject to any relevant international obligations of the Czech State. The acts of the Czech Government, the Czech Parliament or its Commissions are not under scrutiny by the Arbitral Tribunal in these proceedings.

590. The Czech State acted towards the claimant and its predecessors as investors under the Treaty solely by acts of the regulator, the media council. It is not the task of the Arbitral Tribunal to judge whether these acts were in compliance with Czech law and regulations. The only task for this Tribunal is to judge whether the actions and omissions of the media council were in compliance with the Treaty. The Tribunal's considered conclusion is that the actions and failures to act of the media council as described above, affecting CME and ČNTS, were in breach of the Treaty.

13

Umbrella clauses

EXERCISE 23 – MINI MOCK ARBITRATION

Helvetia, a Swiss company, enters into a contract with the Republic of Farawaystan. Under the contract, the company undertakes to provide certain import supervision services to the government. In essence, Helvetia is to assist the Customs Bureau of Farawaystan with inspection of goods before they are shipped to Farawaystan. The contract, which allows Helvetia to perform the customs services globally, includes a jurisdiction clause with the following wording:

> The provisions of this Agreement shall be governed in all respects by and construed in accordance with the laws of the Farawaystan. All actions concerning disputes in connection with the obligations of either party to this Agreement shall be filed at the Regional Trial Courts of Farawaystan City.

After Farawaystan allegedly fails to pay its invoices, Helvetia requests ICSID arbitration pursuant to the Swiss-Farawaystani BIT and argues that the failed payments constitute a breach of the BIT's FET and expropriation clauses. Helvetia also argues a breach of another, separate BIT clause with the following wording:

'Each Contracting Party shall observe any obligation it has assumed with regard to specific investments in its territory by investors of the other Contracting Party.'

The BIT also includes an arbitration clause with, *inter alia*, the following wording:

> For the purpose of solving disputes with respect to investments between a Contracting Party and an investor of the other Contracting Party and without prejudice to Article IX of this Agreement (Disputes between Contracting Parties), consultations will take place between the parties concerned.
>   If these consultations do not result in a solution within six months from the

date of request for consultations, the investor may submit the dispute either to the national jurisdiction of the Contracting Party in whose territory the investment has been made or to international arbitration. In the latter event the investor has the choice between

(a) the International Center for the Settlement of Investment Disputes (ICSID) instituted by the Convention on the settlement of investment disputes between States and nationals of other States, opened for signature at Washington, on 18 March 1965;[...]

The ICSID Tribunal decides to bifurcate the proceedings and holds a hearing on jurisdiction.

 **GROUP**

Group 1

You are the observer group.

Group 2

You are the counsel for Farawaystan. Based on the facts above, your job is to dispute the ICSID Tribunal's jurisdiction.

Group 3

You are the ICSID Tribunal. Do you find that you have jurisdiction?

Group 4

You are the counsel for Helvetia. You have to present arguments that the ICSID Tribunal should accept jurisdiction.

14

Expropriation

Problem 1

Review and study the pages from *Methanex v USA* below. Do you agree with the award? Does it suggest that measures taken in the public interest are not subject to compensation?

Problem 2

After a long public debate, State S grants a concession for gold mining to investor I.

A BIT is applicable to the investment, with a clause that provides for compensation 'in case of an expropriation or measure with similar effect'.

The concession runs for 30 years. After two years, a new government in S revokes the concession even though I has spent $30 million on the project. The reason for the revocation of the licence is that the concession is granted for a piece of tropical forests in which rare birds are living and they are endangered by the mining activities.

Argue that S is obliged to compensate I. Consider *Methanex*.

Problem 3

Based on the facts set out above, argue that S is not obliged to compensate I. Consider *Methanex*.

Problem 4

Review the attached excerpt from the *Yukos v Russia* cases. Do you agree with the Tribunal's findings on indirect expropriation? What problems can you see with the Tribunal's reasoning?

CASE

Methanex v USA

The dispute: Methanex's claim, the US measures and the US's defences

(1) Introduction: MTBE, methanol and ethanol

1. It is here convenient to summarise briefly the essential characteristics of the claim as eventually advanced in Methanex's second amended statement of

claim of November 2002, it being recalled that Methanex's claim was originally set out in its statement of claim of December 1999 and subsequently in drafts of January and February 2001. The Tribunal also here sets out briefly the essential characteristics of the US's amended statement of defence of December 2003, pleaded in response to Methanex's second amended statement of claim.

2. MTBE: As already indicated earlier in this Award, Methanex's claim is brought in relation to the production and sale of a methanol-based source of octane and oxygenate for gasoline which is known as methyl tertiary-butyl ether or, in short, MTBE. According to Methanex, MTBE is a safe, effective and economic component of gasoline; and it is the oxygenate of choice 'in markets where free and fair trade is allowed'. It is also said to produce significant environmental and other benefits; and that it does not pose a risk to human health or the environment.

3. Methanol: Methanex does not produce or sell MTBE. It is Methanex's case that its sole business is the production, transportation and marketing of methanol; and that it is the world's largest producer and marketer of methanol, accounting for approximately 17 per cent of global capacity. It is Methanex's case that approximately one-third of its methanol production is utilised in the fuel sector, principally for use in methanol-based MTBE. According to Methanex, there are no methanol production plants located in California; and, in the period 1993–2001, only a small amount of the methanol directly consumed in California was produced anywhere in the US (an average of 20.2 thousand metric tons out of a total consumption figure of 185.5 thousand metric tons). It is Methanex's case that most of the methanol consumed in that period (72 per cent) was produced in Canada, and that Methanex was the largest supplier to the California marketplace for Methanol.

4. It is uncontested that methanol is the essential oxygenating element of MTBE. According to Methanex, methanol can also be used directly as a fuel oxygenate. This is contested by the US.

5. Ethanol: Ethanol is a source of octane and oxygenate for gasoline, generally manufactured from biomass feedstocks, such as corn. According to Methanex, ethanol is plainly an inferior product to MTBE, both environmentally and economically. It is Methanex's case that the ethanol industry in the US is almost entirely a domestic industry which exists solely as a result of US governmental protection.

6. Interchangeability: It is an important part of Methanex's case that methanol and ethanol are essentially interchangeable with one another as oxygen-

ates, as are their respective ethers MTBE and ETBE. Methanex claims that, as recognised by the US Clean Air Act Amendments 1990, both methanol and ethanol can be used directly as oxygenates. Alternatively, both can be used as a feedstock to produce a derivative ether oxygenate, MTBE and ETBE respectively. Accordingly, Methanex claims that oxygenate consumers have a binary choice between methanol and ethanol. It is Methanex's case that there are three significant groups of oxygenate consumers (i) integrated oil refineries, (ii) merchant ether-oxygenate producers and (iii) wholesale gasoline blenders; and that methanol competes with ethanol for the business of each of these three groups.

(2) The 1997 California Bill and the US 'Measures'

7. During these arbitration proceedings, Methanex has attacked four legislative texts as 'measures'; and it is convenient to list each in turn.

8. *(i) The 1997 California Bill*: In its Statement of Claim of 3 December 1999, Methanex challenged Bill 521 of the California Senate dated 9 October 1997 (the 'California Bill'; also referred to below as 'California Senate Bill 521'). Methanex subsequently withdrew this challenge; and the California Bill is not now a 'measure' impugned by Methanex in these proceedings. (. . .).

9. Nevertheless, the California Bill remains of considerable importance to an understanding of the US measures that Methanex does challenge in these proceedings. Section 2 of the California Bill provided:

> The legislature hereby finds and declares that the purpose of this act is to provide the public and the legislature with a thorough and objective evaluation of the human health and environmental risks and benefits, if any, of the use of methyl tertiary-butyl ether (MTBE), as compared to ethyl tertiarybutyl ether (ETBE), tertiary amyl methyl ether (TAME) and ethanol, in gasoline, and to ensure that the air, water quality, and soil impacts of the use of MTBE are fully mitigated.

10. Section 3(a) of the California Bill appropriated US$500,000 to the University of California to conduct this 'thorough and objective evaluation', to be applied not only to MTBE but also (inter alia) ethanol. The Bill also provided at section 3(d) that a draft of the assessment report would be submitted to the Governor of California for transmittal to the US Geological Survey and the Agency for Toxic Substances and Disease Registry at the Centres for Disease Control. There would then be a series of public hearings on the draft report and the comments of these two bodies.

11. Sections 3(e) and (f) of the California Bill provided as follows:

> (e) Within ten days from the date of the completion of the public hearings
> . . . the Governor shall issue a written certification as to the human health and
> environmental risks of using MTBE in gasoline in this state. The certification shall
> be based solely upon the assessment and the report submitted pursuant to this
> section and any testimony presented at the public hearings. The certification shall
> state either of the following conclusions:
>
> > (1)   That, on balance, there is no significant risk to human health or the
> > environment of using MTBE in gasoline in this state.
> > (2)   That, on balance, there is a significant risk to human health or the
> > environment of using MTBE in gasoline in this state.
>
> (f) If the Governor makes the certification described under paragraph (2) of
> subdivision (e), then, notwithstanding any other provision of law, the Governor
> shall take appropriate action to protect public health and the environment.

The Tribunal has supplied the underlined emphases in this legislative text, points considered later in this Award.

12. In addition, section 4(a) provided: '(a) If the sale and use of gasoline is discontinued pursuant to subdivision (f) of section 3 of this act, the state shall not thereafter adopt or implement any rule or regulation that permits or requires the use of MTBE in gasoline'.

13. Pursuant to the California Bill, the Report of the University of California (the 'UC Report') was completed on 12 November 1998. It was accompanied by the public hearings and scientific peer review required under the California Bill. According to Methanex, the UC Report is one of a series of events leading up to the measures that Methanex challenges; and it is thus on any view highly relevant to Methanex's claims in these proceedings. It is Methanex's case that the UC Report found that replacing MTBE with ethanol would not alleviate all the perceived problems with MTBE, and that it was crucial that ethanol or any other substitutes for MTBE be further evaluated before they were widely used as MTBE substitutes. The UC Report is considered further below, in Part III of this Award.

14. *(ii) The 1999 California Executive Order*: This is now the first US measure impugned by Methanex. The California Executive Order signed by the Governor of California on 25 March 1999 recorded the Governor's certification that 'on balance, there is significant risk to the environment from using MTBE in gasoline in California'. (. . .).

15. This certification was made by Governor Gray Davis pursuant to section 3(e)(2) of the California Bill. As noted by the Tribunal, Governor Davis was obliged by law to make a timely certification under the Bill, within ten days from the completion of the public hearings; and the only alternative for him under the law was either to make a certification of the significant risk to human health or that 'on balance, there is no significant risk to human health or the environment of using MTBE in gasoline' in California, under section 3(e)(1) of the California Bill. The governor had no other discretion in making the statutorily required certification. Moreover, under the California Bill and as appears from the recital to the Executive Order, the governor based his certification on the UC Report, its peer review by other agencies and experts, the public meetings and the ensuing findings and recommendations that: 'while MTBE has provided California with clean air benefits, because of leaking underground fuel storage tanks MTBE poses an environmental threat to groundwater and drinking water . . .'

16. The California Executive Order also provided (inter alia):

'4. The California Energy Commission (CEC), in consultation with the California Air Resources Board, shall develop a timetable by July 1, 1999 for the removal of MTBE from gasoline at the earliest possible date, but not later than 31 December 2002.' (. . .)
'10. The California Air Resources Board and the State Water Resources Control Board shall conduct an environmental fate and transport analysis of ethanol in air, surface water, and groundwater. The Office of Environmental Health Hazard Assessment shall prepare an analysis of the health risks of ethanol in gasoline. . .'
(. . .)
'11. The California Energy Commission (CEC) shall evaluate by December 31, 1999 and report to the Governor and the Secretary for Environmental Protection the potential for development of a California waste-based or other biomass ethanol industry. CEC shall evaluate what steps, if any, would be appropriate to foster waste-based or other biomass ethanol development in California should ethanol be found to be an acceptable substitute for MTBE'
(. . .).

17. In addition, the California Executive Order required the California Air Resources Board to develop regulations that would require that gasoline containing MTBE be labelled prominently at the pump to enable consumers to make an informed choice on the type of gasoline they wished to purchase (para 7).

18. Methanex and methanol did not appear, expressly, in the California Bill and California Executive Order.

19. *(iii) The California Regulations*: The California Phase III Reformulated Gasoline Regulations implemented the California Executive Order. They constitute the second US measure now impugned by Methanex. California Code of Regulations title 13 §§ 2273 required gasoline pumps containing MTBE to be labelled in California as follows: 'Contains MTBE. The State of California has determined that use of this chemical presents a significant risk to the environment.' In particular, §§ 2262.6 provided at sub-section (a)(1) that: 'Starting December 31, 2002, no person shall sell, offer for sale, supply or offer for supply California gasoline which has been produced with the use of methyl tertiary-butyl ether (MTBE).'

20. Methanex alleges that these California Regulations went beyond merely banning MTBE: it claims that the California Regulations provided that only ethanol could be used as an oxygenate in California gasoline. Consequently, by September 2000, the California Regulations banned both MTBE, and (implicitly) methanol from competing with ethanol in the California oxygenate market, with intended legal effect from 31 December 2002.

21. These California Regulations do not refer, expressly, to methanol or Methanex.

22. *(iv) The Amended California Regulations*: Methanex also claims, as set out in its letter dated 13 June 2004, that the California Regulations as amended with effect from 1 May 2003 ('the Amended California Regulations of May 2003') expressly banned the use of methanol as an oxygenate in California.

23. As clarified in its closing oral argument at the main hearing in June 2004, Methanex relies on the amended measure not only as evidence of California's earlier intent to harm methanol producers (including foreign methanol producers, such as Methanex) but also as a new 'measure' in its own right, albeit hitherto unpleaded as such by Methanex. Methanex sought, in so far as it was necessary, permission from the Tribunal to re-amend its claim in this respect. (The application to re-amend Methanex's Second Statement of Claim, and the Amended California Regulations of May 2003, are considered further below in Chapter II F of this Award).

(3) Methanex's allegations as to the true motives behind the US Measures

24. Methanex claims that California's stated concerns over MTBE resulted from the poor regulation of underground storage tanks for gasoline (USTs), which allowed not only MTBE but many other chemicals to escape into the environment via gasoline leaks. Nonetheless, California banned only MTBE. If, as California acknowledged, the true problem was leaking USTs, it was irrational for California to ban only one component of reformulated gasoline (MTBE) whilst allowing dangerous and potentially lethal components, such as benzene, to continue to contaminate California's groundwater. Ethanol has also been detected in California's water supply. According to Methanex, the cost of remedying the leaking USTs was far less than the projected cost of banning MTBE. The fact that California chose its irrational course of action demonstrates its intent to effectuate a discriminatory transfer of the oxygenate market from (a) methanol and MTBE producers to (b) ethanol producers.

25. In brief, Methanex alleges that the US measures came into being because California intended rank protectionism of ethanol and concomitant punishment of methanol, methanol-based MTBE, and indeed Methanex. It claims that the facts, and the inferences that can reasonably be drawn from the facts, establish that California, in enacting the US measures, intended to create a local ethanol industry where no significant industry had previously existed in California; to benefit the US ethanol industry; to accomplish these goals by banning ethanol's competition, namely methanol and MTBE; and that California was motivated to protect ethanol in part by political and financial inducements (but not bribes) provided by the US ethanol industry; and in part because of nationalistic biases, both inherent and overt, to discriminate against and thereby harm Methanex as a Canadian entity and all other foreign methanol producers.

(4) alleged breaches of Articles 1102, 1105 AND 1110 NAFTA

26. *Article 1102*: As to Article 1102 NAFTA, Methanex alleges that California and thereby the US plainly intended to deny foreign methanol producers, including Methanex, the best treatment it has accorded to domestic ethanol investors, thus violating Article 1102.

27. *Article 1105*: As to Article 1105 NAFTA, Methanex alleges that the US measures were intended to discriminate against foreign investors and their investments, and intentional discrimination is by definition unfair and inequitable.

28. *Article 1110*: As to Article 1110 NAFTA, Methanex alleges that a substantial portion of its investments, including its share of the California and larger US oxygenate market, were taken by patently discriminatory measures and handed over to the domestic ethanol industry. Methanex alleges that such a taking is at a minimum tantamount to expropriation under the plain language of Article 1110.

(5) Articles 1116 and 1117 NAFTA

29. Methanex advances its claims under Article 1116 NAFTA 'Claim by an investor of a party on its own behalf'. Methanex claims as an investor of a NAFTA Party (Canada) that another NAFTA Party (the US) has breached obligations under Section A of Chapter 11 (Arts 1102, 1105 and 1110 NAFTA), and that Methanex has suffered grave damage as a result of those breaches, both directly and through its US investments.

30. Methanex also advances its claims under Article 1117 NAFTA 'Claim by an Investor of a Party on Behalf of an Enterprise'. Methanex claims as an investor of a NAFTA Party (Canada), which indirectly owns and controls Methanex-US and Methanex-Fortier which are US enterprises, that another NAFTA Party (the US) has breached obligations under Section A of Chapter 11 (Arts 1102, 1105 and 1110 NAFTA), and that Methanex-US and Methanex-Fortier have suffered grave damage as a result of those breaches.

(6) Methanex's alleged loss and damage

31. A summary of the damages claimed by Methanex is contained at paragraphs 321–327 of the Second Amended Statement of Claim. Methanex claims (inter alia) that the US measures have deprived and will continue to deprive Methanex and Methanex-US of a substantial portion of their customer base, goodwill and market for methanol in California. Methanex claims that California has essentially taken part of the US business of Methanex and Methanex-US and handed it directly to its competitor, the US ethanol industry. It also claims that the US measures have contributed to the continued idling of the Methanex-Fortier plant, and that the measures have reduced the return to Methanex, Methanex-US and Methanex-Fortier on capital investments, increased their cost in capital and reduced the value of their investments. It claims that the immediate damage to Methanex, its investments and its shareholders is evidenced by the direct and immediate drop in Methanex's market value following the issue of the California Executive Order, and that Methanex's share price and capitalisation have never recovered from the damage inflicted by the US measures.

32. Methanex claims damages of approximately US$970 million. It also claims costs and interest. However, in its closing oral argument, and conscious of the fact that issues of quantum were not being decided at the June 2004 hearing, Methanex stated that its current damages calculation would almost certainly be different from the calculation originally made in 1999. (Whilst the precise quantum of Methanex's claim is not an issue here decided in this Award, the parties addressed the Tribunal at the main hearing on issues of causation.)

(7) The US's amended statement of defence

33. The US pursues the jurisdictional objection under Article 1101 NAFTA that was the principal decision in the Tribunal's Partial Award. The US contends that Methanex has still not shown that the US measures 'relate to' methanol producers or Methanex and that, accordingly, the Tribunal lacks jurisdiction pursuant to Article 1101 NAFTA. The US submits that methanol is not interchangeable with MTBE and does not compete with ethanol in the market for oxygenates used in gasoline and that, contrary to Methanex's claims, there is no 'binary choice' between methanol and ethanol. The US also submits that the decision to ban MTBE was firmly grounded in the administrative record and the recommendations and findings of the UC Report.

34. On the merits of Methanex's claim, the US submits that there has been no breach of Articles 1102, 1105 or 1110 NAFTA and, independently, that Methanex has failed to establish to the applicable standard of causation (being 'proximate causation') that the damages it alleges were caused by the US measures. The US also submits that Methanex has in fact suffered no quantifiable loss at all. Finally, it claims that Methanex has failed to establish ownership of Methanex-US and Methanex-Fortier; and that for this reason also Methanex's claim should be dismissed by the Tribunal, with costs. In short, Methanex has not discharged any relevant part of the legal and evidential burden required to prove its pleaded claim against the US.

35. As is apparent from the Partial Award and the Tribunal's order of 2 June 2003, it remains appropriate for the Tribunal to decide together the US's cases on jurisdiction and the merits under Article 21(4) of the UNCITRAL Rules.

[...]

(6) The Tribunal's findings on the scientific evidence

101. Having considered all the expert evidence adduced in these proceedings by both Disputing Parties, the Tribunal accepts the UC Report as reflecting a serious, objective and scientific approach to a complex problem in California. Whilst it is possible for other scientists and researchers to disagree in good faith with certain of its methodologies, analyses and conclusions, the fact of such disagreement, even if correct, does not warrant this Tribunal in treating the UC Report as part of a political sham by California. In particular, the UC Report was subjected at the time to public hearings, testimony and peer-review; and its emergence as a serious scientific work from such an open and informed debate is the best evidence that it was not the product of a political sham engineered by California, leading subsequently to the two measures impugned by Methanex in these arbitration proceedings. Moreover, in all material respects, the Tribunal is not persuaded that the UC Report was scientifically incorrect: the Tribunal was much impressed by the scientific expert witnesses presented by the US and tested under cross-examination by Methanex; and the Tribunal accepts without reservation these experts' conclusions.

102. It is convenient here to summarise the principal findings of fact which the Tribunal has made in regard to the scientific issues relating to MTBE:

(1) The California ban on the oxygenate MTBE began as a policy decision of the California Senate which, as expressed in the California Bill, was contingent on the scientific findings of the UC Report and which was to be implemented by California in the light of its public hearings, testimony and peer review;

(2) This policy was motivated by the honest belief, held in good faith and on reasonable scientific grounds, that MTBE contaminated groundwater and was difficult and expensive to clean up;

(3) There is no credible evidence that, by commissioning or producing the UC Report, the California Senate or the University of California researchers intended to favour the United States ethanol industry or particular companies within it (including ADM); and

(4) There is no credible evidence of any intention on the part of the California Senate or the University of California researchers, by commissioning or producing the UC Report, to injure methanol producers, whether US or foreign companies (including Methanex).

[...]

Part IV – Chapter C Article 1105 NAFTA

(1) Introduction

1. As noted in the previous Chapter, at the outset of the Tribunal's discussion of NAFTA Article 1102, an affirmative finding of a malign intent under NAFTA Article 1101 might satisfy the requirements of a showing of the requisite 'relation' under NAFTA Article 1105. But a failure to find a malign intent under Article 1101 might yet be repaired by an affirmative finding that an investor had not been accorded treatment in accordance with international law. Hence in fairness to Methanex, the Tribunal, as part of the joinder of jurisdictional questions and the merits, will now turn to the material adduced with respect to the claims under Article 1105 to determine whether a possible finding of a violation under Article 1105 could fulfil the requirements of Article 1101.

(2) Methanex's case regarding Article 1105 NAFTA

2. Methanex submits that the US measures were intended to discriminate against foreign investors and their investments and that intentional discrimination is, by definition, inequitable. Thus it is claimed that the US's breach of Article 1102 NAFTA establishes a breach of Article 1105 as well.

3. Methanex's pleaded claim under Article 1105 was commendably succinct. It was developed in three paragraphs in the Second Amended Statement of Claim and consisted of a single assertion: 'the California measures were intended to discriminate against foreign investors and their investments, and intentional discrimination is, by definition, unfair and inequitable'. Methanex went on to state, '[T]his is a straightforward case of raw economic protectionism. On such facts, the United States' breach of Article 1102 'establishes a breach of Article 1105 as well'. Methanex's Reply devoted only four paragraphs to its Article 1105 claim – two of which argued against the validity of the FTC's interpretation of Article 1105 and two of which restated its contention that 'intentional discrimination violates even the minimum standard of treatment required by Article 1105.

4. Both in its written and oral submissions, Methanex contended that the FTC's interpretation of 31 July 2001 is a purported amendment, as opposed to a valid interpretation, of Article 1105; and it is therefore not binding on this Tribunal under Article 1131(2) NAFTA. In oral argument, Methanex assailed the FTC's interpretation as invalid substantively because Article 1131 requires the Tribunal 'to take into account all of international law'; and

invalid procedurally because '[t]hat's too distinct and too important a dele-
tion from the Treaty to be anything other than an amendment'.

5. Accordingly, Methanex contends that the Tribunal should disregard the
interpretation on the basis that it is nothing more than an attempt by the
US retroactively to suppress a legitimate claim. Methanex relies on the legal
opinion of the late Sir Robert Jennings in support of its contentions at the
jurisdictional phase of this case:

> It would be wrong to discuss these three-Party 'interpretations' of what have
> become key words in this arbitration, without protesting the impropriety of
> the three governments making such an intervention well into the process of the
> arbitration, not only after the benefit of seeing the written pleadings of the parties
> but also virtually prompted by them.

Methanex contends that, in any event, the interpretation should have
no material impact on the proceedings as it cannot alter the substance of
NAFTA's investment protections.

6. In response, the US argued that the FTC's interpretation is binding on
this Tribunal and, by its terms, precludes the contention that a breach of
Article 1102 also breaches Article 1105 (or, as the case may be, another
article in Chapter Eleven, such as Article 1110). Even ignoring the FTC's
interpretation, the US argues, nationality-based discrimination was cabined
exclusively under Article 1102. Further, according to the US, Methanex has
not demonstrated the existence of a rule of customary international law that
prohibits a State from differentiating between nationals and aliens.

7. At the main hearing in June 2004, Methanex placed considerable weight
on the description of the general standard emerging for Article 1105(1) set
out in the award in the *Waste Management v Mexico* arbitration:

> 98. The search here is for the Article 1105 standard of review, and it is not
> necessary to consider the specific results reached in the cases discussed above. But
> as this survey shows, despite certain differences of emphasis a general standard
> for Article 1105 is emerging. Taken together, the *S D Myers*; *Mondev*, *ADF*;
> and *Loewen* cases suggest that the minimum standard of treatment of fair and
> equitable treatment is infringed by conduct attributable to the State and harmful
> to the claimant if the conduct is arbitrary, grossly unfair, unjust or idiosyncratic,
> is discriminatory and exposes the claimant to sectional or racial prejudice, or
> involves a lack of due process leading to an outcome which offends judicial
> propriety – as might be the case with a manifest failure of natural justice in judicial

proceedings or a complete lack of transparency and candour in an administrative process. In applying this standard it is relevant that the treatment is in breach of representations made by the host State which were reasonably relied on by the claimant.

99. Evidently the standard is to some extent a flexible one which must be adapted to the circumstances of each case.

8. According to Methanex, California's actions in banning MTBE and methanol and precipitously introducing ethanol were arbitrary, grossly unfair, unjust and idiosyncratic in the sense that there was a pandering to a domestic US industry, i.e., the domestic ethanol industry. These actions were discriminatory because they discriminated against foreign-owned investments such as the investments of Methanex. In addition, Methanex argues that there was a complete lack of transparency because the critical event was not the public hearings held in California, but rather the meeting between Mr Davis and ADM in Decatur, Illinois. Methanex claims that the promotion of ethanol in California was driven by the political debt that Governor Davis felt he owed to ADM in return for its political contributions, which was not in any way apparent in the administrative process. Methanex submits that, whenever a political official implicitly favours one competitor in return for political contributions and shuts another competitor out of the market, that action is arbitrary, grossly unfair, unjust, and idiosyncratic as the decision is not made on the merits.

(3) The Tribunal's decision regarding Article 1105 NAFTA

9. Article 1105 NAFTA provides:

> 1. Each Party shall accord to investments of investors of another party treatment in accordance with international law, including fair and equitable treatment and full protection and security.
>
> 2. Without prejudice to paragraph 1 and notwithstanding Article 1108(7)(b), each party shall accord to investors of another party, and to investments of investors of another party, non-discriminatory treatment with respect to measures it adopts or maintains relating to losses suffered by investments in its territory owing to armed conflict or civil strife.
>
> 3. Paragraph 2 does not apply to existing measures relating to subsidies or grants that would be inconsistent with Article 1102 but for Article 1108(7)(b).

Article 1108(7)(b), to which Article 1105(3) refers, provides: '(b) subsidies or grants provided by a Party or a state enterprise, including government supported loans, guarantees and insurance'. Article 1131(2) provides: '2. An interpretation by the Commission of a provision of this Agreement shall be binding on a Tribunal established under this Section'.

10. As recited earlier in this Award, the FTC issued on 31 July 2001 an interpretation of Article 1105(1), as follows:

> B. Minimum Standard of Treatment in Accordance with International Law
>
> 1. Article 1105(1) prescribes the customary international law minimum standard of treatment of aliens as the minimum standard of treatment to be afforded to investments of investors of another party.
> 2. The concepts of 'fair and equitable treatment' and 'full protection and security' do not require treatment in addition to or beyond that which is required by the customary international law minimum standard of treatment of aliens.
> 3. A determination that there has been a breach of another provision of the NAFTA, or of a separate international agreement, does not establish that there has been a breach of Article 1105(1).

The purport of this FTC interpretation has been discussed in a number of NAFTA arbitral awards, some of which are relevant to this case.

11. The Tribunal in *Mondev*, for example, emphasised that the application of the customary international law standard does not per se permit resort to other treaties of the NAFTA parties or, indeed, other provisions within NAFTA. The *ADF* Tribunal emphasised that recourse to customary international law 'must be disciplined by being based on State practice and judicial or arbitral case law or other sources of customary or general international law'. The *Loewen* Tribunal observed, by way of *obiter dictum*: 'Manifest injustice in the sense of a lack of due process leading to an outcome which offends a sense of judicial propriety is enough, even if one applies the [FTC] Interpretation according to its terms.'

12. Most recently, as more fully cited above from Methanex's argument, the NAFTA Tribunal in *Waste Management* attempted the difficult task of synthesising the post-interpretation jurisprudence of Article 1105, as:

> [T]he minimum standard of treatment of fair and equitable treatment is infringed by conduct attributable to the State and harmful to the claimant if the conduct is arbitrary, grossly unfair, unjust or idiosyncratic, is discriminatory and exposes the claimant to sectional or racial prejudice, or involves a lack of due process leading to an outcome which offends judicial propriety – as might be the case with a manifest

failure of natural justice in judicial proceedings or a complete lack of transparency and candour in any administrative process.

13. Methanex marshals a number of arguments, which are considered below. Ultimately, however, the Tribunal decides that Methanex's claim under Article 1105 fails for a number of reasons.

14. First, even assuming that Methanex had established discrimination under Article 1102, (which the Tribunal has found it did not) and ignoring, for the moment, the FTC's interpretation – the plain and natural meaning of the text of Article 1105 does not support the contention that the 'minimum standard of treatment' precludes governmental differentiations as between nationals and aliens. Article 1105(1) does not mention discrimination; and Article 1105(2), which does mention it, makes clear that discrimination is not included in the previous paragraph. By prohibiting discrimination between nationals and aliens with respect to measures relating to losses suffered by investments owing to armed conflict or civil strife, the second paragraph imports that the preceding paragraph did not prohibit – in all other circumstances – differentiations between nationals and aliens that might otherwise be deemed legally discriminatory: *inclusio unius est exclusio alterius*. The textual meaning is reinforced by Article 1105(3), which makes clear that the exception in paragraph 2 is, indeed, an exception.

15. Elsewhere, when the NAFTA parties wished to incorporate a norm of nondiscrimination, they did so – as one finds in Article 1110(1)(b) which requires that a lawful expropriation must, among other requirements be effected 'on a nondiscriminatory basis'. But Article 1110(1)(c) makes clear that the NAFTA parties did not intend to include discrimination in Article 1105(1). Article 1110(1)(c) establishes that another requirement for a lawful expropriation is that it be effected 'in accordance with due process of law and Article 1105(1)'. If Article 1105(1) had already included a non-discrimination requirement, there would be no need to insert that requirement in Article 1110(1)(b), for it would already have been included in the incorporation of Article 1105(1)'s due process requirement.

16. This is not an instance of textual ambiguity or lacuna which invites a tribunal even to contemplate making law. When the NAFTA parties did not incorporate a nondiscrimination requirement in a provision in which they might have done so, it would be wrong for a Tribunal to pretend that they had. Thus, even if Methanex had succeeded in establishing that it had suffered a discrimination for its claim under Article 1102, it would not be

admissible for it, as a matter of textual interpretation, to establish a claim under Article 1105.

17. This textual analysis places the FTC's interpretation in perspective. The interpretation, it will be recalled, stated in relevant part that: '3. A determination that there has been a breach of another provision of the NAFTA, or of a separate international agreement, does not establish that there has been a breach of Article 1105(1)'. In clarifying that, for purposes of the present case, a determination of 1105(1), the FTC simply confirmed the text.

18. In this respect, the rather severe words of the late Sir Robert Jennings, in his September 2001 legal opinion for Methanex – referring to the 'impropriety' of the FTC Interpretation under the circumstances of the case – lack a predicate in this case. For, as far as Methanex's textual claim under Article 1105(1) was concerned, the interpretation changed nothing. Moreover, as a factual matter, the Tribunal cannot now assume that the three NAFTA Parties had Methanex's claim specifically in mind; the US has observed that every NAFTA claimant in cases pending in 2001 has argued that the FTC interpretation was specifically targeted against it.

19. If there were rules of customary international law prohibiting differentiations by a government between foreign investors or their investments and national investors or their investments, a matter to which the Tribunal will turn in a moment, Sir Robert's opinion might be more understandable; but in oral submissions at the main hearing Methanex cited only one case, which had been delivered a month earlier and whose purport is, on examination, not helpful to its argument.

20. But even if Methanex's assertions of the existence of a customary rule were correct, the FTC interpretation would be entirely legal and binding on a Tribunal seised with a Chapter 11 case. The purport of Article 1131(2) is clear beyond peradventure (and any investor contemplating an investment in reliance on NAFTA must be deemed to be aware of it). Even assuming that the FTC interpretation was a far-reaching substantive change (which the Tribunal believes not to be so with respect to the issue relating to this case), Methanex cites no authority for its argument that far-reaching changes in a treaty must be accomplished only by formal amendment rather than by some form of agreement between all of the parties.

21. Article 39 of the Vienna Convention on the Law of Treaties says simply that '[a] treaty may be amended by agreement between the parties'. No particular mode of amendment is required and many treaties provide for their

amendment by agreement without requiring a re-ratification. Nor is a provision on the order of Article 1131 inconsistent with rules of international interpretation. Article 31(3)(a) of the Vienna Convention provides that: '3. There shall be taken into account, together with the context: (a) any subsequent agreement between the parties regarding the interpretation of the treaty or the application of its provisions.'

22. Nor is Article 1131(2) improper under general principles of law or international constitutional principles. If a legislature, having enacted a statute, feels that the courts implementing it have misconstrued the legislature's intention, it is perfectly proper for the legislature to clarify its intention. In a democratic and representative system in which legislation expresses the will of the people, legislative clarification in this sort of case would appear to be obligatory. The Tribunal sees no reason why the same analysis should not apply to international law.

23. From the time of the *Alabama* award, it has been accepted that States may agree To arbitrate by specifying the principles and rules of law they wish the Tribunal to apply. This is frequently referred to as arbitration on an agreed basis. When the parties wish to arbitrate on an agreed basis, a Tribunal is then bound by law and honour to respect and give effect to the parties's selection of the rules of law to be applied.

24. Nevertheless, the Tribunal agrees with the implication of Methanex's submission with respect to the obligations of an international Tribunal – that as a matter of international constitutional law a Tribunal has an independent duty to apply imperative principles of law or *jus cogens* and not to give effect to parties' choices of law that are inconsistent with such principles. Yet even assuming that the US errs in its argument for an approach to minimum standards that does not prohibit discrimination, this is not a situation in which there is a violation of a *jus cogens* rule. Critically, the FTC interpretation does not exclude non-discrimination from NAFTA Chapter 11, an initiative which would, arguably, violate a *jus cogens* and thus be void under Article 53 of the Vienna Convention on the Law of Treaties. All the FTC's interpretation of Article 1105 does, in this regard, is to confine claims based on alleged discrimination to Article 1102, which offers full play for a principle of non-discrimination.

25. As to the question of whether a rule of customary international law prohibits a State, in the absence of a treaty obligation, from differentiating in its treatment of nationals and aliens, international law is clear. In the absence of a contrary rule of international law binding on the States parties, whether of

conventional or customary origin, a State may differentiate in its treatment of nationals and aliens. As the previous discussion shows, no conventional rule binding on the NAFTA parties is to the contrary with respect to the issues raised in this case. Indeed, the text of NAFTA indicates that the States parties explicitly excluded a rule of non- discrimination from Article 1105.

26. Customary international law has established exceptions to this broad rule and has decided that some differentiations are discriminatory. But the International Court of Justice has held that '[t]he Party which relies on a custom of this kind must prove that this custom is established in such a manner that it has become binding on the other Party'. In his oral submissions at the main hearing, Counsel for Methanex cited only one case. That award, *Waste Management*, in the relevant part of the excerpt quoted above, states that 'the minimum standard of treatment of fair and equitable treatment is infringed by conduct attributable to the State and harmful to the claimant if the conduct is . . . discriminatory and exposes the claimant to sectional or racial prejudice. . .. The Tribunal, presumably deriving this part of its syn-thesis from *Loewen*, opined that the conduct must have been 'discriminatory and expose[d] the claimant to sectional or racial prejudice'. The Tribunal need not comment on the accuracy of the cumulative requirement in this part of the *Waste Management* synthesis, since Methanex failed, as explained in Part III of this Award, to establish that California and the California ban on MTBE was discriminatory or in any way exposed it to 'sectional or racial prejudice'. Methanex offered no other authority for its assertion.

27. For all the above reasons, the Tribunal decides that Methanex's claim under Article 1105 NAFTA fails. The Tribunal also decides that Methanex's case under Article 1101 is not assisted by its arguments under Article 1105. [. . .]

 CASE

Yukos v Russia

C. Article 13 of the ECT

1. Introduction

1528. Article 13(1) of the ECT provides, in relevant part:

> Expropriation
> (1) Investments of Investors of a Contracting Party in the Area of any other Contracting Party shall not be nationalized, expropriated or subjected to a

measure or measures having effect equivalent to nationalization or expropriation (hereinafter referred to as 'Expropriation') except where such Expropriation is:

(a)   for a purpose which is in the public interest;

(b)   not discriminatory;

(c)   carried out under due process of law; and

(d)   accompanied by the payment of prompt, adequate and effective compensation.

Such compensation shall amount to the fair market value of the Investment expropriated at the time immediately before the Expropriation or impending Expropriation became known in such a way as to affect the value of the Investment (hereinafter referred to as the 'Valuation Date'). Such fair market value shall at the request of the Investor be expressed in a Freely Convertible Currency on the basis of the market rate of exchange existing for that currency on the Valuation Date. Compensation shall also include interest at a commercial rate established on a market basis from the date of Expropriation until the date of payment.

1529. The parties analyse Article 13 in two steps, first by addressing what constitutes expropriation or 'measures having effect equivalent to nationalisation or expropriation,' and then by discussing what constitutes a legal expropriation, i.e., an expropriation conducted in accordance with the four conditions set out in Article 13(1): that the expropriation be (a) in the public interest; (b) not discriminatory; (c) carried out under due process of law; and (d) accompanied by the payment of prompt, adequate and effective compensation. The Tribunal will summarise first the parties' principal arguments regarding the legal standards of Article 13 and will then review the facts of the present case in the light of these standards.

2. Applicable legal standards under Article 13 of the ECT

(a) Claimants' position

1530. Claimants note that Article 13(1) of the ECT deals with nationalisation and expropriation, as well as other equivalent measures. Claimants submit that such equivalent measures include 'covert or incidental interference with the use of property which has the effect of depriving the owner . . . of the use or reasonably-to-be- expected economic benefit of property even if not necessarily to the obvious benefit of the host State'.

1531. Claimants submit that the standard for expropriation is objective and that while the showing of intent to expropriate may evidence a measure to be expropriatory, it is not a requirement of expropriation.

1532. Claimants emphasise that, in considering whether respondent expropriated claimants' investment within the meaning of Article 13(1), the Tribunal should look at the totality of respondent's actions and not at each fact in isolation. The question is not, claimants submit, whether each of respondent's individual actions was lawful under Russian law, or was no different than the practice in other jurisdictions, but whether the totality of respondent's conduct was lawful under international law.

1533. Claimants argue that, contrary to respondent's assertion, the standard for expropriation is not limited to the investor's legitimate expectations. Respondent's reference in this regard to the treaty practice of various States is unavailing, as whether or not other treaties refer to legitimate expectations as a criterion to establish expropriation is irrelevant to the interpretation of the ECT.

1534. With regard to the requirement that expropriation be in the public interest, claimants submit that international Tribunals have emphasised that expropriation must have occurred for a 'bona fide public purpose' and not for 'purely extraneous political reasons,' 'amusement and private profit' or 'reprisal.' Claimants submit that a State's broad discretion to determine what constitutes 'public interest' is not unfettered.

1535. Claimants challenge respondent's assertion that States should be afforded a particularly wide margin of discretion when seeking to collect taxes. According to claimants, a State alleging that it has legitimately exercised its powers of taxation is not impervious to scrutiny under international law; 'taxation, like the exercise of any other sovereign power, can be expropriatory'.

1536. With regard to non-discrimination, claimants assert that it is defined as the singling out of a person or group of people without a reasonable basis. Thus, claimants submit, a finding of 'unjustified differential treatment, whether in law or in fact,' has been regarded as discriminatory. Claimants quote a commentary that the 'expropriation of an investment because of animosity between the host-state officials and the investor or in retaliation for lawful, but politically unpopular, conduct of the investment would violate the nondiscrimination condition'. Claimants add that, as in the case of Article 10(1) of the ECT, discrimination under Article 13(1) refers not only to nationality-based discrimination, but to other types of unjustified discriminatory treatment as well.

1537. Claimants also maintain that, by stating that an expropriation must be 'carried out under due process of law,' the ECT, unlike some other investment treaties, requires that expropriations conform not only to local, but also international standards of due process. Claimants argue that due process 'contains both substantive and procedural elements'; implies that 'whenever a State seizes property, the measures taken must be free from arbitrariness' and that the 'administrative or judicial machinery used or available must correspond at least to the minimum standard required by international law;' and requires that the investor must be given 'reasonable advance notice, a fair hearing and an unbiased adjudicator to assess the actions in dispute'.

1538. Finally, claimants submit that the taking of property without compensation engages the international responsibility of States, regardless of the purpose of the taking.

(b) Respondent's position

1539. Respondent submits that the standard for expropriation under Article 13 of the ECT must not be conflated with the standard for fair and equitable treatment under Article 10(1), as otherwise the taxation carve-out of Article 21, pursuant to which a tribunal may lack jurisdiction over fair and equitable treatment claims, while retaining jurisdiction over claims of expropriation, would be rendered meaningless.

1540. Respondent also contends that the absence of one or more of the four requirements of Article 13(1) (i.e., public purpose, non-discrimination, due process and compensation) 'is not in itself indicative of expropriation'.

1541. Respondent submits that, to show expropriation or equivalent measures under Article 13(1), claimants must (in addition to showing that the challenged actions are attributable to respondent and constitute an exercise of *puissance publique*), demonstrate firstly that the challenged measures 'proximately' caused a total or substantial deprivation of their investment; and secondly that they interfered with their legitimate expectations.

1542. The importance of the causal link between the challenged measures and the investors' investment, argues respondent, has been confirmed by international Tribunals in *Otis Elevator v Iran*; *Elettronica, Link-Trading Joint Stock Company v Moldova*; and *El Paso v Argentina*. By applying the standard resulting from these precedents to the present case, respondent submits that claimants must prove that the loss of their shares was the 'only possible, unavoidable consequence of conduct attributable to respondent, conduct that is *iure imperii* and not excluded under Article 21 ECT'. Therefore, claimants cannot base a claim for expropriation on damages suffered as a result of their own conduct or the conduct of their investment.

1543. As regards investors' legitimate expectations, respondent submits that they are a 'central element of claims' under Article 13(1) of the ECT. Respondent argues that this is in accordance with the treaty practice of both ECT and non-ECT Contracting Parties, which, in turn, reflects customary international law. Respondent then submits that:

> [P]roperty rights have inherent limitations. The host State has the power to accept and define the rights acquired by an investor at the time of the making of the investment. And a foreign investor acquires rights in an investment, subject to the existing regulatory framework. So absent a specific commitment from the host State to the investor, an expropriation may occur only where the State measure does not reflect a pre-existing lawful limitation inherent in private property.

1544. Thus, argues respondent, without a specific commitment from the host State, an investor has no right or legitimate expectation to non-enforcement or exemption from taxes and associated penalties, regardless of any earlier knowledge or tolerance of the tax authorities. Moreover, legitimate expectations cannot be based on host State commitments when the investor has provided the State with incomplete and inaccurate information. Nor can legitimate expectations be premised on illegal conduct. Respondent also submits that legitimate expectations include an expectation of 'the evolution of the regulatory regime, including through interpretation or application of the law, even if without precedent, and changes through legislative amendment'.

1545. In addition, respondent submits that a distinction must be made between expropriatory measures that breach a host State's obligations under the ECT and the legitimate exercise of a State's regulatory power, including for the imposition and enforcement of taxes. Factors which distinguish one from the other include the compatibility of the measures with international and comparative standards, as well as their compatibility with national law and review by domestic courts. Applying the latter criterion, respondent submits that States cannot usually incur international responsibility through the actions of their tax authorities so long as domestic courts are available to resolve disputes between the tax authorities and taxpayers.

1546. Thus, in the present case, to establish a violation of Article 13(1) of the ECT, claimants must demonstrate that the decisions of the Russian courts that upheld the challenged taxation measures, as well as the decisions issued in the context of Yukos' bankruptcy, are themselves 'measures having effect equivalent to nationalisation or expropriation'. Accordingly, respondent says, claimants must demonstrate that these decisions were the result of a systemic failure of the Russian judicial system or, at a minimum, are manifestly improper, abusive, extraordinarily excessive or arbitrary, in manifest violation of Russian law, and in violation of international and comparative standards, so as to place them outside Russia's wide margin of discretion in taxation matters. Respondent emphasises that this Tribunal cannot sit as an appellate court reviewing the decisions of the Russian courts.

1547. Finally, respondent submits that claimants must establish a violation of the requirements in Article 13(1) of the ECT.2046. Regarding the non-discrimination requirement, respondent submits that Article 13(1) calls for proof that similar cases were, without reasonable justification, treated differently on the basis of nationality. Accordingly, claimants must allege differential treatment based on foreign ownership.

3. Did respondent's actions constitute expropriation (or 'measures having effect equivalent to nationalisation or expropriation') within the meaning of Article 13(1) of the ECT?

(a) Claimants' position

1548. According to claimants, respondent completely and totally deprived claimants of their investments in Yukos through a series of 'coordinated and mutually reinforcing actions', which were motivated by a political and economic agenda and not any legitimate tax collection purpose.

1549. Claimants submit that respondent expropriated their investments by:

(a) seizing, in October 2003, approximately 99 per cent of the shares held by Hulley and YUL in Yukos, thus preventing claimants from disposing of their shares before they lost all value;

(b) causing the unwinding of the Yukos–Sibneft merger, allowing the State-owned company Gazprom to acquire Sibneft;

(c) 'fabricat[ing] massive tax debts' against Yukos, while simultaneously freezing or seizing the company's assets and interfering with its day-to-day management through the harassment of executive officers, employees and other related persons, 'thereby engineering the circumstance of non-payment';

    (d) selling YNG in a sham auction that allowed State-owned company Rosneft to acquire Yukos' 'crown jewel' for an 'absurdly low price'; and

    (e) initiating and controlling the Yukos bankruptcy so as to obtain, either directly or through State-owned Rosneft, Yukos' main production assets, as well as almost all of the bankruptcy proceeds.

1550. Claimants submit that the liquidation of Yukos on 21 November 2007 'marked the final act in the expropriation of Yukos'.

1551. Finally, claimants argue that, even viewed individually, the harassment campaign against Yukos and its associates, the sale of YNG and the bankruptcy of Yukos each constitute an act of expropriation.

(b) Respondent's position

1552. Respondent submits that claimants have failed to establish that any of the challenged measures constitute expropriation or 'measures having effect equivalent to nationalisation or expropriation' within the meaning of Article 13(1) of the ECT.

1553. Firstly, respondent maintains that claimants have failed to establish that conduct that is attributable to respondent and an exercise of its sovereign power proximately caused claimants' total or substantial deprivation of their investment. Respondent argues that the actions that directly caused Yukos' liquidation and the ensuing loss of claimants' Yukos shares – the bankruptcy petition and the decision to liquidate Yukos – are either not attributable to respondent, or not an exercise of its sovereign power. The Moscow Arbitrazh Court's acceptance of the bankruptcy petitions and ratification of the creditors' decision to liquidate Yukos does not change this conclusion, as loss resulting from a court's enforcement of legal limitations inherent in private property is not compensable under Article 13 of the ECT, irrespective of whether the court proceedings were instituted by a State organ.

1554. According to respondent, it is therefore not responsible for the loss of claimants' investment unless 'claimants can prove that respondent is responsible for Yukos' financial situation that led to its liquidation'. Yet, argues respondent, Yukos' financial situation was actually 'the result of claimants' and their owners' decision to siphon off billions of dollars from Yukos and its subsidiaries to further their own financial interests, at the expense of Yukos' creditors and minority shareholders'.

1555. Respondent emphasises that claimants could have avoided Yukos' insolvency, which, in respondent's view, led to Yukos' bankruptcy and eventual liquidation, by paying the taxes assessed against it for years 2000–03 in the first quarter of 2004; filing amended VAT and other tax returns; and petitioning for a refund of any amounts paid that it believed not to be legally due.

1556. As for the criminal proceedings against Messrs Khodorkovsky and Lebedev and certain Yukos officials, as well as the searches, seizures and arrests carried out in support of those proceedings, respondent submits that these events did not cause Yukos' liquidation. According to respondent, the evidence establishes that these measures did not impair Yukos' operations.

1557. Respondent further contends that claimants have failed to establish that the measures they challenge interfered with claimants' legitimate expectations.

1558. With regard to the tax assessments, respondent argues that claimants had no 'legitimate expectation that the tax authorities would not apply the substance-over-form, proportionality, and bad-faith taxpayer doctrines to attribute the income nominally earned by Yukos' sham trading shells to Yukos', because respondent had never made any specific representation, based upon full disclosure, that respondent would allow Yukos to operate its tax schemes with impunity. Nor had claimants ever sought or obtained a formal tax ruling on the legality of Yukos' tax scheme. In fact, prior to the 2000 Tax Audit Report, according to respondent, Yukos sought, but was unable to obtain, a legal opinion supporting the legality of its tax scheme.

1559. In addition, respondent submits that claimants had no legitimate expectation that Yukos would not be held liable for the taxes assessed. According to respondent, the attribution for tax purposes of revenues nominally earned by sham entities to a company that sought to evade taxes was a proper application of legal doctrines that were well-settled in Russia, and are employed by many other States. Yukos itself, argues respondent, was well aware that its tax schemes, if discovered or disclosed, would result in substantial tax liabilities.

1560. Respondent also argues that the Russian legislation on which the enforcement measures (including the asset freezes, fines, default interest, enforcement fees and the forced sales of Yukos' assets) were based was already extant in the 1990s. These enforcement measures were thus foreseeable consequences of Yukos' failure to pay.

1561. Respondent then submits that the measures taken for the imposition and enforcement of taxes were well within the range of a State's generally accepted regulatory powers. This is shown by the fact that these measures were in conformity with Russian law and were upheld by national courts, and were in accordance with international and comparable standards and practices of other countries.

1562. According to respondent, claimants have failed to show that the Russian courts contributed to any 'measures having effect equivalent to nationalisation or expropriation' through any of the decisions they issued in the context of the enforcement of the tax demands, the Yukos–Sibneft demerger, the criminal proceedings against Messrs Khodorkovsky and Lebedev, or the Yukos bankruptcy proceedings.

1563. Finally, respondent submits that the ECtHR unanimously determined that the challenged tax assessments were a legitimate exercise of respondent's regulatory powers. According to respondent, given that the vast majority of the ECT Contracting States (including the Russian Federation, the United Kingdom, and Cyprus) are also ECHR Contracting States and that the ECHR enshrines the common *ordre public* of the European States in terms of democracy and the rule of law, the 'ECtHR's interpretation and application of the ECHR to the measures at issue, through a final and binding judgment, must be taken into account under Article 31(3)(c) VCLT in assessing whether they are within the bounds of generally recognised regulatory Powers'.

4. If respondent's actions constitute expropriation, has respondent met the criteria for a lawful expropriation under Article 13(1) of the ECT?

(a) Claimants' position

1564. Claimants submit that respondent did not meet any of the four requirements under Article 13(1) of the ECT for a lawful expropriation (i.e., public interest, non-discrimination, due process and adequate compensation).

1565. According to claimants, the expropriation of claimants' investment was not in the public interest. In fact, 'the facts of the case unmistakably show that the actions of the Russian Federation had nothing to do with the legitimate exercise of sovereign power, whether taxation, law enforcement or otherwise but were rather a blatant confiscation of strategic assets and the elimination of a potential political opponent'. Claimants invoke the finding of the *RosInvestCo* Tribunal that the Russian Federation's actions were 'linked to the strategic objective to return assets to the control of the Russian State and to an effort to suppress a political opponent'. According to claimants, respondent's justification that it only sought to enforce its laws is without any basis.

1566. Claimants also submit that the expropriation of their investments was discriminatory and was not carried out under due process of law. Nor was the expropriation accompanied by compensation, let alone 'prompt, adequate and effective compensation'.

1567. Claimants conclude that the Russian Federation's actions are in breach of Article 13(1) and constitute an internationally wrongful act for which respondent is responsible.

(b) Respondent's position

1568. Even if claimants could establish expropriation, which respondent contends they cannot, respondent maintains that the requirements in Article 13(1) of the ECT have not been breached.

1569. Respondent submits that no lack of public interest has been established. Respondent states that its actions were legitimate, as 'the purposes justifying imposition and enforcement of taxes, including severe penalties, fines and other sanctions in case of non-compliance of taxpayers with their obligations to pay taxes, are firmly recognized in international law'. Respondent asserts that claimants have not addressed the ECtHR's rejection of Yukos' 'political motivation' charge.

1570. Respondent also contends that claimants have failed to establish discrimination under Article 13(1)(b) of the ECT because claimants do not allege any discrimination based on foreign ownership or residence, which respondent contends is the intended scope of the term 'discriminatory' in this provision. Respondent submits that selective tax enforcement is not discriminatory within the meaning of Article 13(1)(b) of the ECT.

1571. According to respondent, Yukos 'was a visible and logical candidate for tax assessments, penalties, and enforcement actions' as its abuses of the low-tax region policy were particularly egregious and the amounts of taxes it evaded unprecedented. Other Russian oil companies, argues respondent, cannot be compared. Some companies, such as Rosneft, Tatneft and Surgutneftegaz did not resort to tax minimisation schemes involving the use of low-tax regions. While some other companies, such as Lukoil, did use such schemes, they abandoned them much earlier than Yukos. Other companies, which continued to rely on the low-tax regions programme, for example Sibneft, satisfied the 'proportionality of investments' requirement of the Russian anti-avoidance rules. Finally, tax arrears, default interest and fines were in fact assessed against some companies, including TNK-BP, Sibneft and Lukoil.

1572. Respondent also submits that claimants have failed to establish due process violations cognisable under Article 13(1)(c) of the ECT. For this assertion, respondent relies on its own articulation of the requisite legal standard, namely that 'administrative authorities cannot be faulted for conduct upheld by their own courts unless the court system is disavowed at the international level', which respondent argues is not the case here.

1573. Respondent contends that in the present case most of the due process violations raised by claimants have been reviewed by Russian courts and dismissed on the merits, while the due process arguments raised by claimants for the first time in this arbitration are 'specious'.

1574. Respondent specifically submits that the pace of the court proceedings that led to decisions upholding the Tax Ministry's tax demands against Yukos was in conformity with Russian procedural law and practice. Respondent notes that, pursuant to Article 215(1) of the Arbitrazh Procedure Code, first instance judgments in tax disputes must be rendered no later than two months after institution of the court proceedings. Respondent denies that Yukos was not provided with sufficient time to review documents during the collection proceedings pertaining to the 2000 Decision conducted by Judge Grechishkin. Respondent also argues that the removal of Judge Cheburashkina and the recusal of Judge Mikhailova were proper, as there was cause to doubt the impartiality of these two judges. Finally, respondent argues that Yukos' challenges to Judges Korotenko and Dzuba (who were charged with reviewing Yukos' challenges to the 2001 Decision and 2002 Decision, respectively) on the ground that they had previously been involved in other proceedings for the collection of taxes against Yukos, were soundly rejected, as Yukos was not able to point to any rule of Russian law that would prevent a judge from hearing similar or related cases.

D. Tribunal's decision on breach of the ECT

1575. As set out in Section X.C.2 above, the parties are in sharp disagreement about the place and content of the legitimate expectations that Yukos had or could have had in devising and implementing its tax avoidance arrangements. Claimants maintain, as Mr Dubov testified, that the most senior officials of the Russian Federation were informed of and approved Yukos' plans in respect of low-tax jurisdictions. Claimants point to the legislation of those jurisdictions which, while requiring a specified level of local investment by a trading company, for the most part did not refer to or require the presence of trading company personnel in the low-tax jurisdiction or specify that the activities of the trading company take place in that jurisdiction. Respondent stresses that virtually all the significant work of the trading companies was done not in the low-tax jurisdictions by a small number of low-level and uninformed functionaries but in and by Yukos' Moscow offices, facts that led two panels of the ECtHR to conclude that the trading companies were a 'sham'. Respondent emphasises that Yukos never secured and apparently was unable to secure a legal opinion upholding the lawfulness of its tax planning arrangements and operations.

1576. The Tribunal accepts that federal legislation and the legislation of the low-tax jurisdictions did not provide, or at any rate, uniformly provide, that the trading companies actually conduct their trading operations in the territory of the low-tax jurisdictions. Such a provision in any event would have been increasingly deprived of its force in view of the advent of electronic communications. Nevertheless there are indications in the record that Yukos itself had doubts, or at least apprehensions, about the legality of aspects of its *modus operandi*. Internal Yukos communications noted above at paragraph 491 so suggest, as may the unwillingness of Mr Khodorkovsky to sign papers required for SEC registration. Yukos was able to advance no convincing explanation for the 'Lesnoy shuffle', which may well have been carried out to frustrate investigation of perceived tax improprieties. While both PwC (Yukos' tax consultants) and Mr Pepeliaev (Yukos' tax lawyer) opined in early January 2004, after the initial tax assessment was issued, that the tax assessment against Yukos itself was not well-founded, the absence of a prior legal opinion supporting the propriety of Yukos' arrangements in the low-tax jurisdictions is striking and may be suggestive. So also is the inability of Yukos to explain immense payments to former Yukos employees and its inability to sustain the claim that certain of its primary trading companies (the BBS companies) were not controlled by it. There is also the issue of the questionable use by claimants of the Cyprus-Russia DTA, which the Tribunal addresses in Chapter X.E on contributory fault.

1577. The Tribunal has not overlooked or discounted the foregoing and other weaknesses in the contentions of claimants. But are they sufficient to support what the Tribunal understands to be a central contention of respondent, namely, that claimants should have expected that the Russian Federation would react as it did to what it claims were violations of Russian tax law and practice as its courts had interpreted that law and practice to be?

1578. In the view of the Tribunal, the expectations of claimants may have been, and certainly should have been, that Yukos' tax avoidance operations risked adverse reaction from Russian authorities. It is common ground between the parties that Yukos and its competitors viewed positions taken by the tax authorities on issues of tax liability to be exigent, erratic and unpredictable. The Tribunal however is unable to accept that the expectations of Yukos should have included the extremity of the actions which in the event were imposed upon it. Not only did Mikhail Khodorkovsky not appear to expect to be arrested even after the arrest of Platon Lebedev, he and his colleagues surely could not have been expected to anticipate the rationale and immensity of the tax assessments and fines. They could not have been expected to anticipate that their legal counsel would labour under the disabilities imposed upon them. They could not have been expected to anticipate the sale of YNG for so low a price under such questionable circumstances. They could not have been expected to anticipate that more than $13 billion in unpaid taxes and fines would be imposed on Yukos for unpaid VAT on oil exports when that oil had in fact been exported. They could not have been expected to anticipate that they risked the evisceration of their investments and the destruction of Yukos.

1579. The Tribunal has earlier concluded that 'the primary objective of the Russian Federation was not to collect taxes but rather to bankrupt Yukos and appropriate its valuable assets'. For the reasons that emerge in Part VIII, if the true objective were no more than tax collection, Yukos, its officers and employees, and its properties and facilities, would not have been treated, and mistreated, as in fact they were. Among the many incidents in this train of mistreatment that are within the remit of this Tribunal, two stand out: finding Yukos liable for the payment of more than $13 billion in VAT in respect of oil that had been exported by the trading companies and should have been free of VAT and free of fines in respect of VAT; and the auction of YNG at a price that was far less than its value. But for these actions, for which the Russian Federation for reasons set out above and in preceding chapters was responsible, Yukos would have been able to pay the tax claims of the Russian Federation justified or not; it would not have been bankrupted and liquidated (unless the Russian Federation were intent on its liquidation and found still additional grounds for achieving that end, as the second criminal trial of Messrs Khodorkovsky and Lebedev indeed suggests).

1580. Respondent has not explicitly expropriated Yukos or the holdings of its shareholders, but the measures that respondent has taken in respect of Yukos, set forth in detail in Part VIII, in the view of the Tribunal have had an effect 'equivalent to nationalisation or expropriation'. The four conditions specified in Article 13(1) of the ECT do not qualify that conclusion.

1581. As to condition (a), whether the destruction of Russia's leading oil company and largest taxpayer was in the public interest is profoundly questionable. It was in the interest of the largest State-owned oil company, Rosneft, which took over the principal assets of Yukos virtually cost-free, but that is not the same as saying that it was in the public interest of the economy, polity and population of the Russian Federation.

1582. As to condition (b), the treatment of Yukos and the appropriation of its assets by Rosneft (and to a much lesser extent, another State-owned corporation, Gazprom), when compared to the treatment of other Russian oil companies that also took advantage of investments in low-tax jurisdictions, may well have been discriminatory, a question that was inconclusively argued between the parties and need not be and has not been decided by this Tribunal.

1583. As to condition (c), Yukos was subjected to processes of law, but the Tribunal does not accept that the effective expropriation of Yukos was 'carried out under due process of law' for multiple reasons set out above, notably in Section VIII.C.3. The harsh treatment accorded to Messrs Khodorkovsky and Lebedev remotely jailed and caged in court, the mistreatment of counsel of Yukos and the difficulties counsel encountered in reading the record and conferring with Messrs Khodorkovsky and Lebedev, the very pace of the legal proceedings, do not comport with the due process of law. Rather the Russian court proceedings, and most egregiously, the second trial and second sentencing of Messrs Khodorkovsky and Lebedev on the creative legal theory of their theft of Yukos' oil production, indicate that Russian courts bent to the will of Russian executive authorities to bankrupt Yukos, assign its assets to a State-controlled company, and incarcerate a man who gave signs of becoming a political competitor.

1584. As to condition (d), what in any event is incontestable is respondent's failure to meet its prescription, because the effective expropriation of Yukos was not 'accompanied by the payment of prompt, adequate and effective compensation', or, in point of fact, any compensation whatsoever. In order for the Russian Federation to be found in breach of its treaty obligations under Article 13 of the ECT, the foregoing violations of the conditions of Article 13 more than suffice.

1585. It follows that respondent stands in breach of its treaty obligations under Article 13 of the ECT. Accordingly, respondent's liability under international law for breach of treaty is established. The Tribunal reaches this conclusion based on its consideration of the totality of the extensive evidence before it. Having found respondent liable under international law for breach of Article 13 of the ECT, the Tribunal does not need to consider whether respondent's actions are also in breach of Article 10 of the Treaty.

1586. The establishment of liability under international law is at the heart of its doctrine and jurisprudence. The Statute of the PCIJ, in Article 36(2), referred to '(c) the existence of any fact which, if established, would constitute a breach of an international obligation; (d) the nature or extent of the reparation to be made for the breach of an international obligation'. The identical provision is found in Article 36(2) of the Statute of the ICJ.

1587. The PCIJ held in the *Factory at Chorzów* case that:

> It is a principle of international law that the breach of an engagement involves an obligation to make reparation in an adequate form. Reparation therefore is the indispensable complement of a failure to apply a convention and there is no necessity for this to be stated in the convention itself.2103

1588. In a subsequent phase of the *Factory at Chorzów* case, the Court specified the content of the obligation of reparation in the following oft-quoted terms:

> The essential principle contained in the actual notion of an illegal act – a principle which seems to be established by international practice and in particular by the decisions of arbitral tribunals – is that reparation must, so far as possible, wipe out all the consequences of the illegal act and re-establish the situation which would, in all probability, have existed if that act had not been committed. Restitution in kind, or, if this is not possible, payment of a sum corresponding to the value which a restitution in kind would bear; the award, if need be, of damages for the loss sustained which would not be covered by restitution in kind or payment in place of it – such are the principles which should serve to determine the amount of compensation due for an act contrary to international law.

1589. The ILC Articles on State Responsibility provide, in Article 31, an article entitled 'Reparation', that '[t]he responsible State is under an obligation to make full reparation for the injury caused by the internationally wrongful act'. In support of this conclusion the Articles quote the foregoing holdings in the *Factory at Chorzów* case.

1590. Article 36 of the Articles, entitled 'Compensation', provides that: '1. The State responsible for an internationally wrongful act is under an obligation to compensate for the damage caused thereby. . .'. The commentary to the Articles states that: 'the function of compensation is to address the actual losses incurred as a result of the internationally wrongful act. Compensation corresponds to the financially assessable damage suffered . . . it is not concerned to punish . . . nor does compensation have an expressive or exemplary character'.

1591. Article 13 of the ECT specifies, in the event of expropriation, that, 'compensation shall amount to the fair market value of the Investment expropriated at the time immediately before the Expropriation . . . the Valuation Date'.

1592. Article 39 of the ILC Articles on State Responsibility, entitled 'Contribution to the injury,' provides that '[i]n the determination of reparation, account shall be taken of the contribution to the injury by wilful or negligent action or omission of the injured . . . entity in relation to whom reparation is sought'. The ILC's commentary to the Articles refers to notions of 'contributory negligence' and 'comparative fault'.

1593. The Tribunal will assess damages in the light of the foregoing accepted principles of international law. [. . .]

15

Fair and equitable treatment

EXERCISE 25 – SEMINAR

DISCUSSION QUESTIONS

Problem 1
Review and analyse *Total v Argentina* (majority opinion, dissent not published). Would you agree with the majority? On what weak points may the dissent have been based?

Problem 2
Study *Tecmed v Mexico*, in particular paragraph 154. Did the Tribunal explain how it reached its position on FET? In your view, how should the Tribunal have argued to explain its view? Which points are the most debatable ones?

Problem 3
Consider the following hypothetical fact pattern.

Between 2010 and 2015 company A invested hundreds of millions of US$ into the renewable infrastructure of country X. It did so on the basis of the legal framework existing at the time of its investments in 2010. The legal framework included a system of favourable electricity tariffs so as to encourage and entice foreign investment into country X. Without these tariffs no foreign investor would have made the high-cost, up-front investments required in the renewable sector, since the tariffs were the only way for the investor to make a profitable return on the investment.

In 2016 the Government of X radically changed the legal framework for investments in the renewable energy sector, affecting not only future investments, but also existing investments in the sector. The tariffs under the new system were calculated in a completely different manner than under the old system, resulting in considerably lower income for company A.

The Government of X explains that the changes are necessary because the favourable treatment of renewable energy is becoming too costly for the country. Government funds are needed for other socially important areas, such as education and healthcare. Also, the government states that it is not reasonable to treat renewable energy more favourably than other forms of energy.

Do the measures taken by the Government of X violate Fair and Equitable Treatment under the ECT, in particular with respect to the legitimate expectations of company A?

Problem 4
To what extent, and under what circumstances, if any, does the violation of a stabilisation clause amount to a breach of the FET standard?

CASE

Total SA v Argentine Republic (ICSID Case No. ARB/04/1) Decision on Liability International Centre for Settlement of Investment Disputes Washington, DC

Part I – Introduction

1. Procedural background

1. On October 12, 2003, Total SA ('Total' or the 'claimant') submitted before the Secretary-General of the International Centre for Settlement of Investment Disputes ('ICSID' or the 'Centre') a request for arbitration against the Argentine Republic ('Argentina' or the 'respondent'), pursuant to the Convention on the Settlement of Investment Disputes between States and Nationals of other States ('ICSID Convention') and the Treaty between France and Argentina concerning the Reciprocal Promotion and Protection of Investment of July 3, 1991 (BIT).

2. In accordance with Rule 5 of the ICSID Rules of Procedure for the Institution of Conciliation and Arbitration Proceedings (the 'Institution Rules'), the Centre acknowledged receipt of the request for arbitration on November 3, 2003. On November 4, 2003, the Centre transmitted a copy of the request for arbitration to the Argentine Republic and to the Argentine Embassy in Washington, DC. On January 22, 2004 the Secretary-General registered Total's request for arbitration and gave notice thereof to the parties, pursuant to Article 36(3) of the ICSID Convention. Pursuant to Rule 7(d) of the Institution Rules, the Secretary-General also invited the parties to proceed as soon as possible to constitute an Arbitral Tribunal in accordance with Articles 37–40 of the ICSID Convention.

3. On March 29, 2004, the claimant appointed Mr Henri C Alvarez, a Canadian national, as arbitrator. On April 14, 2004, the Argentine Republic appointed Dr Luis Herrera Marcano, a national of Venezuela, as arbitrator. On August 20, 2004, in accordance with Rule 4 of the Rules of Procedure for Arbitration Proceedings (the 'Arbitration Rules'), the Chairman of the Administrative Council of ICSID appointed Professor Giorgio Sacerdoti, a national of Italy, as President of the Tribunal. On August 24, 2004, the Deputy Secretary-General of ICSID informed the parties that all members of the Tribunal had accepted their appointments and that, in accordance with Arbitration Rule 6(1), the Tribunal was deemed to have been constituted on that same day.

4. The first session of the Arbitral Tribunal was held on November 15, 2004. During the session, the parties confirmed that the Tribunal had been properly constituted pursuant to the ICSID Convention and the Arbitration Rules and that they did not have any objections in this respect.

5. During the course of the first session, the parties agreed on a number of procedural matters as reflected in the written minutes of the session which were signed by the President and the Secretary of the Tribunal. Among other matters, it was agreed that, in accordance with Arbitration Rule 22, the languages of the proceedings would be English and Spanish. It was confirmed that the claimant would file its pleadings in English and Argentina would file its pleadings in Spanish, without a subsequent translation of the written pleadings into the other party's chosen procedural language. After hearing the parties, the Tribunal decided by Procedural Order No 1 that the claimant would file its memorial on the merits within five months of the date of the first session. The Tribunal also decided that, if the respondent wished to raise any objections to jurisdiction, it should do so within 45 days of the receipt of the claimant's memorial on the merits. In the event of an objection to jurisdiction, the claimant would file its counter-memorial on jurisdiction within 45 days of the receipt of the respondent's memorial on jurisdiction. in the same procedural order, the Tribunal further decided that: if the respondent did not raise any objections to jurisdiction, it would file its counter-memorial on the merits within five months of receipt of the claimant's memorial on the merits; the claimant would then file its reply on the merits within 60 days of receipt of the respondent's counter-memorial on the merits; and the respondent would file its rejoinder on the merits within 60 days of receipt of the claimant's reply on the merits.

6. The claimant filed its memorial on the merits ('CMM') on April 11, 2005; Argentina filed its 'Memorial sobre objeciones a la jurisdicción del Centro y a la competencia del Tribunal' on June 3, 2005. In accordance with Arbitration Rule 41(3), the proceeding on the merits was thereby suspended. In conformity with Procedural Order No 1, the claimant then submitted its counter-memorial on jurisdiction on August 1, 2005.

7. The hearing on jurisdiction was held in Washington DC on September 5, 2005. Ms Cintia Yaryura, Ms María Victoria Vitali and Mr Ariel Martins addressed the Tribunal on behalf of Argentina. Mr Nigel Blackaby, Mr Georgios Petrochilos and Mr Luis A Erize addressed the Tribunal on behalf of the claimant. During the course of the hearing, the Tribunal posed questions to the parties, as provided for in Arbitration Rule 32(3).

8. The Tribunal issued its Decision on Objections to Jurisdiction ('Decision on Jurisdiction') on August 25, 2006, rejecting Argentina's objections to jurisdiction and deciding that the parties' dispute was within the jurisdiction of ICSID and the competence of the Tribunal. In the Decision on Jurisdiction, the Tribunal stated that the matter of costs relating to the jurisdictional phase of the proceeding would be considered as part of the merits phase.

9. On the same date, the Tribunal confirmed that pursuant to Procedural Order No 1, the respondent would submit its counter-memorial on the merits within five months of the date of the Decision on Jurisdiction i.e., by January 26, 2007. The claimant would thereafter file its reply on the merits within 60 days of receipt of the respondent's counter-memorial on the merits and the respondent would file its rejoinder on the merits 60 days of receipt of the claimant's reply on the merits. According to the schedule, Argentina filed its counter-memorial on the merits on January 26, 2007.

10. On February 9, 2007, the claimant proposed a revised schedule for the submission of the claimant's reply and the respondent's rejoinder. By letter of February 16, 2007, Argentina indicated that it did not oppose the claimant's proposal to modify the schedule. Taking into consideration the parties' views in this respect, the Tribunal decided to modify the deadlines established in Procedural Order No 1, which had been issued on August 25, 2006. Accordingly, the Tribunal ordered the claimant to file its reply on the merits by May 15, 2007 and the respondent to file its rejoinder on the merits within 102 days of receipt of the claimant's reply.

11. By letter of March 16, 2007, the respondent requested a one-month extension for the submission of both the claimant's reply and the respondent's rejoinder. On March 16, 2007, the claimant submitted its observations on the respondent's extension request. By letter of April 9, 2007, the Tribunal decided to grant the one month extension requested by Argentina. The Tribunal decided that the claimant's reply on the merits should be filed by June 15, 2007 and the respondent's rejoinder on the merits within 102 days of receipt of the claimant's reply on the merits.

12. By letters of May 9 and 18, 2007, the claimant informed the Tribunal that it would submit its reply on May 18, 2007, and that it expected Argentina's rejoinder to be submitted around August 28, 2007. By letter of May 14, 2007, Argentina requested the Tribunal to maintain the one-month extension that it had requested and to order the submission of its rejoinder by October 1, 2007. As indicated by the claimant, the reply on the merits was submitted on May 18, 2007.

13. By letter of May 22, 2007, the Tribunal stated that the respondent was entitled to rely on the one-month extension granted by the Tribunal. The Tribunal also confirmed that the claimant was free to file its reply before the deadline established by the Tribunal in its letter of April 9, 2007. Accordingly, the Tribunal ordered that the Secretariat should not forward the claimant's reply to the respondent until June 15, 2007, and that the respondent should file its rejoinder within 102 days of receipt of the reply.

14. By letter of September 25, 2007, the respondent filed a request for production of documents and requested a 15-day extension for the filing of its rejoinder on the merits. By letter of September 30, 2007, the claimant submitted its observations on the respondent's letter of September 25, 2007. By letter of October 3, 2007, the Tribunal granted the extension requested by the respondent and ordered the submission of the Rejoinder of the merits by October 15, 2007.

15. By letter of October 9, 2007, the respondent requested the deadline to be moved to October 16, 2007, as October 15, 2007 was an official holiday in Argentina. By letter of October 10, 2007, the Tribunal granted the respondent until October 16, 2007 to submit its rejoinder on the merits. The Tribunal also indicated that it would fix a deadline for the respondent to file comments on certain financial valuation issues as the respondent had not yet received some documents that the claimant had been ordered to produce. The respondent filed its rejoinder on the merits on October 16, 2007. The parties exchanged a number of communications regarding the production of documents dealing with financial valuation matters. Having considered the parties' positions in this respect, the Tribunal, by letter of November 5, 2007, ordered the respondent to submit its report on quantum by November 20, 2007. The respondent filed its expert report on damages on the date ordered by the Tribunal.

16. On December 10, 2007, the Tribunal held a pre-hearing conference call with the parties and, on December 13, 2007, it issued procedural directions for the organisation of the hearing on the merits.

17. The Tribunal held a hearing on the merits at the seat of the Centre in Washington DC from January 7 through January 18, 2008. [. . .]

19. On April 11, 2008, the parties filed their post-hearing briefs. On May 26, 2008, the parties filed their submissions on costs. In its submission, Argentina claimed that the cost incurred by Argentina amounted to US$1,215,222.99. In its submission on costs the claimant: 'request[ed] that the Tribunal:

(i)   Order Argentina to reimburse to Total an amount of US$431,500, which is the present total of the costs-advances made by Total, with interest at a rate to be determined by the Tribunal from the date of the Award until final payment; and

(ii) Order Argentina to pay Total an amount of € 10,264,735.62 and US$4,368,881.87, which is the present total of 'the costs reasonably incurred' by the claimant in this arbitration, with interest at a rate to be determined by the Tribunal from the date of the Award until final payment'.

20. On May 9, 2008, the respondent requested the Tribunal's authorisation to produce certain documents. On May 15, 2008, the claimant filed observations on the respondent's request. By letter dated May 21, 2008, Ms Natalí Sequeira, Secretary of the Tribunal, informed the parties that the Tribunal had determined that the new exhibit RA-299, which Argentina sought to place on the record of the case, as well as exhibits RA 294-297 already introduced by the respondent as annexes to its post-hearing brief, were inadmissible. By the same letter, the parties were informed that, as a matter of due process and in view of the stage of the proceedings, the Tribunal had decided not to take into consideration new evidence and arguments submitted subsequent to the post-hearing briefs.

21. On February 20, 2009, the claimant requested the Tribunal's authorisation to produce a number of documents concerning developments involving certain Argentine authorities that had affected TGN. On March 20, 2009, the respondent filed observations on the claimant's request and requested authorisation to produce documents on the same issue concerning TGN. On April 9, 2009, the Tribunal issued a further decision on production of documents. Recalling its previous decision of May 21, 2008, the Tribunal restated that it would not take into consideration new evidence and arguments submitted subsequent to the post-hearing briefs and that it would rely solely on the evidence and the parties' submissions already on the record of the case.

22. On October 23, 2009, Argentina wrote to the Centre in order to inform the Tribunal about facts related to a labour dispute between Total and one of its former employees. According to Argentina's letter, the facts on which the aforementioned labour dispute are based are of particular relevance to these arbitration proceedings. The Tribunal expresses its doubts that the facts outlined by the respondent in its letter are relevant to the ongoing arbitration proceedings. The Tribunal notes that the respondent is seeking to place new documents and arguments on the record of the case, contrary to the previous decisions taken by the Tribunal relating to the production of documents.

The respondent's request was absolutely out of time in view of the stage of the proceedings. The Tribunal determines, therefore, that it cannot either admit these documents as evidence or take into consideration the legal arguments based thereon.

2. General overview of the subject matter of the dispute and of Total's claims and request for relief

23. The Tribunal considers it useful to sum up briefly at the outset the subject matter of the dispute, in fact and in law, as presented by the claimant in its 'Request for Arbitration' and subsequently particularised.

24. In its Request for Arbitration, Total submits that it is a company incorporated in accordance with the laws of France, having its registered office in France and, therefore, that it qualifies as a French 'investor' within the meaning of Article 1.2(b) of the BIT. Total has made a number of investments in Argentina in the gas transportation, hydrocarbons exploration and production and power generation industries. According to Total, its investments in Argentina include majority and minority shareholding interests in companies operating in the gas transportation, exploration and production and power generation sectors, as well as various licences, rights, concessions and loans, each of which qualifies as an 'investment' in accordance with the meaning of this term in Article 1.1 of the BIT.

25. Total maintains that it made its investments in each of the various areas on the basis of the representations and promises made by the Argentine government about the legal and regulatory framework for privatised gas transmission companies, the oil and gas exploration and production industry and the power generation industry. Total alleges that a number of measures taken by the Argentine Government, most of which derived from or followed Law 25.561/02 (the 'Emergency Law'), together with the Emergency Law itself, breached or revoked the commitments made to attract investment and upon which Total relied in making its investments. More specifically, Total indicates that these measures include:

- the forced conversion of dollar-denominated public service tariffs into pesos (or 'pesification') at a rate of one to one;
- the abolition of the adjustment of public service tariffs based on the US Producer Price Index ('PPI') and other international indices;
- the 'pesification' of dollar-denominated private contracts at a rate of one to one;

- the freezing of the gas consumer tariff (which is the sum of the: (a) well-head price of gas; (b) gas transportation tariff; and (c) gas distribution tariff);
- the imposition of: (a) export withholding taxes on the sale of hydrocarbons; and (b) restrictions on the export of such hydrocarbons;
- the abandonment of the uniform marginal price mechanism in the power generation market by price caps and other regulatory measures;
- the pesification, at a one-to-one rate, of all other payments to which power generators are entitled; and
- the refusal to pay power generators their dues, even at the dramatically reduced values resulting from the measures.

26. The claimant claims that the measures adopted by Argentina have resulted in several breaches of the BIT. As to Total's gas transmission assets, Total argues that the measures: expropriated Total's investment in TGN in breach of Article 5(2) of the BIT; resulted in unfair and inequitable treatment of Total's investment in TGN in breach of Article 3 of the BIT; discriminated against Total's investment in TGN in breach of Articles 3 and 4 of the BIT; and are in breach of Argentina's obligation to respect specific undertakings contrary to Article 10 of the BIT.

27. As to Total's investments in the exploration and production of crude oil and natural gas, Total claims that the measures: revoked Total's right freely to dispose of its hydrocarbons in breach of the duty of fair and equitable treatment pursuant to Article 3 of the BIT; affected Total's hydrocarbon production in an arbitrary and discriminatory manner contrary to Articles 3 and 4 of the BIT by benefiting domestic, industrial, commercial or residential consumers to the detriment of Total; and restricted Total's export of hydrocarbons in further breach of the duty to accord fair and equitable treatment pursuant to Article 3 of the BIT.

28. In relation to Total's investments in the power generation sector, Total claims that Argentina, through the measures: failed to observe its obligation to refrain from taking measures equivalent to expropriation without prompt, adequate and effective compensation in breach of Article 5(2) of the BIT; breached the duty of fair and equitable treatment in Article 3 of the BIT; and discriminated against Total's investments in Central Puerto and HPDA in breach of Article 4 of the BIT.

29. Based on the above, the claimant asks the Tribunal to declare that Argentina, by its various acts and the conduct specified in claimant's Request for Arbitration and Memorials, breached the above-mentioned Articles of

the BIT. In its Request for Arbitration, the claimant seeks compensation for the alleged damages caused to its investment by Argentina's violations of the BIT 'in an amount to be assessed and which is provisionally assessed to be no less than US$ 940 million', in addition to interest, additional reparation to be further specified and payment by Argentina of all arbitration costs and expenses.

30. To support its request for damages, during the arbitral proceedings, Total filed three reports by its experts Mr Spiller and Mr Adbala (LECG, LLC). Based on the data contained in these reports, in its post-hearing brief, Total claimed damages in the aggregate amount, as of 31 December 2006 of US$1,292,100,000, divided as between each of its various claims of breach of the BIT by Argentina as set forth below.

31. In its post-hearing brief, Total submitted the following Request for Relief to the Tribunal:

> On the basis of the foregoing and the claimant's prior written pleadings, the claimant respectfully requests that the Tribunal, dismissing all contrary requests and submissions by Argentina:
>
> (i) Declare that Argentina has breached Article 5(2) of the Treaty by taking measures which deprived the claimant's investment in TGN of substantially all of its value without provision for the payment of the prompt and adequate compensation required under Article 5(2) of the Treaty;
>
> (ii) Declare that Argentina has breached Article 3 of the Treaty by failing to accord fair and equitable treatment to the claimant and its investments in TGN, the hydrocarbons exploration and production sector and the claimant's equity participations in Central Puerto and HPDA;
>
> (iii) Declare that Argentina has breached Article 5(1) of the Treaty by failing to 'fully and completely protect[] and safeguard[]' the claimant's investments in TGN, in the hydrocarbons exploration and production sector, and as an equity investor in Central Puerto and HPDA;
>
> (iv) Declare that Argentina has breached Article 4 of the Treaty by taking discriminatory measures to the detriment of the claimant in respect of its investments in TGN, in the hydrocarbons exploration and production sector, and in respect of its equity participations in Central Puerto and HPDA;
>
> (v) Order Argentina to compensate the claimant for the foregoing breaches of the Treaty and international law, in the aggregate amount as of 31 December 2006 of US$1,292,100,000;

(vi) Order Argentina to pay compound pre-judgment interest on all amounts awarded under (v) above, accruing from 1 January 2007 until the date of the Award, at a rate of:

  i.   13.5 per cent per annum for damages with respect to TGN;

  ii. 12.18 per cent per annum for damages with respect to Total Austral; and

  iii. the current six-month US Treasury bond rate for damages with respect to HPDA and Central Puerto;

(vii) Order Argentina to pay compound interest, from the date of the Tribunal's Award to the date of Argentina's final payment to the claimant, at the six-month US Treasury bond rate on any and all amounts of compensation ordered by the Tribunal;

(viii) Order Argentina to pay all of the costs and expenses of this arbitration, including the fees and expenses of the Tribunal, the fees and expenses of any experts appointed by the Tribunal and the claimant, the fees and expenses of the claimant's legal representation in respect of this arbitration, and any other costs of this arbitration, to be specified in the claimant's costs submissions, to follow, plus interest; and

(ix) Award such other relief as the Tribunal considers appropriate.

32. On the basis of the facts and legal arguments set forth in its briefs, as well as the statements and reports made and documents submitted by its witnesses and experts, Argentina asks the Arbitral Tribunal to dismiss each and every one of Total's claims and to order the claimant to pay all of the expenses and legal costs deriving from this arbitration, including Argentina's own costs amounting to US$1,215,222.99.

[. . .]

6. Legal evaluation by the Tribunal of Total's claims

99. The first issue for the Tribunal is to determine whether the legislation, regulation and provisions invoked by Total constitute a set of promises and commitments towards Total whose unilateral modifications entail a breach of the legitimate expectations of Total and, as a consequence, are in breach of the fair and equitable treatment standard in the BIT. The opposite view held by Argentina is that Argentina has not breached any promise or guarantee made to Total because '[T]he Argentine State did not execute any contract with Total' nor did it induce Total to invest in TGN. The provisions invoked by Total as 'guarantees' are in Argentina's

view nothing other than the totality of the regulatory framework effective from time to time.

100. It is undisputed that Total did not enter into a contractual relationship with Argentina's authorities in 2000–01 when it acquired an indirect share in TGN by buying a share of Gasinvest from TransCanada, one of the various foreign shareholders of TransCanada. All of the laws and regulations, which Total invokes as a source of the promises that it relies upon (the Gas Law and the Gas Decree of 1992), are instruments of general application, enacted by the Congress or the Executive branch of Argentina pursuant to the powers vested in these bodies under the Constitution of Argentina. Further, Total does not submit that it had participated in any way in the privatisation of the gas transportation utilities of Argentina in 1991–92 through which the first private investors in TGN had become its shareholders.

101. As concerns Total's reliance on TGN's Licence as a contractual commitment undertaken by Argentina, it is clear that this instrument establishes the rights and obligations of the parties (namely TGN and Argentina's authorities) to that licence. Specifically, the TGN Licence sets forth the obligations of the Argentine authorities vis-à-vis the concessionaire. These obligations encompass details of how those authorities may (and should) exercise, with respect to the concessionaire, the regulatory powers granted to them by the Gas Law and Gas Decree in order to preserve the general interest underlying the performance of the public service. Since Total is not a party to the concession, a more accurate description of the situation would be that Total has invested in a public utility (namely TGN) which operated a public service activity regulated by a defined legal regime set forth (also) in the concession. Therefore TGN Licence cannot be regarded as a source of contractual legal obligations of a specific character assumed directly by Argentina towards Total. Accordingly, it is not correct to qualify and treat the TGN Licence provisions as stabilisation clauses agreed between Total and Argentina. Stabilisation clauses are clauses, which are inserted in State contracts concluded between foreign investors and host States with the intended effect of freezing a specific host State's legal framework at a certain date, such that the adoption of any changes in the legal regulatory framework of the investment concerned (even by law of general application and without any discriminatory intent by the host State) would be illegal. For the reasons stated above, this characterisation does not fit the relationship between Total and Argentina as to Total's investment in TGN.

102. Total submits that legitimate expectations with respect to the stability of the legal framework under which a foreign company makes an investment

may derive not only from contractual undertakings, but also from legislation and regulation that was precisely meant to attract foreign investment. Total points out that the gas regulatory framework was devised and enacted in order to attract long-term private foreign investments in utilities, which until then had been run by the State, that were badly in need of modernisation through massive investment by competent operators and others, especially in view of the past record of high inflation in Argentina. This regime was based on a sound economic underpinning, an integral part of which was the overarching commitment to reasonable and fair tariffs for the operators and specifically the US dollar peg.

103. Subjectively, Total submits that the existence of such a framework, which had been in place for almost nine years when it decided to become a shareholder of TGN, was a major consideration in carrying out such an investment.

104. To the contrary, Argentina points to the agreed suspensions of the PPI, which were in place when Total made its acquisition of the shareholding in TGN from TransCanada, that should have put Total on notice that the Gas Regulatory Framework was being undermined. Argentina also submits that Total was careless in making its investment in that it did not carry out the due diligence analysis that is commonly undertaken before making such a large direct investment abroad. Had Total carried out proper due diligence, it would have been aware of the looming economic difficulties of Argentina and of their possible impact on the future stability of the Gas Regulatory Framework.

105. The legal issue for the Tribunal is thus to determine whether the fair and equitable treatment standard of Article 3 of the BIT, in particular as far as it includes the 'protection of legitimate expectations' of the foreign investor, has been breached by the unilateral changes of legislation and regulation effected by Argentina and challenged by Total.

6.1 Applicable standard: the fair and equitable treatment standard in general

106. The undertaking of the host country to provide fair and equitable treatment to the investors of the other party and their investments is a standard feature in BITs, although the exact language of such undertakings is not uniform. The generality of the fair and equitable treatment standard distinguishes it from specific obligations undertaken by the parties to a BIT in respect of typical aspects of foreign investment operations such as those concerning monetary transfers, visas, etc. At the same time, the fair and

equitable treatment standard can be distinguished from other general standards included in BITs, namely the national and the most-favoured nation treatment standards, which guarantee a variable protection that is contingent upon the treatment given by the host State to its own nationals or to the nationals of the best treated third State.

107. The fair and equitable treatment standard is, by contrast, an autonomous standard, although its exact content is not predefined, except in cases where a treaty provides additional specifications, which is not the case for the France-Argentina BIT. Since this standard is inherently flexible, it is difficult, if not impossible, 'to anticipate in the abstract the range of possible types of infringements upon the investor's legal position'. Its application in a given case must take into account relevant State practice and judicial or arbitral case law as well as the text of the BIT and other sources of customary or general international law.

108. The meaning of various fair and equitable treatment clauses has been tested in several investment disputes and the issue has been dealt with by a number of academic writings, including by the most prominent scholars in the field of international investment law. Some Tribunals have started from the ordinary meaning of the term, in accordance with Article 31(1) of the Vienna Convention of the Law of Treaties ('VCLT'), recalling the dictionary definitions of just, even-handed, unbiased, legitimate. On the other hand, one cannot but agree with Judge Higgins' observation in the *Oil Platforms* case, that 'the key terms "fair and equitable treatment to nationals and companies" . . are legal terms of art well known in the field of overseas investment protection'.

109. On the premise that a 'judgement of what is fair and equitable cannot be reached in the abstract; it must depend on the fact of the particular case' and that 'the standard is to some extent a flexible one which must be adapted to the circumstances of each case', Tribunals have endeavoured to pinpoint some typical obligations that may be included in the standard, as well as types of conduct that would breach the standard, in order to be guided in their analysis of the issue before them.

110. A breach of the fair and equitable treatment standard has been found in respect of conduct characterised by 'arbitrariness' and of 'acts showing a wilful neglect of duty, an insufficiency of action falling far below international standards, or even subjective bad faith'. It has been also held that the standard requires 'treatment in an even-handed and just manner, conducive to fostering the promotion of foreign investment', thereby condemning conduct that

is arbitrary, grossly unfair, unjust or idiosyncratic or that 'involves a lack of due process leading to an outcome which offends judicial propriety – as might be the case with a manifest failure of natural justice in judicial proceedings or a complete lack of transparency and candour in administrative process'. Awards have found a breach in cases of discrimination against foreigners and 'improper and discreditable' or 'unreasonable' conduct. This does not mean that bad faith is necessarily required in order to find a breach: 'A State may treat foreign investment unfairly and inequitably without necessarily acting in bad faith.'

111. In determining the scope of a right or obligation, Tribunals have often looked as a benchmark to international or comparative standards. Indeed, as is often the case for general standards applicable in any legal system (such as 'due process'), a comparative analysis of what is considered generally fair or unfair conduct by domestic public authorities in respect of private firms and investors in domestic law may also be relevant to identify the legal standards under BITs. Such an approach is justified because, factually, the situations and conduct to be evaluated under a BIT occur within the legal system and social, economic and business environment of the host State. Moreover, legally, the fair and equitable treatment standard is derived from the requirement of good faith which is undoubtedly a general principle of law under Article 38(1) of the Statute of the International Court of Justice.

112. UNCTAD has followed such an approach in its publication on the topic, besides referring to arbitral practice, in order:

> to identify certain forms of behaviour that appear to be contrary to fairness and equity in most legal systems and to extrapolate from this the type of State action that may be inconsistent with fair and equitable treatment, using the plain meaning approach. Thus, for instance, if a State acts fraudulently or in bad faith, or capriciously and wilfully discriminates against a foreign investor, or deprives an investor of acquired rights in a manner that leads to the unjust enrichment of the State, then there is at least a prima facie case for arguing that the fair and equitable standard has been breached.

6.2. The notion of legitimate expectations of foreign investors

113. We turn now to the more specific concept, which Total asserts forms part of the fair and equitable treatment standard, of the protection of 'legitimate expectations' on the part of an investor concerning the stability of the legal framework under which it has made its investment.

114. Tribunals have often referred to the principle of the protection of the investor's legitimate expectations, especially with reference to the 'stability' of the legal framework of the host country applicable to the investment, as being included within the fair and equitable treatment standard. However, case law is not uniform as to the preconditions for an investor to claim that its expectations were 'legitimate' concerning the stability of a given legal framework that was applicable to its investment when it was made. On the one hand, stability, predictability and consistency of legislation and regulation are important for investors in order to plan their investments, especially if their business plans extend over a number of years. Competent authorities of States entering into BITs in order to promote foreign investment in their economy should be aware of the importance for the investors that a legal environment favourable to the carrying out of their business activities be maintained.

115. On the other hand, signatories of such treaties do not thereby relinquish their regulatory powers nor limit their responsibility to amend their legislation in order to adapt it to change and the emerging needs and requests of their people in the normal exercise of their prerogatives and duties. Such limitations upon a government should not lightly be read into a treaty which does not spell them out clearly nor should they be presumed. In fact, even in those BITs where stability of the legal framework for investment is explicitly mentioned, such as in the BIT between the United States and Argentina of 1991 (in accordance with the US Model BIT of the time) such a reference appears only in the preamble.

116. In various disputes between US investors and Argentina under that BIT, Tribunals have relied on the explicit mention in its preamble of the desirability of maintaining a stable framework for investments in order to attract foreign investment as a basis for finding that the lack of such stability and related predictability, on which the investor had relied, had resulted in a breach of the fair and equitable treatment standard. This reference is justified because, although such a statement in a preamble does not create independent legal obligations, it is a tool for the interpretation of the treaty since it sheds light on its purpose. However, the BIT between France and Argentina does not contain any such reference, following the French BIT model. This absence indicates, at a minimum, that stability of the legal domestic framework was not envisaged as a specific element of the domestic legal regime that the Contracting Parties undertook to grant to their respective investors. The operative provisions of the France-Argentina BIT must in any case be read taking into account, within the object and purpose of the treaty, the reference in the preamble to the

desire of the parties to create favourable conditions for the investments covered.

117. In the absence of some 'promise' by the host State or a specific provision in the bilateral investment treaty itself, the legal regime in force in the host country at the time of making the investment is not automatically subject to a 'guarantee' of stability merely because the host country entered into a bilateral investment treaty with the country of the foreign investor. The expectation of the investor is undoubtedly 'legitimate', and hence subject to protection under the fair and equitable treatment clause, if the host State has explicitly assumed a specific legal obligation for the future, such as by contracts, concessions or stabilisation clauses on which the investor is therefore entitled to rely as a matter of law.

118. The situation is similar when public authorities of the host country have made the private investor believe that such an obligation existed through conduct or by a declaration. Authorities may also have announced officially their intent to pursue a certain conduct in the future, on which, in turn, the investor relied in making investments or incurring costs. As stated within the NAFTA framework:

> the concept of 'legitimate expectations' relates [. . .] to a situation where a
> Contracting Party's conduct creates reasonable and justifiable expectations on the
> part of an investor (or investment) to act in reliance on said conduct, such that a
> failure by the NAFTA party to honour those expectations could cause the investor
> (or investment) to suffer damages.

119. In fact, when relying on the concept of legitimate expectations, arbitral Tribunals have often stressed that 'specific commitments' limit the right of the host State to adapt the legal framework to changing circumstances. Representations made by the host State are enforceable and justify the investor's reliance only when they are specifically addressed to a particular investor.

> Where a host State which seeks foreign investment acts intentionally, so as to
> create expectations in potential investors with respect to particular treatment or
> comportment, the host State should, we suggest, be bound by the commitments
> and the investor is entitled to rely upon them in instances of decision.

120. In other words, an investor's legitimate expectations may be based:

> on any undertaking and representations made explicitly or implicitly by the host
> State. A reversal of assurances by the host State which have led to legitimate

expectations will violate the principle of fair and equitable treatment. At the same time, it is clear that this principle is not absolute and does not amount to a requirement for the host State to freeze its legal system for the investor's benefit. A general stabilisation requirement would go beyond what the investor can legitimately expect.

121. The balance between these competing requirements and hence the limits of the proper invocation of 'legitimate expectations' in the face of legislative or regulatory changes (assuming that they are not contrary to a contractual, bilateral or similar undertaking, binding in its own right) has been based on a weighing of various elements pointing in opposite directions. On the one hand, the form and specific content of the undertaking of stability invoked are crucial. No less relevant is the clarity with which the authorities have expressed their intention to bind themselves for the future. Similarly, the more specific the declaration to the addressee(s), the more credible the claim that such an addressee (the foreign investor concerned) was entitled to rely on it for the future in a context of reciprocal trust and good faith. Hence, this accounts for the emphasis in many awards on the government having given 'assurances', made 'promises', undertaken 'commitments', offered specific conditions, to a foreign investor, to the point of having solicited or induced that investor to make a given investment. Total itself described the acts of Argentina on which it relies in this way. As a result of such conduct by the host authorities, the expectation of the foreign investor may 'rise to the level of legitimacy and reasonableness in light of the circumstances'. When those features are not present, a cautious approach is warranted based on a case specific contextual analysis of all relevant facts.

122. Indeed, the most difficult case is (as in part in the present dispute) when the basis of an investor's invocation of entitlement to stability under a fair and equitable treatment clause relies on legislation or regulation of a unilateral and general character. In such instances, investor's expectations are rooted in regulation of a normative and administrative nature that is not specifically addressed to the relevant investor. This type of regulation is not shielded from subsequent changes under the applicable law. This notwithstanding, a claim to stability can be based on the inherently prospective nature of the regulation at issue aimed at providing a defined framework for future operations. This is the case for regimes, which are applicable to long-term investments and operations, and/or providing for 'fall backs' or contingent rights in case the relevant framework would be changed in unforeseen circumstances or in case certain listed events materialize. In such cases, reference to commonly recognised and applied financial and economic principles to be followed for the regular operation of investments of that type (be they domestic

or foreign) may provide a yardstick. This is the case for capital-intensive and long-term investments and operation of utilities under a license, natural resources exploration and exploitation, project financing or Build Operate and Transfer schemes. The concept of 'regulatory fairness' or 'regulatory certainty' has been used in this respect. In the light of these criteria when a State is empowered to fix the tariffs of a public utility it must do so in such a way that the concessionaire is able to recover its operations costs, amortise its investments and make a reasonable return over time, as indeed Argentina's gas regime provided.

123. On the other hand, the host State's right to regulate domestic matters in the public interest has to be taken into consideration as well. The circumstances and reasons (importance and urgency of the public need pursued) for carrying out a change impacting negatively on a foreign investor's operations on the one hand, and the seriousness of the prejudice caused on the other hand, compared in the light of a standard of reasonableness and proportionality are relevant. The determination of a breach of the standard requires, therefore, 'a weighing of the claimant's reasonable and legitimate expectations on the one hand and the respondent's legitimate regulatory interest on the other'. Thus an evaluation of the fairness of the conduct of the host country towards an investor cannot be made in isolation, considering only their bilateral relations. The context of the evolution of the host economy, the reasonableness of the normative changes challenged and their appropriateness in the light of a criterion of proportionality also have to be taken into account. Additional criteria for the evaluation of the fairness of national measures of general application as to services are those found in the WTO General Agreement on Trade of Services (GATS). The Tribunal recalls that Article VI of the GATS of 1994 on 'Domestic regulation' provides that 'In sectors where specific commitments are undertaken, each member shall ensure that all measures of general application affecting trade in services are *administered in a reasonable, objective and impartial manner*' (emphasis added). This reference concerning services (as undoubtedly Total's operations in the gas transportation and electricity were) in a multilateral treaty to which both Argentina and France are parties offers useful guidance as to the requirements that a domestic regulation must contain in order to be considered fair and equitable. The Tribunal refers to the requirements found in Article VI GATS just as 'guidance' because it has not been submitted that the GATS is directly applicable here. This would require that Argentina had admitted Total's investment in the electricity sector on the basis of a specific commitment in respect of the opening of electricity generation to investors from other WTO Members.

124. Besides such an objective comparison of the competing interests in context, the conduct of the investor in relation to any undertaking of stability is also, so to speak 'subjectively', relevant. Tribunals have evaluated the investor's conduct in this respect, highlighting that BITs 'are not insurance policies against bad business judgments' and that the investor has its own duty to investigate the host State's applicable law.

6.3 The content of Article 3 of the Argentina-France BIT

125. The commitment to fair and equitable treatment in Article 3 of the BIT relates to a treatment that must be in conformity with the principles of international law ('*conforme a los principios de Derecho International / en conformité des principes du droit international*'). The parties have discussed whether this reference is to a minimum standard, as suggested by Argentina, or whether it sets forth an autonomous standard, as submitted by Total. For the reasons stated hereunder the Tribunal is of the opinion that the phrase 'fair and equitable in conformity with the principles of international law' cannot be read as 'treatment required by the minimum standard of treatment of aliens/investors under international law'. This is irrespective of the issue of whether today there really is a difference between this traditional minimum standard and what international law generally requires as to treatment of foreign investors and their investments.

126. In order to elucidate the content of the treatment required by Article 3 in conformity with international law, a tribunal is directed to look not just to the BIT in isolation or the case law of other arbitral tribunals in investment disputes interpreting and applying similarly worded investment protection treaties, but rather to the content of international law more generally.

127. The Tribunal will, therefore, proceed to further interpret the 'fair and equitable treatment' standard looking also at general principles and public international law in a non-BIT context. This approach is consistent with the interpretation of Article 3 of the France-Argentina BIT by the '*Vivendi II*' Tribunal which has expressed the view we have developed above, namely, that: 'The Tribunal sees no basis for equating principles of international law with the minimum standard of treatment . . . the reference to principles of international law supports a broader reading that invites consideration of a wider range of international law principles than the minimum standard'. The views expressed by commentators on the French model BIT, from which the phrase derives, are consistent with these conclusions.

6.4 Comparative analysis

128. Since the concept of legitimate expectations is based on the requirement of good faith, one of the general principles referred to in Article 38(1)(c) of the Statute of the International Court of Justice (ICJ) as a source of international law, the Tribunal believes that a comparative analysis of the protection of legitimate expectations in domestic jurisdictions is justified at this point. While the scope and legal basis of the principle varies, it has been recognised lately both in civil law and in common law jurisdictions within well-defined limits.

129. In domestic legal systems the doctrine of legitimate expectations supports 'the entitlement of an individual to legal protection from harm caused by a public authority retreating from a previous publicly stated position, whether that be in the form of a formal decision or in the form of a representation'. This doctrine, which reflects the importance of the principle of legal certainty (or rule of law), appears to be applicable mostly in respect of administrative acts and protects an individual from an incoherent exercise of administrative discretion, or excess or abuse of administrative powers. The reasons and features for changes (sudden character, fundamental change, retroactive effects) and the public interest involved are thus to be taken into account in order to evaluate whether an individual who incurred financial obligations on the basis of the decisions and representations of public authorities that were later revoked should be entitled to a form of redress. However it appears that only exceptionally has the concept of legitimate expectations been the basis of redress when legislative action by a State was at stake. Rather a breach of the fundamental right of property as recognised under domestic law has been the basis, for instance, for the European Court of Human Rights to find a violation of the First Protocol to the European Convention on Human Rights protecting the peaceful enjoyment of property.

130. From a comparative law perspective, the tenets of the legal system of the European Community (now European Union), reflecting the legal traditions of 27 European countries, both civil and common law (including France, the home country of the claimant) are of relevance, especially since the recognition of the principle of legitimate expectations there has been explicitly based on the international law principle of good faith. Based on this premise, the Tribunal of the European Union has upheld the legitimate expectations of importers that the Community would respect public international law. According to the Court of Justice of the European Union private parties cannot normally invoke legitimate expectations against the exercise of normative powers by the Community's institutions, except under the most

restrictive conditions (which the Court has never found in any case submitted to it).

6.5 Public international law

131. Under international law, unilateral acts, statements and conduct by States may be the source of legal obligations which the intended beneficiaries or addressees, or possibly any member of the international community, can invoke. The legal basis of that binding character appears to be only in part related to the concept of legitimate expectations – being rather akin to the principle of 'estoppel'. Both concepts may lead to the same result, namely, that of rendering the content of a unilateral declaration binding on the State that is issuing it. According to the ICJ, only unilateral acts that are unconditional, definitive and 'very specific' have binding force, which derives from the principle of good faith. This fundamental principle requires a State to abide by its unilateral acts of such a character and to follow a line of conduct coherent with the legal obligations so created.

132. The recent 'Guiding Principles applicable to unilateral declarations of States capable of creating legal obligations' ('the Guidelines'), which were formulated by the International Law Commission in 2006 as a restatement of international (interstate) case law in the subject matter, are of interest here. We are aware that the Guidelines deal with the legal effects of unilateral acts of States addressed to other subjects of international law, and not with domestic normative acts relied upon by a foreign private investor. Still, we believe that the conditions required for unilateral declarations of a State to give rise to international obligations are of relevance here since the issue before the Tribunal has to be resolved by application of international law.

133. Relevant provisions for our analysis are found in Article 7 of the Guidelines:

> A unilateral declaration entails obligations for the formulating State only if it is stated in clear and specific terms. In case of doubt as to the scope of the obligations resulting from such a declaration, such obligations must be interpreted in a restrictive manner. In interpreting the content of such obligation, weight shall be given first and foremost to the text of the declaration, together with the context and the circumstances in which it was formulated.

Also of relevance is the final article of the Guidelines. Article 10 on revocation provides that:

[a] unilateral declaration that has created legal obligations for the State making the declaration cannot be revoked arbitrarily. In assessing whether a revocation would be arbitrary, consideration should be given to: (i) Any specific terms of the declaration relating to revocation; (ii) The extent to which those to whom the obligations are owed have relied on such obligations; (iii) The extent to which there has been a fundamental change of circumstances.

134. International law on the binding nature of unilateral commitments, as evidenced by the Guidelines, relies on concepts found in investment arbitral practice and in comparative law concepts, such as the importance of factual circumstances, the relevance of content and intent, non-arbitrariness in case of revocation and the restrictive interpretation of unilateral acts invoked as a source of commitments for the issuing party. The cautious approach that emerges appears to be consistent, *mutatis mutandis*, with that of domestic legal systems, European Union legal system and the European Court of Human Rights case law.

7. Application of the fair and equitable treatment standard

135. We turn now to apply the legal principles that we have highlighted to the facts of the case so as to evaluate Total's various claims of breach by Argentina. In this respect we find it appropriate to distinguish and sub-divide the three distinct claims made by Total, as follows:

- the elimination of the calculation of the tariffs in US dollars;
- the elimination of the automatic adjustments of the US dollar tariffs every six months in accordance with the US PPI, distinguishing in this respect the six-month automatic adjustment in itself from its pegging to the US dollar based PPI;
- the non-application or elimination of the promises of economic equilibrium and a reasonable rate of return through the ongoing suspension of the Five-Year and Extraordinary Reviews, thus freezing the tariffs since 2002.

7.1 The elimination of the calculation of gas tariffs in US dollars

136. The Tribunal recalls that the calculation of the gas transportation tariffs in US dollars was provided for by Article 41 of the Gas Decree as an element of the 'normal and periodic adjustment of the tariffs authorised by the body' [ENARGAS]. The provision established further that the tariffs ('*el cuadro tarifario*') would be expressed in convertible pesos in conformity with Law 23.928, that is, Argentina's convertibility law of March 1991 (the

'Convertibility Law'), with the reconversion to pesos to be made in accord-ance with the parity established in Article 3 of Decree 2.198/91.148.

137. Under the Convertibility Law and generally the Currency Board system that Argentina had adopted in 1991, the peso was pegged to the US dollar at par and there was free convertibility between the peso and the US dollar. As described by the IMF:

> The Convertibility Law, which pegged the Argentine currency to the US dollar in April 1991, was a response to Argentina's dire economic situation at the beginning of the 1990s. Following more than a decade of high inflation and economic stagnation, and after several failed attempts to stabilise the economy, in late 1989 Argentina had fallen into hyperinflation and a virtual economic collapse [...]. The new exchange rate regime, which operated like a currency board, was designated to stabilise the economy by establishing a hard nominal peg with credible assurances of non-reversibility. The new peso (set equal to 10,000 australes) was fixed at par with the US dollar and autonomous money creation by the central bank was severely constrained, though less rigidly than in a classical currency board. The exchange rate arrangement was part of a larger Convertibility Plan, which included a broader agenda of market-oriented structural reforms to promote efficiency and productivity in the economy. Various service sectors were deregulated, trade was liberalised, and anticompetitive price-fixing schemes were removed; privatisation proceeded vigorously, notably in oil, power, and telecommunications, yielding large capital revenues.

138. As described by another ICSID Tribunal:

> In more precise legal terms, the convertibility regime entailed that the national currency (the peso that replaced the Austral at one peso for each 10,000 Australes on January 1, 1992) was freely convertible with the U.S. dollar at 1:1, and the external value of the peso being pegged to the dollar under a currency board type arrangement. Transactions in convertible currencies were permitted. Authorised banks could open accounts in pesos or foreign currencies so that Argentines and foreigners in Argentina were allowed to hold and use any currency. This possibility led in time to the 'dollarisation' of Argentina's economy to a notable degree: contracts, especially medium- and long-term contracts such as rents, loans, supply contracts were expressed in dollars, rather than in pesos, and bank deposits were opened and maintained in dollars. Specifically, a large proportion of the banking system's assets and liabilities were denominated in dollars. The level of dollarisation, which had been growing steadily since 1991, increased substantially in the second half of 2000: more than 70 per cent of the private sectors deposits and almost 70 per cent of the

banking system credit to private sector were denominated in dollars by the end of 2000.

139. However, as reported officially by the IMF, in legal terms 'the currency of Argentina is the Argentine peso', and only the peso. 'Transactions in convertible currencies are permitted, and contracts in these currencies are legally enforceable, although the currencies are not legal tender'.

140. As outlined by the Tribunal above at paragraph 81, all calculation of public utility tariffs in US dollars, as well as their indexation to foreign currencies, was rendered ineffective by the Emergency Law. According to Article 8, all of those tariffs would be fixed in pesos at the conversion rate of 1:1. Other provisions of the same law abolished the convertibility at par of the peso with the US dollar provided for under the Convertibility Law, and provided that all private dollar-denominated contracts would be converted to pesos at 1:1, with the possibility of renegotiation of the indebtedness between the parties concerned. Through the various provisions of the Emergency Law, Argentina de-linked its currency and its economy from the US dollar. For the conversion, the law established generally the existing parity of 1:1,152 so that the existing nominal value of all monetary values would go on expressing those values in pesos, although the peso had ceased to be convertible at par to the US dollar.

141. The pesification of the gas tariffs, as well as the tariffs of all other utilities and public contracts, and the cessation of their adjustment according to foreign indices, was carried out via the Emergency Law as an integral part of the complete de-linking in legal terms of the peso from the US dollar (and, as a consequence, marked the end of the pegging at par that had been in force since 1991 under Argentina's currency board system) taking place after the run on Argentina's reserves and the massive devaluation of the peso in the international market.

142. Total submits that it is not challenging the pesification of Argentina's economy as effected by the Emergency Law. Total objects only to the pesification of the gas tariffs (and the connected abandonment of the PPI adjustment). Total claims that the pegging of the gas tariffs to the US dollar was neither connected with nor part of the convertibility system, and, accordingly, should not have been abolished as part of such pesification in view of the promises and assurances given by Argentina under the Gas Regulatory Framework about the stability of the tariff denomination in US dollars. According to Total, the calculation of the gas tariffs in US dollars and the automatic adjustment of the tariffs according to the US PPI

were specific promises given by Argentina in order to maintain TGN's gas tariffs in real dollar terms. In other terms, these two 'additional commitments' were stabilisation clauses exactly designed to operate in the event of a devaluation. On this premise, according to Total, even in the case of a massive devaluation (entailing a radical change in the Convertibility regime):

> the onus would be on the regulator to call an Extraordinary Tariff Review in order to reduce the dollar-calculated tariff to reflect the reduction in peso-based costs and restore the licensee's equilibrium. Therein lies the principal benefit of the dollar tariff: it protects the licensee whilst this review is carried out; whereas with a peso tariff, the licensee is exposed to a devaluation and there is no immediate incentive for the regulator to carry out a review promptly. However, in either case, the principal commitment in the Gas Regulatory Framework is that the licensee's economic equilibrium is maintained through an Extraordinary Tariff Review.

143. Argentina points out that, in terms of devalued post-2001 pesos, this would have meant an increase in tariffs of about 200–300 per cent. In response, Total states that it would have been feasible to maintain those tariffs in US dollars through an Extraordinary Tariff review, notwithstanding that the rest of the economy had been pesified. According to Total, had Argentina not pesified the tariffs and had ENARGAS carried out the Extraordinary Review *sua sponte* on the consumers' request according to Articles 46 and 47 of the Gas Law, by taking into account the reduced value in US dollar terms of those components of the tariff that were incurred in (devalued) pesos, the tariff in US dollar terms would have decreased by almost 25 per cent (equivalent in peso terms to a 130 per cent tariff increase). More specifically, after the Extraordinary Review the tariffs of US$11 would have been equivalent to AR$33 (after the devaluation) and would have amounted to US$8.33 (equivalent to AR$25).

144. Recalling its previous legal analysis of the applicable principles regarding government promises and undertakings made to foreign investors, i.e., the requirement of specificity and the freedom that States generally have to amend their laws, particularly when a fundamental change of factual circumstances occurs, the Tribunal is not convinced by Total's arguments for the following reasons

7.2 No 'promise' of dollar denominated tariffs and their adjustment was made to Total

145. The Tribunal considers that the provisions according to which the gas tariffs were to be calculated in US dollars and adjusted in line with the US

PPI cannot properly be construed as 'promises' upon which Total could rely, since they were not addressed directly or indirectly to Total. They were provided for in the Gas Decree and in TGN's license as a means of implementing the core principle of the Gas Law, namely, that of guaranteeing to efficient licensees sufficient revenue to cover all reasonable operating costs and ensuring a reasonable rate of return (Arts 38 and 39), in accordance with the dollar-based convertibility system then in force in Argentina. Total contends that, under the Gas Regulatory Framework, dollar tariffs were not linked to the Convertibility Law and invokes section 9.2 of TGN's Licence, Article 41 of the Gas Decree and section 7.1, Annex F of the Bidding Rules of 1992. The Tribunal notes, however, that section 9.2 of TGN's Licence and Article 41 of the Gas Decree expressly refer to the Convertibility Law. This reference thus supports the opposite conclusion, namely, that the dollar denomination of the tariffs was closely linked to the Convertibility Law. In addition, another linkage is shown by the fact that the Convertibility Law prohibited indexation in pesos, in order to reinforce the stabilisation aim of the Convertability regime, while indexation of dollar values through reference to foreign prices was instead not prohibited.

146. Total claims that the denomination of the tariff in US dollars was meant to protect the distributors in case of devaluation. Total supports this argument by reference to the TGN Offering Memorandum of 1995 pursuant to which the shares still belonging to the government were offered for sale in the market. According to Total, the warnings to investors contained therein concerning the consequences of a peso devaluation on TGN's operation did not include a warning that the US dollar tariffs might be pesified. The Tribunal is, however, of the opinion that this document rather points in the contrary direction. The 1995 Offering Memorandum drafted for the sale of the 25 per cent stake held by the government warned potential investors of the risk of a great devaluation under the heading 'Convertibility and risks of the exchange rate.' More precisely, according to the Memorandum:

> Since the coming into force of the Convertibility Law in April, 1991, the peso/dollar exchange rate has suffered strict variations. The Central Bank, which in accordance with this Law is obliged to sell dollars to a price which does not exceed a peso per unit, has adopted the policy to buy dollars also at the rate of 1 peso per dollar. The persistence of the free convertibility of pesos into dollars cannot be ensured. In the event a great devaluation of the peso against the dollar takes place, the financial position and results of operations of the Company might be negatively affected, as well as its capacity to make payments in foreign currency (including cancellation of debt denominated in foreign currency) and dividend distribution in dollars at acceptable levels.

In the light of this text, the Tribunal is of the view that the Memorandum, besides warning potential investors of the general commercial risk of TGN's default and of decreasing demand for TGN caused by a devaluation of peso, also warned potential investors in TGN that a great devaluation of the peso and/or an abandonment of convertibility would affect the calculation of the tariffs in US dollar terms resulting in prejudice to 'the financial position and results of operations of the Company'. This reflected the fact that, as Total points out, TGN's regulated tariffs represented 98 per cent of its revenue.

147. Finally, Total supports its argument that the US dollar tariffs and the PPI adjustment were 'commitments' on which it could legally rely, invoking section 7.1, Annex F, Bidding Rules. We recall that with a view to obtaining foreign participation in the privatisation of the various Argentine State-owned utilities, the government made specific commitments towards such interested foreign parties for the purposes of inducing them to participate in the bidding process and to bring additional capital, technical and other know-how to modernise and efficiently run those utilities. More specifically, Total refers to section 7.1 of the Bidding Rules. Under the heading '*Ajuste Futuro de Tarifas*' (Annex F section 7), section 7.1. provided that:

> Tariffs are expressed in pesos, convertible as per Law No. 23.928 at par 1=1 with the United States dollar. . . . tariffs would be adjusted immediately and automatically in the event of a modification of the exchange rate. To all effects, the amount of Argentine currency necessary to buy one US dollar in the New York market shall be considered.

Moreover, the Bidding Rules at section 7.5. went on to indicate that:

> The Distribution tariff . . . shall be adjusted semi-annually, from the taking of possession, in accordance with the variation operated in the wholesale price index of industrial commodities of the US, taken by the Board of Governors of the Federal Reserve system, within the second month prior to the beginning of each semester after the Taking of Possession, as established in the corresponding licence and the remaining requirements established in the Tariff Rules and General Conditions of Service. The Regulating Authority shall determine the mechanism for adjustment.

148. The Tribunal does not need to analyse the import of those provisions because Total did not take part in the bidding process in December 1992. Therefore, on the basis of the legal principles highlighted above, Total cannot invoke the Bidding Rules as a promise on which it could have relied when it invested in the gas sector in 2001. The situation of Total is, therefore,

different from that of foreign investors who had participated in the privatisation and, consequently, invoked their reliance on the bidding rules in other disputes.

149. No assurance about such stability – that is the maintenance of the tariffs in US dollars and the associated US PPI adjustment, irrespective of the Convertibility Law being in force – had been given by Argentina's authorities to Total when Total was considering the investment or was carrying out the transaction. Moreover, such assurances had not been sought by Total. In making its investment Total properly considered (or should have considered) the totality of the relevant legal regime as it existed in 2001 (including the suspension of the US PPI adjustment). Within this framework, the Gas Decree and TGN's Licence (to which Total was not party) incorporated as a matter of law and regulation the US dollar and US PPI pegs.

150. Summing up, the Tribunal concludes that the denomination of the tariffs in US dollars was not the object of a promise or a commitment to Total but rather was an integral element of the Gas Regulatory Framework in place in Argentina when Total made its investment. The automatic adjustment of the tariffs to the US PPI was part of this framework and was closely linked to and reflected the denomination and calculation in US dollars of those tariffs, which in turn was correlated to the convertibility monetary system in force in Argentina since 1991.

7.3 Relevance of the PPI adjustment suspension being in place when Total invested in TGN

151. The Tribunal now must examine the conduct of Total with respect to its alleged reliance on the stability of the operation of the gas regime in US dollars as was the case when Total made its investment, taking into account the suspension(s) of the US PPI adjustments that were in place at that time.

152. The Tribunal recalls that Total agreed to buy the shares of TransCanada Group in May 2000 and that it closed the deal in January 2001. Thus, on this second date, Total became a French foreign investor in Argentina whose investment in TGN was protected by the BIT. As recalled above at paragraphs 62 ff., at that time the PPI adjustments had been suspended twice by agreement between the ENARGAS (and the government) and the licensees: first, in January 2000, for six months and subsequently, on August 4, 2000, for two years. Moreover, on August 18, 2000, a judge had suspended the application of the second adjustment and the subsequent recovery of the increases due to accrue during the suspension.

153. Argentina submits that Total could not have legitimate expectations about the stability of the tariff regime as laid down in the Gas Regulatory Framework since it had been undermined by those suspensions. Argentina suggests that, in analysing the Gas Regulatory Framework, Total had not exercised the diligence that it should have done as a foreign investor intending to make a long-term investment in a country such as Argentina. In this regard, Total explained in its submissions that Total's management, even if aware of this development, 'did not consider that TGN's right to the adjustment of its tariffs in accordance with the US PPI to be in jeopardy'.

154. The Tribunal notes that Total's management considered the first Acta Acuerdo as a 'favour' to Fernando De la Rúa's new administration; the second suspension for two years as immaterial because of the subsequent recovery provided for by Decree, and the suspension of the Decree by injunction as irrelevant because Total believed the injunction was based on weak legal grounds (the injunction had been challenged by the government), notwithstanding, however, the admission of Mr François Faurès (one of Total's managers in Argentina and a witness called by Total) that 'there are always doubts in a legal dispute, since it depends on an independent power'.

155. The Tribunal notes that while all of these developments affecting the tariff adjustment based on the US PPI were considered as irrelevant by Total's management in making its investment in TGN, another foreign company (CMS Gas Transmission Company) that had already invested in TGN considered them relevant enough to start a dispute against Argentina under the U.S.-Argentina BIT based on the opposite conclusion that TGN's right to adjust its tariffs in accordance with the US PPI was in jeopardy.

156. The Tribunal is of the view that, although the various Actas Acuerdo and judicial acts at the time were temporary, they affected the future existence of the PPI adjustment mechanism. From a business point of view, an experienced international investor such as Total could not have considered these developments as irrelevant to the future stability of the PPI-adjusted US dollar gas tariffs. An objective risk analysis of the situation should have alerted Total that the stability of the gas regime was being undermined in practice from various directions. This was happening at the very moment when, for the first time, the PPI would have provided greater protection to the utilities than if a peso-based adjustment had been in place. Expecting that, after a two-year suspension, the government would have been willing and able to impose on the users (usuarios) an obligation to pay the PPI increase retroactively for that period appears contrary to common sense or

experience. This is especially the case since a judge, at the request of the Ombudsman, issued an injunction in the interest of those users.

157. Total also claims that it did not weigh these negative developments because it was focusing on a long-term perspective in making its investment, as stated by one of its managers in oral testimony. This is quite possible, but then Total contradicts itself when it complains that its legitimate expectations based on the stability of this very regime have been frustrated.

158. In conclusion, therefore, the Tribunal is of the view that Total's alleged full reliance on the mechanism for adjusting tariffs based on the US PPI was misplaced, especially in light of the growing difficulties experienced by Argentina's economy that were at the root of the US PPI tariff adjustment suspension.

7.4 Reasons for Argentina's abandonment of US dollar tariffs and their adjustment according to US PPI

159. The Tribunal has already highlighted above that the reasons for, and modalities and context of, a change to a national legal system (specifically, in this case, the change affecting the Gas Regulatory Framework) are also relevant and important in light of the requirement that a host State act in good faith, which underpins the fair and equitable treatment standard.

160. In this respect the Tribunal considers that Argentina's emergency at the end of 2001, taking into account its political and social fall-out, justified Argentina's abandonment of the convertibility regime, including the pesification of tariffs. Leaving utilities tariffs in US dollars, while the rest of the economy had been de-dollarised, would have lacked any reasonable basis and would have entailed a form of reverse discrimination or a privilege for the beneficiaries. This is particularly true taking into account that TGN's gas transportation activity is not an ordinary business operation but is qualified by law as a 'national public service' (Article 1, Gas Law). The principle that the gas transportation and distribution activities are to be regulated so as to ensure that just and reasonable tariffs are applied (Article 2(d), Gas Law), which Total has specifically emphasised, cannot justify any one-sided interpretation in favour of public service providers. Rather, the Tribunal considers that a more balanced interpretation is called for, taking into account that consumer protection is one of the primary objectives of the Gas Law, which provides that the tariffs shall be just and reasonable for consumers and at the same time that ensure that utilities can earn a reasonable rate of return. Total suggests that while maintaining the tariffs in US dollars, an Extraordinary

Review could have reduced the tariff to reflect the pesification of the local components of the costs. However, this would have transferred most of the impact of the peso devaluation to Argentina's consumers and only the gas tariffs would have remained in dollars, while the rest of the economy had been pesified.

161. In the case of a 'normal' devaluation of the peso, the de-dollarisation of the gas tariffs would not have been economically justified nor socially necessary, and might thus be objectionable under the fair and equitable treatment clause of the BIT (Art. 3). In contrast, the 'bankruptcy' of Argentina in 2001–02, the forced abrupt abandonment of the US dollar parity and the devaluation of the peso by more than 300 per cent, support the conclusion that the pesification of the tariffs and their de-linkage from the US PPI were not unfair or inequitable.

162. The balancing test recalled above, requires an assessment of the existence of a breach of the fair and equitable treatment standard taking into account the purposes, nature and objectives of the measures challenged, and an evaluation of whether they are proportional, reasonable and not discriminatory. In other terms, the changes to the Gas Regulatory Framework brought about by the measures have to be judged in the context of the severe economic emergency that Argentina was facing in 2001–02.

163. The pesification was a measure of general application to all sectors of Argentina's economy and to all legal obligations expressed in monetary terms within the country. It was a devaluation and redenomination of the national currency within the monetary sovereignty of the State. Moreover, this measure was taken in good faith in a situation of recognised economic emergency of an exceptional, even catastrophic, nature. In this context, a series of harsh measures was imposed on the population (such as blocking withdrawals from banks – the *corralito*) to avoid a general collapse of the economy, and hence of the State and society, and to foster a progressive recovery. The complete reversal of Argentina's monetary policies and system was made inevitable by the impossibility for the country to maintain the exchange rate after having lost almost all of its reserves, leading to the massive, rapid devaluation of the peso on the free exchange markets, while the IMF had withdrawn its support. In this context, the pesification of the economy – the elimination of the fixed link to the US dollar – necessarily also entailed the de-dollarisation of the public utilities' tariff regimes on the same terms, so that all tariff-related dollar-denominated debt as well as future prices were converted into pesos at the previously fixed and official exchange rate of 1:1. Utilities were treated

the same as all other holders of contractual rights, salary holders, etc. in Argentina. The 1:1 rate reflected the impossibility for holders of debt in US dollars to pay the market rate for the US dollar when all of their claims, income, etc., had been converted forcibly and inevitably at the official rate. The de-dollarisation of the tariffs was thus a non-discriminatory measure of general application, parallel to those applied to other sectors of the economy and to all inhabitants of Argentina. The mechanism for tariff adjustment in accordance with the US PPI was also a part of the tariff dollarisation scheme connected with convertibility at par; accordingly, it was an exception to the prohibition of indexation of any peso-denominated obligations under the convertibility, reflecting the pegging of the tariffs to the US dollar rather than to the evolution of prices in Argentina. The US PPI adjustment was not abolished by cutting this link in isolation, but as part of the delinkage of the Argentine monetary system from the US dollar that was effected by the general pesification via the Emergency Law in the exercise of Argentina's monetary sovereignty.

164. The Tribunal finds that this measure and its application cannot be considered unfair in the circumstances, considering the inherent flexibility of the fair and equitable standard. Unfairness must be evaluated in respect of the measures challenged, both in the light of their objective effects but also in the light of the reasons that led to their adoption (subjective good faith, proportionality to the aims and legitimacy of the latter according to general practice). It is therefore not possible to share Total's view, developed especially in the LECG Report on Damages, that the pesification breached Total's treaty rights and that its effects must be included in the calculation of damages suffered by Total for which it claims compensation under the BIT. Such changes to general legislation, in the absence of specific stabilisation promises to the foreign investor, reflect a legitimate exercise of the host State's governmental powers that are not prevented by a BIT's fair and equitable treatment standard and are not in breach of the same. The untouchability ('*intangibilidad*') of those foreign currency peg provisions invoked by Total cannot be the object of legal expectation in a case of monetary and economic crisis such as that experienced by Argentina in 2001–02.

165. The general character, the good faith and absence of discrimination by Argentina, as well as the exceptional circumstance that 'forced' Argentina to adopt the measures at issue, viewed objectively, preclude the Tribunal from finding that Argentina breached the fair and equitable obligations of treatment under the BIT with respect to the dollar denomination of the tariff and the six-month US PPI adjustment.

7.5 The freezing of tariffs since 2002

166. Having examined the measures taken by Argentina to address the crisis by enacting the Emergency Law (i.e., the pesification of the tariffs and abolition of adjustments based on the variations of the US PPI), the Tribunal now addresses the de facto freezing of tariffs since 2002, which was caused by the failure of the renegotiation mechanisms proposed by Argentina after the enactment the Emergency Law.

167. We recall that the Tribunal has concluded above that pesification of the utility tariffs was reasonable in the circumstances due to the crisis in Argentina and the general de-dollarisation of Argentina's economy. No expectations could reasonably be maintained (even less 'legitimately') that only the tariffs would be excepted from such a pesification, especially as Total was not a beneficiary of any specific promise. The situation is, however, different concerning the absence of any readjustment of the gas tariffs since 2002. We recall that the principle that tariffs of privatised gas utilities should be sufficient to cover their reasonable costs and a reasonable rate of return was enshrined in the Gas Regulatory Framework. As a means to ensure this 'economic equilibrium', a variety of adjustments over time were provided for by the Gas Regulatory Framework. These included the six-month US PPI adjustment, the five-year Tariff Review and the Extraordinary Review. This framework is consistent with sound management of utilities in a market economy, where private entrepreneurs must be able to cover their costs and make a reasonable return in order to operate and to raise capital to provide an efficient service, especially considering that investments in such utilities are based on long-term planning. The gas transportation tariffs were accordingly to be determined and adjusted in a way reflecting those criteria. The expectation of foreign investors in the gas sector about the long-term maintenance of the above-mentioned principle was reinforced by the existence of Argentina's BITs. Irrespective of their specific wording, undoubtedly these treaties are meant to promote foreign direct investment and reflect the signatories' commitments to a hospitable investment climate. Imposing conditions that make an investment unprofitable for a long-term investor (for instance, compelling a foreign investor to operate at a loss) is surely not compatible with the underlying assumptions and purpose of the BIT regime (i.e., 'to create favourable conditions for French investments . . .' in accordance with the Preamble to the Argentina-France BIT).

168. An operator-investor such as Total was entitled, therefore, to expect that the gas regime would respect certain basic features. This did not mean

that Total could rely on BIT protection to ensure the stability of the gas law regime without any possibility of change to that regime by Argentina in the light of the dramatic developments. The basic principles of economic equilibrium and business viability enshrined in the Gas Law were protected from a forward-looking perspective by the mechanisms of readjustment, namely the ordinary and extraordinary reviews whose benefits were not restricted to the participants in the initial privatisation.

169. The Tribunal notes that these principles and mechanisms were restated forcefully in the Emergency Law and in the subsequent decrees of early 2002 that were based on that law, which established a single commission for all renegotiations of utilities contracts and set short deadlines to complete these processes.

170. Moreover, since this process was moving slower than anticipated, the Ministry of Economy authorised ENARGAS to proceed with an Extraordinary Review that had been blocked by the Emergency Law. Thus, while pesifying the tariffs and suppressing the US PPI adjustment, the Emergency Law restated the principle that tariffs could be readjusted, a future undertaking that gained special importance after the devaluation and the complete overturn of the US dollar basis of the gas regulatory regime. We note moreover that the Gas Law enshrining the fundamental principles mentioned above was not amended and is still in force.

171. However, the Extraordinary Review, as well as a 7 per cent tariff increase proposed by Argentina's Executive in December 2002 and January 2003 (Decrees 2.437/02, 146/03, and 120/03), were blocked by a judicial intervention. When President Kirchner took office in May 2003, no adjustment of TGN's tariffs had yet taken place. By this point, Argentina had emerged from the crisis as commentators, international organisations and other arbitral tribunals in investment disputes against Argentina have recognised. The failure of the renegotiation process in 2002 to lead to re-adjustments, notwithstanding the legal provisions enacted for that purpose, might be understandable in view of the political and economic emergency of that period.

172. This is not true after President Kirchner's election and the creation through UNIREN of a general mechanism to carry out tariff re-adjustments. It is generally recognised that Argentina's economy quickly recovered from the crisis – by the end of 2003 and the beginning of 2004. Moreover, in February 2004 a 450 per cent increase in the gas price was imposed on industrial users. This increase did not go, however, to the benefit of TGN, but

rather financed the trust fund for new investments in the gas transportation network. Total has also submitted that the government treated the gas sector differently than other sectors in this respect.

173. The Tribunal recalls here that UNIREN was required to conclude the renegotiation process by 31 December, 2004, this being the new term set out after the ineffective expiration of the latest term fixed by MoE Resolution No. 62/03. However, this did not happen. Negotiations with utilities had been dragging. As late as April 2007, UNIREN proposed to TGN a Final Acta Acuerdo entailing a 15 per cent staggered tariff increase, that would not have remedied the lack of readjustments in the past. Moreover, Article 17 of the proposal imposed on TGN, as a precondition for the agreement to come into force, the obligation to obtain from its shareholders: (i) an immediate suspension of any claim against Argentina; and (ii) their agreement to entirely withdraw those claims after the full tariff review was held and the new tariffs published. As outlined by Total, under Article 17, TGN needed to secure the relevant undertakings from 99.9 per cent of its shareholders (including CMS and Total). Without the above-mentioned suspensions and withdrawals, the Acta Acuerdo would be terminated and thus TGN would not receive tariff increase, the licence could be revoked and TGN would be obliged to indemnify the government for any damages payable as a result of a claim brought by a TGN minority shareholder. Total submits that these conditions represent an additional breach of the fair and equitable treatment required under Article 3 of the BIT.

174. In sum, from the passage of Emergency Law onwards, Argentina's public authorities repeatedly established new deadlines, causing protracted delays in the renegotiation of concessions and licences (the tariff regime included) in the public utility sector for almost six years. At the same time, any automatic semi-annual adjustment (such as the one originally provided linked to the US PPI) had been discontinued.

175. As mentioned above, the failure to promptly readjust the tariffs when the Emergency Law was enacted and during the height of the crisis could have been justified, provided that Argentina subsequently had pursued successful renegotiations to re-establish the equilibrium of the tariffs as provided by law. This, however, has not happened due to the inconclusive results of the renegotiation process entrusted by Argentina to UNIREN. Therefore, the Tribunal cannot but conclude that, in this respect, Argentina is in breach of its BIT obligation to grant fair and equitable treatment to Total under Article 3 in respect of Total's investment in TGN.

7.6 Analysis of previous arbitral decisions

176. At this point, before concluding on this claim, the Tribunal considers it appropriate to recall previous arbitral decisions that have dealt with the impact of the Emergency Law and related measures on Argentina's legal framework governing, generally, the public utilities sectors and, more specifically, the gas sector. The Tribunal shares the opinion that judicial consistency in the field of international investment law is as far as possible desirable, notwithstanding the absence of a rule of precedent.

177. The Tribunal notes that, among the disputes against Argentina raised by foreign investors in Argentina's public utilities sectors, those involving Enron (a US investor in TGS, one of the two gas transportation companies subject to the privatisation process of 1991–92), British Gas (a UK investor in MetroGAS, one of the eight gas distribution companies subject to the privatization process of 1991–92) and National Grid Transco plc (a UK investor in Transener, an electricity transmission company subject to the privatisation process of 1992–93) concerned investors who had been original participants in the privatisation process. By finding that the enactment of the Emergency Law breached the relevant fair and equitable treatment clause by Argentina, these tribunals emphasise the Bidding Rules that regulated participation in the privatisation of the various public utilities concerned (as well as the various related Information Memoranda prepared by Argentina's financial advisers for this purpose). In order to find that Argentina had breached the relevant BIT, these Tribunals have referred explicitly to these rules as specific commitments of Argentina towards foreign investors and as specific promises made to them on which they had relied on in making their investment. According to these Tribunals, Argentina (through the pesification of gas tariffs and the removal of the US PPI tariff adjustment mechanism as a consequence of the Emergency Law) frustrated the expectations of those investors who legitimately relied upon the provisions of the Bidding Rules and breached the fair and equitable treatment obligation of the relevant BIT.

178. The Tribunal recalls that the position of Total is different from that of the claimants in the above-mentioned cases who took part in the privatisation process, as Total invested in Argentina's gas sector in 2001, almost ten years after the privatisation process took place. We have explained above why this Tribunal believes that this different factual situation warrants different legal conclusions as to the presence or lack of 'specific commitments' by Argentina and as to the issue of 'legitimate expectations' based thereon.

179. On the other hand, the Tribunals in *Sempra*, *LG&E* and *CMS*, have found breaches of the fair and equitable treatment standard because of the pesification of tariffs (and the connected abolition of tariff adjustments to the US PPI), where the investors involved had invested after the original privatisation process. As Total did here, these investors had subsequently acquired their interests in the gas distribution and transmission utilities from Argentina itself, or from other investors. According to these Tribunals, the US dollar denomination of gas tariffs and their automatic adjustment to the US PPI variations should have remained unaffected by the general pesification adopted by Argentina through the Emergency Law pursuant to the fair and equitable treatment standard protection under the relevant BITs. This Tribunal has explained above the basis upon which it reached the partly different conclusion that neither the pesification of gas tariffs nor the abolition of their linkage to the US PPI variations are in breach of the fair and equitable clause of the Argentina-France BIT. The Tribunal believes that its conclusions are firmly rooted in relevant international law, as reviewed above, taking into account the features of the Argentina-France BIT and the specific circumstances of Total's investment, and in the light of the exceptional nature of Argentina's crisis.

180. As explained above, in following this different approach, this Tribunal has distinguished the abandonment of the US dollar denomination of tariffs and their linkage to the US PPI (found not to be in breach of the BIT in view of their connection to the Convertibility Law and the exceptional crisis of Argentina that led to the pesification) from the subsequent failure to readjust the tariffs. The Tribunal has found that this latter conduct by Argentina constitutes a breach of the fair and equitable treatment standard, also because it is contrary to the very principles spelled out by Argentina's law and authorities, both before and after the Emergency Law. This Tribunal thus shares the view of previous Tribunals that have found Argentina to be in breach of the fair and equitable treatment standard because of the persistent lack of any tariff readjustment.

181. Finally, the Tribunal notes that many of the previous awards dealing with the same matter, while following a different approach, mitigated the impact of their holdings that Argentina acted in breach of the fair and equitable treatment standard, by giving weight, on different bases, to the emergency situation of Argentina that brought about the pesification of public service tariffs. In this respect, such tribunals have relied on the defence of necessity under customary international law, or on specific provisions in the relevant BITs, and have considered that Argentina's breach of the fair and equitable treatment standard did not occur when the measures challenged were taken

through the Emergency Law on January 6, 2002, but rather at a later date (such as June 2002), recognising that the BIT protection could not have insulated an investor completely from the emergency situation of Argentina in 2001–02.

[...]

 CASE

Technicas Medioambientales Tecmed SA v The United Mexican States ('Tecmed'), excerpt

A. Procedural history

[...]

C. Summary of facts and allegations presented by the parties

26. The claimant's claims are related to an investment in land, buildings and other assets in connection with a public auction called by Promotora Inmobiliaria del Ayuntamiento de Hermosillo (hereinafter referred to as 'Promotora'), a decentralised municipal agency of the Municipality of Hermosillo, located in the State of Sonora, Mexico. The purpose of the auction was the sale of real property, buildings and facilities and other assets relating to 'Cytrar', a controlled landfill of hazardous industrial waste. Tecmed was the awardee, pursuant to a decision adopted by the Management Board of Promotora on February 16, 1996. Later on, the holder of Tecmed's rights and obligations under the tender came to be Cytrar, a company organised by Tecmed for such purpose and to run the landfill operations.

27. The landfill was built in 1988 on land purchased by the Government of the State of Sonora, in the locality of Las Víboras, within the jurisdiction of the Municipality of Hermosillo, State of Sonora. The landfill had a renewable license to operate for a five-year term as from December 7, 1988, issued by the Ministry of Urban Development and Ecology (SEDUE) of the Federal Government of Mexico to Parques Industriales de Sonora, a decentralised agency of the Government of the State of Sonora. During this period, the landfill operator was not this agency but another entity, Parque Industrial de Hermosillo, another public agency of the State of Sonora. Ownership of the landfill was then transferred to a decentralised agency of the Municipality of Hermosillo, Confinamiento Controlado Parque Industrial de Hermosillo

OPD; in this new phase, it had a new authorisation to operate for an indefinite period of time. Such authorisation had been granted on May 4, 1994, by the Hazardous Materials, Waste and Activities Division of the National Ecology Institute of Mexico (hereinafter referred to as INE), an agency of the Federal Government of the United Mexican States within the Ministry of the Environment, Natural Resources and Fisheries (SEMARNAP), which cancelled the previous authorization, granted on December 7, 1988. INE – both within the framework of SEDUE as well as of its successor SEMARNAP – is in charge of Mexico's national policy on ecology and environmental protection, and is also the regulatory body on environmental issues.

28. Upon the liquidation and dissolution of the above-mentioned decentralised agency, ordered by the Governor of the State of Sonora on July 6, 1995, in mid-1995, the assets of the landfill became the property of the Government of the State of Sonora. Subsequently, on November 27, 1995, through a donation agreement entered into between that Government and the Municipality of Hermosillo, the property was transferred to Promotora.

29. In a letter dated April 16, 1996, confirmed by letters of June 5, August 26 and September 5, 1996, Tecmed made a request to INE for the operating license of the landfill – then in the name of Confinamiento Controlado Parque Industrial de Hermosillo OPD – to be issued in the name of Cytrar. The Municipality of Hermosillo supported this request in its note to INE dated March 28, 1996, requesting INE to provide all possible assistance in connection with the name-change procedure in the operating license in favour of Tecmed or of the company organised by it. In an official letter of September 24, 1996, INE notified Cytrar, in connection with the application to change the name of the entity from Promotora to Cytrar, that Cytrar had been registered with INE. The official letter was then returned by Cytrar to INE as requested by INE after having been issued, and replaced by another one of the same date to which the authorisation relating to the landfill was attached, dated November 11, 1996, stating the new name of the entity. Such authorisation could be extended every year at the applicant's request 30 days prior to expiration. It was so extended for an additional year, until November 19, 1998.

30. The arbitration claim seeks damages, including compensation for damage to reputation, and interests in connection with damage alleged to have accrued as of November 25, 1998, on which date INE rejected the application for renewal of the authorisation to operate the landfill, expiring on November 19, 1998, pursuant to an INE resolution on the same date, whereby INE further requested Cytrar to submit a programme for the clo-

sure of the landfill. Subsidiarily, the claimant has requested restitution in kind through the granting of permits to the claimant enabling it to operate the Las Víboras landfill until the end of its useful life, in addition to compensation for damages.

31. The claimant further argues that the successive permits granted by INE to Cytrar in connection with the operation of the landfill constitute a violation of the conditions on which the claimant made its investment because: (i) such permits, both as regards their duration as well as the conditions to which they were subject, were different from the permit given for operation of the landfill at the time the investment was made; and (ii) the price paid by Cytrar included the acquisition of intangible assets which involved the transfer to Cytrar of existing permits to operate the landfill and under which such landfill was being operated at the time of making the investment, and not the ones ultimately granted to it. The claimant argues that such a violation of conditions also involves a violation of, among other provisions, Articles 2 and 3(1) of the Agreement and a violation of Mexican law. However, the claimant states that it is not seeking in these arbitration proceedings a pronouncement or declaration regarding the lawfulness or unlawfulness, legality or illegality of acts or omissions attributable to the respondent in connection with permits or authorisations relating to the operation of the Las Víboras landfill prior to the INE resolution of November 19, 1998, which terminated Cytrar's authorisation to operate the landfill, considered in isolation, although it highlights the significance of such acts or omissions as preparatory acts for subsequent conduct attributable to the respondent which, according to the claimant, is in violation of the Agreement or facilitated such conduct.

32. The claimant argues that the refusal to renew the landfill's operating permit, contained in the INE resolution of November 25, 1998, constitutes an expropriation of its investment, without any compensation or justification thereof, and further constitutes a violation of Articles 3(1), 3(2), 4(1), 4(5), 5(1), 5(2) and 5(3) of the Agreement, as well as a violation of Mexican law. According to the claimant, such refusal would frustrate its justified expectation of the continuity and duration of the investment made and would impair recovery of the invested amounts and the expected rate of return.

33. The claimant alleges that the conditions of the tender and the invitation to tender, the award or sale of the landfill or of the assets relating thereto and the investment made by the claimant were substantially modified after the investment was made for reasons attributable to acts or omissions of Mexican municipal, State and federal authorities. The claimant claims that such modifications, with detrimental effects for its investment and which

allegedly led to the denial by the Federal Government of an extension to operate the landfill, are, to a large extent, due to political circumstances essentially associated to the change of administration in the Municipality of Hermosillo, in which the landfill is physically situated, rather than to legal considerations. Specifically, the claimant attributes such changes to the result of the election held in Mexico in July 1997, one of the consequences of which was the taking of office of a new Mayor of the Municipality of Hermosillo and similar changes in other municipal governments in the State of Sonora. According to the claimant's allegations, the new authorities of Hermosillo encouraged a movement of citizens against the landfill, which sought the withdrawal or non-renewal of the landfill's operating permit and its close-down, and which also led to confrontation with the community, even leading to blocking access to the landfill. The authorities of the State of Sonora, where the Municipality of Hermosillo is located, are alleged to have expressly supported the position adopted by the Municipality.

34. The claimant argues that the Federal Government yielded to the combined pressure of the municipal authorities of Hermosillo and of the State of Sonora along with the community movement opposed to the landfill, which, according to the claimant, led to the INE Resolution of November 25, 1998, referred to above. This Resolution denied Cytrar authorisation to operate the landfill and ordered its closedown. The claimant argues that INE's refusal to extend the authorisation to operate the landfill is an arbitrary act which violates the Agreement, international law and Mexican law. It further denies any misconduct or violation on its part of the terms under which the landfill permit was granted and which could justify a refusal to extend the authorisation. The claimant alleges that certain breaches of the conditions of the permit that expired on November 19, 1998, which was subsequently not extended by INE, did not warrant such an extreme decision. The claimant points out that such breaches had been the subject matter of an investigation conducted by the Federal Environmental Protection Attorney's Office ('PROFEPA'), which, like INE, is an agency within the purview of SEMARNAP, but with powers, among other things, to monitor compliance with federal environmental rules and to impose sanctions, which may include a revocation of the operating license. It also stresses that PROFEPA had not found violations of such an extent that they might endanger the environment or the health of the population or which justified more stringent sanctions than the fines eventually imposed on Cytrar by PROFEPA as a result of its investigations.

35. The claimant stresses the commitment of Cytrar, with the support of Tecmed, as from July 3, 1998, to relocate the hazardous waste landfill operation to another site on the basis of agreements reached with federal, state

and municipal authorities as of such date, and denies the allegation that the fact that such relocation had not yet taken place at the time the extension of Cytrar's permit was refused could be validly argued among the grounds referred to by INE in its resolution of November 1998 denying the extension. The claimant points out that Cytrar, with the support of Tecmed, subsequently added to its commitment to relocate the landfill another commitment to pay the costs and economic consequences involved in such relocation, and further denies that the delay or failure to relocate was attributable to it. The claimant insists that the only condition to which Cytrar subjected its relocation commitment was that, pending such relocation, operation by Cytrar of the Las Víboras landfill and the relevant operating permit should continue, and that such condition is a part of the relocation agreement entered into with the federal, state and municipal authorities of the respondent. At any rate, the respondent argues that Cytrar unsuccessfully applied to INE for a limited extension of its permit to operate the Las Víboras landfill (five months as from November 19, 1998), in order to come to an agreement, within such term, on the identification of the site to which the landfill operation would be relocated and to carry out the relocation.

36. According to the claimant, the expropriation act and other violations of the Agreement which it deems to have suffered, have caused the claimant to sustain a complete loss of the profits and income from the economic and commercial operation of the Las Víboras landfill as an ongoing business. Therefore the damage sustained includes the impossibility of recovering the cost incurred in the acquisition of assets for the landfill, its adaptation and preparation and, more generally, the investments relating to or required for this kind of industrial activity, including, but not limited to, constructions relating to the landfill; lost profits and business opportunities; the impossibility of performing contracts entered into with entities producing industrial waste, thus leading to termination of such contracts and to possible claims relating thereto; and the injury caused to the claimant and to its subsidiaries in Mexico due to the adverse effect on its image in that country, with the consequent negative impact on the claimant's capacity to expand and develop its activities in Mexico.

37. The respondent, after pointing out that it does not consider that the powers of INE to deny the landfill's operating permit are regulated but discretionary, denies that such denial was a result of an arbitrary exercise of such discretionary powers. The respondent claims that denial of the permit is a control measure in a highly regulated sector and which is very closely linked to public interests. Accordingly, the respondent holds that such denial seeks to discourage certain types of conduct, but is not intended to penalise. The

respondent stresses that the matters debated in these arbitration proceedings are to be solved in a manner consistent with the provisions of the Agreement and of international law.

38. The respondent denies that the subject matter of the tender and subsequent award to Tecmed was a landfill, understood as a group or pool of tangible and intangible assets including licenses or permits to operate a controlled landfill of hazardous waste. The respondent argues that the assets tendered and sold by Promotora solely include certain facilities, land, infrastructure and equipment, but no permits, authorisations or licenses. With regard to the documents signed by Promotora, Tecmed and Cytrar in connection with the public auction of the assets relating to the landfill, the respondent further argues that: (i) the obligation or responsibility to obtain permits, licenses or authorisations to operate the landfill was vested in Cytrar; (ii) Promotora did not attempt to obtain or provide such permits, licenses and authorizations for the benefit of or in the name of Cytrar, of the claimant or of Tecmed, nor did it guarantee that they would be obtained; (iii) Promotora's only commitment in this regard was to ensure that Cytrar could operate the landfill under the existing permits, authorisations or licenses, which remained vested in Confinamiento Parque Industrial de Hermosillo O.P.D. until Cytrar obtained its own permits, authorisations or licenses; (iv) it was always clear to Cytrar that it would require its own licenses, authorisations or permits in order to operate the landfill; and (v) neither Cytrar nor Tecmed contacted the competent federal authorities for information regarding the possibility of transferring existing authorizations or permits. The respondent denies the claim that the amount of $24,047,988.26 (Mexican Pesos) was paid as price for the permits or authorisations to operate the landfill, or that Promotora's related invoice reflects the reality of the tender and of the subsequent sales transaction.

39. The respondent challenges the Arbitral Tribunal's jurisdiction to decide in connection with conduct attributable or attributed to the respondent which occurred before the entry into force of the Agreement, or that any interpretation thereof – particularly Article 2(2), which extends the application of the Agreement to investments made prior to its entry into force – could lead to a different conclusion. Likewise, based on Title II.5 of the Appendix to the Agreement, the respondent rejects the Arbitral Tribunal's jurisdiction over acts or omissions attributed or attributable to the respondent which were or could have been known to the claimant, together with the resulting damages, prior to a fixed three-year period, calculated as from the commencement date of this arbitration pursuant to the Agreement. The respondent further denies that the conduct allegedly in violation of the Agreement attributed

to the respondent caused any damage to the claimant, so the claimant's claims would not fulfil the requirements of Title II.4 of the Appendix to the Agreement.

40. The respondent claims that the granting and conditions of the license of November 11, 1996, were within the statutory powers of INE, and that such conditions were similar to the ones governing other permits granted by INE at the time. The respondent stresses the negative attitude of the community towards the landfill due to its location and to the negative and highly critical view taken by the community with regard to the way Cytrar performed its task of transporting and confining the hazardous toxic waste originating in the former lead recycling and recovery plant of Alco Pacífico de México, SA de CV (hereinafter referred to as 'Alco Pacífico'), located in Tijuana, Baja California, which would highlight the importance of demanding strict compliance with the new operating permit granted by INE to Cytrar on November 19, 1997.

41. The respondent alleges that the municipal, state and federal authorities, as well as the security forces and courts of law addressed by Cytrar, acted diligently and in a manner consistent with the respondent's obligations under the Agreement to offer protection to Cytrar, to its personnel and to the claimant's investment relating to the landfill, in view of the different forms of social pressure exercised by groups or individuals opposed to the landfill, as well as to finding solutions to the problems resulting from such social pressure. The respondent further denies that any acts or omissions on the part of such groups or individuals or any liability arising out of such acts or omissions are attributable to the respondent under the Agreement or under international law. The respondent underscores the distinct duties performed by PROFEPA and INE, and points out that only INE is competent to decide whether or not to renew an expired permit, based on an assessment of different elements and circumstances exclusively pertaining to INE. The respondent therefore argues that it is irrelevant that PROFEPA did not revoke Cytrar's permit relating to the landfill or that it did not close it down due to considerations taken into account by INE in order to decide not to extend the authorisation, or that PROFEPA did not find that such matters were significant enough to justify more serious sanctions other than a fine.However, the Respondent highlights the growing number of violations committed by PROFEPA in Cytrar's operation of the landfill.

42. The respondent ultimately concludes that there is no conduct on the part of municipal, state or federal authorities of the United Mexican States in connection with Cytrar, Tecmed, the claimant, the landfill or the claimant's

investments which constitutes a violation of the Agreement pursuant to its provisions or to the provisions of Mexican or international law. It specifically denies that refusing to give a new permit to Cytrar to operate the landfill is in the nature of an expropriation or that there has been a violation of Article 5 of the Agreement. The respondent also denies that the claimant suffered discrimination or that it was denied national treatment in violation of Article 4 of the Agreement. The respondent denies having violated Article 2(1) of the Agreement regarding promotion or admission of investments or having committed any violation of Article 3 of the Agreement. Finally, the respondent challenges the calculation basis for the compensation sought by the claimant, which it considers absolutely inappropriate and inordinate.

D. The merits of the dispute

[...]

Fair and equitable treatment

152. According to Article 4(1) of the Agreement: 'Each Contracting Party will guarantee in its territory fair and equitable treatment, according to International Law, for the investments made by investors of the other Contracting Party.'

153. The Arbitral Tribunal finds that the commitment of fair and equitable treatment included in Article 4(1) of the Agreement is an expression and part of the *bona fide* principle recognised in international law, although bad faith from the State is not required for its violation: 'To the modern eye, what is unfair or inequitable need not equate with the outrageous or the egregious. In particular, a State may treat foreign investment unfairly and inequitably without necessarily acting in bad faith.'

154. The Arbitral Tribunal considers that this provision of the Agreement, in light of the good faith principle established by international law, requires the Contracting Parties to provide to international investments treatment that does not affect the basic expectations that were taken into account by the foreign investor to make the investment. The foreign investor expects the host State to act in a consistent manner, free from ambiguity and totally transparently in its relations with the foreign investor, so that it may know beforehand any and all rules and regulations that will govern its investments, as well as the goals of the relevant policies and administrative practices or directives, to be able to plan its investment and comply with such regulations. Any and all State actions conforming to such criteria should relate not

only to the guidelines, directives or requirements issued, or the resolutions approved thereunder, but also to the goals underlying such regulations. The foreign investor also expects the host State to act consistently, i.e., without arbitrarily revoking any pre-existing decisions or permits issued by the State that were relied upon by the investor to assume its commitments as well as to plan and launch its commercial and business activities. The investor also expects the State to use the legal instruments that govern the actions of the investor or the investment in conformity with the function usually assigned to such instruments, and not to deprive the investor of its investment without the required compensation. In fact, failure by the host State to comply with such pattern of conduct with respect to the foreign investor or its investments affects the investor's ability to measure the treatment and protection awarded by the host State and to determine whether the actions of the host State conform to the fair and equitable treatment principle. Therefore, compliance by the host State with such pattern of conduct is closely related to the above-mentioned principle, to the actual chances of enforcing such principle, and to excluding the possibility that State action be characterised as arbitrary; i.e., as presenting insufficiencies that would be recognised 'by any reasonable and impartial man', or, although not in violation of specific regulations, as being contrary to the law because: '(it) shocks, or at least surprises, a sense of juridical propriety'.

16

International investment law and taxation

 EXERCISE 26 – MINI MOCK ARBITRATION

In January 2011, the Nordic Kingdom of Calaska ('Calaska') introduced a new investment programme to incentivise both domestic and foreign direct investment in renewable energy. Under the banner 'Fly with the Wind' (Gov. Bill 32359/2011), the Energy Ministry introduced several generous tax breaks and tariff programmes that made it attractive for foreign companies to invest in the country's sole profitable renewable energy, the wind. The programme was far more successful than expected: it subsequently led to intense competition from foreign companies that adversely affected existing domestic actors.

Around the same time, a local businessman, Matt Entrysmith, acquired a controlling interest in the State's national wind monopoly, Vent, after the company was privatised. The acquisition was made possible with the support and via the investment made by several foreign companies, Vind Investment AB (Sweden), OOO Veter (Kazakhstan) and Vento Investissmento SA (Malta) all subsequently becoming minority shareholders in Vent Ltd.

Two years ago, after becoming concerned with the negative effect that the tax incentives have had on domestic producers, the government slashed all incentives programmes to roughly half of the initial amounts (Gov. Bill 17891/2014). This change in policy has caused all foreign players, except for those connected to Vent, to gradually leave Calaska. In part due to a rise in his fortune and due to his sense of patriotic obligation, Mr Entrysmith has entered politics and challenged President Pathway's policies on economy, domestic and foreign policy.

In his political campaign, President Pathway announced that he will clean up the mess that his predecessors made by selling the country to foreigners and an example will be made of all the profiteers. Earlier this year, government authorities (under the control of President Pathway) conducted a raid on Mr Entrysmith's property and on Vent's premises. In the raid, several sensitive documents were discovered that revealed a complex tax planning scheme involving Mr Entrysmith and Vent's subsidiaries, where purchases of raw materials were rerouted to claim VAT relief. Furthermore, a lower tax base was assessed via off-shore accounts based in Kazakhstan and Malta. Mr Entrysmith was subsequently arrested, convicted and sentenced to ten years in prison on charges of tax evasion, aggravated fraud and bribery. The National Tax Authority conducted a prompt audit of Vent's holdings, following which it assessed a tax bill for US$25 billion (125 per cent of the companies' total earnings) payable within 30 days. While Vent's Board was negotiating an extension for the tax bill, the National Tax Authority moved before the Calaskian court to set Vent Ltd in bankruptcy. Vent was declared bankrupt 24 hours later; its assets were sold in a forced-sale to a shadow company; the latter being acquired 48 hours later by the State-controlled company, EnergyBall. President Pathway later appeared on public television distancing himself from the actions of the National Tax Authority asserting that the Agency's actions were legal, reasonable and well-justified in accordance with Calaskian law.

The Boards of Vind Investment AB (Sweden), OOO Veter (Kazakhstan) and Vento Investissmento SA (Malta) have met and agreed on commencing an investment arbitration against the Kingdom of Calaska, under the Energy Charter Treaty pursuant to the UNCITRAL Rules. The SCC, as the appointing authority, has appointed the arbitral tribunal, which decided in the first procedural order that Stockholm will be the seat of the arbitration.

Assumption: Malta, Sweden, Kazakhstan and Calaska are signatories to, and have ratified, the Energy Charter Treaty.

 GROUP

Group 1
You represent the respondent in the arbitration, i.e., the Government of Calaska. Argue why the claims should not be admissible under the Energy Charter Treaty and even if these claims were admissible, that they should not succeed on the merits.

Group 2
You are the observer group. Were the best arguments presented? Did the Tribunal reach a well-reasoned decision?

Group 3
You represent claimant(s) in this dispute, i.e., the investors Vind Investment AB (Sweden), OOO Veter (Kazakhstan) and Vento Investissmento SA (Malta). Argue for why any relief should be

granted. When presenting your arguments, make sure to explain why the claims surrounding tax matters is admissible under the ECT.

Group 4
You are the arbitral tribunal charged with resolving the dispute under the Energy Charter Treaty. Decide whether the issues raised are admissible and if so, whether relief should be granted. Motivate your decision.

For the purpose of the mini mock arbitration, please ignore the other jurisdictional issues (the definition of investor, investment and any temporal element(s)). You should only focus on the admissibility and substantive issues related to taxation matters under the Energy Charter Treaty (ECT).

17

International investment law and the environment

 EXERCISE 27 – SEMINAR

Problem 1

In the ICSID case *Compañía Del Desarollo De Santa Elena, SA v Republic of Costa Rica* the Tribunal stated the following:

> While an expropriation or taking for environmental reasons may be classified as a taking for a public purpose, and thus may be legitimate, the fact that the property was taken for this reason does not affect either the nature or the measure of the compensation to be paid for the taking. That is, the purpose of protecting the environment for which the property was taken does not alter the legal character of the taking for which adequate compensation must be paid. The international source of the obligation to protect the environment makes no difference.
>
> Expropriatory environmental measures – no matter how laudable and beneficial to society as a whole – are, in this respect, similar to any other expropriatory measures that a State may take in order to implement its policies: where property is expropriated, even for environmental purposes, whether domestic or international, the State's obligation to pay compensation remains.

Do you agree with this statement? Are there any problems with it?

Problem 2

To what extent may conflicts arise between environmental law and international investment law? Do these concerns undermine the legitimacy of international investment treaty arbitration? How can these concerns be addressed by States?

Problem 3

To what extent should arbitration tribunals take environmental considerations into account? In what ways can principles of environmental law and sustainable development be incorporated into arbitral decision making?

Problem 4

An ICSID case emanating from the mining sector is brought under both an investment treaty and the domestic investment law of the host State, but the Tribunal only accepts jurisdiction under the latter. In essence, the investor argues that it was '*de facto*' subjected to a mining ban on behalf of the host State, while the State cites heavy opposition in the local community and environmental concerns as the reason for rejecting certain mining permits to the investor.

A handful of domestic NGOs petition to the Tribunal to participate in the proceedings as *amici curiae*. One of them, NGO X, is an international advocacy organisation that is generally opposed to mining in the relevant region and works on many levels to prevent it. Discuss the extent to which NGO X can be said to be impacted by the dispute. Which rights and interest do they represent? Are the local communities among them? If not, how else are the concerns of these communities represented in the arbitration?

Is your analysis affected by the fact that the State's consent to arbitration is located in its own legislation, rather than in a treaty?

18

Emergency and necessity

EXERCISE 28 – SEMINAR

Review *CMS v Argentina* Award 12 May 2005 and *LG&E v Argentina*, Decision on Liability, 30 October 2006.

DISCUSSION QUESTIONS

Problem 1
Explain how/why the two Tribunals came to different conclusions concerning necessity.

Problem 2
What arguments should the losing parties have put forward to convince the respective Tribunal with respect to necessity?

Problem 3
Are the two awards compatible with customary international law on necessity?

Problem 4
Use Articles XIX, XX AND XXI of GATT 1994 to present arguments in support of 'necessity' against the factual background of *CMS v Argentina*.

CASE

CMS v Argentina (Case No. ARB/01/8) International Centre for Settlement of Investment Disputes Washington, DC, excerpt from Award

D. State of necessity contended in the alternative

304. The Government of Argentina has contended in the alternative that in the event the Tribunal should come to the conclusion that there was a breach of the Treaty the respondent should be exempted from liability in light of the existence of a state of necessity or state of emergency. *Force majeure*, emergency and other terms have also been used by the respondent in this context.

305. This contention is founded on the severe economic, social and political crisis described above and on the belief that the very existence of the Argentine State was threatened by the events that began to unfold in 2000. The respondent asserts in this respect that economic interest qualifies as an essential interest of the State when threatened by grave and imminent peril.

306. It is argued that the Emergency Law was enacted with the sole purpose of bringing under control the chaotic situation that would have followed the economic and social collapse that Argentina was facing. State of necessity based on this crisis would exclude, in the respondent's argument, any wrongfulness of the measures adopted by the government and in particular would rule out compensation.

307. In support of its argument the respondent invokes first the existence of the state of necessity under Argentine law and its acceptance under the Constitution and the decisions of courts. The Tribunal has already discussed the meaning of the state of necessity and the state of emergency under Argentine law and its interpretation by the Supreme Court, with particular reference to its temporary nature and the requirement not to upset the rights acquired by contract or judicial decision. These issues will not be discussed here again.

308. The respondent has also invoked in support of its contention the existence of a state of necessity under both customary international law and the provisions of the Treaty. In so doing, the respondent has raised one fundamental issue in international law.

28. The respondent's view of the state of necessity under customary international law

309. The respondent has mainly based its argument on this question on the ruling of the International Court of Justice in the *Gabcikovo-Nagymaros* case which held that the state of necessity is recognised by customary international law for 'precluding the wrongfulness of an act not in conformity with an international obligation'.

310. The *French Company of Venezuelan Railroads* case is invoked so as to justify that the government's duty was to itself when its 'own preservation is paramount'. Further support is found in the *Dickson Car Wheel Co* case where it was decided that the 'foreigner, residing in a country which by reasons of natural, social or international calamities is obliged to adopt these measures,

must suffer the natural detriment to his affairs without any remedy, since Governments . . . are not insurers against every event'.

311. In addition to the discussion of these and other cases, the Government of Argentina also relies on the work of the International Law Commission under the leadership of the Special Rapporteurs F V García-Amador, Roberto Ago and James Crawford. In particular the respondent argues that it meets the criteria set out in Article 25 of the Articles on International Responsibility. The specific terms of Article 25 will be discussed further below.

312. In the respondent's view the Argentine State was not only facing grave and imminent peril affecting an essential interest, but it did not contribute to the creation of the state of necessity in a substantive way. This situation, it is argued, was prompted for the most part by exogenous factors. It is further asserted that the measures adopted, particularly the specification of contractual relations, were the only measures capable of safeguarding the essential economic interests affected. By introducing the measures, the respondent argues, the essential interests of another State that was a beneficiary of the obligation breached or, for that matter, those of the international community as a whole were not affected and foreign investors were also not treated in a discriminatory manner.

29. The claimant's view of the state of necessity under customary international law

313. The claimant first argues in connection with the state of necessity that the respondent has not met the heavy burden of proof required by the International Court of Justice in the *Gabcikovo-Nagymaros* case. The claimant notes that the Court made reference to the work and views of the International Law Commission in so far [as] the latter explained that 'the state of necessity can only be invoked under certain strictly defined conditions which must be cumulatively satisfied; and the State concerned is not the sole judge of whether those conditions have been met. . .Those conditions reflect customary international law'.

314. The claimant asserts next that neither has the respondent complied with the conditions set down for the operation of state of necessity under Article 25 of the Articles on State Responsibility. In the claimant's view, severe as the crisis was, it did not involve 'grave' or 'imminent' peril nor has it been established that the respondent State did not contribute to the emergency as most of the causes underlying the crisis were endogenous. Moreover, it is asserted that the respondent has not shown that the measures adopted were the only means available to overcome the crisis.

30. The Tribunal's findings in respect of the state of necessity under customary international law

315. The Tribunal, like the parties themselves, considers that Article 25 of the Articles on State Responsibility adequately reflect the state of customary international law on the question of necessity. This Article, in turn, is based on a number of relevant historical cases discussed in the Commentary, with particular reference to the *Caroline*, the *Russian Indemnity*, *Société Commerciale de Belgique*, the *Torrey Canyon* and the *Gabcikovo-Nagymaros* cases.

316. Article 25 reads as follows:

1. Necessity may not be invoked by a State as a ground for precluding the wrongfulness of an act not in conformity with an international obligation of that State unless the act:

    (a) is the only way for the State to safeguard an essential interest against a grave and imminent peril; and
    (b) does not seriously impair an essential interest of the State or States towards which the obligation exists, or of the international community as a whole;

2. In any case, necessity may not be invoked by a State as a ground for precluding wrongfulness if:

    (a) the international obligation in question excludes the possibility of invoking necessity; or
    (b) the State has contributed to the situation of necessity.

317. While the existence of necessity as a ground for precluding wrongfulness under international law is no longer disputed, there is also consensus to the effect that this ground is an exceptional one and has to be addressed in a prudent manner to avoid abuse. The very opening of the Article to the effect that necessity 'may not be invoked' unless strict conditions are met, is indicative of this restrictive approach of international law. Case law, State practice and scholarly writings amply support this restrictive approach to the operation of necessity. The reason is not difficult to understand. If strict and demanding conditions are not required or are loosely applied, any State could invoke necessity to elude its international obligations. This would certainly be contrary to the stability and predictability of the law.

318. The Tribunal must now undertake the very difficult task of finding whether the Argentine crisis meets the requirements of Article 25, a task not rendered easier by the wide variety of views expressed on the matter

and their heavy politicisation. Again here the Tribunal is not called upon to pass judgment on the measures adopted in that connection but simply to establish whether the breach of the Treaty provisions discussed is devoid of legal consequences by the preclusion of wrongfulness.

319. A first question the Tribunal must address is whether an essential interest of the State was involved in the matter. Again here the issue is to determine the gravity of the crisis. The need to prevent a major breakdown, with all its social and political implications, might have entailed an essential interest of the State in which case the operation of the state of necessity might have been triggered. In addition, the plea must under the specific circumstances of each case meet the legal requirements set out by customary international law.

320. In the instant case, the respondent and leading economists are of the view that the crisis was of catastrophic proportions; other equally distinguished views, however, tend to qualify this statement. The Tribunal is convinced that the crisis was indeed severe and the argument that nothing important happened is not tenable. However, neither could it be held that wrongfulness should be precluded as a matter of course under the circumstances. As is many times the case in international affairs and international law, situations of this kind are not given in black and white but in many shades of grey.

321. It follows that the relative effect that can be reasonably attributed to the crisis does not allow for a finding on preclusion of wrongfulness. The respondent's perception of extreme adverse effects, however, is understandable, and in that light the plea of necessity or emergency cannot be considered as an abuse of rights as the claimant has argued.

322. The Tribunal turns next to the question whether there was in this case a grave and imminent peril. Here again the Tribunal is persuaded that the situation was difficult enough to justify the government taking action to prevent a worsening of the situation and the danger of total economic collapse. But neither does the relative effect of the crisis allow here for a finding in terms of preclusion of wrongfulness.

323. A different issue, however, is whether the measures adopted were the 'only way' for the State to safeguard its interests. This is indeed debatable. The views of the parties and distinguished economists are wide apart on this matter, ranging from the support of those measures to the discussion of a variety of alternatives, including dollarisation of the economy, granting of direct subsidies to the affected population or industries and many others. Which of these policy alternatives would have been better is a decision

beyond the scope of the Tribunal's task, which is to establish whether there was only one way or various ways and thus whether the requirements for the preclusion of wrongfulness have or have not been met.

324. The International Law Commission's comment to the effect that the plea of necessity is 'excluded if there are other (otherwise lawful) means available, even if they may be more costly or less convenient', is persuasive in assisting this Tribunal in concluding that the measures adopted were not the only steps available.

325. A different condition for the admission of necessity relates to the requirement that the measures adopted do not seriously impair an essential interest of the State or States towards which the obligation exists, or of the international community as a whole. As the specific obligations towards another State are embodied in the Treaty, this question will be examined in the context of the applicable treaty provisions. It does not appear, however, that the essential interest of the international community as a whole was affected in any relevant way, nor that a peremptory norm of international law might have been compromised, a situation governed by Article 26 of the Articles.

326. In addition to the basic conditions set out under paragraph 1 of Article 25, there are two other limits to the operation of necessity arising from paragraph 2. As noted in the Commentary, the use of the expression 'in any case' in the opening of the text means that each of these limits must be considered over and above the conditions of paragraph 1.

327. The first such limit arises when the international obligation excludes necessity, a matter which again will be considered in the context of the Treaty.

328. The second limit is the requirement for the State not to have contributed to the situation of necessity. The Commentary clarifies that this contribution must be 'sufficiently substantial and not merely incidental or peripheral'. In spite of the view of the parties claiming that all factors contributing to the crisis were either endogenous or exogenous, the Tribunal is again persuaded that similar to what is the case in most crises of this kind the roots extend both ways and include a number of domestic as well as international dimensions. This is the unavoidable consequence of the operation of a global economy where domestic and international factors interact.

329. The issue, however, is whether the contribution to the crisis by Argentina has or has not been sufficiently substantial. The Tribunal, when reviewing

the circumstances of the present dispute, must conclude that this was the case. The crisis was not of the making of one particular administration and found its roots in the earlier crisis of the 1980s and evolving governmental policies of the 1990s that reached a zenith in 2002 and thereafter. Therefore, the Tribunal observes that government policies and their shortcomings significantly contributed to the crisis and the emergency and while exogenous factors did fuel additional difficulties they do not exempt the respondent from its responsibility in the matter.

330. There is yet another important element which the Tribunal must take into account. The International Court of Justice has in the *Gabcikovo-Nagymaros* case convincingly referred to the International Law Commission's view that all the conditions governing necessity must be 'cumulatively' satisfied.

331. In the present case there are, as concluded, elements of necessity partially present here and there but when the various elements, conditions and limits are examined as a whole it cannot be concluded that all such elements meet the cumulative test. This in itself leads to the inevitable conclusion that the requirements of necessity under customary international law have not been fully met so as to preclude the wrongfulness of the acts.

31. The emergency clause of the Treaty

332. The discussion on necessity and emergency is not confined to customary international law as there are also specific provisions of the Treaty dealing with this matter. Article XI of the Treaty provides:

> This Treaty shall not preclude the application by either party of measures necessary for the maintenance of public order, the fulfilment of its obligations with respect to the maintenance or restoration of international peace or security, or the protection of its own essential security interests.

333. Article IV(3) of the Treaty reads as follows:

> Nationals or companies of either party whose investments suffer losses in the territory of the other party owing to war or other armed conflict, revolution, state of national emergency, insurrection, civil disturbance or other similar events shall be accorded treatment by such other party no less favourable than that accorded to its own nationals or companies or to nationals or companies of any third country, whichever is the more favourable treatment, as regards any measures it adopts in relation to such losses.

334. The meaning and extent of these clauses has prompted an important debate between the parties and the legal experts requested by them to discuss the issue, namely Dean Anne-Marie Slaughter and Professor José E Alvarez.

335. The Tribunal will now consider the views of the parties and the experts on this matter, beginning with those of the claimant.

32. The claimant's view of the Treaty's emergency clauses

336. The claimant argues that the Treaty clauses provide very narrow and specific exceptions to liability that do not allow the respondent to invoke the operation of the state of necessity or emergency.

337. The claimant asserts first that under Article 25(2) of the Articles on State Responsibility necessity may not be invoked if the international obligation in question excludes the possibility of invoking necessity. This, in the claimant's view, is the case here as the object and purpose of the Treaty, which is to provide protection to investors in circumstances of economic difficulty, exclude reliance on such difficulties for non-performance of the obligations established under the Treaty. Moreover, the claimant argues, both under the Treaty umbrella clause embodied in Article II(2)(c) and Article X the respondent has the duty to observe obligations entered into with regard to investments.

338. The claimant invokes in support of its views the *Himpurna* case where *force majeure* was not accepted as precluding the wrongfulness of acts of devaluation and the contractual obligations were upheld even in circumstances of economic adversity. *Socobelge*, on which the *Himpurna* Tribunal relied in part, is also invoked by the claimant as an example of contract enforcement in spite of an economic crisis. To the same effect the claimant invokes the *Martini* case.

339. In connection with the specific clause of Article XI of the Treaty the claimant, following the expert opinion of Professor José E Alvarez, argues first that this clause is not self-judging, and therefore requires the Tribunal and not the respondent to decide when or to what extent essential security interests were at stake. The claimant makes the further point that if the State were to have discretion in this regard, such discretion should be provided expressly. Provisions of this kind include Article XXI of the GATT as well as provisions in the bilateral investment treaties concluded by the United States with Russia and with Bahrain. It is further affirmed, that this requirement was also the conclusion of the International Court of Justice in the *Nicaragua* case, and the *Oil Platforms* case.

340. The claimant argues next that economic crises do not fall within the concept of 'essential security interests', which is limited to war, natural disaster and other situations threatening the existence of the State. In its view, this is also the meaning of Article 25 of the Articles on State Responsibility, the interpretation given to Article XXI of the GATT and the scope of the *Russian Indemnity* case.

341. A third argument made by the claimant is that, in any event, Article XI does not exempt the respondent from liability as this provision does not allow for the denial of benefits under the Treaty.

342. The claimant discusses in this context the meaning of Article IV(3) of the Treaty which, it is argued, is not intended to reduce the obligations of the host State to investors but rather to reinforce such obligations, and cannot be read to include economic emergency. The ICSID cases *American Manufacturing v Zaire* and *AAPL v Sri Lanka* are invoked as precedents supporting this interpretation.

343. It is further argued in this regard that even if the Article were to include economic difficulties the claimant would still be entitled to full protection under the most favoured nation clause (MFNC) of both Articles and IV(3) of the Treaty, and certainly nothing less than the treatment local investors or those from other countries have received from the respondent. The MFNC is also invoked in support of the argument that other bilateral investment treaties concluded by the respondent do not contain provisions similar to Article XI and thus the claimant is entitled to the better treatment resulting from the absence of such exceptions.

33. The respondent's view of the Treaty's emergency clauses

344. Articles IV(3) and XI of the Treaty provide, in the respondent's view, for the *lex specialis* governing emergency situations which the government has implemented in order to maintain public order, protect its essential security interests and re-establish its connections with the international economic system, all with a view to granting investors treatment not less favourable than that granted to nationals.

345. The respondent argues first that the object and purpose of the Treaty do not exclude the operation of necessity or emergency, which are expressly provided for in periods of distress. To this effect, the respondent further argues, the decisions invoked by the claimant in support of its views are not relevant to the present case.

346. The respondent particularly rejects the reliance by the claimant on the Tribunal's decision in the *Himpurna* case. The claimant invoked that decision to draw a comparison with the Indonesian crisis and to show that the Tribunal in that case had held that necessity was excluded by specific commitments undertaken by contract and treaty. The present dispute, the respondent argues, has emerged under circumstances very different from those that prevailed in Indonesia and the *Himpurna* case in no way contradicts the position taken by Argentina in light of extraordinary circumstances.

347. The respondent also rejects the relevance of the situation of Greece in the 1930s as taken into account in the decision in the *Socobelge* case. This decision was also invoked by the claimant to show that the obligations under a contract were upheld in spite of financial hardship, in the case of Greece. The respondent believes the Argentine crisis to have been much worse and deeper and that *force majeure* as discussed in that case was held to be beyond the powers of the Permanent Court of International Justice.

348. As to the *Martini* case, invoked by the claimant as an example of state of necessity not having been accepted as an excuse and of contractual commitments having been strictly enforced, the respondent does not consider it relevant to the present case as it did not deal with a case of institutional abnormality.

349. The expert opinions of Dean Anne Marie Slaughter, introduced by the respondent on December 15, 2003 and June 23, 2004, elaborate on the meaning and the coverage of the relevant Treaty articles. It is first asserted in this respect that Article XI of the Treaty needs to be interpreted broadly and this in fact was the intention of the parties.

350. Since the very outset of the United States' model bilateral investment treaties it has been apparent, in the expert's view, that this country desired to safeguard certain sovereign interests by means of 'non-precluded measures' such as those of Article XI. This trend was strengthened after the decision in the *Nicaragua* case which held that similar provisions of another treaty could not be understood to be self-judging. At the time the Treaty was signed with Argentina, it is further argued, this trend had become manifest as evidenced by the treaties negotiated with other countries and debates in the United States Congress.

351. On the basis of the principle of reciprocity, it is explained next, Argentina should be accorded the benefit of a similar understanding when invoking

necessity and emergency. The self-judging character of these provisions, in the expert's view, should not be understood as precluding their submission to arbitration as the Tribunal must determine whether Article XI applies and whether measures taken thereunder comply with the requirements of good faith.

352. The expert's opinions also emphasise that security interests include economic security, particularly in the context of a crisis as severe as that of Argentina, and that, as in many instances of *force majeure*, the State should be released from Treaty obligations. It is held, moreover, that the claimant has not been treated differently from nationals or other investors under Article IV(3) of the Treaty.

34. The Tribunal's findings in respect of the Treaty's clauses on emergency

353. The first issue the Tribunal must determine is whether the object and purpose of the Treaty exclude necessity. There are of course treaties designed to be applied precisely in the case of necessity or emergency, such as those setting out humanitarian rules for situations of armed conflict. In those cases, as rightly explained in the Commentary to Article 25 of the Articles on State Responsibility, the plea of necessity is excluded by the very object and purpose of the treaty.

354. The Treaty in this case is clearly designed to protect investments at a time of economic difficulties or other circumstances leading to the adoption of adverse measures by the government. The question is, however, how grave these economic difficulties might be. A severe crisis cannot necessarily be equated with a situation of total collapse. And in the absence of such profoundly serious conditions it is plainly clear that the Treaty will prevail over any plea of necessity. However, if such difficulties, without being catastrophic in and of themselves, nevertheless invite catastrophic conditions in terms of disruption and disintegration of society or are likely to lead to a total breakdown of the economy, emergency and necessity might acquire a different meaning.

355. As stated above, the Tribunal is convinced that the Argentine crisis was severe but did not result in total economic and social collapse. When the Argentine crisis is compared to other contemporary crises affecting countries in different regions of the world it may be noted that such other crises have not led to the derogation of international contractual or treaty obligations. Renegotiation, adaptation and postponement have occurred but the essence of the international obligations has been kept intact.

356. As explained above, while the crisis in and of itself might not be characterised as catastrophic and while there was therefore not a situation of *force
majeure* that left no other option open, neither can it be held that the crisis
was of no consequence and that business could have continued as usual,
as some of the claimant's arguments seem to suggest. Just as the Tribunal
concluded when the situation under domestic law was considered, there
were certain consequences stemming from the crisis. And while not excusing liability or precluding wrongfulness from the legal point of view they
ought nevertheless to be considered by the Tribunal when determining
compensation.

357. A second issue the Tribunal must determine is whether, as discussed
in the context of Article 25 of the Articles on State Responsibility, the act
in question does not seriously impair an essential interest of the State or
States towards which the obligation exists. If the Treaty was made to protect
investors it must be assumed that this is an important interest of the States
parties. Whether it is an essential interest is difficult to say, particularly at a
time when this interest appears occasionally to be dwindling.

358. However, be that as it may, the fact is that this particular kind of treaty is
also of interest to investors as they are specific beneficiaries and for investors
the matter is indeed essential. For the purpose of this case, and looking at the
Treaty just in the context of its States parties, the Tribunal concludes that it
does not appear that an essential interest of the State to which the obligation
exists has been impaired, nor have those of the international community as
a whole. Accordingly, the plea of necessity would not be precluded on this
count.

359. The third issue the Tribunal must determine is whether Article XI of
the Treaty can be interpreted in such a way as to provide that it includes
economic emergency as an essential security interest. While the text of the
Article does not refer to economic crises or difficulties of that particular
kind, as concluded above, there is nothing in the context of customary international law or the object and purpose of the Treaty that could on its own
exclude major economic crises from the scope of Article XI.

360. It must also be kept in mind that the scope of a given bilateral treaty,
such as this, should normally be understood and interpreted as attending
to the concerns of both parties. If the concept of essential security interests
were to be limited to immediate political and national security concerns,
particularly of an international character, and were to exclude other interests,
for example, major economic emergencies, it could well result in an unbal-

anced understanding of Article XI. Such an approach would not be entirely consistent with the rules governing the interpretation of treaties.

361. Again, the issue is then to establish how grave an economic crisis must be so as to qualify as an essential security interest, a matter discussed above.

362. It is true that Paragraph 6 of the Protocol attached to the Treaty qualifies the reference to maintenance or restoration of international peace and security as related to obligations under the Charter of the United Nations. Similarly, the letter of submission of the Treaty to Congress in Argentina and the Report of the pertinent Congressional Committee, refer in particular to situations of war, armed conflict or disturbance. However, this cannot be read as excluding altogether other qualifying situations.

363. Since the Security Council assumes to be many times the law unto itself, and since there is no specific mechanism for judicial review under the Charter, it is not inconceivable that in some circumstances this body might wish to qualify a situation of economic crisis as a threat to international peace and security and adopt appropriate measures to deal with a given situation. This would indeed allow for a broad interpretation of Article XI.

364. As explained by Professor Alvarez, in practice the Security Council has, to a limited extent, adopted decisions connecting economic measures with security matters, for example, in the formulation of the sanctions programme enacted as a consequence of the 1991 Gulf War and other instances. In such cases, it is explained, there could be a treaty breach under the authority of the Security Council. However, this sort of situation does not have to do with the present case.

365. It is also important to note that in Dean Slaughter's understanding of the reference to the United Nations in the Treaty Protocol, such clause should not be considered as self-judging to the extent that the issue relates to the maintenance or restoration of international peace and security, involving a broader understanding of the concept as opposed to a nation's own security interest. The latter would in her view allow for self-judging in so far as the security interest is not a part of the maintenance or restoration of international peace and security. The question of the self-judging character of these provisions will be discussed next.

366. The fourth issue the Tribunal must determine is whether the rule of Article XI of the Treaty is self-judging, that is if the State adopting the measures in question is the sole arbiter of the scope and application of that rule,

or whether the invocation of necessity, emergency or other essential security interests is subject to some form of judicial review.

367. As discussed above, three positions have emerged in this context. There is first that of the claimant, supporting the argument that such a clause cannot be self-judging. There is next that of the respondent, who believes that it is free to determine when and to what extent necessity, emergency or the threat to its security interests need the adoption of extraordinary measures. And third, there is the position expressed by Dean Slaughter to the effect that the Tribunal must determine whether Article XI is applicable particularly with a view to establishing whether this has been done in good faith.

368. The Tribunal notes in this connection that, as explained by Dean Slaughter, the position of the United States has been evolving towards the support of self-judging clauses in so far as security interests are affected. This policy emerged after the *Nicaragua* decision, which will be discussed below, and was expressly included in the US-Russia bilateral investment treaty, which has incidentally not been ratified. With some changes it was also included in the US-Bahrain investment treaty, the precise meaning of which is debated by the experts. The GATT self-judging clause was also mentioned above. Other treaties have not included a self-judging clause but this again is debated by the experts, and in any event such policy would also be reflected in the 2004 US Model bilateral investment treaty.

369. The discussion of these treaties in the US Congress allows for a variety of interpretations but does not clearly support the conclusion that all such clauses are self-judging. The record shows that during the discussion of the first round of bilateral investment treaties in 1986 a proposal to allow for the termination of treaties in light of security needs was not accepted, although this discussion apparently did not address specifically the question of self-judging clauses. The expert discussion of the Exon-Florio law has also generated much debate on its meaning.

370. The Tribunal is convinced that when States intend to create for themselves a right to determine unilaterally the legitimacy of extraordinary measures importing non-compliance with obligations assumed in a treaty, they do so expressly. The examples of the GATT and bilateral investment treaty provisions offered above are eloquent examples of this approach. The first does not preclude measures adopted by a party 'which it considers necessary' for the protection of its security interests. So too, the US-Russia Treaty expressly confirms in a Protocol that the non-precluded measures clause is self-judging.

371. The International Court of Justice has also taken a clear stand in respect of this issue, twice in connection with the *Nicaragua* case and again in the *Oil Platforms* case noted above. Referring to the 1956 Treaty of Friendship, Commerce and Navigation between the United States and Nicaragua, the Court held:

> Article XXI defines the instances in which the Treaty itself provides for exceptions to the generality of its other provisions, but it by no means removes the interpretation and application of that article from the jurisdiction of the Court. . . The text of Article XXI of the Treaty does not employ the wording which was already to be found in Article XXI of the General Agreement on Tariffs and Trade. This provision of GATT, contemplating exceptions to the normal implementation of the General Agreement, stipulates that the Agreement is not to be construed to prevent any contracting party from taking any action 'which it considers necessary for the protection of its essential security interests', in such fields as nuclear fission, arms, etc. The 1956 Treaty, on the contrary, speaks simply of 'necessary' measures, not of those considered by a party to be such.

372. As explained above, in the *Gabcikovo-Nagymaros* case the International Court of Justice, referring to the work and views of the International Law Commission, notes the strict and cumulative conditions of necessity under international law and that 'the State concerned is not the sole judge of whether those conditions have been met'.

373. In light of this discussion, the Tribunal concludes first that the clause of Article XI of the Treaty is not a self-judging clause. Quite evidently, in the context of what a State believes to be an emergency, it will most certainly adopt the measures it considers appropriate without requesting the views of any court. However, if the legitimacy of such measures is challenged before an international tribunal, it is not for the State in question but for the international jurisdiction to determine whether the plea of necessity may exclude wrongfulness. It must also be noted that clauses dealing with investments and commerce do not generally affect security as much as military events do and, therefore, would normally fall outside the scope of such dramatic events.

374. The Tribunal must conclude next that this judicial review is not limited to an examination of whether the plea has been invoked or the measures have been taken in good faith. It is a substantive review that must examine whether the state of necessity or emergency meets the conditions laid down by customary international law and the treaty provisions and whether it thus is or is not able to preclude wrongfulness.

375. The Tribunal must still consider the question of the meaning and extent of Treaty Article IV(3) in light of the discussion noted above. The plain meaning of the Article is to provide a floor treatment for the investor in the context of the measures adopted in respect of the losses suffered in the emergency, not different from that applied to nationals or other foreign investors. The Article does not derogate from the Treaty rights but rather ensures that any measures directed at offsetting or minimising losses will be applied in a non-discriminatory manner.

376. As noted above, the Tribunal is satisfied that the measures adopted by the respondent have not adversely discriminated against the claimant.

377. Although the MFNC contained in the Treaty has also been invoked by the claimant because other treaties done by Argentina do not contain a provision similar to that of Article XI, the Tribunal is not convinced that the clause has any role to play in this case. Thus, had other Article XI type clauses envisioned in those treaties a treatment more favourable to the investor, the argument about the operation of the MFNC might have been made. However, the mere absence of such provision in other treaties does not lend support to this argument, which would in any event fail under the *ejusdem generis* rule, as rightly argued by the respondent.

378. The Tribunal must finally conclude in this section that the umbrella clauses invoked by the claimant do not add anything different to the overall Treaty obligations which the respondent must meet if the plea of necessity fails.

35. Temporary nature of necessity

379. The Tribunal is also mindful that Article 27 of the Articles on State Responsibility provides that the invocation of a circumstance precluding wrongfulness is without prejudice to '(a) compliance with the obligation in question, if and to the extent that the circumstance precluding wrongfulness no longer exists'.

380. The temporary nature of necessity is thus expressly recognised and finds support in the decisions of courts and tribunals. The Commentary cites in this connection the *Rainbow Warrior* and *Gabcikovo-Nagymaros* cases. In this last case the International Court of Justice held that as soon 'as the state of necessity ceases to exist, the duty to comply with treaty obligations revives'.

381. This does not appear to be contested by the parties as various witness statements did in fact clearly establish that the crisis had been evolv-

ing toward normalcy over a period of time. The claimant invokes to this effect the statements of Ambassador Remes Lenicov and Doctor Folgar, who explained how the crisis was subsiding by the end of 2002. This was also the view of the Argentine Supreme Court and the *Procurador General* noted above. It may be observed that this positive trend continued to evolve thereafter.

382. Even if the plea of necessity were accepted, compliance with the obligation would re-emerge as soon as the circumstance precluding wrongfulness no longer existed, which is the case at present.

36. Necessity and compensation

383. Article 27 also expressly provides that any circumstance precluding wrongfulness is without prejudice to '(b) the question of compensation for any material loss caused by the act in question'. Again this conclusion finds support in the *Gabcikovo-Nagymaros* case, where the Court noted that 'Hungary expressly acknowledged that, in any event, such a state of necessity would not exempt it from its duty to compensate its partner.'

384. This criterion was also the basis for the decisions in earlier cases, such as the *Compagnie Générale de l'Orinocco* case and the *Properties of the Bulgarian Minorities in Greece* case invoked by the claimant, or the *Orr & Laubenheimer* case. In these cases the concept of damages appears to have been broader than that of material loss in Article 27.

385. The respondent has argued in this connection that the *Compagnie Générale de l'Orinocco* dealt with a totally different set of issues, all involving illicit acts, and is therefore not relevant to the present case. The respondent further invokes the *Gould Marketing, Inc* case, where the Iran-United States Tribunal held that injuries caused as a result of social and economic forces beyond the power of the State to control through due diligence are 'not attributable to the state for purposes of its responding for damages'.

386. The claimant, however, contends that '[i]n any event, Article XI does not exempt Argentina from liability', since it 'provides only a temporary and limited suspension of benefits, and Argentina is still therefore obliged to provide compensation for the permanent losses [. . .]'. It recalls that the Treaty shows a difference between clauses that (a) 'do not preclude or do not impede certain measures', (b) 'permit a Party clearly to deny treaty

benefits', or (c) 'permit treaty termination' – Articles XI, I (2) and XIV (2), respectively.

387. Because the Argentine crisis, as explained above, gradually subsided, the claimant asserts that '[e]ven assuming that at the beginning of 2002 Argentina was experiencing an emergency of the sort covered by Article XI, Argentina has not demonstrated that the crisis persists today. Argentina's measures promise to remain in effect indefinitely, and [the respondent] must therefore compensate CMS for the harm it has suffered, regardless of the applicability of Article XI'.

388. The claimant's reasoning in this respect is supported by Article 27 and the decisions noted above, as well as by the principle acknowledged even in the generality of domestic legal systems: the plea of state of necessity may preclude the wrongfulness of an act, but it does not exclude the duty to compensate the owner of the right which had to be sacrificed. Still more stringent are the requirements of emergency under Argentine case law as discussed above.

389. The respondent contends to the contrary that no compensation is due if the measures in question were undertaken in a state of necessity, under the rule contained in Article XI of the Treaty, and that the norm which prescribes that the parties shall avoid uneven treatment of investors does not otherwise establish a duty to compensate even if the investor had been submitted to unfair or unequal treatment.

390. The Tribunal is satisfied that Article 27 establishes the appropriate rule of international law on this issue. The respondent's argument is tantamount to the assertion that a party to this kind of treaty, or its subjects, are supposed to bear entirely the cost of the plea of the essential interests of the other party. This is, however, not the meaning of international law or the principles governing most domestic legal systems.

391. The Tribunal's conclusion is further reaffirmed by the record. At the hearing the Tribunal put the question whether there are any circumstances in which an investor would be entitled to compensation in spite of the eventual application of Article XI and the plea of necessity.

392. The answer to this question by the respondent's expert clarifies the issue from the point of view of both its temporary nature and the duty to provide compensation: while it is difficult to reach a determination as long as the crisis is unfolding, it is possible to envisage a situation in which the

investor would have a claim against the government for the compliance with its obligations once the crisis was over; thereby concluding that any suspension of the right to compensation is strictly temporary, and that this right is not extinguished by the crisis events.

393. The Tribunal also notes that, as in the *Gaz de Bordeaux* case, the International Law Commission's Commentary to Article 27 suggests that the States concerned should agree on the possibility and extent of compensation payable in a given case.

394. It is quite evident then that in the absence of agreement between the parties the duty of the Tribunal in these circumstances is to determine the compensation due. This the Tribunal will do next.

 CASE

LG&E v Argentina (ICSID Case No ARB/02/1) International Centre for Settlement of Investment Disputes Washington, DC, excerpt from Decision on liability

[. . .]

E. State of necessity

1. Parties' positions

201. Respondent contends in the alternative that, if Argentina would have breached its Treaty obligations, the state of political, economic and social crisis that befell Argentina allowed it to take action contrary to the obligations it had assumed with respect to the gas-distribution licensees. Thus, even if the measures adopted by the State in order to overcome the economic crisis suffered during the years 1998 through 2003, resulted in a violation of the rights guaranteed under the Treaty to foreign investments, such measures were implemented under a state of necessity and therefore, Argentina is excused from liability during this period.

202. Respondent pleads its defence as a 'state of necessity' defence, available under Argentine law, Treaty in Articles XI and IV(3), as well as customary international law.

203. Claimants reject respondent's contentions regarding the alleged state of necessity defense. Claimants contend that Article XI is not applicable in

the case of an economic crisis because the public order and essential security interests elements are intentionally narrow in scope, limited to security threats of a physical nature.

2. General comments on Article XI

(i) Preliminary considerations

204. Article XI of the Bilateral Treaty provides:

> This Treaty shall not preclude the application by either Party of measures necessary for the maintenance of public order, the fulfillment of its obligations with respect to the maintenance or restoration of international peace or security, or the protection of its own essential security interests.

205. The Tribunal's analysis to determine the applicability of Article XI of the Bilateral Treaty is twofold. First, the Tribunal must decide whether the conditions that existed in Argentina during the relevant period were such that the State was entitled to invoke the protections included in Article XI of the Treaty. Second, the Tribunal must determine whether the measures implemented by Argentina were necessary to maintain public order or to protect its essential security interests, albeit in violation of the Treaty.

206. The Tribunal reiterates that to carry out the two-fold analysis already mentioned, it shall apply first, the Treaty, second, the general international law to the extent that is necessary and third, the Argentine domestic law. The Tribunal underscores that the claims and defences mentioned derive from the Treaty and that, to the extent required for the interpretation and application of its provisions, the general international law shall be applied (. . .).

(ii) The question of whether Article XI is self-judging

207. Before turning to its substantive analysis of Article XI, the Tribunal must determine whether Article XI is self-judging.

208. Respondent has argued that because Article XI is a self-judging provision, it is for the State to make a good faith determination as to what measures are necessary for the maintenance of public order, or the protection of its essential security interests. According to respondent, under this self-judging exception, the Tribunal must decide only whether Argentina acted in good faith or not. Respondent has not relied upon the third element of Article XI,

Emergency and necessity · **425**

'the fulfillment of its obligations with respect to the maintenance or restoration of international peace or security'.

209. Respondent considers Article XI is ambiguous and characterises such ambiguity as a 'strategic ambiguity' on the part of the US, since it does not clearly define who should determine if the measures to maintain public order or protect essential security interests are necessary. Respondent recognises that the US' 1987 Model BIT, upon which the Argentina-US BIT was based, does not clarify the US' position, nor does any of the documentation related to the negotiation or ratification of the Argentina-US BIT. However, respondent contends that subsequent to the conclusion of the Argentina-US BIT, the US shifted its position permanently with regard to essential security clauses, stating in 1992 that the US considered such clauses to be self-judging, presently and retroactively (Slaughter Witness Statement, ¶¶ 12–31).

210. Claimants disagree that Article XI is self-judging and argue instead that its application requires that the Tribunal conduct its own analysis of whether the conditions necessitated measures to maintain public order or protect Argentina's essential security interests within the meaning of Article XI.

211. Claimants contend that neither the plain meaning of Article XI, nor the context or purpose of the Treaty suggest that Article XI is self-judging, and that the position of the US at the time the parties signed the Treaty was that such clauses were not self-judging (Hearing on the Merits, 28 January 2005, Alvarez, Spanish Transcript, p. 925 et seq.). Claimants argue that respondent has not proven that the parties to the Treaty intended Article XI to be self-judging, which they characterise as 'an exceptional thing'. (Hearing on the Merits, 28 January 2005, Alvarez, Spanish Transcript, pp. 932 et seq.). Claimants contend that the US did not consider essential security clauses as self-judging until the Russia-US BIT of 1992 and the 1992 US Model BIT, both of which post-date the Argentina-US BIT, and both of which noted explicitly the change in the US' policy that these provisions were to be self-judging.

212. Certainly, the language of the BIT does not specify who should decide what constitutes essential security measures – either Argentina itself, subject to a review under a good faith standard, or the Tribunal. Based on the evidence before the Tribunal regarding the understanding of the parties in 1991 at the time the Treaty was signed, the Tribunal decides and concludes that the provision is not self-judging.

213. The provisions included in the international treaty are to be interpreted in conformity with the interpretation given and agreed upon by both parties

at the time of its signature, unless both parties agreed to its modification. In that case, the date to be considered is November 1991. It is not until 1992, with the ratification of the Russia-US BIT, that the US begins to consider that the application of the essential security measures are self-judging; both instruments post-date the bilateral treaty between the US and the Argentine Republic and, in both cases, this change was explicitly clarified.

214. Were the Tribunal to conclude that the provision is self-judging, Argentina's determination would be subject to a good faith review anyway, which does not significantly differ from the substantive analysis presented here.

(iii) Necessary nature of the measures adopted

a. Parties' positions   215. Argentina defends the measures it implemented as necessary to maintain public order and protect its essential security interests. It contends that under any interpretation, the financial crisis, riots and chaos of the years 2000 through 2002 in Argentina constitute a national emergency sufficient to invoke the protections of Article XI (Slaughter Witness Statement, ¶ 45).

216. Concerning 'public order', respondent reinforces its arguments on the necessary nature of the measures it had implemented by pointing to numerous reports of waves of sudden economic catastrophe, massive strikes involving millions of workers, fatal shootings, the shut-down of schools, businesses, transportation, energy, banking and health services, demonstrations across the country, and a plummeting stock market, culminating in a 'final massive social explosion' in which five presidential administrations resigned within a month (Slaughter Witness Statement, ¶¶ 46–49). Under these circumstances, Argentina argues that price controls by the Argentine Government would have been fully justifiable under the public order provisions of Article XI. Additionally, Respondent argues that actions to freeze price increases in the gas-distribution sector were justifiable to maintain the country's basic infrastructure, which was dependent on natural gas energy.

217. Argentina also defends its measures as necessary to protect its essential security interests. Argentina asserts that Article XI's 'essential security interests' element encompasses economic and political interests, as well as national military defense interests. Respondent cites several US officials who have propounded a broad interpretation of 'essential security interests' (Slaughter Witness Statement, ¶ 38).

218. Respondent attacks claimants' basis for asserting that the clause is narrow, reserved only for military actions. Furthermore, in all of the cases cited by claimants, the point was whether the use of military force was justifiable under international law – a narrow reading of essential security clauses in these cases would be expected.

219. Because economic stability, in respondent's view, falls within a State's essential security interests, respondent defends the measures it took as necessary to protect its economic interests. Respondent argues that during the crisis period, the health, safety and security of the Argentine State and its people were threatened, and that the economic melt-down had the potential to cause catastrophic State failure. Thus, the public emergency that Argentina declared and the Emergency Law the government passed altering its financial arrangements were necessary to protect the State's essential security interests.

220. Claimants identify the four measures at issue here – suspension and abolishment of the PPI adjustment, freezing the gas-distribution tariffs, and abandonment of the calculation of the tariffs in dollars, all taken unilaterally – and contend that respondent must prove that each measure was necessary in order to maintain public order and protect Argentina's essential security interests (Reply, ¶ 209). By the term 'necessary', claimants contend that these measures must have been the only option available to Argentina in order to invoke protection under Article XI.

221. Claimants define public order measures as 'actions taken pursuant to a State's police powers, particularly in respect of public health and safety'. Based on this definition, claimants state that the measures in dispute in this case were not aimed at bringing calmness to the collapse that was threatening the country. Consequently, such measures cannot be deemed necessary to maintain public order.

222. With respect to 'essential security interests', claimants reiterate that such interests do not include economic interests – only defence or military concerns. They compare a State's interest in essential security to a national security threat, while a 'national emergency', the alleged circumstance in which respondent invokes the protection, has an entirely different meaning. In claimants' view, economic crises should not be elevated to an essential security interest, and that doing so would disregard the object and purpose of the Treaty. They argue that an economic crisis is precisely when investors need the protections offered by a BIT.

223. Claimants argue that in any event, Article XI does not relieve Argentina of its obligations to compensate claimants for damages suffered as a result of breaches of the Treaty.

224. Claimants also reject the possibility of applying the rule provided by Article IV(3) of the Treaty. They are of the opinion that this provision does not apply to economic crises, and it does not authorise the host State to revoke or suspend the protections given to foreign investors (Reply, ¶ 229).

225. Claimants invoke Article 27 of the International Law Commission's Draft Articles on State Responsibility. Claimants contend that even if the state of necessity defense is available to Argentina under the circumstances of this case, Article 27 of the Draft Articles makes clear that Argentina's obligations to claimants are not extinguished and Argentina must compensate claimants for losses incurred as a result of the government's actions. Article 27 provides that 'invocation of a circumstance precluding wrongfulness in accordance with this chapter is without prejudice to (a) compliance with the obligation in question. . . (b) the question of compensation for any material loss caused by the act in question' (Reply, ¶¶ 226–228).

b. Tribunal's analysis   226. In the judgment of the Tribunal, from 1 December 2001 until 26 April 2003, Argentina was in a period of crisis during which it was necessary to enact measures to maintain public order and protect its essential security interests.

227. The Tribunal does not consider that the initial date for the state of necessity is the effective date of the Emergency Law, 6 January 2002, because, in the first place, the emergency had already started when the law was enacted. Second, should the Tribunal take as the initial date the day when the Emergency Law became effective, it might be reasonable to take as its closing date the day when the state of emergency is lifted by the Argentine State, a fact that has not yet taken place since the law has been extended several times.

228. It is to be pointed out that there is a factual emergency that began on 1 December 2001 and ended on 26 April 2003, on account of the reasons detailed below, as well as a legislative emergency, that begins and ends with the enactment and abrogation of the Emergency Law, respectively. It should be borne in mind that Argentina declared its state of necessity and has extended such state until the present. Indeed, the country has issued a record number of decrees since 1901, accounting for the fact that the emergency periods in Argentina have been longer than the non-emergency periods.

Emergency periods should be only strictly exceptional and should be applied exclusively when faced with extraordinary circumstances. Hence, in order to allege state of necessity as a State defence, it will be necessary to prove the existence of serious public disorders. Based on the evidence available, the Tribunal has determined that the situation ended at the time President Kirchner was elected.

229. Thus, Argentina is excused under Article XI from liability for any breaches of the Treaty between 1 December 2001 and 26 April 2003. The reasons are the following:

230. These dates coincide, on the one hand, with the government's announcement of the measure freezing funds, which prohibited bank account owners from withdrawing more than one thousand pesos monthly and, on the other hand, with the election of President Kirchner. The Tribunal marks these dates as the beginning and end of the period of extreme crisis in view of the notorious events that occurred during this period.

231. Evidence has been put before the Tribunal that the conditions as of December 2001 constituted the highest degree of public disorder and threatened Argentina's essential security interests. This was not merely a period of 'economic problems' or 'business cycle fluctuation' as claimants described (claimants' post-hearing brief, ¶ 14). Extremely severe crises in the economic, political and social sectors reached their apex and converged in December 2001, threatening total collapse of the government and the Argentine State.

232. All of the major economic indicators reached catastrophic proportions in December 2001. An accelerated deterioration of Argentina's Gross Domestic Product (GDP) began in December 2001, falling 10 to 15 per cent faster than the previous year. Private consumption dramatically dropped in the fourth quarter of 2001, accompanied by a severe drop in domestic prices. Argentina experienced at this time widespread decline in the prices and in the value of assets located in Argentina. The Merval Index, which measures the share value of the main companies of Argentina listed on the Buenos Aires Stock Exchange, experienced a dramatic decline of 60 per cent by the end of December 2001. By mid-2001, Argentina's country risk premium was the highest premium worldwide, rendering Argentina unable to borrow on the international markets, and reflecting the severity of the economic crisis.

233. At this time, capital outflow was a critical problem for the government. In the fourth quarter of 2001, the Central Bank of Argentina lost US$ 11

billion in liquid reserves, amounting to 40 per cent. The banking system lost 25 per cent of its total deposits.

234. While unemployment, poverty and indigency rates gradually increased from the beginning of 1998, they reached intolerable levels by December 2001. Unemployment reached almost 25 per cent, and almost half of the Argentine population was living below poverty. The entire healthcare system teetered on the brink of collapse. Prices of pharmaceuticals soared as the country plunged deeper into the deflationary period, becoming unavailable for low-income people. Hospitals suffered a severe shortage of basic supplies. Investments in infrastructure and equipment for public hospitals declined as never before. These conditions prompted the government to declare the nationwide health emergency to ensure the population's access to basic health care goods and services. At the time, one-quarter of the population could not afford the minimum amount of food required to ensure their subsistence. Given the level of poverty and lack of access to healthcare and proper nutrition, disease followed. Facing increased pressure to provide social services and security to the masses of indigent and poor people, the government was forced to decrease its per capita spending on social services by 74 per cent.

235. By December 2001, there was widespread fear among the population that the government would default on its debt and seize bank deposits to prevent the bankruptcy of the banking system. Faced with a possible run on banks, the government issued on 1 December 2001 Decree of Necessity and Emergency No. 1570/01. The law triggered widespread social discontent. Widespread violent demonstrations and protests brought the economy to a halt, including effectively shutting down transportation systems. Looting and rioting followed in which tens of people were killed as the conditions in the country approached anarchy. A curfew was imposed to curb lootings.

236. By 20 December 2001, President De la Rúa resigned. His presidency was followed by a succession of presidents over the next days, until Mr. Eduardo Duhalde took office on 1 January 2002, charged with the mandate to bring the country back to normal conditions.

237. All of these devastating conditions – economic, political, social – in the aggregate triggered the protections afforded under Article XI of the Treaty to maintain order and control the civil unrest.

238. The Tribunal rejects the notion that Article XI is only applicable in circumstances amounting to military action and war. Certainly, the conditions in Argentina in December 2001 called for immediate, decisive action

to restore civil order and stop the economic decline. To conclude that such a severe economic crisis could not constitute an essential security interest is to diminish the havoc that the economy can wreak on the lives of an entire population and the ability of the government to lead. When a State's economic foundation is under siege, the severity of the problem can equal that of any military invasion.

239. Claimants contend that the necessity defence should not be applied here because the measures implemented by Argentina were not the only means available to respond to the crisis. The Tribunal rejects this assertion. Article XI refers to situations in which a State has no choice but to act. A State may have several responses at its disposal to maintain public order or protect its essential security interests. In this sense, it is recognised that Argentina's suspension of the calculation of tariffs in US dollars and the PPI adjustment of tariffs was a legitimate way of protecting its social and economic system.

240. The Tribunal has determined that Argentina's enactment of the Emergency Law was a necessary and legitimate measure on the part of the Argentine Government. Under the conditions the government faced in December 2001, time was of the essence in crafting a response. Drafted in just six days, the Emergency Law took the swift, unilateral action against the economic crisis that was necessary at the time (Hearing on the Merits, 25 January 2005, Ratti, Spanish Transcript, pp. 415–419).

241. In drafting the Emergency Law, the government considered the interests of the foreign investors, and concluded that it 'could not leave sectors of the economy operating with the brutally dollarised economy – [the] system was in crisis, so we had to cut off that process, and we had to establish a new set of rules for everybody'. (Hearing on the Merits, 25 January 2005, Ratti, Spanish Transcript, p. 417). Argentina's strategy to deal with the thousands of public utility contracts that could not be individually assessed during the period of crisis was to implement 'across-the-board solutions' and then renegotiate the contracts (Hearing on the Merits, 26 January 2005, Roubini, Spanish Transcript, p. 635). The Tribunal accepts the necessity of approaching enactment of a stop-gap measure in this manner and therefore rejects claimants' objection that Argentina's unilateral response was not necessary.

242. The Tribunal accepts that the provisions of the Emergency Law that abrogated calculation of the tariffs in US dollars and PPI adjustments, as well as freezing tariffs were necessary measures to deal with the extremely serious economic crisis. Indeed, it would be unreasonable to conclude that

during this period the government should have implemented a tariff increase pursuant to an index pegged to an economy experiencing a high inflationary period (the US). The severe devaluation of the peso against the dollar renders the government's decision to abandon the calculation of tariffs in dollars reasonable. Similarly, the government deemed that freezing gas tariffs altogether during the crisis period was necessary, and claimants have not provided any reason as to why such measure would not provide immediate relief from the crisis.

243. The Tribunal will now turn to Article IV(3) of the Treaty, which provides:

> Nationals or companies of either Party whose investments suffer losses in the territory of the other Party owing to war or other armed conflict, revolution, *state of national emergency*, insurrection, civil disturbance or other similar events shall be accorded treatment by such other Party no less favorable than that accorded to its own nationals or companies or to nationals or companies of any third country, whichever is the more favorable treatment, as regards any measures it adopts in relation to such losses (emphasis added)

244. Article IV(3) of the Treaty confirms that the States Party to the Bilateral Treaty contemplated the state of national emergency as a separate category of exceptional circumstances. That is in line with the Tribunal's interpretation of Article XI of the Treaty. Furthermore, the Tribunal has determined, as a factual matter that the grave crisis in Argentina lasted from 1 December 2001 until 26 April 2003. It has not been shown convincingly to the Tribunal that during that period the provisions of Article IV(3) of the Treaty have been violated by Argentina. On the contrary, during that period, the measures taken by Argentina were 'across the board'

245. In the previous analysis, the Tribunal has determined that the conditions in Argentina from 1 December 2001 until 26 April 2003 were such that Argentina is excused from liability for the alleged violation of its Treaty obligations due to the responsive measures it enacted. The concept of excusing a State for the responsibility for violation of its international obligations during what is called a 'state of necessity' or 'state of emergency' also exists in international law. While the Tribunal considers that the protections afforded by Article XI have been triggered in this case, and are sufficient to excuse Argentina's liability, the Tribunal recognises that satisfaction of the state of necessity standard as it exists in international law (reflected in Article 25 of the ILC's Draft Articles on State Responsibility) supports the Tribunal's conclusion.

246. In international law, a state of necessity is marked by certain characteristics that must be present in order for a State to invoke this defence. As articulated by Roberto Ago, one of the mentors of the Draft Articles on State Responsibility, a state of necessity is identified by those conditions in which a State is threatened by a serious danger to its existence, to its political or economic survival, to the possibility of maintaining its essential services in operation, to the preservation of its internal peace, or to the survival of part of its territory. In other words, the State must be dealing with interests that are essential or particularly important. Article 25 of the Draft Articles on Responsibility of States for Internationally Wrongful Acts provides:

> 1. Necessity may not be invoked by a State as a ground for precluding the wrongfulness of an act not in conformity with an international obligation of that State unless the act:
>
> (a)   Is the only way for the State to safeguard an essential interest against a grave and imminent peril; and
>
> (b)   Does not seriously impair an essential interest of the State or States towards which the obligation exists, or of the international community as a whole.
>
> 2. In any case, necessity may not be invoked by a State as a ground for precluding wrongfulness if:
>
> (a)   The international obligation in question excludes the possibility of invoking necessity; or
>
> (b)   The State has contributed to the situation of necessity.

The ILC's Draft Articles, after some debate regarding the original prepared under the auspices of the Society of Nations in 1930, was abandoned and then resumed by the General Assembly in 1963. Its definitive version, due mainly to the works of Mssrs Roberto Ago, Willem Riphagen and Gaetano Arangio-Ruiz, was approved in 1981 and subject to a revision in 1998, which was approved in 2001, during the 85th plenary session of the United Nations' General Assembly. Similarly, the ILC has defined the state of necessity as that situation where the only means of safeguarding an essential interest of the State against a grave and imminent peril is an act that is not in conformity with an international obligation binding that State with another State. In shaping the concept of state of necessity, one must make a compulsory reference to the Russian seal furs case. There, the Russian Government banned the hunting of seals near the Russian shorelines.

247. The United Nations Organization has understood that the invocation of a state of necessity depends on the concurrent existence of three circumstances, namely: a danger to the survival of the State, and not for its interests, is necessary; that danger must not have been created by the acting State; finally, the danger should be serious and imminent, so that there are no other means of avoiding it.

248. The concept of state of necessity and the requirements for its admissibility lead to the idea of prevention: the State covers itself against the risk of suffering certain damages. Hence, the possibility of alleging the state of necessity is closely bound by the requirement that there should be a serious and imminent threat and no means to avoid it. Such circumstances, in principle, have been left to the State's subjective appreciation, a conclusion accepted by the International Law Commission. Nevertheless, the Commission was well aware of the fact that this exception, requiring admissibility, has been frequently abused by States, thus opening up a very easy opportunity to violate the international law with impunity. The Commission has set in its Draft Articles on State Responsibility very restrictive conditions to account for its admissibility, reducing such subjectivity.

249. James Crawford, who was rapporteur of the Draft Articles approved in 2001, noted that when a State invokes the state of necessity, it has full knowledge of the fact that it deliberately chooses a procedure that does not abide an including international waters and founded such decision on the absolute need to adopt immediate provisional measures. In a communication addressed, on the occasion of this incident, by the Russian Foreign Minister, Chickline, to the British Ambassador, Morier, the main elements of the state of necessity were established: the absolutely exceptional nature of the alleged situation; the imminent character of the threat against an important State interest; the impossibility of avoiding the risk with other means, and the necessarily temporary nature of this justification, linked to the due danger's persistence. See United Nations, Report of the International Law Commission on the work performed during its 32nd session, p. 87. This deliberate action on the part of the State is therefore subject to the requirements of Article 25 of the Draft Articles, which must concur jointly and without which it is not possible to exclude under international law the wrongfulness of a State's act that violates an international obligation.

250. Taking each element in turn, Article 25 requires first that the act must be the only means available to the State in order to protect an interest. According to S P Jagota, a member of the Commission, such requirement implies that it has not been possible for the State to 'avoid by any other means, even a much

more onerous one that could have been adopted and maintained the respect of international obligations. The State must have exhausted all possible legal means before being forced to act as it does'. Any act that goes beyond the limits of what is strictly necessary 'may not be considered as no longer being, as such, a wrongful act, even if justification of the necessity may have been admitted'.

251. The interest subject to protection also must be essential for the State. What qualifies as an 'essential' interest is not limited to those interests referring to the State's existence. As evidence demonstrates, economic, financial or those interests related to the protection of the State against any danger seriously compromising its internal or external situation, are also considered essential interests. Roberto Ago has stated that essential interests include those related to 'different matters such as the economy, ecology or other'. Julio Barboza affirmed that the threat to an essential interest would be identified by considering, among other things, 'a serious threat against the existence of the State, against its political or economic survival, against the maintenance of its essential services and operational possibilities, or against the conservation of internal peace or its territory's ecology'.

252. James Crawford has stated that no opinion may be offered *a priori* of 'essential interest', but one should understand that it is not the case of the State's 'existence', since the 'purpose of the positive law of self-defence is to safeguard that existence'. Thus, an interest's greater or lesser essential, must be determined as a function of the set of conditions in which the State finds itself under specific situations. The requirement is to appreciate the conditions of each specific case where an interest is in play, since what is essential cannot be predetermined in the abstract.

253. The interest must be threatened by a serious and imminent danger. The threat, according to Roberto Ago, 'must be "extremely grave" and "imminent"'. In this respect, James Crawford has opined that the danger must be established objectively and not only deemed possible. It must be imminent in the sense that it will soon occur.

254. The action taken by the State may not seriously impair another State's interest. In this respect, the Commission has observed that the interest sacrificed for the sake of necessity must be, evidently, less important than the interest sought to be preserved through the action. The idea is to prevent against the possibility of invoking the state of necessity only for the safeguard of a non-essential interest.

255. The international obligation at issue must allow invocation of the state of necessity. The inclusion of an article authorising the state of necessity in a Bilateral Investment Treaty constitutes the acceptance, in the relations between States, of the possibility that one of them may invoke the state of necessity.

256. The State must not have contributed to the production of the state of necessity. It seems logical that if the State has contributed to cause the emergency, it should be prevented from invoking the state of necessity. If there is fault by the State, the exception disappears, since in such case the causal relationship between the State's act and the damage caused is produced. The Tribunal considers that, in the first place, claimants have not proved that Argentina has contributed to cause the severe crisis faced by the country; secondly, the attitude adopted by the Argentine Government has shown a desire to slow down by all the means available the severity of the crisis.

257. The essential interests of the Argentine State were threatened in December 2001. It faced an extremely serious threat to its existence, its political and economic survival, to the possibility of maintaining its essential services in operation, and to the preservation of its internal peace. There is no serious evidence in the record that Argentina contributed to the crisis resulting in the state of necessity. In this circumstance, an economic recovery package was the only means to respond to the crisis. Although there may have been a number of ways to draft the economic recovery plan, the evidence before the Tribunal demonstrates that an across-the-board response was necessary, and the tariffs on public utilities had to be addressed. It cannot be said that any other State's rights were seriously impaired by the measures taken by Argentina during the crisis. Finally, as addressed above, Article XI of the Treaty exempts Argentina of responsibility for measures enacted during the state of necessity.

258. While this analysis concerning Article 25 of the Draft Articles on State Responsibility alone does not establish Argentina's defence, it supports the Tribunal's analysis with regard to the meaning of Article XI's requirement that the measures implemented by Argentina had to have been necessary either for the maintenance of public order or the protection of its own essential security interests.

259. Having found that the requirements for invoking the state of necessity were satisfied, the Tribunal considers that it is the factor excluding the State from its liability vis-à-vis the damage caused as a result of the measures adopted by Argentina in response to the severe crisis suffered by the country.

260. With regard to Article 27 of the United Nations' Draft Articles alleged by claimants, the Tribunal opines that the article at issue does not specifically refer to the compensation for one or all the losses incurred by an investor as a result of the measures adopted by a State during a state of necessity. The commentary introduced by the Special Rapporteur establishes that Article 27 'does not attempt to specify in what circumstances compensation would be payable'. The rule does not specify if compensation is payable during the state of necessity or whether the State should reassume its obligations. In this case, this Tribunal's interpretation of Article XI of the Treaty provides the answer.

261. Following this interpretation the Tribunal considers that Article XI establishes the state of necessity as a ground for exclusion from wrongfulness of an act of the State, and therefore, the State is exempted from liability. This exception is appropriate only in emergency situations; and once the situation has been overcome, i.e., certain degree of stability has been recovered; the State is no longer exempted from responsibility for any violation of its obligations under the international law and shall reassume them immediately.

(iv) Consequences of the state of necessity

262. Three relevant issues arise with respect to the Tribunal's finding Argentina is entitled to invoke the state of necessity as contemplated by Article XI, and general international law.

263. The first issue deals with the determination of the period during which the state of necessity occurred. As previously indicated, in the view of the Tribunal, the state of necessity in this case began on 1 December 2001 and ended on 26 April 2003, when President Kirchner was elected (see the Tribunal's analysis). All measures adopted by Argentina in breach of the Treaty before and after the period during which the state of necessity prevailed, shall have all their effects and shall be taken into account by the Tribunal to estimate the damages.

264. The second issue related to the effects of the state of necessity is to determine the subject upon which the consequences of the measures adopted by the host State during the state of necessity shall fall. As established in the Tribunal's Analysis, Article 27 of ILC's Draft Articles, as well as Article XI of the Treaty, does not specify if any compensation is payable to the party affected by losses during the state of necessity. Nevertheless, and in accordance with that expressed under paragraphs 260 and 261 *supra*, this Tribunal

has decided that the damages suffered during the state of necessity should be borne by the investor.

265. The third issue is related to what Argentina should have done, once the state of necessity was over on 26 April 2003. The very following day (27 April), Argentina's obligations were once again effective. Therefore, respondent should have re-established the tariff scheme offered to LG&E or, at least, it should have compensated claimants for the losses incurred on account of the measures adopted before and after the state of necessity.

(v) Conclusions of the Tribunal

266. Based on the analysis of the state of necessity, the Tribunal concludes that, first, said state started on 1 December 2001 and ended on 26 April 2003; second, during that period Argentina is exempt of responsibility, and accordingly, the claimants should bear the consequences of the measures taken by the host State; and finally, the respondent should have restored the tariff regime on 27 April 2003, or should have compensated the claimants, which did not occur. As a result, Argentina is liable as from that date to claimants for damages.

19

International investment law and EU law

EXERCISE 29– MINI MOCK ARBITRATION

In November 2012, an arbitration based on the Netherlands-Romania BIT was registered by the Permanent Court of Arbitration under the 1976 UNCITRAL Rules. The Dutch company Althea had invested in the Romanian health insurance market in 2007, following liberalisations made as part of Romania's accession to the EU. In the fall of 2009, about the time when Althea's investments had started to produce revenue, there was a government change in Romania. The new government had run on a policy that would once again regulate health insurance and, among other things, prohibit the for-profit sale of such insurance. In its request for arbitration in November 2012, Althea argues that its investments in Romania have been rendered worthless under the new policies and claims damages for breach of the fair and equitable standard, as well as for what it sees as an unlawful expropriation. The tribunal determined that the legal seat of arbitration should be in Vienna, Austria.

Romania raises various jurisdictional objections based on the relationship between investment law and EU law. The State argues (i) that the BIT was implicitly terminated when Romania joined the EU; (ii) the BIT's arbitration clause is incompatible with EU law, because it constitutes discrimination towards EU investors that are not from the Netherlands; and (iii) the fair and equitable treatment and expropriation provisions in the BIT are not compatible with EU law, which means that Althea has no legitimate claim before the tribunal.

GROUP

Group 1
You are the Arbitral Tribunal. You have to determine your own jurisdiction based on the parties' arguments.

Group 2
You are the observer group. Have the best arguments been presented? Was the Tribunal right in its decision? What could the parties and the Tribunal have done differently?

Group 3

You represent Romania, which objects to the Tribunal's jurisdiction. You are to base your arguments exclusively on the various aspects of EU law that are raised by the fact pattern.

Group 4

You represent the claimant Althea and have to argue that EU law does not prohibit the Tribunal from finding that it has jurisdiction.

 CASE

Agreement on encouragement and reciprocal protection of investments between the Government of the Kingdom of the Netherlands and the Government of Romania

The Government of the Kingdom of the Netherlands and the Government of Romania, (hereinafter referred to as the contracting parties), desiring to strengthen the traditional ties of friendship between their countries, to extend and intensify the economic relations between them particularly with respect to investments by the investors of one contracting party in the territory of the other contracting party, recognising that agreement upon the treatment to be accorded to such investments will stimulate the flow of capital and technology and the economic development of the contracting parties and that fair and equitable treatment of investment is desirable, have agreed as follows:

Article 1

For the purposes of this Agreement:

(a) the term 'investments' means every kind of asset invested by investors of one contracting party in the territory of the other contracting party, in conformity with the laws and regulations of the latter, and more particularly, though not exclusively:

i. movable and immovable property as well as any other rights in rem in respect of every kind of asset;

ii. rights derived from shares, bonds and other kinds of interests in companies and joint ventures;

iii. title to money, to other assets or to any performance having an economic value;

iv. rights in the field of intellectual property, technical processes, goodwill and know-how;

v. rights granted under public law or contract, including rights to prospect, explore, extract and win natural resources.

(b) the term 'investors' shall comprise with regard to either contracting party:

i. natural persons having the citizenship or the nationality of that contracting party in accordance with its laws;

ii. legal persons constituted under the law of that contracting party;

iii. legal persons owned or controlled, directly or indirectly, by natural persons as defined in i. or by legal persons as defined in ii. above.

(c) the term 'territory' includes the maritime areas adjacent to the coast of the State concerned, to the extent to which that State exercises sovereign rights or jurisdiction in those areas according to international law.

Article 2

Either contracting party shall, within the framework of its laws and regulations, promote economic cooperation through the protection in its territory of investments of investors of the other contracting party. Subject to its right to exercise powers conferred by its laws or regulations, each contracting party shall admit such investments.

Article 3

(1) Each contracting party shall ensure fair and equitable treatment of the investments of investors of the other contracting party and shall not impair, by unreasonable or discriminatory measures, the operation, management, maintenance, use, enjoyment or disposal thereof by those investors. Each contracting party shall accord to such investments full physical security and protection.

(2) More particularly, each contracting party shall accord to such investments treatment, including with respect to fiscal matters, which in any case shall not be less favourable than that accorded either to investments of its own investors or to investments of investors of any third State, whichever is more favourable to the investor concerned. Fiscal matters refer to taxes, fees,

charges and to fiscal deductions and exemptions, other than those covered by paragraph 3.

(3) If a contracting party has accorded special advantages to investors of any third State by virtue of agreements establishing customs unions, economic unions, monetary unions or similar institutions, or on the basis of interim agreements leading to such unions or institutions, that contracting party shall not be obliged to accord such advantages to investors of the other contracting party. Nor shall such treatment relate to any advantage, which either contracting party accords to investors of a third state by virtue of an agreement for the avoidance of double taxation or other agreement on a reciprocal basis regarding fiscal matters.

(4) Each contracting party shall observe any obligation it may have entered into with regard to investments of investors of the other contracting party.

(5) If the provisions of law of either contracting party or obligations under international agreements existing at present or established hereafter between the contracting parties in addition to the present Agreement contain a regulation, whether general or specific, entitling investments by investors of the other contracting party to a treatment more favourable than is provided for by the present Agreement, such regulation shall to the extent that it is more favourable prevail over the present Agreement.

Article 4

The contracting parties shall guarantee that payments relating to an investment may be transferred. The transfers shall be made in a freely convertible currency, without restriction or delay. Such transfers include in particular though not exclusively:

(a) profits, interest, dividends and other current income;

(b) funds necessary:

i. for the acquisition of raw or auxiliary materials, semi-fabricated or finished products, or

ii. to replace capital assets in order to maintain the continuity of an investment;

(c) additional funds necessary for the development of an investment;

(d) funds in repayment of loans;

(e) royalties or fees;

(f) earnings to which persons are entitled;

(g) the proceeds of sale or liquidation of the investment;

(h) payments arising under Article 6.

Article 5

Neither contracting party shall take any measures, such as nationalisation, expropriation, requisition or other measures of similar effect, depriving investors of the other contracting party of their investments, unless the following conditions are complied with:

(a) the measures are taken in the public interest and under due process of law;

(b) the measures are not discriminatory or contrary to any undertaking which the contracting party which takes such measures may have given;

(c) the measures are taken against just compensation. Such compensation shall represent the fair market value of the investments affected, immediately before the measures were taken or became known, shall include interest at a normal commercial rate until the date of payment and shall, in order to be effective for the claimants, be paid and made transferable, without delay, to the country designated by the claimants concerned and in the currency of the country of which the claimants are investors or in any freely convertible currency accepted by the claimants.

Article 6

Investors of the one contracting party who suffer losses in respect of their investments in the territory of the other contracting party owing to war or other armed conflict, revolution, a state of national emergency, revolt, insurrection or riot shall be accorded by the latter contracting party treatment, as regards restitution, indemnification, compensation or other settlement, no less favourable than that which that contracting party accords to its own investors or to investors of any third State, whichever is more favourable to the investors concerned.

Article 7

If the investments of an investor of the one contracting party are insured against non-commercial risks under a system established by law or regulation, any subrogation of the insurer or re-insurer to the rights of the said investor pursuant to the terms of such insurance shall be recognised by the other contracting party.

Article 8

(1) For the purpose of solving disputes with respect to investments between a contracting party and an investor of the other contracting party, consultations will take place between the parties concerned.

(2) If these consultations do not result in a solution within three months, the investor may submit the dispute, at his choice, for settlement to:

(a) the competent court of the contracting party in the territory of which the investment has been made; or

(b) the International Centre for Settlement of Investment Disputes (ICSID) provided for by the Convention on the Settlement of Investment Disputes between States and Nationals of other States, of 18 March 1965; or

(c) an ad hoc arbitral tribunal which, unless otherwise agreed upon by the parties to the dispute, shall be established under the arbitration rules of the United Nations Commission on International Trade Law (UNCITRAL).

(3) In case the dispute is not resolved pursuant to paragraph 2(a) within a period of ten months the investor may, subject to withdrawing his claim from the courts of the Contracting Party concerned, submit the dispute to arbitration under paragraph 2(b) or (c).

(4) Each contracting party hereby consents to the submission of an investment dispute to international conciliation or arbitration.

(5) The contracting party which is a party to the dispute shall at no time whatsoever during the procedures involving investment disputes, assert as a defence its immunity or the fact that the investor has received compensation under an insurance contract covering the whole or part of the incurred damage or loss.

(6) A legal person which is an investor of one contracting party and which before such a dispute arises is controlled by investors of the other contracting party shall in accordance with Article 25, paragraph 2(b) of the Convention for the purpose of the Convention be treated as an investor of the other Contracting Party.

Article 9

The provisions of this Agreement shall, from the date of entry into force thereof, also apply to investments, which have been made before that date. However, disputes that have arisen before its entry into force are to be settled in accordance with the Agreement on Reciprocal Encouragement and Protection of Investments concluded between the Contracting Parties on October 27, 1983.

Article 10

Either contracting party may propose the other party that consultations be held on any matter concerning the interpretation or application of the Agreement. The other party shall accord sympathetic consideration to the proposal and shall afford adequate opportunity for such consultations.

Article 11

(1) Any dispute between the contracting parties concerning the interpretation or application of the present Agreement, which cannot be settled within a reasonable lapse of time by means of diplomatic negotiations, shall, unless the parties have otherwise agreed, be submitted, at the request of either party, to an arbitral tribunal, composed of three members. Each party shall appoint one arbitrator and the two arbitrators thus appointed shall together appoint a third arbitrator as their chairman who is not a national of either party.

(2) If one of the parties fails to appoint its arbitrator and has not proceeded to do so within two months after an invitation from the other party to make such appointment, the latter party may invite the President of the International Court of Justice to make the necessary appointment.

(3) If the two arbitrators are unable to reach agreement, in the two months following their appointment, on the choice of the third arbitrator, either party may invite the President of the International Court of Justice, to make the necessary appointment.

(4) If, in the cases provided for in the paragraphs 2 and 3 of this Article, the President of the International Court of Justice is prevented from discharging the said function or is a national of either Contracting Party, the Vice-President shall be invited to make the necessary appointments. If the Vice-President is prevented from discharging the said function or is a national of either party the most senior member of the Court available who is not a national of either party shall be invited to make the necessary appointments.

(5) The Tribunal shall decide on the basis of respect for the law, including the provisions of this Agreement and other relevant agreements between the contracting parties, the general principles of international law and relevant domestic legislation. Before the Tribunal decides, it may at any stage of the proceedings propose to the parties that the dispute he settled amicably. The foregoing provisions shall not prejudice the power of the tribunal to decide the dispute *ex aequo et bono* if the parties so agree.

(6) Unless the parties decide otherwise, the Tribunal shall determine its own procedure.

(7) The Tribunal shall reach its decision by a majority of votes. Such decision shall be final and binding on the parties.

(8) Each contracting party shall bear the cost of the arbitrator it has appointed and of its representation in the arbitral proceedings. The cost of the chairman and the remaining costs shall be borne in equal parts by the contracting parties.

Article 12

As regards the Kingdom of the Netherlands, the present Agreement shall apply to the part of the Kingdom in Europe, the Netherlands Antilles and to Aruba, unless the notification provided for in Article 13, paragraph 1 provides otherwise.

Article 13

(1) The present Agreement shall enter into force on the first day of the second month following the date on which the contracting parties have notified each other in writing that the procedures constitutionally required therefor in their respective, countries have been complied with, and shall remain in force for a period of 15 years.

(2) Unless notice of termination has been given by either contracting party at least six months before the date of the expiry of its validity, the present Agreement shall be extended tacitly for periods of ten years, whereby each contracting party reserves the right to terminate the Agreement upon notice of at least six months before the date of expiry of the current period of validity.

(3) In respect of investments made before the date of the termination of the present Agreement the foregoing Articles shall continue to be effective for a further period of 15 years from that date.

(4) Subject to the period mentioned in paragraph 2 of this Article, the Government of the Kingdom of the Netherlands shall be entitled to terminate the application of the present Agreement separately in respect of any of the parts of the Kingdom.

(5) Upon entry into force of this Agreement, the Agreement on Reciprocal Encouragement and Protection of Investments between the Kingdom of the Netherlands and the Socialist Republic of Romania, signed on 27 October 1983, shall be replaced by this Agreement except in case of disputes as referred to in Article.

(6) This Agreement shall replace the Agreement of 1983 only in relations between Romania and those parts of the Kingdom of the Netherlands to which the present Agreement applies in conformity with Article 12 of this Agreement.

In Witness Whereof, the undersigned representatives, duly authorised thereto, have signed the present Agreement.

the Kingdom of the Netherlands

Protocol to the agreement on encouragement and reciprocal protection of investments between the Government of the Kingdom of the Netherlands and the Government of Romania.

On the signing between the Government of the Kingdom of the Netherlands and the Government of Romania of the Agreement on Encouragement and Reciprocal Protection of Investments, the undersigned representatives have agreed on the following provision which constitutes an integral part of the Agreement:

Ad Article 4

Without prejudice to the requirements of Article 4, the Government of Romania shall take appropriate steps to improve the efficiency of the procedures for the transfer of payments related to investments. In any case investors of the Netherlands shall be treated no less favourably than investors of any third State.

20
Compensation

EXERCISE 30 – SEMINAR

 DISCUSSION QUESTIONS

Problem 1

What different concepts of valuation exist for compensation of expropriations – historically and currently? What interests lie behind these models? What considerations do you think should be decisive when assessing the level of compensation? What role does the loss of future profits play in these considerations of yours? To what extent may the actions of the investor influence the valuation of compensation in an investment treaty case? Is there a duty on behalf of the investor to mitigate its losses?

Problem 2

Review the *Chorzow Factory* judgment (*Germany v Poland*) from the Permanent Court of International Justice from September 13, 1928 (easily available online). What standard of compensation does the Court express? Do you see any problems with applying this standard in modern-day investor-state disputes?

Problem 3

Compare the *Yukos Case* with *The Gold Reserve Case*. Which valuation dates did the respective Tribunals use? Explain the differences, if any.

Problem 4

Explain the valuation methods used by the Tribunals in *Yukos* and in *Gold Reserve*. How did the respective Tribunals deal with the burden of proof?

 CASE

Yukos Universal Ltd (Isle of Man) v The Russian Federation, UNCITRAL, PCA Case No. AA 227, excerpt

XII. The quantification of claimants' damages

1693. The Tribunal will now determine the damages caused to claimants by respondent's breach of Article 13 of the ECT. The parties' positions in this regard can be summarised as follows.

A. Claimants' position

1694. Claimants assert that they are entitled to full reparation for respondent's breach of its obligations under the ECT 'through financial compensation measured at the date of expropriation or at the date of the award, whichever is the greatest' and seek damages in 'an amount to be determined by the Arbitral Tribunal', but estimated at 'no less than US$ 114.174 billion'. Claimants maintain that, while Article 13(1) of the ECT provides a specific rule of compensation, this rule applies only to legal expropriations (i.e., expropriations satisfying the conditions contained in Article 13(1)), and that, where one or more of the conditions of Article 13(1) have not been met, the rules of customary international law apply to the issue of reparation. According to claimants, in order to achieve full reparation in the event of an unlawful expropriation, an investor must be able to choose between a valuation of the damages it has suffered as at the date of the breach and a valuation as at the date of the award.

1. Valuation date

1695. Claimants submit that there are two potentially relevant dates with regard to the assessment of damages, namely the moment when a treaty breach occurs and the moment when an award is rendered. Claimants take the view that 'an investor should be compensated in the highest amount between the valuation of the damages it has suffered as at the date of the breach and that at the date of the award'. The reason for this alternative valuation, according to claimants, is that 'to the extent the assets expropriated have increased in value during the arbitration process, this increase must accrue for the benefit of the claimants, not to the Russian Federation'. Claimants refer to a number of legal authorities to support the conclusion that, in cases of unlawful expropriations, investors are entitled to choose between a valuation as at the date of the breach and a valuation as at the date of the award.

1696. Claimants assert that the date of the expropriation of their investment in this case was 21 November 2007, the date on which Yukos was struck off the Russian register of legal entities. The justification for choosing this date, according to claimants, is that '[i]n cases involving expropriations through a series of coordinated interferences by the State, the date of expropriation corresponds to the date on which the governmental interference ripened into an irreversible deprivation of the investor's property', and that striking Yukos from the register of legal entities constituted 'a point of no return'.

2. Causation

1697. With regard to causation, claimants assert that they do not need to establish a link between individual actions of respondent and the damages suffered, but that it suffices for them to show that the sum of respondent's actions caused those damages. Claimants argue that:

> [T]he Russian Federation sought and achieved the dismantlement and destruction of Yukos, and the claimants' investments therein, through a series of cumulative actions. . . .The breach, and the respondent's responsibility, arises from the Russian Federation's actions taken as a whole and not from each and every one of these actions. It is the cumulative effect of these acts that is criticised by the claimants.

1698. Claimants also argue that: '[A] causal link needs only be established between the actions of the Russian Federation taken as a whole and the claimants' damages, namely the destruction of their investments. This causal link is obvious. . .'

1699. According to claimants, there is ample authority to support their position that the Tribunal need only consider 'the totality of the Russian Federation's actions and their result: the inexcusable treatment of the Claimants' investments and, ultimately, their outright expropriation'.

3. Calculations performed by claimants and Mr Kaczmarek

1700. Claimants have submitted two expert reports on damages authored by Mr Brent Kaczmarek of Navigant Consulting, dated 15 September 2010 and 15 March 2012, together with their Memorial and their Reply, respectively. The calculations contained in these reports and referred to in claimants' pleadings can be summarised as follows.

(a) The 'scenarios' presented by claimants 1701. Claimants perform calculations based on three different 'scenarios.' Within each of these scenarios, claimants also differentiate between a number of sub-scenarios.

1702. The first scenario developed by claimants is based on two fundamental assumptions, namely (a) that the tax assessments against Yukos constituted a breach of the ECT, and (b) that this breach caused the merger between Yukos and Sibneft to be cancelled. In addition, claimants call in aid an optional assumption in the context of this scenario, namely (c) that Yukos would have had a 70 per cent chance of obtaining a listing on the NYSE, which would have further increased its value. Claimants' first scenario can thus be subdivided into two sub-scenarios: sub-scenario 1a, which is based only on assumptions (a) and (b); and sub-scenario 1b, which is based on all three assumptions (a), (b), and (c).

1703. Claimants' second scenario is based on assumption (a) described above, namely that the tax assessments against Yukos constituted a breach of the ECT, whilst excluding assumption (b) (thus not seeking damages for the demerger between Yukos and Sibneft). Here again two sub-scenarios can be distinguished: sub-scenario 2a is based solely on assumption (a), whereas sub-scenario 2b is based on both assumptions (a) and (c).

1704. Claimants' third scenario assumes that the tax assessments against Yukos did not constitute a breach of the ECT, but that the subsequent enforcement of the tax claims did. Accordingly, claimants calculate the 'damages arising out of the 2004 and 2007 auctions, regardless of the merits of the alleged tax claims imposed on Yukos'. Within this third scenario, claimants distinguish five sub-scenarios (subsequently referred to as 3a, 3b, 3c, 3d and 3e), all of which assume that Yukos should have been allowed to settle its alleged tax debts one way or another (thus avoiding the liquidation of the company), but propose different modalities as to how this could have been done.

1705. Sub-scenario 3a assumes that Yukos would have been allowed a grace period of five years and would then have 'been able to pay off the entire amount of its alleged tax liabilities out of its operating cash-flows only by 2009'.

1706. Sub-scenario 3b assumes that Yukos would have been granted a grace period of three years and would then have been able to pay off its alleged tax liabilities with a combination of its free cash flows and the sale of non-core assets during that period.

1707. Sub-scenario 3c assumes that Yukos would have been granted a grace period of one year and would then have been able to pay off its alleged tax liabilities with a combination of its free cash flows, the sale of non-core assets and debt financing during that period.

1708. Sub-scenario 3d also assumes that Yukos would have been granted a grace period of only one year, but then assumes (in contradistinction to sub-scenario 3c) that Yukos would have paid off its alleged tax liabilities with a combination of free cash flows, the sale of certain core assets and (limited) debt financing.

1709. Finally, sub-scenario 3e assumes that, while Yukos would have had to sell YNG to settle its alleged tax obligations, the auction 'would have been conducted in a manner ensuring a fair, rather than grossly undervalued, price', generating proceeds of USD 19.703 billion, with the result that Yukos would have paid off its alleged tax liabilities with these proceeds as well as its cash flows in 2004 and 2005, while remaining a going concern.

1710. In accordance with claimants' submissions regarding the relevant valuation dates, claimants base their damages calculations in the first place on a valuation date of 21 November 2007. Accordingly, claimants provide calculations for all three scenarios based on this date. In addition, claimants also carry out a number of calculations based on the date of 1 January 2012, as a proxy for the date of the award, 'for comparison purposes'. Claimants provide calculations based on this date for scenarios 1 and 2, but not for scenario 3.

(b) Methodology used for calculations based on scenarios 1 and 2 1711. Claimants' calculations for scenarios 1 and 2 as of November 2007 are in principle based on the following methodology: the total of the damages claimed corresponds to the sum of claimants' share in a hypothetical Yukos entity as of the valuation date plus the hypothetical cash flows that claimants would have received in the form of dividends based on claimants' share-holding in Yukos from 2004 to November 2007. In addition, in scenarios 1b and 2b, claimants also include the value they attribute to the 'lost chance' of listing Yukos' shares on the NYSE. The total amount thus obtained is then 'brought forward' to a date close to the date of Mr Kaczmarek's report by adding pre-award interest. Each one of these steps is set out in more detail below.

i. Value of shares 1712. With regard to the valuation date of 21 November 2007, claimants calculate the value of their shares in Yukos as follows:

1713. *(a) Valuation of Yukos.* As a first step, claimants calculate the value of the relevant Yukos entity, as defined by the assets that claimants assume Yukos would have owned in November 2007 in the absence of respondent's alleged breaches. The assets taken into account depend on the scenario. For the purposes of scenario 1, both Yukos' and Sibneft's original assets are taken into account, whereas for scenario 2 the calculations are based only on Yukos' assets. Claimants use three different methods for valuing Yukos, namely the DCF method, the comparable companies method and the comparable transactions method.

1714. With regard to the DCF method, claimants describe their approach as an attempt to reconstruct the 'pro-forma financial statements' that the relevant Yukos entity would have presented in November 2007, based on the financial and operational data published by Rosneft and Gazprom Neft, which held the majority of Yukos' assets at that point in time. Where no such data is available, claimants rely on 'historical financial statements and operating information published by Yukos and Sibneft . . . as well as a benchmark of indicators from Yukos' and Sibneft's industry peers in Russia'. Based on this data, claimants estimate cash flows between 2007 and 2015 as well as a 'terminal value' of the entity in 2015. Claimants then bring the above estimates to their November 2007 value by applying a discount rate based on Yukos' cost of capital. This operation leads them to Yukos' enterprise value as of November 2007.

1715. Claimants also use a comparable companies approach, based on data available for a pool of Russian (Rosneft, Gazprom Neft, Lukoil, TNK-BP and Surgutneftegaz) and international (BP, Chevron, Conoco-Philips, Exxon-Mobil, Royal Dutch Shell and Total SA) oil companies. This approach identifies companies with characteristics similar to Yukos (notably in terms of production, reserves, profitability, revenue growth and financing structure), establishes the ratios between the enterprise value of these companies and relevant operating or financial metrics (EBITDA, reserves and production), and then applies these ratios to the relevant metrics of Yukos in order to estimate the latter's enterprise value. The net income, EBITDA, reserves and production of Yukos are derived from the 'pro-forma financial statements' established in the context of the DCF method.

1716. Finally, claimants use a comparable transactions approach based on public purchase transactions of comparable companies. In this regard, claimants apply a 'sum of the parts valuation', in which they select transactions that are meant to match the upstream and downstream business of Yukos separately. Here again, the operating and financial metrics of Yukos as determined in the context of the DCF method are used to calculate the value of the company.

1717. Claimants then calculate a synthesised enterprise value of Yukos based on the results of the three approaches, weighing the DCF approach at 50 per cent, the comparable companies approach at 40 per cent and the comparable transactions approach at 10 per cent. By then subtracting Yukos' assumed debt, they arrive at Yukos' synthesised equity value.

1718. *(b) Calculation of the value of claimants' shareholding.* In a final step, for each of the scenarios considered, claimants calculate the value of claimants' shareholding in Yukos by multiplying the company's equity value by claimants' share in the company – 53 per cent (corresponding to the dilution of claimants' shareholding associated with the creation of YukosSibneft) for scenario 1 and 70.5 per cent (corresponding to claimants' original shareholding in Yukos) for scenario 2.

ii. ADDITIONAL INDICATORS RELIED ON BY CLAIMANTS TO CONFIRM THE VALUE OF YUKOS SHARES   1719. With regard to scenario 1, Mr Kaczmarek avers that he confirmed his valuation with a number of additional indicators. Claimants calculate Yukos' enterprise value based on the market capitalisation of Rosneft in November 2007, with a number of adjustments made in order to take into account the differences between Rosneft's assets and Yukos' (fictitious) assets as of that date. The result of this calculation is an enterprise value that is about US$4.5 billion lower than the enterprise value calculated on the basis of the above-described methodology.

1720. Mr Kaczmarek also confirms his valuation of Yukos' enterprise value as of November 2007 based on the increase of three benchmarks (Urals blend prices, the RTS Oil and Gas index an Lukoil's market capitalisation) between October 2003 and November 2007. These calculations lead to an enterprise value of Yukos that is approximately halfway between US$14.4 billion lower (RTS Oil and Gas) and US$46.5 billion higher (Lukoil market capitalisation) than the enterprise value of Yukos calculated on the basis of claimants' basic methodology.

1721. Finally, claimants calculate Yukos' enterprise value on the basis of a share swap involving YNG shares that would have taken place between Rosneft and Yukos in October 2006, which Claimants say implies a valuation of YNG's equity at US$46.2 billion at that point in time. On that basis, Claimants calculate an enterprise value of Yukos as of 21 November 2007 that is approximately US$12.8 billion lower than the value calculated on the basis of their basic methodology.

iii. HYPOTHETICAL CASH FLOWS FROM DIVIDENDS   1722. The second component of claimants' damages calculation is the cash flows from dividends that claimants argue would have been paid to them in the first and second scenarios but for respondent's treaty breaches. Claimants assume that, without the alleged breaches of the ECT by respondent, Yukos would have paid dividends to its shareholders between 30 September 2003 and 21 November 2007. Accordingly, claimants say that they would have received a pro rata share of these dividends, calculated on the basis of their shareholding in the company.

iv. Loss of chance   1723. The third component of claimants' damages calculation is based on claimants' valuation of what they refer to as the loss of a chance to obtain a listing of Yukos on the NYSE. Claimants submit that, without the breaches of respondent, Yukos would likely have been listed on the NYSE, and that this listing would have decreased the company's costs of capital and thus increased Yukos' share value. Claimants quantify the value of the loss of this chance by multiplying the assumed increase in share value with the probability of a successful listing, which they assume to be 70 per cent. This loss for claimants is the amount thus obtained, multiplied by claimants' shareholding in Yukos.

v. Pre-award interest   1724. In a final step for purposes of their calculations with regard to scenarios 1 and 2, claimants bring forward the total amount thus obtained to a date close to the date of their last submissions and add pre-award interest of LIBOR plus 4 per cent on a compound basis.

(c) Methodology used for calculations based on scenario 3   1725. Claimants' calculations for scenarios 3a to 3d are based on their calculations for the second scenario, but are adjusted to take into account the settlement of Yukos' tax liabilities through Yukos' cash flow, the sale of certain assets and/or debt financing. These scenarios do not assume any payment of dividends to Yukos' shareholders or the loss of a chance of obtaining a listing of Yukos on the NYSE. Rather, claimants determine Yukos' equity value as of November 2007 and derive the value of their ownership interest in Yukos from that figure. They then bring forward the amount thus obtained to a date close to the date of their last submissions again by adding compound pre-award interest at a rate of LIBOR plus 4 per cent.

1726. Claimants' calculations for scenario 3e (which assumes the sale of YNG at a price higher than that achieved in the 2004 auction) are somewhat more complex. In this scenario, claimants estimate the enterprise value of YNG as of November 2007, and then subtract this amount from their estimate of the enterprise value of Yukos as of the same date. This leaves claimants with a figure for the enterprise value of Yukos' assets without YNG. Claimants then subtract the assumed debt of this smaller Yukos entity and thus arrive at the equity value of Yukos (without YNG) in November 2007. Claimants calculate their losses as a pro rata share (based on their 70.5 per cent shareholding in Yukos) of the sum of this equity value, their estimate of free cash flows that a diminished Yukos (without YNG) would have achieved between January 2005 and November 2007, and pre-award interest brought forward to a date close to the date of their last submissions.

(d) Methodology used for calculations based on 2012 valuation date   1727. The position of claimants is that, because of the unlawful taking by respondent of Yukos, they are entitled to select the evaluation of the damages either at the date of respondent's breach or at the date of the award, whichever is the highest. Thus, claimants, in their reply, also quantify their damages in scenarios 1 and 2 based on a valuation date of 1 January 2012. Claimants state they chose this date for practical purposes since it is close to the date of submission of Mr Kaczmarek's second expert report and that, if need be, calculations 'can subsequently be updated at a date closer to the award'.

1728. While Mr Kaczmarek does not set out the methodology used in this regard in any great detail, it can be inferred from some of the appendices to his second report. In these appendices, Mr. Kaczmarek estimates Yukos' cash flows for the years 2004 to 2011 as well as the terminal value of Yukos as of 1 January 2012 for scenarios 1 and 2 and then applies pre-award interest of LIBOR plus four percent to bring these figures to the present (i.e., 15 March 2012) value and thus obtain Yukos' total damages. For scenarios 1b and 2b, claimants also add the incremental value of the chance of obtaining a listing on the NYSE. Claimants then calculate their damages as a percentage of Yukos' damages, based on their shareholding in the relevant entity.

(e) Summary of results of claimants' calculations   1729. The valuation by Mr Kaczmarek of each of the scenarios described above (including pre-award interest through 15 March 2012) is summarised in the following table (amounts in USD billion) [removed].

4. Failure of claimants to mitigate

1730. In response to respondent's contention that claimants should promptly have paid the original taxes assessed against Yukos (as well as those Yukos should have anticipated would be imposed for succeeding years on the same grounds) to avoid massive damages, claimants aver that there is no 'duty to appease' and that 'a victim of extortion is not to blame if the threats against it are carried out after it refuses to pay'.

1731. Claimants also argue that Yukos had no reason to concede the validity of the Russian authorities' position with regard to the initial tax assessments 'in circumstances where its objections to the December 29, 2003 Audit Report were still under consideration' and where it had received advice from its lawyers that the Audit Report was 'totally inconsistent with the Russian tax law'. In any event, claimants say that Yukos did not have enough cash to settle an alleged tax debt of US$9 billion in the first quarter of 2004.

1732. In addition, claimants assert that, to apply respondent's argument, 'the Tribunal would need to ignore the most salient facts – the respondent's breaches – and assume . . . that the very same Russian authorities who committed those breaches would have acted differently if only Yukos had taken the actions specified by the respondent'. In particular, with regard to respondent's argument that Yukos could have significantly reduced its tax burden by filing corrected VAT returns during the first quarter of 2004, claimants contend that the actual conduct of the Russian authorities demonstrates that any amended returns that Yukos might have submitted would, in any event, have been either ignored or rejected.

5. Windfall and double-recovery

1733. Finally, claimants also reject respondent's arguments that any award of damages should avoid presenting claimants with a windfall and take into account the risk of double-recovery. According to claimants, these arguments of respondent merely seek to 'repackage its so-called 'unclean hands' theory in the context of damages' and respondent, they say, 'has failed to articulate any basis on which alleged collateral illegalities could . . . be relevant to an assessment of damages'. In any event, conclude claimants, any benefits they may have received through their investments prior to respondent's breaches of the ECT are irrelevant for the calculation of the damages in the present arbitration and, furthermore, any assets located outside Russia have been excluded from Mr Kaczmarek's valuations.

B. Respondent's position

1734. Respondent argues that, even if it were held to be liable for a breach of the ECT, claimants should not be awarded any damages in this case. Respondent has submitted two expert reports on damages by Professor James Dow, one dated 1 April 2011 and the other 15 August 2012, with their Counter-Memorial and their Rejoinder, respectively. These reports and respondent's arguments with regard to claimants' damages calculations can be summarised as follows.

1. Valuation date

1735. Respondent disagrees with both valuation dates proposed by claimants.

1736. With regard to claimants' valuation as of the date of expropriation, respondent invokes the principle that 'the valuation date should be when the purported substantial deprivation of the investor's investment has occurred'.

Respondent objects, however, to claimants' assessment that in this case a substantial deprivation of their investment occurred on 21 November 2007, a date which respondent considers 'arbitrary'. Respondent argues that 'the hallmark of an appropriate valuation date is the loss of effective control over the investor's investment' and concludes that 'claimants have repeatedly averred that they lost control of their investment and that it lost all value long before November 21, 2007'.

1737. As a result, respondent disputes that the date of 21 November 2007 chosen by claimants has any relevance. As Professor Dow explained at the Hearing:

> I am very clear in stating that the 2007 date has no economic relevance, in my view. And I say that because at the end of 2004 Yukos shares had lost essentially all of their value. Yukos was a penny stock. It wasn't expected to recover, the market did not expect it to recover; that was reflected in the share price. . . So from an economic point of view, the date of delisting in 2007 is a bureaucratic event, not an event at which value was lost.

1738. While respondent does not propose any specific alternative date when claimants lost control of their investments, Professor Dow suggested at the Hearing that such a date would, in any event, have to be before the end of 2004.

1739. Respondent also rejects claimants' submission that the date of an award can be used as an alternative valuation date. In this regard, respondent argues that the 'standard theoretical framework economists typically use to calculate damages is an "*ex ante*" one' where damages are assessed at the moment of the relevant breaches and then brought to present value with prejudgment interest. By contrast, an '*ex post*' approach would, according to respondent, use information based on hindsight, provide no principled basis for choosing a date and therefore be vulnerable to error. In addition, respondent claims that, 'with each passing day after the alleged takings date, it becomes increasingly speculative to value the asset taken as of some later date'.

1740. In his first report, Professor Dow writes that there is a 'general preference among economists for the *ex ante* approach when evaluating damages in commercial matters' and refers, in this connection, to an article published in the 1990 *Journal of Accounting, Auditing and Finance*. Relying on this article, respondent submits that 'an expropriation relieves the owner not only of the value of the asset on the date of expropriation, but also of the risk associated with owning it' and that, as a consequence, '[t]he only way to recognise both aspects is to assess the value of the asset on the date of expropriation, when neither its owner nor the State knows whether the asset will increase or decrease in value.'

2. Causation

1741. Respondent also disagrees with claimants with respect to causation. In particular, respondent emphasises the need to establish 'a sufficient causal link' between breach and damage, where the latter is the 'proximate result' of the former. Respondent advocates the following methodology:

> [I]f the damages are caused by a series of harmful actions . . . each violation can be treated as a new action and the corresponding incremental change can be estimated at the time of the action, . . . [t]he incremental damage figures for each violation can then be added together to obtain a total damage figure.

1742. According to respondent, claimants' approach to damages fails 'to connect any of the alleged treaty violations to a specific amount of damages' and provides 'no mechanism for determining the incremental damages allegedly caused by any specific alleged violation'. As a consequence, respondent alleges that claimants' valuations 'do not accommodate the situation where the Tribunal finds that fewer than all of the scores of alleged "bad acts" were violations'.

3. Specific aspects of the calculations performed by claimants criticised by respondent

1743. Principally, respondent criticises claimants' damages claims as being 'based on inherently incorrect or speculative assumptions'. According to Professor Dow, Mr Kaczmarek's various calculations are 'riddled with errors' and the obvious result of 'reverse engineering to a desired result'. Respondent and its expert raise numerous arguments in support of their criticism, the most important of which are summarised below.

(a) Credibility of claimants' DCF analysis   1744. One of respondent's main criticisms with regard to claimants' valuation is directed at Mr Kaczmarek's DCF analysis. In particular, in his first expert report, Professor Dow identifies what respondent claims are 'three obvious and significant errors' regarding the valuation of YNG. Respondent points out that, while Mr Kaczmarek admitted to two of these errors in his second expert report, the valuation of YNG remained virtually unchanged. As a consequence, respondent claims that Mr Kaczmarek's 'main task' in his second report must have been to 'find

a way to make up for gaping holes in his initial valuation that he concedes were the result of readily identifiable errors that he realized had to be corrected, after Professor Dow had identified them'. Respondent points out that, while the necessary corrections identified by Professor Dow caused claimants' expert to make adjustments of over US$10 billion to his valuation of YNG, Mr Kaczmarek still ended up with virtually the same figure as in his first report as a consequence of a series of simultaneous 'discretionary' upward adjustments.

1745. Respondent also claims that claimants' expert 'did the same thing in his other two DCF models, correcting mistakes that reduce his valuation of Yukos and YukosSibneft by US$40 billion and US$90 billion, respectively, and then adjusting other elements to bring his conclusions back up to where he started'. According to respondent, 'Mr Kaczmarek confirmed . . . that his DCF model is simply a device for justifying an *a priori* conclusion, conceding repeatedly that his focus was not on critically analysing the inputs to his model, but rather on whether the output met pre-conceived notions that were never disclosed in his reports.' As a result, respondent concludes that claimants' results have been 'reverse engineered' and are 'made-up numbers around which models were built'.

(b) Claimants' selection of comparable companies for purposes of the comparable companies analysis   1746. With regard to claimants' use of the comparable companies method, respondent criticises claimants' valuation as being based on an 'unsupportable decision to weigh Rosneft as 70 per cent of the analysis, when Rosneft's market metrics never resembled Yukos' or those of other private Russian oil companies'. Professor Dow, provides a 'corrected' comparable companies analysis that excludes the data with regard to Rosneft, Gazprom Neft and the international major oil companies from the analysis, and leads to an enterprise value for Yukos in 2007 that is approximately USD 32 billion lower than the enterprise value calculated by Mr Kaczmarek based on the comparable companies method.

(c) Claimants' reliance on comparable transactions   1747. With regard to claimants' calculations based on comparable transactions, respondent asserts that claimants' expert, Mr Kaczmarek, admits that no truly comparable transactions exist. In addition, Professor Dow criticises Mr Kaczmarek's selection criteria for identifying comparable upstream and downstream transactions as 'indefensible from an economic perspective'.

(d) Claimants' calculations of hypothetical cash flows from dividends   1748. Respondent does not explicitly address claimants' calculations of hypothetical dividends that would have been paid by Yukos to its shareholders if there

had been no breach of the ECT as alleged by claimants. However, when criticising Mr Kaczmarek's calculations with regard to scenario 3, Professor Dow does comment on the free cash flows of Yukos that, according to claimants, would have been the basis for the payment of dividends. Thus, according to Professor Dow, the free cash flows identified by Mr Kaczmarek in this context are 'inflated because they are based on his . . . grossly erroneous [. . .] Yukos DCF model that overstates Yukos cash flows'. Professor Dow provides an alternative set of figures that he refers to as the 'corrected' cash flows from Mr Kaczmarek's model.

(e) Claimants' calculations based on the loss of a chance to obtain a listing on the New York Stock Exchange 1749. Professor Dow also criticises claimants' assumption that Yukos would have benefited from a listing on the NYSE as 'thrice wrong because it assumes an event that did not happen, that was entirely within Yukos' control, and overstates the economic benefit that would be expected were the event to have come to pass'. In addition, Professor Dow states that there is no basis for the assumption that, without respondent's actions, Yukos would have had a 70 per cent chance of being listed on the NYSE.

(f) Claimants' calculations based on the assumption of a completed Yukos–Sibneft merger 1750. Professor Dow criticises claimants' calculations based on a completed Yukos–Sibneft merger arguing that such a merger was never completed and that the valuation of a combined YukosSibneft entity is therefore utterly speculative. In particular, Professor Dow claims that Mr Kaczmarek's calculations largely ignore 'the effects of the merger on operational costs, any impact on costs as a result of changed regulatory requirements, and the combined entity's creditworthiness and cost of borrowing'.

(g) Claimants' scenarios 3a–3d 1751. With regard to claimants' scenarios 3a to 3d, which assume payment of Yukos' tax liabilities over a period of one, three or five years, respondent asserts that Russian law did not allow the Tax Ministry to enter into any such arrangements as postulated by claimants and that it was, in any event, not obligated to do so. In addition, respondent claims that, based on the knowledge available regarding the development of oil prices in 2004, claimants' calculations in relation to expected cash flows are not realistic. Respondent also disputes that claimants would have been able to negotiate a loan of USD 16 billion, as assumed in claimants' scenario 3c.

(h) Claimants' scenario 3e and the valuation of YNG 1752. With regard to claimants' scenario 3e (which assumes that the auctioning of YNG was

necessary, but should have been realised at a fair price) and the valuation of YNG in Mr Kaczmarek's first expert report, respondent claims that Mr Kaczmarek made three 'obvious and significant errors' relating to the application of the inflation rate, the export duty rate and the mineral extraction tax rate. Adjusting for these errors, the valuation of YNG would have been USD 12.5 billion, with the consequence that Yukos would not have been able to pay its taxes by the end of 2005, even if YNG had been sold at a higher price.

(i) Claimants' calculation of pre-award interest   1753. As described in Part XI above, respondent submits that claimants are not entitled to claim pre-award interest.

4. Failure of claimants to mitigate

1754. Respondent asserts that claimants had 'repeated opportunities to mitigate the damage caused', and that, in particular, by paying its taxes in early 2004, Yukos could have 'halved the total amount to be paid' rather than 'subject[ing] itself to . . . US$ 12 billion in additional 2000–2003 Avoidable Taxes and Fees'. If Yukos had paid its taxes and filed appropriate returns during the first quarter of 2004, respondent says it 'would have survived as a going concern and still could have pursued a claim for a refund of any amounts the courts found it did not need to pay'. Accordingly, the 'loss of all value of Yukos' would be 'the consequence of the contributory fault and the failure to mitigate of Yukos, under the control of claimants'.

1755. Respondent claims that, as a consequence, 'claimants' maximum damage claim is for their proportion of the harm (if any) Yukos would have suffered if the assessment and payment of the 2000–2003 Unavoidable Taxes were deemed to constitute a violation of the ECT'. Respondent calculates this 'maximum damage' as amounting to USD 6.27 billion.

5. Windfall and double-recovery

1756. In addition, respondent claims that any calculation of damages should take into account any previous benefits obtained by claimants from their investments in Russia, so as to prevent any 'double-recovery'. Respondent contends that granting claimants the damages sought 'would be a massive windfall to claimants, who have already received far more from their investment in Yukos than they would have received had they invested in a comparable Russian oil company during the same period'. Respondent also suggests that, had the market known of

> Yukos' lack of transparency, its disregard of minority interests, and its failures of corporate governance, not to mention its internal documents acknowledging the civil and criminal exposure it faced from its massive tax fraud, Yukos would not have experienced the share appreciation . . . on which claimants' damages claim depends.

As a consequence, respondent claims that 'the market metrics . . . are not fair indicators of value and cannot be relied upon by the Tribunal'.

1757. Respondent concludes that 'any damages award should provide for no more than a reasonable rate of return'. Since claimants would 'have already gained that return through Yukos' dividends and share repurchases, . . . hundreds of millions of dollars worth of Russian taxes.

C. Tribunal's analysis and decision

1758. Having reviewed and considered the parties' submissions and their experts' reports, the Tribunal will now determine the damages suffered by claimants as a result of respondent's unlawful expropriation of Yukos' assets in breach of Article 13 of the ECT.

1. Valuation date

1759. With regard to the date of valuation, the Tribunal needs to address two issues, namely (a) the date of the expropriation of claimants' investment by respondent, and (b) whether claimants are entitled to choose between a valuation based on that date of expropriation and a valuation based on the date of the award. Each of these questions is addressed in turn.

(a) The date of the expropriation 1760. As noted earlier, claimants have advanced the date of 21 November 2007, the day on which Yukos was struck off the Russian register of legal entities, as the date of the expropriation of their investment, and have performed their main damages analysis based on a valuation of their shares in Yukos as of that date.

1761. The Tribunal agrees with respondent that the date of 21 November 2007 cannot be the date of Yukos' expropriation. The Tribunal observes that both parties are agreed that, in principle, in the event of an expropriation through a series of actions, the date of the expropriation is the date on which the incriminated actions first lead to a deprivation of the investor's property that crossed the threshold and became tantamount to an expropriation. This is the date that is relevant for the determination of the Tribunal.

1762. The Tribunal finds that the threshold to the expropriation of claimants' investment was crossed earlier than in November 2007. On the basis of the record, it is clear to the Tribunal that a substantial and irreversible deprivation of claimants' assets occurred on 19 December 2004, the date of the YNG auction. YNG was Yukos' main production asset and its loss, with the conclusion of the auction on that date, marked a substantial and irreversible diminution of claimants' investment. This conclusion of the Tribunal is confirmed by statements made by claimants in December 2004 to the effect that they had 'lost the power to govern the financial and operating policies of Yukos so as to obtain the benefits from its activities' and that Yukos had become 'incapable of operating as a business'. The date of the expropriation of claimants' investment is therefore determined by the Tribunal to be 19 December 2004.

(b) The possibility for claimants to choose between a valuation as of the date of expropriation and a valuation as of the date of the award   1763. The Tribunal also holds that, in the case of an unlawful expropriation, as in the present case, claimants are entitled to select either the date of expropriation or the date of the award as the date of valuation.

1764. As the Tribunal noted earlier, respondent, relying on the opinion of its expert on damages, maintains that claimants may not make such a choice and that there is a preference amongst economists for what he refers to as an '*ex ante*' approach to the evaluation of damages. In support of his opinion, Professor Dow relies on a single article published in an economics journal in 1990.

1765. Neither the text of Article 13 of the ECT nor its *travaux* provide a definitive answer to the question of whether damages should be assessed as of the date of expropriation or the date of the award. The text of Article 13, after specifying the four conditions that must be met to render an expropriation lawful, provides that for 'such' an expropriation, that is, for a lawful expropriation, damages shall be calculated as of the date of the taking. *A contrario*, the text of Article 13 may be read to import that damages for an unlawful taking need not be calculated as of the date of taking. It follows that this Tribunal is not required by the terms of the ECT to assess damages as of the time of the expropriation. Moreover, conflating the measure of damages for a lawful taking with the measure of damages for an unlawful taking is, on its face, an unconvincing option.

1766. In the view of the Tribunal, and in exercise of the latitude that the terms of Article 13 of the ECT afford it in this regard, the question of whether an expropriated investor is entitled to choose between a valuation as of the expropriation date and the date of an award is one best answered by considering which party should bear the risk and enjoy the benefits of unanticipated events leading to a change in the value of the expropriated asset between the time of the expropriatory actions and the rendering of an award. The Tribunal finds that the principles on the reparation for injury as expressed in the ILC Articles on State Responsibility are relevant in this regard. According to Article 35 of the ILC Articles, a State responsible for an illegal expropriation is in the first place obliged to make restitution by putting the injured party into the position that it would be in if the wrongful act had not taken place. This obligation of restitution applies as of the date when a decision is rendered. Only to the extent where it is not possible to make good the damage caused by restitution is the State under an obligation to compensate pursuant to Article 36 of the ILC Articles on State Responsibility.

1767. The consequences of the application of these principles (restitution as of the date of the decision, compensation for any damage not made good by restitution) for the calculation of damages in the event of illegal expropriation are twofold. First, investors must enjoy the benefits of unanticipated events that increase the value of an expropriated asset up to the date of the decision, because they have a right to compensation in lieu of their right to restitution of the expropriated asset as of that date. If the value of the asset increases, this also increases the value of the right to restitution and, accordingly, the right to compensation where restitution is not possible.

1768. Second, investors do not bear the risk of unanticipated events decreasing the value of an expropriated asset over that time period. While such events decrease the value of the right to restitution (and accordingly the right to compensation in lieu of restitution), they do not affect an investor's entitlement to compensation of the damage 'not made good by restitution' within the meaning of Article 36(1) of the ILC Articles on State Responsibility. If the asset could be returned to the investor on the date where a decision is rendered, but its value had decreased since the expropriation, the investor would be entitled to the difference in value, the reason being that in the absence of the expropriation the investor could have sold the asset at an earlier date at its previous higher value. The same analysis must also apply where the asset cannot be returned, allowing the investor to claim compensation in the amount of the asset's higher value.

1769. It follows for the several reasons stated above that in the event of an illegal expropriation an investor is entitled to choose between a valuation as of the expropriation date and as of the date of the award. The Tribunal finds support for this conclusion in the fact that this approach has been adopted by tribunals in a number of recent decisions dealing with illegal expropriation. One of these tribunals, in *Ioannis Kardassopoulous and Ron Fuchs v The Republic of Georgia*, so interpreted the ECT.

2. Causation

1770. The parties disagree with regard to the requirements for showing the causation of damages. The Tribunal finds it useful to address the parties' views on this matter in two steps. First, the Tribunal will address the requirements for showing the causation of damages where several actions are invoked at the same time. Second, it will deal with the consequences of damage being caused by several actions, only some of which are breaches attributable to the respondent party.

(a) Causation and reliance on multiple actions   1771. Claimants assert that 'a causal link needs only be established between the actions of the Russian Federation taken as a whole and claimants' damages' and that '[t]his causal link is obvious'. Respondent takes the view that, by simply asserting a link between the totality of a number of 'bad acts' and the damage, claimants put themselves in a position where they have to show that 'all of the scores of alleged "bad acts" were [treaty] violations'.

1772. The Tribunal holds that claimants do, in fact, establish that a specific series of actions of respondent, consisting of the 2000–04 tax assessments against Yukos and the subsequent enforcement measures (including the forced auction of YNG), constituted an illegal expropriation of claimants' investment, and that this expropriation caused claimants damage. In particular, the 2000–04 tax assessments were actions that contributed to the expropriation of claimants' investment, and without these assessments, the damage to claimants would not have occurred. While other actions taken by respondent may or may not have contributed to a violation of the ECT's standards, showing that they did is not required for establishing causation with regard to the damage suffered by claimants. All of the heads of damage subsequently identified by the Tribunal are consequences of the 2000–04 tax assessments that led to the expropriation of claimants' investment, and this expropriation was clearly a breach of Article 13 ECT.

(b) Multiple causes for the same damage   1773. The parties also do not agree with regard to the consequences of damage being caused by several events, where only some of those events are breaches attributable to a respondent party. Respondent appears to suggest that concurrent causation

of a particular line of damage by claimants' own conduct, the conduct of third parties and conduct of respondent that is not wrongful should exclude respondent's responsibility for that damage, and that claimants bear the burden of showing that no such causation exists. The Tribunal does not agree with that argument.

1774. In this regard, the Tribunal finds it instructive to look to the ILC Articles on State Responsibility. Article 31 of the ILC Articles provides that '[t]he responsible State is under an obligation to make full reparation for the injury caused'. The official commentary to this provision notes that '[o]ften two separate factors combine to cause damage', before pointing out that:

> Although, in such cases, the injury in question was effectively caused by a combination of factors, only one of which is to be ascribed to the responsible State, international practice and the decisions of international tribunals do not support the reduction or attenuation of reparation for concurrent causes, except in cases of contributory fault. . . Such a result should follow *a fortiori* in cases where the concurrent cause is not the act of another State. . . but of private individuals . . ..
> [U]nless some part of the injury can be shown to be severable in causal terms from that attributed to the responsible State, the latter is held responsible for all the consequences, not being too remote, of its wrongful conduct.

1775. As the commentary makes clear, the mere fact that damage was caused not only by a breach, but also by a concurrent action that is not a breach does not, as such, interrupt the relationship of causation that otherwise exists between the breach and the damage. Rather, it falls to the respondent to establish that a particular consequence of its actions is severable in causal terms (due to the intervening actions of claimants or a third party) or too remote to give rise to respondent's duty to compensate. As the Tribunal considers that respondent has not demonstrated this with regard to any of the heads of damage identified in the remainder of this Chapter, the Tribunal holds that causation exists between the damage and respondent's expropriation of claimants' investment.

3. Failure of claimants to mitigate

1776. Respondent asserts that claimants could have significantly mitigated their damages by taking a few simple steps in the first quarter of 2004, namely by paying the taxes then assessed against Yukos, filing amended VAT returns in Yukos' name, and filing amended tax returns for the years 2000–02 and a tax return for 2003 recognising all of Yukos' income without assigning it to its trading entities. The Tribunal has considered each of the actions respondent suggests claimants should have taken (set out in paras 679–80, 745–48 and 934–35 above) and has concluded that the suggested actions would not ultimately have made a difference to the enforcement measures subsequently taken by the Russian Federation. As seen in Part VIII above, the measures taken by the Russian Federation demonstrate that its primary objective was to bankrupt Yukos and appropriate its assets and that it was determined to do whatever was necessary to achieve this purpose. In light of this finding, the Tribunal cannot accept that by paying the taxes then assessed or re-filing VAT and tax returns in early 2004, claimants could have deterred respondent in the pursuit of its objective.

4. The methodology followed by the Tribunal

1777. Having made these determinations in respect of the valuation dates, causation and mitigation, the Tribunal now turns to the specific methodology of establishing the damages in this arbitration. As an initial matter, the Tribunal observes that, since it has decided that claimants are entitled to the higher of the damages determined as of the date of expropriation and as of the date of the award, the Tribunal must establish the total amount of damages caused by respondent's actions on each of the two valuation dates identified, namely the date of the YNG auction and the date of this Award. For purposes of the Tribunal's calculations, the date of the Award will be deemed to be 30 June 2014. Claimants will be entitled to the higher of these two figures, subject to the deduction of 25 per cent for contributory fault.

1778. On each of these valuation dates, claimants are entitled to the following heads of damages: (1) the value of claimants' shares in Yukos valued as of the valuation date; (2) the value of the dividends that the Tribunal determines would have been paid to claimants by Yukos up to the valuation date but for the expropriation of Yukos; and (3) pre-award simple interest on these amounts.

1779. By contrast, the Tribunal considers that a potential listing of Yukos on the NYSE and the benefits that claimants might have derived from such a listing are too uncertain to be taken into account for purposes of calculating claimants' damages. This element of claimants' damages case is therefore rejected.

1780. The Tribunal also finds that the assessment of claimants' damages must be based on their shareholding in Yukos, without taking into account the potential effects of a completed merger between Yukos and Sibneft. The Tribunal has not been convinced, on the balance of probabilities, that in the absence of respondent's expropriatory actions, the envisaged merger would have been completed; indeed, the Tribunal considers that assuming a completed merger in the 'but for' scenario is too speculative. As a consequence, the Tribunal rejects claimants' first damages scenario, notably the valuation of claimants' share in YukosSibneft.

1781. Before turning to the calculation of the damages components for the two relevant valuation dates, the Tribunal explains in the following subsections the methodology it has decided to adopt for valuing Yukos on each of the given dates, and the basis on which it has determined the amount of dividends that would likely have been paid to claimants, in the 'but for' scenario, prior to each of the valuation dates.

(a) Valuation of Yukos   1782. As set out earlier in this chapter, for purposes of the damages calculation, the Tribunal has decided that the relevant valuation dates are the date of the YNG auction and the date of this Award. However, the starting point for the Tribunal's analysis must be the calculations done by claimants as of their suggested valuation date of 21 November 2007. Claimants have put forward alternative valuations of Yukos as of that date calculated on the basis of various valuation methods. These methods and the valuations of Yukos derived from them (in USD billion) are summarised in the following table [removed].

1783. Respondent has not put forward a methodology for valuating Yukos or any valuation figures of its own. However, Professor Dow has provided a 'corrected' version of claimants' comparable companies analysis, making adjustments for what he considered to be the principal errors contained therein. Based on these adjustments, respondent's expert arrives – in orally advancing what 'could be' a 'useful' evaluation – at a 'corrected' enterprise value of Yukos, as of 21 November 2007, in the amount of US$67.862 billion. Assuming a 90/10 equity/debt capital structure of Yukos, this corresponds to an equity value of Yukos, as of 21 November 2007, of approximately US$61.076 billion.

1784. Having considered the extensive expert evidence presented by Mr Kaczmarek and Professor Dow, including the written evidence in the two expert reports that each submitted (with detailed accompanying annexes and appendices), and the testimony that was elicited from them during the Hearing, the Tribunal concludes, for the reasons set out below, that the 'corrected' comparable companies figure is the best available estimate for what Yukos would have been worth on 21 November 2007 but for the expropriation.

1785. The Tribunal finds that neither of the other two primary valuation methods put forward by claimants is sufficiently reliable to ground a determination of damages for this case. On balance, the Tribunal was persuaded by Professor Dow's analysis of claimants' DCF model, and is compelled to agree that little weight should be given to it. The Tribunal observes that claimants' expert admitted at the Hearing that his DCF analysis had been influenced by his own pre-determined notions as to what would be an appropriate result. Similarly, the Tribunal can put little stock in claimants' calculations based on the comparable transactions method, since both parties agree that, in fact, there were no comparable transactions and thus no basis that would allow a useful comparison.

1786. As for the remaining valuation methods put forward by claimants, and the valuations of Yukos generated by them, the Tribunal notes that claimants use these secondary valuations primarily in support of their main valuation. Moreover, some of these figures were only introduced by claimants at a very late stage of the proceedings (through demonstrative exhibits at the Hearing and in claimants' post-hearing brief) and could therefore not be properly addressed by respondent. Accordingly, the Tribunal finds that none of these secondary valuation methods can serve as a suitable independent basis for determining the value of Yukos.

1787. By contrast to all of the other methods canvassed above, the Tribunal does have a measure of confidence in the comparable companies method as a means of determining Yukos' value. While Professor Dow stated at the Hearing that he had not performed an analysis sufficient to fully endorse the figure resulting from his corrections to claimants' comparable companies approach, he agreed that it 'could be a useful valuation'. The Tribunal for its part finds that the comparable companies method is, in the circumstances, the most tenable approach to determine Yukos' value as of 21 November 2007, and therefore the starting point for the Tribunal's further analysis.

1788. The next step for the Tribunal consists in determining the value of Yukos as of the relevant valuation dates by adjusting Yukos' value as of November 2007 on the basis of the development of a relevant index. Having considered the various options in this regard, the Tribunal finds that the RTS Oil and Gas index is the most appropriate index for that purpose. The RTS Oil and Gas index is based on prices of trades executed in securities admitted to trading on the Moscow Stock Exchange and presently includes preferred or common shares of nine Russian oil and gas companies, the most important of which are Gazprom, Lukoil, Novatek, Rosneft and Surgutneftegas. The methodology for establishing the index as well as its current and historical values are transparent and publicly available on the webpage of the Moscow Stock Exchange. Both parties have referred to the RTS Oil & Gas index as a reliable indicator reflecting the changes in the value of Russian oil and gas companies and have used it in their calculations to carry forward certain valuations from one date to another.

1789. In order to determine the value of Yukos on each of the two valuation dates, the Tribunal will now adjust Yukos' value as of 21 November 2007 (US$61.076 billion) by multiplying it by a factor that reflects the change in the RTS Oil and Gas index between 21 November 2007 and each of the two valuation dates. This adjustment factor is calculated and applied for each of the two valuation dates in subsections 5(a) and 5(b) below.

1790. Having explained the Tribunal's methodology in respect of the first head of damage (the valuation of Yukos on each of the valuation dates), the Tribunal will now explain the basis on which it has determined the value of 'lost' dividends, namely the dividends that would likely have been paid to claimants, in the 'but for' scenario, prior to each of the valuation dates.

(b) Valuation of lost dividends   1791. A second element of the damages suffered by claimants as a result of respondent's expropriation of their investment is the loss of dividends that would otherwise have been paid to them as Yukos shareholders. For each valuation calculated as of the two valuation dates, the Tribunal must determine the value of the lost dividends up to each date, since the value of Yukos as of that date, while it captures the expectations of future profit, does not capture any of the past profit that the company would likely have generated.

1792. The Tribunal recalls that the two valuation dates are the date of the YNG auction (19 December 2004) and the date of this Award (deemed to be 30 June 2014 for valuation purposes). For the first valuation date, the Tribunal must therefore determine the value of the lost dividends up to 19 December 2004; for the second valuation date, the Tribunal must determine the value of the lost dividends up to 30 June 2014.

1793. The starting point for the Tribunal's analysis are the "Yukos lost cash flows" (i.e., free cash flow to equity) that claimants' expert calculated with respect to his valuation of claimants' damages. In his first report, Mr. Kaczmarek values Yukos as of 21 November 2007 only, and therefore produces a model of 'lost cash flows' that does not extend beyond that date. The 'lost cash flows' between 2004 and 21 November 2007 are presented as being based on actual historical information, as opposed to the cash flows included in Mr Kaczmarek's DCF model for the period 21 November 2007 through the end of 2015, which are based on forecasts and projections built up from information available prior to the period.

1794. In his second report, Mr Kaczmarek updates his valuation of Yukos as of November 2007 (including his presentation of 'lost cash flows' to that date), but also presents, for the first time, a valuation of Yukos as of 1 January 2012 (as a proxy for the valuation of Yukos as of the date of the Award). For purposes of the valuation as of 1 January 2012, Mr Kaczmarek produces a model of 'lost cash flows' that extends from 2004 through to the end of 2011. The 'lost cash flows' between 2004 and 2011 are presented as being based on actual historical information, as opposed to the cash flows included in Mr Kaczmarek's DCF model for the period 2012 through the end of 2019, which are based on forecasts and projections built up from information available prior to the period.

1795. The Tribunal observes that no free cash flow to equity figures are provided by claimants' expert for the years 2012 to 2014. While claimants offered to update their damages calculations at a date closer to the Award, the Tribunal has been able to establish the relevant figures on the basis of Mr Kaczmarek's methodology, using data provided elsewhere in Mr Kaczmarek's reports. The Tribunal's calculations are set out in Tables T4 to T6 [removed], attached to the Award, and explained in greater detail in the following paragraphs.

1796. To calculate Yukos' free cash flow to equity, Mr Kaczmarek uses the following formula: Free cash flow to equity = Free cash flow to the firm – Tax-adjusted interest payments + Change in net debt + 20 per cent of Sibneft dividends. Mr Kaczmarek provides figures regarding the free cash flow to the firm and the tax-adjusted interest payments for the relevant time period in Appendix AJ.2 to his second report. In addition, in note (5) to Appendix AJ.1 to his second report, Mr Kaczmarek defines Yukos' annual change in net debt as the annual change in 19 December 2004; for the second valuation date, the Tribunal must determine the value of the lost dividends up to 30 June 2014.

1797. The starting point for the Tribunal's analysis are the 'Yukos lost cash flows' (i.e., free cash flow to equity) that claimants' expert calculated with respect to his valuation of claimants' damages. In his first report, Mr Kaczmarek values Yukos as of 21 November 2007 only, and therefore produces a model of 'lost cash flows' that does not extend beyond that date. The 'lost cash flows' between 2004 and 21 November 2007 are presented as being based on actual historical information, as opposed to the cash flows included in Mr Kaczmarek's DCF model Yukos' long-term debt plus its short-term debt less its cash. Mr Kaczmarek provides these figures in Appendix AJ.4 to his second report. With regard to the Sibneft dividends, Mr Kaczmarek provides figures for years 2004 through 2011 in Appendix AJ.1 to his second report. For the years 2012 through 2014, the Tribunal has assumed that the Sibneft dividends would have been equal to those paid in 2010, the last year for which Mr Kaczmarek has provided an annual figure (his figure for 2011 being based on annualised third quarter figures).

1798. With these additional numbers calculated by the Tribunal, on the basis of data and formulas set out in Mr Kaczmarek's reports, the Tribunal is able to arrive at numbers for Yukos' 'lost cash flows' (i.e., free cash flows to equity) for the entire period extending from 2004 through 2014. The Tribunal then, in principle, has the input it needs in order to determine the lost dividends for each of the valuation dates: for the first valuation date (the date of the YNG auction), the Tribunal can therefore arrive at a value (based on Mr. Kaczmarek's model) for the lost dividends up to 19 December 2004; and for the second valuation date (the date of the Award), the Tribunal can also arrive at a value (based on Mr Kaczmarek's model) of the lost dividends up to 30 June 2014. The Tribunal notes that the total amount of lost dividends, based on Mr Kaczmarek's model, for the period from 2004 to 30 June 2014, is US\$67.213 billion. 1798. As mentioned earlier, however, claimants' calculation of Yukos' lost cash flows is merely a starting point for the Tribunal's determination of what it views as the correct estimate of the dividends that claimants would have earned from Yukos in the 'but for' scenario. As explained in the following paragraphs, several fundamental considerations lead the Tribunal to modify the calculations of claimants' expert.

1799. Firstly, although Yukos' lost cash flows determined by Mr Kaczmarek are based in part on actual historical information (i.e., largely information about the performance of Yukos' former assets disclosed by Rosneft in its financial reports), the Tribunal is unable to dissociate them from claimants' DCF model, which was convincingly criticised by respondent's expert and its counsel.

1800. In his second report, Professor Dow identifies and explains a 'series of errors' embedded in claimants' DCF valuation of Yukos. His 'corrections' of those errors result in a very substantial reduction (51 per cent) in the valuation of Yukos generated by the DCF model. Although not all of those 'corrections' apply to the cash flows discussed above, which are based in part on actual historical information (and thus are not plagued by some of the errors associated with forecasts and projections), some of the 'corrections' – notably those related to the interpretation of the historical information – in the view of the Tribunal, do impact the cash flows.

1801. For example, the Tribunal accepts Professor Dow's opinion that claimants have underestimated Yukos' transportation costs (by implicitly assuming that, in the 'but for' scenario, 'Yukos would have been able to capture the efficiencies of Rosneft's proprietary pipeline network'). The Tribunal also accepts Professor Dow's opinion that claimants' model overlooks certain operating expenses of Yukos, thus evidencing a 'basic flaw' in claimants' DCF model, namely that there is 'no systematic attempt' to ensure that all of Yukos' costs have been accounted for.

1802. Although, for the reasons stated above, the Tribunal does not consider it appropriate to accept all of Professor Dow's 'corrections' for purposes of the valuation of the dividends, the Tribunal notes that the spreadsheets submitted by respondent's expert with his Second Report allow the Tribunal to calculate 'corrected' free cash flow to equity figures for the relevant years. While respondent's expert has not explicitly endorsed this 'corrected' version as representing his views with regard to Yukos' free cash flow to equity, it is evident to the Tribunal that it represents a figure that is more in line with his views. According to this 'corrected' methodology, Yukos' dividends in 2004 would have been US$3.218 billion (instead of US$3.645 billion), and the sum of Yukos' dividends over the period from 2004 through the first half of 2014 would have been US$49.293 billion (instead of US$67.213).

1803. The Tribunal has formed the view that Professor Dow's corrections, however, do not take into account all the risks that Yukos would have had to contend with in carrying on business during the period 2004 through to the present if the company had not been expropriated. The Tribunal agrees with respondent that 'an expropriation relieves the owner not only of the value of the asset on the date of expropriation, but also of the risk associated with owning it'. Accordingly, in any model of the cash flows that would have been generated by Yukos had it not been expropriated (i.e., the cash flows in a 'but for' scenario), it is necessary to take into account the risks to those cash flows that were eliminated by the expropriation. Those risks must be factored back into the cash flow model in the 'but for' scenario.

1804. The Tribunal observes that Mr Kaczmarek's cash flow model does not factor in those risks in his calculations. To the contrary, Mr Kaczmarek models Yukos' financial performance after the date of expropriation based, in large measure, on the results achieved by Yukos' assets in the hands of

Rosneft. As respondent rightly submits, 'Mr Kaczmarek effectively valued Yukos as if it were a State-owned strategic enterprise, which it never was'.

1805. The first significant risk that, in the Tribunal's view, is not adequately accounted for in the cash flow models of either expert is the real risk of substantially higher taxes. Since taxes other than income taxes (also referred to as 'non-income taxes') consistently account for well over 50 per cent of Yukos' net income from year to year, Yukos' cash flows could be significantly affected by any increases in the tariffs and rates relating to the non-income taxes. In Mr Kaczmarek's model, the taxes that are established annually by legislation (such as the export customs duty and domestic excise tax for refined products) are based on actual historical data (if available) and, for the forecast period, are based on the prior year's tax rate plus an adjustment to account for annual inflation. In other words, there is no accounting for the possibility – even likelihood– that had Yukos remained in private hands, the State would have increased taxes, perhaps even substantially, in order to capture a greater share of the rent earned from the exploitation of Russia's natural resources. Yet, the record shows that this is precisely what the Russian Federation did in 2002 and 2003, when Yukos was still in private hands. In paragraph 188 of his first report, for example, Mr Kaczmarek explains that large tax increases in 2002 and 2003 caused surging profits at Yukos to level off during that period.

1806. In this connection, the Tribunal notes that Yukos, in its 2002 Annual Report, disclosed the following concerns about taxation:

> We are subject to numerous taxes that have had a significant effect on our results of operations. Russian tax legislation is and has been subject to varying interpretations and frequent changes. . . .
>   In the context of the significant regulatory changes related to Russia's transition from a centrally planned to a market economy over the past ten years and the general instability of the new market institutions introduced in connection with this transition, taxes, tax rates and implementation of taxation in Russia have experienced numerous changes. Although there are signs of improved political stability in Russia, further changes to the tax system may be introduced which may adversely affect the financial performance of our Company.
>   In addition, uncertainty related to Russian tax laws exposes us to enforcement measures and the risk of significant fines and could result in a greater than expected tax burden.

1807. The 2002 Annual Report also alerted the Yukos shareholders to risks related to the Company's dividend policy:

Reserves available for distribution to shareholders are based on the statutory accounting reports of YUKOS Oil Company, which are prepared in accordance with Regulations on Accounting and Reporting of the Russian Federation and which differ from US GAAP.

Russian legislation identifies the basis of distribution as net income. For 2002, the current year statutory net income for YUKOS Oil Company as reported in the annual statutory accounting reports was RR 40,701 million. However, current legislation and other statutory laws and regulations dealing with distribution rights are open to legal interpretation and, consequently, actual distributable reserves may differ from the amount disclosed.

1808. Finally, and perhaps most significantly, there are the risks associated with the complex and opaque structure set up by claimants, or by others on their behalf, in order to transfer money earned by Yukos out of the Russian Federation through a vast offshore structure. This structure is well documented in the reports of Professor Lys. An organisational chart attached as an appendix to a letter from PwC Cyprus to PwC Moscow dated 10 April 2003 shows the complexity of the structure as of that date, and the fact that Yukos' control over it was established by means of call options. With this structure, Yukos was able to consolidate the profits of the trading companies and offshore holding companies (entities within its 'consolidation perimeter') into its results while remaining 'free to segregate these profits from minority shareholder claims whenever it served the majority shareholders' or management's interests'.

1809. As respondent rightly points out, Yukos' claim of corporate governance reforms, Western standards of transparency and protection of minority interests, which Mr Kaczmarek highlighted in his first report (and which was a recurring theme heard from claimants in this case), 'was a façade'. Notably, even the company's President, Mr Theede, testified that they had no knowledge that Yukos was using offshore structures that it did not own.

1810. The Tribunal notes that even after the tax assessments at issue in the present arbitration were issued, claimants and their owners were able to divert money earned by Yukos out of Yukos, and into the two Stichtings, and therefore away from the tax authorities. The Tribunal cannot exclude the possibility that, but for the expropriation, the very same mechanism would have been resorted to by claimants under different circumstances to divert some of the money earned by Yukos.

1811. In light of all the circumstances, and taking into account: (a) the figures based on Mr Kaczmarek's calculations; (b) the figures based on Professor

Dow's 'corrections'; and (c) the additional risks described above, which the Tribunal finds must be factored into its damages analysis, the Tribunal, in the exercise of its discretion, concludes that it is appropriate to determine and fix the dividend payments that it assumes Yukos would have paid to its shareholders in the 'but for' scenario in the amounts set out in the far right column of the following table (in USD billion) [removed].

1812. Accordingly, the Tribunal concludes that Yukos' dividends in 2004 would have been US$2.5 billion, and the sum of Yukos' dividends over the period from 2004 through the first half of 2014 would have been US$45 billion.

5. Application of the methodology followed by the Tribunal

1813. The Tribunal, applying the methodology outlined above to the two valuation dates of 19 December 2004 and 30 June 2014, can now proceed to the valuation of the expropriated company as of those two dates.

(a) Calculations based on 19 December 2004 valuation date   1814. The damages suffered by claimants based on a valuation date of 19 December 2004 are determined as follows.

i. VALUATION OF SHARES IN YUKOS   1815. As explained earlier, the Tribunal will determine the equity value of Yukos as of 19 December 2004 by adjusting what it considers, based on the parties' submissions, to be the best available estimate of this value as of 21 November 2007, i.e., an amount of US$61.076 billion, with a factor that reflects the development of the RTS Oil and Gas index between 19 December 2004 and 21 November 2007. The value of the RTS Oil and Gas index on 19 December 2004 was 92.85, whereas on 21 November 2007 it had a value of 267.8. The adjustment factor to be applied to determine Yukos' value as of the earlier date is therefore $x=92.85/267.8=0.3467$. By applying this factor to the amount of USD 61.076 billion, the Tribunal arrives at an equity value of Yukos as of 19 December 2004 in the amount of US$21.176 billion.

1816. The value of claimants' 70.5 per cent share in Yukos, calculated as a pro rata share of this amount, corresponds to $US\$(70.5/100)*21.176=14.929$ billion.

ii. DIVIDENDS   1817. According to the Tribunal's methodology outlined above, the dividends that would have been paid to Yukos' shareholders throughout 2004 will be assumed to be US$2.5 billion. Since the valuation date is 19 December 2004, there are 12 days missing for the full year which must be taken into consideration. Accordingly, this amount must be multiplied by a factor $x=(365-12)/365$, corresponding to approximately 97 per cent. This gives a total amount of free cash flow to equity based on a valuation date of 19 December 2004 of US\$2.418 billion. Claimants' share of this amount corresponds to dividends of US\$$(70.5/100)*2.418=1.705$ billion.

iii. INTEREST   1818. By applying an annual interest rate of 3.389 percent, the total amount of interest payable on the equity value of Yukos and the dividends that would have been paid to its shareholders from 1 January 2005 to 30 June 2014 is 7.596 billion. The total amount of interest payable to claimants on this basis is 70.5 percent of this figure, i.e., US\$5.355 billion.

iv. TOTAL DAMAGES SUFFERED BY CLAIMANTS   1819. The damages suffered by claimants due to the breach by respondent of Article 13 of the ECT based on a 19 December 2004 valuation date is the sum of the claimants' share of these components calculated above, i.e., 70.5 per cent of $(21.176 + 2.418 + 7.596)$, which amounts to US\$21.988 billion.

(b) Calculations based on 2014 valuation date   1820. The damages suffered by claimants based on a valuation date of 30 June 2014 are determined as follows.

i. VALUATION OF CLAIMANTS' SHARE IN YUKOS   1821. As for the calculations based on the date of the expropriation, the Tribunal will determine the equity value of Yukos as of 30 June 2014 by adjusting what it considers, based on the parties' submissions, the best available estimate of this value as of 21 November 2007, i.e., the amount of US\$61.076 billion, with a factor that reflects the development of the RTS Oil and Gas index between 21 November 2007 and 30 June 2014. For practical purposes, and in order to eliminate the effects of random fluctuations of the index on the amount to be awarded, the Tribunal has chosen to use the average of the values of the index over the period from 6 January 2014 to 24 June 2014 as the basis for its calculations. This average value of the RTS Oil and Gas index is 186.90. The adjustment factor to be applied to determine Yukos' value as of the later date is therefore $x=186.90/267.8=69.79$ percent. By applying this factor to the amount of US\$61.076 billion the Tribunal arrives at an equity value of Yukos as of 30 June 2014 in the amount of US\$42.625 billion.

1822. The value of claimants' 70.5 per cent share in Yukos, calculated as a pro rata share of this amount, corresponds to US\$$(70.5/100)*42.625=30.049$ billion.

ii. DIVIDENDS AND INTEREST ON DIVIDENDS   1823. According to the Tribunal's methodology outlined earlier, the dividends that would have been paid to Yukos' shareholders from the beginning of 2004 to 30 June 2014 will be assumed to correspond to US$45 billion. Together with interest, the total amount for this period is US$51.981 billion.

1824. Claimants' share of this amount corresponds to US$(70.5/100)* 51.981=36.645 billion.

iii. TOTAL DAMAGES SUFFERED BY CLAIMANTS   1825. The damages suffered by claimants due to the breach by respondent of Article 13 of the ECT, based on a valuation date of 30 June 2014, is the sum of the claimants' share of the two components calculated above, i.e., 70.5 per cent of (42.625 + 51.981), which amounts to US$66.694 billion.

(c) Comparison of the results based on the two different valuation dates   1826. The total amount of claimants' damages based on a valuation date of 19 December 2004 is US$21.988 billion, whereas the total amount of their damages based on a valuation date of 30 June 2014 is US$66.694 billion. Since the Tribunal has concluded earlier that claimants are entitled to the higher of these two amounts, the total amount of damages to be awarded before taking into account any deductions necessary as a consequence of claimants' contributory fault is US$66.694 billion.

6. Deductions due to claimants' contributory fault

1827. As determined earlier, the Tribunal has concluded that the claimants contributed to the extent of 25 per cent to the prejudice they suffered at the hands of the Russian Federation. As a consequence, the amount of damages to be paid by respondent to claimants will be reduced by 25 per cent to US$50,020,867,798 and the Tribunal so finds.

7. Windfall and double recovery

1828. The Tribunal sees no reason to make any further deductions beyond those set out above. In particular, any advantages that claimants may have obtained through their investments prior to respondent's expropriatory actions cannot have any impact on the damages they have suffered. The Tribunal sees no risk of 'double-recovery' in this regard.

1829. Finally, the rate of return that claimants may realise on their original investment in Yukos as a result of the damages that the Tribunal has awarded to them for the expropriation of their shares is irrelevant. It is the value of the expropriated investment on the date of the Award rather than the amount originally invested by claimants that is the basis for the calculation of the damages awarded.

 CASE

Gold Reserve Inc v Bolivarian Republic of Venezuela, ICSID Case No. ARB(AF)/09/1, excerpt

A. Applicable legal framework

[. . .]

Tribunal's analysis

674. The Tribunal begins its analysis of applicable legal framework by noting that, although other solutions could have been adopted, both parties contend that, even in the case of no expropriation, the appropriate measure of damages in the present circumstances is fair market value. Both parties have also used April 2008 as the valuation date for assessing the fair market value of the investment.

675. Article XII(9) of the BIT provides the Tribunal with the power to award monetary damages or restitution in the case of breach of an obligation contained therein. This provision provides the tribunal with a wide discretion when assessing damages for breach of FET. Article XII(7) of the BIT also requires the Tribunal to decide the issues in dispute in accordance with the treaty and the applicable rules of international law. Therefore, the Tribunal is empowered to award monetary damages or restitution in accordance with principles of international law and the provisions in the BIT. There is no suggestion in the present case that restitution is an appropriate remedy. Therefore, the Tribunal now considers the international law principles applicable to the award of monetary damages for breach of FET, as well as any relevant provisions of the treaty. Both parties have devoted considerable argument to whether the reference to 'prompt, fair and adequate compensation' in Article VII provides a *sui generis* remedy for expropriation (and for breaches of other provisions which result in total deprivation of property), such that principles of international law would not apply. The Tribunal does not find it necessary to determine whether prompt, fair and adequate compensation is the appropriate remedy for expropriation, given no breach of Article VII has been found. Concerning its application to breaches other

than expropriation, the Tribunal is not convinced that even if prompt fair and adequate compensation could correctly be categorised as a *sui generis* remedy under Article VII, that it should be considered a *sui generis* remedy for other breaches where a total deprivation of the investment has resulted.

676. Respondent has produced no evidence to support such a claim, nor is it an approach that, as far as the Tribunal is aware, has been taken in previous investment treaty cases. Finally, there is nothing in language of the treaty itself that would support such an interpretation. Therefore, the Tribunal concludes that the appropriate course of action is that it award monetary compensation under Article XII(9) in accordance with applicable rules of international law.

677. In any case, the discussion regarding whether Article VII provides a *sui generis* remedy may be somewhat academic, at least in the present circumstances, as its primary relevance (given that respondent acknowledges that prompt, adequate and fair compensation is equivalent to fair market value) is to arguments advanced by claimant that, in some circumstances, more than fair market value could be awarded by a tribunal. The Tribunal acknowledges that, in some circumstances, changing the date of valuation may be appropriate, but does not consider that those circumstances exist here. The Tribunal therefore finds that the valuation date to be applied to the assessment of damages is 14 April 2008.

678. Turning now to the relevant principles of international law applicable to the award of damages for breach of FET, the Tribunal begins with an analysis of the *Chorzów Factory* principles. It is true that this was a case involving State-to-State liability and, as respondent correctly noted, cannot therefore automatically be applied to a State-Investor situation. However, it is well accepted in international investment law that the principles espoused in the *Chorzów Factory* case, even if initially established in a State-to-State context, are the relevant principles of international law to apply when considering compensation for breach of a BIT. It is these well-established principles that represent customary international law, including for breaches of international obligations under BITs, that the Tribunal is bound to apply. Even a cursory analysis of previous ICSID cases considering this issue confirms as much. As stated in *Impregilo v Argentina*:

> As regards compensation, the basic principle to be applied is that derived from the judgment of the Permanent Court of International Justice in the *Chorzów Factory* case. According to this principle, reparation should as far as possible eliminate the consequences of the illegal act and re-establish the situation which would, in

all probability, have existed if that act had not been committed. In other words, Impregilo should in principle be placed in the same position as it would have been, had Argentina's unfair and inequitable treatment of Impregilo's investment not occurred.

679. The above principles complement those found in the ILC Articles on State Responsibility, particularly in Article 31 to make full reparation for injury caused through violating an international obligation. This, in turn, reflects customary international law. Respondent rightly cautioned that the ILC Articles on State Responsibility primarily concern internationally wrongful acts against States, not individuals or other non-State actors, and some prominent commentators have warned against an uncritical conflation of the two.

680. This Tribunal has given due consideration to these arguments. Nevertheless, the serious nature of the breach in the present circumstances and the fact that the breach has resulted in the total deprivation of mining rights suggests that, under the principles of full reparation and wiping-out the consequences of the breach, a fair market value methodology is also appropriate in the present circumstances. As noted above, both parties have taken this position in the submissions.

681. In summary, this Tribunal is empowered to award monetary compensation in accordance with the principles of international law. The relevant principles of international law applicable in this situation are derived from the judgment of the Permanent Court of International Justice in the *Chorzów Factory* case that reparation should wipe-out the consequences of the breach and reestablish the situation as it is likely to have been absent the breach. As the consequence of the serious breach in the present situation was to deprive the investor totally of its investment, the Tribunal considers it appropriate that the remedy that would wipe-out the consequences of the breach is to assess damages using a fair market value methodology. This conclusion accords with the submissions of the parties, both of whom have acknowledged that a fair market value methodology is an appropriate way of providing effective compensation in the present circumstances. The Tribunal therefore finds that this methodology should be applied, with a valuation date as at 14 April 2008.

682. Finally, the fair market value of the investment is influenced by a number of different factors that each party's experts have addressed. As noted above, the Tribunal has already found that the Brisas Project did not include the North Parcel of land to which no legal title existed. The Tribunal therefore

considers that the fair market value should be calculated without reference to that parcel. While a willing buyer might have thought it could have acquired rights to this land in the future, it could not be certain of doing so and therefore it would be speculative of the Tribunal to assume a buyer would have valued the Brisas Project as if the legal right had been acquired. As such, the Tribunal will value the Project using a 'no layback' scenario. As noted above, no compensation is due in relation to the Choco 5 investment.

Burden and standard of proof

683. Claimant acknowledges that it carries the burden of proof for proving its damages. It argues that while damages cannot be speculative, they also do not need to be certain. The appropriate standard of proof is the balance of probabilities and the 'certainty principle' relates to the fact of loss rather than the quantum.

684. Respondent similarly contends that claimant has the burden of proving damages and that such damages cannot be speculative. However, respondent submits that damages must be proved with 'a sufficient degree of certainty' rather than being more probable than not. Respondent also devoted considerable argument seeking to demonstrate that lost profits claimed in situations where the investment was not yet operational are inherently speculative and do not meet the required standard of proof.

685. The Tribunal agrees with the parties that claimant bears the burden of proving its claimed damages. The Tribunal finds no support for the conclusion that the standard of proof for damages should be higher than for proving merits, and therefore is satisfied that the appropriate standard of proof is the balance of probabilities. This, of course, means that damages cannot be speculative or merely 'possible', as both parties acknowledge. In the Tribunal's view, all of the authorities cited by the parties – including by respondent in relation to its claim that a degree of certainty is required – accord with the principle that the balance of probabilities applies, even if some tribunals phrase the standard slightly differently. In particular, those cases that discuss the requirement for 'certainty' do so in the context of distinguishing 'proven' damages from speculative damages, rather than suggesting that a higher degree of proof is applied to damages than to liability.

686. The Tribunal further notes that, while a claimant must prove its damages to the required standard, the assessment of damages is often a difficult exercise and it is seldom that damages in an investment situation will be able to be established with scientific certainty. This is because such assess-

ments will usually involve some degree of estimation and the weighing of competing (but equally legitimate) facts, valuation methods and opinions, which does not of itself mean that the burden of proof has not been satisfied. Because of this element of imprecision, it is accepted that tribunals retain a certain amount of discretion or a 'margin of appreciation' when assessing damages, which will necessarily involve some approximation. The use of this discretion should not be confused with acting on an *ex aequo et bono* basis, even if equitable considerations are taken into account in the exercise of such discretion. Rather, in such circumstances, the Tribunal exercises its judgment in a reasoned manner so as to discern an appropriate damages sum which results in compensation to claimant in accordance with the principles of international law that have been discussed earlier.

B. Approach to calculating fair market value

687. As explained above, the parties agreed that if any damages were awarded by the Tribunal, the calculation of these damages should be done using a fair market value approach. Each party presented a number of experts on both mining and valuation issues to assist the Tribunal in determining the fair market value of the Brisas Project as at April 2008. The following experts presented written expert reports to the Tribunal:

For claimant:

RPA: Mr Richard Lambert (mining and metallurgical experts)

Navigant: Mr Brent Kaczmarek (valuation expert)

For respondent:

SRK: Dr Neal Rigby (mining expert)

CRA: Dr Francis Brown and Mr Leonard Kowal (metallurgical experts)

CRA: Dr James Burrows (valuation expert)

Boliden: Mr Pekka Tuokkola (saleability)

688. At the hearing of 15–16 October 2013, the above experts gave evidence, together with the following persons who had assisted in preparing the experts reports:

For claimant:

RPA: Dr Kathleen Altman (metallurgical issues)

Tetra Tech: Mr Mike Henderson and Mr Dave Hallman (mining issues), Mr Erik Spiller (metallurgical issues)

For respondent:

SRK: Mr Bret Swanson, Mr John Tinucci (mining issues)

689. It is noted that, in this Chapter, the Tribunal refers to positions taken in the expert's written reports by stating the name of the expert followed in brackets by the relevant firm. This is because in the Parties' submissions experts were sometimes referred to by name and at other times by firm. Where the Tribunal references something said during the oral hearing, the Tribunal references the relevant expert's name only.

690. Both valuation experts used the Discounted Cash Flow ('DCF') method as the primary method for assessing the quantum of damages payable if claimant succeeded on liability (as explained at para. 822 below, Mr Kaczmarek (Navigant) also used the comparable transactions and market capitalisation methods). Dr Burrows (CRA) did not provide a separate DCF calculation on behalf of respondent, but critiqued and made adjustments to the DCF calculation advanced by Mr Kaczmarek (Navigant) on behalf of claimant.

691. Clearly, any DCF calculation is dependent upon an assessment of the quantum of the mineral deposits likely to be extracted over the 20-year period of the extended concession. The DCF valuation by both Mr Kaczmarek (Navigant) and Dr Burrows (CRA) was initially based on reserves estimated using a layback on the North Parcel of land. Pursuant to Procedural Order No. 2, the experts adjusted the valuation for a no-layback scenario which excluded the North Parcel. This revision required a re-estimation of mineral deposits which in turn required examination of the following issues by the mining and metallurgical experts: (i) pit shape and design; (ii) need for a buffer zone; (iii) impact of stockpiling; (iv) likely delays for obtaining permits in the no-layback scenario; (v) metallurgical issues including ramp-up, mill capacity, and metal recovery rates and concentrate grades; and (vi) their saleability.

692. The Tribunal addresses each of the above issues in the paragraphs that follow. The Tribunal then considers a number of financial issues which were

disputed by the valuation experts, whether the with-layback or the no-layback scenario applied. These issues include: (i) fair market value methodology; (ii) metal prices; (iii) inflation rate; (iv) discount rate; (v) delay in receiving revenues; and (vi) fuel and electricity costs.

693. It is only after considering all of the above issues that the Tribunal has been able to reach a conclusion as to the damages owed to claimant as a result of respondent's breach of its FET obligations under the BIT. This conclusion is set out in paragraphs 848 and 849 below.

C. Mine plan issues

694. The following section considers the issues relating to the mine plan, as follows: Mine Pit Design; Buffer Zone; Stockpiles; and Delays. It concludes by assessing the impact on the estimate of mineral deposits available to be mined under the no-layback scenario.

695. The experts that provided evidence at the hearing on these issues were: Mr Lambert (RPA), Mr Henderson and Mr Hallman (both of Tetra Tech) for claimant and Dr Rigby, Mr Swanson and Mr Tinucci (all of SRK) for respondent.

696. While all experts were well qualified on the issues at hand, the Tribunal found the RPA Reports and the witnesses from RPA and Tetra Tech to be more convincing on the mine plan issues. Respondent's experts, as might be expected, challenged certain aspects of the RPA optimal mine plan but, as noted below, some of these challenges were formulated in a general way without providing any supporting analysis as to the specific effect of the alleged impact on the overall calculation.

D. Mine pit design – shape of pit and placement of ramps

Claimant's position

697. So as to determine the optimal shape of the mine pit in the various possible no-layback scenarios (0 meter, 25 meter and 100 meter buffer), Mr Lambert (RPA) used a software program known as 'Whittle' to design the shape of the mine pit in the no-layback scenario. Claimant stated that:

> Due to the parties' disagreement as to whether a 100-meter buffer was needed in the north, the parties agreed to generate alternative 'Whittle pits,' with different

geographic boundaries to the north, from which alternative mine plan scenarios could be considered. For all scenarios, the parties agreed to use the pit slope parameters included in the 2008 Marston mine plan. The parties also agreed that for all scenarios, they would use the metal prices assumed in the NI 43-101 Technical Report prepared for the Brisas Project and the mining cost assumptions set forth in the 2008 Marston mine plan.

698. Mr Lambert (RPA) adopted the shape of the pit produced by the Whittle program with a zero meter buffer as his 'optimal scenario'. He stated that this design maximised access to high quality ore in the northern section of the pit. In doing so, Mr Lambert (RPA) considered that he was not bound under Procedural Order No. 2 to retain the original shape of the with-layback pit used in the 2008 Marston mine plan and rejected Dr Rigby's (SRK) assertions on this point. During the hearing, Mr Lambert noted that Dr Rigby had not in fact adopted the Marston shape without modification as SRK had adjusted the pit shape in the south-east side in order to access what was termed a 'bullseye' (an area that had not been included in the Marston plan).

699. Regarding the ramps, Mr Lambert (RPA) placed them along the eastern wall of the no-layback mine pit, so as to allow maximum access to the high-quality ore on the northern boundary. He used the ramp locations suggested by Pincock, Allen & Holt in 2004 for their no-layback design which did not include ramps on the north wall.

700. Mr Lambert (RPA) contended that the ramp design – which mirrored the with-layback Marston design – used by Dr Rigby (SRK) did not make sense in the case of a no-layback scenario. Using the same design as the with-layback scenario meant that the ramps were placed over key mineral deposits. Mr Lambert (RPA) said that given the amount of high grade copper in the area, it would be irrational to place ramps on the northern wall.

701. Mr Lambert (RPA) rejected Dr Rigby's (SRK) analysis that the dual ramp system on the north wall was required due to the unstable nature of the wall. In particular, it rejected the suggestion that this instability was known, but not specifically included, in the Marston Report. Indeed, Mr Lambert (RPA) said that his design made the northern wall safer as including ramps on the northern wall would have placed additional stress on that wall, which would have been undesirable had it been unstable.

702. During oral evidence, Mr Lambert suggested that the haulage times for his ramp design would be the same as estimated in the Marston Report as

the ramps would have exited the pit at approximately the same point as the Marston ramps and the length of the ramps were similar.

Respondent's position

703. Dr Rigby (SRK) did not agree with Mr Lambert (RPA) that adjusting the mine pit shape to maximize access to mineral deposits was the preferable option. He considered that the original Marston pit shape should be retained so as to retain the statistical accuracy of the Marston Report to a feasibility level (+/- 15 per cent) and to be consistent with Procedural Order No. 2. He suggested that using the original pit shape would allow statistics in the Marston Report to remain valid for the no-layback design. He therefore simply moved the position of the pit to adjust for the required buffer zone and did not change its shape.

704. Dr Rigby (SRK) also retained the ramp positions used in the original Marston mine plan – placing a dual ramp system on the north wall. He said that Mr Lambert's (RPA) new design left the mine vulnerable if a wall collapsed because (i) the dual ramp system in place on the northern wall in the with-layback design provided alternative access in case of a wall collapse or slip and (ii) it provided a geotechnical catch bench on the northern wall of around 70 meters to catch sloughage that may fall from the unstable saprolite rock in the upper section of the north wall.

705. According to Dr Rigby (SRK), the dual ramp system was desirable for safety reasons and addressed poor geotechnical conditions, as indicated by the Marston Report when it stated: '[t]wo haul roads were designed into phases 5 and 6 and the ultimate pit to provide greater flexibility in ore and waste haulage routes and pit access. This also provides alternative access in the event of slope failures.'

706. In its Joint Expert Procedure Post-Hearing Brief, Respondent also said that moving the ramps had an effect on haulage times for transporting ore out of the pit, even if the ramp length and exit points were similar, because the entry points were different. It criticised Mr Lambert (RPA) for estimating costs based on haulage times that had been calculated using the dual ramp system, and therefore did not take into account any increase in costs. Respondent also emphasised that the mine design would affect the stripping ratio which would in turn affect the costs of producing saleable metal. It said that even if the amount of metal itself increased, the economics of carting all the extra waste, would not make it worthwhile.

Tribunal's analysis

707. The initial issue that the Tribunal must consider is whether the experts were confined to using the Marston 2008 mine design when considering the impact of a no-layback scenario or whether the experts were able to redesign the pit to optimise value in a no-layback scenario. Claimant's expert took the latter position, using the Whittle tool to create an optimal design. The Tribunal concludes that nothing in Procedural Order No. 2 required the experts to retain the with-layback pit design to value the concession absent the North Parcel. Indeed, just the opposite – Procedural Order No. 2 specifically asked the experts to estimate 'the changes required to adjust the Brisas Project's mine plan due to the absence of a layback agreement within the North Parcel'. While the Tribunal agrees with the parties that it is desirable to maintain the Marston parameters so far as possible, there is no reason to do so where the particular no-layback circumstances suggest otherwise, including adjusting the pit shape to maximize access to mineral deposits.

708. Indeed, all experts agreed that the Marston pit was not optimal for a no-layback scenario and both experts made adjustments for this. Given that Dr Rigby (SRK) accepted a so-called 'bullseye' in the south-eastern corner of the original pit, there is no clear rationale not to accept a reshaping along the northern boundary so as to access to high-quality mineral deposits in this area. Similarly, Procedural Order No. 2 did not prevent the experts from re-locating ramps if there is sound rationale for doing so. The Tribunal regrets that the experts did not request clarification from the Tribunal on this point, as provided by the Order, at the time of producing the joint expert report, as it may have facilitated additional agreement.

709. Based on the foregoing analysis, the Tribunal considers that the Whittle program produces the optimum mine pit shape in a no-layback scenario. Moreover, a reasonable investor would seek to adjust the pit to ensure access to key mineral deposits and therefore changes to the both the Southern and Northern corners of the pit were rational in accordance with sound mining practice. The Tribunal therefore adopts the pit shape proposed by claimant's expert.

710. In relation to ramp location, the Tribunal accepts Mr Lambert's evidence that it would not make 'logical sense' for an investor to place the ramps on the north wall and therefore lose access to valuable ore, unless there was a specific reason (for example, a safety reason) for doing so.

711. The Tribunal discusses safety concerns regarding the north wall in more detail at paragraphs 726–734 below. It is sufficient to note here that the Tribunal finds no evidence of safety concerns regarding the north wall. Moreover, the Tribunal finds it unlikely that the Marston Report would have failed to refer to safety concerns regarding the stability of the north wall, had Marston been aware of any such concerns at the time. This is especially so if Marston had deliberately designed the dual ramp system to address such safety concerns. The Tribunal therefore finds, in the absence of any evidence to the contrary, that no such concerns existed at the time of the Marston Report. The Tribunal also notes Dr Rigby's comments that a mine designer would not place a main haulage road directly underneath an unstable slope. This also supports the conclusion that Marston had no significant concerns about the safety of the northern wall. Aside from the erroneous factor of safety calculations discussed above, Dr Rigby adduced no evidence to suggest that safety concerns were discovered by Marston or otherwise after the Marston Report was issued. Consequently, the Tribunal finds that claimant's ramp locations are to be preferred and accordingly they are adopted for the purpose of calculating damages.

712. On this topic, there are three matters which, for completeness, should be mentioned at this point. First, as to haulage times, Mr Lambert said that there would be no increase in haulage times using his ramp design from those used in the Marston Report because the ramps would be about same length and would exit the pit at same location. In its Joint Expert Procedure Post-Hearing Brief, respondent stated that even if this were so, the entry point for the ramp would differ which would 'necessarily result in different haul times, thus requiring adjustments to project plans and potentially increasing production costs'. However, this assertion was not accompanied by any attempt at calculating the additional haulage time specific to reaching the entry point of the ramp (respondent refers to a difficulty in calculating haulage times to stockpiles given uncertainty of their location, but this is a separate issue). The Tribunal accepts Mr Lambert's evidence that the length and exit points for his proposed ramp were the same as the previous ramps, and notes that respondent did not contest this. The Tribunal is not in a position to speculate on whether any additional haulage time would have been incurred due to a varying entry point and if so what the cost impact may have been. If respondent wished to pursue this point it should have offered a costing calculation and, as it did not, the Tribunal finds that no adjustment is required to the DCF calculation on account of haulage times relating to ramp location.

713. Secondly, in its Joint Expert Procedure Post-Hearing Brief, respondent suggested that the stripping ratio for mining the additional sectors of the pit

that would be mined pursuant to claimant's optimal no-layback pit design would be very high at 16:1 (compared to an average project ratio of 3:1), which would increase costs. This assertion is problematic for two reasons. First, although this was an issue raised with Mr Lambert during the hearing in relation to the shape of the mine pit, it was referred to be Dr Rigby and Mr Swanson in relation to accessing 'additional resources' rather than reserves. The Tribunal addresses additional resources separately below and does not consider that a high stripping ratio generated by accessing resources (rather than reserves) is of relevance to the more general issues of pit shape. In addition, aside from asserting that a high stripping ratio would be uneconomic (which was refuted by Mr Lambert), once again no calculations have been provided to the Tribunal regarding the effect on the DCF calculation, assuming a Whittle pit shape. Without costing calculations, the Tribunal is unable to speculate as to the cost impact of any increased stripping ratio on the DCF calculation, if indeed an increase would result in relation to reserves (rather than resources).

714. Finally, Dr Rigby suggested at the hearing that retaining the original pit shape was required so that the Marston figures, which were accurate to a feasibility level (within 15 per cent) could be retained. He considered that changing the pit shape resulted in a loss of accuracy, such that the figures might be accurate within 40 per cent, which was not at feasibility study level. Mr Lambert refuted this, maintaining that the figures proposed in his expert report were accurate to a feasibility level. The Tribunal has carefully considered Dr Rigby's concerns, but is not convinced that this provides sufficient reason not to adjust the mine plan where it is reasonable to do so. A loss of accuracy was always inevitable when the Tribunal issued Procedural Order No. 2 and requested the experts to estimate the impact of a no-layback scenario, which clearly entailed deviating from the Marston figures where required. Claimant has an obligation to meet its burden of proof. As noted earlier, the Tribunal found Mr Lambert to be more persuasive and there is no basis on which to assert that a reasoned and well-founded adjustment to the shape of the mine pit would suddenly render claimant's damages calculations speculative.

E. 100 meter buffer zone

Claimant's position

715. Mr Lambert's (RPA) optimal no-layback pit design did not include a buffer zone between the northern wall of the pit and the northern boundary of the concession.

716. The original with-layback pit design had contained a 100 meter buffer zone. Mr Lambert (RPA) noted that this buffer had been inserted to ensure that there would be no water seepage issues resulting from the planned water diversion channel in the Las Cristinas concession (as required by Venezuelan law). However, in April 2008, the planned location for the channel had been moved north so it necessarily followed that the reason for the buffer was removed.

717. Mr Lambert (RPA) rejected Dr Rigby's (SRK) assertion that a 100 meter buffer remained necessary for safety reasons. He submitted that the contemporaneous pit design took account of the unstable top layer of rock with flatter slopes at the top than at the bottom. Using these gradients, all of the independent experts who contemporaneously analysed the design for claimant prior to 2008 (Vector, Marston and Micon) had confirmed that the northern wall was sufficiently stable. Mr Lambert (RPA) used these gradients from the original design in his no-layback scenario.

718. Regarding safety, all experts agreed that calculating a factor of safety of 1.3 or above would indicate a stable wall. To do this calculation, Mr Lambert (RPA) requested the assistance of Tetra Tech (previously Vector Colorado a firm specialising in geochemical and geotechnical analysis and engineering) to conduct a new safety analysis of the no-layback scenario. Vector Colorado had conducted the original safety analysis for Claimant. Using Vector's contemporaneous data taken from six hard rock boreholes and four saprolite boreholes, as well as geotechnical data gathered from other drilling holes in the area, Tetra Tech calculated the safety factor of various parts of the north wall in Mr Lambert's (RPA) no-layback pit design. The lowest factor of safety recorded was 1.3.

719. Mr Lambert (RPA) rejected Dr Rigby's (SRK) calculation of much lower factors of safety and during the hearing claimant questioned Dr Tinucci, Dr Rigby's colleague, about apparent errors in SRK's factor of safety calculations. Claimant suggested that incorrect data had been entered into the relevant software program which resulted in a significantly lower safety of factor being generated. Claimant also suggested that Dr Rigby had overestimated the depth of the saprolite and 'weak rock' layers at the northern boundary, thereby inferring a less stable wall than would have existed had the pit been mined.

Respondent's position

720. Dr Rigby (SRK) asserted that a 100 meter buffer zone between the edge of the northern boundary and the start of the pit wall was required to ensure

safety and guard against slope failure. This was because the upper portion of the rock face at the northern wall was inherently unstable. The inclusion of a buffer zone would prevent the pit from encroaching into neighbouring property in the event of a slope failure. Alternatively, Dr Rigby (SRK) stated that the slope gradient could be flatter so as to prevent slope failure (both Parties had adopted the Marston slope gradients).

721. Dr Rigby (SRK) performed a factor of safety calculation based on the contemporaneous data provided by Vector for claimant's. He calculated a range of local and global safety factors, the lowest being a local safety factor of 0.87, well below the required 1.3.

722. Dr Rigby (SRK) stated that the instability at the northern wall was caused by the 'saprolite' rock layer which extended for approximately 225 meter below the surface. It was this upper portion of the wall for which the 'local' factor of safety of 0.87 was calculated. Dr Rigby (SRK) stated that he had checked his results using the 'more robust finite element method' which calculated a safety factor for the upper portion of the wall of 1.12, still below 1.3.

723. Dr Rigby (SRK) criticised the amount of data available for the northern section of the wall, stating that fewer boreholes were drilled than would be expected, and data from other drill holes could not be relied upon. Dr Rigby (SRK) also rejected Tetra Tech's analysis, suggesting that Tetra Tech was not independent as it was formally Vector – the company that performed the original analysis.

724. Due to the alleged paucity of data, Dr Rigby (SRK) made a comparison between the north wall and the M1 sector of the pit for which more contemporaneous data was available. Dr Rigby (SRK) considered that the M1 sector most closely resembled the geotechnical nature of the northern wall. However, Dr Rigby (SRK) acknowledged that this sector had a safety factor of 1.32, which claimant noted was still above the required 'safe' level (1.3).

725. Dr Rigby (SRK) also made a number of comparisons with other pits, such as the Cleo pit in Australia where one of the walls collapsed following significant rainfall.

Tribunal's analysis

726. The original mine plan used by Marston for the with-layback scenario included a 100 meter buffer zone between the northern wall of the mine pit

and the proposed diverted water channel in the Crystallex project. As the position of the channel had been moved to a more northern location, both parties agreed that there was no water seepage issue on April 2008 and, consequently, the original reason for the buffer zone had disappeared.

727. The experts also agreed that a stability buffer zone is not required by industry standards generally and therefore it is only needed if there is a specific reason for it in a given scenario, such as slope stability. Consequently, the central issue to be addressed here is whether or not there was a specific safety risk in the no-layback scenario which would suggest that a buffer zone was required.

728. Again, the Tribunal starts from the position that the rational investor would wish to adopt the mine plan which maximises access to mineral deposits, unless there is a technical, legal or safety reason which would prevent this. Dr Rigby's (SRK) inclusion of a buffer zone was based on his safety analysis which he said demonstrated that the northern wall was unstable and therefore a risk of slope failure existed. Indeed, with regard to the buffer, the difference in the factor of safety calculated by the experts appears to be the key issue. The Tribunal therefore addresses that now.

729. The experts agreed that a factor of safety of 1.3 or above is considered stable. In Mr Lambert's (RPA) calculation, the lowest factor for any portion of the north wall was 1.3, whereas Dr Rigby (SRK) calculated a lowest factor of 0.87 (which related specifically to the upper portion of the wall and was a so-called 'local' safety factor). Both parties relied upon the contemporaneous rock strength information provided by Vector to claimant.

730. During the hearing it became evident that some errors had occurred in respondent's safety calculations. In particular, it appears that certain data inputs were entered erroneously resulting in a significantly lower factor of safety being generated. Dr Tinucci (a colleague of Dr Rigby) could not explain why the Young's Modulus figures that had been entered into SRK's model were incorrect and that, as a result, the 'value is probably low'. Moreover, the Tribunal was not convinced by Dr Tinucci's explanation that a typographical error had been made in the heading of the certain columns, but that the figures were still correct. Due to the fact that the headings generated by the computer program could not have been changed manually (as Dr Tinucci acknowledged) and the fact that the data inputted corresponded to other data available, the Tribunal finds that a number of unintentional data entry errors occurred, resulting in an incorrect calculation. As such, the Tribunal cannot rely on the data presented by respondent. It therefore accepts the calculations provided by claimant which it finds to be robust.

731. The use of claimant's data is further compelled by Mr Hallman's (of Tetra Tech) explanation that claimant ran approximately 5,000 tests (including both local and global factors of safety) and reported the lowest factor of 1.3 in its submissions.

732. The only remaining issue is whether the Vector data is sufficient to be able to be relied upon. The Tribunal considers it is in no position to question this data when it was relied upon in the original Marston Report which did not question its reliability, nor did the various independent experts who reviewed that Report at the time. Moreover, the Tribunal accepts claimant's explanation that ten boreholes (six in hard rock and four in saprolite) together with geotechnical data gather the from over 800 other drill holes provided sufficient data. Claimant also explained that Vector had conducted an analysis of Sector I stability but, in line with industry practice, only included four sectors in its report (which did not include Sector I). As such, the Tribunal finds no basis on which it should reject calculations that rely on the contemporaneous Vector data.

733. The above findings lead the Tribunal to conclude that the lowest factor of safety applicable at the North wall was 1.3 and that therefore there is no safety reason for including a buffer zone at the Northern boundary. The Tribunal will accordingly calculate fair market value using the zero buffer scenario.

734. Before leaving this topic, the Tribunal recalls the question put by Professor Dupuy to the experts during the confrontation at the hearing in relation to the effect of climate and specifically of heavy rainfall on the safety of the northern wall. It is evident that heavy rainfall may have had a considerable effect on the stability of the saprolite material in the upper portion of the northern wall. However, the Tribunal is satisfied that RPA has taken adequate account of this in its pit design and that the contemporaneous testing provided was satisfactory. In particular, the Tribunal considers that it is unable to ignore the site-specific testing done for the Brisas Project on the basis of the experience at the Cleo pit in Australia cited by Respondent. The Tribunal does not have sufficient information to satisfy itself that the conditions and the design at the Cleo pit were so similar that it could reasonably equate the two mines, nor of the specific climatic circumstances that occurred to cause to slope failure and whether they could reasonably be expected to be replicated. There are simply too many uncertainties involved in such a comparison. The Tribunal finds it appropriate to rely on the test results at the Brisas mine, especially given that no clear evidence has been provided that such tests were deficient or failed to reach industry standards.

F. Stockpiles

735. In the no-layback scenario, the parties agreed that hard rock stockpiles not included in the original mine plan would be needed which would then be blended to ensure a more consistent copper head grade was fed into the processing plant. The experts disagreed on a number of issues regarding these stockpiles including size, location, management, costs, environmental impacts and the effect of oxidation.

Claimant's position

736. Mr Lambert (RPA) proposed the use of large blending stockpiles (one for low grade and one for high-grade ore) in order to smooth out fluctuations in the head grade ore being fed into the processing plant. Large variability in the copper grade of ore would affect mill performance and the quality of the product and blending would help to counter this. As such, blending would assist in maintaining the average copper head grade in a no-layback scenario (with no buffer zone) of 0.10 per cent. This would be lower than the average copper head grade predicted in the with-layback scenario but, Mr Lambert (RPA) explained, it would be within acceptable limits.

737. Mr Lambert (RPA) proposed the use of two stockpiles which would have a combined capacity of up to 68 million tonnes and would reach a maximum height of 96 meters each. Mr Lambert (RPA) claimed that this size was not unusual and that the use of temporary stockpiles such as these were standard industry practice. One stockpile would be for low-grade ore (0.02–0.03 per cent) and the other for higher grade ore.

738. Mr Lambert (RPA) contended that the preferable location for the stockpiles would be on the NLSAV1 parcel where saprolite stockpiles were already planned. Mr Lambert (RPA) suggested replacing the saprolite stockpiles (which would be depleted in the early years of the Project) with hard rock stockpiles which would only be needed several years into the project. This location option was based on an estimated maximum height for the stockpiles of 96 meters, which Mr Lambert (RPA) said was lower than the waste rock stockpiles already included in the Marston mine plan. Alternatively, if more space were required as per respondent's argument below, space would be available north of the waste rock dump (Esperanza parcel).

739. Claimant said that the additional costs involved in establishing and managing these stockpiles would be minimal, noting that the main cost would be in supplying some additional haulage trucks and loaders. On this

basis, claimant's financial experts, Mr Kaczmarek (Navigant), included an additional $53 million in capital for the stockpile expenditure – $20 million for new equipment and $33 million for replacement capital expenditure over the life of the mine.

740. Regarding mining costs, Mr Lambert (RPA) estimated that the use of the stockpiles would result in a 1 per cent increase in mining costs, but that the increased mining rate would yield a 2 per cent decrease in costs. Because these figures essentially cancelled each other out, Mr Lambert (RPA) made no adjustments to Marston figures. In response to criticism that the mining rate departed too far from the original Marston figures, Mr Lambert (RPA) noted that respondent's mining rate (as predicted by the production schedules) was even higher. Mr Lambert (RPA) also emphasized that only 17 per cent of the hard rock would be stockpiled and therefore averred that the change to the mine plan was not as significant as respondent was suggesting.

741. Regarding environmental impacts, Mr Lambert (RPA) contended that testing done for the VESIA showed that there was little potential for generating acid rock drainage or for deteriorating copper concentrate. In particular, the high carbonate component in the rock would neutralize acid and effectively create a buffer against leakage. He also said that waste rock and saprolite stockpiles were included in the original mine plan, so environmental concerns had already been addressed. In particular, Mr Lambert (RPA) noted that water treatment equipment had already been factored into the original mine plan at the site where stockpiles were planned. He also highlighted that contemporaneous assessments concluded that no geomembrane liner was required for the other stockpiles, as the compacting of the saprolite rock by trucks/diggers preparing the site would create an effective liner that would prevent any acid leaching.

742. Mr Lambert (RPA) also dismissed oxidation concerns. He cited tests which showed that over the course of two years there was very little oxidation of the copper content in stockpiled ore. He also emphasised that (i) the stockpile would be composed primarily of large pieces of rock minimising surface exposure of the ore; (ii) the high stockpiles in its optimal design would also minimise such exposure; and (iii) the hard rock has low permeability. Therefore, oxidation (if any) would be negligible. Finally, Mr Lambert (RPA) noted that evidence of potential oxidation referred to by respondent's experts was based on crushed ore stockpiles which would inevitably be more susceptible to oxidation. It also pertained to a different type of rock and was based on much wetter conditions than would be the case with the proposed stockpiles. At the hearing, Mr Lambert gave evidence regarding the location

and management of the stockpiles and Mr Henderson (from Tetra Tech) gave evidence regarding environmental issues.

Respondent's position

743. Dr Rigby (SRK) submitted that the inclusion of new large hard rock stockpiles introduced speculation into the valuation and were a significant change. He criticised Mr Lambert (RPA) for failing to provide sufficient detail as to the management and operation of these stockpiles. In particular, Dr Rigby (SRK) considered that Mr Lambert (RPA) had insufficiently addressed the costs and management issues surrounding the stockpiles, and had simply assumed that everything in the stockpile could be accessed and used.

744. Dr Brown and Mr Kowal (CRA) acknowledged that stockpiles were possible, but that 'it requires very close control and co-ordination of both mining and stockpile construction and management operations to be efficient and effective'. Dr Rigby (SRK) stated that to ensure an average head grade of 0.10 per cent, rock within each stockpile would need to be classified into high/low grades. Respondent's experts proposed a design for the stockpile that they contended would ensure this access and would segregate incoming ore into recordable areas so that operators could select the exact grade of ore required for blending.

745. Respondent's experts contended that lower stockpiles were necessary because (i) the practicalities of managing the blending process meant that the ore needs to be accessible at all times; and (ii) it had load-bearing concerns regarding the saprolite rock. Lower stockpiles with a maximum height of 10 meter were advocated by respondent, although this would require significantly more area. Dr Rigby (SRK) estimated approximately 300 hectares would be required.

746. Regarding Mr Lambert's (RPA) suggestion that the hard rock stockpiles could replace the saprolite stockpiles (already included in the original mine plan) over time, Dr Brown and Mr Kowal (CRA) said that this was not possible. They concluded that the hard rock stockpiles could not effectively be sequenced to utilise space vacated by saprolite stockpiles, as they would need to be built up faster than the saprolite stockpiles would be depleted. Respondent's experts said that Mr Lambert (RPA) was wrong to suggest that hard rock stockpiling would begin several years into production; rather claimant would need to blend north and south rock from early years of the Project to ensure a copper head-grade of 0.10 per cent.

747. Dr Rigby (SRK) noted that the alternative locations suggested by Mr Lambert (RPA) would significantly increase the haulage times for mined rock, which would have implications for operational costs. Mr Lambert (RPA) used the cycle times in the original Marston Report, but Dr Rigby (SRK) said that these would be inapplicable for many of the suggested stockpile locations. Dr Burrows (CRA) instead estimated costs based on an 18-minute cycle time, rather than the seven-minute cycle time used by Mr Kaczmarek (Navigant).

748. In relation to environmental impacts, Dr Rigby (SRK) contended that the testwork undertaken by claimant was insufficient and inadequate to support its conclusion that acid rock drainage/metal leaching would not occur. It remained an environmental risk to the project and therefore a geomembrane liner should be inserted, as well as a collection system for any water seepage through the stockpiles into the underlying rock and a treatment plant for such water if it were acidic.

749. Dr Brown and Mr Kowal (CRA) also contended that oxidation may be an issue in the stockpiles, which would deplete the copper content that is recoverable from the ore. They estimated that the ore would be in stockpiles for up to 6.75 years (depending on procedure adopted for managing the stockpile), and therefore Mr Lambert (RPA) could not rely on two-year tests undertaken contemporaneously. Respondent did not state definitively that oxidation would in fact occur, rather that there was insufficient evidence to conclude that it would not occur – and that no proper verification was done.

750. Regarding the costs involved in introducing such stockpiles, Dr Burrows (CRA) said that many of the management costs were not 'hard coded' as claimant had assumed, but would increase with the volume of rock mined, transported and stockpiled. This meant that, in most years, costs would increase from the original layback design. Dr Burrows (CRA) also noted that claimant had kept most costs the same for the no-layback scenario as for the with-layback scenario which he concluded 'makes no sense. The two mine plans are very different'. He calculated that stockpile costs (including the geomembrane liner and additional haulage time) would reduce Mr Lambert's (RPA) DCF valuation by $107 million. Dr Burrows (CRA) noted that the geomembrane liner would be a 'big item' within this cost, however no precise break-down was provided. The Tribunal also understands this figure to include contingency and indirect costs.

Tribunal's analysis

751. It is evident that the use of hard rock stockpiles for blending purposes is not uncommon and that both parties agree that they could, and should,

be used as part of a no-layback mine plan to smooth out fluctuating copper grades.

752. The Tribunal found the oral evidence provided at the hearing and the parties' post-hearing briefs useful in distilling the key areas of difference between experts. It appears to the Tribunal that there are two key issues that need to be addressed initially, with a number of more minor issues to consider thereafter. The first of these key issues concerns the purpose of the blending process itself. This in turn will determine the size and management of the stockpiles. The second issue concerns the environmental effects on the ore as a result of exposure to air and rain.

753. Turning to the first issue, claimant contended that only blending would be required to smooth out, but not eliminate, the fluctuations in head grade. Respondent considers that to consistently produce a head grade of 0.10 copper more precise blending is required. For the rough blending advocated by claimant, two large stockpiles – one containing low-grade ore and one containing high-grade ore – would be sufficient. Whereas, for more precise blending, it is evident that greater access to ore would be required, hence respondent's preferred plan of ten-meter high stockpiles where ore could be separated according to the specific grade of copper contained therein.

754. The first point that the Tribunal notes is that Mr Lambert stated at the hearing that the low-grade stockpile would have very little variation and would contain 0.02–0.03 per cent copper. Respondent did not challenge this at the hearing or in its Joint Expert Procedure Post-Hearing Brief. Indeed, it seemed to recognise this when it stated 'Mr Lambert acknowledges that there will be variations in grade, especially in the higher grade pile. . ..'

755. As a result, subject to safety concerns addressed below, the Tribunal considers that whether or not rough blending or more precise blending is required, it is clear that the low-grade stockpile could be of a larger size and would not need to be spread into ten-meter high piles for the purpose of accessing ore.

756. Regarding the high-grade stockpiles, the Tribunal accepts claimant's explanation that, unlike gold blending, where precision is important, there would be no need for such precision for copper blending. As such, the aim of the blending is to avoid extreme fluctuations, rather than to eliminate fluctuations altogether to ensure that a constant head grade is consistently fed into the mill. Respondent has not provided any evidence or explanation

as to why precise blending would be necessary for copper, as the examples it used as comparables related to gold blending only.

757. Nonetheless, even claimant seems to have acknowledged it would be preferable to have slightly more precise blending than can be delivered by two large stockpiles in which ore is simply placed anywhere. At the very least, as Mr Lambert said, regarding 'the higher grade stockpile, you may put in three or four areas that have a slight variation in grade'. This suggests that two large stockpiles in which ore is placed indiscriminately within each pile would not work in the case of the high grade ore. This would lead credence to the argument that slightly flatter, or a few more, stockpiles are required.

758. Overall, the Tribunal finds that claimant's mine plan that includes larger stockpiles is credible and should be preferred. However, as noted above, the high-grade pile may need to be spread over a slightly larger area than initially anticipated so to allow for the separation of ore into three or four areas. The impacts of this in terms of costs and location of the stockpiles are discussed further below.

759. For completion, the Tribunal notes that it is satisfied that there would be no stability issues with locating the stockpiles of the saprolite surface, as similar height stockpiles for waste rock were already included in the original mine plan.

760. The only remaining issue with regard to the height of the stockpiles is whether safety concerns dictate that smaller piles are required. Respondent contended that 96-meter high stockpiles would pose a risk to those working at their base. However, this concern appeared more relevant where precise blending was required, as attempting to select ore buried deep within such a high pile would no doubt create issues. Claimant provided a number of examples of other stockpiles which had a similar height to those proposed here, including stockpiles that would be depleted over the life of the mine. Given that it does not seem unusual to build stockpiles of this height, and in a scenario where the selection of precise ore grades from within the piles is not necessary, the Tribunal finds no evidence that safety would require stockpiles to be limited to 10 meter in height.

761. Regarding management costs, the Tribunal is sympathetic to respondent's concerns that claimant's experts have not fully considered the detail of the management or operation of the stockpiles. Mr Lambert himself said during the hearing that the Tribunal only asked the experts to 'estimate' and therefore he had not gone into the detail. While it is true that the Tribunal

asked the experts to 'estimate' design changes in a no-layback scenario, claimant still has a burden of proof to satisfy. Because of the limited analysis of the detail of the stockpiles undertaken by claimant's experts, the Tribunal considers that the costs of operating such stockpiles could indeed be higher than claimant suggests.

762. The Tribunal has studied the parties and expert submissions in detail with regard to the costs of managing stockpiles. It considers that the suggested deduction by Dr Burrows of $107 million is too high, especially as it includes environmental issues. It also included contingency costs. However, as noted above, the Tribunal considers that Mr Lambert's estimate of an additional $52million in capital costs may not be sufficient to cover all costs associated with the stockpiles. On balance, looking at the issue overall, the Tribunal finds that a deduction of US$ 80 million from claimant's DCF calculation would be fair and reasonable, taking into account any need to store higher grade ore in three of four different areas and general costs that will likely arise in establishing and managing such stockpiles.

763. This deduction would also take account of any increase in haulage time required if claimant's preferred stockpile location is not possible. As with the consideration of management costs, the Tribunal finds that claimant's experts have not sufficiently analyzed whether the saprolite stockpiles could actually be depleted at a rate that would allow the hard rock stockpiles to replace them. The Tribunal has built in the additional costs in paragraph 848 below to allow for extra haulage time if another location is required.

Environmental concerns

764. The Tribunal now considers the second key issue regarding stockpiles: the potential for Acid Rock Drainage ('ARD') and oxidation of the ore. Claimant asserts that ore will be in the stockpiles for approximately three years, while respondent considered that it could there for up to six years.

765. Based on contemporaneous testing, RPA asserted that neither ARD nor oxidation is of significant concern. In particular, Mr Henderson noted that the carbonate levels in the rock would ensure that any acidity is countered so to keep the pH neutral, and Dr Rigby acknowledged this buffering potential. It also seems to be accepted that much of the rock in the temporary stockpiles would be in the form of large boulders, rather than crushed ore making it less susceptible to ARD or oxidation. The minimal risk indicated by the contemporaneous testing, even if over a shorter period than the ore would be stored for on either claimant's or respondent's estimates, is persuasive.

The Tribunal finds that it has no evidence before it to suggest that ARD or oxidation would be in issue and, indeed, all evidence points to the contrary.

766. This conclusion is not at odds with respondent's position: Dr Rigby was careful to clarify at the hearing that his position was not that the ore would oxidise, rather that it 'might' and that he did not consider he had enough evidence to state that it would not. Respondent's concern was that the contemporaneous testing did not mirror the exact time period or conditions that would exist in the stockpiles and therefore one could not be sure that such environmental hazards would not occur. This may be true, but given that all the evidence suggests that the risk of ARD or oxidation is very low, the Tribunal is satisfied that no additional cost needs to be built into the valuation to allow for the building to geomembrane liners etc. or that the recoverability of metal would be significantly lowered by oxidation. The Tribunal notes that any evidence that did suggest that environmental concerns may exist was based on crushed ore studies and is therefore not sufficiently analogous to the present situation in which larger portions of rock would predominantly be stored.

G. Delay

Parties' positions

767. Respondent incorporated into its DCF calculation a two-year delay to allow for obtaining new permits and undertake any further feasibility studies associated with a no-layback scenario, and in particular with the hard rock stockpiles.

768. Claimant disagreed with incorporating time to get additional permits. Its position was that the parties should assess the no-layback scenario as if it had always been the preferred option – i.e., an alternative, hypothetical world. It also stated that, even if some delay may have occurred, respondent had not provided any rationale to explain why a two-year period is appropriate.

769. Claimant's valuation expert, Mr Kaczmarek (Navigant), stated that the two-year delay has a significant financial impact, being worth $221 million. Mr Burrows (CRA) calculated that this would be $217million, if additional resources were excluded.

Tribunal's analysis

770. The issue of delay is important due to its financial impact. Claimant noted that '[d]ue to the significant impact on a DCF measure of value of

reducing early revenues, this . . . assumption represents the largest difference between the experts' valuations specific to the no-layback scenario'.

771. Given the delays that had occurred in the Project prior to 2008 in relation to the granting of permits and the approval of feasibility and environmental studies, it is reasonable to factor in some time allowance for relevant approvals. The Tribunal does not agree with claimant that the valuation should be assessed as an 'alternative world' scenario, as if the no-layback plan had always been in place. The task of the experts was to value the Brisas Project as it was at April 2008. As no lay-back agreement was in place and claimant had no legal right to use the North Parcel, this must be factored into the valuation. It would therefore be reasonable to assume that some additional approvals would have been required to implement the no-layback design.

772. The Tribunal is not, however, convinced that a two-year delay is necessary. In the Tribunal's view, the changes to the mine plan, while important, are not so significant that they would have required extensive additional work in order to be approved. The Tribunal therefore finds that a one-year delay is reasonable and will take this into account in its calculations. Consequently, the Tribunal shall deduct US$108,500,000 from the DCF calculation (being half of Dr Burrows' estimated cost of a two-year delay). The Tribunal notes that the experts agreed that, although it is only an approximation of the financial impact, this figure would be roughly correct for a one-year delay.

H. Impact on Resources

773. The parties and their experts agreed that 'mineral reserve' is a defined term that identifies proven and probable resources that are demonstrated to be economic to extract. 'Mineral resources' are made up of the 'measured and indicated' and 'inferred' resources that may become profitable to mine in the future if metals prices were to increase. Mineral reserves are said to be more geologically certain, with 'inferred resources' being the least geologically certain.

Parties' positions

774. Mr Lambert (RPA) calculated that the optimal no-layback design would result in mineral reserves would be 9.087 million ounces of gold and 985 million pounds of copper. This represented a reduction of reserves by approximately 11 per cent in the case of gold and 29 per cent in the case of copper, as compared to a with-layback scenario.

775. In its Joint Expert Procedure Post-Hearing Brief, respondent stated that:

> There is no disagreement as to this process, and both experts discussed at the hearing how mineral resources undergo a technical process, through which they are converted to become reserves with demonstrated economic value. And although there is disagreement as to the amount of gold and copper ore reserves that will be lost under the no-layback scenario, there is general agreement that this is due to the different mine design plans.

776. Mr Lambert (RPA) also estimated 'additional resources' using prices of US$ 800/oz gold and US$ 3.25/lb copper to be 3,384,356 ounces of gold and 473,184,949 pounds of copper. Dr Rigby (SRK) disputes the inclusion of additional resources in any valuation, stating that by definition such resources would have been uneconomic to mine as at April 2008 unless metals prices significantly changed. Respondent argues that these resources are speculative and would not be included in securities filings such as the NI 43-101.

Tribunal's analysis

777. As indicated by Respondent's Joint Expert Procedure Post-Hearing Brief quoted above, and by the discussion between the experts at the hearing, the experts agreed upon the definition and process for measuring reserves and resources. The fundamental differences came down to pit shape/location (which has already been addressed by the Tribunal) and whether additional resources were to be included. Dr Rigby stated at the hearing that he accepted the estimate provided by Mr Lambert for claimant's 'optimal' zero buffer scenario. Because the Tribunal has determined that no buffer is required and has therefore adopted Claimant's preferred mine design, the mineral reserves estimate provided by Mr Lambert (RPA) should be used when calculating fair market value. That is, mineral reserves are estimated to be 9.087 million ounces of gold and 985 million pounds of copper.

778. In relation to additional resources, the Tribunal understands that additional resources can and often are reported for different purposes and, in some scenarios, might be ascribed value. However, for other purposes and reports, such as the NI 43-101 Technical Report filed by Claimant with the Toronto Stock Exchange, no value is ascribed to additional resources.

779. Mr Lambert (RPA) concluded that certain additional resources may become economic to mine at a metals price of US$ 800/oz gold and US$

3.25/lb copper – it is at this point that they may have value. The Tribunal understands that it is industry practice to estimate resources at a higher price.

780. However, the Tribunal must consider what the value that a willing buyer would have been likely to ascribe to such resources as at April 2008. Given that, as described by respondent, these resources have the 'lowest level of geological confidence' and that the Canadian Institute of Mining, Metallurgy and Petroleum on Valuation of Mineral Properties ('CIMVal') Guidelines, to which claimant refers, acknowledges the 'higher risk or uncertainty' associated with these resources and cautions that they should only be used with great care, the Tribunal finds the additional resources to be too speculative to include in the present valuation. The Tribunal concludes in this case that for the purposes of a fair market valuation, it will not ascribe any value to the additional resources in its calculations.

781. The Tribunal also finds that the valuation should not include silver resources. As noted by Mr Kaczmarek (Navigant), 'Gold Reserve applied for concession rights to exploit silver, but the Ministry of Mines never acted on this application' and Gold Reserve itself acknowledged silver was not covered by the corresponding mining titles. No evidence has been presented of any inferred right to mine silver and therefore any value ascribed to this metal would be on the speculative basis that such a right be granted in the future. The Tribunal does not find this convincing and considers that no value should be ascribed to any silver reserves in the DCF valuation.

782. Consequently, the Tribunal shall reduce claimant's DCF valuation by US$31 million to account for silver included in claimant's valuation and by a further US$ 162 million to amount for additional resources included in claimant's valuation.

I. Metallurgical issues

783. A number of metallurgical issues were raised by the parties as impacting on the valuation. The most important of these issues involved the processing plant performance and the resulting metal recovery rates and concentrate grades. Before addressing this significant issue, the Tribunal considers two more minor issues – ramp up rates and mill capacity.

784. The Tribunal heard evidence at the October 2013 hearing on metallurgical issues from Dr Altman (RPA) and Mr Spiller (Tetra Tech) on behalf of Claimant and from Dr Brown (CRA) on behalf of respondent. The Tribunal

found Dr Brown's evidence to be particularly convincing and helpful in the determination of these very technical issues.

J. Ramp-up rates

785. Ramp-up refers to the time it takes for the processing plant to 'ramp-up' to its full capacity. This is not an issue specific to a no-layback scenario, but was addressed by the experts in the Joint Expert Procedure reports and therefore the issue is addressed here by the Tribunal.

Claimant's position

786. Mr Lambert (RPA) stated that he used the ramp-up figures from the Marston Report of 2008 in both the with-layback and no-layback scenarios. This Report determined that the plant would operate at 87.5 per cent of capacity in the first year, made up of 60 per cent capacity in first quarter, rising to 90 per cent in second and full capacity after that. Micon had independently verified the Marston figures at the relevant time.

787. Mr Lambert (RPA) criticised Dr Rigby's (SRK) use of comparisons with other mining projects, stating that they used 'selective and skewed sampling' which were not truly comparable with the Brisas Project. Mr Lambert (RPA) also countered that many of those mines actually performed better than anticipated, and ended up with ramp-up rates higher than 87.5 per cent. Mr Lambert (RPA) also submitted that the calculations used by Dr Rigby (SRK) to estimate ramp-up were incorrect.

Respondent's position

788. Dr Rigby (SRK) submitted that the ramp-up figures in the Marston Report, and used by Mr Lambert (RPA), were too high. It used other 'comparable' processing plants to demonstrate that the figures should be lower and stated that the resultant lower predicted income in the early years would impact the DCF valuation. However, Dr Burrows (CRA) said that modeling the impact of slower ramp-up times is very complex, so to be conservative, he did not include any adjustment to the DCF to account for slower ramp-up times.

Tribunal's analysis

789. As respondent did not include any financial impact for slower ramp-up rates in its DCF adjustments, the Tribunal understands that this is not an

issue that will affect any damages to be awarded hereunder. It is also not an issue on which the parties concentrated at the hearing or in their post-hearing briefs. As such, the Tribunal will only address this issue briefly.

790. The Tribunal is persuaded by claimant's evidence that the comparable processing plants referred to by Dr Rigby (SRK) are not sufficiently reliable to conclude that a move away from the Marston figures is warranted. The Tribunal is also persuaded that Mr Lambert's use of the Marston rampup rates is the correct approach in the present case. Moreover, the Tribunal accepts Mr Lambert's submission that Dr Rigby (SRK) made crucial errors in his ramp-up calculations which prevents the Tribunal from placing any weight on the conclusions which might otherwise be drawn from those calculations. The Tribunal notes that, as this is not an issue that is affected by the no-layback scenario, strong evidence would be required for the Tribunal to depart from the figures adopted in the Marston Report, as approved and reviewed by Micon and Pincock, Allen & Holt, and on which the parties have frequently placed reliance in other areas. Given no such evidence exists, the Tribunal finds that the ramp-up rates in the Marston Report should be applied in a fair market valuation.

K. Mill capacity

Parties' positions

791. Respondent's experts submitted that the processing mill had a processing capacity of 25.2 million tonnes of ore per year. Claimant's expert said that this estimated capacity was for the 'SNC Lavalin' mill design in 2006, but the mill was subsequently redesigned so that its processing capacity increased to 27 metric tons of ore in early years and up to 29.2 metric tons later for the Brisas Project. In particular, Mr Lambert (RPA) said that he used Marston's contemporaneous mill capacity data, which was independently verified at the time by Pincock Allan & Holt and Micon.

Tribunal's analysis

792. The Tribunal notes once again that this is not an issue specific to the no-layback scenario. Therefore, as with the ramp-up issue above, the Tribunal finds that the figures used in the Marston Report should apply, unless convincing evidence to the contrary is provided. No such evidence exists in the present case and therefore the Marston figures should apply as per claimant's analysis. The Tribunal accepts that the processing capacity changed and therefore using the original figures from the SNC Lavalin mill would not be appropriate.

L. Metal recovery rates and concentrate grades

793. This is the central issue regarding the metallurgical analysis. The grade of the gold-copper concentrate coming out of the processing plant is dependent upon (i) the plant's average metal recovery rate; and (ii) the 'mass' recovery, referring to the density of the recovered concentrate. Density depends on how successful the plant is at separating waste rock from valuable metal.

794. Contemporaneous testing in 2008 for the with-layback scenario predicted that, with an assumed 0.10 per cent copper head-grade:

(a)   the average copper concentrate grade would be 24 per cent;
(b)   the average metal recovery rate would be 87.4 per cent for copper and 83.2 cent for gold; and
(c)   the average mass recovery would be 0.36 per cent.

795. These results were based on a number of tests carried out by Gold Reserve before the dispute arose. The most reliable of these tests for the purposes of recovery rates were the Locked-Cycle Tests ('LCTs'), of which eight were performed (although only seven were relevant to the issues discussed here). Both experts accepted the accuracy of the LCTs, although respondent disputed whether a sufficient number of LCTs had been carried out so as to produce reliable data.

796. The experts agreed that the head grade of the ore fed into the plant in a no-layback scenario is likely on average to be lower than in the with-layback scenario. The experts agreed that the mill itself would be able to handle lower head grade ore. The fundamental disagreement appears to be how this would then affect mill performance.

Claimant's position

797. Mr Lambert (RPA) contended that the contemporaneous test results could still be applied to the no-layback scenario to predict metal recovery rates because, although in some years the average copper head-grade would be below 0.1 per cent, there was nothing to indicate that the metal recovery rate would materially reduce with the slightly expanded range of copper head-grade expected in a no-layback scenario. Moreover, Mr Lambert (RPA) suggested that the mineralogy of the deposit was more important than the head grade when considering mill performance. This would not change in the no-layback scenario and the type of ore is easy to process.

798. According to claimant, LCT No. 8 most closely reflected the process to be adopted for the processing plant. Although the LCTs were used as the primary basis to design the processing plant and determining average metal recovery rate, claimant suggested that a certain amount of professional judgment was also used in the design which should in turn be used when assessing the impact of the no-layback scenario.

799. The contemporaneous data was based on an assumed head grade feed range of 0.083–0.176 per cent (with average grade of 0.131 per cent). RPA contended that in its optimal no buffer scenario the head grade feed range would be between 0.075– 0.182 per cent, with an overall average of 0.1 per cent. It was therefore not substantially different from the head grade range predicted in a with-layback scenario and therefore the contemporaneous testing could be relied upon to predict metal recovery rates. Accordingly, Mr Lambert (RPA) predicted that the average copper recovery rate in the no-layback scenario (assuming zero meter buffer) would be the same as for the with-layback scenario tested contemporaneously – 87.4 per cent for copper and 83.2 per cent of gold. He said that only in the 100-meter buffer zone scenario would the contemporaneous testing become unreliable.

800. Mr Lambert (RPA) also stressed that the processing plant had sufficient flexibility to cope with slightly lower head grades and only significantly lower head grades would likely reduce recovery rates. This was also consistent with the fact that the LCTs did not show a significant correlation between head grade and metal recovery, with some lower head grades producing high metal recoveries.

801. While contemporaneous data could be used to estimate metal recovery rate, this is not so for the average concentrate grade of the copper that would result from different head grades below 0.1 per cent. For the years in which the head grade is 0.1 per cent or above, Mr Lambert (RPA) said that the average of 24 per cent copper concentrate used in the contemporaneous testing was appropriate. In years when the average head grade falls below 0.1 per cent, the anticipated concentrate was based on the 'definitional relationship between concentrate grade, metal recovery, head grade and mass recovery and the processing plant design criteria'. More specifically, Mr Lambert (RPA) used an equation whereby the concentrate grade is equal to the (head grade x metal recovery rate) / mass recovery. Claimant contended that this equation is more accurate than relying on the 'assumed' concentrate grade used in the testing. Using the equation, Mr Lambert (RPA) predicted concentrates of between 18–22 per cent for ten years of the project's life and above 22 per cent for seven years.

802. In relation to Dr Brown and Mr Kowal's (CRA) analysis, Mr Lambert (RPA) contended that they had used test data inappropriately and consequently that their analysis generated flawed and unrealisable results. This was because the model chosen required more data points than were available from the LCTs. In particular, Respondent's model used tests that were conducted for other purposes and under different conditions than would exist in the processing plant as designed.

Therefore, the tests also involved samples that were unrepresentative of the general ore content put through the processing plant. Mr Lambert (RPA) said that the LCTs are the best indicator and that one should use only these tests when analysing metal recovery rates.

803. Mr Lambert (RPA) and Mr Kaczmarek (Navigant) stated that this issue was worth US$ 175 million.

Respondent's position

804. Dr Brown and Mr Kowal (CRA) used a 'non-linear exponential' model to predict metal recovery rates and concentrate grades. They too relied on contemporaneous data in their model, but from a wider range of tests than just the LCTs. They opined that this wider range of data points demonstrated that metal recovery rates fell as the head grade fell and that this reflected standard expectation in the industry. Using this model, Dr Brown and Mr Kowal (CRA) predicted copper concentrate grades of between approximately 15–23 per cent in the no buffer scenario (i.e., claimant's optimal scenario).

805. Dr Brown and Mr Kowal (CRA) noted that for recovery of gold, test data at pilot plant for the Brisas Project Feasibility Study showed differing gold recovery results from that used by Mr Lambert (RPA). Hence, they said that Mr Lambert (RPA) had overestimated gold recovery, making the concentrate appear more valuable than it would have been in reality.

806. Dr Brown and Mr Kowal (CRA) criticised Mr Lambert's (RPA) analysis as overly-simplistic and based on too many assumptions to be reliable. They said that the assumption that the concentrate grade would be 24 per cent at head grades above 0.1 per cent is not consistent with other available information which would suggest the head grade would need to be at least 0.15 per cent to produce a 24 per cent concentrate. Micon reported that material from the North (high copper) and the South (low copper) should be blended to produce concentrate 24 per cent from ore containing 0.13–0.15 per cent

copper. Dr Brown and Mr Kowal (CRA) pointed out that other documents say marketable concentrates could not be produced from head grade under 0.1 per cent – this would be lower limit and that the LCT tests at head grades of 0.12–0.13 per cent show percentage recovery at 16–21 per cent. They said that the LCTs were all based on higher copper grades and it is speculative to apply them to mill performance for lower copper grades.

Tribunal's analysis

807. This area is both technical and complex and has been the subject of significant disagreement between the experts. The Tribunal understands the parties to agree that the processing plant performance depends on the range of copper grades fed into the mill and that this range will be lower in the no-layback scenario than it would have been with a layback. The dispute between the experts concerns first the percentage that the head grade would drop and secondly the impact that this drop would have on metal recovery rates.

808. The experts appeared to agree that the mill as designed would be capable of processing the ore at lower head grades. It is the performance of the mill in terms of metal recoveries and concentrates that is at issue. Claimant's basic position was that the both the average head grade of the ore and the range of head grade to be fed into the mill – while lower than the with-layback scenario – is not so significantly lower to affect mill performance. Therefore the data obtained in the LCTs can be reasonably relied upon to predict performance. Respondent's position is that the head grade of the ore would be 'significantly lower' and therefore a mathematical model should be used to extrapolate from the available test data what mill performance would be at these lower head grades.

809. The Tribunal notes that both parties accepted the accuracy of the tests performed by SGS Lakefield, as reported in the Marston Report and reviewed by Micon, Pincock Allan & Holt and SNC Lavalin. However, respondent's experts considered that insufficient LCT data was available for lower head grades to confidently predict mill performance. This is especially so, claimed respondent, because the head grade of ore fed into the mill would be below an average of 0.10 per cent in the first 13 years of the life of the mine.

810. The importance of using the contemporaneous data wherever possible is undisputed, as is the fact that the LCTs provided the most reliable indication of mill performance. However, given that the LCTs did not provide sufficient data to run a statistical model for estimating performance in the no-layback

scenario, the Tribunal considers it both practical and preferable to use the next best data available – that generated by other tests including batch flotation tests and pilot plant data. The Tribunal prefers such a statistical analysis over the use of 'professional judgment' which is subjective and, as has been demonstrated by the substantial disagreement between the highly qualified experts involved in the present case, can legitimately produce widely variable results. The Tribunal notes that both parties relied on data gathered from these other tests for various parts of their analysis and the key, as Mr Spiller noted during the hearing, was to use that data 'carefully'.

811. Moreover, the Tribunal is not convinced that metal recovery rates predicted by the LCTs would remain the same at lower head grades. The Tribunal is not persuaded by claimant's experts' assertions that mineralogy rather than head grade is more important in determining metal recovery or that there would be no correlation between head grade and metal recovery evident from the testing. The Tribunal notes Dr Brown's observation that industry standard practice would expect metal recovery to reduce with lower head grades, and considers that claimant has not provided any convincing rationale for why the Brisas mine would behave differently. The Tribunal consequently prefers the statistical model advocated by respondent for predicting metal recovery rates and lower grades, rather than simply assuming that metal recovery would stay the same.

812. In relation to concentrate grades, the Tribunal also finds respondent's statistical approach to be more convincing and reliable than the pull model adopted by claimant which incorporated a number of assumptions. The Tribunal accepts the criticisms made by respondent's experts as to incorrect nature of the assumptions made by claimant's experts on which the pull model relied for its accuracy. In particular, the Tribunal notes respondent's criticism that:

> [The pull model] can only be used as a predictive model if one knows the dependence of recovery on head grade, as well as the dependence of pull on head grade. Since evaluations of the data regarding recovery and pull were not made, the pull 'model' is wholly dependent on the assumptions that claimant's experts make in this regard.

813. Moreover, at the hearing, Dr Altman was unable to answer Dr Brown's criticisms of her assumptions simply stating 'we know that plant will operate that way'. In the absence of evidence that would support claimant's assumptions, the Tribunal does not consider the pull model appropriate in the present circumstances.

814. Consequently, the Tribunal finds that claimant's DCF valuation should be adjusted to reflect that respondent's mill performance analysis. This requires a reduction of US$101 million as reflected in paragraph 848 below.

M. Saleability of concentrates

Parties' positions

815. The experts agreed that the concentrate produced under a no-layback scenario would be saleable. The issue therefore was whether the copper content would fall below agreed levels such that the draft commercial terms that had been agreed with three smelters in 2005 would need to be renegotiated. The three smelters were Aurubis (Germany), Sumitomo (Japan), and Boliden (Sweden).

816. Respondent contended that smelters would seek to maintain their margin by negotiating higher treatment and refining charges in the case of lower copper concentrates (which cost the smelters more to treat). It estimated the cost to be approximately $50 million. Respondent introduced evidence from Mr Tuokkola who was the Vice-President of Operations at the Boliden smelter at the time the draft terms were negotiated with claimant.

817. Claimant submitted that, even if concentrate grades fell below agreed levels, it was unlikely that the smelters would seek to renegotiate terms because the market had shifted significantly between 2005–08 against the smelters. In particular, treatments and refining charges had halved by 2008 as regards those agreed in the 2005 terms and smelters were no longer able to charge price participation. Claimant contended that the smelters would not risk losing these benefits by reopening the terms to negotiation. However, if a renegotiation did occur, it would result in a DCF deduction of no more than US$5 million.

Tribunal's analysis

818. The experts agreed that market conditions had changed since the negotiation of the smelter agreement in favour of the mines, particularly in relation to treatment/refining charges and the inclusion of price participation provisions. The Tribunal is not persuaded that, given the significant drop in average treatment and refining charges which had effectively halved between 2005 and 2008, that the smelters would risk renegotiation. Even if renegotiation were sought, the Tribunal is not convinced that it would have any material impact on the DCF calculation as, in the market that existed in 2008,

Gold Reserve would be as likely to benefit from the renegotiation as it would to be disadvantaged by it – indeed, more likely to benefit than not. As such, the Tribunal considers that there is no need to make any further adjustment to the DCF valuation to account for any potential renegotiation.

N. Valuation / financial issues

Claimant's position

819. Claimant's primary position was that the absence of a formal legal right to the North Parcel of land as at April 2008 would not have had any material effect on damages. This is because, according to claimant and its valuation expert, Mr Kaczmarek (Navigant), a 'reasonably informed buyer' would have assumed the good faith application of Venezuelan law which, in turn, would mean that the buyer would have been able to obtain the right to use the North Parcel as a layback. Thus, the Brisas Project would be purchased on this assumption. Therefore, the fact that the legal right had not been acquired as at April 2008 did not affect the value, as the right would be acquired in the future.

820. To support this conclusion, claimant cited the following reasons for assuming a layback would be granted in the future: it was required to max-imise the concession; laybacks are common in the industry; laybacks and easements were being approved at the time; Crystallex's filings indicated it expected the layback agreement to be implemented; third-party valuations at the time assumed a layback; those minerals were included in claimant's reserves in the 2008 NI 43-101 Technical Report filed with the Toronto Stock Exchange (in which a qualified person independently reported reserves to the public). Finally, Claimant contended that the owner of the Brisas Project had a right to obtain use of the North Parcel and a layback agreement onto the Cristinas 4 parcel by Court order if necessary.

821. However, claimant also provided (as requested under Procedural Order No. 2) an alternative valuation based on the assumption that no layback existed (i.e., the no-layback scenario). Mr Kaczmarek (Navigant) determined the value of the Brisas Project on this alternative basis to be US$1,374,492,000 (which was 21 per cent drop in value from the with-layback scenario).

822. To calculate this value, Mr Kaczmarek (Navigant) used same methodol-ogy as it did in the original reports, adjusted for the new mine plan with no layback. This methodology comprised the weighted average of (i) DCF method; (ii) comparable publically traded company method; and (iii) com-parable transaction method. The weightings attached to each methodology

were 50 per cent, 35per cent and 15 per cent respectively. Mr Kaczmarek (Navigant) contended that using a weighted average of these three methods meant that the valuation was not over-sensitive to changes in inputs and that including a comparable transaction method ensures the valuation is not too far removed from the market.

823. Mr Kaczmarek (Navigant) criticized Dr Burrows' (CRA) zero-dollar valuation, stating that there was clearly economic value in the significant gold and copper mineral deposits at Brisas (as shown by the mineral reserves which are by definition economic to mine). It also cited a number of errors in Dr Burrows' (CRA) methodology including use of an incorrect base value and discount rate. Most of these criticisms are not specific to the no-layback scenario and were also made during the initial quantum phase. Differences that were specific to the no-layback scenario stem primarily from the differences between the mining experts already addressed above.

Respondent's position

824. Respondent's position, based on the analysis by Dr Burrows (CRA), is that the Brisas Project had a zero-dollar fair market value (with or without layback) as at April 2008.

825. Respondent rejected claimant's assertion that a willing buyer would assume a future layback, even if no legal right had been granted at that time, and therefore would value the concession on this basis. Respondent stated that the absence of a layback had a significant effect on value, noting that, in March 2008, Pincock Allen & Holt wrote 'in the event an agreement [on the layback] is not reached, the reserve estimate will have to be reduced significantly.'

826. Dr Burrows (CRA) assessed the value of the Brisas Project based on the DCF method only, stating that a comparables-based methodology is inappropriate because nature of the geology and mineralisation varies so much from site to site that no valid comparables exist.

827. For the no-layback scenario (as for the with-layback scenario), Dr Burrows did not produce his own DCF calculation, but began with Mr Kaczmarek's (Navigant) DCF valuation for its optimum no-layback scenario (i.e., zero-meter buffer and large stockpiles). He then made a number of 'fundamental corrections' to allow for lower metals recovery, higher smelter charges, revisions to reflect better the revised mine plan (ramps etc.), and a two-year delay to obtain additional permits etc. (i.e., all the corrections that respondent's mining experts suggested). He also corrected the assumed

speed at which claimant would receive revenue which reduced the value by a further $43million. In total, these corrections significantly decreased the DCF value to $614 million.

828. Dr Burrows (CRA) then went on to make a number of further corrections to the value regarding gold/copper prices, inflation, cost of capital etc. These corrections reflected criticisms previously made of Mr Kaczmarek's (Navigant) model and were not specific to the no-layback scenario. The key points in Mr Kaczmarek's (Navigant) methodology with which Dr Burrows (CRA) took issue were summarized at paragraphs 24 and 26. The result of making all of these adjustments is a zero-dollar value attributed to the Brisas Project. In effect, his view was that the concession would have been uneconomical to mine.

Tribunal's analysis

Claimant's primary case

829. The Tribunal does not accept claimant's primary position that the absence of a legal right to use the North Parcel of land would have no effect on the value of the Project. There is no doubt that any reasonable purchaser would take into account the possibility that it would not acquire the right to use the North Parcel, especially given that claimant had failed to secure the right or reach an agreement on a layback by April 2008. Moreover, the Tribunal simply cannot compensate claimant for the deprivation of a right that it never possessed.

830. Claimant's experts have modelled an alternative value based on a weighted average of a DCF valuation, comparable publically traded company and comparables transactions. Although the Brisas Project was never a functioning mine and therefore did not have a history of cashflow which would lend itself to the DCF model, the Tribunal accepts the explanation of both Dr Burrows (CRA) and Mr Kaczmarek (Navigant) that a DCF method can be reliably used in the instant case because of the commodity nature of the product and detailed mining cashflow analysis previously performed. The Tribunal also notes that the experts agreed on the DCF model used, and it is only the inputs that are contested. Many of these have already been discussed above, with the remaining variables discussed below.

Comparables

831. With regard to the use of comparables, respondent contended that there were simply no comparable companies or transactions close enough

to be used as a measure of value. The Tribunal notes that the DCF method is a preferred method of valuation where sufficient data is available. This conclusion is supported by the CIMVal Guidelines (referred to at para. 780 above) to which both experts referred. In the present cases, many of the arguments in favour of a DCF approach (a commodity product for which data such as reserves and price are easily calculated) mitigates against introducing other methods such as comparable transactions or market capitalization, unless close comparables can be found. On several occasions in this Award, the Tribunal has rejected a comparable with other mines on the basis that many variables are specific to each mine (such as climatic and geological conditions) all of which have an impact on value. Dr Burrows observed in relation to the comparables used by Mr Kaczmarek (Navigant) that '[t]he characteristics of these deposits vary widely. They were in very different locations with different geopolitical risks, different types of deposits, different kinds of mining technologies, different process technologies, different stages of production and different stages of development'. He also noted that no adjustments were made to take account of differences. Although the Tribunal appreciates claimant's concern that the DCF model can be over-sensitive to changes in inputs, the Tribunal is not convinced that the comparables offered are sufficiently similar to enable then to be used in a weighted valuation calculation. Because of this uncertainty, the Tribunal prefers to use the DCF model only.

832. This does not mean, however, that the comparables analysis conducted should be ignored completely. However, rather than ascribed a weighted value to each methodology, the Tribunal prefers to use the DCF value to assess compensation and refer to comparable companies and transactions as a cross-reference as to the reasonableness of the DCF valuation. It is noted that, at least for the original DCF valuation advanced by claimant, the comparables were in a close range, suggesting the DCF value was reasonably accurate. Similarly, contemporaneous valuation reports prepared by independent analysts from JP Morgan, RBC Capital, and Trevor Ellis are useful references to ensure that the compensation awarded is reasonable. Once again, these analyses produced values reasonably similar to that derived from Mr Kaczmarek's (Navigant) DCF valuation.

Dr Burrows' negative valuation

833. Turning now to the specific DCF values advanced by the parties, the Tribunal did not find Dr Burrows' (CRA) negative valuation, resulting in no compensation, convincing. This would essentially mean that the mine was completely uneconomic to operate – a highly unlikely proposition given

the effort and expense to which Gold Reserve had committed to get the mine operational. The detailed feasibility study and various impact studies all demonstrated that the level of analysis that had gone into the mine was significant. Moreover, claimant demonstrated that its valuation was consistent with other independent valuations in 2006 and 2007 by Trevor Ellis, JP Morgan and RBC Capital. To suggest that all of these independent valuations are worthless is simply not credible. If mining the concessions had been uneconomic, claimant would have been aware of this and no doubt would not have been proceeding with the venture. In addition, Mr Pingle (who provided expert evidence on behalf of claimant for the first hearing) confirmed the financing that had been arranged for the project, indicating that a convincing business case had been made to obtain the debt. The absence of a layback on the North Parcel is hardly likely to be such a significant change as to turn a highly profitable investment into an unprofitable one.

834. The Tribunal's rejection of Dr Burrows' negative valuation, together with the endorsement of Mr Kaczmarek's (Navigant) valuation by its reasonable proximity to the comparables methodologies and to independent valuations conducted during the relevant period, strongly suggests that claimant's DCF analysis is to be preferred to that of Dr Burrows. However, as indicated in the previous sections of this damages chapter, the Tribunal finds it appropriate to make certain adjustments to the DCF valuation to account for some of the no-layback specific valuation issues. These adjustments are set out in paragraph 848 below. However, in relation to other disputes between the experts on issues not specific to the no-layback scenario, the Tribunal generally prefers the methodology and evidence advanced by Mr Kaczmarek (Navigant). For the sake of completeness, the Tribunal briefly addresses each of these additional issues below.

Metal prices

835. The first issue is the appropriate metal prices to be used. In relation to gold, both experts used the futures prices available through to the end of 2012 for calculating prices up until this date. Thereafter, Mr Kaczmarek (Navigant) continued to apply the last known futures price (as at December 2012) through to the end of the project. Dr Burrows (CRA) instead used long-term price forecasts from analysts to calculate the price of metals after December 2012. The dispute therefore regards the price to be applied from the beginning of 2013.

836. In relation to copper, Mr Kaczmarek (Navigant) used the futures price through June 2010 and assumed that the price would stay constant (at $3.55

per pound) thereafter. Dr Burrows (CRA) used Mr Kaczmarek's (Navigant) projection of the copper price through 2014 and the analysts' expectations thereafter.

837. The Tribunal accepts claimant's explanation that the approach adopted by Mr Kaczmarek (Navigant) is conservative and holding the last futures contract price constant in a forecast is a common forecasting methodology in commodity sectors. Dr Burrows' (CRA) approach results in a sudden and significant price drop as at the beginning of 2013 and in turn creates an 'unrealistic pricing pattern'. As noted by Mr Kaczmarek (Navigant), Dr Burrows' (CRA) analysis is the result of mixing two quite different types of forecasts which in turn have predicted vastly different prices. In the Tribunal's view, this mixing of methodologies which creates a pricing prediction that is clearly at odds with normal price patterns is inappropriate. Given that holding the final futures prices is a both a common and conservative methodology in the instant case, and appears more consistent with a realistic (albeit conservative) pricing pattern, the Tribunal does not consider that any adjustment needs to be made to Claimant's DCF valuation regarding the prices of copper or gold. Although not relevant to the analysis, the Tribunal notes that actual pricing patterns since 2008 confirm that conservative nature of the metal prices used by claimant, reinforcing the Tribunal's decision not to adjust the valuation further.

Inflation rate

838. Regarding the inflation rate to be applied, Mr Kaczmarek (Navigant) calculated a 2.39 per cent inflation rate based on the difference between the yield on 20-year treasury inflation protected securities ('TIPs') and the yield on standard treasury bonds of a similar maturity. Dr Burrows (CRA) used 20-year US dollar inflation swap rates to project inflation of 2.89 per cent. Mr Kaczmarek (Navigant) stated that its methodology provided a market estimate for the expected rate of inflation and, while acknowledging that debate exists on the topic, said that 'many well-regarded valuation texts relied on by valuation practitioners advocate the use of TIPs'. It is evident that the use of inflation swaps to predict inflation is also a valid method of predicting inflation. Faced therefore with two valid methodologies for estimating inflation over the relevant 20-year period, the Tribunal is persuaded by the five alternative predictions of long-term US dollar inflation presented by claimant at paragraph 178 of Mr Kaczmarek's Second Expert Report of July 2011 (which provided a range between 2 and 2.5 per cent) that vlaimant's inflation rate should be adopted in the present case.

Discount rate

839. The experts calculated the discount rate to be applied in the present case using the weighted average cost of capital (or 'WACC'). Mr Kaczmarek's (Navigant) calculation yielded a WACC of 8.22 per cent made up of the cost of equity; equity/total capital; cost of debt; and debt/total capital. Dr Burrows (CRA) agreed with the formula to calculate the WACC, put not with the specific inputs used by Mr Kaczmarek (Navigant) in the calculation. Dr Burrows (CRA), using different inputs, calculated a WACC discount rate of between 16.5 per cent and 23.8 per cent.

840. Of the different inputs used by Dr Burrows (CRA), the largest discrepancy concerned the country risk premium applied as part of the cost of equity. Mr Kaczmarek's (Navigant) uses a country risk premium of 1.5 per cent which he says was confirmed by assessments by independent analysts in 2008. Dr Burrows' (CRA) country risk premium, unlike Mr Kaczmarek's (Navigant), was based on both full and 'generic' country risk for an investment in Venezuela in April 2008. He used a figure of between 6.7 and 16.4 per cent. Thus, it took account of Venezuela's policies at the time, including the President's policy of ousting North American companies from the mining sector, thus increasing the risk significantly.

841. The Tribunal agrees with Mr Kaczmarek's (Navigant) contention that it is not appropriate to increase the country risk premium to reflect the market's perception that a State might have a propensity to expropriate investments in breach of BIT obligations. As such, the Tribunal finds the range of country risk premiums offered by Dr Burrows (CRA) to be too high, as all of these include some element reflective of the State policy to nationalise investments which has been discussed in earlier sections of this Award. However, the Tribunal also considers that the country risk premium adopted by Mr Kaczmarek (Navigant) is too low, as it takes into account only labour risks and not other genuine risks that should be accounted for – including political risk, other than expropriation. The Tribunal considers that Mr Kaczmarek (Navigant) has not taken adequate account of these other risks when estimating his country risk premium. The Tribunal is also mindful of the fact that it has found that no expropriation occurred in the present case and that claimant's failure to exploit the Concessions within the required timeframes provided the legal basis on which Respondent terminated the Concessions (albeit inconsistently with its FET obligations). This fact further detracts from Mr Kaczmarek's position that expropriation concerns were the cause of the higher risk premiums estimated by other analysts in 2008. The Tribunal therefore

finds that the country risk premium should be increased to properly reflect the risks involved.

842. Having considered the various premiums used by analysts in 2008, the Tribunal decides to adopt a country risk premium of 4 per cent as used in the RBC Capital Markets Report, which was one of the reports referenced by Mr Kaczmarek (i.e., a 2.5 per cent increase). The Tribunal accepts Dr Burrows' (CRA) explanation that this premium appropriately considers political risks, together with other risks, but has not been over-inflated on account of expropriation risks. The Tribunal calculates that using a 4 per cent country risk premium results in a cost of equity of 11.92 per cent, with a resulting WACC rate of 10.09 per cent (rather than 8.22 per cent as used by claimant). This results in an increase to the WACC rate of 1.87 per cent. The Tribunal recalls that it asked Dr Burrows and Mr Kaczmarek at the October 2013 Hearing whether it could calculate approximate adjustments to the DCF based on the information provided by the experts to date. In relation to the discount rate, Dr Burrows noted that although a little complicated, 'you could make a back-of-the-envelope calculation and probably come up with a reasonable adjustment factor without having to actually rewind the model'. While acknowledging that its estimate might be 'rough' the Tribunal finds it appropriate to deduct US$130 million from claimant's DCF total to reflect the fact that Mr Kaczmarek's country risk premium was too low.

843. With regard to the other inputs used to calculate the cost of equity, the Tribunal prefers those used by Mr Kaczmarek (Navigant). The Tribunal is convinced that the use of a geometric mean to calculate the equity market risk premium is appropriate in the present case and also agrees that a proxy beta rate was required given that Gold Reserve's beta rate had been affected by respondent's policies. These inputs, as well as the country risk premium are reaffirmed by the fact that Mr Kaczmarek's (Navigant) calculation resulted in a WACC that is consistent with those applied by independent experts both to Gold Reserve and other similar companies at the time. As such, no change is made to the discount rate and no reduction to the overall valuation on account of this issue is required.

844. The Tribunal accepts the cost of debt calculated by Mr Kaczmarek (Navigant) and finds that his methodology was sound. Mr Kaczmarek (Navigant) applied the interest rate that had been negotiated by Gold Reserve with the Mandatory Lead Arrangers for $425 million debt, being 6.24 per cent (or LIBOR plus 3.55 per cent). He demonstrated that this rate was unlikely to change thus suggesting it is an appropriate indicator of cost of debt. He also convincingly rebutted the concerns raised by Dr Burrows

(CRA) and demonstrated why each of these concerns did not invalidate the rate applied, nor did they support the much higher rate that Dr Burrows (CRA) had proposed instead. The exception was Dr Burrows' (CRA) suggestion that the interest rate include an additional 0.72 per cent premium to convert the floating LIBOR rate into a fixed rate. Mr Kaczmarek (Navigant) agreed and adjusted its cost of debt to 6.96 per cent to include this premium. The Tribunal therefore finds that no further adjustment is required to Navigant's WACC rate on account of cost of debt. Consequently, subject to the country risk premium adjustment set out in paragraph 843 above, the Tribunal determines that the discount rate calculated and applied by Mr Kaczmarek (Navigant) was appropriate and no further adjustments are required.

Capital and operating costs

845. In its quantum submissions prior to the Joint Expert Procedure, respondent advocated a number of capital adjustments that were based primarily on assessments by Dr Rigby (SRK) which in turn were based on a number of errors in Dr Rigby's original report summarised in claimant's (original) post-hearing brief at paragraph 106. Given the seminal nature of these errors, the Tribunal considers that it cannot rely on Dr Rigby's evidence in this regard. Conversely, the Tribunal considers the evidence provided by claimant's experts supports the conclusion that capital costs adopted by Mr Kaczmarek (Navigant) were reasonable and appropriately supported. The Tribunal therefore finds that no adjustments should be made to Claimant's DCF valuation on account of capital or operating costs.

Delay in receiving revenues

846. Dr Burrows (CRA) suggested that the 2008 NI 43-101 Report failed to account for a delay in receiving revenues and although he admitted the delay and its financial impact were uncertain, he advocated that some account should be taken of this in the DCF valuation. He estimated a delay of delayed 75 days for concentrate and 30 days for ore would be appropriate. Dr Burrows (CRA) acknowledged that some delay would be offset by a delay in payables. Given that the 2008 NI 43-101 Report does not include such a delay and that the smelting agreements for concentrate included a highly favourable terms which would have allowed Gold Reserve to receive 90 per cent of the sales proceeds when the ship was loaded, the Tribunal does not consider that it would be justified to reduce the DCF in this regard. As such, the Tribunal accepts Mr Kaczmarek's conclusion his calculation is conserva-

tive on this point and that the favourable terms in the relevant smelting agreements 'would allow Gold Reserve to collect revenues faster than it would need to pay many of its operating costs and to reduce its overall cost of debt by using some of the cash advances to pay down debt principle'.

Fuel and electricity costs

847. Finally, the Tribunal also accepts Mr Kaczmarek's (Navigant) calculations regarding fuel and electricity costs, which is consistent with the 2008 NI 43-101 Report. Moreover, given 'Venezuela's long-standing policy of subsidising low electricity and fuel prices', the Tribunal does not consider it reasonable to double such prices over the forecast period as Dr Burrows (CRA) did in his analysis. The prices adopted by Mr Kaczmarek (Navigant) are inflation adjusted and consistent, or even conservative, in the light of historical trends demonstrating prices had previously tracked downwards. Therefore, the Tribunal finds that no adjustment to claimant's DCF calculation is required regarding fuel and electricity costs.

O. Damages calculation

848. Taking all of the foregoing considerations into account and doing its conscientious best on the evidence presented to it, the Tribunal finds it appropriate to award claimant damages in the sum of US$713,032,000 calculated as follows:

Adjustments Amount

Claimant's DCF value 1,325,532,000

- Less Additional Resources (162,000,000)
- Less Metal Recovery and Concentrate Grades (101,000,000)
- Less Stockpiles (80,000,000)
- Less Delay (108,500,000)
- Less Silver (31,000,000)
- Less Country Risk Premium (130,000,000)
- Total 713,032,000

849. The Tribunal has attempted to keep the sequence of the deductions the same as the order used by the experts so as to minimise any impact from making adjustments for some issues, but not others. It has based its figures and the sequence on Dr Burrows' analysis at Table 1 and Table 3 of his Rebuttal Joint Expert Procedure Report dated 3 July 2013. The Tribunal

recognises that these figures are estimates of financial impact, but as the experts acknowledged at the hearing, these 'rough' calculations can be used to 'come up with a reasonable adjustment factor without having to actually rerun the model'. This is what the Tribunal has done and it considers that the overall damages figure resulting from the calculation reflects a fair and reasonable level of compensation to claimant and has the effect of wiping out the consequences of the breach of FET.

Part III

International investment arbitration

21

Jurisdiction

 EXERCISE 31 – JURISDICTION I – MINI MOCK ARBITRATION

The US company Big Oil has made an investment in the Republic of Ecuador.

In the view of Big Oil, the Republic has taken measures which constitute expropriation of the investment. Big Oil therefore initiates an ICSID arbitration pursuant to the USA-Ecuador BIT (enclosed).

Ecuador raises a jurisdictional objection to the effect that Big Oil has commenced arbitration prior to the expiry of the cooling-off period stipulated in the BIT. The ICSID Tribunal agrees with Ecuador and issues a decision dismissing Big Oil's claim for lack of jurisdiction.

Upon the expiry of the cooling-off period, Big Oil again commences an ICSID arbitration. Meanwhile, however, Ecuador has withdrawn from the ICSID Convention. As a consequence, Ecuador takes the position that it is no longer bound by the ICSID Convention and does not accept ICSID arbitration.

Big Oil then withdraws its (second) request for ICSID arbitration. A few months later, Big Oil commences an UNCITRAL Arbitration based on the BIT.

In response thereto, Ecuador again raises a jurisdictional objection, arguing that Big Oil has exhausted its possibilities for going to arbitration. In essence Ecuador is saying: 'You can only have one bite of the apple.'

 GROUP

Group 1
You are the observer group.

Group 2
You are the UNCITRAL Tribunal and must decide this jurisdictional issue.

Group 3

Based on the BIT, and its proper interpretation pursuant to the Vienna Convention, present the best arguments in support of Big Oil's position that the UNCITRAL Tribunal does indeed have jurisdiction to try the dispute.

Group 4

Based on the BIT, and its proper interpretation pursuant to the Vienna Convention, present the best arguments in support of Ecuador's position.

 CASE

Treaty between The United States of America and The Republic of Ecuador concerning the encouragement a reciprocal protection of investment

The United States of America and the Republic of Ecuador hereinafter the 'parties'; desiring to promote greater economic cooperation between them, with respect reinvestment by nationals and companies of one party in the territory of the other party; ecognising that agreement upon the treatment to be accorded such investment will stimulate the flow of private capital and the economic development of the parties; agreeing that fair and equitable treatment of investment is desirable in order to maintain a stable framework for investment and maxim effective utilisation of economic resources; recognising that the development of economic and business ties can contribute to the well-being of workers in both parties and promote respect for internationally recognised worker rights; and having resolved to conclude a Treaty concerning the encouragement and reciprocal protection of investment; have agreed as follows:

Article I

1. For the purposes of this Treaty,

(a) 'investment' means every kind of investment in the territory of one Party owned or controlled directly or indirectly by nationals or companies of the other Party, such as equity, debt, and service and investment contracts; and includes:

   (i)   tangible and intangible property, including rights, such as mortgages, lions and pledges;
   (ii)   a company or shares of stock or other interests in a company or interests in the assets thereof;
   (iii)   a claim to money or a claim to performance having economic value, and associated with an investment;

      (iv)   intellectual property which includes, inter alia, rights relating to:

- literary and artistic works, including sound recordings;
- inventions in all fields of human endeavor;
- industrial designs;
- semiconductor mask works;
- trade secrets, know-how, and confidential business information; and
- trademarks, service marks, and trade names; and

      (v)   any right conferred by law or contract, and any license and permits pursuant to law;

(b) 'company' of a party means any kind of corporation, company, association, partnership, or other organisation, legally constituted under the laws and regulations of a party or a political subdivision thereof whether or not organised for pecuniary gain, or privately or governmentally owned or controlled;

(c) 'national' of a party means a natural person who is a national of a party under its applicable law;

(d) 'return' means an amount derived from or associated with an investment, including profit; dividend; interest; capital gain; royalty payment; management, technical assistance or other fee; or returns in kind;

(e) 'associated activities' include the organisation, control, operation, maintenance and disposition of companies, branches, agencies, offices, factories or other facilities for the conduct of business; the making, performance and enforcement of contracts; the acquisition, use, protection and disposition of property of all kinds including intellectual property rights; the borrowing of funds; the purchase, issuance, and sale of equity shares and other securities; and the purchase of foreign exchange for imports.

(f) 'State enterprise' means an enterprise owned, or controlled through ownership interests, by a party.

(g) 'delegation' includes a legislative grant, and a government order, directive or other act transferring to a State enterprise or monopoly, or authorising the exercise by a State enterprise or monopoly, of governmental authority.

2. Each party reserves the right to deny to any company the advantages of this Treaty if nationals of any third country control such company and, in the case of a company of the other party, that company has no substantial business activities in the territory of the other party or is controlled by nationals

of a third country with which the denying party does not maintain normal economic relations.

3. Any alteration of the form in which assets are invested or reinvested shall not affect their character as investment.

Article II

1. Each party shall permit and treat investment, and activities associated therewith, on a basis no less favourable than that accorded in like situations to investment or associated activities of its own nationals or companies, or of nationals or companies of any third country, whichever is the most favourable, subject to the right of each party to make or maintain exceptions falling within one of the sectors or matters listed in the Protocol to this Treaty. Each party agrees to notify the other party before or on the date of entry into force of this Treaty of all such laws and regulations of which it is aware concerning the sectors or matters listed in the Protocol. Moreover, each party agrees to notify the other of any future exception with respect to the sectors or matters listed in the Protocol, and to limit such exceptions to a minimum. Any future exception by either party shall not apply to investment existing in that sector or matter at the time the exception becomes effective. The treatment accorded pursuant to any exceptions shall, unless specified otherwise in the protocol, be not less favourable than that accorded in like situations to investments and associated activities of nationals or companies of any third country.

2. (a) Nothing in this Treaty shall be construed to prevent a party from maintaining or establishing a State enterprise.

   (b) Each party shall ensure that any State enterprise that it maintains or establishes acts in a manner that is not inconsistent with the party's obligations under this Treaty wherever such enterprise exercises any regulatory, administrative or other governmental authority that the party has delegated to it, such as the power to expropriate, grant licenses, approve commercial transactions, or impose quotas, fees or other charges.

   (c) Each party shall ensure that any State enterprise that it maintains or establishes accords the better of national or most favoured nation treatment in the sale of its goods or services in the party's territory.

3. (a) Investment shall at all times be accorded fair and equitable treatment, shall enjoy full protection and security and shall in no case be accorded treatment less than that required by international law.

   (b) Neither party shall in any way impair by arbitrary or discriminatory measures the management, operation, maintenance, use, enjoyment, acquisition, expansion, or disposal of investments. For purposes of dispute resolution under Articles VI and VII, a measure may be arbitrary or discriminatory notwithstanding the fact that a party has had or has exercised the opportunity to review such measure in the courts or administrative tribunals of a party.

(c)   Each party shall observe any obligation it may have entered into with regard to investments.

4. Subject to the laws relating to the entry and sojourn of aliens, nationals of either party shall be permitted to enter and to remain in the territory of the other party for the purpose of establishing, developing, administering or advising on the operation of an investment to which they, or a company of the first party that employs them, have committed or are in the process of committing a substantial amount of capital or other resources.

5. Companies which are legally constituted under the applicable laws or regulations of one party, and which are investments, shall be permitted to engage top managerial personnel of their choice, regardless of nationality.

6. Neither party shall impose performance requirements as a condition of establishment, expansion or maintenance of investments, which require or enforce commitments to export goods produced, or which specify that goods or services must be purchased locally, or which impose any other similar requirements.

7. Each party shall provide effective means of asserting claims and enforcing rights with respect to investment, investment agreements, and investment authorisations.

8. Each party shall make public all laws, regulations, administrative practices and procedures, and adjudicatory decisions that pertain to or affect investments.

9. The treatment accorded by the United States of America to investments and associated activities of nationals and companies of the Republic of Ecuador under the provisions of this Article shall in any State, Territory or possession of the United States of America be no less favourable than the treatment accorded therein to investments and associated activities of nationals of the United States of America resident in, and companies legally constituted under the laws and regulations of other States, Territories or possessions of the United States of America.

10. The most favoured nation provisions of this Treaty shall not apply to advantages accorded by either party to nationals or companies of any third country by virtue of:

(a) that party's binding obligations that derive from full membership in a free trade area or customs union; or
(b) that party's binding obligations under any multilateral international agreement under the framework of the General Agreement on Tariffs and Trade that enters into force subsequent to the signature of this Treaty.

Article III

1. Investments shall not be expropriated or nationalised either directly or indirectly through measures tantamount to expropriation or nationalisation ('expropriation') except: for a public purpose; in a nondiscriminatory manner; upon payment of prompt, adequate and effective compensation; and in accordance with due process of law and the general principles of treatment provided for in Article II(3). Compensation shall be equivalent to the fair market value of the expropriated investment immediately before the expropriatory action was taken or became known, whichever is earlier; be calculated in a freely usable currency and the basis of the prevailing market rate of exchange at that time; be paid without delay; include interest at a commercially reasonable rate from the date of expropriation; be fully realisable; and be fully transferable.

2. A national or company of either party that asserts that all or part of its investment has been expropriated shall have a right to prompt review by the appropriate judicial or administrative authorities of the other party to determine whether any such expropriation has occurred and, If so, whether such expropriation, and any associated compensation, conforms to the principles of international law.

3. Nationals or companies of either party whose investments suffer losses in the territory of the other party owing to war or other armed conflict, revolution, state of national emergency, insurrection, civil disturbance or other similar events shall be accorded treatment by such other party no less favourable than that accorded to its own nationals or companies or to nationals or companies of any third country, whichever is the most favorable treatment, as regards any measures it adopts in rotation to such losses.

Article IV

1. Each party shall permit all transfers related to an investment, to be made freely and without delay into and out of its territory. Such transfers include: (a) returns; (b) compensation pursuant to Article III; (c) payments arising out of an investment dispute; (d) payments made under a contract, including amortisation of principal and accrued interest payments made pursuant to a loan agreement; (e) proceeds from the sale or liquidation of all or any part of an investment; and (f) additional contributions to capital for the maintenance or development of an investment.

2. Transfers shall be made in a freely usable currency at the prevailing market rate of exchange on the date of transfer with respect to spot transactions in the currency to be transferred.

3. Notwithstanding the provisions of paragraphs 1 and 2, either party may maintain laws and regulations (a) requiring reports of currency transfer; and (b) imposing income taxes by such means as a withholding tax applicable to dividends or other transfers. Furthermore, either party may protect the rights of creditors, or ensure the satisfaction of judgments in adjudicatory proceedings, through the equitable, nondiscriminatory and good faith application of its law.

Article V

The parties agree to consult promptly, on the request of either, to resolve any disputes in connection with the Treaty, or to discuss any matter relating to the interpretation or application of the Treaty.

Article VI

1. For purposes of this Article, an investment dispute is a dispute between a party and a national or company of the other party arising out of or relating to (a) an investment agreement between that party and such national or company; (b) an investment authorization granted by that party's foreign investment authority to such national or company; or (c) an alleged broach of any right conferred or created by this Treaty with respect to an investment.

2. In the event of an investment dispute, the parties to the dispute should initially seek a resolution through consultation and negotiation. If the dispute cannot be settled amicably, the national or company concerned may choose to submit the dispute, under one of the following alternatives, for resolution:

(a) to the courts or administrative tribunals of the party that is a party to the dispute; or

(b) in accordance with any applicable, previously agreed dispute-settlement procedures; or

(c) in accordance with the terms of paragraph 3.

3. (a) Provided that the national or company concerned has not submitted the dispute for resolution under paragraph 2 (a) or (b) and that six months have elapsed from the date on which the dispute arose, the national or company concerned may choose to consent in writing to the submission of the dispute for settlement by binding arbitration:

(i) to the International Centre for the Settlement of Investment Disputes ('Centre') established by the Convention on the Settlement of Investment Disputes between States and Nationals of other States, done at Washington, March 18, 1965 (IICSID Convention'), provided that the party is a party to such Convention; or

(ii) to the Additional Facility of the Centre, if the Centre is not available; or

(iii) in accordance with the Arbitration Rules of the United Nations Commission on International Trade Law (UNCITRAL), or

(iv) to any other arbitration institution, or in accordance with any other arbitration rules, as may be mutually agreed between the parties to the dispute.

(b) Once the national or company concerned has so consented, either party to the dispute may initiate arbitration in accordance with the choice so specified in the consent.

4. Each party hereby consents to the submission of any investment dispute for settlement by binding arbitration in accordance with the choice specified in the written consent of the national or company under paragraph 3. Such consent, together with the written consent of the national or company when given under paragraph 3 shall satisfy the requirement for:

(a) written consent of the parties to the dispute for purposes of Chapter II of the ICSID Convention (jurisdiction of the Centre) and for purposes of the Additional Facility Rules; and

(b) an 'agreement in writing' for purposes of Article II of the United Nations Convention on the Recognition and Enforcement of Foreign Arbitral Awards, done at New York, June 10, 1958 ('New York Convention').

5. Any arbitration under paragraph 3(a)(ii), (iii) or (iv) of this Article shall be held in a State that is a party to the New York Convention.

6. Any arbitral award rendered pursuant to this Article shall be final and binding on the parties to the dispute. Each party undertakes to carry out without delay the provisions of any such award and to provide in its territory for its enforcement.

7. In any proceeding involving an investment dispute, a party shall not assert, as a defence, counterclaim, right of set-off or otherwise, that the national or company concerned has received or will receive, pursuant to an insurance or guarantee contract, indemnification or other compensation for all or part of its alleged damages.

8. For purposes of an arbitration held under paragraph 3 of this Article, any company legally constituted under the applicable laws and regulations of a party or a political subdivision thereof that, immediately before the occurrence of the event or events giving rise to the dispute, was an investment of nationals or companies of the other party, shall be treated as a national or company of such other party in accordance with Article 25(2)(b) of the ICSID Convention.

Article VII

1. Any dispute between the parties concerning the interpretation or application of the Treaty which is not resolved through consultations or other diplomatic channels, shall be submitted, upon the request of either party, to an arbitral tribunal for binding decision in accordance with the applicable rules of international law. In the absence of an agreement by the parties to the contrary, the arbitration rules of the United Nations commission on international Trade Law (UNCITRAL), except to the extent modified by the parties or by the arbitrators, shall govern.

2. Within two months of receipt of a request, each party shall appoint an arbitrator. The two arbitrators shall select a third arbitrator as chairman, who is a national of a third State. The UNCITRAL Rules for appointing members of three-member panels shall apply *mutatis mutandis* to the appointment of the arbitral panel except that the appointing authority referenced in those rules shall be the Secretary General of the Centre.

3. Unless otherwise agreed, all submissions shall be made and all hearings shall be completed within six months of the date of selection of the third

arbitrator, and the Tribunal shall render its decisions within two months of the date of the final submissions or the date of the closing of the hearings, whichever is later.

4. Expenses incurred by the Chairman, the other arbitrators, and other costs of the proceedings shall be paid for equally by the parties. The Tribunal may, however, at its discretion, direct that a higher proportion of the costs be paid by one of the parties.

Article VIII

This Treaty shall not derogate from:

(a) laws and regulations, administrative practices or procedures, or administrative or adjudicatory decisions of either party;
(b) international legal obligations; or
(c) obligations assumed by either party, including those contained in an investment agreement or an investment authorisation,

that entitle investments or associated activities to treatment more favourable than that accorded by this Treaty in like situations.

Article IX

1. This Treaty shall not preclude the application by either party of measures necessary for the maintenance of public order, the fulfillment of its obligations with respect to the maintenance or restoration of international peace or security, or the protection of its own essential security interests.

2. This Treaty shall not preclude either party from prescribing special formalities in connection with the establishment of investments, but such formalities shall not impair the substance of any of the rights set forth in this Treaty.

Article X

1. With respect to its tax policies, each party should strive to accord fairness and equity in the treatment of investment of nationals and companies of the other party.

2. Nevertheless, the provisions of this Treaty, and in particular Article VI and VII, shall apply to matters of taxation only with respect to the following:

(a)   expropriation, pursuant to Article III;

(b)   transfers, pursuant to Article IV; or

(c)   the observance and enforcement of terms of an investment agreement or authorisation as referred to in Article VI (1) (a) or (b), to the extent they are not subject to the dispute settlement provisions of a Convention for the avoidance of double taxation between the two parties, or have been raised under such settlement provisions and are not resolved within a reasonable period of time.

Article XI

This Treaty shall apply to the political subdivisions of the parties.

Article XII

1. This Treaty shall enter into force 30 days after the data of exchange of instruments of ratification. It shall remain in force for a period of ten years and shall continue in force unless terminated in accordance with paragraph 2 of this Article. It shall apply to investments existing at the time of entry into force as well as to investments made or acquired thereafter.

2. Either party may, by giving one year's written notice to the other party, terminate this Treaty at the end of the initial ten-year period or at any time thereafter.

3. With respect to investments made or acquired prior to the date of termination of this Treaty and to which this Treaty otherwise applies, the provisions of all of the other Articles of this Treaty shall thereafter continue to be effective for a further period of ten years from such date of termination.

4. The Protocol and Side Letter shall form an integral part of the Treaty.

In witness whereof, the respective plenipotentiaries have signed this Treaty.

Done in duplicate at Washington on the twenty-seventh day of August, 1993, in the English and Spanish languages, both texts being equally authentic.

EXERCISE 32 – JURISDICTION II – SEMINAR

 DISCUSSION QUESTIONS

Problem 1

Review the *Generation Ukraine* award and argue against the Tribunal's interpretation of the requirement to exhaust local remedies as part of the merits of the claim.

Problem 2

Review the *Generation Ukraine* award and defend the Tribunal's interpretation of the requirement to exhaust local remedies as part of the merits of the claim.

Problem 3

Explain the *Helnan v Egypt* Annulment Decision and the Committee's interpretation of the requirement to exhaust local remedies. How did it differ from that in *Generation Ukraine*?

Problem 4

The investor Graceful Burials from State X runs a medium-sized funeral business in State Y. A local competitor sues Graceful Burials in a local court in State Y for $10 million, claiming that Graceful Burials has engaged in various unlawful acts in order to dominate the funeral market in State Y. After a heated main hearing – which featured many anti-foreign sentiments and improper language on behalf of the local competitor – a jury orders Graceful Burials to pay $500 million, including punitive damages.

Graceful Burials appeals the jury verdict to an appeals court. In order to proceed with the appeal, the appeals court orders (in compliance with domestic law in State Y) that Graceful Burials must post a bond equal to the damages ordered ($500 million), despite Graceful Burial's claims that this would bankrupt the company. Graceful Burial considers appealing the bond decision to the Supreme Court in State Y, but the company's lawyers advise that such an appeal would be pointless. Unable to post the bond, Graceful Burial instead settles the case for $100 million.

After the settlement, Graceful Burial requests ICSID arbitration against State Y under a bilateral investment treaty, alleging denial of justice on behalf of State Y. How does the factual background affect the Graceful Burial's chance to pursue the ICSID claim?

 CASE

Generation Ukraine, Inc v Ukraine, (ICSID Case No. ARB/00/9), excerpt from award

3. Exhaustion of local remedies

13.1 The respondent maintains that it had the right to insist upon the exhaustion of local remedies by the claimant as a precondition to the submission of the dispute to ICSID arbitration. The source of this right, according to the respondent, is Article 26 of the ICSID Convention, which reads:

Consent of the parties to arbitration under this Convention shall, unless otherwise stated, be deemed consent to such arbitration to the exclusion of any other remedy. A Contracting State may require the exhaustion of local administrative or judicial remedies as a condition of its consent to arbitration under this Convention.

13.2 The respondent submits that the second sentence of Article 26 of the ICSID Convention prevails over Article VI(4) of the BIT, which contains no reference to the local remedies rule, by reason of the *lex specialis* character of the ICSID Convention vis-à-vis the BIT.

13.3 It is not necessary for the Tribunal to consider the relationship between Article 26 of the ICSID Convention and Article VI(4) of the BIT because there is no conflict between these provisions. Article 26 of the ICSID Convention does not assist the respondent in its attempt to impose a procedural obstacle for the claimant's submission to arbitration.

13.4 The first sentence of Article 26 secures the exclusivity of a reference to ICSID arbitration vis-à-vis any other remedy. A logical consequence of this exclusivity is the waiver by Contracting States to the ICSID Convention of the local remedies rule, so that the investor is not compelled to pursue remedies in the respondent State's domestic courts or tribunals before the institution of ICSID proceedings. This waiver is implicit in the second sentence of Article 26, which nevertheless allows [the] Contracting State to reserve its right to insist upon the prior exhaustion of local remedies as a condition of its consent.

13.5 Any such reservation to the Ukraine's consent to ICSID arbitration must be contained in the instrument in which such consent is expressed, i.e., the BIT itself. As the Tribunal put it in *Lanco International Inc v Argentina*:

> A State may require the exhaustion of domestic remedies as a prior condition for its consent to ICSID arbitration. This demand may be made (i) in a bilateral investment treaty that offers submission to ICSID arbitration, (ii) in domestic legislation, or (iii) in a direct investment agreement that contains an ICSID clause.

The United States and Ukraine have elected to omit any requirement that an investor must first exhaust local remedies before submitting a dispute to ICSID arbitration in the BIT. In any case, once the investor has accepted the State's offer to arbitrate in the BIT by filing its Notice of Arbitration, no further limitations or restrictions on the reference to arbitration can be imposed unilaterally, whether by the State or by the investor.

13.6 For these reasons, the respondent's reliance on Article 26 is unfounded. The claimant was under no constraint to exhaust any remedies in the Ukrainian courts before filing its Notice of Arbitration to the ICSID Centre.

[…]

20. First alleged expropriation

20.1 The claimant submits that the 'indirect ("first") global expropriation of the company's rights and property' occurred on 31 October 1997 'by virtue of the [Kyiv City State Administration]'s failure to produce revised land lease agreements with valid site drawings'. This is characterised by the claimant as the beginning of the dispute.

20.2 The claimant relies on the Yalovoy Protocol as creating a legal obligation upon Kyiv City State Administration and the Kyiv City Department of Land Resources to issue Heneratsiya with a new set of land lease agreements that incorporated corrected site plans by 31 October 1997. The background to the Yalovoy Protocol has been explained previously at paragraphs 18.47 et seq. The claimant submits that new land lease agreements were required to reflect changes in its design that were necessitated by the SBU's demands. Hence the inclusion of point 13 of the Yalovoy Protocol which reads:

> To change the boundaries of the land parcels of Heneratsiya Ltd, SB Ukraine, the Financial Directorate, and the International Business Centre by taking into account the situation which developed around these approved projects and with the consent of the landholders.

20.3 Responsibility for implementation of point 13 was placed on the Kyiv City Department of Land Resources. The 'authentic' (as the claimant would have it) version of the Yalovoy Protocol imposed a deadline of 31 October 1997 for this amendment, whereas the 'falsified' (idem) version extended the date to 1 February 1998.

20.4 The claimant also submits that, even in the absence of the Yalovoy Protocol, the Kyiv City State Administration and Kyiv City Department of Land Resources 'could not lawfully escape the obligation to prepare new site plans approved for the new building by the Kyiv Architectural Council that was designed especially for the SBU/KGB'.

20.5 The source of the obligation to provide amended lease agreements was therefore either the Yalovoy Protocol or Ukrainian law relating to land use.

20.6 The claimant submits that the Kyiv City State Administration's failure to comply with this obligation effectively put an end to the Parkview Project because it created an insurmountable obstacle for any construction work to lawfully proceed. Mr Laka explained the ramifications of this omission as follows:

> The Land Code of Ukraine requires that any land lease agreement correctly and properly reflect the territory to which the land user has lawful access. Our old land lease agreements did not correctly and properly reflect the territory to which we were now being given access, so they became unlawful.

20.7 It is important first to identify the object of the alleged expropriation. The claimant has persistently asserted that this omission on the part of the Kyiv City State Administration constitutes the final and irreparable destruction of the Parkview Project. Hence the issue becomes the precise nature of the 'Parkview Project' on 31 October 1997.

20.8 It will be recalled that the claimant interprets Certificate B issued by the State Agency of Ukraine for Author's and Joint Rights on 5 June 1998 as giving effect to the claimant's ownership rights over the Parkview Project in its entirety. This interpretation of the scope of the rights contemplated by Certificate B has been rejected by the Tribunal. Independently of this finding, it is important to point out the contradiction in the claimant's pleadings, for if its interpretation were to be accepted, it would not be possible for the entire Parkview Project to be expropriated before the point in time at which the claimant's rights to the project were perfected. The truth of the matter is that, as of 31 October 1997, the claimant had a very limited bundle of rights arising under the Order on Land Allocation, Lease Agreements, Foundation Agreement and Construction Permit. Thus, if the Kyiv City State Administration's omission on 31 October 1997 did constitute an expropriation, it could only have deprived the claimant of these legal interests and them alone.

20.9 The claimant's reliance on Certificate B as the penultimate and definitive source of its rights in the Parkview Project gives rise to another contradiction. The claimant invokes the Yalovoy Protocol as the source of the legal obligation upon the Kyiv City State Administration to provide a set of amended lease agreements. The beneficiary of this obligation was Heneratsiya as the signatory to the Yalovoy Protocol and the named leasee pursuant to the Lease Agreements. According to the claimant's submissions, however, the 'entire' Parkview Project was not transferred from Generation Ukraine to Heneratsiya until the Act of Property Transfer was signed on 21

July 1998. Thus it is difficult to see how the Kyiv City State Administration's omission vis-à-vis Heneratsiya on 31 October 1997 could have the effect that the claimant alleges if the claimant's interpretation of Certificate B were to be accepted.

20.10 It is necessary to consider some facts surrounding the Kyiv City State Administration's failure, by 31 October 1997, to provide a set of amended lease agreements to properly reflect changes to the boundaries of the territory to which the claimant, through Heneratsiya, had a leasehold interest.

20.11 According to the claimant, these changes were necessitated by reason of the SBU's demands for a buffer zone around their building on the neighbouring property. Such demands were first communicated by the SBU on 20 February 1997, by which time Heneratsiya had obtained Construction Permit No.103-Rd to commence construction at its site.

20.12 The SBU's demands necessitated corrections to the design of the Parkview Office building. These corrections were approved by the relevant Ukrainian authorities and a new Construction Permit No.189-P(d) was issued on 17 July 1998. The Yalovoy Protocol was drafted to regulate this and several other outstanding issues following the meeting on 11 July 1997.

20.13 In recognition of the additional expense incurred by the claimant in modifying its existing architectural plans to comply with SBU's demands, amendments were made to the Foundation Agreement which, inter alia, exempted Heneratsiya from land payments until the date a construction permit is obtained for the revised design. The payments envisaged under clause 4.1 of the Foundation Agreement were also reduced significantly. Concomitantly, the date of the commencement of construction was postponed to December 1998. These amendments were signed by Mr Laka on behalf of Heneratsiya on 25 August 1998 and by Mr Omelchenko of Kyiv City State Administration on 4 December 1998. The latter issued a Ruling by the Kyiv City State Administration on the same day to give administrative effect to these changes.

20.14 At a meeting attended by Mr Yalovoy, Mr Omelchenko and Mr Laka on 25 December 1998, Mr Laka was informed that there was no longer any administrative obstacle to the commencement of construction. Mr Yalovoy reiterated this position in letters to Mr Laka and the US Ambassador in Kyiv dated 20 January 1999 and 28 January 1999 respectively. Mr Laka wrote to the US Ambassador on 4 February 1999 to challenge the Kyiv City State Administration's position that there were no further obstacles preventing construction at Heneratsiya's site and cited the following 'major problems' that remained outstanding:

- the uncertainty concerning Heneratsiya's liability in the event that the roof of a neighbouring derelict building collapses during construction on Heneratsiya's site;
- Heneratsiya's unjustified prepayment of 15 months' rent instead of three Months' rent, amounting to an 'interest free loan' of USD 12,145.53;
- the failure of the Kyiv City State Administration to procure the temporary use of the neighbouring property (leased by IBC) for Heneratsiya as a construction staging area in accordance with point 10 of the Yalovoy Protocol;
- the failure of the Kyiv City State Administration to release a copy of the order granting a section of Heneratsiya's territory covered by its three-year lease to the SBU;
- the failure of a neighbouring occupant to gain a 'technical exemption Approval' for a sewage line encroaching on the property of Heneratsiya;
- the fact that the same neighbouring occupant commenced construction on a portion of Heneratsiya's territory preventing the installation of hot water, electricity and water lines;
- the failure of the Kyiv City State Administration to 'produce a pair of simple, two-page documents' to effect amendments to Heneratsiya's two land lease agreements;
- the failure of Mr Omelchenko to reprimand Mr Karminsky for attempting to invalidate Heneratsiya's construction permit;
- the fact that Heneratsiya must have guaranteed access to Mr Omelchenko 'when it needs it to resolve critical issues';
- the fact that Heneratsiya must have 'Mr Omelchenko's guarantee to the company regarding his personal protection of [Heneratsiya's] project..'

20.15 Mr Laka concluded this letter with the following statement, the first sentence of which appeared in bold, underlined and in capital letters:

> The Kyiv City State Administration, in the past, has repeatedly left matters unresolved resulting in persistent interruptions in the company's project. Therefore, the company is unwilling to move forward at any level of effort on its project until each and every outstanding problem is fully resolved.

20.16 This letter has been summarised in detail because it is the most comprehensive contemporaneous account of the types of grievances that, according to the claimant, prevented the realisation of its Parkview Project following its receipt of a Construction Permit. In its pleaded case, the claimant has attached particular significance to the Kyiv City State Administration's failure to execute amended land lease agreements by labelling this as an expropriatory act for the purpose of Article III of the BIT.

20.17 In its defence to this alleged act of expropriation, the respondent denies that the Kyiv City State Administration was under any obligation to issue amended land lease agreements pursuant to the Yalovoy Protocol or otherwise. Furthermore, the respondent submits that Heneratsiya did not itself comply with its own obligations under the Yalovoy Protocol by failing to procure the requisite approvals for the relevant version of its design of the Parkview Project office building, which in turn would have prevented the Kyiv City State Administration from issuing the aforementioned amended land lease agreements. Finally, the respondent contests the necessity of amending the leases at all in order for Heneratsiya to proceed with construction.

20.18 The Tribunal notes that there is serious disagreement between the parties about the existence of an obligation on the part of the Kyiv City State Administration, whether pursuant to the Yalovoy Protocol or arising under general Ukrainian law, to issue amended land lease agreements. There is also serious disagreement about whether or not the claimant was in a position to proceed with the construction of its Parkview Office Building in the absence of these amended lease agreements.

20.19 In order to analyse the respondent's international obligations under the BIT, the Tribunal will put this controversy to one side and accept the facts as pleaded by the claimant in order to test the respondent's conduct against the standard of investment protection encapsulated in Article III of the BIT. Article III provides:

> 1. Investments shall not be expropriated or nationalised either directly or indirectly through measures tantamount to expropriation or nationalisation (expropriation) except: for a public purpose; in a nondiscriminatory manner; upon payment of prompt, adequate and effective compensation; and in accordance with due process of law and the general principles of treatment provided for in article II(2). Compensation shall be equivalent to the fair market value of the expropriated investment immediately before the expropriatory action was taken or become known, whichever is earlier; be calculated in a freely usable currency on the basis of the prevailing market rate of exchange at that time; be paid without delay; include interest at a commercially reasonable rate, such as LIBOR plus an appropriate margin, from the date of expropriation; be fully realisable; and be freely transferable.
>
> 2. A national or company of either party that asserts that all or part of its

investment has been expropriated shall have a right to prompt review by the appropriate judicial or administrative authorities of the other party to determine whether such expropriation has occurred and, if so, whether such expropriation, and any associated compensation, conforms to the principles of international law.

20.20 The formulation in the first sentence of Article III(1) is somewhat circular by prohibiting an expropriation by measures tantamount to expropriation. Nevertheless, it is perfectly clear that the State Parties to the BIT envisaged that both direct and indirect forms of expropriation are to be covered by Article III.

20.21 The alleged final expropriatory act or measure, as previously mentioned, is said to be the failure by the Kyiv City State Administration to issue amended lease agreements. The disputed measure cannot possibly constitute a direct expropriation of the claimant's investment because the Kyiv City State Administration never purported to transfer Heneratsiya's proprietary rights in its investment to the State or to a third party. Quite properly, the claimant has never sought to characterise the disputed measure as a direct expropriation. Instead, the claimant has, in its written and oral pleadings, contended that this disputed measure was the culmination of a series of other prejudicial acts that ultimately deprived the claimant of its rights to its investment, due to the level of resulting interference. The various measures of the respondent thus, according to the claimant, amounted to a 'creeping expropriation'.

20.22 Creeping expropriation is a form of indirect expropriation with a distinctive temporal quality in the sense that it encapsulates the situation whereby a series of acts attributable to the State over a period of time culminate in the expropriatory taking of such property. The case of German Interests in Polish Upper Silesia is one of many examples of an indirect expropriation without a 'creeping' element – the seizure of a factory and its machinery by the Polish Government was held by the PCIJ to constitute an indirect taking of the patents and contracts belonging to the management company of the factory because they were so closely interrelated with the factory itself. But although international precedents on indirect expropriation are plentiful, it is difficult to find many cases that fall squarely into the more specific paradigm of creeping expropriation.

20.23 The *Tippetts, Abbett, McCarthy, Stratton v TAMS-AFFA Consulting Engineers of Iran, et al.* case before the Iran/US Claims Tribunal might be said to demonstrate the possibility of a taking through the combined effect of several acts. The Iranian Government appointed a temporary manager of the joint venture investment company in which the claimant had a 50 per cent stakehold with the 50 per cent owned by an Iranian entity. The temporary manager commenced his duties in August 1979 and immediately breached the partnership agreement that regulated the joint venture by signing cheques on the partnership's accounts by himself and making other decisions without consulting the claimant. The claimant managed to rectify these violations of the partnership agreement. Thus, for instance, the practice of two signatures on cheques was restored. The hostage crisis at the US Embassy in Tehran then intervened in November 1979 and the working relationship that had developed between the temporary manager and the claimant came to an end. The claimant's representatives left Iran in December 1979 and thereafter the management of the joint venture ceased all communication with the claimant with respect to its business operations. The Iran/US Claims Tribunal reflected upon the nature of the indirect taking in light of these facts in the following oft-cited passage:

> A deprivation or taking of property may occur under international law through interference by a State in the use of that property or with the enjoyment of its benefits, even where legal title to the property is not affected. While assumption of control over property by a government does not automatically and immediately justify a conclusion that the property has been taken by the government, thus requiring compensation under international law, such a conclusion is warranted whenever events demonstrate that the owner was deprived of the fundamental rights of ownership and it appears that this deprivation is not merely ephemeral. The intent of the government is less important than the effects of the measures on the owner, and the form of the measures of control or interference is less important than the reality of their impact.

20.24 The Tribunal held that the taking of the claimant's property was consummated not when the temporary manager was first appointed in August 1979, but in March 1980 by which time the tentative co-operation between the claimant and the temporary manager had come to an end.

20.25 The *Tippetts* case was cited with approval in a recent ICSID arbitration in *Compañia del Desarrollo de Santa Elena, SA v The Republic of Costa Rica*. The following statement of principle provides useful guidance in the analysis of the claimant's plea of creeping expropriation in the circumstances of the present case:

> As is well known, there is a wide spectrum of measures that a State may take in asserting control over property, extending from limited regulation of its use to a complete and formal deprivation of the owner's legal title. Likewise, the period of

time involved in the process may vary – from an immediate and comprehensive taking to one that only gradually and by small steps reaches a condition in which it can be said that the owner has truly lost all the attributes of ownership. It is clear, however, that a measure or series of measures can still eventually amount to a taking, though the individual steps in the process do not formally purport to amount to a taking or to a transfer of title. . ..

There is ample authority for the proposition that a property has been expropriated when the effect of the measures taken by the state has been to deprive the owner of title, possession or access to the benefit and economic use of his property. . ..

20.26 The claimant's submissions on its plea of creeping expropriation have been seriously flawed due to the absence of a coherent analysis of the timing and the nature of its investments in Ukraine and how the acts and omissions of the Kyiv City State Administration have affected the claimant's investment in the form it existed at the time of those acts and omissions. A plea of creeping expropriation must proceed on the basis that the investment existed at a particular point in time and that subsequent acts attributable to the State have eroded the investor's rights to its investment to an extent that is violative of the relevant international standard of protection against expropriation. It is conceptually possible to envisage a case of creeping expropriation where the investor's interests in its investment develop in parallel with the commission of the acts complained of. But such a plea, in order to be successful, would demand a high level of analytical rigorousness and precision that is absent from the submissions before this Tribunal.

20.27 The claimant's pleadings assume that the claimant had a vested right to a commercial return on a completed office building, on or before the alleged final act of expropriation on 31 October 1997. This cannot possibly be so. As of 31 October 1997, not a single brick had been laid, nor had the foundations for the building been excavated, nor indeed had the claimant definitively secured financing for the construction phase of the Parkview Project. The materialisation of the claimant's legal interests – evidenced by the Order on Land Allocation, Lease Agreements, Foundation Agreement and Construction Permit – translate not to a right to a commercial return, but simply to proceed with the construction of the Parkview Office building on land over which Heneratsiya had a 49-year-leasehold interest.

20.28 The Kyiv City State Administration's omission on 31 October 1997 did not have the express intention of depriving the claimant of the legal basis of this right to proceed to construction. The question is, therefore, whether on this date the alleged cumulative interference on the part of the Kyiv City

State Administration nevertheless constituted an 'indirect' expropriation for the purposes of Article III of the BIT.

20.29 Predictability is one of the most important objectives of any legal system. It would be useful if it were absolutely clear in advance whether particular events fall within the definition of an 'indirect' expropriation. It would enhance the sentiment of respect for legitimate expectations if it were perfectly obvious why, in the context of a particular decision, an arbitral tribunal found that a governmental action or inaction crossed the line that defines acts amounting to an indirect expropriation. But there is no checklist, no mechanical test to achieve that purpose. The decisive considerations vary from case to case, depending not only on the specific facts of a grievance but also on the way the evidence is presented, and the legal bases pleaded. The outcome is a judgment, i.e., the product of discernment, and not the printout of a computer programme.

20.30 The fact that an investment has become worthless obviously does not mean that there was an act of expropriation; investment always entails risk. Nor is it sufficient for the disappointed investor to point to some governmental initiative, or inaction, which might have contributed to his ill fortune. Yet again, it is not enough for an investor to seize upon an act of maladministration, no matter how low the level of the relevant governmental authority; to abandon his investment without any effort at overturning the administrative fault; and thus to claim an international delict on the theory that there had been an uncompensated virtual expropriation. In such instances, an international tribunal may deem that the failure to seek redress from national authorities disqualifies the international claim, not because there is a requirement of exhaustion of local remedies but because the very reality of conduct tantamount to expropriation is doubtful in the absence of a reasonable – not necessarily exhaustive – effort by the investor to obtain correction.

20.31 As stated earlier, the claimant's pleadings do not disclose an analysis of the acts attributable to the respondent, occurring between 16 November 1996 and 31 October 1997, that purportedly interfered with its right to proceed with the construction of the Parkview office building (leaving aside the question of whether such a right existed throughout this entire period commencing from the date of the Tribunal's jurisdiction *ratione temporis*). Nevertheless, Mr Laka's letter to the US Ambassador in Kyiv dated 4 February 1999 (see para 20.14) provides a detailed account of all the obstacles (mostly in the form of administrative omissions) that he alleged prevented him from proceeding with the construction of his Parkview Office Building. Although it is far from certain that all these purported obstacles existed on or before 31

October 1997, Mr Laka's list of outstanding grievances nevertheless gives a flavour of the other acts that could form the series of measures constituting a creeping expropriation. The final alleged act of expropriation that was identified was the Kyiv City State Administration's failure to issue amended lease agreements.

20.32 The Tribunal finds that the conduct of the Kyiv City State Administration in the period 16 November 1996 to 31 October 1997 does not come close to creating a persistent or irreparable obstacle to the claimant's use, enjoyment or disposal of its investment. The Tribunal's conclusion would be no different if the relevant period were to be extended to the date when the claimant instituted these proceedings.

20.33 No act or omission of the Kyiv City State Administration during this period, whether cumulatively or in isolation, transcends the threshold for an indirect expropriation. This Tribunal does not exercise the function of an administrative review body to ensure that municipal agencies perform their tasks diligently, conscientiously or efficiently. That function is within the proper domain of domestic courts and tribunals that are cognisant of the minutiae of the applicable regulatory regime. In the circumstances of this case, the conduct cited by the claimant was never challenged before the domestic courts of Ukraine. More precisely, the claimant did not attempt to compel the Kyiv City State Administration to rectify the alleged omissions in its administrative management of the Parkview Project by instituting proceedings in the Ukrainian courts. There is, of course, no formal obligation upon the claimant to exhaust local remedies before resorting to ICSID arbitration pursuant to the BIT. Nevertheless, in the absence of any per se violation of the BIT discernable from the relevant conduct of the Kyiv City State Administration, the only possibility in this case for the series of complaints relating to highly technical matters of Ukrainian planning law to be transformed into a BIT violation would have been for the claimant to be denied justice before the Ukrainian courts in a bona fide attempt to resolve these technical matters.

20.34 In *Feldman v Mexico*, the arbitral tribunal found that although 'the claimant, through the respondent's actions, is no longer able to engage in his business' as a result of the elimination of a tax rebate on export resales of cigarettes, and although 'it is undeniable that the claimant has experienced great difficulties in dealing with [Ministry] officials, and in some respects has been treated in a less than reasonable manner', the Mexican Government's regulatory actions were, on balance, not equivalent to an expropriation. In declining to find that the claimant's allegations of unlawful administrative actions constituted expropriation, the Tribunal took account of the availability of court review of those administrative actions. The claimant contended that those actions violated both Mexican judicial precedents and a specific agreement between governmental officials and the claimant. The arbitral tribunal summarised its rationale under four points which may be paraphrased as follows: (1) 'not every business problem experienced by a foreign investor in an expropriation', (2) neither general international law nor the relevant treaty required the State to permit the kind of activity which was impeded by adverse regulation, (3) local law did not create the right to engage in such activity and (4) control of the corporate vehicle for the investment remained in the hands of the claimant, with the 'apparent right' to pursue its activities in conformity with Mexican regulations. The arbitral tribunal concluded: 'while none of the factors alone is necessary conclusive, in the Tribunal's view taken together they tip the expropriation/regulation balance away from a finding of expropriation'. The parallels with the precedent case where the claimant argues that the Kyiv authorities violated both Ukrainian law and specific agreements with the investor, are evident.

20.35 In *Feldman v Mexico*, although the Tribunal recognised that use of the power of taxation could constitute acts tantamount to expropriation, it was influenced by the victim's failure to seek 'formal, binding rulings' with respect to what he viewed as the irregular denial of certain tax benefit which had motivated his investment. The arbitrators wrote:

> It is unclear why he refrained from seeking clarification, but he did so at his peril, particularly given that he was dealing with tax laws and tax authorities, which are subject to extensive formalities in Mexico and in most other countries of the world.

20.36 In *Middle East Cement Shipping and Handling Co SA v Arab Republic of Egypt*, the act found to be 'tantamount to expropriation' was a decree, signed by the competent Minister and published in the Egyptian Gazette, and containing the following simple resolution: 'To prohibit the import of all kinds of Gray Portland Cement either through the Public Governmental Sector or the Private Sector.' The decree was found to contradict the terms of an import license in reliance upon which the relevant investment had been made. Moreover, the respondent conceded that the decree had deprived the claimant of rights under the license for 'at least a period of four months'. It did not agree to the ten-year duration allegation by the claimant. The difference with the present case is palpable, both with respect to the clear and categorical effect of the governmental measure, and the level of government at which it was taken.

20.37 Finally, it is relevant to consider the vicissitudes of the economy of the State that is host to the investment in determining the investor's legitimate expectations, the protection of which is a major concern of the minimum standards of treatment contained in bilateral investment treaties. The claimant was attracted to the Ukraine because of the possibility of earning a rate of return on its capital in significant excess to the other investment opportunities in more developed economies. The claimant thus invested in the Ukraine on notice of both the prospects and the potential pitfalls. Its investment was speculative. Perhaps for this very reason, the claimant was cautious about contributing substantial sums of its own money to the enterprise, preferring to seek capital from third parties to finance the construction of the building. By 31 October 1997, the claimant had undoubtedly experienced frustration and delay caused by bureaucratic incompetence and recalcitrance in various forms. But equally, the claimant had managed to secure a 49-year leasehold over prime commercial property in the centre of Kyiv without having participated in a competitive tender and without having made any substantial payment to the Ukrainian authorities.

20.38 For these reasons, the Tribunal rejects the claimant's submission that an 'indirect ... global expropriation of the company's rights and property' occurred on 31 October 1997 'by virtue of the [Kyiv City State Administration]'s failure to produce revised land lease agreements with valid site drawings'.

 CASE

Helnan International Hotels A/S and Arab Republic of Egypt (ICSID Case No ARB/05/19) annulment proceeding

[. . .]

I. Procedural history

1. On 30 October 2008, the International Centre for the Settlement of Investment Disputes ('ICSID' or 'the Centre') received from Helnan International Hotels A/S (formerly Scandinavian Management Co AlS) ('Helnan' or 'the applicant'), an Application for Annulment of the Award rendered on 3 July 2008 in the arbitration proceeding between Helnan and the Arab Republic of Egypt ('Egypt' or 'the respondent'), by the Arbitral Tribunal comprised of Mr Yves Derains (Chairman), Professor Rudolf Dolzer and Mr Michael Lee (the Tribunal), in a dispute arising under the

Bilateral Investment Treaty dated 24 June 1999 between the Arab Republic of Egypt and the Kingdom of Denmark (the BIT).

2. The Application for Annulment was submitted within the time period provided for by Article 52(2) of the Convention on the Settlement of Investment Disputes between States and Nationals of Other States (the ICSID Convention). On 10 November 2008, the Centre registered the Application for Annulment.

3. On 22 December 2008, an ad hoc Committee composed of Judge Stephen M Schwebel (President), Judge Bola A Ajibola, and Professor Campbell A McLachlan, was constituted to pass upon that application. Ms Natali Sequeira was designated by ICSID to serve as Secretary of the Committee.

4. The Committee held its first procedural session with the parties at the seat of the Centre in Washington, DC on 6 February 2009. During the session, the parties confirmed that they did not have any objections to the proper constitution of the Committee and that its members had been validly appointed in accordance with the arbitration agreement, the ICSID Convention and the ICSID Rules of Procedure for Arbitration Proceedings (the Arbitration Rules). During the session the parties also agreed on a number of procedural matters reflected in the minutes signed by the President and the Secretary of the Committee. In particular, these matters concerned:

(i)   the representation of the parties;
(ii)   the advance payments to the Centre;
(iii)   the fees and expenses of the Committee Members;
(iv)   the applicable Arbitration Rules;
(v)   the place of proceedings;
(vi)   the procedural language;
(vii)   the records of the hearings;
(viii)   the means of communication and copies of instruments;
(ix)   the presence and quorum for meetings of the Committee;
(x)   the decisions of the Committee by correspondence;
(xi)   the delegation of power to the President of the Committee to fix time limits;
(xii)   the written and oral phases of the proceeding;
(xiii)   number, sequence and schedule of written pleadings;
(xiv)   scheduling of a pre-hearing conference;
(xv)   the production of evidence and witnesses' testimony;
(xvi)   the dates and nature of subsequent hearings; and
(xvii)   publication of decisions related to the proceeding.

5. Helnan's Memorial on its Application for Annulment (Memorial) was filed on 21 April 2009. Egypt's Counter-Memorial (Counter-Memorial) was filed on 22 June 2009. Helnan's Reply Memorial (Reply) was filed on 22 July 2009 and Egypt's Rejoinder (Rejoinder) was filed on 13 August 2009. A Hearing was held in the Peace Palace at The Hague on 19 October 2009.

II. Background

6. The dispute addressed in the Award concerned Helnan's eviction from the management of the Shepheard Hotel in Cairo (the Hotel), following:

(a) a decision on the part of the Ministry of Tourism to downgrade the hotel's classification from the five-star status required under Helnan's long-term Management Contract (the Management Contract) with the Egyptian Organisation for Tourism and Hotels (EGOTH); and,

(b) an award of 20 December 2004 by an arbitral tribunal appointed under the aegis of the Cairo Regional Centre for International Commercial Arbitration to decide the contractual dispute between Helnan and EGOTH (the Cairo Arbitration).

That latter award, in the making of which appointees of the parties took part, unanimously terminated the Management Contract on the ground that it was impossible to execute, and that both parties were responsible for failing to execute the contract. The tribunal awarded a sum to Helnan in settlement of debts, which Helnan encashed. The Cairo tribunal did not consider any claims for breach of treaty, no such claims having been submitted to it.

7. During the ICSID arbitration proceeding, the Tribunal decided that it had jurisdiction over Helnan's claims, and that those claims were admissible. However, it dismissed all of Helnan's claims on the merits.

8. Helnan now seeks annulment of the ICSID Award, invoking three grounds specified under Article 52(1) of the ICSID Convention: (a) that the award has failed to state the reasons on which it is based; (b) that the Tribunal has manifestly exceeded its powers and (c) that there has been a serious departure from a fundamental rule of procedure. It challenges four findings made in the Award as meriting annulment:

(a) the finding that Egypt's plan to terminate the Management Contract cannot constitute a treaty violation;

(b) the finding that all Helnan's claims are disqualified because it did not challenge the downgrade in the Egyptian courts;

(c) the finding that conduct of EGOTH and Ministry of Tourism officials did not go beyond contractual matters and commercial motivation; and,

(d) the finding that Helnan's claims fail due to lack of legal causality.

9. For the reasons set out below, arguments (a), (c) and (d) do not justify annulment of the Award. The position is different in relation to argument (b) (failure to challenge the decision in the Egyptian courts). The Tribunal's finding on this issue (principally found in the Award at para 148) was a manifest excess of its powers. An ICSID Tribunal may not decline to make a finding of breach of treaty on the ground that the investor ought to have pursued local remedies or otherwise validated the substance of its claims by recourse to the courts of the host State. Although this part of the Award must be annulled, it was not essential to the Tribunal's decision to dismiss Helnan's claims. Therefore, there is no ground to set aside the Tribunal's decision on the merits of the dispute as provided in operative paragraphs 169 and 170 of the Award.

Memorial. Part V.

10. This Decision sets out the reasons for this conclusion, taking each of the impugned bases of the Tribunal's Award in turn, and summarising the parties' respective submissions, followed by the Committee's evaluation of them.

HI. Treaty consequences of plan to terminate the management contract

(a) Helnan's case

11. Helnan seeks annulment of the Award on the ground that the Tribunal characterised the inspection of the hotel on 4 September 2003 as 'a semblance', conceived as a mere formality deprived of any substance, and part of the implementation of an already taken decision to immediately downgrade the Shepheard Hotel. The Tribunal found the circumstances of the September inspection to be 'very suspicious'. Nevertheless the Tribunal held that Egypt had not breached its treaty obligations, relying for this purpose on the June 2003 inspection. The Tribunal held that:

> This does not necessarily lead to the conclusion that because of this suspicious inspection and the following downgrade, Egypt is responsible for breaches of the Treaty provisions. It must be recognised that the decision to downgrade the hotel could as well have been taken after the 14 June 2003 inspection, as suggested by the subsequent Memorandum submitted to the Minister of Tourism. . ..
>
> This was not done and, instead, the Egyptian administration decided that it had to organise a semblance of an inspection to produce a report which reached

the same result as the June report. The Tribunal cannot ignore that after the 28 June letter of the Ministry of Tourism, Helnan never seriously challenged the conclusions in favour of the downgrading of the hotel. Its main line of argument was to put the responsibility on EGOTH. As already pointed out, the allocation of the responsibility for the downgrading was of a contractual nature outside the scope of jurisdiction of this Arbitral Tribunal. Under these circumstances, the downgrading as such cannot amount to a breach of Egypt's obligations under the Treaty, even if the procedure followed was rather suspicious.

12. Helnan contends that the foregoing holding was a serious departure from a fundamental rule of procedure, since the legal status and consequences of the June 2003 inspection was not an issue submitted by either party for decision. A tribunal is not entitled to adjudge a dispute on a ground not argued by either of the parties. Second, the Tribunal failed to state the reasons on which its conclusion in this respect was based; its reasoning in this respect being inconsistent and contradictory. Third, the Tribunal manifestly exceeded its powers. Helnan relies in this respect on the foregoing points. It also submits that the Tribunal exceeded its powers by applying Egyptian law rather than international law as an excuse for non-compliance with the Treaty. Helnan criticises in this respect the Tribunal's reliance on the June 2003 Memorandum of the Ministry of Tourism as an instrument of Egyptian law, contending that it should instead have considered and applied the treaty standard.

(b) Egypt's reply

13. Egypt replies to Helnan's arguments by submitting that in fact the Tribunal's reflections on the September inspection were superfluous, since it had already legitimately found that grounds existed for the downgrade following the June inspection. Egypt's approach in organising the September inspection was unsurprising since '[c]ountless parties around the world every day consider how they might put their co-contractants formally in breach when they are confident that material grounds therefore are extant'. It argues that Helnan's submission on failure to be heard on the import of the June inspection mistakes the nature of the Award's findings. The Award did not find that the June inspection was itself a breach of the Treaty. It rather held that Helnan's loss of the Management Contract resulted from the contractual termination ordered in the Cairo Arbitration.

(c) The Tribunal's approach

14. The Tribunal dealt with the relationship between the June and September inspections in the following way in its Award:

(a) It observed that the essence of Helnan's claim was that Egypt had orchestrated a series of events which ultimately led to Helnan's eviction from the hotel, because Egypt considered that the Management Contract was an obstacle to the privatisation of the hotel. Both the June and September inspections were alleged by Helnan to be part of that single strategy. As a result of it, Helnan claimed that its investment had been expropriated and that it had been treated unfairly and inequitably.

(b) As to the June inspection itself, the Tribunal recorded Helnan's observation that this inspection did not follow customary practice. But the Tribunal also found that the inspection had concluded that the hotel was not of a five-star standard. This finding was not challenged by Helnan at the time – a fact that was unsurprising since the problems with the hotel had persisted for some years, there being an outstanding and longstanding dispute between Helnan and EGOTH as to which of them was financially responsible for the investments required to upgrade and maintain the hotel at a five-star standard. Given this broader context, the June inspection did not violate the principle of fair and equitable treatment.

(c) Against this background, the September inspection was a 'mere formality', since the decision to downgrade could have been taken after the June inspection. Helnan never challenged the substantive findings of the June inspection, since its real dispute was a contractual one – that EGOTH and not Helnan had financial responsibility for the necessary works.

(d) The Committee's analysis

15. Helnan's argument takes the June inspection out of the context in which the issue arose for decision and was decided by the Tribunal. Helnan invited the Tribunal to consider the June inspection as part of its narrative of complaint as to an orchestrated campaign by Egypt to evict Helnan from the hotel. It figures as part of Helnan's allegation of an orchestrated 2003 inspection and downgrade in its Memorial on the Merits (paras 119–121). In Helnan's Post-hearing Memorial, the June and September inspections are dealt with collectively under the heading: 'The Summer 2003 inspections and downgrade breached Egypt's treaty obligations' (paras 68–79). After devoting some ten paragraphs to the June inspection and report, Helnan then adds a section under the heading: 'The September inspection also did not conform to standard procedure.'

16. Thus, Helnan correctly accepted before the ad hoc Committee that the parties did refer to the June inspection in their arguments. But the June

inspection evidently played a role in Helnan's submissions which went beyond it being merely part of a sequence of facts which led ultimately to the September inspection. Rather, the June inspection was itself part of Helnan's claim of unfair and inequitable treatment.

17. Egypt, for its part, denied that the downgrade was collusive, claiming instead that it was 'the culmination of a long series of inspectoral condemnations stretching over several years'. Helnan's objections to the June and September 2003 reports and the alleged failure to provide a reasonable opportunity to cure the violations referred to in them was 'self-defeating because the 2003 reports basically reiterate violations already reported in previous years'.

18. The report on the June inspection of the hotel, which was part of the evidence before the Tribunal concludes at paras 3(d)–(e):

(d)   The management of the hotel previously received a notice and it was notified several times with remarks in order to act accordingly. However, the management of the hotel does not respond and does not observe such remarks. *Consequently, the hotel will be downgraded to four stars*
. . ...

(e)   Because the hotel is owned by the State (Egoth Company) and because there was a contract between the owning company and the management company, we suppose the following:
To consider the hotel position with the owning company before imposing penalties (by downgrading its class), so that such penalties are not used for the benefit of one of the parties in such a manner as to adversely impact the public interest. (emphasis added.)

19. Helnan devoted extensive evidence and submissions to rebutting this element of Egypt's defence, arguing that the July and September 2003 reports were different in kind from those rendered in 2002 and further contending that the hotel was of a five-star standard.

20. It is no part of the function of an annulment committee to reconsider findings of fact made by an ICSID arbitral tribunal. Rather the issues for this Committee are circumscribed by the terms of Article 52(1) of the ICSID Convention and relate to the Tribunal itself: its powers; its process; and the reasoning of its Award.

21. The above exposition demonstrates that the June 2003 inspection and report was the subject of detailed submissions and evidence, because Helnan

had included it as part of its complaint of failure to provide fair and equitable treatment under the Treaty.

22. Each of the parties presented a very different theory to the Tribunal as to the significance of the June inspection. For Helnan, it was another instance of its allegation of Egypt's orchestrated campaign to oust it from the hotel in order to prepare for privatisation. For Egypt, it was merely confirmatory of the inadequate standard of the hotel, which was the subject of an ongoing and unresolved contractual dispute between Helnan and EGOTH.

23. The task for the Tribunal was thus to decide upon its own interpretation of the significance of factual events in order to decide the claims of breach of Treaty before it. In this context, the observations of the ad hoc committee in the first decision on annulment in *Vivendi v Argentina*, paras 84–85, are apposite:

> It may be true that the particular approach adopted by the Tribunal in attempting to reconcile the various conflicting elements of the case before it came as a surprise to the parties, or at least to some of them. But even if true, this would by no means be unprecedented in judicial decision-making, either international or domestic.

From the record, it is evident that the parties had a full and fair opportunity to be heard at every stage of the proceedings. They had ample opportunity to consider and present written and oral submissions on the issues, and the oral hearing itself was meticulously conducted to enable each party to present its point of view. The Tribunal's analysis of the issues was clearly based on the materials presented by the parties and was in no sense *ultra petita*.

24. In the present case, the June inspection was plainly within the ambit of the dispute. Indeed, it was central to each party's larger case. As a consequence, the Tribunal cannot be said to have exceeded its powers in giving dispositive weight to its interpretation of the evidence presented. Nor did it fail to afford the parties an opportunity to present their case.

25. The Tribunal was obliged to reach a view as to whether it accepted Helnan's claim or Egypt's defence in this respect. In summary, it rejected Hernan's claim of an orchestrated campaign. Instead, it accepted Egypt's defence that the hotel had for long failed to reach a five-star standard, in view of the contractual dispute between EGOTH as owner and Helnan as manager over which of them bore financial responsibility for investing in the hotel's maintenance.

26. In explaining why it came to that view, the Tribunal was not obliged simply to choose en bloc between each of the rival theories and the evidence in support of them adduced by the parties. It was itself 'the judge' of the probative value of any evidence adduced: ICSID Arbitration Rule 34(1). It was therefore entitled to reach the view, relying as it expressly on the Inspection Report, that the September 2003 was a mere formality, because it was already clear in June that the hotel did not meet five-star standard and should be downgraded.

27. This was not a matter of applying Egyptian law to a question of international law. It was simply a matter of determining on the evidence which of the two rival arguments as to the overall significance of the summer 2003 inspections should be preferred. The Tribunal is not to be faulted for reaching its own conclusions as to the correct interpretation and significance of the evidence before it.

IV. Effect of failure to challenge the downgrade in the Egyptian courts

(a) Helnan's case

28. Helnan seeks annulment of the finding in paragraph 148 of the Award that: The ministerial decision to downgrade the hotel, not challenged in the Egyptian administrative courts, cannot be seen as a breach of the Treaty by Egypt. It needs more to become an international delict for which Egypt would be held responsible under the Treaty.

29. Helnan alleges that this finding is unsupported by reasons; fails to mention its pleadings and therefore seriously departs from a fundamental rule of procedure; and fails to apply the relevant Treaty standard to the measures, thereby manifestly exceeding the Tribunal's powers.

30. Helnan pleads that the impugned paragraph in the Award fails to explain why if, as both parties accepted, and as the Tribunal records; there is no requirement to exhaust local remedies, Helnan was nevertheless obliged, in order to have a valid treaty claim, to challenge the ministerial decision before the Egyptian administrative courts. It submits that the Tribunal does not give reasons to explain why the sale legal authority which it relied upon for its proposition (*Generation Ukraine Inc v Ukraine*) was applicable to the instant case, when on a proper analysis it was not. Helnan submits that, by failing to refer to Helnan's submissions on the point (contained in its Post-Hearing Memorial, paras 321–342) the Tribunal failed to observe the fundamental rule of procedure requiring each party to have an opportunity to present its

case, which must include the reasonable consideration by the tribunal of the party's arguments.

31. Finally, Helnan submits that the Tribunal's failure to apply the clear provisions of the applicable law (the BIT and the ICSID Convention) in imposing such a requirement on Helnan constituted a manifest excess of power. Citing the First Decision on Annulment in Vivendi v. Argentina, para 102, Helnan submits that: [I]t is not open to an ICSID tribunal having jurisdiction under a BIT in respect of a claim based upon a substantive provision of that BIT, to dismiss the claim on the ground that it could or should have been dealt with by a national court.

(b) Egypt's reply

32. Egypt replies that this point was merely confirmatory rather than decisive in the Tribunal's reasoning. The duty to give reasons does not, in its submission, require the Tribunal to give express consideration in its Award to Helnan's arguments. Helnan was heard on the point, even if its arguments did not ultimately persuade the Tribunal.

33. In its oral pleading before the ad hoc Committee, Egypt developed its explanation of the Tribunal's approach on this point. It submitted that the Tribunal was entitled to reject the investor's complaints of unfair and inequitable treatment if it had not resorted to the local courts as the obvious form of recourse for a disputed downgrading of the hotel. Such a finding went to the materiality of the investor's complaint – whether it could amount to a breach of the international obligation if no step had been taken locally to correct the act of maladministration. In any event, such a finding by the Tribunal was not reviewable on annulment.

(e) The Committee's analysis

34. Paragraph 148 of the Award (and the subsequent repetition of the same point at paras 159 and 162) raises a question of importance to the arbitration of investment treaty claims under the ICSID Convention, namely the extent to which an investor may be required, as a matter of substance rather than jurisdiction, to pursue local remedies in order to sustain a valid claim for breach of treaty.

35. In the context of the present annulment application, Helnan's objections that there has been a failure to give reasons and failure to observe a fundamental rule of procedure are not persuasive.

36. Article 52(1)(e) of the ICSID Convention permits annulment on the ground 'that the award has failed to state the reasons on which *it* is based'. (emphasis added). Thus, the object of this ground is the reasoning which leads to the Tribunal's Award. It does not permit annulment simply because the Tribunal has not deemed it necessary to discuss every argument raised by one of the parties.

37. In the light of this standard, paragraph 148 of the Award does enable the reader to follow the process of the Tribunal's reasoning. The paragraph may not deal with every contrary argument raised by Helnan. It may not resolve every further question which the Tribunal's formulation raises. But the factor which the Tribunal regarded as germane to its reasoning is clear enough, as is the legal basis and authority upon which it relied.

38. By the same token, there was no failure to observe a fundamental rule of procedure in this regard. Although Egypt did not apparently raise the point until its rejoinder, Helnan was afforded an opportunity to advance its arguments on the point, both at the hearing and in its written Post-hearing Memorial. Its arguments were plainly considered by the Tribunal. They are summarised in the Award at paragraphs 87–88, The right to be heard does not require a Tribunal to consider *seriatim* and evaluate expressly in its award every argument raised by each party. Helnan's essential submissions on this point were heard by the Tribunal, but they were rejected in favour of those advanced by Egypt.

39. However, the rejection of each of these grounds for annulment does not dispose of this issue. It leaves the question whether the Tribunal's finding in paragraph 148, in reliance on a passage of the Award in Generation Ukraine, constituted a manifest excess of its powers.

40. The question whether an ICSID arbitral tribunal has exceeded its powers is determined by reference to the agreement of the parties. It is that agreement or *compromis* from which the Tribunal's powers flow, and which accordingly determines the extent of those powers. In the case of an investment treaty claim, this agreement is constituted by the BIT and by the ICSID Convention (which the agreement to arbitrate incorporates by reference) as well as by the filing of the investor's claim. Read together, these three elements constitute the arbitration agreement and therefore prescribe the parameters of the Tribunal's powers. As the International Law Commission put it in formulating its seminal Draft Rules on Arbitral Procedure, from which Article 52 was derived: The question of excess of power or jurisdiction is, in essence, a question of treaty interpretation. It is a question which is to

be answered by a careful comparison of the award or other contested action by the Tribunal with the relevant provisions of the *compromis*. A departure from the terms of submission or excess of jurisdiction should be clear and substantial and not doubtful and frivolous.

41. The concept of the 'powers' of a tribunal goes further than its jurisdiction, and refers to the scope of the task which the parties have charged the Tribunal to perform in discharge of its mandate, and the manner to which the parties have agreed that task is to be performed. That is why, for example, a failure to apply the law chosen by the parties (but not a misapplication of it) was accepted by the Contracting States of the ICSID Convention to be an excess of powers, a point also accepted by annulment committees. Further, a failure to decide a question entrusted to the Tribunal also constitutes an excess of powers, since the Tribunal that event failed to fulfil the mandate entrusted to it by virtue of the parties' agreement.

42. By virtue of Article 9 of the BIT in the present case, the parties agree to submit '[a]ny dispute which may arise between an investor of one Contracting Party and the other Contracting Party in connection with an investment' to international arbitration, inter alia, under the ICSID Convention. Article 9 does not refer such disputes to host State courts.

43. The parties having chosen arbitration under the ICSID Convention pursuant to Article 9 of the BIT, the jurisdiction of the Centre is determined under Chapter II of the ICSID Convention (arts 25–27) Article 26 within that Chapter expressly provides:

> Consent of the parties to arbitration under this Convention shall, unless otherwise stated, be deemed consent to such arbitration to the exclusion of any other remedy. A Contracting State may require the exhaustion of local administrative or judicial remedies as a condition of its consent to arbitration under this Convention.

44. The Report of the Executive Directors of the World Bank on the Convention explains the purpose of this provision in para 32 as follows:

> Arbitration as an exclusive remedy It may be presumed that when a State and an investor agree to have recourse to arbitration, and do not reserve the right to have recourse to other remedies or require the prior exhaustion of other remedies, the intention of the parties is to have recourse to arbitration to the exclusion of any other remedy. This rule of interpretation is embodied in the first sentence of Article 26. In order to make clear that it was not intended thereby to modify the rules of international law regarding the exhaustion of local remedies, the second

sentence explicitly recognises the right of a State to require the prior exhaustion of local remedies.

45. Thus, by Article 26, the Contracting States agreed upon a fundamental reversal of the local remedies rule as it applies in customary international law, unless the relevant State expressly imposed such a condition. Article 26 represents one of the singular progressive advantages of the ICSID Convention. It 'create[s] a rule of priority vis-à-vis other systems of adjudication in order to avoid contradictory decisions and to the preserve the principle of *ne bis in idem*'. Article 26 operates as a key element of the parties' agreement to arbitrate – confirming the exclusivity of ICSID arbitration as the means of dispute resolution, where the parties have agreed to that forum for the resolution of their dispute.

46. The Tribunal accepts in paragraph 148 of its Award that there was no requirement for Helnan to exhaust local remedies before starting the arbitration. But it then proceeds, relying on a passage in *Generation Ukraine*, to find as a matter of substance that the failure of Helnan to challenge the ministerial decision in the administrative courts means that that decision 'cannot be seen as a breach of Treaty'.

47. The problem with the Tribunal's reasoning is that this is to do by the back door that which the Convention expressly excludes by the front door. Many national legal systems possess highly developed remedies of judicial review. Yet it would empty the development of investment arbitration of much of its force and effect, if, despite a clear intention of States parties not to require the pursuit of local remedies as a pre-condition to arbitration, such a requirement were to be read back in as part of the substantive cause of action.

48. In numerous ICSID cases, tribunals have rendered awards in favour of the claimants as a result of administrative decisions, in which no such application to the local courts had been made. Of course, a claimant's prospects of success in pursuing a treaty claim based on the decision of an inferior official or court, which had not been challenged through an available appeal process, should be lower, since the Tribunal must in any event be satisfied that the failure is one which displays insufficiency in the system, justifying international intervention. But that is a very different matter to imposing a requirement on the claimant to pursue local remedies before there can be said to have been a failure to provide fair and equitable treatment.

49. In the light of these precedents and considerations, the Award in *Generation Ukraine* – at any rate, as applied in these proceedings – stands

somewhat outside the *jurisprudence constante* under the ICSID Convention in the review of administrative decision-making for failure to provide fair and equitable treatment. On its facts, the decision of the Tribunal in that case is understandable. The impugned decision was that of an inferior official in the Kyiv City State Administration in omitting to grant a lease agreement and construction permit, which it was alleged amounted to expropriation. In these circumstances, it is unsurprising that the tribunal in *Generation Ukraine* should observe that:

> Yet again, it is not enough for an investor to seize upon an act of maladministration, no matter how low the level of the relevant governmental authority; to abandon his investment without any effort at overturning the administrative fault; and thus to claim an international delict on the theory that there had been an uncompensated virtual expropriation. In such instances, an international tribunal may deem that the failure to seek redress from national authorities disqualifies the international claim, not because there is a requirement of exhaustion of local remedies but because the very reality of conduct tantamount to expropriation is doubtful in the absence of a reasonable; – not necessarily exhaustive – effort by the investor to obtain correction.

50. But it does not at all follow from this conclusion that, in order to succeed in a claim of failure to provide fair and equitable treatment based upon a ministerial decision, the investor must challenge that decision in the local administrative courts. To be sure, the Treaty standard of fair and equitable treatment is concerned with consideration of the overall process of the State's decision making. A single errant decision of a low-level official is unlikely to breach the standard unless the investor can demonstrate that it was part of a pattern of State conduct applicable to the case or that the investor took steps within the administration to achieve redress and was rebuffed in a way which compounded, rather than cured, the unfair treatment.

51. But it is an entirely different matter to impose upon an investor, as a condition 'to become an international delict for which [the Contracting State] would be held responsible under the Treaty', a requirement that the decision of a government Minister, taken at the end of an administrative process, must in turn be challenged in the local courts. Such a decision is one for which the State is undoubtedly responsible at international law, in the event that it breaches the international obligations of the State. Moreover, the characterisation of such an act as unlawful under international law is not affected by its characterisation as lawful under internal law. Thus a decision by a municipal court that the Minister's decision was lawful (a judgment which such a court could only reach applying its own municipal administrative law) could

not preclude the international tribunal from coming to another conclusion applying international law.

52. The consequences of the adoption of the approach of the Tribunal in question in investment treaty law could be serious. It would inject an unacceptable level of uncertainty into the way in which an investor ought to proceed when faced with a decision on behalf of the Executive of the State, replacing the clear rule of the Convention which permits resort to arbitration. As Schreuer has rightly observed:

> Once it is accepted that the investor should make an attempt at local remedies it is only a small step to require that the attempt should not stop at the level of the lowest court. Once we require that reasonable appeals be taken we are close to demanding that these be exhaustive.

53. A requirement to pursue local court remedies would have the effect of disentitling a claimant from pursuing its direct treaty claim for failure by the Executive to afford fair and equitable treatment, even where the decision was taken at the highest level of government within the host State. It would leave the investor only with a complaint of unfair treatment based upon denial of justice in the event that the process of judicial review of the ministerial decision was itself unfair. Such a consequence would be contrary to the express provisions of Article 26, incorporated into the parties' *compromis*, since it would have the effect of [. . .] substituting another remedy for that provided under the BIT and the ICSID Convention.

54. Such a requirement would also have the effect of leading to the dismissal of claims precisely on the ground that they should have been submitted to a national court. It was the unjustified imposition of such a requirement which led to the annulment of the first Award in *Vivendi v Argentina*, cited above.

55. In order to annul this part of the Award, the ad hoc Committee must of course be satisfied that the Tribunal's excess of powers is manifest. This means that the excess must be obvious or clear. An ad hoc Committee will not annul an award if the Tribunal's disposition is tenable, even if the Committee considers that it is incorrect as a matter of law. But in the present case, the requirements of the parties as to the powers of the Tribunal in this respect are manifest. They are 'stated in the plain words of Article 9 of the BIT and Article 26 of the ICSID Convention, being provisions which confer jurisdiction upon the Tribunal, and thus describe the mandate or powers conferred upon the Tribunal by the agreement of the parties'. Accordingly, in failing to

observe those clear requirements, the Tribunal has manifestly exceeded its powers within the terms of Article 52(1)(b) of the ICSID Convention.

56. An ad hoc Committee is expressly empowered to annul any part of an Award on the grounds specified in Article 52(1) by virtue of Article 52(3), a power which Committees have used in other annulment applications. The consequence of such a finding is that 'severable parts of an award which are not themselves annulled will stand'.

57. In the instant case, it is clear from the text of the Award that the ratio of the Tribunal's decision was that the allocation of responsibility for the downgrading of the hotel was a contractual matter and, as a result, Egypt's actions in this regard could not amount to a breach of Treaty. The impugned passage at para 148 opens with the word '[m]oreover', which, as Egypt correctly observed in its submissions, demonstrated that the paragraph was merely –confirmatory not decisive. In these circumstances, the annulment of the Tribunal's finding in para 148 can have no effect on the rest of the Award, including the dismissal of the claimant's claims in paragraph 3 of the *dispositif*, which must continue to stand.

[…]

VIII. Decision of the ad hoc Committee

73. For the foregoing reasons, the Committee decides:

(1) To annul the holding of the Arbitral Tribunal in paras 148 and 162 of its Award which, while disclaiming a requirement of exhaustion of local remedies before ICSID arbitral recourse may be implemented, nevertheless accepts that challenge by Helnan of the decision to terminate its Management Contract in competent Egyptian administrative courts was required in order to demonstrate the substantive validity of its claims.

(2) To deny the claims of Helnan otherwise to annul the Arbitral Tribunal's Award of July 3, 2008.

(3) To require the parties equally to share the costs and expenses of ICSID and the fees of the members of the ad hoc Committee, each party being left to meet the costs of its representation in the annulment proceedings.

EXERCISE 33 – JURISDICTION III – SEMINAR

Review the excerpts from *CME v Czech Republic* and *Lauder v Czech Republic* (background attached to Exercise 22) and the judgment of the Svea Court of Appeal (in so far as it deals with *res judicata* and *lis pendens*).

DISCUSSION QUESTIONS

Problem 1

Explain how the Tribunals in *CME* and *Lauder* dealt with the issues of *res judicata* and *lis pendens*.

Problem 2

Was the Svea Court of Appeal right in its analysis of *res judicata* and *lis pendens*? Could the Czech Republic have presented better arguments to the Court?

Problem 3

What can an Arbitral Tribunal do to prevent parallel investment treaty arbitrations?

Problem 4

Is there/should there be a *sui generis* approach to *res judicata/lis pendens* in international arbitration, including investment treaty arbitration?

CASE

CME v Czech Republic, excerpt from final award

C. The London Tribunal's Award does not control this arbitration

1. Respondent refused co-ordination of the two arbitral proceedings

426. The respondent, in the First Phase of these proceedings, expressly and repeatedly refused any coordination of the London Arbitration and this arbitration. At the procedural hearing on November 17, 2000 the issue of coordination of the two proceedings was examined on the basis of the claimant's letter to the Tribunal dated November 10, 2000, which communicated to the Tribunal the parties' Joint Agenda for the procedural hearing and the claimant's proposals for co-ordination.

427. At the hearing the respondent declined anew to accept any of the claimant's alternative proposals, which were recapitulated in the claimant's letter to the Tribunal of November 10, 2000, under the heading 'Co-ordination of this proceeding with *Lauder v Czech Republic*'.

(i) to have the two arbitrations consolidated into a single proceeding;

(ii) to have the same three arbitrators appointed for both proceedings;

(iii) to accept the claimant's nomination in this proceeding of the same arbitrator that Mr Lauder nominated in the London proceeding;

(iv) to agree that the parties to this arbitration are bound by the London Tribunal's determination as to whether there has been a treaty breach;

(v) that after the submission of the parties' respective reply memorials and witness statements in this arbitration, the hearing be postponed until after the issuance of an award in the London Arbitration.

428. By letter November 15, 2000 the respondent wrote to the Tribunal:

> We refer to Debevoise & Plimpton's faxed letter of November 10 and the joint proposed agenda. We comment below on those matters where we disagree with the claimant.
>
> 1. Co-ordination of CME proceedings with Lauder arbitration.
>
> As noted by Debevoise & Plimpton, the Czech Republic does not agree to the consolidation of the CME and Lauder arbitrations, and does not agree to be bound in the CME arbitration by determinations of the Lauder Tribunal. If Mr Lauder and CME are concerned by duplicative proceedings, clearly the proper course for them would be to discontinue the Lauder proceedings. Mr Lauder provides no explanation as to why he is unwilling to do so. This is inexplicable given that his explanation for bringing the CME proceedings is that 'a damage award (and other potential forms of remedy) to Mr. Lauder would not fully compensate all of CME's shareholders for the harms CME has claimed' (Debevoise letter, November 10) and that an award in favour of Mr Lauder 'would not, however, make CME itself whole' (statement of claim, para 77). It is respectfully submitted that the continuation of separate proceedings both by CME and Mr Lauder – who purports to have voting control over CME – amounts to an abuse of the bilateral investment treaty regime.
>
> The Czech Republic opposes CME's application that the substantive hearing in this arbitration be postponed until the Lauder Tribunal has issued its award.
>
> The Czech Republic does not consider it appropriate that claims brought by different claimants under separate Treaties (which give rise to obligations of the Czech Republic to two different sovereign States – the United States and the Netherlands – under international law) should be effectively consolidated and *the Czech Republic asserts the right that each action be determined independently and promptly* (emphasis supplied)

429. By letter dated November 10, 2000 the respondent already had stated that it would 'not agree to be bound by in the CME arbitration by determinations of the US Tribunal'.

430. The Tribunal's conclusion is that if the London Arbitration Award arguably would have had any res judicata effect on this arbitration, the Respondent waived that defense by refusing to accept any of the Claimant's proposals to coordinate the two proceedings.

2. Respondent explicitly waived lis pendens or res judicata defences

431. As stated in the Partial Award the respondent expressly and impliedly waived any *lis pendens* or *res judicata* defence. The Tribunal decided this question in the Partial Award in passing upon its jurisdiction pursuant to UNCITRAL Rule Art. 21(2). The respondent in its pleadings expressly stated that it is not seeking to rely upon technical doctrines of *lis alibi pendens* or *res judicata*. It invoked the argument of 'abuse of process' by Mr. Lauder for initiating two parallel proceedings, which argument was dealt with and rejected by the Tribunal in the Partial Award (paragraphs 412, 419).

3. Res judicata does not apply in substance

432. The Tribunal further is of the view that the principle *of res judicata* does not apply in favour of the London Arbitration for more than one reason. The parties in the London Arbitration differ from the parties in this arbitration. Mr Lauder is the controlling shareholder of CME Media Ltd, whereas in this arbitration a Dutch holding company being part of the CME Media Ltd Group is the claimant. The two arbitrations are based on differing bilateral investment treaties, which grant comparable investment protection which, however, is not identical. Both arbitrations deal with the Media Council's interference with the same investment in the Czech Republic. However, the Tribunal cannot judge whether the facts submitted to the two tribunals for decision are identical and it may well be the facts and circumstances presented to this Tribunal have been presented quite differently to the London Tribunal.

433. Because the two bilateral investment treaties create rights that are not in all respects exactly the same, different claims are necessarily formulated. As an international tribunal recognised, 'the application of international law rules on interpretation of treaties to identical or similar provisions of different treaties may not yield the same results, having regard to, inter alia, differences in the respective contexts, objects and purposes, subsequent practice of parties and *travaux préparatoires*'. *The Mox Plant Case (Ireland v United Kingdom)*, Request for Provisional Measures, ITLOS, Case No. 10, December 3, 2001, § 51.

434. This Tribunal decided this issue with binding effect in the Partial Award (Partial Award 419). This holding of the Tribunal is supported by the London Tribunal's findings, according to which the respondent's recourse in the London Arbitration to the principle of *lis alibi pendens* was held to be of no use, since all the other court and arbitration proceedings involved different parties and different causes of action. The London Tribunal considered the risk that the two tribunals may decide differently. It identified the risk that damages could be concurrently granted by more than one court or arbitral tribunal, in which case the amount of damages granted by the second deciding court or arbitral tribunal could take this fact into consideration when addressing the final damage (London Award, paras 171–172, 174). It did not see an issue in differing decisions, which is a normal fact of forensic life, when different parties litigate the same dispute (which is not necessarily the case in all respects of this arbitration).

435. The principle of *res judicata* requires, for the 'same' dispute, identical parties, the same subject matter and the same cause of action. This is accepted by international tribunals. Moreover, the fact that one tribunal is competent to resolve the dispute brought before it does not necessarily affect the authority of another tribunal, constituted under a different agreement, to resolve a dispute – even if it were the 'same' dispute. *Certain German Interests in Polish Upper Silesia, Jurisdiction* (1925), P.C.I.J., Series A, No. 6, at 20 (PCIJ jurisdiction not barred by the existence of separate proceeding); *American Bottle Company (US v Mexico, April 2, 1929)*, 4. R.I.A.A 435, 437 (submission to another tribunal of identical dispute between the same parties has no effect on tribunal's jurisdiction); *SSP (ME) Ltd v Egypt* (First Decision on Jurisdiction, Nov 27, 1985) 106, I.L.R 502, 509.

436. Only in exceptional cases, in particular competition law, have tribunals or law courts accepted a concept of a 'single economic entity', which allows discounting of the separate legal existences of the shareholder and the company, mostly, to allow the joining of a parent of a subsidiary to an arbitration. Also a 'company group' theory is not generally accepted in international arbitration (although promoted by prominent authorities) and there are no precedents of which this Tribunal is aware for its general acceptance. In this arbitration the situation is even less compelling. Mr Lauder, although apparently controlling CME Media Ltd, the claimant's ultimate parent company, is not the majority shareholder of the company and the cause of action in each proceeding was based on different bilateral investment treaties. This conclusion accords with established international law (*Barcelona Traction Case, (Belgium v Spain)* Second Phase, I.C.J Rep. 1970, 3, 48–50, §§95–100, *Holiday Inns SA et al v Morocco* in P Lalive, The

First World Bank Arbitration – Some Legal Problems, I ICSID Reports 645, 664, (1993)).

4. 'Common position' in respect to res judicata

437. The agreed minutes of the Common Position of the Netherlands and the Czech Republic, adopted in pursuance of the consultation procedure under Art. 9 of the Treaty, support the Tribunal's view that the London Award does not govern this arbitration. According to the agreed minutes, at p. 3, the Netherlands position is that:

> Claims of different legal entities, even though they may be controlled by the same economic entity, are not necessarily the same claims and difference in legal personality has been recognized by tribunals (see, e.g. the ICJ *Barcelona Traction* Case). For instance, subsidiaries can operate rather independently from the parent company.

In conclusion, the Tribunal is of the view that, even disregarding the respondent's waiver in respect to *lis pendens* and *res judicata*, the principle of *res judicata* cannot apply in relation to the London Award.

 CASE

Lauder v Czech Republic, excerpt from final award

4.2 The same dispute is submitted to State courts and to other Arbitral Tribunals

156. The respondent argues that Article VI(3)(a) of the Treaty precludes the Arbitral Tribunal from exercising jurisdiction on the ground that the same dispute was submitted to Czech courts and to another Arbitral Tribunal before the present proceedings were initiated. Those proceedings arise from the same circumstances and seek the same substantive remedy, so that the issue in dispute is the same in all cases. As a result, Mr Lauder has removed the dispute from any Arbitral Tribunal under the Treaty (Response, pp 47–8).

157. The claimant argues that the present proceeding is the only one in which he claims that the Czech Republic violated obligations under the Treaty. Article VI(3)(a) actually sets forth a limited form of the principle of *lis alibi pendens*, whose elements are not met (Reply Memorial, pp 50–62).

158. Article VI(3)(a) of the Treaty reads as follows:

> (. . .) Once the national or company concerned has so consented, either party to the dispute may institute such proceeding provided:
>
> (i) the dispute has not been submitted by the national or the company for resolution in accordance with any applicable previously agreed dispute settlement procedures; and
>
> (ii) the national of company concerned has not brought the dispute before the courts of justice or administrative tribunals or agencies of competent jurisdiction of the party that is a party to the dispute. (. . .)

159. The Arbitral Tribunal considers that the word 'dispute' in Article VI(3)(a) of the Treaty has the same meaning as the words 'investment dispute' in Article VI(1), which reads as follows:

> For the purposes of this Article, an investment dispute is defined as a dispute involving (a) the interpretation or application of an investment agreement between a Party and a national or company of the other Party; (b) the interpretation or application of any investment authorisation granted by a Party's foreign investment authority to such national or company; or (c) an alleged breach of any right conferred or created by this Treaty with respect to an investment.

160. It is undisputed that the claimant's allegations concern an investment dispute under Article VI(1)(c) of the Treaty, i.e., 'an alleged breach of any right conferred or created by this Treaty with respect to an investment'.

161. The purpose of Article VI(3)(a) of the Treaty is to avoid a situation where the same investment dispute ('the dispute') is brought by the same the claimant ('the national or the company') against the same respondent (a party to the Treaty) for resolution before different arbitral tribunals and/or different State courts of the party to the Treaty that is also a party to the dispute.

162. The resolution of the investment dispute under the Treaty between Mr Lauder and the Czech Republic was not brought before any other arbitral tribunal or Czech court before – or after – the present proceedings was initiated. All other arbitration or court proceedings referred to by the respondent involve different parties, and deal with different disputes.

163. In particular, neither Mr Lauder nor the Czech Republic is a party to any of the numerous proceedings before the Czech courts, which opposed or are opposing CNTS or the various CME entities, on the one side, and CET 2.1

or Mr Železný, on the other side. The respondent has not alleged – let alone shown – that any of these courts would decide the dispute on the basis of the Treaty.

164. The ICC arbitration proceeding was between CME and Mr Železný, and dealt with the latter's alleged breach of the 11 August 1997 Share Purchase Agreement pursuant to which CME acquired a 5.8 per cent participation in CNTS held by Nova Consulting, a.s., an entity owned by Mr Železný.

165. The parallel UNCITRAL arbitration proceeding (hereinafter: 'the Stockholm Proceedings') is between CME and the Czech Republic, and is based on the bilateral investment treaty between the Netherlands and the Czech Republic.

166. Therefore, the Arbitral Tribunal holds that Article VI(3)(a) of the Treaty does not preclude it from having jurisdiction in the present proceedings.

4.3 The same remedies are sought in different fora

167. The respondent argues that, independently of Article VI(3)(a) of the Treaty, the claimant cannot seek the same remedies in multiple parallel actions.

168. At first the respondent asserted that if the claimant chooses to pursue a contractual remedy in the local courts or in an Arbitral Tribunal, he should not be allowed to concurrently pursue a remedy under the Treaty. The claimant could indeed not complain of any mistreatment of his investment by the State until that State's courts had finally disposed of the case. In addition, by initiating proceedings under the Treaty, the claimant deprives the other party to the court proceedings of the opportunity to argue its case before the Treaty Tribunal. Here, the existence of multiple proceedings creates a risk of incompatible decisions, a prospect of disorder 'that the principle of *lis alibi pendens* is designed to avert' (Response, pp 46–7).

169. Later the respondent indicated that it was not seeking 'to rely upon technical doctrines of *lis alibi pendens* or *res judicata*', but on a new 'important issue of principle, not yet tested (. . .) in previous court or arbitral proceedings'. The multiplicity of proceedings involving, directly or indirectly, the State 'amounts to an abuse of process', in that no court or Arbitral Tribunal would be in a position to ensure that justice is done and that its authority is effectively upheld. The respondent added that there is 'an obvious risk of conflicting findings between the two Treaty tribunals' (Sur-Reply, pp 14–15).

170. The claimant argues that no principles of *lis alibi pendens* are applicable here. Should such principles apply, it would not deprive the Arbitral Tribunal of jurisdiction, since the other court and arbitration proceedings involve different parties, different claims, and different causes of action. However, if CNTS could obtain any recovery from the Czech courts, this may reduce the amount of damage claimed in the present proceedings (Reply Memorial, pp 50–62).

171. The Arbitral Tribunal considers that the respondent's recourse to the principle of *lis alibi pendens* to be of no use, since all the other court and arbitration proceedings involve different parties and different causes of action (see 4.2 above). Therefore, no possibility exists that any other court or arbitral tribunal can render a decision similar to or inconsistent with the award which will be issued by this Arbitral Tribunal, i.e., that the Czech Republic breached or did not breach the Treaty, and is or is not liable for damages towards Mr Lauder.

172. It is to be noted that the risk of conflicting findings is even less possible since the claimant withdrew his two reliefs on the imposition of conditions to the License and the enforcement of such conditions, and only maintained its relief for damages. Assuming that the Arbitral Tribunal would decide that the respondent breached the Treaty and that the claimant is entitled to damages, such findings could not be contradicted by any other court or arbitral decision. The damages which could be granted in the parallel proceedings could only be based on the breach by CET 21 and/or Mr Železný of their contractual obligations towards CNTS or any CME entity (decision by Czech courts or the ICC arbitral tribunal) or on the breach by the Czech Republic of its obligations towards CME pursuant to the Dutch/Czech bilateral investment treaty (decision by the parallel UNICTRAL arbitral tribunal). The only risk, as argued by the claimant, is that damages be concurrently granted by more than one court or arbitral tribunal, in which case the amount of damages granted by the second deciding court or arbitral tribunal could take this fact into consideration when assessing the final damage.

173. There might exist the possibility of contradictory findings of this Arbitral Tribunal and the one set up to examine the claims of CME against the Czech Republic under the Dutch-Czech Bilateral Investment treaty. Obviously, the claimants in the two proceedings are not identical. However, this Arbitral Tribunal understands that the claim of Mr Lauder giving rise to the present proceeding was commenced before the claims of CME was raised and, especially, the respondent itself did not agree to a *de facto* consolidation of the two proceedings by insisting on a different Arbitral Tribunal to hear CME's case.

174. Finally, there is no abuse of process in the multiplicity of proceedings initiated by Mr Lauder and the entities he controls. Even assuming that the doctrine of abuse of process could find application here, the Arbitral Tribunal is the only forum with jurisdiction to hear Mr Lauder's claims based on the Treaty. The existence of numerous parallel proceedings does in no way affect the Arbitral Tribunal's authority and effectiveness, and does not undermine the parties' rights. On the contrary, the present proceedings are the only place where the parties' rights under the Treaty can be protected.

175. Therefore, the Arbitral Tribunal holds that the seeking of the same remedies in a different fora does not preclude it from having jurisdiction in the present proceedings.

 CASE

Excerpt from Svea Court of Appeal, Case no T 8735-01

[The Czech Republic's claim] *lis pendens* and *res judicata*

The principles of *lis pendens* and *res judicata* are a part of the *ordre public* and the principles are applicable between arbitration proceedings in different countries and which are carried out under different bilateral investment treaties. The Stockholm award is thereby invalid. In any event, the Stockholm Tribunal committed a procedural error by not dismissing CME's claim during the proceedings with reference to the principle *of lis pendens*, and after the issuance of the London award with reference to the principle of *res judicata*.

The identity criteria between the London proceedings and the Stockholm proceedings were fulfilled. The London proceedings and the Stockholm proceedings concerned the same investment, the same alleged treaty violations, the same facts, the same damage, the same claims for, firstly, restitution and, secondly, damages, the same parties, and the same legal grounds.

Both *Lauder* and *CME* invoked the same legal grounds based on their respective bilateral investment treaties. The two investment treaties provide the same protection and notwithstanding that they are variously drafted there is no great difference between them. The linguistic differences are insignificant. The obligations of the Republic pursuant to the two investment protection treaties are essentially identical.

A claim pursuant to any of the treaties leads to the same legal consequences. CME did not in any of the arbitration proceedings claim that the treaties were different. In a letter of March 10, 2000 from CME's counsel to the London Tribunal, it was stated that the treaties were indistinguishable documents, which was also stated in CME's Notice of Arbitration and Statement of Claim in the Stockholm proceedings.

Notwithstanding that Lauder and CME were not formally the same legal entity, they were to be regarded as the same party with respect to the issue of *lis pendens* and *res judicata*. Lauder and CME constitute shareholders at different levels in the chain of companies which Lauder used to make his investment in ČNTS. Lauder owned and owns a minority of the shares in the parent company, Central Media Enterprises Ltd, which, in turn, through inactive wholly-owned subsidiaries, owns 99 per cent of the shares in ČNTS. Lauder was and is the controlling shareholder of the parent company, which made it possible for him to exercise control over CME and over the companies in the CME group. Such control was also a necessary condition in order for Lauder to be able to bring his claim pursuant to the American Investment Treaty.

Lauder was the only shareholder who was, the entire time, a constant in the chain of companies which controlled ČNTS from 1993 until the Stockholm proceedings.

CME revealed the identity between CME and Lauder when CME's counsel, in both proceedings, proposed that the London proceedings and the Stockholm proceedings be consolidated. It was the same representative for Lauder and CME, Frederic T Klinkhammer, who instructed the same lawyers to represent Lauder in the London proceedings and CME in the Stockholm proceedings and who also participated during both proceedings.

It would not have been possible to resolve the problem of two awards against the Republic merely by setting off the amount which the Republic was to pay, inter alia, due to company and tax law rules.

Also according to English law, the *res judicata* effect does not only extend to the same party in a strict sense, but can also be extended and, by the application of English law, the *res judicata* effect of the London award affects the Stockholm proceedings.

The Republic immediately and persistently objected to parallel proceedings by invoking various grounds during the Stockholm proceedings, and took the position that either the London or Stockholm proceedings would have to be discontinued. It is true that the Republic did not invoke the legal-technical import of the doctrines of *lis pendens* and *res judicata* when it objected, but the Republic moved for dismissal and stay. This was due, inter alia, to the existence of the large number of disputes regarding CME, CET 21, ČNTS, and Železný, in addition to the disputes between Lauder/CME and the Republic which the Republic also referred to in the Stockholm proceedings. This is apparent, inter alia, from the Republic's Statement of Defence, Sur-Reply, and its opening statement in the Stockholm proceedings. The Republic invoked all circumstances in the Stockholm proceedings which are invoked in the present case regarding *lis pendens* and *res judicata* notwithstanding that the Republic did not use the same legal labels in the Stockholm proceedings.

The Republic did not raise any new objection regarding *res judicata* after the London award was issued since the proceedings at that time had been concluded and the Stockholm Tribunal had deliberated for four months. The Stockholm Tribunal was aware the entire time of the London proceedings. On a number of occasions, Kühn telephoned the parties' legal counsel to find out whether the London Tribunal had issued its award. The arbitrators in the Stockholm Tribunal learned of the London award when it was issued. When the London award was issued, the Stockholm Tribunal should have stayed the proceedings to consult the parties.

Immediately after CME had requested the Stockholm proceedings, CME wanted the proceedings to be consolidated. The Republic was of the opinion that it was not lawful to allow both proceedings to proceed, and that it was not possible to consolidate the cases pursuant to the respective treaties but, rather, that CME/Lauder should choose which proceeding they wanted to pursue. The Republic was left only to continue to object and hope that one of the proceedings would be terminated. Consolidating the proceedings was also incompatible with the Republic's position that neither of the proceedings could be pursued according to the respective Investment Treaties. The Republic did not state that its actions constituted a waiver of the right to assert the principles of *lis pendens* and *res judicata* in subsequent proceedings.

[. . .]

[CME'S response] *lis pendens* and *res judicata*

None of the parties in the arbitration proceedings, their legal counsel, nor the arbitrators, were Swedish. It is clear from the award that it was not written on the basis of Swedish principles of *lis pendens* and *res judicata*. The parties in the case argued on the basis of international *lis pendens* and *res judicata* and it may be stated that there was some form of silent agreement between the parties to apply certain types of international principles in the proceedings. However, this probably did not extend as far as to the criteria for *lis pendens* and *res judicata*, or to the application thereof in cases before Swedish courts of law.

The principles of *lis pendens* and *res judicata* do not fall under section 33 of the Arbitration Act but, rather, are to be assessed on the basis of the rules in section 34 of the same Act. Nor are the principles of *lis pendens* and *res judicata* applicable in the instant case between two different international arbitration proceedings in accordance with two different bilateral investment protection treaties.

Nor was there any identity between Lauder and CME. Lauder did not own more than 30 percent of the controlling company, Central Media Entertainment Ltd – a Bermuda registered company which is listed on the New York Exchange and has approximately 3,000 shareholders – nor was such the case when the arbitration proceedings were pending. Lauder controlled the company through a majority of the voting capital, but did not own a majority of the share capital. The companies, which were structured as the parent company Central Media Enterprises Ltd and CME, were wholly owned.

Nor was there identity between the bases for CME's and Lauder's claims. CME's and Lauder's claims were based on two different bilateral investment protection treaties between the Republic and Holland, and the USA respectively. The investment protection treaties are in all essential regards identical but there are differences between the treaties. These are, inter alia, that it is not obvious that CME's right as successor to a previous investor should be assessed equally under both treaties; that Lauder, in accordance with the American Investment Treaty, could claim compensation as a controlling shareholder; and that there are differences in the treaties with respect to the time in which a party may claim compensation. In addition, Lauder would not have been able to pursue a claim based on the Treaty and CME would not have been able to pursue its claim in accordance with the American Investment Treaty.

The injuries were not the same for Lauder and CME. In the London proceedings, Lauder could only claim damages in an amount corresponding to his loss, while CME claimed injury as owner of 99 per cent of the ČNTS. The injury and the calculation of damages would have been different. Nor would the Stockholm Tribunal have ordered different damages with the consequences that the Republic would have to pay twice.

The Stockholm Tribunal also discussed the question of the Republic's different behavior in different cases with respect to the jurisdiction issue and came to the conclusion that the jurisdiction of the Tribunal was not affected.

If CME cannot have a claim tried in accordance with the Treaty since Lauder brought a claim in accordance with the American Investment Treaty, the consequence is that CME and other shareholders, apart from Lauder, are being denied the possibility to have their claims tried.

In the Stockholm proceedings, the Republic explicitly stated that the Republic refrained from raising any objection regarding *lis pendens*, a matter which the Stockholm Tribunal and CME seized on. This is evident, inter alia, from the Republic's Statement of Defence, Sur-Reply, and the opening statement in the Stockholm proceedings. The Republic argued on the basis of a concept of 'abuse of process' in the Stockholm proceedings. Abuse of process is a concept which exists within the English legal tradition and an objection on the basis thereof does not include an objection based on *lis pendens*. There was no illegitimate purpose behind Lauder and CME commencing separate proceedings. Lauder was obliged to use the American Investment Treaty and the Treaty prescribes a waiting time which meant that Lauder could commence arbitration proceedings six months earlier than CME, which he also did.

The Stockholm Tribunal did not find that there existed any abuse of process and that the overlapping awards could be handled when the amount of the damages was to be determined; on the other hand, an assessment could not be made as to whether there existed a breach of the Treaty.

The London Tribunal also found the co-ordination could take place on the damages level when determining an amount and that there was no abuse of process. In any event, the Republic was the cause of the parallel proceedings. CME made a large number of attempts to co-ordinate the London and Stockholm proceedings in order to avoid a situation such as the instant one. CME proposed that the proceedings be consolidated, that they should have the same arbitrators, that the arbitrator appointed by CME should be the same in both proceedings, that the Stockholm Tribunal should stay its proceedings, and that the London Tribunal's award with a respect to the issue whether there existed a breach of the American Investment Treaty should be binding on the Stockholm Tribunal in its assessment whether there was a violation of the Treaty. Both the Stockholm and the London Tribunals referred to the aforementioned facts in their reasons for their awards.

[Reasons for the judgment] *lis pendens* and *res judicata*

When deciding whether the arbitral award should be set aside on the grounds of alleged *lis pendens* and *res judicata*, an assessment must first be made whether the stated grounds at all are applicable with respect to arbitral awards issued by two different Arbitral Tribunals following arbitration proceedings in accordance with the UNCITRAL rules under two different bilateral investment treaties. In this regard, the parties have different opinions. The issue whether *lis pendens* and *res judicata* may be applicable in a situation such as the instant one has not, as far as is known, arisen previously. The mere fact that the arbitrations were initiated under different investment treaties which were entered into between different States, the Czech Republic and the United States in the one treaty and the Czech Republic and the Netherlands in the other, militates against these legal principles being applicable at all. However, a couple of arbitral awards have been invoked from which it at least is evident, that the dispute has been considered to be the same in different arbitration proceedings which were brought under two different treaties.

Since, in any event, it cannot be ruled out entirely that the principles of *lis pendens* and *res judicata* may become applicable as between two different international arbitrations, the Court of Appeal will proceed with its assessment.

The UNCITRAL rules contain no provisions which shed light on the issue. The Republic has argued that English law might be applicable. However, the claim has not been based on any investigation which clarifies in detail the position under English law and the legal opinions that have been submitted do not contribute to a clarification of the legal situation. Taking the aforesaid into consideration, and since the issue whether English law is applicable to some extent is unclear, the Court of Appeal will disregard this matter for the time being.

To begin with, the Court of Appeal notes that, according to Swedish law, in arbitration proceedings *lis pendens* and *res judicata* constitute bars to substantive adjudication which are taken into account only after a party has raised an objection with respect thereto. Since the parties are free to raise, or not raise, an objection of *lis pendens* and *res judicata*, any violation thereof should not violate *ordre public*.

Consequently, a violation based on the aforesaid cannot result in invalidity in accordance with section 33 of the Arbitration Act. Instead, the matter is to be adjudged as a ground for challenge in accordance with section 34 of the same

Act (see Government Bill, p. 236). From section 34, second paragraph it is evident that a party is not entitled to invoke a circumstance which, through participating in the arbitration proceedings without objection or otherwise, he may be deemed to have waived. Thus, in such a case, the right to invoke a circumstance is barred. The Court of Appeal will now proceed to determine whether this is the case.

In the arbitration proceedings, the Republic expressly stated in its 'Sur Reply' that it did not rely on the doctrines of *lis pendens* and *res judicata*. The statement was made in connection with the Republic's claim that the Arbitral Tribunal should declare that CME's claim was not acceptable and should not be adjudicated. Instead, the Republic argued that – even excluding the arbitration proceedings in London – it had been exposed to or affected by a large number of actions brought by Lauder and the CME companies and that this constituted a type of abuse of process by the initiation of similar cases.

Accordingly, the Republic expressly waived raising an objection of *lis pendens* or *res judicata*. The aforesaid strongly supports the view that the right to challenge the Stockholm award is barred with respect to the allegation that the Stockholm Tribunal acted erroneously in failing to take into consideration the principles of *lis pendens* and *res judicata*.

In the present case, however, the Republic has argued that the objection during the arbitration proceedings regarding abuse of process constitutes an objection with a special meaning which also includes the principles of *lis pendens* and *res judicata*. By invoking abuse of process the Republic has, so it is argued, nevertheless not waived an objection of *lis pendens* and *res judicata*. Thus, the Republic claims that it is still entitled to invoke such grounds in the challenge proceedings.

The concept of abuse of process has no direct equivalent in Swedish law and it has also been questioned whether it can be applied in conjunction with international arbitration proceedings. Taking into consideration what has come to light in the case, it appears to be unclear whether an objection of abuse of process includes or does not include an objection regarding *lis pendens* and *res judicata*.

In light of the aforesaid, the Court of Appeal elects, for reasons of judicial economy, not to adopt a definite position regarding the issue of a bar but, rather, will determine whether the conditions are otherwise fulfilled in order for *lis pendens* and *res judicata* to be applicable. The Court of Appeal will, in this context, first determine whether identity may be deemed to exist between the claimant parties in the different arbitration proceedings, namely Lauder and CME.

It has come to light in the case that Lauder, a private person who is a citizen of the United States, holds not more than 30 per cent of the share capital in CME's parent company and is the controlling shareholder in such company. CME is a legal entity with its registered office in the Netherlands. It has not even been argued that identity in the formal sense exists between Lauder and CME. However, the Republic has argued that, in reality, they may nevertheless be deemed to be the same party. Based on the fact that the Court, primarily bearing in mind the international dimension of the case, should not adopt a too restrictive approach when making its assessment, the Republic has in support of its position referred, inter alia, to principles regarding piercing the corporate veil, which for example may entail, in certain circumstances, that a shareholder may be equated with the company, and to the concept of privy in English law.

CME has called into question the application of English law and denied that there exists a situation in which any form of piercing of the corporate veil is applicable. CME has, inter alia, further argued that Lauder would not have been able to bring his claim under the Treaty even if he had been a citizen of the Netherlands and that CME would not have been able to bring its claim based on the US and Czech Investment Treaty even if the company had a registered office in the United States.

The Court of Appeal notes that the concept of 'privy', and what it might be deemed to entail – the meaning of the concept has not been clarified entirely – lacks any direct equivalent in Swedish law. There is no reason to take this concept into consideration in conjunction with the assessment.

With respect to piercing the corporate veil, no international cases have been presented in the case in which, in an actual situation of *lis pendens* and *res judicata*, a controlling minority shareholder has been equated with the company.

According to Swedish law, one of the fundamental conditions for *lis pendens* and *res judicata* is that the same parties are involved in both cases. As far as is known, the same condition applies in other legal systems which recognise the principles in question. Identity between a minority shareholder, albeit a controlling one, and the actual company cannot, in the Court of Appeal's opinion, be deemed to exist in a case such the instant one. This assessment would apply even if one were to allow a broad determination of the concept of identity.

Thus, since Lauder and CME cannot be deemed to be the same party, one of the prerequisites *for lis pendens* and *res judicata* is lacking. Based on the aforesaid, the Republic's claim cannot be accepted based on the ground now considered.

EXERCISE 34 – JURISDICTION IV – MINI MOCK ARBITRATION

Review the Award on Preliminary Objections in SCC Arbitration V (02412007): *SVSA, et al v The Russian Federation,* including the dissenting opinion (attached to Exercise 18).

It is now being the subject of a declaratory action according to section 2 of the 1999 Swedish Arbitration Act.

 GROUP

Group 1
You represent the claimants in the arbitration, i.e., the respondents before the District Court. Your job is to find arguments to support that the MFN clause can be used to give the Tribunal jurisdiction.

Group 2
You are the observer group. Were the best arguments presented? Did the District Court reach a reasonable decision?

Group 3
You represent the respondent in the arbitration, i.e., the claimants before the District Court. Your job is to argue that the MFN clause in the BIT does not give the Tribunal jurisdiction.

Group 4
You are the Stockholm District Court. You have to decide whether or not the Tribunal has jurisdiction according to the MFN clause in the BIT.

For the purpose of the mini mock arbitration, please ignore the other jurisdictional issues in the decision. You should only focus on the most-favoured-nation clause.

22

Applicable law

 DISCUSSION QUESTIONS

Problem 1
Read the *Wena Hotels v Egypt* Annulment Decision. Do you agree with the Committee's view on the relationship between municipal law and international law?

Problem 2
Explain and defend the Tribunal's reasoning on the relationship between EU law and international law in *Electrabel v Hungary*, Decision on Jurisdiction, Applicable Law and Liability.

Problem 3
Argue against the Tribunal's finding on applicable law in *Electrabel v Hungary*, Decision on Jurisdiction, Applicable Law and Liability.

Problem 4
Which law should the arbitrators apply to resolve the issues discussed in the following paragraphs from *RosInvestCo UK Ltd*?

 CASE

RosInvestCo UK Ltd v The Russian Federation, SCC Case No. 079/2005, excerpt from Final Award, 12 September, 2010

International condemnation of the respondent's treatment of Yukos

91. The actions of the respondent in respect of the expropriation and re-nationalisation of Yukos' assets has (sic) been uniformly condemned. The Council of Europe passed a resolution on 25 January 2005 recognising the non-conformity of the proceedings with the rule of law. The Houston Bankruptcy Court also found that the assessments against Yukos deviated from established Russian law when it enjoined Gazprom and Western banks from participating in the auction of YNG. The Amsterdam District Court

declared on 31 October 2007, that the Russian proceedings violated the principle of due process and that therefore the Dutch courts would not recognise the Russian bankruptcy. Even before the auction of YNG, the International Commission of Jurists, a non-profit non-governmental agency raised its concerns with President Putin himself. The English courts also recognised the politicised nature of the processes against a Yukos board member and refused to extradite him. Other courts around the world have also refused judicial assistance to the Russian Federation in relation to the extradition of defendants and collection of documents.

Claimant's purchase of Yukos shares

92. Claimant, RosInvestCo, an investment company incorporated under English law and based in London, England, purchased a total of seven million shares in Yukos, then traded on the Moscow and other stock exchanges, on two occasions on 17 November and 1 December of 2004.

93. Claimant is specialises (sic) in purchasing shares at such moments of market distress, judging that the market has overreacted to transient events and has undervalued a company's underlying assets. Some of these investments turn out to be profitable, and some do not, and the investor may be presumed to understand the market risks when it makes the investment. But when an investment becomes worthless, not because of market movements, but because of unlawful government action, an investor does not lose its rights under treaties such as the IPPA simply because it bought its shares at a moment of uncertainty.

94. Claimant is an indirect subsidiary of Elliott Associates, LP, as openly disclosed in claimant's published English accounts, which state: 'The company's ultimate parent undertaking is Elliott Associates L.P., a limited partnership organised under laws of Delaware, United States.'

95. Elliott Associates, founded in 1971, has been described, together with its sister fund, Elliott International, L.P. (Elliott International), as one of the oldest funds of its kind under continuous management. Elliott is said to manage in excess of US$14 billion in assets for large institutional investors and individuals. Elliott has been described as preferring to invest in 'situations that are complex', because those 'may have greater discounts and fewer participants'. Elliott's reported investments cover a wide range of asset classes, many of which meet the 'complex, greater discounts, fewer participants' formula.

[...]

Contentions in respondent's Surreply R-II

305. In its Surreply (R-II) respondent argues that claimant was neither the legal nor was it the economic owner of the Yukos shares before 2007. Respondent also rebuts claimant's arguments that respondent's reliance on customary international law is irrelevant.

Claimant not the legal owner

306. With regard to its claim that claimant was not the legal owner, respondent argues that the law under which the Tribunal must evaluate claimant's assertion that it is the legal owner of the Yukos shares is Russian law. Under applicable Russian law, CSFB was the legal owner of the Yukos shares. Under Russian law, specifically the Federal Law 'On the Securities Market' only persons listed (in so-called 'depo-accounts') on the books and records of a licensed securities depository are legally recognised as the owners of the relevant shares, and no other person has any legally recognised rights as a shareholder in relation to the company.

307. CSFB was registered with the depository as the holder of the Yukos shares and therefore was at all relevant times the only person with legal ownership of the shares and therefore the only person entitled to legal rights as a shareholder in relation to the company as a matter of Russian law.

308. Under the Russian Joint Stock Companies Law, and confirmed by the Supreme Arbitrazh Court (in a case cited in RM-851), CSFB, as the legal owner of the shares, was the only person entitled to receive notices of shareholders' meetings, attend shareholders' meetings and to vote the Yukos shares. CSFB is also the only person entitled to receive dividends and other distributions from Yukos. Accordingly, claimant's allegation that it 'alone had the power to vote the shares and to receive any dividends or residual funds upon liquidation' is unsupported and false. Claimant had no rights in relation to the Yukos shares and was only a financial intermediary standing between the legal (or nominal owner) CSFB and the economic owner Elliott International.

Claimant's arguments on ownership under Russian law rejected

309. Respondent continues its argument that the legal owner under Russian law was CSFB. In CPHB-I, claimant actually concedes that CSFB was the legal owner on the basis of the same Law on the Securities Market which

respondent cites as the basis for its argument claimant's arguments that the shares were held for administrative reasons through its 'global custodian' CSFB is of no basis. Under the Russian system, CSFB would have been entitled to all dividends and would have the right to vote the shares, the rights of the depositary was minor.

310. Claimant's argument that nonetheless it was the 'true owner' of the shares is deficient: It ignores that claimant actually sold 100 per cent of its interest to Elliott International. The argument has been invented for the purposes of this arbitration and effectively acknowledges that claimant was never the legal owner, nor the beneficial owner until March 2007 of the Yukos shares. Furthermore, under Russian law there can only be one owner of the shares, any other outcome would amount to chaos. Claimant's 'true ownership' argument is also based on a misreading of Russian law, and is not supported by the facts in this case. According to claimant, (a) the Yukos shares were acquired by CSFB as a 'commission agent' on behalf of claimant, (b) 'title' to the Yulcos shares passed to RosInvestCo as 'principal' under Article 996 of Russia's Civil Code and (c) the provisions of Russia's Civil Code take precedence over Russian civil law statutes such as the Law on the Securities Market, pursuant to which CSFB, claimant now acknowledges, was the legal owner of the shares.

311. The 'true ownership' argument is wrong for the following four reasons:

a. The relationship between claimant (UK company) and CSFB (US company) was governed by an agreement under New York law, therefore any arguments claimant makes citing the Russian Civil Code are irrelevant. There was (and is) no provision of Russian law that would require their relationship to be governed by Russian law.
b. Respondent has established that Russian law determines the relationship between a Russian company and its shareholders. The Law on the Securities Market sets out in Article 28 that for a company such as Yukos, the owner of the shares is the person registered as the owner on the books of the company's depositary.
c. A 2006 Moscow Arbitrazh Court decision (RM-85 1) involving a broker and the broker's client held that the broker (and not the client) was entitled to the dividends because the broker was listed on the depo account as the owner. This decision, discussed at the hearing, remains unchallenged, and confirms that a Russian company's relationship with its shareholders is governed by the Law on the Securities Market and the Joint Stock Companies Law, a conclusion now acknowledged by claimant.
d. Even if Russian law governed the relationship between claimant

and CSFB, and even if CSFB had acted as claimant's 'commission agent', claimant would in fact have been acting as the agent for Elliott International, the principal and beneficial owner of the shares for as long as the Participation Agreements were in effect.

Claimant was not the economic owner – the participation agreements

312. Claimant was not the economic owner even during the supposed brief period between initial acquisition of the shares and the entering into force of the participation agreements. Claimant sold its entire economic interest even before claimant first acquired any interest in those shares.

313. Respondent contends that in order to determine the rights retained by claimant under the participation agreements, reference must be made to their terms and to New York law, applicable in this case pursuant to Russian private international law rules. Those participation agreements (RM-16 and RM-19) provide that claimant 'hereby irrevocably participates and sells to [Elliott International], and [Elliott International] hereby purchases, the Participated Interest', defined as 'a 100 per cent interest in and to Highberry's Interest.' (Highberry later became RosInvestCo, the claimant). Furthermore, in section 6 of each participation agreement, claimant undertook to pay to Elliott International all the cash and other payments and property received by claimant in respect of the Yukos shares (less any related expenses and taxes), and in section 7 to vote the participated Yukos shares only in accordance with Elliott International's instructions. The participation agreements transferred 100 per cent of the economic ownership and beneficial interest in the Yukos shares to Elliott International.

314. Claimant retained none of the basic rights of an ordinary shareholder and rights to receive dividends under Russian law. Furthermore, under New York law the Yukos shares were the property of Elliott International. As long the participation agreements were in force Elliott International was the sole beneficial owner of the Yukos shares, the Yukos shares as property of Elliott International, were not an asset of claimant, and had claimant become insolvent, would not have been included in claimant's bankruptcy estate; and claimant was either Elliott International's uncompensated collection agent or an uncompensated constructive trustee acting on behalf of Elliott International, and was obligated, in either of those capacities, to collect the Yukos dividends paid to CSFB, and to pay those dividends over to Elliott International.

315. Claimant contends it was not a mere nominal owner because claimant retained the right under Section 5 of the Participation Agreements, to bar Elliott International from transferring or encumbering the shares without the prior written consent of RosInvestCo. This argument is fundamentally mistaken. First, claimant was not even 'a mere nominal owner' of the Yukos shares. Second, the contractual limitation in Section 5 was not an expression of claimant's continuing ownership of the Yukos shares and did not bestow upon claimant any right having an economic value. Rather, Section 5 was an attempt by claimant to avoid the potentially serious US securities law consequences that might otherwise have resulted from claimant's sale of the economic interest in the Yukos shares to Elliott International, (pp 11–17 Annex DR-II) And third, the free assignability of a company's shares is not an essential right of a Russian shareholder. Banks and other creditors, for example, routinely prohibit the transfer of shares pledged as security, without calling into question the debtor's continuing ownership of the encumbered shares.

316. From the claimant's perspective the participation agreement were at all times a strictly cash-in, cash-out arrangement. Claimant was not entitled to retain any dividends. This in underlined by the fact that the claimant's interest in the Yukos shares did not appear on claimant's balance sheet in its financial statements until those statements for the year ended 31 December 2007 (RM-856), the year when the participation agreements were terminated.

 CASE

Wena Hotels Ltd v Arab Republic of Egypt (ICSID Case No. ARB/98/4), excerpt from the annulment decision

A. Did the Tribunal manifestly fail to apply the applicable law?

26. Article 42(1) of the ICSID Convention provides that:

> The Tribunal shall decide a dispute in accordance with such rules of law as may be agreed by the parties. In the absence of such agreement, the Tribunal shall apply the law of Contracting State party to the dispute (including its rules on the conflict of laws) and such rules of international law as may be applicable.

27. The first aspect the Committee must establish is whether the parties agreed to the rules of law to be applied by the Tribunal in the light of the first sentence of the Article. In fact, the question touches upon a prior determin-

ation of the proper subject of the dispute brought before the Tribunal and the parties concerned by it.

(i) The dispute brought before the Tribunal

28. It is undisputed that the lease contracts were concluded between Wena and EHC. It is also undisputed that the two leases were subject to Egyptian law. However, there is disagreement about the meaning of this submission to Egyptian law. In the applicant's view this was the choice of law required by the first sentence of Article 42(1). Accordingly, the Tribunal was under the obligation to apply such law.

29. The respondent believes otherwise. Egyptian law was indeed applicable, but only in the context of the disputes concerning those parties and for the commercial aspects specifically arising from the contracts. The dispute before the Tribunal involved different parties, namely the investor and the Egyptian State, and concerned a subject matter entirely different from the commercial aspects under the leases. The dispute before the Tribunal is, in the respondent's view, about the role of the State in the light of its obligations under the IPP A. Accordingly, the respondent is of the view that the parties to the instant case made no choice of law under Article 42(1).

30. It is not disputed that EHC is a State-owned company with its own legal personality. Neither is it disputed that its functions are essentially commercial and not governmental in nature. In fact, none of the parties has claimed that the acts of EHC could be attributed to the State. Therefore, EHC is to be dealt with as an entity different from the Egyptian State, with a legal personality of its own, the functions of which cannot be confused with those of the State.

31. The leases deal with questions that are by definition of a commercial nature. The IPPA deals with questions that are essentially of a governmental nature, namely the standards of treatment accorded by the State to foreign investors. It is therefore apparent that Wena and EHC agreed to a particular contract, the applicable law and the dispute settlement arrangement in respect of one kind of subject, that relating to commercial problems under the leases. It is also apparent that Wena as a national of a Contracting State could invoke the IPPA for the purpose of a different kind of dispute, that concerning the treatment of foreign investors by Egypt. This other mechanism has a different and separate dispute settlement arrangement and might include a different choice of law provision or make no choice at all.

32. The issue was also raised during the jurisdictional phase of the case before the Tribunal. In fact, Egypt objected to the jurisdiction of the Tribunal on the basis that there was no legal dispute between Wena and Egypt. This objection was denied by the Tribunal.

33. The parties appear to be in agreement that the acts of self-help undertaken by EHC in respect of the hotels were wrongful and that the initiative to undertake those acts is not to be attributed to the State. Indeed, this case involves a claim not against the acts of EHC but against those acts or omissions of the State that the investor considers to be in violation of the IPPA. It is the latter acts that were considered by the Tribunal on the merits as amounting to measures having effects equivalent to expropriation of the investment.

34. However, the parties again here differ as to the consequences of such dual relationship, existing between Wena and EHC on one hand, and between Wena and Egypt on the other hand. For the applicant the resolution of the dispute brought before the Tribunal cannot be separated from the leases and the rights of the parties to those contracts. The applicant has in fact argued that the relationship between Wena and Egypt under the IPPA is entirely dependent upon and a function of the relationship between Wena and EHC under the leases. The respondent believes that the failure of the State to adopt measures in protection of the investor is a violation of the IPPA independently of any questions arising under the leases.

35. The Committee cannot ignore of course that there is a connection between the leases and the IPPA since the former were designed to operate under the protection of the IPPA as the materialisation of the investment. But this is simply a condition precedent to the operation of the IPPA. It does not involve an amalgamation of different legal instruments and dispute settlement arrangements. Just as EHC does not represent the State nor can its acts be attributed to it because of its commercial and private function, the acts or failures to act of the State cannot be considered as a question connected to the performance of the parties under the leases. The private and public functions of these various instruments are thus kept separate and distinct.

36. This Committee accordingly concludes that the subject matter of the lease agreements submitted to Egyptian law was different from the subject matter brought before ICSID arbitration under the IPPA. It follows that it cannot be held that the parties to the instant case have made a choice of law under the first sentence of Article 42(1) of the ICSID Convention.

(ii) The role of international law

37. The second sentence of Article 42(1) of the ICSID Convention provides that, in the absence of an agreement on the applicable rules of law, the Tribunal shall apply the law of the host State, including its rules on the conflict of laws, and such rules of international law as may be applicable. It is therefore necessary for the Committee to examine the meaning of this second sentence and the question of the interrelation between domestic and international law in this context.

38. This discussion brings into light the various views expressed as to the role of international law in the context of Article 42(1). Scholarly opinion, authoritative writings and some ICSID decisions have dealt with this matter. Some views have argued for a broad role of international law, including not only the rules embodied in treaties but also the rather large definition of sources contained in Article 38(1) of the Statute of the International Court of Justice. Other views have expressed that international law is called in to supplement the applicable domestic law in case of the existence of *lacunae*. In *Klöckner I* the ad hoc Committee introduced the concept of international law as *complementary* to the applicable law in case of *lacunae* and as *corrective* in case that the applicable domestic law would not conform on all points to the principles of internationallaw. There is also the view that international law has a controlling function of domestic applicable law to the extent that there is a collision between such law and fundamental norms of international law embodied in the concept of *jus cogens*.

39. Some of these views have in common the fact that they are aimed at restricting the role of international law and highlighting that of the law of the host State. Conversely, the view that calls for a broad application of international law aims at restricting the role of the law of the host State. There seems not to be a single answer as to which of these approaches is the correct one. The circumstances of each case may justify one or another solution. However, this Committee's task is not to elaborate precise conclusions on this matter, but only to decide whether the Tribunal manifestly exceeded its powers with respect to Article 42(1) of the ICSID Convention. Further, the use of the word 'may' in the second sentence of this provision indicates that the Convention does not draw a sharp line for the distinction of the respective scope of international and of domestic law and, correspondingly, that this has the effect to confer on to the Tribunal a certain margin and power for interpretation.

40. What is clear is that the sense and meaning of the negotiations leading to the second sentence of Article 42(1) allowed for both legal orders to have

a role. The law of the host State can indeed be applied in conjunction with international law if this is justified. So too international law can be applied by itself if the appropriate rule is found in this other ambit.

41. In particular, the rules of international law that directly or indirectly relate to the State's consent prevail over domestic rules that might be incompatible with them. In this context it cannot be concluded that the resort to the rules of international law under the Convention, or under particular treaties related to its operation, is antagonistic to that State's national interest.

42. Particular emphasis is put on this view when the rules in question have been expressly accepted by the host State. Indeed; under the Egyptian Constitution treaties that have been ratified and published 'have the force of law'. Most commentators interpret this provision as equating treaties with domestic legislation. On occasions the courts have decided that treaty rules prevail not only over prior legislation but also over subsequent legislation. It has also been held that *lex specialis* such as treaty law prevails over *lex generalis* embodied in domestic law. A number of important domestic laws, including the Civil Code and Code of Civil Procedure of Egypt, provide in certain matter for a 'without prejudice clause' in favour of the relevant treaty provisions. This amounts to a kind of *renvoi* to international law by the very law of the host State.

43. Most prominent among this treaty law is that embodied in investment treaties. As from 1953 Egypt has been a leader in the field. Examples of this leadership are the Convention on Payments on Current Transactions and the Facilitation of Transfer of Capital among the States of the Arab League of 1953, the Convention on the Investment and Transfer of Arab Capital of 1971, the Convention Establishing the Arab Investment Guarantee Corporation, the ICSID Convention and numerous bilateral investment treaties.

44. This treaty law and practice evidences that when a tribunal applies the law embodied in a treaty to which Egypt is a party it is not applying rules alien to the domestic legal system of this country. This might also be true of other sources of international law, such as those listed in Article 38(1) of the Statute of the International Court of Justice mentioned above.

45. Therefore, the reliance of the Tribunal on the IPPA as the primary source of law is not in derogation or contradiction to the Egyptian law and policy in this matter. In fact, Egyptian law and investment policies are fully supportive of the rights of investors in that country. The ICSID Convention and

the related bilateral investment treaties are specifically mentioned in Egypt's foreign investment policy statements.

46. In the light of the above this Committee concludes that in applying the rules of the IPPA in the instant case the Tribunal did not exceed its powers.

 CASE

Electrabel SA v Republic of Hungary (ICSID Case No. ARB/07/19), excerpt from the Decision on Jurisdiction, Applicable Law and Liability

(5) The Tribunal's analysis

4.111 The necessary starting point for this arbitration is that the Tribunal has been seized as an international tribunal by a Request for Arbitration made by the claimant against the respondent under the ECT and the ICSID Convention. As pleaded in paragraph 1.1 of the claimant's request:

> This Request for Arbitration is served pursuant to Article 26(3) of the Energy Charter Treaty (the 'ECT'), Article 36(1) of the Convention on the Settlement of Investment Disputes between States and Nationals of Other States (the 'ICSID Convention'), and Rule 1 of the Rules of Procedure for the Institution of Conciliation and Arbitration Proceedings pursuant to the ICSID Convention (the 'ICSID Institution Rules').

4.112 Under Article 26 ECT and Article 42 of the ICSID Convention, the Tribunal is required to apply the ECT and 'applicable rules and principles of international law'. In other words, this Tribunal is placed in a public international law context and not a national or regional context. Moreover, this ICSID arbitration does not have its seat or legal place of arbitration in Hungary or elsewhere in the European Union. Such an arbitral seat could trigger the application of the *lex loci arbitri* and give rise to the jurisdiction of the local courts in regard to the arbitral process, including challenges to the award. This ICSID arbitration is a dispute resolution mechanism governed exclusively by international law. As a result of the Tribunal's international status under the ECT and the ICSID Convention, several of the Commission's submissions cannot be taken into account in this arbitration, because they are based on a hierarchy of legal rules seen only from the perspective of an EU legal order applying within the EU, whereas this Tribunal is required to operate in the international legal framework of the ECT and the ICSID Convention, outside the European Union.

4.113 Before entering any further into the analysis of the applicable law(s), the Tribunal is minded to set the stage in a general manner. Two important and potentially competing values are here at stake: the substantive and procedural protections of the rights of a foreign investor and the economic integration of EU Member States into the European Union operating under the rule of law. The task of this Tribunal is to ascertain the correct legal balance between these values, as required by the ECT, the ICSID Convention and the applicable rules and principles of international law.

4.114 The texts of the ECT and of the ICSID Convention raise relatively little difficulty. The more difficult step is to identify the applicable rules and principles of international law and, more precisely, whether and, if so, to what extent, EU law forms part of such rules and principles. The relationship between the ECT and EU law, as was submitted by the claimant in its post-hearing submissions, is '(a) question which features prominently in this arbitration' (claimant's post-hearing submissions, para. 69). It is a question with potentially far reaching consequences for the present case, both on the question of jurisdiction and on the merits of the parties' dispute.

4.115 As far as jurisdiction is concerned, the Tribunal notes that the respondent has not raised any like objection to jurisdiction as that made by the European Commission. It is however the Tribunal's duty independently to check whether or not it has jurisdiction to decide the parties' dispute, particularly when such jurisdiction is contested by the European Commission based on the interpretation and application of EU law. In other words, in this case and as already indicated, the Tribunal must consider its jurisdiction under Article 26 ECT and the effect of EU law. It does so in Part V of this Decision.

4.116 As far as the merits are concerned, it is equally important for the Tribunal to ascertain the effect of EU law, particularly as submitted by the respondent (here supported by the European Commission), in the following words: '(i)n evaluating these legal arguments, the Tribunal should bear in mind the very real practical consequences of any ruling under the Energy Charter Treaty that requires Hungary to act inconsistently with EC mandatory law' (Respondent's Counter-Memorial, para. 301).

4.117 *(i) The multiple nature of EU Law:* EU law is a *sui generis* legal order, presenting different facets depending on the perspective from where it is analysed. It can be analysed from the perspectives of the international community, individual Member States and EU institutions.

4.118 Given those perspectives, EU law has a multiple nature: on the one hand, it is an international legal regime; but on the other hand, once introduced in the national legal orders of EU Member States, it becomes also part of these national legal orders. It is in that latter sense that the claimant submits that EU law has to be considered as part of the national Hungarian legal order. In the *Kadi* case, Advocate-General Maduro's Opinion also described EU law as a 'municipal legal order of transnational dimension'. It is more accurately expressed in the French version: '*un ordre juridique interne d'origine internationale*'.

4.119 The Tribunal accepts that EU law forms part of the Hungarian legal order; but it considers that the claimant is wrong to so limit its nature. In the international setting in which this Tribunal is situated and from which it necessarily derives its perspective, EU law has to be classified first as international law, as explained below.

4.120 *(ii) EU law is based on international treaties*: EU law is international law because it is rooted in international treaties; and both Parties accepted, of course, that the EU Treaties are legal instruments under public international law. EU law flows from the Treaty of Rome, as amended many times, creating the European Union, as was submitted by the respondent:

> Both Belgium and Hungary are parties to this multinational treaty and are
> bound by it, just as they are parties to another multinational treaty, the ECT.
> The intersection of these two treaties is thus not one of 'international' law versus
> 'internal' law, but rather one of two multinational treaties on the same plane in the
> hierarchy of international law, as between the State Parties who are bound to both.
> (counter-memorial, para. 551)

4.121 The claimant likewise accepts that the EU Treaties are international treaties:

> Should the Tribunal conclude that Article 26(6) ECT may extend the applicable
> law to include EU law in a dispute between an Investor from one EU Member State
> and another Member State, Electrabel submits that only EU Treaty law is relevant.
> (claimant's post-hearing submissions, para. 81).

4.122 *(iii) The whole of EU Law as an international legal order*: Moreover, the Tribunal considers that EU law as a whole is part of the international legal order; and it does not draw a material distinction, as proposed by the claimant, between the EU Treaties (which the claimant acknowledges as international law) and the '*droit dérivé*' (which the claimant does not acknowledge as international law). In the Tribunal's view, all EU legal rules are part of a regional system of international law and therefore have an international legal character. This was stated clearly by the ECJ many years ago, in the famous case *Van Gend en Loos*: 'The Community constitutes a new legal order of international law for the benefit of which the states have limited their sovereign rights. . ..'

4.123 In the Tribunal's view, it would be artificial to categorise, as an international legal rule, Article 87 EC (precluding 'any aid granted by a Member State or through State resources. . .incompatible with the internal market'), and refuse that same status to the necessary implementation of that international rule by the non-national organ created by the same EU treaty. A contrary analysis would result in a situation where the international rule would remain free-floating, as a mere theoretical aspiration. For this international rule to be translated into legal obligations binding on EU Member States, decisions have to be taken by the European Commission. A typical example of such a decision is the European Commission's Final Decision of 4 June 2008 in the present case. For these reasons, the Tribunal does not accept the claimant's proposition.

4.124 *(iv) EU law as national law*: In the Tribunal's view, the fact that EU law is also applied within the national legal order of an EU Member State does not deprive it of its international legal nature. EU law remains international law; EU law is not limited to a treaty but includes a body of law flowing from the EU Treaties. Legal rules created under the Treaties can apply directly within the different national legal orders, without any further procedural step taken by EU Member States.

4.125 From the perspective of international law, it does not matter whether such application within a national legal order take effect directly or indirectly. The Tribunal recognises that international law is applied within national legal orders more or less directly in monist countries and by reception in dualist countries. As a result, in many countries, international law is considered part of national law. As regards treaties, by virtue of Article 26 of the Vienna Convention ('*Pacta sunt servanda*'), States have a duty to perform in good faith obligations binding on them under international law. This duty requires, amongst other matters, an obligation to introduce treaties into their national legal order. In France, for example, international law is part of the national legal order with a status superior to legislation under Article 55 of the 1958 Constitution, which provides that treaties or agreements duly ratified or approved 'shall, upon publication, prevail over Acts of Parliament, subject, with respect to each agreement or treaty, to its application by the other party'. In contrast to France, the United Kingdom introduced the Treaty of Rome into its law by the European Communities Act 1972 (as amended), but with the same result that English law includes EU law.

4.126 Accordingly, in the Tribunal's view, there is no fundamental difference in nature between international law and EU law that could justify treating EU law, unlike other international rules, differently in an international arbitration requiring the application of relevant rules and principles of international law.

4.127 *(v) EU Law as fact*: In the Tribunal's view, when it is not applied as international rules under the ECT, EU law must in any event be considered as part of the respondent's national legal order, i.e., to be treated as a 'fact' before this international tribunal.

4.128 The importance of rules contained in a national legal order, as a factual element to be taken into account, has long been acknowledged by international tribunals. For example, in *Azurix Corporation v The Argentine Republic*, the ICSID Tribunal stated the following:

> Azurix's claim has been advanced under the BIT and, as stated by the Annulment Committee in Vivendi II, the Tribunal's inquiry is governed by the ICSID Convention, by the BIT and by applicable international law. While the Tribunal's inquiry will be guided by this statement, this does not mean that the law of Argentina should be disregarded. On the contrary, the law of Argentina should be helpful in the carrying out of the Tribunal's inquiry into the alleged breaches of the Concession Agreement to which Argentina's law applies, but it is only an element of the inquiry because of the treaty nature of the claims under consideration.

A similar approach was later taken by the ICSID tribunal in *El Paso v The Argentine Republic*.

4.129 Accordingly, where a binding decision of the European Commission is concerned, even when not applied as EU law or international law, EU law may have to be taken into account as a rule to be applied as part of a national legal order, as a fact.

4.130 *(vi) The relationship between the ECT and EU law*: The Tribunal does not accept that there is a general principle of international law compelling the harmonious interpretation of different treaties. This may be a desirable outcome; but the end does not establish the means to that end. However, the situation here is somewhat special, with the European Union and its Member States so closely involved in and parties to the ECT. In the Tribunal's view, the ECT's historical genesis and its text are such that the ECT should be interpreted, if possible, in harmony with EU law.

4.131 The Tribunal acknowledges that, as a matter of legal, political and economic history, the European Union was the determining actor in the creation of the ECT. As noted above, the respondent submitted that 'the ECT was the brainchild of the European Union' (counter-memorial, para. 404); and, according to the European Commission, the EU 'played a key role in negotiating the . . . Energy Charter Treaty, signed in December 1994' (European Commission's submission, para. 32). The claimant did not contradict these historical statements in its different submissions; nor could it on the materials before the Tribunal.

4.132 This historical account has been developed by legal specialists of the ECT, including the late Professor Thomas Wälde. He noted that tribunals in ECT cases should consider an 'interpretative strategy of reciprocal consistency' in circumstances where both the ECT and another international treaty apply, 'i.e., to interpret the [two treaties] to minimise conflict and enhance consistency'. This is particularly the case where the 'other' applicable treaty involves the competition provisions of the EU Treaties, given the ECT's historic origins (at least as between EU Member States) as a vehicle to 'implement the principles enunciated in the European Energy Charter', including the central principle of 'promoting market-oriented reforms'. More precisely, the same scholar applied this interpretative approach to the relationship between the ECT and EU law:

> The ECT is largely a product of EU external political, economic and energy policy. It is meant to integrate the formerly Communist countries, provides an antechamber and preparation area for EU accession for many of them; it is intended to promote EU investment in these countries and energy flows from these countries to the EU. It is therefore linked more closely to EU integration, accession to the EU and EU external relations law than the 'run-of the mill' BIT.

4.133 Taking this background into consideration, the Tribunal considers that, in the circumstances, the two texts should be reconciled if possible, for three important legal reasons. The first derives from the ECT's genesis: it would have made no sense for the European Union to promote and subscribe to the ECT if that had meant entering into obligations inconsistent with EU law. The second derives from one of the ECT's objectives: it is an instrument clearly intended to combat anti-competitive conduct, which is the same objective as the European Union's objective in combating unlawful State aid. The third derives from the ECT's implicit recognition that decisions by the

European Commission are legally binding on all EU Member States which are party to the ECT. It is necessary to explain these three reasons and their effect separately below.

4.134 The ECT's genesis: In the Tribunal's view, the ECT's genesis generates a presumption that no contradiction exists between the ECT and EU law. As regards the respondent, the historical chronology indicates that the ECT entered into force for the respondent (in 1978) before the EC Treaty (in 2004). However, the ECT was negotiated and ratified after the coming into existence of the Rome Treaty, by its Member States. The interpretation of the ECT's text should therefore take into account such circumstances, in accordance with Article 32 of the Vienna Convention (which provides that, in order to interpret a treaty '(r)ecourse may be had to supplementary means of interpretation, including . . . the circumstances of its conclusion'). This means, in the Tribunal's view, that the ECT's conclusion by the European Union and its Member States at that time (including Belgium) should be presumed, in the absence of clear language or cogent evidence otherwise, to have been made in conformity with EU law.

4.135 The legal basis on which the European Union became a party to the ECT is set out in Council Decision 94/998/EC (as to signature) and Council and Commission Decision 98/181/EC, ECSC, Euratom (as to ratification). When treaties concern a matter for which the European Union is competent (as here, regarding the ECT), the relevant EU rule is contained in Article 133 EC (now Article 207(3) TFEU). Article 207(3) TFEU provides that '(t)he Council and the Commission shall be responsible for ensuring that the agreements negotiated are compatible with internal Union policies and rules'.

4.136 This EU rule most probably does not impose an absolute obligation, i.e., it is an '*obligation de moyens*' and not an '*obligation de résultat*'. Nonetheless, its existence confirms the Tribunal's conclusion that EU law can be presumed not to conflict or otherwise be inconsistent with the ECT. It also confirms the strong legal relationship between the ECT and EU law: EU law, being based on a treaty, forms part of international law; and the ECT, being a treaty adopted by EU institutions, forms part of EU law.

4.137 ECT and EU objectives: In the Tribunal's view, the ECT and the EC Treaty share the same broad objective in combating anti-competitive conduct. One of the obligations undertaken by States under the ECT was to protect investors, but another was to combat anti-competitive conduct, as provided in Article 6 ECT:

Article 6 – Competition
(1) Each Contracting Party shall work to alleviate market distortions and barriers to competition in Economic Activity in the Energy Sector.
(2) Each Contracting Party shall ensure that within its jurisdiction it has and enforces such laws as are necessary and appropriate to address unilateral and concerted anti-competitive conduct in Economic Activity in the Energy Sector.

4.138 The importance of this objective was acknowledged by one of the claimant's expert witnesses, Professor Amkhan. In his expert report, Professor Amkhan stated that one of the ECT's objectives was: 'to promote the development of an efficient energy market throughout Europe, and a better functioning global market, in both cases based on the principle of non-discrimination and on market-oriented price formation . . .' (First Report, para. 16).

4.139 The fact that both the ECT and EU law have common objectives was likewise emphasised in the Advocate-General's opinion of 15 March 2011 in *Commission v Slovakia*, where it was stated: 'The aim of EU energy policy is the opening up of markets, increase competition and the [sic] create a level playing field by no longer giving preferential treatment to former monopolies' (para. 50).

4.140 It was clear in 1993 when the Europe Agreement was signed between the European Union (then the Community) and the respondent that 'any public aid which distorts or threatens to distort competition by favouring certain undertakings or the production of certain goods' was not compatible with EU law.

4.141 For all these reasons, the Tribunal concludes that the objectives of the ECT and EU law were and remained similar as regards anti-competitive conduct, including unlawful State aid. Foreign investors in EU Member States, including Hungary, cannot have acquired any legitimate expectations that the ECT would necessarily shield their investments from the effects of EU law as regards anti-competitive conduct.

4.142 ECT and EU decisions: The framework of the ECT recognises that EU Member States will be legally bound by decisions of the European Union under EU law. Article 1(3) ECT acknowledges:

A 'Regional Economic Integration Organisation' means an organisation constituted by States to which they have transferred competence over certain matters a number of which are governed by this Treaty, including the authority to take decisions binding on them in respect of those matters.

It is common ground that the European Union (including the European Commission) was and remains, of course, such a Regional Economic Integration Organisation ('REIO'). As regards protection under the ECT, investors can have had no legitimate expectations in regard to the consequences of the implementation by an EU Member State of any such decision by the European Commission. In other words, the possible interference with a foreign investment through the implementation by an EU Member State of a legally binding decision of the European Commission was and remains inherent in the framework of the ECT itself.

4.143 *(vii) Harmonious interpretation:* It is noteworthy that both parties (albeit to differing extents) and the European Commission have argued for a harmonious interpretation of the ECT and EU law. The respondent considers that the Tribunal should seek to harmonise its interpretation of the ECT with EU law, in disputes between EU companies and EU Member States; and it has argued for an 'axiomatic' principle of harmony (respondent's counter-memorial, para. 410):

> In fact, international law suggests that where two States (such as Belgium and Hungary) have each entered into two different multinational treaties with one another, neither Treaty should be presumed to be automatically dominant over the other. Rather, the Tribunal should start from a presumption that no conflict exists, and seek to determine whether application of the treaty norms to the particular facts of the case might result in an outcome that reflects harmony. (respondent's counter-memorial, para. 411)

4.144 The European Commission submits that there exists a general principle of harmonious interpretation:

> More generally, the principle of harmonious interpretation is based on the principles of customary law on the interpretation of international treaties, as codified in Article 31 of the Vienna Convention on the Law of Treaties (VCLT).' (European Commission's submission, para. 125)

4.145 The claimant conditionally acknowledged that a harmonious interpretation could be made (see for example, claimant's post-hearing submissions, para. 98), although the result of its harmonious interpretation was somewhat different from that advanced by the respondent and the European Commission.

4.146 In the Tribunal's view, there is no need to harmonise the ECT's provisions for the settlement of investor-state disputes by international arbitration with EU law because there is no inconsistency. The Tribunal understands that the main concern of the European Commission is to protect the ECJ's monopoly over the interpretation of EU law, operating as its ultimate guardian and also its gate-keeper. With this concern, so it is said, there must be a unique EU court entrusted with the final word on what EU law means, whereas the existence of arbitral tribunals interpreting EU law could jeopardise its uniform application.

4.147 The ECJ's monopoly is said to derive from Article 292 EC (now Article 344 TFEU) which grants to the ECJ exclusive jurisdiction to decide disputes amongst EU Member States on the application of EU law. Article 292 states: 'Member States undertake not to submit a dispute concerning the interpretation or application of the Treaties to any method of settlement other than those provided for therein.' However, as is well known and recognised by the ECJ, such an exclusive jurisdiction does not prevent numerous other courts and arbitral tribunals from applying EU law, both within and without the European Union. Given the widespread relevance and importance of EU law to international trade, it could not be otherwise.

4.148 First, as far as the courts and tribunals of EU Member States are concerned (but not private arbitration tribunals), a certain uniformity of interpretation is made possible by their capacity (by any such court or tribunal) and their obligation (by a court or tribunal against whose decisions there is no judicial remedy under national law) to refer preliminary questions of interpretation of EU law to the ECJ under Article 234 EC (now Article 267 TFEU).17 The Tribunal notes the fact that EU national courts retain a certain degree of discretion in their decision to refer a question of interpretation to the ECJ and that the courts of last resort may use the legal theory of *acte clair* to retain also a further element of discretion. In other words, there is no automatic reference to or seizure by the ECJ, as soon as any question of EU law arises in a dispute before an EU national court. This factor leaves open the possibility, if not even probability, of divergent interpretations or applications of EU law to similar disputes by courts and tribunals within the European Union.

4.149 Second, as far as the courts and tribunals of non-EU Member States are concerned, there is no possibility for them to refer to the ECJ any question of interpretation of EU law. In other words, to take only one example, a Japanese court deciding a dispute between an EU company and a Japanese company might have to interpret and apply a mandatory rule of EU law relevant to the parties' transaction: in such a case, this exercise cannot be controlled by the ECJ if there is no later enforcement of the Japanese judgment within the European Union. Only if there were such enforcement proceedings before the national court of an EU Member State could the possibility arise of a reference to the ECJ, but the same discretions would then apply as described above, meaning that control by the ECJ would remain only a possibility and not a certainty. This factor leaves open the further probability of divergent interpretations or applications of EU law to similar disputes by courts and tribunals outside the European Union.

4.150 Third, as far as arbitration is concerned, Article 234 EC (now Article 267 TFEU) prevents arbitration between EU Member States. This was ostensibly decided in the *Mox Plant* case between the United Kingdom and the Republic of Ireland, where the ECJ held that EU Member States are prevented from submitting their disputes to 'any other method of dispute settlement' than the method provided by EU law; and that, as a result, the ECJ has exclusive jurisdiction to resolve any dispute between two EU Member States that at least partially raises an issue of EU law. It is however doubtful whether this decision of the ECJ would prevent, for example, the International Court of Justice (ICJ) from deciding any issue of EU law, if raised in a dispute involving two or more EU Member States. It is not however necessary to interpret any further the ECJ's decision in the *Mox Plant* case, given that the parties' dispute does not here involve two EU Member States.

4.151 Fourth, as regards an international or national arbitration tribunal in a dispute not involving two or more EU Member States as parties, there is no provision equivalent to Article 292 EC (now Article 344 TFEU) dealing with arbitration between two or more private parties, nationals of Member States, or with mixed disputes settlement mechanisms such as investor-state arbitration between individuals, nationals of EU Member States and an EU Member State under the ICSID Convention or other international instruments. Article 292 EC is not applicable to these arbitration tribunals. If the submissions made by the European Commission were correct, this would seem to be an extraordinary omission.

4.152 As regards arbitrations between private parties, it has long been recognised by the ECJ that such arbitrations are frequently held within the EU, interpreting and applying EU law, and do not thereby infringe the monopoly of interpretation of EU law by the ECJ, as illustrated (for example) by the *Eco Swiss* case.

4.153 However, the Tribunal recognises that one reason why the ECJ did not find such an arbitration objectionable under EU law in the *Eco Swiss* case was because the award made in that arbitration (with its arbitral seat in the Netherlands) remained subject to the control of the Dutch national courts; and these Dutch courts could seek an interpretation of EU law from the ECJ under Article 234 EC. The ECJ long ago decided that a private arbitration tribunal is not a national court or tribunal under Article 234 EC, with no capacity itself to refer any question of EU law to the ECJ. This recognition necessarily extends not only to arbitration tribunals seated within the European Union but also to tribunals seated outside the European Union. The present case concerns an international arbitration between a private party – a national of an EU Member State – and an EU Member State, held outside the EU. It also concerns an arbitration subject to the ICSID Convention, as incorporated in Hungary and in the laws of almost all EU Member States. In the Tribunal's view, this arbitration does not come under Article 292 EC and cannot therefore infringe EU law. There is indeed no rule in EU law that provides, expressly or impliedly, that such an international arbitration is inconsistent with EU law. Again, if the submissions made by the European Commission were correct, this would also seem to be an extraordinary omission.

4.154 The Tribunal's conclusion is confirmed by the Opinion 1/09 of the ECJ (Full Court) of 8 March 2011, delivered pursuant to Article 218(11) TFEU (formerly Art 300(6) EC). The issue there was whether the creation of a Patent Court ('PC') by an international agreement to be made by the European Union infringed the exclusive status of the ECJ:

> 1. The request submitted for the Opinion of the Court by the Council of the European Union is worded as follows: 'Is the envisaged agreement creating a Unified Patent Litigation System (currently named European and Community Patents Court) compatible with the provisions of the Treaty establishing the European Community?'

4.155 On the question of whether Article 292 EC (now Art 344 TFEU) applied to settlement mechanisms for disputes involving private parties, the ECJ's answered this question without ambiguity in the negative:

> 63. Nor can the creation of the PC be in conflict with Article 344 TFEU [formerly Art 292 EC], given that that article merely prohibits Member States from submitting a dispute concerning the interpretation or application of the Treaties to any method of settlement other than those provided for in the Treaties. The jurisdiction which the draft agreement intends to grant to the PC relates only to disputes between individuals in the field of patents.

4.156 The Tribunal notes, of course, that the ECJ also decided that the creation of this Patent Court would violate the ECJ's monopoly of rendering judgments on significant issues of EU law, such as the interpretation of the EC Treaties and the validity of decisions made by EU institutions provided by Article 230 (now Art 263 TFEU). This was so because the Patent Court 'may be called upon to determine a dispute pending before it in the light of the fundamental rights and general principles of European Union law, or even to examine the validity of an act of the European Union' (para 78). In this respect, the ECJ can be understood to have been protecting its traditional roles as the ultimate guardian of EU law and as its ultimate gate-keeper. It is therefore an important decision, which has generated much interest. It is however unnecessary for the Tribunal here to address this decision any further because it is clear that the ECJ was not applying its decision on the proposed Patent Court to the settlement of disputes by private or mixed arbitrations.

4.157 Moreover, as explained by the Tribunal elsewhere in this Decision, this case does not turn on the interpretation of the EC Treaties or the validity of decisions made by EU institutions. It has already been stated above that the parties' dispute is about alleged violations of the ECT by the respondent; it does not include any attack by the claimant on the legal validity of any decision by the European Commission (including its Final Decision of 4 June 2008); and it does not concern any alleged violations of EU law by the Respondent or the European Union.

4.158 Moreover, the Tribunal notes the important legal fact that the European Commission itself, in signing the ECT, accepted the possibility of international arbitrations under the ECT, both between a non-EU investor and an EU Member State or between an EU investor and a non-EU Member State, without any distinction or reservation. This factor reinforces the Tribunal's conclusion. It is also noteworthy that this acceptance applied to both ICSID and non-ICSID arbitrations, in other words (i) non-ICSID arbitration awards whose recognition or enforcement within the European Union could entail possible control by EU national courts (under the *lex loci arbitri* or the New York Convention) with a possible reference to the ECJ, and (ii) ICSID arbitration awards equivalent under the ICSID Convention to judgments of national courts which are not equally susceptible to like control by EU national courts, if enforced within the EU.

4.159 The apparent absence of control by the EU national courts over ICSID awards may lie behind the concerns of the European Commission expressed in this ICSID arbitration as regards applicable law and therefore jurisdiction.

The Tribunal considers that such concerns lack any juridical basis under EU law because there remains the possibility to ensure a uniform application of EU law by the ECJ in proceedings involving an EU Member State, regardless of any arbitration or award under the ICSID Convention.

4.160 This possibility was explained by Professor Thomas Eilmansberger in his scholarly article:

> If the fallacious application of EC law by the arbitral tribunal, or its failure to apply EC law at all, however, results in EC law being rendered ineffective in a given case, again nothing prevents the Commission from initiating proceedings against a Member State which, in execution of the award, would be acting in violation of EC law (e.g., by paying out an illegal subsidy promised to the investor).

4.161 It is useful to cite here Article 226 EC (now Art 258 TFEU) and Article 228 EC (now Art 260 TFEU) 25:

> Article 226: If the Commission considers that a Member State has failed to fulfil an obligation under the Treaties, it shall deliver a reasoned opinion on the matter after giving the State concerned the opportunity to submit its observations. If the State concerned does not comply with the opinion within the period laid down by the Commission, the latter may bring the matter before the Court of Justice of the European Union.
>
> Article 228:
> (1) If the Court of Justice of the European Union finds that a Member State has failed to fulfil an obligation under the Treaties, the State shall be required to take the necessary measures to comply with the judgment of the Court.
> (2) If the Commission considers that the Member State concerned has not taken the necessary measures to comply with the judgment of the Court, it may bring the case before the Court after giving that State the opportunity to submit its observations. It shall specify the amount of the lump sum or penalty payment to be paid by the Member State concerned which it considers appropriate in the circumstances.
> If the Court finds that the Member State concerned has not complied with its judgment it may impose a lump sum or penalty payment on it.
> This procedure shall be without prejudice to Article 259.
> [Article 259 EC addresses remedies available to an EU Member State against another Member State].

4.162 In other words, even when disputes raising issues of EU law are decided by international arbitration, if the resulting award is honoured voluntarily by the EU Member State or enforced judicially within the European Union against that Member State, the ECJ retains the possibility, through different mechanisms for both ICSID and non-ICSID awards under the EU Treaties, to exercise its traditional role as the ultimate guardian of EU law.

4.163 The Tribunal notes the still more important fact that the European Union also accepted in signing the ECT to submit itself to international arbitration, thereby accepting the possibility of an arbitration between the European Union and private parties, whether nationals of EU or Non-EU Member States and whether held within or without the EU. This acceptance did not and could not include ICSID arbitrations, given the inability of the European Union (not being a State) to sign the ICSID Convention and its reservation to such effect. There is however no reason to infer that, if the European Union had been able to accede to the ICSID Convention, its acceptance of international arbitration would not have extended to arbitrations under the ICSID Convention.

4.164 In the Tribunal's view, if the European Union has itself accepted to submit to arbitration a dispute with a private investor concerning the application of the ECT (as it did), it cannot properly argue that such an arbitration is not similarly available to the same private investor advancing a claim under the ECT against an EU Member State, including an arbitration under the ICSID Convention.

4.165 The Tribunal also notes that EU law has been interpreted and applied by several ICSID Tribunals, without raising any insuperable problems for the European Union. By way of only one example, in the *Maffezini* case, the arbitral tribunal interpreted and applied an EEC Directive in order to analyse the extent of the investor's rights, as appears from the following extract from its award:

> Particularly noteworthy is the legislation on EIA. Strict procedures in this
> respect are provided in EEC Directive 85/337 of June 27, 1985 and in Spain's
> Royal Legislative Decree No. 1302/1986 of June 28, 1986. Chemical industries
> are specifically required under both measures to undertake an EIA. Public
> information, consultation with pertinent authorities, licensing and other
> procedures are also a part thereof. The EEC Directive, like the one that later
> came to amend it, requires 'that an EIA is undertaken before consent is given to
> certain public and private projects considered to have significant environmental
> implications'.

4.166 In conclusion, the Tribunal has found no legal rule or principle of EU law that would prevent this Tribunal from exercising its functions in this arbitration under Article 26 of the ECT. In the Tribunal's view, there is no inconsistency between the ECT and EU law as regards the rules and principles of international law applicable to the parties' arbitration agreement contained in the ECT and the ICSID Convention (including the Tribunal's jurisdiction thereunder) or applicable to the merits of the Claimant's claims and the Respondent's defences under the ECT.

4.167 *(viii) Possible inconsistency between the ECT and EU law*: The Tribunal has decided that there is no material inconsistency between the ECT and EU law. The Tribunal has also concluded that if there were any material inconsistency between the ECT and EU law, the ECT and EU law should, if possible, be read in harmony. It is nonetheless appropriate to address further the parties' submissions (with the European Commission's submission) on the hypothesis that the Tribunal is mistaken, i.e., that there could in fact be a material inconsistency not subject to harmonisation, and whether there are international rules that can be used to clarify the relationship between the ECT and EU law. This issue arises in regard to the European Commission's Final Decision of 4 June 2008.

4.168 The ECT acknowledges the authority of the European Union (as an REIO) to take decisions binding under EU law on EU Member States which have signed the ECT, including the respondent. Neither party refutes this binding character of such decisions under EU law. That is acknowledged by the claimant's response, confirming its earlier written and oral submissions, where the claimant does not complain at the enforcement by the respondent of the European Commission's Final Decision, but rather impugns the respondent for not correctly enforcing that Decision within its permitted margin of appreciation under EU law:

> Hungary did have a discretion, afforded to it by EU law, to decide how to respond to the Commission Decision (Exhibit C-106), i.e. whether to outright terminate the PPA and whether to compensate Electrabel and in what amount. As addressed in detail in the Claimant's Post-Hearing Brief, this case is about whether Hungary's exercise of that discretion was in conformity with its obligations towards Electrabel under the ECT. . . . the key issue is whether Hungary breached the ECT when exercising the discretion afforded to it by EU law.

4.169 In the Tribunal's view, the acts of the respondent implementing such a binding decision under EU law have to be taken into account in the evaluation of its conduct under the ECT. This means, in the present case, that there can be no practical contradiction between the ECT and EU law in regard to the Final Decision. It also means that the ECT does not protect the claimant, as against the respondent, from the enforcement by the respondent of a binding decision of the European Commission under EU law.

4.170 This analysis leaves open the responsibility of the European Union under the ECT for decisions of the European Commission which violate the rights of investors under the ECT. This factor was readily acknowledged in the European Commission's submission:

> . . .within the Community's legal order, the Energy Charter Treaty is binding on the institutions of the Community and the Member States under Article 300(7) EC. In particular, any act adopted by the institutions may thus not violate the international obligations assumed by the Community (para. 33).

In the European Commission's submission, the responsibility for preventing unlawful State aid lies with the European Union and not with EU Member States; and therefore the respondent is the wrong party named by the claimant for its PPA Termination Claim. However, as the Commission asserts, it 'would trigger the [European Union's] responsibility if contrary to the ECT' (para. 41).

4.171 The Tribunal considers that the Commission's analysis is correct, but only if and to the extent that the relevant dispute engages the legal responsibility of the European Union under the ECT for a decision of the European Commission. However, this is manifestly not what this case is all about: the European Union is not a named party to this arbitration; the claimant here makes no complaint against the European Union or the European Commission; it does not impugn the legal validity of the Commission's Final Decision; and its claims are not made under EU law. The claimant's claims under the ECT relate only to certain measures taken by the Respondent, some resulting from the Final Decision under EU law and some with no link with the Commission or EU law.

4.172 Accordingly, for the purposes of this case, the Tribunal concludes that the two legal orders are not in fact inconsistent or otherwise contradictory. However, as a courtesy to the elaborate and extensive arguments advanced by the parties and the European Commission, the Tribunal next considers, assuming the two legal orders did produce different results in this case, whether there are any legal rules providing for a hierarchy between such applicable laws.

4.173 *Hierarchy of legal orders*: The Tribunal has already concluded above that there is no general principle under international law compelling the harmonious interpretation of all existing legal rules. If different rules deal with the same subject matter in a way that seems contradictory, there is no general hierarchical system, but certain tools of interpretation regarding chronology (*lex posterior derogat priori*), specificity (*lex specialis generalibus derogat*) and identity of the parties to the agreements (same or different parties) can assist in solving the conflict. However, these rules do not always apply or can only be applied with difficulty. For this reason, international instruments often contain their own rules concerning the relationship with other agreements, as is the case here with Article 16 ECT and Article 307 EC (Art 351 TFEU).

4.174 *Article 16 ECT*: The claimant submits that Article 16 ECT is applicable, whereas the respondent submits that it is inapplicable, whether or not the ECT and the EC Treaty are considered as having the same subject matter.

4.175 First, it is necessary to note again that the EU law is not incompatible with the provision for investor-state arbitration contained in Part V of the ECT, including international arbitration under the ICSID Convention. The two legal orders can be applied together as regards the parties' arbitration agreement and this arbitration, because only the ECT deals with investor-state arbitration; and nothing in EU law can be interpreted as precluding investor-state arbitration under the ECT and the ICSID Convention.

4.176 As regards the substantive protections in Part III of the ECT, the Tribunal does not consider that the ECT and EU law share the same subject matter; and, accordingly, it considers that Article 16 ECT is inapplicable.

4.177 However, the two legal orders share much in common: the protection of foreign investors is clearly addressed by both the ECT and EU law, although from different perspectives. There are a large number of rules in EU law which protect foreign investors, even if differently formulated from the rules in the ECT. Accordingly, the Tribunal next considers possible solutions to resolve any inconsistency, if (contrary to its decision above) the ECT and the EC Treaties concerned the same subject matter.

4.178 *Article 307 EC (Art 351 TFEU)*: Assuming the same subject matter, the Tribunal decides that Article 16 ECT would still be inapplicable because the conflict rule of the later treaty would apply, namely Article 307 EC. Both parties submit that Article 307 EC is inapplicable to the present case; but the Tribunal does not consider that Article 307 can so easily be dismissed.

4.179 The Tribunal notes that, as stated by Professor Jan Klabbers, 'Article 307 is the only article in the entire edifice of the EU relating to the status of treaties concluded by the EU's member states vis-à-vis EU law.' In particular, there is no other specific article in the EU Treaties dealing with the fate of treaties concluded between EU Member States. However, the effect of Article 307 EC is not straightforward under EU law.

4.180 From its wording, it is clear that Article 307 EC cannot apply to treaties made between EU Member States. Article 307 deals only with relations between EU Members and Non-EU Members that survive the entry of the EU Member into the European Union; and it does not address relations between EU Member States. The Tribunal concludes that Article 307 EC, as a 'survival clause', does not apply to the relations between the two EU Member States in this case, Belgium as the home State of the claimant and the respondent, as the host State of the claimant's alleged investment.

4.181 The meaning of Article 307 EC was considered by the ECJ in a case dealing with the protection of investments under a treaty between Switzerland (a Non-EU State) and Slovakia (an EU Member State), which had entered into force before the entry of Slovakia into the European Union. The opinion of the Advocate-General dated 15 March 2011 reads as follows:

> Under Article 307(1) EC, the rights and obligations arising from an agreement concluded before the date of accession of a Member State between it and a third country are not affected by the provisions of the Treaty. Hence that provision resolves the conflict between the two incompatible obligations in favour of the earlier obligation, and thus codifies the international law principle that a subsequent treaty that conflicts with an earlier one cannot legally affect the rights of a State that is a party only to the earlier treaty.

According to the Advocate-General (as also adopted by the ECJ), Article 307 EC is only the expression in the EC Treaties of the general international rule contained in Article 30(4)(b) of the Vienna Convention, to the effect that if there are two successive treaties not having the same parties, the applicable treaty is the one (whether the first or the second one) to which both States are parties.

4.182 However, the Tribunal notes that the ECJ has interpreted Article 307 EC not only positively for what it does say, but also, 'negatively', for what it does not say. If two States are both parties to a pre-accession treaty and the EC Treaties, in case of incompatibility between the two legal orders, it is the later treaty which applies, in conformity with Article 30(3) of the Vienna Convention, to which Article 30(4)(b) of the Vienna Convention refers.

4.183 Under this 'negative' interpretation, Article 307 EC means that between EU Member States, EU law prevails in case of inconsistency with another earlier treaty. Article 307 EC has been interpreted to mean that relations between EU Members differ, by a logical implication, from relations between Non-EU Members, i.e., that inconsistent earlier treaties between Member States do not survive entry into the European Union. If Article 307 EC provides that treaty rights between Non-EU Members cannot be jeopardised by the subsequent entry of a Non-EU State into the European Union, it appears logical, taking into account the integration processes of the European Union, that the opposite consequence should be implied, i.e., the non-survival of rights under an earlier treaty incompatible with EU law as between EU Member States.

4.184 It has to be stressed that these two different consequences have been considered as being applicable at the same time to the same treaty, when both EU Members and Non-EU Members were parties to the treaty. Another analysis was possible, as advanced by Professor Klabbers in his work 'Treaty Conflict and the European Union' (p. 120):

> . . . (o)n one reading, Article 307 EC could be interpreted as simply giving priority to anterior treaties over the later EC Treaty, even to the extent that such anterior treaties would have to be applied between member states inter se, as long as the treaties concerned would also count non-members among their parties. This was the argument made by Italy in the first case to invoke Article 307 EC (Art 234, as it then was) before the Court of Justice.

In *Commission v Italy*, the issue concerned treaty rights under the GATT which conflicted with EU customs rules. In its judgment, the ECJ distinguished between (i) the reciprocal rights between EU Members and Non-EU Members under the GATT that survived the entry of a State into the European Union and (ii) the reciprocal rights between EU Members that were superseded, in case of incompatibility, by EU customs rules. The ECJ decided in no uncertain terms that: '[i]n matters governed by the [EC] Treaty, that treaty takes precedence over agreements concluded between Member States before its entry into force'.

4.185 In the same manner, in *Commission v Austria*, the ECJ confirmed that it is 'settled case-law' that, 'whilst Article 307 EC allows Member States to honour obligations owed to non-member States under international agreements preceding the Treaty, it does not authorise them to exercise rights under such agreements in intra-Community relations'.

4.186 The Tribunal considers this interpretation of Article 307 to accord with international rules relating to the interpretation of successive treaties.

It notes that the preeminence of EU law applies not only to pre-accession treaties between EU Members, but also to post-accession treaties between EU Members, as EU Members cannot derogate from EU rules as between themselves. There is therefore a significant coherence between EU law and treaties between EU Member States.

4.187 When the respondent and Belgium acceded to the ECT in 1998, Belgium was an EU Member State, but the respondent was not. In 2004, the respondent became and remains an EU Member State. Accordingly, Article 307 EC (as interpreted by the ECJ) means that, if any inconsistency existed between the ECT and EU law, the ECT would apply in relations between EU Members and Non-EU Members, but that EU law would prevail over the ECT in relations between EU Members themselves (including Belgium and the respondent). This was aptly summarised in Professor Klabbers' work on 'Treaty conflict and the European Union', already cited above ([para. 4.184]):

> Article 307 TEC has a limited protective role: it protects only the rights of third parties under anterior treaties; the rights of member states themselves under such treaties are to be considered renounced by virtue of concluding the EC Treaty.

4.188 A last point should be clarified by the Tribunal. The claimant submits that the rights of investors under the ECT are different from the rights of EU Member States; and thus that investors should be treated in a way analogous to the rights of a non-EU Member State, i.e., that those rights should survive membership of the European Union. The claimant relies on Professor Klabbers' suggestion that Article 307(1) EC might apply to protect not only the rights of States, but also to individual rights conferred by earlier treaties. In the Tribunal's view, this analysis cannot disconnect the rights of individual investors from the rights of their home States, with the effect that all individual rights pre-dating the EU Treaties would survive, for both nationals of Non-EU States and nationals of EU States. The Tribunal agrees with the respondent's submission in its reply response that the protection of the rights of individuals 'must necessarily be limited to protecting individual rights of nationals of *non-Member States*' (para. 13, original emphasis).

4.189 Subject to the several assumptions above (being contrary to the Tribunal's own decisions), the Tribunal concludes that Article 307 EC precludes inconsistent preexisting treaty rights of EU Member States and their own nationals against other EU Member States; and it follows, if the ECT and EU law remained incompatible notwithstanding all efforts at harmonisation, that EU law would prevail over the ECT's substantive protections and that the ECT could not apply inconsistently with EU law to such a national's claim against an EU Member State.

4.190 Article 30 of the Vienna Convention: The Tribunal can deal summarily with Article 30 of the Vienna Convention, because it has the same consequences as the 'negative' interpretation of Article 307 EC decided by the ECJ and Advocate General in *Commission v Slovakia* (where, as described above, Art 307 was treated as the expression under EU law of Article 30(4)(b) of the Vienna Convention).

Accordingly, even in situations where Article 307 EC would not have applied, the same result would have followed under Article 30, on the hypothesis that the two treaties related to the same subject matter.

4.191 In summary, from whatever perspective the relationship between the ECT and EU law is examined, the Tribunal concludes that EU law would prevail over the ECT in case of any material inconsistency. That conclusion depends, however, upon the existence of a material inconsistency; and the Tribunal has concluded that none exists for the purpose of deciding the parties' dispute in this arbitration.

(6) The Tribunal's conclusions

4.192 In summary, the Tribunal concludes that it is required to apply to the parties' arbitration agreement and to the merits of the parties' dispute in this case the rules of international law agreed by the parties under Article 42(1) of the ICSID Convention; and that under Article 26(6) ECT, these rules comprise the ECT and rules and principles of international law.

4.193 As regards the law applicable to its jurisdiction to decide the parties' dispute, the Tribunal likewise concludes that it is required, as an international tribunal, to apply the ECT and the ICSID Convention, together with rules and principles of international law.

4.194 The Tribunal also concludes that the ECT and the ICSID Convention were and remain valid treaties under international law legally binding upon the respondent and validly invoked by the claimant in this arbitration. In particular, the Tribunal decides that Article 42 of the ICSID Convention and Article 26 ECT are not in any way invalidated, suspended or terminated under international law; nor has the respondent withdrawn from either treaty. Indeed the claimant and the respondent have not contended otherwise before this Tribunal.

4.195 The Tribunal further concludes that EU law (not limited to EU Treaties) forms part of the rules and principles of international law applicable to the parties' dispute under Article 26(6) ECT. Moreover EU law, as part of the respondent's national law, is also to be taken into account as a fact relevant to the parties' dispute.

4.196 As regards the parties' arbitration agreement and the merits of their dispute, the Tribunal concludes that there is in this case no material inconsistency between the ECT and EU law.

4.197 The Tribunal recognises the special status of EU law operating as a body of supranational law within the EU. It also recognises the roles undertaken by the ECJ as the arbiter and gate-keeper of EU law comprising, in the words of ECJ Opinion 1/09, 'the fundamental elements of the legal order and judicial system of the EU' (para. 54). However, these important features do not arise in the present case.

4.198 Although the Tribunal is required in this arbitration to interpret the European Commission's Final Decision of 4 June 2008, and in that sense, to apply EU law to the parties' dispute, the Tribunal is not required to adjudicate here upon the validity of that decision, as the claimant has consistently confirmed to the Tribunal during the course of these arbitration proceedings. That adjudication remains a decision for the EU courts alone, within the pending legal proceedings brought against the European Commission by Dunamenti (but not the claimant). This Tribunal is not therefore required to review and does not here review the legality of any act of any EU institution, including the European Commission.

4.199 Lastly, the Tribunal recognises that it is an international tribunal established under the ECT and the ICSID Convention, in an international arbitration with no seat or legal place within the European Union and with its award potentially enforceable under the ICSID Convention both within and without the European Union. The Tribunal does not consider that any of these factors affect its conclusions as regards the law applicable to the parties' arbitration agreement, the Tribunal's jurisdiction and the merits of their dispute.

23
Remedies

EXERCISE 36 – SEMINAR

Review *Enron Corporation and Ponderosa Assets LP v The Argentine Republic,*
Decision on Jurisdiction dated 14 January 2004.

 DISCUSSION QUESTIONS

Problem 1
What limitations, if any, exist with respect to remedies that a claimant can request in an investment treaty arbitration? Does it matter if the remedy sought is enforceable or not?

Problem 2
To what extent do Arbitral Tribunals in investment treaty disputes have the authority to order interim measures? Is there a difference between ICSID and non-ICSID arbitration? Should there be a difference?

Problem 3
What remedies are available to an investor who is a minority shareholder in a company, incorporated in the host State, whose business has allegedly been expropriated? What lessons in this respect can be learnt from the Enron case?

Problem 4
Does it matter, as far as available remedies are concerned, if an expropriation is legal or illegal?

 CASE

Enron Corporation and Ponderosa Assets LP v The Argentine Republic, excerpt from Decision on Jurisdiction

A. Procedure

[...]

Shareholders' rights under the Bilateral Investment Treaty

42. As the ICSID Convention did not attempt to define 'investment', this task was left largely to the parties to bilateral investment treaties or other expressions of consent. It has been aptly commented that there is, however, a limit to this discretion of the parties because they could not validly define as investment in connection with the Convention something absurd or entirely incompatible with its object and purpose. The definition of investment relevant to this case is set out in Article I (1) of the Bilateral Investment Treaty, which provides in part:

> (a) 'investment' means every kind of investment in the territory of one Party owned or controlled directly or indirectly by nationals or companies of the other Party, such as equity, debt, and service and investment contracts; and includes without limitation:
> (...)
> (ii) a company or shares of stock or other interests in a company or interests in the assets thereof. . ..

43. As noted above, in the view of the Argentine Republic neither TGS nor CIESA qualify as an investment or as investor under the Bilateral Investment Treaty. While it is admitted that the investment made by the claimants is protected under the Treaty this would only allow for claims affecting their rights *qua* shareholders. This view, as also noted, is contested by the claimants.

44. The Tribunal notes, as did the Tribunal in *Lanco* and also the Committee on Annulment in *Compañía de Aguas del Aconquija* or *Vivendi*, the latter in respect of a different but comparable bilateral investment treaty, that the definition of investment set out above is broad indeed. It is apparent that this definition does not exclude claims by minority or non-controlling shareholders. Neither is there anything unreasonable in this definition that would make it incompatible with the object and purpose of the ICSID Convention.

45. The Argentine Republic has made in this context the argument that when treaties have wished to include within their scope indirect damages of the sort claimed in this case, they have done so expressly. The North American Free Trade Agreement (NAFTA) and the Algiers Claims Settlement Declaration establishing the jurisdiction of the Iran-United States Claims Tribunal have been invoked as examples of this express reference. This, it is further explained, is also the case of the Argentina-United Kingdom Bilateral Investment Treaty. Most treaties, in the respondent's view, allow for claims of locally incorporated companies only when controlled by foreign nationals, a

situation not given in the instant case. The silence of the Bilateral Investment Treaty on the question of claims for indirect damage cannot be held, in the respondent's argument, against the principles established in the legislation of Argentina or international law.

46. The fact that a treaty may have provided expressly for certain rights of shareholders does not mean that a treaty not so providing has meant to exclude such rights if this can be reasonably inferred from the provisions of such treaty. Each instrument must be interpreted autonomously in the light of its own context and in the light of its interconnections with international law. Moreover, the United States model investment treaties are based on a rather broad interpretation of investment that was included with the express intention of overriding the eventual restrictive effects that could result from the *Barcelona Traction* decision.

47. The rules governing the interpretation of treaties under the Vienna Convention on the Law of Treaties lead to a similar conclusion in so far as the parties to the treaties concerned are different. Indeed, the interpretation of a bilateral treaty between two parties in connection with the text of another treaty between different parties will normally be the same, unless the parties express a different intention in accordance with international law. A similar logic is found in Article 31 of the Vienna Convention in so far as subsequent agreement or practice between the parties to the same treaty is taken into account regarding the interpretation of the treaty. There is no evidence in this case that the intention of the parties to the Argentina-United States Bilateral Treaty might be different from that expressed in other investment treaties invoked.

48. The parties in this case have also discussed the meaning and extent of the *Mondev* case where, as indicated by the Argentine Republic, the United States held the view that shareholders cannot claim for injury to a corporation and can claim only for direct injuries suffered in their capacity as shareholders. The claimants have argued that what matters is the conclusion of the tribunal in that case, which dismissed the United States' arguments and upheld the claimant's standing. The Tribunal must note in this connection that what the State of nationality of the investor might argue in a given case to which it is a party cannot be held against the rights of the investor in a separate case to which the investor is a party. This is precisely the merit of the ICSID Convention in that it overcame the deficiencies of diplomatic protection where the investor was subject to whatever political or legal determination the State of nationality would make in respect of its claim.

49. This Tribunal must accordingly conclude that under the provisions of the Bilateral Investment Treaty, broad as they are, claims made by investors that are not in the majority or in the control of the affected corporation when claiming for violations of their rights under such treaty are admissible. Whether the locally incorporated company may further claim for the violation of its rights under contracts, licences or other instruments, does not affect the direct right of action of foreign shareholders under the Bilateral Investment Treaty for protecting their interests in the qualifying investment.

50. But this conclusion is not the end of the matter. It was explained above that the claimants made their investment in various companies participating in CIESA and only marginally in TGS. That is, they invested in a string of locally incorporated companies that in turn made the investment in TGS. The Argentine Republic has rightly raised a concern about the fact that if minority shareholders can claim independently from the affected corporation, this could trigger an endless chain of claims, as any shareholder making an investment in a company that makes an investment in another company, and so on, could invoke a direct right of action for measures affecting a corporation at the end of the chain.

51. Counsel for the Argentine Republic have addressed this issue by describing the case as one in which 'certain investor who is the owner of the shares in certain corporations which, in turn, own shares of an Argentine corporation, that does not qualify either as investor or as an investment, alleges that the treaty was breached as a consequence of certain tax claims over the latter corporation'.

52. The Tribunal notes that while investors can claim in their own right under the provisions of the treaty, there is indeed a need to establish a cut-off point beyond which claims would not be permissible as they would have only a remote connection to the affected company. As this is in essence a question of admissibility of claims, the answer lies in establishing the extent of the consent to arbitration of the host State. If consent has been given in respect of an investor and an investment, it can be reasonably concluded that the claims brought by such investor are admissible under the treaty. If the consent cannot be considered as extending to another investor or investment, these other claims should then be considered inadmissible as being only remotely connected with the affected company and the scope of the legal system protecting that investment.

53. This issue was discussed, but not actually decided, in the ICSID case of *Gruslin v Malaysia*, where the respondent government raised as an objection

to jurisdiction the question that 'the claimant has made no investment in Malaysia, and has no legal relationship with Malaysia that falls within the scope of the investment treaty'. The Tribunal in that case ruled that it lacked jurisdiction on another ground, namely that the investment was not made in an approved project as required under the pertinent bilateral investment treaty, thus making unnecessary a determination of the first issue. It is also interesting to note that the objection raised relied on the argument that the claimant was not the 'owner' of the investment and that its rights in respect of the management company involved were no more than rights of a contractual nature.

54. At the hearing on jurisdiction held in the present case, the Tribunal put a question to the parties as to whether the claimants had been invited by the Government of Argentina to participate in the investment connected to the privatisation of TGS. It turned out that this had been precisely the case.

55. In fact, the Information Memorandum issued in 1992 and other instruments related to the privatisation of the gas industry had specifically invited foreign investors to participate in this process. A 'road show' followed in key cities around the world and specific meetings with the claimants were held in this context. Successful bidders were required to establish an investment company in Argentina 'which will hold their interest in the licensed operating company'. Moreover, the technical expertise of the claimants was one of the elements required to materialise their participation in the process. This explains why EPCA was required to execute the Transfer Agreement and to enter into a Technical Assistance Agreement with TGS. The requirements of the Technical Assistance Agreement referred not only to the Technical Operator but also to the 'company participating in the same Economic Group providing the necessary technical support'. The investors also had certain decision-making power in the management of TGS. The pertinent officials of the Argentine Government were kept abreast of the various corporate arrangements organized to materialise the investment sought.

56. The conclusion that follows is that in the present case the participation of the claimants was specifically sought and that they are thus included within the consent to arbitration given by the Argentine Republic. The claimants cannot be considered to be only remotely connected to the legal arrangements governing the privatisation, they are beyond any doubt the owners of the investment made and their rights are protected under the Treaty as clearly established treaty rights and not merely contractual rights related to some intermediary. The fact that the investment was made through CIESA and related companies does not in any way alter this conclusion.

57. The Tribunal accordingly decides that the claim in the present case is admissible under the Bilateral Investment Treaty or, stated in another way, that the claimants have *jus standi* under this Treaty in their capacity as protected investors.

[. . .]

Jurisdictional objection concerning injunctive relief and other remedies

75. The Argentine Republic has made two objections to the jurisdiction of this Tribunal concerning the remedies requested by the claimants. The first objection relates to the question that any remedy would really have its effect on TGS, which cannot benefit from the claim as not being in the respondent's view an investment or an investor under the Treaty. This part of the objection has been dealt with above in the context of the determination that the claimants are exercising a right in their own capacity under the Treaty which is separate from any rights appurtenant to TGS. Whether a remedy, in addition to protecting the investors' rights, benefits a separate but related corporate entity is not a ground for objection to jurisdiction.

76. The second objection to jurisdiction made under this heading is more complex. It concerns the power of the Tribunal to order injunctive relief. In the respondent's view the Tribunal lacks such a power under the Convention and the Treaty, and it could only either issue a declaratory statement that might satisfy the investor or else determine the payment of compensation based on a finding that a certain measure is wrongful. In particular it is argued that an ICSID Tribunal cannot impede an expropriation that falls exclusively within the ambit of State sovereignty; that Tribunal could only establish whether there has been an expropriation, its legality or illegality and the corresponding compensation.

77. The claimants agree on the point that a Tribunal has the power to issue a declaratory statement, but in addition they believe that it can order injunctive relief concerning the performance or non-performance of certain acts. To this end, an award can deal both with pecuniary and non-pecuniary determinations, including specific performance and an injunction. In the present case the claimants have indeed requested that the taxes assessed be declared expropriatory and in breach of the Treaty and unlawful, and that they be annulled and their collection permanently enjoined.

78. The parties have discussed in this context the decisions of ICSID Tribunals and other courts and tribunals. For the claimants, the ICSID

case of *Goetz v Burundi*, like the cases decided by other tribunals in *Martini* (*Italy v Venezuela*), the *Trail Smelter* (*United States v Canada*), the *La Grand* (*Germany v United States*) and the *Arrest Warrant* (*Democratic Republic of Congo v Belgium*), amply support their view about tribunals having a broad power to order injunctive relief and other non-pecuniary measures. The respondent argues that these various cases are not relevant here, either because they involve inter-State disputes or because they are based on the agreement of the parties, concern contractual relations or the tribunals have been specifically empowered to adopt measures of the kind requested. Neither is the subject matter of this case, the respondent further argues, in any way related to recent decisions of the International Court of Justice.

79. An examination of the powers of international courts and tribunals to order measures concerning performance or injunction and of the ample practice that is available in this respect, leaves this Tribunal in no doubt about the fact that these powers are indeed available. The claimants have convincingly invoked the authority of the *Rainbow Warrior*, where it was held:

> The authority to issue an order for the cessation or discontinuance of a wrongful act or omission results from the inherent powers of a competent tribunal which is confronted with the continuous breach of an international obligation which is in force and continues to be in force. The delivery of such an order requires, therefore, two essential conditions intimately linked, namely that the wrongful act has a continuing character and that the violated rule is still in force at the time in which the order is issued.

80. The same holds true under the ICSID Convention. In *Goetz v Burundi* such a power was indeed resorted to by the Tribunal, and the fact that it was based on a settlement agreement between the parties does not deprive the decision of the Tribunal of its own legal force and standing. A scholarly opinion invoked by the claimants is also relevant in this context, having an author concluding that it is 'entirely possible that future cases will involve disputes arising from ongoing relationships in which awards providing for specific performance or injunctions become relevant'.

81. The Tribunal accordingly concludes that, in addition to declaratory powers, it has the power to order measures involving performance or injunction of certain acts. Jurisdiction is therefore also affirmed on this ground. What kind of measures might or might not be justified, whether the acts complained of meet the standards set out in the *Rainbow Warrior*, and how the issue of implementation that the parties have also dis-

cussed would be handled, if appropriate, are all matters that belong to the merits.

[...]

Jurisdiction affirmed

99. The fact that the claimants have argued and demonstrated *prima facie* that they have been adversely affected by the tax measures complained of is sufficient for the Tribunal to consider that the claim, as far as this matter is concerned, is within its jurisdiction to examine such claim on the merits under the provisions of the Bilateral Investment Treaty.

100. The Tribunal must note in concluding that counsel for both parties have performed their duties with outstanding professionalism and have at all times fully cooperated with the work of the Tribunal.

C. Decision

101. For the reasons stated above the Tribunal decides that the present dispute is within the jurisdiction of the Centre and the competence of the Tribunal. The Order necessary for the continuation of the procedure pursuant to Arbitration Rule 41(4) has, accordingly, been made.

So decided.

24
Challenges and annulments

EXERCISE 37 – CHALLENGES AND ANNULMENTS I – SEMINAR

Review the judgment of the Svea Court of Appeal in the *CME v Czech Republic* (attached to Exercise 33) and the Annulment Committee Decision in *Sempra Energy v Argentina*.

DISCUSSION QUESTIONS

Problem 1

Discuss the *pros* and *cons* of allowing national courts to hear challenges of investment treaty awards.

Problem 2

Are there any differences in the approaches taken by the Svea Court of Appeal and the Annulment Committee to the various grounds relied upon by the challenging parties? Discuss and explain.

Problem 3

What review standard should be adopted by courts and annulment committees when they try challenges to the jurisdiction of an investment treaty tribunal?

Problem 4

Do you think there is a need for any improvement of the ICSID annulment system? Discuss in what ways it can be changed and how/if this can be achieved.

CASE

Sempra Energy v Argentina (ICSID Case No. ARB/02/16) Annulment Proceeding

Introduction

1. On 25 January 2008, the Argentine Republic filed with the Secretary General of the International Centre for Settlement of Investment Disputes an application requesting annulment of the 28 September 2007 Award, rendered by the Tribunal in the arbitration proceeding between Sempra and Argentina (hereinafter jointly referred to as 'the parties'). The Application

for Annulment was made within the time period provided in Article 52(2) of the ICSID Convention.

2. In its Application, Argentina sought annulment of the Award on four of the five grounds set out in Article 52(1) of the ICSID Convention, specifically claiming that:

(i)   The Tribunal was not properly constituted (ICSID Convention, Article 52(1)(a));

(ii)   The Tribunal manifestly exceeded its powers (ICSID Convention, Article 52(1)(b);

(iii)   There had been a serious departure from a fundamental rule of procedure (ICSID Convention, Article 52(1)(d)); and

(iv)   The Award had failed to state the reasons on which it was based (ICSID Convention, Article 52(1)(e)).

3. The Application for Annulment also contained a request, under Article 52(5) of the ICSID Convention and ICSID Arbitration Rule 54(1), for a stay of enforcement of the Award until the Application for Annulment was decided.

4. The Secretary-General of ICSID registered the Application on 30 January 2008 and on the same date, in accordance with ICSID Arbitration Rule 50(2), transmitted a Notice of Registration to the parties. The parties were also notified that, pursuant to ICSID Arbitration Rule 54(2), enforcement of the Award was provisionally stayed.

5. By letter of 15 September 2008, in accordance with ICSID Arbitration Rule 52(2), the parties were notified by the Centre that an ad hoc Committee (the Committee) had been constituted, composed of Mr Christer Söderlund, from Sweden, Sir David A O Edward, QC, from the United Kingdom, and Ambassador Andreas J Jacovides, from Cyprus, each of them appointed by their respective countries to the ICSID Panel of Arbitrators. On the same date the parties were informed that Mr Gonzalo Flores, Senior Counsel, ICSID, would serve as Secretary of the Committee.

6. On 16 September 2008, Sempra filed a request to lift the provisional stay of enforcement of the Award.

7. By letter of 25 September 2008, the parties were notified that Mr Christer Söderlund had been designated President of the Committee.

8. By letter of 10 October 2008, the Committee proposed to hold a first session by telephone conference on 21 October 2008. A provisional agenda for the session was attached to the letter. The parties were also notified that the Committee had decided to continue the provisional stay of enforcement of the Award until 8 December 2008, the date fixed by the Committee to hear the parties' oral pleadings on stay.

9. The first session of the Committee was held, as proposed, on 21 October 2008 by telephone conference. At the session, Sempra was represented by Messrs Craig S Miles and Roberto Aguirre Luzi and by Ms Kerrie A Nanni, from the law firm of King & Spalding LLP (Houston). The Argentine Republic was represented by Dr Gabriel Bottini and Dra Gisela Makowski from Procuración del Tesoro de la Nación Argentina.

10. During the first session: (a) the parties expressed their agreement that the Committee had been duly constituted, in accordance with the ICSID Convention and the ICSID Arbitration Rules, and confirmed that they had no objections to any of its members; (b) several issues of procedure were agreed and decided; and (c) the Committee informed the parties of its decision to continue the provisional stay of enforcement of the Award until a decision on this matter was taken by the Committee. Scheduling arrangements which could not be agreed during the course of the first session were resolved by the parties shortly after.

11. In accordance with the parties' agreement, Argentina filed its observations on the continuation of the stay of enforcement of the Award on 7 November 2008 and Sempra filed its observations on 21 November 2008.

12. On 8 December 2008, a hearing was held at the seat of the Centre in Washington DC, at which the parties presented oral arguments on the matter of stay of enforcement. Present at the hearing were: [. . .].

13. On 18 December 2008, Sempra wrote to the Committee, claiming that Argentina had 'again refused to change its interpretation of its obligations under Articles 53 and 54 of the ICSID Convention', referring to the *Vivendi* ad hoc Committee's request for a 'comfort letter' and to Argentina's response to that committee of 28 November 2008. By letter of 29 December 2008 Argentina declared its readiness to provide comments on Sempra's 18 December submission while, at the same time, describing its letter to the *Vivendi* ad hoc Committee as 'self-explanatory'.

14. By letter of 30 January 2009, Argentina notified the Committee of its intent to adduce additional written testimony into the proceeding. By letter dated 6 February 2009, Sempra objected, emphasising that the proposed testimony had been presented to the Sempra Tribunal which had conclusively disposed of it. In a reply letter of 20 February 2009, Argentina opined that the proposed testimony should be admitted as it had a bearing on the allegation that a serious departure from a fundamental rule of procedure had occurred in the Sempra arbitration.

15. On 3 March 2009, Argentina filed its Memorial on Annulment.

16. The Committee issued its *Decision on the Argentine Republic's Request for a Continued Stay of Enforcement of the Award* on 5 March 2009. In its decision, the Committee granted a continuation of the stay of enforcement of the Award subject to the condition that Argentina place in escrow an amount of USD 75 million. The Committee's decision further provided that, if Argentina failed to place the sum required in escrow within 120 days from the date of the issuance of the decision, the Committee might – at the request of Sempra – order termination of the stay of enforcement with or without providing an opportunity for Argentina to make up for any failure in payment.

17. The Committee further decided on Argentina's request to adduce additional evidence on 31 March 2009. In its decision, the Committee, invoking ICSID Arbitration Rule 34(1), according to which '[t]he tribunal shall be the judge of the admissibility of any evidence [. . .]' and ICSID Arbitration Rule 53, according to which:

> [t]the provisions of *Compañía de Aguas del Aconquija S A and Vivendi Universal S A v Argentine Republic* (ICSID Case No. ARB/97/3), Decision on the Argentine Republic's Request for a Continued Stay of Enforcement of the Award rendered on 20 August 2007 (4 November 2008) these Rules shall apply mutatis mutandis to any procedure relating to [. . .] annulment of an award and to the decision of the [. . .] Committee,

confirmed its power to rule on the admissibility of any evidence invoked by a party to annulment proceedings.

18. The Committee, however, noting that the ambit of its review was strictly limited to questions of law relating to the grounds for annulment exhaustively listed in the Convention, rejected Argentina's application to adduce additional testimony. Specifically, the Committee considered that the proposed

evidence could not contribute to elucidating whether or not the Tribunal dealt with certain evidentiary matters in such a manner as to constitute a serious departure from a fundamental rule of procedure.

19. On 4 May 2009, Sempra filed its Counter-Memorial on Annulment.

20. By letter of 13 May 2009, Sempra requested that the stay of enforcement be lifted. The reason invoked for the request was that Argentina had not agreed to, let alone offered, any escrow agreement, as provided in the Committee's 5 March decision.

21. In particular, Sempra referred to paragraph 119 of the Committee's decision, which provided:

> In the event where Sempra considers the escrow arrangement offered by Argentina as unsatisfactory, Sempra may bring this matter to the Committee's attention by submitting a notice at the relevant time, but no later than 30 (thirty) days before expiry of the time limit set forth above. Argentina shall be entitled to submit comments and take corrective action by reason of such notice. If the Committee considers that the escrow arrangement is unsatisfactory – despite corrective action, if any – the Committee may terminate the stay pursuant to Rule 54(3) of the ICSID Arbitration Rules.

22. By letter of 22 May 2009, the Committee invited Argentina to offer comments on Sempra's letter of 13 May 2009.

23. In a communication of 1 June 2009, Argentina made reference to discussions said to have taken place between Argentina and 'counsel for Sempra' in the *Enron* case, inter alia, concerning a proposal to put an escrow agreement in place as a condition for continuing the stay in [those] annulment proceedings. Argentina had explained that such an arrangement as proposed would create 'unacceptable risks of attachment' to Argentina, pointing to the contingency of other creditors attaching Argentina's entitlement to lift the amount in escrow, should its application for annulment be granted. Argentina noted, in particular, that the ad hoc Committee in the *Enron* annulment proceedings had, for reasons given in paragraph 42 of that committee's decision of 20 May 2009, granted a continuation of the stay without conditions. Argentina requested this Committee to do likewise.

24. By letter of 10 June 2009, Sempra expressed its disagreement with the *Enron* Committee's reasoning on the point of third-party attachment risk, emphasising that, taking such a risk into account 'encourages recalcitrant debtors [. . .]

to continue repudiating their international monetary obligations', and questioning why Sempra should suffer the consequences of 'Argentina's unilateral decision to renege on its prior international monetary obligations'.

25. In the same letter, Sempra reiterated its request that the Committee lift the stay of enforcement, noting that Argentina had not only failed to 'offer' an escrow arrangement but had not even responded to a draft escrow agreement proposed by Sempra, let alone committed any funds into such escrow.

26. By letter of 17 June 2009, the Committee stated that it would consider the parties' arguments on the matter of the ongoing stay and issue a decision in respect of the Sempra's request that the stay now be lifted. Further, the Committee invited the parties to communicate 'any new development or other circumstances, which may be relevant for the matters presently pending'.

27. On 29 June 2009, the Argentine Republic filed its Reply on Annulment.

28. By letter of 16 July 2009, Sempra asked the Committee to lift the stay of enforcement of the Award. Argentine immediately filed a response on 17 July 2009.

29. The Committee issued its *Decision on Sempra Energy International's Request for the Termination of the Stay of Enforcement of the Award (Rule 54 of the ICSID Arbitration Rules)* on 7 August 2009. The Committee terminated the stay of enforcement of the Award, dismissing Argentina's argument that the placing of funds in escrow (or issuing a letter of credit) would cause prohibitive cost and create an 'unacceptable risk of attachment to Argentina'. In doing so, the Committee noted that: (a) the circumstances invoked by Argentina did not amount to economic hardship that would constitute a valid consideration when deciding whether to continue or terminate the stay (as already decided in its 5 March decision; paras 77–79); and (b) that it does not 'see as its function to create safeguards against the possibility of third-party creditors generally obtaining satisfaction in respect of outstanding claims.[. . .] [s]uch contingencies are outside the scope of considerations which an ad hoc committee should take into account'. Argentina not having complied with the condition imposed by the Committee for continuing the stay for the duration of this proceeding, the stay of enforcement of the Award was terminated.

30. On 13 August 2009, Sempra filed its Rejoinder on annulment.

31. A three-day hearing was held at the seat of the Centre in Washington, D C on 1–3 September 2009, at which counsel for both parties presented their

arguments and submissions, and responded to questions from the Members of the Committee. [. . .].

32. The Committee declared the proceeding closed on 7 May 2010. During the course of the proceedings, the Members of the Committee deliberated by various means of communication, including a meeting at The Hague on 14–16 December 2009, and have taken into account all pleadings, documents and testimony before them.

The dispute

33. In 1989 Argentina introduced a privatisation programme in order to revitalise its economy and put an end to the then ongoing economic crisis. An important facet of this programme was the introduction of a legal and regulatory framework by way of the Convertibility Law, introduced in 1991, together with an implementing decree, fixing the Argentine peso (ARS) to the US Dollar (USD) at the exchange rate of one to one.

34. In 1992, the natural gas industry was restructured, and the government-owned company Gas del Estado was privatised. In this connection, the Gas Law was introduced together with its implementing regulations in the form of the Gas Decree. Within the framework of this regulatory regime, a number of companies were formed for purposes of distribution of gas for residential and commercial users. Sempra invested in two of these gas companies by acquiring an indirect shareholding amounting to 43.09 per cent of Sodigas Pampeana's and Sodigas Sur's shares, which, in turn, are the holders of 90 per cent and 86.09 per cent, respectively, of the shares of Camuzzi Gas Pampeana S A (CGP) and Camuzzi Gas del Sur (CGS), i.e., the 'Licensees', two Argentine companies which have been granted licenses for the distribution of gas (hereinafter the 'License(s)') in 1996.

35. In December 2001 a financial crisis erupted in Argentina, and in the period 2001–02 the Government of Argentina undertook a number of measures which, in the view of Sempra, constituted a wholesale abrogation and repudiation of significant rights and entitlements under the Licenses and other entitlements under the regulatory environment, that had been established within the framework of the Argentine privatisation program. Essentially, these rights concerned the Licensees' entitlement to calculation of tariffs in USD and their semi-annual adjustment on the basis of the US Producer Price Index (PPI).

36. In January 2002, the Emergency Law was enacted, the currency board system was abrogated, the Argentine economy was pesified – including

public service agreements and licences – and all contracts and relationships then in force were, according to the Emergency Law, to be adapted to the new context.

37. On the basis of the above-stated circumstances, Sempra filed, on 11 September 2002, a Request for Arbitration under the ICSID Convention, invoking the US-Argentina Bilateral Investment Treaty (BIT).

38. On 31 December 2003, Argentina filed objections to the Centre's jurisdiction and the competence of the Tribunal. On 11 May 2005 the Tribunal issued its *Decision on Jurisdiction*, wherein it held that the dispute fell under the jurisdiction of the Centre and the competence of the Tribunal.

39. A merits phase in the arbitration followed, and the Award on the merits was dispatched to the parties on 28 September 2007. In the Award it was held that Argentina had breached the fair and equitable standard and the Umbrella Clause of the BIT. On these bases, Sempra was awarded damages.

40. On 25 January 2008 Argentina requested the annulment (and stay of enforcement) of the Award.

The grounds for annulment

A brief summary of Argentina's annulment application

41. In this annulment proceeding, Argentina has raised a number of issues with regard to the arbitral proceeding and the Award, each of which, on Argentina's case, have been dealt with in such a way as to constitute one or more grounds for annulment of the Award in its entirety. The issues raised by Argentina concern the *jus standi* of Sempra to bring claims relating to the Licenses and related rights; alleged impropriety in dealing with Argentina's proposal for the disqualification of the members of the Tribunal; matters relating to the admission of certain fact witnesses in the arbitration proceeding; interpretation of various terms of the Licenses; and the way in which the Tribunal dealt with the fair and equitable treatment standard and the Umbrella Clause of the BIT.

42. Finally, as explained in greater detail below, Argentina raised arguments in respect of the way that the Tribunal dealt with emergency under Argentine law, necessity under customary international law and preclusion on the basis of Article XI of the BIT.

43. In its application for annulment, Argentina invoked (as already noted in para 2 above) the following grounds for annulment as provided for in the ICSID Convention:

1. The Tribunal was not properly constituted (Article 52(1)(a) of the ICSID Convention).
2. The Tribunal manifestly exceeded its powers (Article 52(1)(b) of the ICSID Convention).
3. There has been a serious departure from a fundamental rule of procedure (Article 52(1)(d) of the ICSID Convention).
4. The Award failed to state the reasons on which it was based. (Article 52(1)(e) of the ICSID Convention).

The arbitral proceeding

44. In the arbitration Sempra argued that the measures adopted by Argentina in the period 2000–02, initiated by the enactment of the Emergency Law and leading to the pesification of tariffs under that law, the abrogation of the PPI adjustment of tariffs, the unilateral modification of the Licenses without compensation and related matters, amounted to abrogation and repudiation of most of the rights it had under the regulatory framework.

45. On this basis, Sempra claimed that Argentina was in breach of specific commitments made to the investors in violation of the applicable legal regulatory norms and the specific guarantees provided under the BIT, seriously impairing the value of its investments.

46. The conduct of Argentina constituted, in Sempra's view, wrongful expropriation of its investment as well as breach of the fair and equitable treatment standard, including legitimate expectations, by measures characterised by arbitrary and discriminatory treatment and failure to provide full protection and security, as well as also breaching the BIT's Umbrella Clause. In sum, according to Sempra, all of the protections offered under the BIT had been breached.

47. Argentina denied that there had been any breach in respect of the measures it undertook and which have been complained of by Sempra. The legal and regulatory framework governing the privatisation provided for the Licensees' right to fair and reasonable tariffs and the right to calculate tariffs in USD could be applied only as long as the Convertibility Law was in force. Moreover, information that the investors relied on when making their

investments was conveyed by private consulting firms and was not attribut-able to Argentina, which had expressly disclaimed responsibility for such information.

48. In Argentina's view, the legal and regulatory framework had also been strictly upheld when adopting the measures complained of and none of those measures amounted to a breach of the Licenses or the BIT. In any event, Argentina maintained that its responsibility, both under domestic as well as international law concerning necessity, whether customary or treaty-based, is excluded.

49. Against the overall scenario described above, Sempra dealt with a number of specific measures undertaken by Argentina in the context of the economic, social and political difficulties gradually emerging in Argentina at the end of the 1990s and the measures undertaken by Argentina com-mencing in December of 2001 and gathering momentum in the following year.

The first claim: PPI adjustment of tariffs

50. According to Sempra, adjustments of the tariffs based on the PPI ('PPI adjustments') were suspended from 1 July 2000, and permanently.

51. Argentina denied that the measures undertaken were in any way in breach of any undertaking, but simply represented a reasonable adjustment to the Argentine economy in a situation of recession and deflation, making the adjustments to the license terms justified.

52. The Tribunal held that the Licensees had been entitled to PPI adjust-ments, and that these adjustments had been abrogated by Argentina.

The second claim: pesification of tariffs under the Emergency Law

53. On 6 January 2002 Argentina enacted the Emergency Law, which essen-tially entailed the abrogation of the Licensees' right to calculate tariffs in USD and the conversion of tariffs at a fixed rate of exchange of one USD to one ARS.

54. According to Argentina, the calculation of tariffs in USD was linked to the Convertibility Law, which, in turn, was subordinated to the overreaching policy goal that tariffs should be fair and reasonable.

55. Sempra contends that the abrogation of these rights constituted violations of the protections offered by Argentina, in particular, in respect of the fair and equitable treatment standard and the Umbrella Clause.

56. The Tribunal, basing itself on an examination of the legal and the regulatory framework, concluded that there was indeed a right for Sempra to calculate tariffs in USD, that this was a central feature of the tariff regime, and that this right was abrogated.

The third claim: The breach of the licenses' stability clauses

57. Sempra's claim in this respect refers, in particular, to contractual provisions of the Licenses prohibiting the freezing of prices, and the duty of the Licensor not to amend the basic rules of the Licenses without written consent of the Licensees. The non-observance of these commitments constituted, in Sempra's view, a breach of the Umbrella Clause in the BIT.

58. Argentina argued that the prohibitions referred to were binding only for the executive branch of government and that any measure arising from congressional action would not fall foul of this prohibition.

59. The Tribunal, noting that the matter at hand did not concern the State's right to adjudicate or legislate, but whether the terms of the Licenses gave a right to damages, dismissed Argentina's argument

The fourth claim: failure to reimburse subsidies

60. The fourth claim advanced by Sempra concerns the failure of Argentina to reimburse certain subsidies promised to the Licensees, essentially CGS. Additionally, Sempra considered that such subsidies were to be calculated in USD as being in lieu of higher tariffs.

61. Argentina denied the claim invoking its attempts to regularise the payments of subsidies and the proposition that the situation now is back to normal. As the subsidies, in Argentina's view, have always been paid in ARS, no conversion into USD is warranted.

62. The Tribunal concluded that Argentina recognised the amount of subsidies owing before 31 December 2001, and that the monies due must be compensated with the parity exchange value of the ARS to USD at that time.

The fifth claim: interference with the collection of bills and related matters

63. Sempra argued that a number of measures have caused interference in collection of bills and that other suspensions and impositions have impacted negatively on the operations of the local companies.

64. Argentina rejected the significance of any such measure as being limited and exceptional and, in any event, later reversed.

65. The Tribunal considered that it did not find much merit in these 'peripheral' claims, but that it was prepared to consider them in the context of Sempra's overall claim for compensation.

The matter of treaty breaches

66. The Tribunal held, essentially, that Argentina had not breached the standard of protection established in Article IV(1) of the BIT (expropriation or equivalent).

The Tribunal held, however, that '[t]he measures in question' had, beyond any doubt, substantially changed the legal and business framework, under which the investment was decided and implemented and that, as a consequence, the fair and equitable treatment standard of Article II(2)(a) of the BIT had been breached.

67. As for Sempra's argument relating to breach of the Umbrella Clause, the Tribunal, opining that the Licenses were 'the ultimate expression of a series of complex investment arrangements made with a specific intention of channeling the influx of capital', concluded that, indeed, the Umbrella Clause in Article II(2)(c) of the BIT was also breached.

68. As for Sempra's assertion that it had been the victim of arbitrary and discriminatory action from the side of Argentina, the Tribunal concluded that the treatment afforded to Sempra did not appear to have been discriminatory or arbitrary in comparison to measures meted out to other entities or sectors in Argentina and did not, therefore, constitute a breach of the BIT's protection from arbitrariness and discrimination (Article II(2)(b)).

69. As for the claim concerning full protection and security, the Tribunal noted that this particular standard has evolved in the context of physical protection but that also, in given cases, a broader interpretation could be

justified. However, the Tribunal saw no reason on the basis of the circumstances of the present case to thus extend this standard of protection and, therefore, rejected Sempra's claim under Article II(2)(a) of the BIT.

Argentina's defence based on necessity and preclusion under Article XI of the BIT

70. In the course of the arbitration, Argentina also raised the defence of necessity under Argentine law and customary international law as well as the question of preclusion under Article XI of the BIT (in that order).

71. The Tribunal held that the conditions under which emergency might be exercised and legally validated under Argentine law were not present, based on Argentine court precedents, and that 'the very constitutional provisions which were subject to judicial control and which led to the definition of those conditions cannot be invoked to preclude a finding of wrongfulness'. Nor did the Tribunal – applying Article 25 of the ILC Articles as an expression of customary international law – find that the cumulative requirements set up by that provision were present in order to excuse wrongfulness. As for preclusion under Article XI of the BIT, the Tribunal held, as will be discussed in greater detail below, that the cumulative requirements for exoneration under Article 25 of the ILC Articles were not satisfied, making it unnecessary, in the view of the Tribunal, to undertake further judicial review under Article XI.

72. In summing up, the Tribunal held that Argentina had incurred liability for breach of the fair and equitable treatment standard as well as the Umbrella Clause, and ordered Argentina to pay compensation.

Proceedings before the Committee – introductory comments

The scope of review to be undertaken by the Committee

73. An ad hoc Committee may only determine whether (a) to annul the Award in whole or in part – rendering the Award (or part thereof) null and void for all intents and purposes, cancelling its *res judicata* effect – or (b) let the Award stand. Annulment is distinct from an appeal. An ad hoc Committee cannot substitute its own judgement on the merits for the decision of the Tribunal. Following a decision to annul an ICSID Award, the dispute may be resubmitted to new tribunal to obtain a decision on the merits.

74. Annulment review is limited to a specific set of carefully defined grounds (listed exhaustively in Art. 52(1) of the ICSID Convention). New arguments or evidence on the merits will therefore be irrelevant for the annulment process, and therefore not admissible. It cannot be excluded, however, that evidence, particularly expert evidence, may exceptionally be accepted in annulment proceedings in so far as it is specifically relevant for the annulment grounds listed in Article 52(1) of the Convention (in so far as invoked by a party).

75. As for the interpretation of grounds for annulment there is compelling support for the view that neither a narrow nor a broad approach is to be applied.

76. Nor is there any preponderant inclination '*in favorem validitatis*', i.e., a presumption in favour of the Award's validity. In line with the consistent, but not invariable, practice of ad hoc committees, this Committee will not express any views on aspects of the Tribunal's reasoning on the merits.

77. It is standard practice for applicants seeking annulment to invoke more than one ground for annulment – as has been done in the present case. The Committee sees it as its task to gauge the circumstances invoked in support of each ground independently. The fact that a particular set of facts may have a bearing on more than one ground of annulment does not, as such, render any error alleged in support of anyone of those grounds of annulment any the more manifest.

78. Once an ad hoc Committee has concluded that there is one instance of manifest excess of powers (or any other ground for annulment), which warrants annulment of the Award in its entirety, this will be the end of the ad hoc Committee's examination. Since annulment of an award in its entirety necessarily leads to the loss of the *res judicata* effect of all matters adjudicated by the Tribunal, it is unnecessary to consider whether there are other grounds – whether in respect of the same matter or other matters – that may also lead to annulment.

79. On the other hand, an ad hoc Committee will need to proceed differently where it decides not to annul the Award or decides to annul the Award only in part. In those instances it will be necessary for the ad hoc Committee to examine all of the grounds invoked by the applicant in support of its application.

80. The question arises whether different considerations apply where the matters of the Centre's jurisdiction and the Tribunal's competence have been

put in issue. In other words, if the affirmation of jurisdiction by the Tribunal is alleged to constitute a manifest excess of powers (or any other ground for annulment), does this question have to be addressed as a preliminary issue (and dismissed), before considering grounds of annulment invoked by the applicant in respect of other aspects of the Award or the arbitral proceedings? The argument for taking this course would be that, if the dispute fell outside the jurisdiction of the Centre and, therefore, outside the competence of the Tribunal, the conduct of the Tribunal in procedural and substantive respects would not be relevant.

81. The contrary argument would be that, since no decision of an ad hoc Committee (or any reasoning underlying it) can have no effect other than upholding or (partially) annulling the Award, the reasons given by the ad hoc Committee for its decision, while decisive for its conclusions, will not be binding on a new Tribunal upon resubmission of the case. Thus, if an ad hoc Committee has found that a Tribunal's assertion of jurisdiction is the result of an error justifying annulment of the Award, a new tribunal may nevertheless declare itself competent to deal with the case.

82. In the present case, although the Committee has come to the conclusion that the Award must be annulled on another ground, it considers that, on balance, it is desirable that it should deal with Argentina's argument on jurisdiction as a preliminary matter.

Jurisdiction

Introduction

83. In the arbitration, Argentina disputed the Tribunal's jurisdiction on a number of grounds, inter alia, Sempra's lack of *jus standi*, arguing, essentially, that Sempra's claims were connected to the Licensees and not directly to its investment, as any alleged violation complained of was susceptible of affecting the Licensees only.

84. Sempra contended that all requirements under the ICSID Convention and the BIT for the Tribunal's jurisdiction were present, i.e., essentially, that there was a legal dispute between a national of the United States and Argentina concerning losses, that these affected the interest of Sempra in the Licensees, and that both parties have consented to ICSID arbitration.

85. Argentina, referring to the second part of Article 42(1) of the ICSID Convention, further argued that of the Tribunal should apply 'domes-

tic legislation and international law'. Sempra argued that it is the ICSID Convention and the BIT that should be applied to determine jurisdiction.

86. The Tribunal confirmed that Article 42(1) applies to the merits of the dispute only, so only Article 25 of the Convention and the terms of the BIT should be applied.

87. The Tribunal also found that also a non-controlling shareholder is an investor under the terms of the BIT. Further, the Tribunal held that Article 25(2)(b) of the Convention establishes an optional jurisdictional alternative and not, as argued by Argentina, an autonomous jurisdictional requirement.

88. Furthermore, the Tribunal noted that, contrary to Argentina's argument, Sempra alleged that it had suffered a direct loss. The Tribunal also concluded that there was an (alleged) loss, arising directly to Sempra's investment, giving Sempra a cause of action under the BIT.

89. As for Argentina's claim that Sempra lacks *jus standi*, i.e., that it is bringing a derivative action on behalf of the Licensees, the Tribunal concluded that, on Sempra's case, it was pursuing its own rights under the BIT. The Tribunal concluded that a cause of action also accrues to a minority shareholder, and that a cause of action lies under the BIT.

90. The Tribunal held that claims submitted by Sempra were founded 'on both the contract and the BIT'. In its *Decision of Jurisdiction*, it concluded that the dispute fell within the jurisdiction of the Centre and the competence of the Tribunal.

Argentina's request to annul in respect of jurisdiction

91. In this annulment proceeding, Argentina has raised two fundamental issues in support of its claim that the Tribunal has engaged in a manifest excess of powers in declaring jurisdiction to be vested in the Centre and itself competent to deal with the dispute. Firstly, the Tribunal accepted 'the claim of a shareholder with respect to the alleged damage to rights belonging to the companies in which it held and holds shares'. Secondly, Argentina raised the 'potential problem that, in both situations, might arise in the event of double compensation'. In this latter respect, Argentina referred to the contingency that the subsidiaries themselves might have actionable claims, premised on the Licenses and other contractual rights, claims which are also comprised by the present claim by Sempra under the BIT. Argentina further contended

that the Tribunal failed to appreciate the fact that the Licenses and other contractual rights were entered into between the Licensees and Argentina, and not with Sempra when considering Sempra's claims, while, at the same time, disregarding agreements between Argentina and the Licensees as *res inter alios acta*.

92. The fact that the Tribunal failed to state grounds for its *Decision on Jurisdiction* by which it accepted the jurisdiction of ICSID and its own competence also amounts, in the view of Argentina, to a failure to state reasons on which these decisions were based, which warrants annulment of the Award.

Sempra's position

93. Sempra has rejected Argentina's affirmations related to alleged absence of *jus standi* mainly on the following grounds.

94. The question whether a particular investment qualifies for protection is determined by the relevant instrument on investment protection, in this case the BIT. According to the Article I(ii) of the BIT, 'shares of stock or other interests in a company or interests in the assets thereof' constitute, inter alia, investments within the meaning of that BIT.

95. According to Article 25(1) of the ICSID Convention 'a national of another Contracting State' constitutes an investor under the Convention; hence, Sempra qualifies as such.

96. Sempra is claiming for its own rights under the BIT and is not pursuing a derivative action for the account of the Licensees. From this follows that Sempra is an investor which has made an investment under the BIT.

97. The potential of double recovery is not relevant for the question of jurisdiction. In any event, this risk is not present.

98. Damages claimed by Sempra, and awarded by the Tribunal, concern its own damages and not those of the Licensees.

99. The Tribunal's reasoning on the matter of jurisdiction is firmly based on the provisions of the Convention and the BIT; there is no excess of powers, let alone manifest, or failure to state reasons.

The Committee's conclusion on jurisdiction

100. The jurisdiction of the Centre is determined by Article 25 of the ICSID Convention, and is governed by the terms of the instrument expressing the parties' consent to arbitration. In the present case, the relevant instruments are, in the case of Argentina, the BIT, and in the case of Sempra, its request for arbitration.

101. Because Article 25 of the Convention does not define 'investment', that task was 'left largely to the terms of bilateral investment treaties or other instruments on which jurisdiction is based'. The BIT provides in its Article I(i), inter alia:

> For the purposes of this Treaty,
> (a) 'investment' means every kind of investment in the territory of one party owned or controlled directly or indirectly by nationals or companies of the other party, such as equity, debt and service and investment contracts; and includes without limitation:
> [. . .]
> (ii) a company or shares of stock or other interests in a company or interests in the assets thereof;
> (iii) a claim to money or a claim to performance having economic value and directly related to an investment;
> [. . .]
> (v) any right conferred by law or contract, and any licenses and permits pursuant to law.

102. The plain language of the BIT is evidence of the broad meaning of the term 'investment' envisaged by the contracting parties when entering into the BIT. Notably, the definition explicitly includes 'investment contracts', 'shares of stock or other interests in a company', and 'any right conferred by law or contract', 'owned or controlled directly or indirectly'.

103. The Committee is clearly of the opinion that Sempra is entitled to bring a claim under the ICSID Convention against Argentina in respect of damage allegedly caused to Sempra's 'investment' in Argentina, i.e., its indirect, minority shareholdings in the local companies. The *Barcelona Traction* case, and the principle confirming the recognition under international law of the personality of juridical entities under municipal law, are irrelevant in the present BIT context. Shareholders may claim under the BIT – as distinct from what was the case in the *Barcelona Traction* case – simply because this BIT extends such rights to 'investors' as defined therein, a right which does not exist under customary international law.

104. In the opinion of the Committee, the arguments advanced by Argentina in support of its objection to jurisdiction confuse two distinct issues. The first issue is whether Sempra is entitled to bring a claim under the ICSID Convention and the BIT in respect of alleged damage to its investment through loss caused to its partly and indirectly owned local companies, CGP and CGS, by impairment of Licenses and other valuable rights held by those subsidiaries. The second is whether acts or omissions on the part of Argentina with respect to CGP or CGS have in fact caused damage to Sempra's investment and, if so, what is the proper measure of that damage. The first issue is one of jurisdiction, while the second issue relates to the merits of the dispute. In the present case, if Sempra were to be found entitled to reparation for damage to its investment, the measure of damages would not necessarily be directly proportionate to any pecuniary loss or deficit suffered by CGP or CGS. That being an issue on the merits, the Committee does not consider it further.

105. For these reasons, the Committee concludes that the Tribunal has neither engaged in any manifest excess of powers nor failed to state reasons on the matter of the *jus standi* of Sempra.

Emergency under international law – Argentina's position

Article XI of the BIT

106. Argentina has submitted that the Tribunal committed a manifest excess of powers by failing to apply Article XI of the BIT. Argentina has based its position on, essentially, the following circumstances.

107. In the Award, the Tribunal determined that Article XI is not self-judging and, consequently, it was incumbent on the Tribunal to carry out a substantial review of its applicability. However, the Tribunal held that Article XI does not establish conditions other than those that follow from the state of necessity under customary international law as enunciated in Article 25 of the ILC Articles. The Tribunal concluded – as follows from its Award – that, having previously determined that the Argentine crisis did not meet the requirements of the state of necessity under customary international law, it would not undertake further judicial review under Article XI.

108. From this follows that the Tribunal failed to distinguish between Article XI of the BIT and the state of necessity under customary international law.

Differences between Article XI of the BIT and the state of necessity

109. Argentina has developed its position on the question of the Tribunal's alleged failure to apply Article XI of the BIT in the following way.

110. In the Award, the Tribunal considered that '[t]he BIT provision is inseparable from the customary law standard insofar as the definition of necessity and the conditions for its operation are concerned' and that Article XI 'does not set out conditions different from customary law in such regard'.

111. However, Article XI of the BIT differs significantly from the state of necessity under customary international law, which is substantially contained in Article 25 of the ILC Articles. This fact requires that this difference is observed in view of the potentially different outcomes of an evaluation of Article XI as opposed to Article 25 of the ILC Articles, and more importantly, it makes it manifest that the Tribunal has failed to embark on an interpretation of Article XI.

112. The main differences between Article XI and the state of necessity under customary international law relate to the sphere of operation of these rules, to their nature and operation, their content, scope, and, as well as to their effects.

113. Article XI is a special conventional rule, while the state of necessity is a general rule of customary international law. Therefore, Article XI may only be invoked within the framework of the BIT. It is a specific provision, bilaterally agreed upon by the contracting States, which delimits the scope of the protections contained in that BIT. On the other hand, the state of necessity 'can be invoked in any context against any international obligation', except for obligations excluding the possibility of invoking the state of necessity.

114. The plea of necessity under customary international law is subsidiary to that of Article XI of the BIT. Article XI is a provision that delimits the scope of application of that BIT: 'if it applies, the substantive obligations under the BIT do not apply'. By contrast, 'Article 25 is an excuse, which is relevant only if it has been decided that there has otherwise been a breach of those substantive obligations under the BIT'.

115. Article XI is a primary rule, since it delimits the scope of the substantive obligations of the BIT itself. If the requirements under Article XI are met,

there is no breach of the BIT. Article 25 is a secondary rule, since it provides discharge from responsibility of the State for internationally wrongful acts. It is a '"ground for precluding the wrongfulness of an act not in conformity with an international obligation", under certain strict conditions'. The state of necessity does not extinguish or terminate the obligation, but excludes responsibility for its non-performance.

116. Therefore, only if conduct violates the BIT by infringing a standard of treatment and such conduct is not precluded under Article XI, can the question arise whether the responsibility of the State is excluded by virtue of the state of necessity.

117. Article XI does not include the stringent requirements of the state of necessity. There is no equivalent to the Article 25 standard of 'grave and imminent peril' amongst the exceptions provided for in Article XI or to the requirement that the measure be 'the only way for the State to safeguard' its interests, or that the State invoking the exception must not have contributed to the situation of necessity.

118. Finally, the preclusion under Article XI and the state of necessity differ as to their effects. In the case of the state of necessity, Article 27 of the ILC Articles provides that '[T]he invocation of a circumstance precluding wrongfulness . . . is without prejudice to . . . [t]he question of compensation for any material loss caused by the act in question'. If, however, Article XI is found to apply, no compensation is payable since such provision excludes 'the operation of the substantive provisions of the BIT'.

Grounds for annulment

119. There are, in Argentina's view, three grounds for annulment in connection with the manner in which the Tribunal dealt with Article XI of the BIT, namely: (a) manifest errors of law; (b) manifest excess of powers; and (c) failure to state reasons.

120. Firstly, the Tribunal made manifest errors of law in equating Article XI of the BIT with the state of necessity under customary international law, in assuming that these provisions were on the same footing, and in applying the rule of Article 27 of the ILC Articles to Article XI. Secondly, the Tribunal manifestly exceeded its powers by its failure to apply Article XI. Finally, the Tribunal failed to explain the reasons why it could refrain from applying Article XI and instead apply rules on state of necessity under customary international law.

Manifest errors of law

121. The Tribunal made manifest errors of law when dealing with Article XI by declaring that:

> [s]ince the Tribunal has found above that the crisis invoked does not meet the customary law requirements of Article 25 of the Articles on State Responsibility, it concludes that necessity or emergency is not conducive in this case to the preclusion of wrongfulness, and that there is no need to undertake a further judicial review under Article XI, given that this Article does not set out conditions different from customary law in such regard.

122. By equating Article XI of the BIT with ILC Article 25, and assuming they were on the same footing, the Tribunal committed manifest errors of law.

123. In addition, the Tribunal also made another manifest error of law by applying the rule of ILC Article 27 to Article XI of the BIT.

124. Although Argentina admits, in principle, that a mere error of law is not a ground for annulment under Article 52 of the ICSID Convention, in certain circumstances, an error of law may be sufficiently serious to qualify as a manifest excess of powers for failure to apply the proper law.

125. The manifest errors of law that are present in the Award in the instant case, are sufficiently serious to amount to a manifest excess of powers in accordance with Article 52(1)b of the ICSID Convention for failure to apply the proper law.

Manifest excess of powers

126. Not only did the Tribunal make manifest errors of law in connection with Article XI of the BIT, but it also engaged in a manifest excess of powers by its failure to apply that provision. Applying Article XI entailed recognising its self-judging nature, thus respecting the decision of Argentina to take measures under cover of that article. However, if such article was deemed not to be self-judging, it would call for a substantive review of the measures adopted by Argentina in order to verify whether those measures satisfied the substantive standards for preclusion that are enunciated in this provision. The Tribunal did not accept the self-judging nature of Article XI of the BIT, nor did it perform a substantive review. The Tribunal simply replaced Article XI of the BIT with the state of necessity under customary

international law which, as explained, differs substantially from the former as to its sphere of operation, nature and functioning, content, scope and effects. The Tribunal did not apply Article XI of the BIT, thus manifestly exceeding its powers.

The self-judging nature of the Article XI of the BIT

127. The Tribunal was called to apply Article XI, which provision, in Argentina's view, would apply in a situation such as the one that evolved in Argentina as from late 2001. This imposed on the Tribunal a duty to defer to Argentina's decision to take measures to maintain public order and protect its essential security interests, since Article XI is self-judging. The State invoking a provision such as Article XI of the BIT is the sole judge of its applicability to the contested measures. By disregarding the self-judging nature of Article XI, the Tribunal manifestly exceeded its powers.

Replacing Article XI with the state of necessity

128. In the Award the Tribunal concluded that Article XI of the BIT was not self-judging and that a substantive review was required.

129. Such a substantive review would have, as its object, an examination of the standards contained in Article XI in order to ascertain whether the requirements of that provision were present. However, instead of proceeding to such substantive review, the Tribunal decided not to apply Article XI and replaced that provision with Article 25 of the ILC Articles, i.e., by a rule of customary international law.

130. The Tribunal even acknowledged explicitly that it would not apply Article XI by stating that there was no 'need to undertake a further judicial review under Article XI'. This declaration represents a conclusive indication of the manifest excess of powers, in which the Tribunal engaged in abstaining from applying this BIT provision.

131. The fact that Argentina also invoked the state of necessity in the arbitration did not allow the Tribunal to disregard Article XI of the BIT and to apply, in its place, Article 25 of the ILC Articles. The Tribunal should have undertaken an examination of the requirements of the state of necessity as a ground for precluding wrongfulness only if Article XI of the BIT was held not to apply, and a violation under that BIT had been established.

Failure to state reasons

132. The Tribunal failed to state reasons pursuant to Article 52(1)(e) of the ICSID Convention in respect of two fundamental issues regarding Article XI of the BIT. The Tribunal did not explain why the lack of a definition in that BIT of the substantive standard of 'essential security interests' made it necessary to rely on the requirements of the state of necessity under customary international law. Nor did the Tribunal explain why Article XI did not establish conditions different from the requirements under customary international law set forth in Article 25 of ILC Articles.

133. In the Award, the Tribunal stated that in the absence of a definition of what is to be understood by an 'essential security interest', the requirements of a state of necessity under customary international law, as expressed in Article 25 of the ILC Articles, become relevant to the matter of establishing whether the necessary conditions have been met for its invocation under the BIT.

134. The Tribunal did not explain in the Award why the lack of a definition of 'essential security interests' of Article XI led to the application of the requirements of the state of necessity under customary international law in place of the BIT provision.

135. In conclusion, by failing to explain why the lack of a definition of 'essential security interests' in Article XI led to application of the requirements of the state of necessity instead of Article XI, the Tribunal failed to state the reasons on which it based its decision in the terms of Article 52(1)(e) of the ICSID Convention. The Award should therefore be annulled on this ground.

Sempra's position

136. Sempra has firmly rejected the notion that the Tribunal committed any excess of powers by any failure to interpret or apply Article XI of the BIT, or failed to state reasons for its conclusions in this regard. Nothing regarding the Tribunal's analysis of Argentina's Article XI and necessity defences constitutes a ground for annulment.

137. The Tribunal correctly interpreted and applied Article XI as well as Argentina's defence of necessity. It found that Argentina had means available other than the Emergency Law to address its economic crisis, and that it substantially contributed to the circumstances which gave rise to the economic crisis. Moreover, Argentina's annulment request is based on new arguments

and material that post-date the Award. Therefore, these objections should be rejected.

138. The Tribunal's mission was to interpret and apply Article XI and Argentina's defence based on state of necessity under customary international law. This the Tribunal did. It analysed Article XI and concluded that because of its lack of clarity, and the fact that it reflects customary international law, a state invoking Article XI must satisfy the same conditions required to invoke the defence of necessity. The Tribunal explained that it reached its interpretation of Article XI because: (i) the BIT's object and purpose requires a narrow interpretation of Article XI; (ii) Article XI does not contain any definition of the terms 'essential security interests' or 'necessary'; (iii) Article XI reflects customary international law; and (iv) relevant rules of international law should be used to interpret BIT provisions that either reflect customary international law or are not defined in the BIT. The Tribunal interpreted Article XI in accordance with relevant rules of treaty interpretation, as codified in Articles 31 and 32 of the VCLT.

139. As follows from the Award, the Tribunal rejected Argentina's defence based on Article XI because: (i) the Emergency Law was not necessary to maintain 'public order' or protect Argentina's 'essential security interests', and (ii) there were other means available to maintain 'public order' and to protect Argentina's 'essential security interests'.

140. The Tribunal found that 'there was a severe crisis', but that this crisis had not 'compromised the very existence of the State and its independence, thereby qualifying as one involving an essential state interest'. The Tribunal stated that '[q]uestions of public order and social unrest could be handled as in fact they were, just as questions of political stabilisation were handled under the constitutional arrangement in force'.

141. The Tribunal concluded that (i) 'there is no convincing evidence that the events were out of control or had become unmanageable' and (ii) that its task under the BIT was to find whether the Emergency Law was the 'only' alternative to address the economic crisis. The Tribunal held that 'this does not appear to have been the case', and therefore, there was more than one alternative to maintain 'public order' or protect its 'essential security interests'.

142. The Tribunal rejected Argentina's argument that it had not contributed to the crisis. The Tribunal first concluded that a 'State cannot invoke necessity if it has contributed to the situation giving rise to a state of neces-

sity'. The Tribunal found this was an 'expression of a general principle of law devised to prevent a party taking legal advantage of its own fault'. Thus, it did not just base its finding on Article XI or customary international law, but on a general principle of law. The Tribunal concluded that Argentina could not succeed in its defence under Article XI or the defence of necessity, if it had contributed to the situation of necessity, and based on the evidence produced by the parties, the Tribunal concluded that in fact Argentina had made a 'substantial contribution' to the state of necessity alleged by Argentina as its basis for invoking Article XI and the defence of necessity.

143. Additionally, in respect of the specific grounds invoked by Argentina for annulment of the Award, Sempra has submitted the following.

A manifest error of law is not a ground for annulment

144. In respect of Argentina's invocation of a manifest error of law, Sempra summarises its case by noting that a manifest error of law is not a ground for annulment. Moreover, Sempra adds, even if manifest error of law could constitute a ground for annulment, it is not present in this context; the Tribunal interpreted the law correctly.

The Tribunal did not manifestly exceed its powers

145. Sempra relies on the fact that the Tribunal agreed that '[t]he requirement for a state of necessity under customary international law, as outlined above in connection with their expression in Article 25 of the ILC Articles, become relevant to the matter of establishing whether the necessary conditions have been met for its invocation under the BIT'.

146. The Sempra Tribunal also rejected the criticism raised by Argentina against the way the CMS Tribunal addressed Article XI and necessity, concluding that the definition of necessity and the conditions for its operations are inseparable, having regard to the fact that it is under customary law that such elements have been defined.

147. As for Argentina's invocation of Article XI as *lex specialis*, the Tribunal accepted that '[i]t is no doubt correct to conclude that a treaty regime specifically dealing with a given matter will prevail over more general rules of customary law'. However, as the BIT text did not provide sufficient guidance, the Tribunal considered customary international law the most appropriate means to interpret the BIT provision.

148. The Tribunal held that the conditions under which Article XI of the BIT and the state of necessity under customary international law may be invoked are the same. The Tribunal reiterated this point when it rejected Argentina's self-judging argument by explaining that:

> The judicial control must be a substantive one, and concerned with whether the requirements under customary law or the BIT have been met and can thereby preclude wrongfulness. [Because the Tribunal rejected the customary international law necessity defence] there is no need to undertake a further judicial review under Article XI given that this Article does not set out conditions different from customary law in such regard.

149. Sempra has also referred to the following circumstances. Article X of the BIT provides that '[t]his Treaty shall not derogate from:. . .b) international legal obligations . . . that entitle investments or associated activities to treatment more favourable than that accorded by this Treaty in like situations'. Thus, the BIT's object and purpose indicate an intent not to interpret particular BIT provisions in a manner that accords investments less protection than that provided under customary international law.

150. In addition, Sempra recalls, the BIT contains several gateways to international law, setting it as the floor below which treatment cannot be afforded, unless required under the BIT. For example, Article II(2)(a) of the BIT, provides that the treatment afforded by the BIT cannot be 'less than that required by international law'. Furthermore, Article 42 of the ICSID Convention imposes on the Tribunal a duty to apply international law. Thus, the BIT cannot be seen as a separate and independent instrument, but as a creature of the international law regime, which at the same time is the applicable law that governs the BIT.

151. Sempra does not agree either that Article XI and the defence of necessity under customary international differ in a number of fundamental ways as argued by Argentina. Moreover, Argentina did not present these arguments to the Tribunal, which should suffice to reject this claim.

152. Sempra does not accept Argentina's affirmation that the content of Article XI and Article 25 are different, and that there is no 'textual link' to customary law in Article XI, on the grounds: (a) that there is no textual equivalent to 'grave and imminent peril'; (b) that Article XI does not require that a 'necessary' measure be the 'only way' to achieve the covered purpose;

and (c) that there is no requirement in Article XI that the State not have contributed to the situation necessitating the measure.

153. Article XI reflects customary international law, a self-contained regime which must be used to interpret Article XI. Also, various elements of Article XI actually reflect international law, and not just the state defence of necessity, but also distress and *force majeure*.

154. Article XI is limited to maintenance of peace, 'essential security interests', and public order. Article 25, on the other hand, only provides that the State interest must be an 'essential interest of the State', meaning that Article XI is not more expansive than customary law.

155. Sempra also does not accept Argentina's assertion that Article XI and Article 25 are different, the latter (but not the former) being without prejudice to compensation. It is, in any event, irrelevant to the question whether the conditions under which Article XI and the customary necessity plea can be invoked are the same or not.

156. The Tribunal did not refrain from applying Article XI, but interpreted this provision as requiring a State invoking it to satisfy the same conditions as required to invoke the plea of necessity under customary law. The Tribunal interpreted one aspect of Article XI – the conditions under which it can be invoked – to be the same as those required by customary international law, and found, as a matter of fact, that Argentina failed to satisfy those conditions. No excess of powers, let alone any manifest excess of powers is involved.

Article XI is not self-judging

157. The Tribunal thoroughly examined Argentina's argument that Article XI is self-judging in character, and that it came to the well-reasoned conclusion that this was not the case. Instead, it found that a substantive review was required. The Tribunal did not exceed its powers, and fully stated reasons for its decision.

There was no failure to state reasons

158. Sempra has emphasised that the Tribunal did not fail to state reasons regarding its analysis of Article XI of the BIT and considers Argentina's position on that issue inconsistent in that Argentina also considers that the Tribunal failed to apply Article XI. Sempra considers, however, that each step in the Tribunal's reasoning in respect of Article XI is lucid and consistent in

that it clearly shows how the Tribunal concluded that: (1) Article XI did not define or provide the legal elements and conditions necessary for its application; (2) it was bound to look to analogous rules of customary law; (3) the conditions for the application of state of necessity under customary law were the same as the elements for the application of the terms of Article XI due to their similarities and the lack of clarity provided by the BIT for its application; and (4) the BIT and Article XI provide treatment that was not less than that of customary law. Therefore, there was no failure to state reasons.

Consideration of the foregoing arguments by the Committee

Application of Article XI of the BIT

159. For reasons which will be discussed in greater detail later, the Committee finds that the Award must be annulled in its entirety on the basis of manifest excess of powers (Article 52(1)(b) of the ICSID Convention) in respect of failure to apply Article XI of the BIT. The question therefore arises whether it is necessary for the Committee to deal with other arguments advanced by Argentina in relation to the way in which the Tribunal dealt with Article XI. The Committee feels that it should deal with these arguments for the sake of completeness.

Manifest error of law

160. Argentina has argued that the Tribunal made 'manifest errors of law' in respect of the way in which it dealt with Article XI. These manifest errors of law consisted in equating Article XI of the BIT with Article 25 of the ILC Articles.

161. Argentina also argued that the Tribunal committed a serious error of law, by considering the application of Article 27 to a possible duty of compensation of the State before, and indeed without, reviewing whether responsibility was precluded under Article XI. Additionally, in this respect, the application of Article 27 under customary international law constituted a manifest error of law. While admitting that a 'mere error of law' is not a ground for annulment under Article 52(1) of the ICSID Convention, Argentina affirms that such error may be serious enough to reach to the level of a manifest excess of powers for failure to apply the proper law.

162. As Argentina itself recognises, a serious error of law is not in itself a ground for annulment under Article 52(1) of the ICSID Convention. It is

instead Argentina's contention that a serious error of law may, in certain circumstances, constitute a manifest excess of powers (and therefore be annullable on that ground).

163. It is correct – as also pointed out by Argentina – that certain ad hoc Committees have dealt with this issue and opined, for instance, that incorrect application of law might constitute a manifest excess of powers if 'it amounts to effective disregard of the applicable law'.

164. As a general proposition, this Committee would not wish totally to rule out the possibility that a manifest error of law may, in an exceptional situation, be of such egregious nature as to amount to a manifest excess of powers.

165. In this case, the Committee has reached the conclusion that the Tribunal – in respect of Article XI of the BIT – has failed altogether to apply the applicable law and, by failing to do so, has committed a manifest excess of powers. This conclusion of the Committee precludes any question of manifest error in applying the applicable law. It is therefore unnecessary for the Committee to engage in any more precise discussion of where that specific line should be drawn between an error of law that justifies annulment and one that does not.

Failure to state reasons

Introduction

166. According to Article 48(3) of the ICSID Convention, '[t]he Award [. . .] shall state the reasons upon which it is based'. The importance of this provision is highlighted by the fact that failure to state reasons constitutes a ground for annulment according to Article 52(1)(e).

167. The fact that a total absence of reasons merits annulment is clear, but such a situation is rarely, if ever, encountered in practice. Rather there will be an (alleged) absence of reasons for a particular aspect of an award, or otherwise insufficient, inadequate or possibly contradictory reasons. Difficulties arise when determining what standard should be applied in deciding whether a defect of reasoning should lead to annulment. While certainly 'frivolous, perfunctory or absurd arguments by a tribunal' may well be subject to annulment, such clear-cut cases do not abound. Ad hoc Committees are faced with making the important distinction between finding, on the one hand, reasons which are reasonably comprehensible and consistent, demonstrating, on the whole, a logical and discernable line of thinking, and, on the other hand,

'circumstances [where] there is a significant lacuna in the Award, which makes it impossible for the reader to follow the reasoning on this point'.

Discussion

168. The Committee observes that the Tribunal dealt with Argentina's defence based on necessity under Argentine law, customary international law, and Article XI of the BIT in that order. In so doing, the Tribunal followed the order in which Argentina argued these defences. It is evident that the Tribunal gave a detailed account of its reasoning in respect of necessity under customary international law. In this regard the Tribunal noted that the ILC Articles, although not constituting a source of customary law still (as was accepted by the Parties) represents a fair expression of such law, and held that the conditions laid down in Article 25 of the ILC Articles were necessary conditions for invoking an 'essential security interest' under the BIT. The Tribunal dedicated considerable attention to the question whether or not Article XI is self-judging (a point also extensively argued by Argentina) and arrived at a reasoned conclusion on that point. Having reasoned so far, the Tribunal held that judicial review of the invocation of Article XI, and the measures adopted, must be a substantive one, and concerned with whether the requirements under customary law or the Treaty were met and could thereby preclude wrongfulness. The Tribunal reasoned that since the BIT itself did not deal with the legal elements necessary for the legitimate invocation of a state of necessity, criteria found in customary international law had to be applied. From the above overview it is clear how the Tribunal reasoned in order to reach the conclusion it did. Hence, there is no failure to state reasons.

Did the Tribunal's rejection of the proposition that Article XI is self-judging constitute an annullable error?

169. Argentina argues that by failing to appreciate that Article XI is self-judging, the Tribunal disregarded Argentina's discretion to take measures in order to maintain public order and protect its essential security interests. Therefore, by ignoring the fact that a State invoking Article XI is the sole judge of the appropriateness of the contested measures, the Tribunal manifestly exceeded its powers.

170. In the Committee's view, it is clear that there was no failure on the part of the Tribunal to consider the matter of whether Article XI is self-judging or not. On the contrary, it applied considerable attention to the subject (as evidently did the parties), reaching the conclusion that Article XI is not self-judging, a conclusion that the Tribunal was perfectly entitled to reach.

171. Argentina censures the Tribunal for having 'dogmatically' asserted what it considered to be the object and purpose of the BIT, without giving reasons and drawing its conclusions from that. Equally seriously, according to Argentina, the Tribunal reversed the logical sequence of the interpretative process by passing over the text of the relevant treaty provision itself in breach of Article 31(1) of the VCLT.

172. In addition, Argentina has argued extensively in favour of the self-judging nature of Article XI of the BIT, referring to a number of sources (expert testimony, official statements and other authorities). These arguments are, however, clearly appropriate to a review of the merits and cannot be considered by an ad hoc Committee.

Manifest excess of powers

Introduction

173. As has been confirmed on numerous occasions there is a fundamental distinction between erroneous application of the law and a failure to apply the law. By way of example, the following statements by ad hoc Committees may be mentioned. The MINE ad hoc Committee stated: 'Disregard of the applicable rules of law must be distinguished from erroneous application of those rules which, even if manifestly unwarranted, furnishes no ground for annulment'.

174. The Amco (I) ad hoc Committee stated:

> The ad hoc Committee will limit itself to determining whether the Tribunal did in fact apply the law it was bound to apply to the dispute. Failure to apply such law, as distinguished from mere misconstruction of that law, would constitute a manifest excess of powers on the part of the Tribunal and a ground for nullity under Article 52(1)(b) of the Convention. The ad hoc Committee has approached this task with caution, distinguishing failure to apply the applicable law as a ground for annulment and misinterpretation of the applicable law as a ground for appeal.

175. On Argentina's case, the Tribunal failed to apply Article XI of the BIT, and, by this failure, apart from a failure to state reasons, committed a manifest excess of powers.

176. It is clear that Argentina in the present case (as well as in CMS) argued the plea of necessity under customary international law before proceeding to the matter of preclusion under Article XI. This sequence of argument is

illogical as the question whether a state of necessity justifies exoneration from State responsibility will become an issue only where liability is not already precluded under Article XI of the BIT. As a general rule, a treaty will take precedence over customary international law.

177. One can certainly discuss Article 25 on the assumption (implicit or explicit) that Article XI does not lead to preclusion. If it is concluded (as in this case) that a justification for wrongfulness is not available under Article 25, the Tribunal would need to go back to Article XI in order to decide whether the assumption under which the Article 25 inquiry was pursued is valid in the circumstances. In this case, however, the Tribunal did not do that.

178. Argentina has argued that the Tribunal made 'manifest errors of law' in respect of its failure to deal with Article XI of the BIT. This manifest error of law consisted in equating Article XI of the BIT with Article 25 of the ILC Articles.

179. Argentina further contends that the Tribunal committed a serious error of law by considering the application of Article 27 concerning a possible duty of compensation of the State before (or indeed without) reviewing whether responsibility was precluded under Article XI of the BIT. Additionally, in this respect, the application of Article 27 under customary international law constituted a manifest error of law. While admitting that a 'mere error of law' is not a ground for annulment under Article 52(1) of the Convention, Argentina affirms that such error may be serious enough to reach to the level of a manifest excess of powers for failure to apply the proper law.

The admissibility of Argentina's arguments

180. In argument before the Committee, Sempra contended that certain of the arguments advanced by Argentina on the first issue were new, in the sense that they had not been advanced before the Tribunal, which had not had an opportunity to consider them. They were therefore inadmissible in these annulment proceedings.

181. Sempra claims that Argentina presented only two arguments concerning (1) the self-judging nature of Article XI, and (2) that the defence of necessity precluded liability and compensation. Further, Argentina did not differentiate between the state of necessity under customary international law, on the one hand, and preclusion under Article XI, on the other.

182. At paragraph 366, having quoted the terms of Article XI, the Tribunal sets out the arguments of Argentina as follows:

> 366. The respondent, relying on the opinion of Dean Slaughter and Professor Burke-White, asserts that public order and national security exceptions have to be interpreted broadly in the context of this Article so as to include considerations of economic security and political stability. Moreover, the respondent's experts understand this Article to be self-judging in so far as each party will be the sole judge of when the situation requires measures of the kind envisaged by the Article, subject only to a determination of good faith by tribunals that might be called upon to settle a dispute on this point. [Footnote omitted]. In the respondent's view, the gravity of the crisis that it faced amply justified resorting to such measures, which can only be considered as having been adopted in good faith.

183. Argentina thus raised two issues. The first concerned the scope and application of Article XI. The second concerned the question whether Article XI is self-judging. The first issue is logically prior to the second.

184. The ad hoc Committee finds that, in so far as the arguments of Argentina can be said to be 'new', they are a permissible development of Argentina's arguments on the first issue identified above and are therefore admissible.

The Tribunal's findings

185. After setting out in greater detail the arguments of Argentina and of Sempra, the Tribunal proceeded to set out its own assessment of the arguments (reproduced here for ease of reference):

> 373. In weighing this discussion, the Tribunal must first note that the object and purpose of the Treaty is, as a general proposition, for it to be applicable in situations of economic difficulty and hardship that require the protection of the internationally guaranteed rights of its beneficiaries. To this extent, any interpretation resulting in an escape route from the defined obligations cannot be easily reconciled with that object and purpose. Accordingly, a restrictive interpretation of any such alternative is mandatory.
> 374. The Tribunal considers that there is nothing that would prevent an interpretation allowing for the inclusion of economic emergency in the context of Article XI. Essential security interests can eventually encompass situations other than the traditional military threats for which the institution found its origins in customary law. However, to conclude that such a determination is self-judging would definitely be inconsistent with the object and purpose noted. In fact, the Treaty would be deprived of any substantive meaning.

375. In addition, in view of the fact that the Treaty does not define what is to be understood by an 'essential security interest,' the requirements for a state of necessity under customary international law, as outlined above in connection with their expression in Article 25 of the Articles on State Responsibility, become relevant to the matter of establishing whether the necessary conditions have been met for its invocation under the Treaty. Different might have been the case if the Treaty had defined this concept and the conditions for its exercise, but this was not the case.

376. The Tribunal notes that in the view of Dean Slaughter and Professor Burke-White, which the respondent shares, the CMS award was mistaken in that it discussed Article XI in connection with necessity under customary law. This Tribunal believes, however, that the Treaty provision is inseparable from the customary law standard in so far as the definition of necessity and the conditions for its operation are concerned, given that it is under customary law that such elements have been defined. Similarly, the Treaty does not contain a definition concerning either the maintenance of international peace and security, or the conditions for its operation. Reference is instead made to the Charter of the United Nations in Article 6 of the Protocol to the Treaty.

377. The expert opinion of Dean Slaughter and Professor Burke-White expresses the view that the treaty regime is different and separate from customary law as it is *lex specialis*. As Professor Burke-White explained at the hearing, the consequence of this approach is that while Article XI requires only a good faith determination, under customary law the whole panoply of requirements laid down in Article 25 of the Articles comes into play. Moreover, Professor Burke-White stated that the US and Argentina had 'decided to accord investors greater protection than they would receive under customary international law, but simultaneously to guarantee to states, the States Parties greater protection to deal with threats to their national security'.

378. It is no doubt correct to conclude that a treaty regime specifically dealing with a given matter will prevail over more general rules of customary law. The problem here, however, is that the Treaty itself did not deal with the legal elements necessary for the legitimate invocation of a state of necessity. The rule governing such questions will thus be found under customary law. As concluded above, such requirements and conditions have not been fully met in this case. Moreover, the view of the respondent's legal expert, as expressed at the hearing, contradicts the respondent's argument that the Treaty standards are not more favourable than those of customary law, and at the most should be equated with the international minimum standard. The Tribunal does not believe that the intention of the parties can be described in the terms which the expert has used, as there is no indication that such was the case. Nor does the Tribunal believe that because Article XI did not make an express reference to customary law, this source of rights and obligations becomes inapplicable. International law is not a fragmented body of law

as far as basic principles are concerned and necessity is no doubt one such basic principle.

379. As explained by Dean Slaughter, the US position has been gradually evolving towards support for self-judging clauses in respect of national security interests, and some bilateral investment treaties reflect this change, albeit not all of them. Yet, this does not necessarily result in the conclusion that such was the intention of the parties in respect of the Treaty under consideration. Truly exceptional and extraordinary clauses, such as a self-judging provision, must be expressly drafted to reflect that intent, as otherwise there can well be a presumption that they do not have such meaning in view of their exceptional nature.

380. In the case of the Treaty, nothing was said in respect of a self-judging character, and the elements invoked in support of this view originate for the most part in US Congressional discussions concerning broader issues, or in indirect interpretations arising mainly with respect to the eventual application of model investment treaties used by the US. The respondent's post-hearing brief has listed a number of discussions and statements which relate to the issue of a self-judging interpretation, but these items are contextual and do not specifically address the case of the Treaty in question.

381. Professor Burke-White also stated at the hearing that, in his understanding, the letter submitting the Treaty to the Argentine Congress did not say 'anything about it being self-judging, nor anything about it being non-self-judging . . . this document does not speak to that issue'. This expert also explained that while he had no evidence about the internal discussions within the Argentine Government as to the intent of the Treaty, there was such evidence in respect of the intent of the US Government, and that given the 'reciprocal nature of the Treaty . . . the intent . . . would be for a self-judging interpretation of Article XI.' This is, however, again a contextual interpretation that does not appear to meet the stricter requirements of Articles 31 and 32 of the Vienna Convention on the Law of Treaties in respect of treaty interpretation in the light of its context, or the resort to supplementary means of interpretation.

382. More to the point is a letter sent by an official of the United States Department of State on September 15, 2006 to a former official asked to testify in the context of a different arbitration, which the respondent brought to the attention of the Tribunal on June 25, 2007. In this letter, it is stated that 'notwithstanding the decision of the ICJ in the *Nicaragua* case, the position of the US Government is that the essential security language in our FCN treaties and Bilateral Investment Treaties is self-judging, i.e., only the party itself is competent to determine what is in its own essential security interests'. The respondent is of the view that this confirms the interpretation given by it of the Treaty in this case. The claimant, however, has opposed this understanding on the argument that the letter refers to an interpretation supposedly adopted as from 2006 and that in any event it does not refer to the Treaty with Argentina nor does it preclude liability or compensation.

383. The discussion noted above concerning the GATT and the *Nicaragua* decision, just like the *Oil Platforms* case, confirms that the language of a provision has to be very precise for it to lead to a conclusion about its self-judging nature. In those decisions, the fact that the language was not express turned out to be crucial to the rejection of arguments favouring a self-judging interpretation. So too, the International Court of Justice held in the *Gabcíkovo-Nagymaros* case, when referring to the conditions defined by the International Law Commission, that 'the State concerned is not the sole judge of whether those conditions have been met'.

384. The Tribunal must also note that not even in the context of GATT Article XXI is the issue considered to be settled in favour of a self-judging interpretation, and the very fact that such article has not been excluded from dispute settlement is indicative of its non-self-judging nature.

385. The same holds true of the US Department of State letter referred to above in that it does not address any specific treaty, least that with Argentina. Furthermore, the fact that arbitration is the compulsory dispute settlement mechanism established in the Treaty in question, like with GATT/WTO, could be rather indicative of the non-self-judging nature of the essential security interest clause. Not even if this is the interpretation given to the clause today by the United States would this necessarily mean that such an interpretation governs the Treaty. The view of one State does not make international law, even less so when such a view is ascertained only by indirect means of interpretation or in a rather remote or general way as far as the very Treaty at issue is concerned. What is relevant is the intention which both parties had in signing the Treaty, and this does not confirm the self-judging interpretation.

386. Moreover, even if this interpretation were shared today by both parties to the Treaty, it still would not result in a change of its terms. States are of course free to amend the Treaty by consenting to another text, but this would not affect rights acquired under the Treaty by investors or other beneficiaries. In fact, Article XIV of the Treaty provides that in case of termination, the investment will continue to be protected under its provisions 'for a further period of ten years'. So too, with reference to rights protected under the Energy Charter Treaty, the tribunal in *Plama* has held that any denial of advantages to which an investor might have rights 'should not have retrospective effect,' as such a situation would result in making legitimate expectations false at a much later date.

387. As an English court has recently held in respect of a claim of non-justiciability relating to a State challenge to the OEPC award, the fact that a treaty is concluded between States cannot allow the derogation of rights that belong to private parties. In that case, the issue concerned dispute settlement, and as a consequence the doctrine of non-justiciability was held not to apply.

388. In the light of this discussion, the Tribunal concludes that Article XI is not self-judging and that judicial review is not limited in its respect to an examination of whether its invocation, or the measures adopted, were taken in good faith.

The judicial control must be a substantive one, and concerned with whether the requirements under customary law or the Treaty have been met and can thereby preclude wrongfulness. Since the Tribunal has found above that the crisis invoked does not meet the customary law requirements of Article 25 of the Articles on State Responsibility, it concludes that necessity or emergency is not conducive in this case to the preclusion of wrongfulness, and that there is no need to undertake a further judicial review under Article XI given that this Article does not set out conditions different from customary law in such regard.

389. A judicial determination as to compliance with the requirements of international law in this matter should not be understood as suggesting that arbitral tribunals wish to substitute their views for the functions of sovereign States. Such a ruling instead simply responds to the Tribunal's duty that, in applying international law, it cannot fail to give effect to legal commitments that are binding on the parties, and must interpret the rules accordingly unless a derogation of those commitments has been expressly agreed to.

390. The Tribunal explained above that it would consider the requirement of Article 25 of the Articles on State Responsibility, to the effect that the act in question not seriously impair an essential interest of the State towards which the obligation exists in the context of the Treaty obligations. In the light of the discussion above about changing interpretations, it does not appear that the Government's invocation of Article XI or of a state of necessity generally would be taken by the other party to mean that such impairment arises.

391. Be that as it may, in the context of investment treaties there is still the need to take into consideration the interests of the private entities who are the ultimate beneficiaries of those obligations, as was explained by the English court in the *OEPC* case noted above. The essential interest of the claimant would certainly be seriously impaired by the operation of Article XI or a state of necessity in this case.

Discussion

186. Investment arbitration under the ICSID regime (or any other type of arbitration whether institutional or ad hoc) is subject to the consent of the parties. The State's consent to arbitration of investment disputes is given, in a very large number of cases, in a treaty, while the investor's consent is normally included in its request for arbitration. The scope, extent and conditions that apply to the procedural means of recourse and substantive protections offered to the investor are exclusively addressed by the treaty.

187. Where the treaty permits or excuses conduct adverse to the investor in specific circumstances enunciated in the treaty, it follows that the terms of the treaty itself exclude the protection to the investor that the treaty would otherwise have provided.

188. According to Article 31(1) of VCLT, the first point of reference for interpretation of a BIT provision is the 'ordinary meaning' of the words of the treaty themselves.

189. In the present case, where the BIT provides the relevant treaty language, it is necessary first and foremost to apply the provisions of the BIT. Indeed, the parties are in agreement that the BIT constitutes the applicable law.

190. Article 38 of the Statute of the ICJ lists 'international conventions' as a primary source of international law. However, it is not primarily for this reason that the BIT has pre-eminence in the investor-state context of arbitration, but because the consent to submit to international dispute resolution is predicated on the very terms of the BIT.

191. Against that background, it is necessary to consider the relevant terms of the BIT and the way in which the Tribunal approached its application.

192. Article XI of the BIT provides as follows:

> This Treaty shall not preclude the application by either party of measures necessary for the maintenance of public order, the fulfilment of its obligations with respect to the maintenance or restoration of international peace or security, or the [p]rotection of its own essential interests.

193. Article XI does not specify who is to be the judge of whether the measures taken are 'necessary' for one or more of the purposes specified – in other words, whether the State Party taking the measures is itself to be the judge of their necessity, in which event the provision is said to be 'self-judging'.

194. The Committee finds that the reasoning of the Tribunal does not distinguish clearly between the question whether Article XI is self-judging and the prior question as to its scope and application. Thus, at the outset in paragraph 374 of the Award, the Tribunal states that 'there is nothing that would prevent an interpretation allowing for the inclusion of economic emergency in the context of Article XI' and that 'essential security interests can eventually encompass situations other than the traditional military threats for which the institution found its origins in customary law'. The Tribunal then goes on directly to say, 'However, to conclude that such a determination is self-judging would definitely be inconsistent with the object and purpose noted. In fact, the Treaty would be deprived of any substantive meaning'.

195. As regards the scope and application of Article XI, the Committee finds the following passages to be central to the reasoning of the Tribunal: (1) in paragraph 376:

> This Tribunal believes . . . that the Treaty provision [i.e. Article XI of the BIT] is inseparable from the customary law standard insofar as the definition of necessity and the conditions for its operation are concerned, given that it is under customary law that such elements have been defined.

(2) in paragraph 378:

> It is no doubt correct to conclude that a treaty regime specifically dealing with a given matter will prevail over more general rules of customary law. The problem here, however, is that the Treaty itself did not deal with the legal elements necessary for the legitimate invocation of a state of necessity. The rule governing such questions will thus be found under customary law. As concluded above, such requirements and conditions have not been fully met in this case. . . . Nor does the Tribunal believe that because Article XI did not make an express reference to customary law, this source of rights and obligations becomes inapplicable. International law is not a fragmented body of law as far as basic principles are concerned and necessity is no doubt one such basic principle.

(3) in paragraph 388:

> In the light of this discussion, the Tribunal concludes that Article XI is not self-judging and that judicial review is not limited in its respect to an examination of whether its invocation, or the measures adopted, were taken in good faith. The judicial control must be a substantive one, and concerned with whether the requirements under customary law or the Treaty have been met and can thereby preclude wrongfulness. Since the Tribunal has found above that the crisis invoked does not meet the customary law requirements of Article 25 of the Articles on State Responsibility, it concludes that necessity or emergency is not conducive in this case to the preclusion of wrongfulness, and that there is no need to undertake a further judicial review under Article XI given that this Article does not set out conditions different from customary law in such regard.

196. In the opinion of the Committee, the reasoning of these passages compels the conclusion that the Tribunal did not deem itself to be required – or even entitled – to consider the applicability of Article XI, both because this provision did not deal with the legal elements necessary for the legitimate invocation of a state of necessity and because the Tribunal found that the Argentine economic crisis did not meet the

customary international law requirements as set out in Article 25 of the ILC Articles.

197. First, as regards paragraph 376, the Committee accepts, of course, that it may be appropriate to look to customary law as a guide to the interpretation of terms used in the BIT. It does not follow, however, that customary law (*in casu*, Article 25 of the ILC Articles) establishes a peremptory 'definition of necessity and the conditions for its operation'. While some norms of customary law are peremptory (*jus cogens*), others are not, and States may contract otherwise, as the Tribunal itself recognises in paragraph 378.

198. Second, Article XI differs in material respects from Article 25, as can be seen from the following comparison of the texts: [Table removed.]

199. It is apparent from this comparison that Article 25 does not offer a guide to interpretation of the terms used in Article XI. The most that can be said is that certain words or expressions are the same or similar.

200. More importantly, Article 25 is concerned with the invocation by a State Party of necessity 'as a ground for precluding the wrongfulness of an act not in conformity with an international obligation of that State'. Article 25 presupposes that an act has been committed that is incompatible with the State's international obligations and is therefore 'wrongful'. Article XI, on the other hand, provides that 'This Treaty shall not preclude' certain measures so that, where Article XI applies, the taking of such measures is not incompatible with the State's international obligations and is not therefore 'wrongful'. Article 25 and Article XI therefore deal with quite different situations. Article 25 cannot therefore be assumed to 'define necessity and the conditions for its operation' for the purpose of interpreting Article XI, still less to do so as a mandatory norm of international law.

201. Third, as regards paragraph 378, it is unclear what the Tribunal means by the statement that 'the Treaty itself [i.e., the BIT] did not deal with the legal elements necessary for the *legitimate* invocation of a state of necessity. The *rule* governing such questions will *thus* be found under customary law' (emphasis added). Invocation of a state of necessity under the terms of a bilateral treaty need not necessarily be 'legitimated' by a 'rule' of international law. There may be no rule governing such questions. Still less is it obvious that the rule is to be found in a provision of customary law dealing with invocation of necessity as a justification for breach of an international obligation.

202. Fourth, again as regards paragraph 378, even if it be the case that 'international law is not a fragmented body of law as far as basic principles are concerned', it does not follow either: (i) that 'necessity is *no doubt* one such basic principle' in the sense that it must be interpreted and applied in exactly the same way in all circumstances, or (ii) that international law will become 'fragmented' if States contract otherwise. While there may be certain norms of international law, including customary law, which would render it unlawful under international law for States to agree to adopt a provision inconsistent with those norms, this is not such a case. *Jus cogens* does not require parties to a bilateral investment treaty to forego the possibility of invoking a defence of necessity in whatever terms they may agree. The terms on which they agree may be thought to be politically or economically unwise, but this does not render them unlawful.

203. Fifth, as regards paragraph 388, for the same reasons, the statement that 'judicial control must be . . . concerned with whether the requirements under customary law or the Treaty have been met and can thereby preclude wrongfulness' begs the question. The prior question is whether there is wrongfulness. As noted above, Article 25 deals with a situation where a State Party is in breach of a Treaty obligation and seeks to justify its breach by a plea of necessity. Article 25 sets out the restrictive conditions in which such a plea may be admitted. Article XI of the BIT, on the other hand, expressly provides that the BIT 'shall not preclude the application by either Party of measures necessary' for certain reasons or purposes.

204. It is true that the BIT does not prescribe who is to determine whether the measures in question are or were 'necessary' for the purpose so invoked – whether, in other words, Article XI is or is not self-judging. But if the measures in question are properly judged to be 'necessary', then there is no breach of any Treaty obligation. In that event, it is not the case that 'judicial control must be . . . concerned with whether the requirements under customary law or the Treaty have been met and can thereby preclude wrongfulness'.

205. So the question arises whether the error in law so identified constitutes an excess of powers. Excess of powers is normally invoked where it is claimed that the Tribunal has failed to apply the applicable law, and a line of decisions in ICSID practice confirms that failure to apply the applicable law may amount to an excess of powers, whereas erroneous application of the law does not constitute a basis for annulment.

206. It will therefore be necessary to determine whether the error in question amounts (i) to a failure to apply the law, in which event the award of the

Tribunal may be annulled, or (ii) to a misapplication of the law, in which event the award, although to that extent defective, will not be annulled.

207. In this case, the Committee finds that the following sentence in paragraph 388 of the Award demonstrates that the Tribunal failed to apply the applicable law:

> Since the Tribunal has found above that the crisis invoked does not meet the customary law requirements of Article 25 of the Articles on State Responsibility, it concludes that necessity or emergency is not conducive in this case to the preclusion of wrongfulness, and that there is no need to undertake a further judicial review under Article XI given that this Article does not set out conditions different from customary law in such regard.

208. The Tribunal has held, in effect, that the substantive criteria of Article XI simply cannot find application where rules of customary international law – as enunciated in the ILC Articles – do not lead to exoneration in case of wrongfulness, and that Article 25 'trumps' Article XI in providing the mandatory legal norm to be applied. Thus, the Tribunal adopted Article 25 of the ILC Articles as the primary law to be applied, rather than Article XI of the BIT, and in so doing made a fundamental error in identifying and applying the applicable law.

209. The Committee is therefore driven to the conclusion that the Tribunal has failed to conduct its review on the basis that the applicable legal norm is to be found in Article XI of the BIT, and that this failure constitutes an excess of powers within the meaning of the ICSID Convention.

210. It remains to be considered whether the excess of powers so found is 'manifest'.

The excess of powers must be 'manifest'

211. In order for excess of powers to require annulment of an Award, the excess must be 'manifest'. In order to ensure that this qualification is satisfied, it should be noted, as a first step, that it is necessary to observe the basic requirement of the VCLT to seek the 'ordinary meaning' of the relevant term. In a literal sense 'manifest' is something which is 'plain', 'clear', 'obvious', 'evident' i.e., easily understood or recognised by the mind.

212. It would appear that ad hoc Committees have applied either a two-step approach determining first whether there is an excess of powers and, if

so, whether that excess was manifest, or an approach starting from a *prima facie* assessment of the presence of any manifest excess and, if the finding is negative, stop the examination there. The Committee favours the two-step approach, as excess of powers is a *sine qua non* for the need to gauge the manifestness of the excess, and allows a more cogent analysis of what constitutes a breach, on one hand, and, on the other, what makes it manifest.

213. Whether an excess of power satisfies the qualitative criterion of being manifest has been the object of scrutiny in a large number of decisions. All of these decisions have, in different language, expressed the opinion that in order for an excess of powers to be manifest, it must be quite evident without the need to engage in an elaborate analysis of the text of the Award.

214. For reasons dealt with above, the Committee has concluded that the Tribunal engaged in an excess of powers by its total failure to apply Article XI of the BIT.

215. Proceeding to the qualitative criterion of 'manifest', the Committee takes the following considerations into account.

216. In paragraph 378 of the Award, the Tribunal opines that because the BIT did not deal with the legal elements necessary for the legitimate invocation of a state of necessity, the rule governing such questions will thus be found under customary law. This implies that, according to the Tribunal's reasoning, where the rules of customary law do not legitimate treaty application, the treaty provision cannot be applied. This conclusion is reinforced by the following sentence in the Award, which explains that 'such requirements and conditions have not been fully met in this case'.

217. In other words, the fact that customary international law, as enunciated by the ILC Articles, does not confer exoneration from wrongfulness was held by the Tribunal to imply that it need not take the inquiry any further. This is further confirmed in the Tribunal's conclusion that for the reasons just mentioned 'there is no need to undertake a further judicial review under Article XI'.

218. On the basis of the above, the Committee considers that it is obvious from a simple reading of the reasons of the Tribunal that it did not identify or apply Article XI of the BIT as the applicable law, and that it failed to do so on the assumption that the language of this provision was somehow not legitimated by the dictates of customary international law.

219. The excess of powers on the part of the Tribunal is therefore manifest.

Articles II(2) (a) and X of the BIT

220. For the sake of completeness, the Committee wishes to address the argument of Sempra relating to Articles II(2)(a) and X of the BIT. Sempra relies on these provisions of the BIT in support of the proposition that the BIT cannot be seen as other than an integral part of the international law regime, the Committee wishes to make the following observations.

221. There is nothing in the materials, and particularly not in the Award, that indicates that the significance, if any, of Articles II (MFN Treatment and a national treatment) and Article X (non-derogation) have been argued by the parties or discussed by the Tribunal in the context of the arbitral proceedings. This is, however, not determinative of the issue. In the present annulment proceeding, the Committee has no reason to discuss whether these provisions could have had a role to play in the application of Article XI (since this provision of the BIT, according to the Committee's finding, was not applied at all). For that reason, Articles II and X simply do not enter into the considerations that the ad hoc Committee needs to take into account in order to reach this conclusion. The reason for annulment is that Article XI was not applied, not that it was applied in any particular way, whether affected or not by the Articles II and X of the BIT.

Exercise of a discretionary right to annul?

222. The effect of the Tribunal's treatment of necessity as a matter solely of customary international law is that Argentina has effectively been deprived of its procedurally assured entitlement to have its right of preclusion laid down in Article XI of the BIT – the applicable law in this respect – subjected to legal scrutiny. For this reason, as annulment may be a matter of discretion, the Committee has concluded that, in this case, the Award must be annulled.

Conclusion

223. Summarising the Committee's discussion above, it arrives at the conclusion that the Award of 28 September 2007 in ICSID Case No. ARB/02/16 shall be annulled on the ground of manifest excess of powers.

Costs

224. According to Article 61(2) of the ICSID Convention, a Tribunal shall (absent party agreement) decide how and by whom fees and expenses of the members of the Tribunal and the charges and fees of the Centre shall be paid,

such decision forming part of the Award. Article 52(4) extends the application of this provision to annulment proceedings.

225. Neither the Convention nor its Rules and Regulations give any guidelines as to the application of this provision. The principal alternatives are (1) the application of the rule that the costs follow the event ('loser pays') or (2) equal sharing of costs.

226. It is fair to say that a majority of ad hoc committees have opted for the latter principle, although a recent tendency towards the former principle may be noted.

227. This ad hoc Committee considers that it is in line with equitable principles to let the rule that the costs-follow-the-event apply to those costs of the annulment proceeding that have been incurred by the Centre, i.e., in respect of the fees and expenses of the members of the ad hoc Committee and the charges, fees, and out-of-pocket expenses incurred by the Centre.

228. For this reason, Sempra shall be ordered to reimburse Argentina the total amount of the costs of the Centre – as finally determined – to the extent that these have been advanced by Argentina, with each party bearing the expenses for its own representation and its related party costs.

Decision

229. In consideration of the foregoing, the Committee unanimously decides to:

> Annul the Award of 28 September 2007 on the ground of manifest excess of powers (Article 52(1)(b) of the Convention) owing to the failure of the Arbitral Tribunal to apply Article XI of the BIT between the United States and the Argentine Republic concerning Reciprocal Encouragement and Protection of Investment of 14 November 1991: such annulment applies necessarily to the Award in its entirety, pursuant to Article 52(3) of the Convention.
>
> Order Sempra to reimburse to the Argentine Republic all of the expenses incurred by the Centre in connection with the Annulment proceeding, including the fees and expenses of the arbitrators.

EXERCISE 38 – CHALLENGES AND ANNULMENTS II – MINI MOCK ARBITRATION

Review the jurisdictional decision in the UNCITRAL proceedings between Venezuela US and the Bolivarian Republic of Venezuela. Now imagine:

I.   that an award on the merits is rendered subsequently, in favour of the investor Venezuela US
II.   that the State wishes to set aside the award on jurisdictional grounds, focusing on the attached jurisdictional decision.

Assume that the UNCITRAL Model Law governs the set-aside proceeding.

 GROUP

Group 1
You represent the Bolivarian Republic of Venezuela. Your task is to attempt to have the award set aside; present the best arguments to that effect.

Group 2
You are the observer group. Have the best arguments been presented? Did the annulment committee come to the best decision?

Group 3
You are the local court at the place of arbitration. After hearing the parties' arguments, your task is to give a reasoned decision on annulment.

Group 4
You represent the investor. You have to argue that the award should not be set aside; present the best arguments to that effect.

 CASE

Venezuela US, SRL v the Bolivarian Republic of Venezuela (PCA Case No. 2013-34)

I. The parties

1. The claimant in these proceedings is Venezuela US, SRL (the claimant), a company organised and existing under the laws of Barbados, with its principal place of business at 1201 Lake Robbins Drive, The Woodlands, Texas 77380, USA.

2. The respondent in these proceedings is the Bolivarian Republic of Venezuela (the respondent or Venezuela), and together with the claimant, (the parties).

II. Procedural history

A. *Commencement of the arbitration*

3. By Notice of Arbitration dated 22 March 2013, the claimant commenced arbitral proceedings against the respondent under the Arbitration Rules of the United Nations Commission on International Trade Law (the UNCITRAL Rules) pursuant to Article 8 of the Agreement between the Government of Barbados and the Republic of Venezuela for the Promotion and Protection of Investments (the "Treaty").1 Article 8 of the Treaty provides, in relevant part:

> Settlement of disputes between one contracting party and nationals or companies of the other contracting party
>
> (1) Disputes between one Contracting Party and a national or company of the other Contracting Party concerning an obligation of the former under this Agreement in relation to an investment of the latter shall, at the request of the national concerned, be submitted to the International Centre for Settlement of Investment Disputes for settlement by arbitration or conciliation under the Convention on the Settlement of Investment Disputes between States and Nationals of other States, opened for signature at Washington on March 18, 1965.
>
> (2) As long as the Republic of Venezuela has not become a Contracting State of the Convention as mentioned in paragraph 1 of this Article, disputes as referred to in that paragraph shall be submitted to the International Centre for Settlement of Investment disputes under the Rules Governing the Additional Facility for the Administration of Proceedings by the Secretariat of the Centre (Additional Facility Rules). If for any reason the Additional Facility is not available the investor shall have the right to submit the dispute to arbitration under the rules of the United Nations Commission on International Trade Law (UNCITRAL).
>
> (3) The arbitral award shall be limited to determining whether there is a breach by the Contracting Party concerned of its obligations under this Agreement, whether such breach of obligations has caused damages to the national concerned, and if such is the case, the amount of compensation.
>
> (4) Each Contracting Party hereby gives its unconditional consent to the submission of disputes as referred to in paragraph 1 of this Article to international arbitration in accordance with the provisions of this Article.

4. The claimant, a company organised under the laws of Barbados, alleges that the respondent, through its acts and omissions, as well as those of State-owned entities acting under its direction and control, breached its

obligations under Articles 2, 3 and 5 of the Treaty with respect to the claimant's investment in the oil and gas industry in Venezuela.

B. Constitution of the Tribunal

5. In its Notice of Arbitration, the claimant appointed The Hon. L. Yves Fortier PC CC OQ QC as the first arbitrator.

6. By letter dated 13 June 2013, the claimant requested that the Secretary-General of the Permanent Court of Arbitration (the PCA) designate an appointing authority pursuant to Articles 6(1) and 6(2) of the UNCITRAL Rules (2010).

7. On 16 July 2013, the Secretary-General of the PCA designated Professor Piero Bernardini as appointing authority.

8. By letter dated 17 July 2013, the claimant requested that Professor Bernardini appoint an arbitrator on behalf of the respondent.

9. By e-mail of 1 August 2013, the respondent advised that it had appointed the law firm of Curtis, Mallet-Prevost, Colt & Mosle LLP to represent it in this case and that the parties had agreed to a two-week extension of time for the respondent to make an appointment.

10. By letter dated 5 August 2013, the respondent appointed Mr Gabriel Bottini as the second arbitrator.

11. By letter dated 13 November 2013, pursuant to the agreement of the parties, H E Judge Peter Tomka was appointed as the Presiding Arbitrator.

C. Initial procedural steps

12. By letter dated 4 December 2013, the Tribunal circulated a Draft Terms of Appointment to the parties for their comments.

13. By letter dated 13 December 2013, the respondent submitted its comments on the Draft Terms of Appointment and asserted that the UNCITRAL Rules (1976) were applicable to the proceedings. By letter of the same date, the claimant submitted its comments on the Draft Terms of Appointment and acknowledged that the original UNCITRAL Rules (1976) were applicable and would govern the arbitration in lieu of the revised UNCITRAL Rules (2010) under which it had commenced the arbitration.

14. By letter dated 18 December 2013, the Tribunal issued a final version of the Terms of Appointment, which were subsequently executed by the parties and the Tribunal (the last signature being on 9 January 2014), and circulated a Draft Procedural Order No. 1 for the parties' comments.

15. By letter dated 7 January 2014, the claimant provided its comments on Draft Procedural Order No. 1 and proposed a procedural calendar for the initial phase of the arbitration. By e-mail dated 8 January 2014, the respondent provided its comments on Draft Procedural Order No. 1. By letter dated 9 January 2014, the Tribunal acknowledged receipt of the parties' comments on Draft Procedural Order No. 1 and invited the claimant to comment on the respondent's proposed modifications to the draft order. By letter dated 15 January 2014, the claimant submitted its comments on respondent's proposed modifications to Draft Procedural Order No. 1.

16. On 17 January 2014, the claimant submitted its Statement of Claim (the statement of claim).

17. On 24 January 2014, the Tribunal issued Procedural Order No. 1.

18. On 3 March 2014, the respondent submitted its statement of defence (the statement of defence), in which it raised objections to jurisdiction and requested the bifurcation of the proceedings.

D. Bifurcation of the proceedings

19. By letter dated 7 March 2014, the Tribunal invited the parties to make submissions on whether to bifurcate the proceedings and whether to hold an in-person procedural meeting to discuss the respondent's request for bifurcation and the timetable for the proceedings.

20. By e-mail of 11 March 2014, the respondent conveyed a request on behalf of both parties that the Tribunal hold a procedural meeting in person.

21. By letter of the same date, the respondent submitted a request for bifurcation of the proceedings (the request for bifurcation) asking the Tribunal to rule upon its first jurisdictional objection relating to the lack of jurisdiction *ratione voluntatis* as a preliminary matter.

22. By letter dated 12 March 2014, the Tribunal confirmed that a procedural meeting would be held in person on 19 March 2014 at the Peace Palace in The Hague, the Netherlands.

23. By letter dated 14 March 2014, the claimant agreed to the bifurcation of the respondent's first jurisdictional objection relating to the Tribunal's jurisdiction *ratione voluntatis* and proposed a timetable for bifurcated proceedings.

24. By e-mail of 14 March 2014, the respondent notified the Tribunal and the claimant of a challenge to Mr Fortier under Articles 10 and 11 of the UNCITRAL Rules for lack of independence and impartiality and requested that the procedural meeting scheduled for 19 March 2014 be postponed.

25. By separate e-mail and letter dated 14 March 2014, the claimant raised certain concerns regarding the disclosures made by Mr Bottini with his statement of independence and impartiality, and opposed the respondent's request to postpone the procedural meeting.

26. The parties exchanged further correspondence on whether to postpone the procedural meeting including the respondent's further e-mail of 14 March 2014, the claimant's e-mail of 15 March 2014, the respondent's e-mail of 16 March 2014, and the claimant's e-mail of 16 March 2014.

27. By letter dated 16 March 2014, the Presiding Arbitrator acknowledged the parties' agreement to bifurcate the respondent's first jurisdictional objection and decided, subject to subsequent revision by the full Tribunal, to cancel the proposed procedural meeting and to establish a procedural calendar for the preliminary jurisdictional phase of the arbitration.

E. Jurisdictional phase

28. By letter dated 17 March 2014, following the claimant's indication that it did not agree to the challenge and Mr. Fortier's refusal to withdraw, the respondent submitted the challenge to Professor Bernardini for a decision pursuant to Article 12 of the UNCITRAL Rules.

29. By letter dated 19 March 2014, Mr Bottini provided further clarifications regarding his declaration of impartiality and independence.

30. By letter dated 25 March 2014, Professor Bernardini resigned as appointing authority.

31. By letter dated 28 March 2014, the claimant requested that the Secretary-General of the PCA designate a substitute appointing authority to decide the challenge to Mr Fortier.

32. On 4 April 2014, the Secretary-General of the PCA designated Mr Jernej Sekolec as appointing authority.

33. On 11 April 2014, the respondent submitted its memorial on the objection to the jurisdiction *ratione voluntatis* of the Tribunal (the memorial).

34. On 9 May 2014, the claimant submitted its counter-memorial on the respondent's objection to the jurisdiction *ratione voluntatis* of the Tribunal (the counter-memorial).

35. On 30 May 2014, the respondent submitted its reply memorial on the objection to the jurisdiction *ratione voluntatis* of the Tribunal (the reply).

36. On 2 June 2014, Mr Sekolec issued a decision in his capacity as appointing authority rejecting the challenge to Mr Fortier.

37. By letter dated 5 June 2014, the Tribunal scheduled a hearing on jurisdiction, to be held on 10 July 2014 at the Peace Palace in The Hague, the Netherlands.

38. On 20 June 2014, the claimant submitted its rejoinder memorial on the objection to the jurisdiction *ratione voluntatis* of the Tribunal (the rejoinder).

39. On 10 July 2014, the hearing on jurisdiction was held at the Peace Palace in The Hague, the Netherlands.

42. By letter dated 23 November 2015, following the respondent's indication that it did not agree to the challenge and Mr Bottini's refusal to withdraw, the claimant submitted the challenge to Mr Sekolec for a decision pursuant to Article 12 of the UNCITRAL Rules.

43. On 22 December 2015, Mr Sekolec issued a decision in his capacity as appointing authority sustaining the challenge against Mr Bottini.

44. By letter dated 18 January 2016, the respondent appointed Professor Marcelo Kohen as substitute arbitrator.

III. Relevant legal provisions

A. *The treaty*

45. The dispute to be decided in the present phase of the proceedings concerns whether the Tribunal has jurisdiction to entertain the claims contained

in the statement of claim. The respondent requests the Tribunal to dismiss the claims 'for lack of jurisdiction *ratione voluntatis*'. The claimant maintains that the Tribunal has jurisdiction to hear the case on the merits and requests the Tribunal to dismiss '[t]he respondent's objection to the jurisdiction of this Tribunal for lack of consent'. The resolution of this disagreement between the parties depends on the proper interpretation of Article 8 of the Treaty, containing the relevant dispute settlement provisions and, depending on the conclusion the Tribunal will reach, possibly also on the application of Article 3 of the Treaty, containing a Most Favored Nation (MFN) clause.

46. Article 8 provides as follows:

> Settlement of disputes between one contracting party and nationals or companies of the other contracting party

> (1) Disputes between one Contracting Party and a national or company of the other Contracting Party concerning an obligation of the former under this Agreement in relation to an investment of the latter shall, at the request of the national concerned, be submitted to the International Centre for Settlement of Investment Disputes for settlement by arbitration or conciliation under the Convention on the Settlement of Investment Disputes between States and Nationals of other States, opened for signature at Washington on March 18, 1965.

> (2) As long as the Republic of Venezuela has not become a Contracting State of the Convention as mentioned in paragraph 1 of this Article, disputes as referred to in that paragraph shall be submitted to the International Centre for Settlement of Investment disputes under the Rules Governing the Additional Facility for the Administration of Proceedings by the Secretariat of the Centre (Additional Facility Rules). If for any reason the Additional Facility is not available the investor shall have the right to submit the dispute to arbitration under the rules of the United Nations Commission on International Trade Law (UNCITRAL).

> (3) The arbitral award shall be limited to determining whether there is a breach by the Contracting Party concerned of its obligations under this Agreement, whether such breach of obligations has caused damages to the national concerned, and if such is the case, the amount of compensation.

> (4) Each Contracting Party hereby gives its unconditional consent to the submission of disputes as referred to in paragraph 1 of this Article to international arbitration in accordance with the provisions of this Article.

47. Article 3 reads as follows:

National treatment and most-favoured-nation provisions

(1)   Neither Contracting Party shall in its territory subject investments or returns of nationals or companies of the other Contracting Party to treatment less favourable than that which it accords to investments or returns of its own nationals or companies or to investments or returns of nationals or companies of any third State.

(2)   Neither Contracting Party shall in its territory subject nationals or companies of the other Contracting Party, as regards their management, maintenance, use, enjoyment or disposal of their investments, to treatment less favourable than that which it accords to its own nationals or companies or to nationals or companies of any third State.

(3)   The treatment provided for in paragraphs (1) and (2) above shall apply to the provisions of Articles 1 to 11 of this Agreement.

B. Vienna Convention on the Law of Treaties

48. In addition to the relevant provisions of the Treaty, it is instructive to reproduce here the rules on the interpretation of treaties set forth in Articles 31 and 32 of the Vienna Convention on the Law of Treaties (the VCLT), which both parties acknowledge govern the interpretation of the Treaty:

Article 31
General rule of interpretation

1.   A treaty shall be interpreted in good faith in accordance with the ordinary meaning to be given to the terms of the treaty in their context and in the light of its object and purpose.

2.   The context for the purpose of the interpretation of a treaty shall comprise, in addition to the text, including its preamble and annexes:

(a)   any agreement relating to the treaty which was made between all the parties in connection with the conclusion of the treaty;

(b)   any instrument which was made by one or more parties in connection with the conclusion of the treaty and accepted by the other parties as an instrument related to the treaty.

3.   There shall be taken into account, together with the context:

(a)   any subsequent agreement between the parties regarding the interpretation of the treaty or the application of its provisions;

(b)   any subsequent practice in the application of the treaty which establishes the agreement of the parties regarding its interpretation;

> (c) any relevant rules of international law applicable in the relations between the parties.
>
> 4. A special meaning shall be given to a term if it is established that the parties so intended.
>
> Article 32
> Supplementary means of interpretation
> Recourse may be had to supplementary means of interpretation, including the preparatory work of the treaty and the circumstances of its conclusion, in order to confirm the meaning resulting from the application of Article 31, or to determine the meaning when the interpretation according to Article 31:
>
> (a) leaves the meaning ambiguous or obscure; or
> (b) leads to a result which is manifestly absurd or unreasonable.

49. The Tribunal notes that, while Barbados is a party to the VCLT, having ratified it on 24 June 1971, Venezuela is not a party to it and has not even signed it. But it is now well accepted that Articles 31 and 32 of the VCLT on interpretation of treaties codify customary rules of international law. In other words, these Articles reflect customary international law, as confirmed on various occasions by the International Court of Justice.

IV. Requests for relief

A. Respondent's request for relief

50. The respondent requests the Tribunal to grant the following relief:

> Respondent respectfully submits that all claims contained in the statement of claim should be dismissed for lack of jurisdiction *ratione voluntatis* and that this Tribunal should allocate the costs of these proceedings to claimant.

B. Claimant's request for relief

51. The claimant requests that the Tribunal grant the following relief:

> For the reasons stated above and in claimant's counter-memorial on jurisdiction, respondent's objection to the jurisdiction of this Tribunal for lack of consent should be dismissed, and this arbitration should proceed on the merits.

V. Issues on jurisdiction

A. Interpretation of Article 8 of the Treaty

1. Respondent's position

52. The respondent objects to the jurisdiction *ratione voluntatis* of the Tribunal on the basis that Article 8 of the Treaty does not provide a valid and effective consent to arbitration under the UNCITRAL Rules in the circumstances of the present case. While the respondent has given its 'unconditional consent' to arbitration in Article 8(4) of the Treaty, it has only done so 'in accordance with the provisions of this Article', which limited its consent to UNCITRAL arbitration to a specific brief period that has long passed.

53. According to the respondent:

> the text and structure of Article 8(2) make it evident that the right to resort to UNCITRAL arbitration was provided only to cover a potential gap in the availability of ICSID jurisdiction under Article 8(1) that might exist '[a]s long as the Republic of Venezuela has not become a Contracting State of the [ICSID] Convention' and '[i]f for any reason the [ICSID] Additional Facility is not available.'

The respondent explains that:

> the possibility of such a gap existed in July 1994, when the Treaty was executed, because while Barbados and Venezuela had both signed the ICSID Convention, the latter had not yet become a Contracting Party which would be subject to ICSID arbitration upon entry into force of the Treaty.

Upon Venezuela's ratification of the ICSID Convention, the above-mentioned interim period ended and Article 8(2) of the Treaty ceased to be applicable.

54. The respondent notes that the parties agree that Venezuela's denunciation of the ICSID Convention on 24 January 2012 rendered ICSID arbitration under Article 8(1) unavailable. The parties further agree that ICSID Additional Facility arbitration under Article 8(2) ceased to be available upon Venezuela's ratification of the ICSID Convention in 1995. The claimant nevertheless seeks to avail itself of UNCITRAL arbitration under the second sentence of Article 8(2), which reads:

> [i]f for any reason the Additional Facility is not available the investor shall have the right to submit the dispute to arbitration under the rules of the United Nations Commission on International Trade Law (UNCITRAL).

55. However, in the respondent's view, the only reasonable interpretation of Article 8(2) of the Treaty is that the entire paragraph was intended to apply only during the pre-ICSID interim period. In particular, the respondent asserts that the specific reference to the ICSID Additional Facility in this second sentence links it to the pre-ICSID period described in the first sentence. According to the respondent, there was significant uncertainty at the time that the Treaty was entered into as to whether the ICSID Additional Facility would continue or be terminated. In addition, the rules of the Additional Facility remained untested and subject to possible modification, the first case under those rules not having been brought until 1997.

56. The respondent supports its interpretation by reference to the 'ordinary contextual interpretation' of treaty terms called for in Article 31(1) of the VCLT and endorsed by international courts and tribunals. This interpretation is also supported by the principles of integration and contemporaneity in treaty interpretation, as well as the object and purpose of the provision in providing an alternative arbitral forum only for the brief period before Venezuela became an ICSID Contracting State. The respondent adds that, given that the ordinary meaning of the terms taken in context is clear, there is no need for resort to further supplementary means of interpretation.

57. The respondent argues that the claimant's interpretation of Article 8(2) ignores the link between the first and second sentence of Article 8(2) and misconstrues the second sentence as a 'catchall', default arbitration provision. The respondent contends that:

> [i]f the Contracting Parties to the Treaty had intended to include UNCITRAL arbitration as a 'catch-all' arbitration option for those cases in which neither ICSID nor the ICSID Additional Facility were available, they would have referred to both ICSID and the ICSID Additional Facility and would have included this option in a new Article 8(3) or otherwise separated it from the ICSID and ICSID Additional Facility provisions, as other Venezuelan BITs do.

According to the respondent, the claimant's interpretation implies that UNCITRAL arbitration would have become equally available alongside ICSID arbitration upon Venezuela's ratification of the ICSID Convention, which clearly was not intended. The respondent also contrasts the instant

Treaty with various other Venezuelan BITs which either (i) provide for ICSID arbitration (and sometimes also for ICSID

Additional Facility arbitration in the interim), but do not contain an alternative arbitral forum in the event that one of the contracting parties withdraws from ICSID, or (ii) clearly include UNCITRAL arbitration as a default, catch-all option in a separate subsection or paragraph. A number of authorities, the respondent submits, endorse the comparison of similar treaties concluded by the Contracting Parties as a useful supplementary means to clarify a treaty text.

58. The respondent notes that, under its interpretation, the investor no longer has access to international arbitration, but retains recourse under Article 23 of the Venezuelan Investment Law, which provides for investment disputes to be submitted to the Venezuelan courts or to domestic arbitration. The respondent adds that denunciation of the ICSID Convention cannot be construed as an act of bad faith, and that 'Venezuela did not denounce the convention for the purpose of frustrating the present claimant's possibility to submit its disputes to arbitration'.

59. In any event, relying on the ICJ's findings in the Interpretation of Peace Treaties case, the respondent stresses that, even if the lack of an international arbitral forum for investment disputes arising under the Treaty were viewed as an undesirable result, 'arguments based on policy considerations cannot justify attributing a meaning to a treaty provision that is contrary to the letter and spirit of that provision'. Nor can the Treaty's object and purpose, the principle of *effet utile*, or good faith be used as 'a source of obligation where none would otherwise exist' in an attempt to rectify the fact that the Contracting Parties did not provide for the possibility of Venezuela's denunciation of the ICSID Convention.

60. The respondent distinguishes the cases cited by the claimant to the contrary. The respondent asserts that, unlike *BG v Argentina*, it is not trying to frustrate access to an international arbitral forum that would otherwise be available to the claimant. In addition, the respondent argues that *Lemire v Ukraine* merely concerned an imprecise description of the agreed dispute settlement mechanism which was resolved by reference to explicit language elsewhere in the arbitration clause, unlike the situation faced with regard to UNCITRAL arbitration under Article 8 of the present Treaty. Lastly, the respondent considers that the result in *Murphy v Ecuador II* is either based on an unduly broad application of the *effet utile* principle or is restricted to the unique facts of that case.

2. Claimant's position

61. The claimant argues that Venezuela has provided, in Article 8(4) of the Treaty, its 'express, irrevocable, and unconditional consent' to arbitrate disputes arising under the Treaty. This essential consent to arbitration, the claimant asserts, cannot be negated by any uncertainty regarding the subsidiary procedural question of which forum and rules apply to a particular dispute In any event, the claimant submits that the text and structure of Article 8 of the Treaty demonstrates that Venezuela consented to submit disputes to UNCITRAL arbitration. According to the claimant, if the respondent's interpretation were adopted, it would render the whole of Article 8 ineffective, contrary to the Contracting Parties' intent and the object and purpose of the Treaty. As such, the claimant contends that it cannot be accepted as a good faith interpretation of the Treaty.

62. Instead, the claimant asserts that Articles 8(1) and 8(2) of the Treaty establish a hierarchy of arbitral fora. In accordance with Article 8(1), ICSID arbitration is the applicable dispute settlement mechanism as long as both parties are Contracting States to the ICSID Convention. Article 8(2) provides that, for the initial period until Venezuela became an ICSID Contracting State, disputes would be submitted to the ICSID Additional Facility. Finally, Article 8(2) also provides that '[i]f for any reason the Additional Facility is not available the investor shall have the right to submit the dispute to arbitration under the [UNCITRAL] rules'. In this case, given Venezuela's ratification (in 1995) and subsequent denunciation of the ICSID Convention (in 2012), arbitration under both the ICSID Convention and Additional Facility Rules is unavailable. As such, in the claimant's view, investors have the right to submit their disputes to UNCITRAL arbitration. The claimant stresses that, unlike the claimant in *Nova Scotia Power v Venezuela* or the other cases on which Venezuela relies, this is not a case where the claimant has failed to observe the hierarchy of arbitral fora or failed to comply with mandatory pre-conditions to arbitration.

63. The claimant contends that its interpretation is supported by the ordinary meaning of the terms used in Article 8. The terms 'unconditional consent' in Article 8(4), and 'for any reason' and 'shall have the right' in Article 8(2), clearly establish that UNCITRAL arbitration is a comprehensive and mandatory fall-back option which 'is not conditioned or limited by whether Venezuela ratified or withdrew from the ICSID Convention'. In particular, the claimant points out that the Contracting Parties added the otherwise superfluous phrase 'for any reason' into the phrase '*if for any reason* the Additional

Facility is not available' (emphasis added). By contrast, in the claimant's view, the respondent's interpretation 'improperly conflates the two separate sentences of Article 8.2 to import a temporal limitation from the first sentence as a condition on the effect of the second', leaving the phrases 'for any reason' and 'shall have the right', as well as the rest of the context of the provision, without meaning or effect.

64. The claimant disputes the relevance of the respondent's comparison of Article 8 of the Treaty with the dispute resolution provisions of other Venezuelan BITs, stating that '[c]omparing the text of one treaty to another between different parties is not a method of interpretation specified by the Vienna Convention, nor is it a favoured interpretive method of arbitral tribunals'. The claimant insists that the Barbados-Venezuela BIT is a standalone agreement negotiated by two sovereign States whose meaning 'cannot be determined in light of unrelated agreements concluded between different parties at different times and in the context of different bilateral relations'.

65. Moreover, the claimant argues that there is no consistent use of language or structure among the Venezuelan BITs cited by the respondent. For example, the claimant states that the Portugal-Venezuela BIT's article on investor-State dispute settlement does not contain an express statement of the States' consent to arbitration and includes all of the provisions for submission to ICSID, ICSID Additional Facility, and – if these are unavailable – UNCITRAL arbitration in the same sub-paragraph. Article 8 of the Czech Republic-Venezuela BIT includes a provision for negotiation, a reference to ICSID arbitration and a secondary reference to the Additional Facility in a single paragraph rather than in separate paragraphs. The dispute settlement clause of the Canada-Venezuela BIT sets out very detailed limitations, conditions, and procedural prerequisites restricting the States' consent to arbitration and omits the Barbados-Venezuela's wording of 'for any reason' and 'shall have the right' or any equivalent broad language. These examples, according to the claimant, contradict the respondent's assertions that, where an UNCITRAL fallback option is included, it is always set out in a separate section or paragraph, that the inclusion of the 'for any reason' and 'shall have the right' language is not significant, and that statements of unconditional consent to arbitration are included as a matter of course.

66. The claimant also rejects the respondent's explanation of the reasons for including the UNCITRAL option. The ICSID Administrative Council decided to continue the ICSID Additional Facility indefinitely in 1984, over

a decade before the conclusion of the Treaty. The claimant further posits that:

> Venezuela's scenario suggests that Barbados and Venezuela were concerned enough about the possibility that an investor might be left without an arbitral forum during the interim period between when Venezuela signed the BIT and when it became an ICSID Contracting State that they not only included the Additional Facility as a temporary, conditional alternative forum to ICSID, but also included UNCITRAL as a conditional, temporary, fall-back alternative to the alternative of the Additional Facility. And yet, under this scenario, the Contracting Parties were ostensibly not concerned with the possibility that at some time during the minimum ten-year term of the BIT, ICSID might not be available, leaving investors without any arbitral forum and Article 8 a nullity.

The claimant asserts that it is far more likely that the Contracting Parties intended the UNCITRAL option as a comprehensive default arbitral forum.

67. Additionally, in the claimant's view, the respondent's construction of Article 8 also runs counter to the requirements of good faith interpretation under Article 31 of the VCLT. The provision of a direct right of investors to arbitrate against the host State is, according to the claimant, one of the main aims of the Treaty, and of BITs in general. However, seeing as Venezuela's withdrawal from the ICSID Convention has foreclosed the option of ICSID arbitration, the respondent's interpretation would deprive Barbadian investors of any arbitral forum whatsoever in which to seek to enforce the Treaty's substantive provisions. This would, the claimant asserts, defeat the Treaty's object and purpose51 and render the whole of Article 8 a dead letter, in violation of the interpretive principle of *ut res magis valeat quam pereat* (alternatively known as *effet utile*) embodied in Article 31(1) of the VCLT. It would also be an absurd and unreasonable result contrary to Article 32 of the VCLT. Moreover, the claimant argues that 'a State should not be allowed to frustrate the investor's access to arbitration to redress treaty violations through a restrictive construction of the consent to arbitration provisions and its own acts in hindrance of that access'. The claimant also points to the case of *Lemire v Ukraine* as a prime example of a tribunal not allowing supervening legal developments to defeat the true intent of Contracting parties, notwithstanding an imprecise arbitration clause. The claimant stresses the seriousness of the present dispute and argues that Venezuela should similarly not be allowed to advance opportunistic interpretations of the Treaty in order to deny the claimant a right to international arbitration and evade its substantive obli-

gations under the Treaty, as it has systematically done with other foreign investors as well.

3. Tribunal's analysis

68. The claimant invokes Article 8 of the Treaty as the basis for the jurisdiction of this Tribunal. It contends that Venezuela, through Article 8 of the Treaty, 'irrevocably consented to arbitration of disputes between it and nationals or companies of Barbados who invested in Venezuela'.

69. Meanwhile, the respondent disputes the Tribunal's jurisdiction to hear the merits of the case, as in the respondent's view, its consent to arbitration under the UNCITRAL Rules ceased to be applicable.

70. To resolve the dispute on jurisdiction, the Tribunal has to interpret Article 8 of the BIT, the full text of which is reproduced above. It consists of four paragraphs. The parties' arguments addressed in particular three of them, namely paragraphs 1, 2 and 4. It seems that paragraph 3 of Article 8, describing what the Tribunal has to determine in its award, is, except in so far as it provides relevant context for the interpretation of the other three paragraphs of the article, of no particular relevance for the task of the Tribunal at the present stage of the proceedings.

71. The Tribunal will therefore focus its attention on paragraphs 1, 2 and 4 in order to determine whether they provide a basis for its jurisdiction to hear and adjudicate the claimant's claim.

72. The consent of Venezuela and Barbados to the submission of investment disputes by nationals of the other party to international arbitration is expressed in Article 8(4) which reads as follows: 'Each Contracting Party hereby gives its unconditional consent to the submission of disputes as referred to in paragraph 1 of this Article to international arbitration in accordance with the provisions of this Article.'

73. This paragraph refers to the other provisions of the same Article as regards the category of disputes which may be submitted to international arbitrations, as well as the available arbitral fora.

74. Paragraph 1 defines the disputes as the ones between a Contracting Party and a national or a company of the other party concerning the investment. It envisages ICSID as the appropriate arbitral forum for resolution of such disputes. It is useful to quote paragraph 1 again. It reads as follows:

> Disputes between one Contracting Party and a national or company of the other Contracting Party concerning an obligation of the former under this Agreement in relation to an investment of the latter shall, at the request of the national concerned, be submitted to the International Centre for Settlement of Investment Disputes for settlement by arbitration or conciliation under the [ICSID] Convention.

75. For the Centre to have jurisdiction under Article 25 of the ICSID Convention, the State which is a party to the dispute and the State whose national is a party to the dispute, must both be Contracting States to the ICSID Convention. As long as this condition is not fulfilled, the Centre has no jurisdiction, even if the applicable BIT in force provides for resolution of investment disputes before a Tribunal to be constituted under the ICSID Convention.

76. Barbados signed the ICSID Convention on 13 May 1981, ratified it on 1 November 1983, and it entered into force in relation to this State on 1 December 1983. Since then Barbados has been a Contracting State to the ICSID Convention. Venezuela signed the ICSID Convention on 18 August 1993, deposited its instrument of ratification on 2 May 1995, and it entered into force for Venezuela on 1 June 1995. On 24 January 2012, Venezuela notified the depositary of the denunciation of the ICSID Convention. This denunciation took effect, in accordance with Article 71 of the ICSID Convention, on 25 July 2012.

77. The parties are in agreement that arbitration under the ICSID Convention was not available before Venezuela became bound by the ICSID Convention on 1 June 1995 and is no longer available after Venezuela ceased to be bound by it on 25 July 2012.

78. Barbados and Venezuela negotiated the Treaty in the early 90s and signed it on 15 July 1994, which is after Venezuela signed the ICSID Convention, but before it deposited its instrument of ratification in May 1995. This explains the inclusion of paragraph 2 in Article 8. That paragraph reads as follows:

> As long as the Republic of Venezuela has not become a Contracting State of the Convention as mentioned in paragraph 1 of this Article, disputes as referred to in that paragraph shall be submitted to the International Centre for Settlement of Investment disputes under the Rules Governing the Additional Facility for the Administration of Proceedings by the Secretariat of the Centre (Additional Facility Rules). If for any reason the Additional Facility is not available the investor shall have the right to submit the dispute to arbitration under the rules of the United Nations Commission on International Trade Law (UNCITRAL).

79. The insertion of this paragraph into Article 8 shows, in the view of the Tribunal, that the parties wished to have an arbitral forum available immediately from the moment of the BIT's entry into force even if the ICSID Convention did not yet bind Venezuela.

80. The parties differ on the interpretation and import of this paragraph.

81. Venezuela contends that paragraph 2 is limited to the temporary period before it became party (a Contracting State) to the ICSID Convention. Only for that period, the argument goes, did it consent to the settlement of a dispute between it and a Barbadian investor through a tribunal established and acting under the Rules Governing the Additional Facility. And only if the Additional Facility, during that pre-ICSID period for Venezuela, was not available for any reason, had Venezuela – according to its interpretation of the provision – consented to the submission of the dispute to arbitration under the UNCITRAL rules. Venezuela denies that the provision expresses its consent to have recourse to arbitration under the UNCITRAL Rules in the period after it denounced the ICSID Convention in 2012.

82. In the claimant's view, UNCITRAL arbitration was not only available in the pre-ICSID period, but is also available now, in the post-ICSID period, after Venezuela withdrew from the ICSID Convention. In support of its interpretation, the claimant invokes the purposes of the BIT, one of which – in its contention – is to provide access to international arbitration. Further support is sought by the claimant in paragraph 4 of Article 8 of the Treaty, according to which '[e]ach Contracting Party hereby gives its unconditional consent to the submission of disputes as referred to in paragraph 1 of this Article to international arbitration in accordance with the provisions of this Article'.

83. In the Tribunal's view, effect should be given to the text of paragraph 2 in its totality, in the context in which it is placed within Article 8. The text is supposed to express the intention of the Contracting Parties when they agreed on it. The introductory words of paragraph 2 clearly describe the timeframe of its applicability. The words '[a]s long as the Republic of Venezuela has not become a Contracting State of the [ICSID] Convention' leave no doubt that the parties had in mind the period prior to Venezuela becoming a party to the ICSID Convention. The fact that only Venezuela, and not Barbados, is expressly mentioned in this paragraph, clearly reveals that this provision contemplated the pre-ICSID period. There is nothing in the formula used by the parties which would suggest that this provision was meant to also deal with the scenario in which one of the parties were to denounce the

Convention and cease to be bound by it (as Venezuela did in 2012). Had this been their intention, they could have easily used the formula 'as long as one of the parties *is not* a Contracting State of the Convention'. It may be, and it is rather very likely, that they had not even considered such a scenario, although under Article 71 of the ICSID Convention any Contracting State has the right to denounce the Convention by written notice. But it is not the task of the Tribunal to speculate, nor to read into the text what it does not say.

84. The key issue in the context of paragraph 2 is the link between the first sentence and the second one. The first provides for arbitration under the Additional Facility Rules 'as long as the Republic of Venezuela has not become a Contracting State of the Convention'. The second specifies that 'if for any reason the Additional Facility is not available the investor shall have the right to submit the dispute to arbitration under the [UNCITRAL] rules'. The second sentence, in the view of the Tribunal, has to be read in relation to the first one. It does not constitute a self-standing provision. The temporal limitation provided for in the first sentence of paragraph 2 thus also applies to the second sentence.

85. The Additional Facility was an option in the pre-ICSID period. And only if 'for any reason' during this period it was not available did arbitration under the UNCITRAL Rules provide a substitute arbitral forum.

86. The claimant accepts that it cannot submit the dispute to arbitration under the Additional Facility Rules because the BIT only provides for arbitration under these rules during the time period prior to Venezuela becoming a Contracting State to the Convention, not after Venezuela denounced it.

87. The claimant nevertheless maintains that UNCITRAL arbitration is available in view of the fact that the Additional Facility is no longer available. It emphasises the words '*if for any reason* the Additional Facility is not available', arguing that in that case, it has the right to submit the dispute to arbitration under the UNCITRAL Rules. In support of its position, it invokes paragraph 4 of Article 8, emphasising that each Contracting Party has given its unconditional consent to arbitration.

88. In the view of the Tribunal, paragraph 4 does not strengthen the claimant's position. The unconditional consent given by the Contracting Parties to the BIT is the consent to submit disputes referred to in paragraph 1 of Article 8 to international arbitration '*in accordance with the provisions of this Article*'. Although consent to international arbitration is expressed in Article 8(4) and is still valid, in order to generate legal consequences in

relation to different arbitral fora, the conditions specified in paragraphs 1 and 2 of Article 8 have to be met. Paragraph 1 envisages ICSID arbitration, which at present is not available as Venezuela ceased to be bound by the ICSID Convention on 25 July 2012. The continued validity of Venezuela's consent to arbitration under Article 8(4) as long as it is a Contracting Party to the BIT would provide for ICSID jurisdiction in the future if Venezuela one day decides to accede once again to the ICSID Convention. Paragraph 2, in the Tribunal's interpretation, envisages situations which might have arisen before Venezuela became a Contracting State to the ICSID Convention.

89. In view of the above, the Tribunal has to conclude that Article 8 alone does not provide a basis for its jurisdiction in the case at hand as arbitration under the UNCITRAL Rules was contemplated by the BIT's Contracting Parties for the period during which Venezuela had not yet become a Contracting State of the ICSID Convention. The present arbitral proceedings were not instituted before Venezuela became a Contracting State to the ICSID Convention, but only after it had ceased to be one, following its denunciation of the Convention.

90. The Tribunal's analysis, however, cannot stop here as the claimant also relies on Article 3 of the BIT, containing the MFN clause, as support for its contention that this Tribunal has jurisdiction to hear the case. It is this issue to which the Tribunal now turns its attention.

B. The application of the MFN clause to the dispute resolution provisions in Article 8

1. Claimant's position

91. Even if the Tribunal were to adopt the respondent's interpretation of Article 8, the claimant argues that the MFN clause contained in Article 3 of the Treaty allows the claimant to take advantage of the dispute settlement provisions of other BITs to which Venezuela is a party, including those which provide for an unrestricted choice of UNCITRAL arbitration or those which the respondent itself acknowledges provide for UNCITRAL arbitration as a catch-all default dispute resolution option. The provisions of these BITs are, according to the claimant, more favourable because they provide investors with a choice of dispute resolution fora.

92. The claimant notes that Article 3(3) of the Treaty expressly states that the MFN clause applies to the dispute resolution provisions under

the Treaty. According to the claimant, the present situation and Treaty are equivalent to those examined in *Garanti Koza v Turkmenistan*, where the Tribunal found that it did not need to grapple with the debate over whether MFN clauses apply to dispute settlement provisions generally, because the language of Article 3(3) required it to apply MFN treatment to the dispute resolution provisions. The *Garanti Koza* Tribunal further found that, even if it were not possible to import consent to arbitration into a BIT that did not provide for arbitration, 'the essential consent of the State – the consent to resolve disputes with UK investors by means of international arbitration – does not in this case need to be imported by operation of the MFN clause, because that consent is contained in Article 8(1) of the BIT', just as it is, the claimant contends, in Article 8(4) of the Barbados-Venezuela BIT.

93. The claimant notes that there is no general rule against importing consent to arbitration through an MFN clause. Even if there were such a rule, however, the claimant emphasises the distinction between consent to arbitration and the kind of arbitration or the conditions under which the investor may submit the dispute to UNCITRAL arbitration, the latter being questions of admissibility or procedure rather than consent. Tribunals which have found the MFN clause under a BIT to apply to the BIT's dispute resolution provisions have, the claimant submits, consistently held that MFN treatment allows an investor to avoid restrictive conditions on an investor's right to submit disputes to arbitration. In the claimant's view, the only effect of MFN treatment in this case would be to remove the temporal condition on the availability of UNCITRAL arbitration, rather than to import a different 'system of arbitration'. Regardless, the claimant argues that Venezuela 'clearly has no objection on principle or in practice to UNCITRAL arbitration', and cites the *Renta 4 v Russia* Tribunal's rejection of similar arguments:

> [D]ispute resolution mechanisms accepted by a State in various international instruments are all legitimate in the eyes of that State. Some may be inherently more efficient. Others may be more reliable in a particular context. Having options may be thought to be more 'favoured' for MFN purposes than not having them. It is not convincing for a State to argue in general terms that it accepted a particular 'system of arbitration' with respect to the nationals of one country but did not so consent with respect to the nationals of another. The extension of commitments is in the very nature of MFN clauses.

2. Respondent's position

94. The respondent insists that the lack of consent to UNCITRAL arbitration in Article 8 of the Treaty cannot be remedied by resort to the MFN clause in Article 3 of the Treaty. In the respondent's view, the claimant relies on a single decision, *Garanti Koza v Turkmenistan*, which was recently rendered by a majority of an ICSID tribunal over the strong dissent of one of the arbitrators, and which is both incorrect and distinguishable from the present case.

95. The respondent agrees with the claimant that the question of the applicability of the MFN standard to dispute settlement is resolved by Article 3(3) of the Treaty, which clarifies that the MFN standards set forth in paragraphs 1 and 2 of Article 3 extend to the dispute settlement provisions in Article 8. However, the respondent asserts that 'even when the MFN standard applies to dispute settlement generally, the system of dispute settlement carefully negotiated by the Contracting Parties cannot be replaced by another, neither negotiated, nor agreed, through the mere invocation of the MFN clause'.

96. According to the respondent, the claimant seeks to impermissibly replace the specific 'system of arbitration' set forth in Article 8 – where UNCITRAL arbitration was only contemplated for a specific contingency – with 'an entirely different mechanism' set forth in other Venezuelan BITs. The respondent argues that the present situation must be distinguished from cases where a claimant is merely attempting to bypass some formalities set forth in a treaty containing indisputable consent to UNCITRAL arbitration. The respondent repeats its earlier arguments that the present Treaty contains no general consent to arbitration, only 'an acceptance of arbitration within the precise terms set out in article 8'. In this context, the respondent notes that the acceptability of UNCITRAL arbitration in other Venezuelan BITs or in general is irrelevant: the MFN clause cannot serve to import consent to arbitration where there is none in the basic treaty.

97. In the respondent's view, this result derives from the principle that MFN clauses do not grant investors rights that do not already exist under the basic treaty. For example, the *Hochtief v Argentina* Tribunal held:

> In the present case, it might be argued that the MFN clause requires that investors under the Argentina-Germany BIT be given MFN treatment during the conduct of an arbitration but that the MFN clause cannot create a right to go to arbitration where none otherwise exists under the BIT. The argument can be put more generally: the MFN clause stipulates how investors must be treated when they are

exercising the rights given to them under the BIT but does not purport to give them any further rights in addition to those given to them under the BIT. [. . .]

In the view of the Tribunal, it cannot be assumed that Argentina and Germany intended that the MFN clause should create wholly new rights where none otherwise existed under the Argentina-Germany BIT. [. . .] The MFN clause is not a *renvoi* to a range of totally distinct sources and systems of rights and duties: it is a principle applicable to the exercise of rights and duties that are actually secured by the BIT in which the MFN clause is found.

98. The respondent also cites the dissenting opinion of Prof Boisson de Chazournes in *Garanti Koza v Turkmenistan*:

In line with what the *Maffezini v Spain* Tribunal held, no investment award or decision has since then decided that an MFN provision would allow the import of consent to ICSID arbitration from another treaty. [. . .] The role of the MFN clause is not to substitute for a lack of consent, but to ensure that the consent given is implemented in the most favourable manner to the individual investor entitled to protection, as compared to the treatment given to other such individuals in treaties with third countries. The *National Grid v Argentina* Tribunal correctly noted that an MFN clause is not a basis for creating consent to ICSID arbitration when none exists.
[. . .]
Granting Article 3(3) of the U.K.-Turkmenistan BIT such extensive effect as to allow for consent to ICSID through incorporation by reference in the frame of a treaty that does not allow this, would have the effect of 'replac[ing] a procedure specifically negotiated by parties with an entirely different mechanism' or 'system of arbitration'. It would involve a forum-shopping attitude that bypasses the consent requirement of the respondent while running against the fundamental principles of international adjudication.

99. According to the respondent, the majority decision in the *Garanti Koza v Turkmenistan* case was wrong, but was in any event premised on the idea that Turkmenistan had provided a general or 'essential consent' to arbitration in Article 8(1) of the UK-Turkmenistan BIT and a standing offer of UNCITRAL arbitration in Article 8(2), neither of which is present in the instant Treaty.

3. Tribunal's analysis

100. The Tribunal begins its analysis of the BIT's provisions in Article 3 on MFN treatment and its implications with respect to Article 8 thereof,

by referring to Article 3, paragraph 3. It leaves no doubt that the MFN provisions under this BIT are applicable to the provisions on settlement of disputes between one Contracting Party and nationals or companies of the other Contracting Party as well. Paragraph 3 reads as follows: 'The treatment provided for in paragraphs (1) and (2) above shall apply to the provision of Articles 1 to 11 of this Agreement'. Article 8 thus features among the Articles to the provisions of which the MFN treatment *shall* apply.

101. This is not disputed by the respondent, who, while observing that 'investment tribunals are divided as to the applicability of MFN [clauses] to dispute settlement provisions', accepts that 'in this case, [. . .] the applicability of the MFN standards to dispute settlement is resolved by the BIT itself'.

102. The Tribunal thus need not pronounce itself on the applicability of MFN clauses to arbitration clauses or dispute settlement provisions in general, in particular in situations when the MFN clause is silent on the scope of its applicability. Arbitral tribunals remain deeply divided on this issue. Nor does the Tribunal have to engage in an analysis as to whether the term 'treatment' in the text of Article 8 of the Barbados-Venezuela BIT covers only substantive standards of treatment, or includes also procedural rights, including the right to initiate arbitral proceedings. Article 3 in its paragraph (3) is clear that '[t]he treatment provided for' in the two paragraphs thereof shall apply also to the provisions of Article 8. As the Study Group of the International Law Commission on the Most-Favoured-Nation Clause, having studied the issue between 2009 and 2015, observed in its Final Report:

> [t]he point [whether MFN provisions are capable of applying to the dispute settlement provisions of the BITs] is essentially one of party autonomy; the parties to a BIT can, if they wish, include the conditions for access to dispute settlement within the scope of coverage of an MFN provision. The question in each case is whether they have done so.

Venezuela and Barbados have done so in their BIT; they have agreed *expressis verbis* that the MFN treatment clause shall apply to Article 8, i.e., to dispute settlement provisions and conditions for resorting to international arbitration thereunder. Therefore, this Tribunal has no other choice than to apply and enforce these provisions 'in accordance with their terms pursuant to the principle of *pacta sunt servanda*'. The majority believes that it must give *bona fide* effect to the provisions agreed by the parties in their BIT, and not to empty Article 3(3) of its meaning, thereby rendering it inapplicable to Article 8 as is the view preferred in the attached dissenting opinion.

103. Article 3(3) of the Barbados-Venezuela BIT is almost identical to the United Kingdom Model BIT (2008), the only difference being that in the UK Model Treaty Article 3(3) starts with the words 'for the avoidance of doubt it is confirmed that' which are then followed by the words identical with the ones used by Barbados and Venezuela in their BIT, namely 'the treatment provided for in paragraphs (1) and (2) above shall apply to the provisions of Articles 1 to 12 of this Agreement'. This kind of provision has been used frequently in the BITs concluded by the United Kingdom since 1990/1991. 81 It may be that this example 'inspired' Barbados and Venezuela during the negotiations of their BIT under consideration in the present case. Be that as it may, what is important is the fact that, as the commentators of the UK Model BIT explain, '[w]here Article 3(3) is included, it therefore provides an answer to the controversial question whether the MFN provision also applies to procedural issues such as investor-State dispute settlement'.

104. The Tribunal observes that Article 3(1) deals with treatment of 'investments', while Article 3(2) deals with treatment of 'nationals or companies of the other Contracting Party' (i.e., investors). The right to submit a dispute to arbitration is a right accorded by Article 8 of the BIT, under the conditions specified therein, to an 'investor'. Article 8(2) uses the expression 'the investor shall have the right to submit the dispute to arbitration'. It follows that MFN treatment can extend to dispute settlement provisions only through the operation of Article 3(2) of the Treaty. 'Investment' as such has no procedural rights, therefore Article 3(1) is without relevance for the purpose of the Tribunal's inquiry into its jurisdiction.

105. It is now for the Tribunal to determine how Article 3(2) impacts the provisions of Article 8 on settlement of disputes between an investor and a State. The Tribunal agrees with the respondent that the MFN clause cannot serve the purpose of importing consent to arbitration when none exists under the BIT between Barbados and Venezuela. It also appears that the claimant is arguing that it does not seek to import consent to arbitration in the present case from another BIT concluded by Venezuela with a third State.

106. The question which has to be answered is whether Venezuela has given its consent to international arbitration for disputes with Barbadian investors in the BIT at hand.

107. It is necessary to recall Article 8(4) of the BIT. It provides that '[e]ach Contracting Party hereby gives its unconditional consent to submission of disputes as referred to in paragraph 1 of this article to international arbitration in accordance with the provisions of this article'. Venezuela thus has given its unconditional consent to international arbitration, but of course, with the caveat 'in accordance with the provisions of Article 8'. The Tribunal earlier analysed Article 885 and reached its conclusion that 'arbitration under UNCITRAL Rules was agreed to by the BIT's Contracting Parties for the period during which Venezuela had not yet become a Contracting State of the ICSID Convention'. Without Article 3 of the BIT, this would have been the end of the exercise.

108. Article 3(3), however, requires the Tribunal to apply 'the treatment provided for in paragraph [. . .] (2) [. . .] to the provisions of' Article 8 of the BIT. The principle of effectiveness calls for giving effect to Article 3(2).

109. There can be no doubt that Venezuela has given its consent, as it is stipulated in Article 8(4) – 'its unconditional consent' – to the submission of investment disputes with Barbadian investors to international arbitration. Article 8(4), by using the expression 'in accordance with the provisions of this Article', makes such submission of disputes to international arbitration subject to the conditions specified in paragraphs (1) and (2) of Article 8. These conditions determine the arbitration forum to which a dispute can be submitted, either ICSID, the ICSID Additional Facility, or arbitration under the UNCITRAL Rules. Yet, the fact remains that Article 8(4) expresses the Contracting Parties' overall 'unconditional consent' to international arbitration. Venezuela has given in Article 8 one consent to international arbitration, not three different consents (one to ICSID arbitration, one to ICSID Additional Facility arbitration and one to ad hoc arbitration under UNCITRAL Rules). That consent covers three different arbitral fora (ICSID, Additional Facility, UNCITRAL) under the conditions specified in Article 8.

110. The Tribunal notes that otherwise Article 8(4) would serve no other useful purpose as it would have been sufficient for the Contracting Parties to limit Article 8 just to its first three paragraphs. Paragraph 1 would have provided for arbitration under the ICSID Convention, while paragraph 2 would have covered scenarios prior to Venezuela's becoming Party to the ICSID Convention. There is a presumption that the parties, by including a specific paragraph in Article 8, namely paragraph 4, by which they give their 'unconditional consent to the submission of disputes ["between one Contracting Party and a national or company of the other Contracting Party concerning an obligation of the former under this [BIT] in relation to an investment of

the latter"] to international arbitration in accordance with the provisions of this Article', intended to give a meaning to this paragraph, or in other words, this paragraph has to produce the legal effects intended by the parties.

111. In the view of the Tribunal, Article 8(4) expresses – as long as the BIT is in force, and it is not disputed that it is still in force – each Contracting Party's consent to submission of investment disputes with nationals or companies of the other Contracting Party to international arbitration. There is thus no question of importing Venezuela's consent to international arbitration with Barbadian investors through the operation of Article 3(2) of the BIT from another of Venezuela's BITs concluded with a third State. The question rather is that of the conditions for resorting to international arbitration. Venezuela, by withdrawing from the ICSID Convention, has not withdrawn its consent to international arbitration, expressed in Article 8(4) of the BIT. The consent is still there and valid. Venezuela's withdrawal from the ICSID Convention prevents Barbadian investors from instituting arbitral proceedings under Article 8(1) of the BIT as doing so is conditioned, pursuant to Article 25(1) of the ICSID Convention, upon Venezuela being a Contracting State to the ICSID Convention. The door to ICSID arbitration has thus been shut by Venezuela. However, if one day Venezuela accepts the Convention anew as it may, the door to ICSID arbitration will reopen since so long as the consent to international arbitration under the BIT has not been withdrawn, it continues to be in place. Without this consent this would not be possible because, as the last preambular paragraph of the ICSID Convention confirms 'no Contracting State shall by the mere fact of its ratification acceptance or approval of this Convention and without its consent be deemed to be under any obligation to submit any particular dispute to . . . arbitration'.

112. Article 8 contains only conditions determining which one of the three arbitral fora mentioned therein may be available. It sets forth no other conditions such as those which are provided for in a number of other BITs, e.g., the requirement that an investor litigate a dispute before the domestic courts of the host State for a specific duration prior to initiating arbitral proceedings or the requirement that an investor make a *bona fide* attempt to settle the dispute through negotiations for a specified period of time (the so-called 'cooling-off' period) before instituting arbitral proceedings. Therefore, in the view of the Tribunal, since Venezuela and Barbados agreed in Article 3 of their BIT that the MFN treatment clause shall apply to dispute settlement procedures under Article 8, and since the respondent admits as much, the MFN treatment is relevant to the application of the conditions under which an arbitral forum may be seised.

113. Recourse to arbitration under the UNCITRAL Rules is subject to a temporal condition, namely that it has been envisaged for the period prior to Venezuela becoming a Contracting State of the ICSID Convention if the Additional Facility was not available for any reason.

114. It is in the nature of an MFN clause that the 'treatment accorded by the granting State to the beneficiary State, or to persons [. . .] in a determined relationship with that State' is 'not lessfavourable than treatment extended by the granting State to a third State or to persons [. . .] in the same relationship with that third State'.

115. The claimant asserts that a number of the BITs concluded by Venezuela with third States provide more favourable terms to investors, including Venezuela's BITs with Belarus, Cuba, Iran, the Russian Federation, Vietnam, Canada, the Czech Republic, Ecuador, Lithuania, Portugal and Uruguay. It is not necessary for the Tribunal to analyse all these BITs. It is sufficient that one of them provides for more favourable treatment of investors in relation to the conditions under which they can have recourse to arbitration under the UNCITRAL Rules than Barbadian investors. If, in one of these BITs, the temporal condition for recourse to arbitration under the UNCITRAL Rules is less stringent, or – in other words – more favourable to investors than the one in the Barbados-Venezuela BIT, then Barbadian investors relying on Article 3(2) of the BIT can claim not to be subjected to the conditions in Article 8(2) of the BIT as they appear therein, but to the conditions more favorable to the investor from the third State.

116. One of the treaties invoked is the BIT which Venezuela concluded with Ecuador on 18 November 1993.90 Article IX, devoted to settlement of disputes between an investor and the Contracting Party in which the investment was made, provides for international arbitration and in that context for three possible arbitral fora, namely ICSID, an ICSID Additional Facility and an ad hoc arbitral tribunal under the UNCITRAL Rules, like Article 8 of the Venezuela-Barbados BIT. It is useful to reproduce here the full text of Article IX of the Venezuela-Ecuador BIT. It reads:

> Article IX
> Settlement of disputes between an investor and the Contracting Party in which the investment was made
>
> 1. Any dispute between an investor of a Contracting Party and the other Contracting Party concerning implementation by the latter of the provisions of this Agreement shall, to the extent possible, be settled by means of amicable consultations.

2. If the dispute cannot be settled within six months of the time it was initiated by one of the Parties, it may be submitted, at the request of the investor, to:

*   The competent courts of the Contracting Party, in whose territory the investment was made; or
*   International arbitration, on the terms laid down in paragraph 3.

Once an investor has submitted the dispute to the courts of the Contracting Party in question or to international arbitration, the choice of one or other of those procedures shall be final.

3. If the investor decides to have recourse to arbitration, the dispute shall be submitted to the International Centre for Settlement of Investment Disputes (ICSID), established by the Convention on the Settlement of Investment Disputes between States and Nationals of Other States, which was opened for signature in Washington, D.C., on 18 March 1965, once both States Parties to this Agreement have acceded to the Convention. Until such condition has been met, each Contracting Party agrees that the dispute shall be submitted to arbitration in accordance with the rules of the Additional Facility of ICSID for the Administration of Conciliation, Arbitration and Fact-Finding Proceedings.

    If for any reason ICSID or its Additional Facility is not available, the dispute shall be submitted, at the request of the investor, to an ad hoc arbitral tribunal established under the Arbitration Rules of the United Nations Commission on International Trade Law (UNCITRAL).

4. The arbitral award shall be limited to determining whether there is a breach of this Agreement by the Contracting Party, whether such breach has caused harm to the investor and, if such is the case, the amount of compensation which is appropriate.

5. Arbitral awards shall be final and binding on the parties to the dispute. Each Contracting Party shall execute them in accordance with itslegislation.

117. The Tribunal notes that paragraph 2 gives the investor a choice, which once made becomes final, to submit a dispute which could not be settled amicably within six months, either to the competent courts of the host State or to international arbitration. In relation to international arbitration the provision specifies that such submission of a dispute shall be 'on the terms laid down in paragraph 3'.

118. In the view of the Tribunal, paragraph 2 of Article IX of the Ecuador-Venezuela BIT expresses the consent of these two States to international (investment) arbitration similarly to how such consent is given in Article 8(4) of the Barbados-Venezuela BIT, albeit in the latter it is expressed in an even more emphatic way ('Each Contracting Party hereby gives its unconditional consent'). Further the Tribunal does not see any material or substantive dif-

ference in the formulas used in Article 8(4) ('consent [...] to international arbitration in accordance with the provisions of this Article') and in Article IX(2) ('[i]nternational arbitration, on the terms laid down in paragraph 3'). Both refer to the conditions specified in the provisions referred to therein.

119. The Tribunal has analysed above the conditions set forth in Article 8 of the Barbados-Venezuela BIT, more precisely in paragraphs 1 and 2 thereof. Moving now to the terms, or in other words the conditions, laid down in paragraph 3 of Article IX of the Ecuador-Venezuela BIT, the Tribunal wishes to make several observations.

120. First, it provides for recourse to ICSID arbitration 'once both States Parties to the [BIT] have acceded to the [ICSID] Convention'. It is worth recalling that the Ecuador-Venezuela BIT was signed on 18 November 1993 when only Ecuador was a party to the ICSID Convention, while Venezuela was only a signatory State but not yet a Contracting Party to the ICSID Convention. The exact same situation of Venezuela not being a Party to the ICSID Convention continued when it signed the BIT with Barbados a few months later, on 15 July 1994.

121. Second, under these same circumstances, both BITs now under the Tribunal's focus, provide for the ICSID Additional Facility. The Tribunal has already interpreted the words '[a]s long as [...] Venezuela has not become a Contracting State of the [ICSID] Convention', in Article 8(2) of the Barbados-Venezuela BIT as 'leav[ing] no doubt that the parties had in mind the period prior to Venezuela becoming a party to the ICSID Convention'. The Tribunal also noted the agreement of the parties to the dispute on this point in relation to the availability of the ICSID Additional Facility only in Venezuela's pre-ICSID period. The Ecuador-Venezuela BIT provides in Article IX(3) that '[u]ntil such condition has been met [i.e., until both Contracting Parties to the BIT "have acceded to the [ICSID] Convention"], each Contracting Party agrees that the dispute shall be submitted to arbitration in accordance with the Additional Facility of ICSID'. In the view of the Tribunal, the expression 'until such condition has been met' means, in the circumstances prevailing at the moment of signing the Ecuador-Venezuela BIT, until Venezuela has become a party to the ICSID Convention, or in other words it covers the pre-ICSID period. Accordingly, the Tribunal does not see any material difference in the temporal scope of the expressions '[a]s long as ... Venezuela has not become a Contracting State of the [ICSID] Convention' and '[u]ntil such condition has been met [i.e., until "both States Parties to the [BIT] have acceded to the [ICSID] Convention"]'.

122. The Tribunal pauses here to observe that investors from Ecuador and from Barbados in Venezuela, in relation to international arbitration with Venezuela before an ICSID Tribunal or under the Additional Facility Rules, were in the same situation. ICSID became available only once Venezuela ratified the ICSID Convention. Until that moment, in the pre-ICSID period for Venezuela, they could have instituted arbitral proceedings under the Additional Facility Rules, but not once that pre-ICSID period was terminated.

123. Third, both BITs also contemplate the possibility of seizing an ad hoc arbitral tribunal under the UNCITRAL Rules. But there the similarity ends. The Barbados-Venezuela BIT provides that '[i]f for any reason Additional Facility is not available the investor shall have the right to submit the dispute to arbitration under the [UNCITRAL Rules]'. This option is envisaged in Article 8(2) which the Tribunal interpreted to the effect that its introductory words '[a]s long as [. . .] Venezuela has not become a Contracting State of the [ICSID] Convention' apply also in relation to the availability of arbitration under the UNCITRAL Rules.

124. The structure of Article IX(3) of the Ecuador-Venezuela BIT differs from paragraph 2 of Article 8 of the Barbados-Venezuela BIT. Article IX(3) is divided into two distinct subparagraphs. The original Spanish text makes this abundantly clear by not only separating the two subparagraphs, but also by opening the second one with a hyphen. The second subparagraph gives a right to the investor to submit a dispute to an ad hoc tribunal under the UNCITRAL Rules not only when the Additional Facility is for any reason not available, but also when ICSID itself is for any reason not available. This is a critical difference in comparison with the Barbados-Venezuela BIT.

125. Ecuador and Venezuela knew when they concluded their BIT that ICSID would be available 'once both States Parties to this [BIT] have acceded to the [ICSID] Convention', i.e., once Venezuela ratified it, as Ecuador had already been a party to the ICSID Convention. For the period prior to Venezuela's ratification of the ICSID Convention, as the words '[u]ntil such condition has been met' used in the second sentence of the first paragraph of Article IX clearly indicate, the Additional Facility was the substitute forum. The words in the separate second subparagraph '[i]f for any reason ICSID [. . .] is not available' cannot be limited just to one single reason, namely to Venezuela becoming a Party to the ICSID Convention through its ratification, since that reason was already specifically addressed in subparagraph 1 of Article IX and the 'remedy' provided for therein in the form of the Additional Facility.

'Any reason' in relation to the ICSID has to have a broader meaning, covering also a situation when the ICSID, having become open to an Ecuadorian investor following Venezuela's ratification of the ICSID Convention, would later be unavailable for 'any reason', for instance as a result of denunciation of that Convention pursuant to its Article 71.

126. The Tribunal reads the condition '[i]f for any reason ICSID or its Additional Facility is not available' for recourse to arbitration under the UNCITRAL Rules as a cumulative one, meaning that neither ICSID nor its Additional Facility is available. The Additional Facility is not available since, in the view of the Tribunal, it was contemplated for the period before Venezuela ratified the ICSID Convention and thus joined Ecuador, among other States, as a Contracting Party thereto. That is, in the Tribunal's view, the meaning of the phrase '[u]ntil such condition has been met' in Article IX(3). In any event, irrespective of the temporal scope of that phrase, the Additional Facility is not available to investors from Ecuador under the Ecuador-Venezuela BIT since both countries denounced the ICSID Convention and are no longer Contracting Parties to it. Ecuador did so on 6 July 2009 with effect, under Article 71 of the ICSID Convention, as of 7 January 2010. Venezuela's denunciation of the ICSID Convention on 24 January 2012 took effect on 25 July 2012. Nor is ICSID available for Ecuadorian investors in investment disputes with Venezuela. However, Ecuadorian investors may still have recourse to UNCITRAL arbitration since neither ICSID nor the Additional Facility is available. Therefore, they benefit from more favorable treatment than investors from Barbados.

127. Venezuela in its BIT with Ecuador in Article IX(2) agreed to international arbitration with Ecuadorian investors, on the terms laid down in paragraph 3. Venezuela, in relation to investors from Barbados, has given in Article 8(4) its unconditional consent to international arbitration in accordance with the provisions of that Article. Both Articles provide for three arbitral fora (ICSID, Additional Facility, UNCITRAL arbitration) under the conditions specified therein. The conditions under which Ecuadorian investors have a right to recourse to an UNCITRAL arbitration are more favourable than the conditions for investors from Barbados.

128. However, in Article 3(2) of its BIT with Barbados Venezuela accepted an obligation not to subject nationals or companies from Barbados to treatment less favorable than that which it accords to nationals or companies of any third State. Ecuador is such a third State. Under Article 3(3) of the Barbados-Venezuela BIT such treatment shall also apply, beyond any doubt, to the settlement of disputes with investors who are nationals of Barbados. Venezuela, having given its consent to international arbitration, shall accept that Barbados'

investors shall have recourse to UNCITRAL arbitration, which is listed in Article 8(2) of the BIT, under conditions which are not less favourable than the conditions under which Ecuadorian investors have such recourse to UNCITRAL arbitration pursuant to Article IX of the Ecuador-Venezuela BIT.

129. It follows that investors from Barbados, relying on Article 3(2) of the Barbados-Venezuela BIT, are entitled to submit their investment disputes with Venezuela in accordance with its Article 8 on the same conditions as investors from Ecuador.

130. Accordingly, the Tribunal comes to the conclusion that, having regard to Article 3(2) of the BIT and Article IX of the Ecuador-Venezuela BIT, the objection of the Respondent that the Tribunal lacks jurisdiction *ratione voluntatis* has to be rejected.

VI. Costs

131. The Tribunal reserves the question of costs until a later stage of these proceedings.

VII. Decision

132. For the reasons set forth above, the Tribunal decides:

(1) By two votes to one, that:

a. The respondent's objection to jurisdiction *ratione voluntatis* is rejected;

b. The proceeding shall continue under a schedule to be established after consultation with the parties;

(2) Unanimously, that:

c. All questions of costs are reserved.

25

Enforcement of investment arbitral awards

EXERCISE 39 – SEMINAR

 DISCUSSION QUESTIONS

Problem 1
(a) Explain the main differences and similarities between the ICSID and the New York Conventions with respect to recognition and enforcement of judgments.
(b) How do the terms 'recognition', 'enforcement', and 'execution' relate to each other?

Problem 2
(a) What are the possible problems with non-ICSID awards that are not rendered under the national arbitration rules of a State?
(b) How do you know which national instance to seize in order to recognise and enforce an ICSID award?
(c) Is it problematic or beneficial if the same State agency or court takes care of cases emanating both from the New York and ICSID Conventions?

Problem 3
(a) How is multiple recovery prevented if recovery is sought in several fora?
(b) Which are the benefits of *recognition* in multiple fora?

Problem 4
(a) What role could the home State play with respect to the enforcement of investment awards?
(b) What role can a host State's reputation play when it comes to enforcement?

26
Sovereign immunity

EXERCISE 40 – MINI MOCK ARBITRATION

This mini-mock arbitration is based on the attached judgment from the Swedish Supreme Court.

GROUP

Group 1
You represent the Russian Federation. Argue that the award should not be enforced due to immunity, including arguments based on the 1961 Vienna Convention on Diplomatic Relations.

Group 2
You represent the investor. Argue that the enforcement is not prevented by immunity, including that the arbitration clause in the BIT constitutes a waiver of immunity.

Group 3
You are the Swedish Supreme Court. Your task is to decide whether the award should be enforced.

Group 4
You are the observer group. Have the best arguments been presented? Did the court reach the correct decision?

CASE

The Russian Federation v Franz J Sedelmayer, Decision of the Swedish Supreme Court Case No. 6170–10

Decision of the Supreme Court

The Supreme Court does not grant the appeal.

The Supreme Court's prior decision on stay of execution shall no longer apply.

The Russian Federation is ordered to compensate Franz J Sedelmayer for his costs in the Supreme Court in the amount of SEK 253,300, out of which SEK

252,600 relates to fees for legal counsel, plus interest pursuant to Section 6 of the Interest Act from the day of the Supreme Court's decision until the date of payment.

Motions before the Supreme Court, etc.

The Russian Federation has moved that the Supreme Court, in reverting the decision of the Court of Appeal, upholds the decision of the District Court. Further, the Russian Federation has moved the Supreme Court to order Franz J Sedelmayer to compensate the Russian Federation for its costs in the District Court as well as in the Court of Appeal.

Franz J Sedelmayer has disputed any changes to the decision of the Court of Appeal.

The parties have claimed compensation for costs incurred during the proceedings before the Supreme Court.

On 8 March 2010, the Supreme Court decided that further measures to enforce the decision of Svea Court of Appeal of 17 December 2009 in the matter 6A 4239-08 should not be taken until further notice.

Grounds

Background and the issue of the present matter

1. After Franz J. Sedelmayer had initiated arbitration proceedings to resolve a dispute that had arisen between him and the Russian Federation and an arbitration award had been rendered in 1998, the Russian Federation initiated challenge proceedings at the Stockholm District Court regarding the validity of the arbitration award. In 2002, the District Court decided in favour of Franz J Sedelmayer and ordered the Russian Federation to compensate Franz J Sedelmayer for his costs. Franz J Sedelmayer requested the Enforcement Authority to enforce the District Court's judgment.

2. On 12 September 2003, the Enforcement Authority ruled that the judgment of the Stockholm District Court could be executed. When investigating the enforcement matter, the Enforcement Authority found, among other things, that the Russian Federation was the registered owner of the real property Lidingo Kostern 5, a multi-family property. Approximately 60 individuals were registered as residents at the property and two companies, Fastighetsmaklare Dick Lindstrom AB and NBN Networks AB (the

business purpose of which was stated as arranging travel tours for tourists in Russia and Sweden etc.), had their respective registered address at the property. The question arose whether or not the rental payments collected by the Russian Federation from lessees at the property could be subject to distraint.

3. In its decision of 9 May 2005, the Enforcement Authority held that the requested execution measure could not be granted. On 25 April 2008, Nacka District Court upheld the Enforcement Authority's decision. Upon Franz J Sedelmayer's appeal of the District Court's decision, Svea Court of Appeal held that distraint of the property and the rental payments paid by the people registered at the property and the company that has its business address there is not barred.

4. The Russian Federation has claimed that it enjoys diplomatic immunity with respect to the jurisdiction of Swedish courts in the enforcement matter, and that enforcement of the judgment of the Stockholm District Court with respect to the currently relevant property is barred. The Russian Federation has, with respect to the matter of enforcement, claimed that the property is used for official purposes of the Russian Federation.

5. The main issue in the matter is whether, due to State immunity with respect to a foreign State's property, distraint of the property Lidingo Kostern 5 and rental payments collected by the Russian Federation from the office and the apartments located at the property is barred or not.

Jurisdiction in the enforcement matter

6. The question of a State's immunity from jurisdiction should not be decided upon separately in matters of enforcement in the foreign State's property.

Immunity from enforcement with respect to a foreign State's property

7. State immunity is deemed as an inherent consequence of the principle that States are sovereign and mutually equal, and consequently do not have jurisdiction over each other. In general, it can be said that the principle of State immunity has evolved from a previous right for States to claim absolute immunity to a current more restrictive practice.

8. The more restrictive practice on States' immunity from jurisdiction has led to the view that immunity currently applies only sovereign acts, i.e., acts by the State as a State. A State's commercial or other actions under private law

are, in the more restrictive theory on immunity, excluded from the right to claim immunity before another State's courts.

9. Immunity from enforcement in State property is a consequence of the view that States are equal. It has been viewed as a bigger intrusion in a State's sovereignty to subject its property to distraint than subjecting the State to the jurisdiction of foreign courts. Internationally, courts have been reluctant to not grant diplomatic immunity from enforcement measures. It appears that the evolution towards a more restrictive scope of the immunity, as is the case with jurisdiction, has not taken place with respect to immunity from enforcement measures. Further, there is a lack of international case law with respect to limitations in the immunity from enforcement measures. In the Government Bill Immunity of States and their property, it is noted that in Western countries also the principle on immunity from enforcement measures in international case law has evolved towards a more restrictive theory, pursuant to which immunity from enforcement applies to State property that is used for official State purposes, but enforcement measures are permitted with respect to property that is used or intended to be used for commercial purposes, even if the State has not rescinded its immunity (Government Bill 2008/09:204 pp 45 and 56; cf. e.g., Hazel Fox, *The Law of State Immunity*, 2nd edn, 2008, pp 599 pp., and August Reinisch, 'European Court Practice Concerning State Immunity from Enforcement Measures', (2006) 17 *European Journal of International* 803.)

10. In its rulings NJA 1999 p. 821 and NJA 2009 p. 905, the Supreme Court has applied the restrictive immunity theory with respect to State immunity from jurisdiction. In the latter ruling, it was held that a State could not claim immunity as a ground for inadmissibility as defence against a claim for rental payments under a lease agreement for the premises of the State's embassy in Sweden.

11. In the rulings NJA 1942 p. 65 and p. 342 on the so-called Sequestration-boats (*Sw. Kvarstadsbatarna*) the Supreme Court stated that the principle of immunity was particularly rigorously upheld with respect to enforcement measures. There are no rulings of later date in which the Supreme Court has had to decide on the issue of immunity from enforcement measures. However, in the ruling NJA 2009 p. 905 the Supreme Court held that a judgment ordering a party to make a payment in general is enforceable, also when the paying party is a State. The Supreme Court also stated that, even if there is great discrepancy in the opinions of States on when immunity can be claimed, it is generally agreed that it is possible to enforce judgments on payment at least with respect to certain State property. However, in said

case it was not necessary for the Supreme Court to rule on the enforcement issue.

12. On 2 December 2004, the General Assembly of the United Nations adopted a convention on immunity of States and their property (United Nations Convention on Jurisdictional Immunities of States and Their Property). The convention is largely – but not entirely – a codification of customary law. On several issues, it forms a compromise between the opinions of different States. In 2009 the Swedish Parliament decided in favour of the government's proposal set out in Government Bill 2008/09:204 mentioned in item 9 above that Sweden should ratify the convention and incorporate it into Swedish law. Neither the convention, nor the Act (2009:1514) on jurisdictional immunities of States and their property has entered into force.

13. The convention provides rules on immunity from enforcement measures in connection with court procedures in Articles 18–21. Articles 18 and 19, that govern State immunity prior to and after a court ruling, provide the main rule that no enforcement measures with respect to State property may be taken other than as provided in the Articles. Under certain circumstances it is possible to use enforcement measures subsequent to a court ruling even if the State has not approved it. The permissibility of the enforcement is in these cases, as far as is relevant for the present matter, dependent on for what purpose the State holds the relevant property. Property that, as far as is now relevant, may be subject to enforcement measures subsequent to a court ruling is described in Article 19 (c) in the English wording as 'property [.] specifically in use or intended for use by the State for other than government non-commercial purposes'. There is no official Swedish language version. A translation is available in the act that has not yet entered into force.

14. The 2004 convention must be considered to state the principle currently accepted by many States that enforcement may be taken with respect to at least some State property, namely with respect to property that is used for other purpose than government non-commercial purposes (see Article 19 (c)). However, there is an apparent disagreement – with respect to subject matter and over time – on what should be considered a holding for government non- commercial purposes. Thus, the meaning of the phrase must be narrowed down. In this context, the phrase must generally be considered to entail that immunity from enforcement measures can be claimed at least with respect to property that is used for a state's official functions. However, the phrase cannot be considered to mean that immunity from enforcement measures can be successfully claimed solely based on the fact that a property is owned by a State and used for government non-commercial purposes.

Enforcement measures should however be held impermissible if the purpose of the holding of the property is of a more specific nature, such as when the property is used for State acts proper and similar purposes of official nature or when the property is of such particular nature as stated in Article 21 of the 2004 UN convention.

15. An individual property may be used for several, various purposes. Through the provisions on State immunity provided under international law in the Vienna Convention, the physical integrity of, inter alia, embassy personnel, the residences of diplomats (and certain other personnel), official vehicles and archives is protected (Arts 22, 24, 30 and 37 of the Vienna Convention on Diplomatic Relations of 18 April 1961, S6 1967:1; Act 1976:661 on immunities and privileges in certain cases). The limits of State immunity and diplomatic immunity do not coincide. Thus, the limits of State immunity cannot be immediately decided by a comparing with the limits of diplomatic immunity. It is clear, however, that the real property of a State, which is to a substantial extent – but not necessarily mainly – used as premises for the State's officials (or for a different official use which is tied to the representation based on a bilateral agreement), should be covered by immunity from enforcement measures, since the property is used for the carrying out of diplomatic functions.

16. However, it is not clearly evident what applies if the real property is used to some extent for official purposes or purposes nearly linked to the official purposes (such as providing apartments to the personnel covered by diplomatic immunity), but is mainly used for other purposes represented by the foreign State, for purposes that are a prerequisite to or consequence of a State-run operation that is commercial or otherwise non-official in nature, or both. In these situations it must be decided whether the different purposes of the use together make up the specific nature that is required to safeguard the property from enforcement measures. When deciding on these matters it is possible that the respect for State immunity with respect to property used for official purposes and that a foreign State cannot be forced to hand over information it does not wish to hand over, may have the consequence that the regular rules on evidence requirements in enforcement matters cannot be fully upheld.

Assessment of the present matter

17. From the agreement of 1927 between the Union of Socialist Soviet Republics and Sweden (as later confirmed to apply between Sweden and the Russian Federation) with respect to the rights and obligations of the

Russian trade delegation's in Stockholm (S6 1928:8) it is clear that the trade delegation is connected to the representation of the Union in Sweden and that it should enjoy exterritorial privileges for its premises in Stockholm. In a written notice from the trade delegation received by the Swedish Ministry for Foreign Affairs on 26 May 1976 the trade delegation informed that it would move from its old premises at the property Lidingo Kostern 5 to new premises at Ringvagen 1, Lidingo. Thus, the property Kostern 5 can no longer be considered to be notified as official premises of the trade delegation pursuant to the agreement of 1927. Nevertheless and as noted above, the Russian Federation has claimed that the property is exclusively used for the official purposes of the Russian Federation and thus enjoys immunity from enforcement measures.

18. The claim that the property is exclusively used for the official purposes of the Russian Federation has been disputed by Franz J Sedelmayer, who has claimed that it is used for commercial purposes. Franz J Sedelmayer has submitted into evidence his own investigation, as well as the investigation of mainly publicly available written sources carried out by the Enforcement Authority, relating to the actual use of the property at the time of the decision of the Enforcement Authority, in order to show that the property was used as residence for approximately 60 people, out of which no one was notified as a diplomat with the Ministry for Foreign Affairs and ten were Swedish citizens, and that two Swedish companies had their address at the property.

19. The Russian Federation has stated, in response to Franz J Sedelmayer's claims, that the ground floor of the building is an archive used both by the trade delegation and the embassy, as well as a garage used for diplomatic vehicles. Before the Svea Court of Appeal, the Russian Federation stated that the property is not a regular commercial housing property, that out of the 48 apartments on the property four were used as residence for diplomats, that 11 apartments were used as residence for other personnel working for the trade delegation or the embassy, that 13 apartments were used by students or researchers as a result of the agreement between the Russian Federation and Sweden on financial and technical-scientific co-operation within the fields of agriculture and foods industry and which can be realised inter alia through exchange students and researchers, that 14 apartments were used as temporary residence and offices for people with official assignments to Sweden and that six apartments were used by people with special needs and the daughter of a former diplomat. The Russian Federation has further claimed that the tenants pay compensation only for actual costs. Before the Supreme Court, the Russian Federation has, among other things, added that the property comprises premises used for official purposes of such nature that they cannot

be further divulged without breaching the Russian Federation's right to integrity and that as from 1 July 2010 all apartments will be used by people who have diplomatic immunity.

20. The assessment as to whether the use of the property is of such specific nature that distraint of the property would be barred should, since the property was not notified as official premises of the trade delegation and since what has been claimed by Franz J Sedelmayer cannot be left without consideration, in this case be based on the actual use of the property. The relevant time of use for this assessment is, in conformity with what must be considered to have been established internationally, when the application was received by the Enforcement Authority. Thus, changes in the use of apartments and premises that have taken place thereafter shall not be taken into consideration.

21. The evidence in the matter provides that the property Lidingo Kostern 5 is a housing property, which at the time relevant for the assessment was not used for official purposes of the representation of the Russian Federation or the trade delegation related thereto. However, according to what the Federation stated before the Court of Appeal, 15 apartments were used for diplomats or personnel at these, and two premises were used as archive and storage of diplomatic vehicles. This use relates to such apartments, premises or property, the physical integrity of which is protected by the Vienna Convention. The question whether this use is sufficient grounds to make distraint of the property inadmissible then turns on the other use of the property.

22. The other use of the property was for purposes under private law but were of non-commercial, but also non-official nature. Some apartments have been let to researchers and students who visit Sweden as a result of a bilateral agreement between the Russian Federation and Sweden, but the provision of the apartments is based on agreements between these individuals and the Russian Federation and not on an official state act between the Russian Federation and the Swedish State. These lease agreements cannot be considered so closely connected to the fulfilment of the agreement that such use is for official purposes.

23. In light of the above, it is clear that the property Lidingo Kostern 5 was not to a substantial part used for the official purposes of the Russian Federation. The nature of the use has not otherwise been of such specific nature as to grant the property immunity from enforcement in the present enforcement matter.

24. A claim for rent is an asset that has arisen through an act that is of a private nature, and typically it is an asset that is of a commercial nature. The fact that the rent is meant to only cover or assist in covering the costs for the administration of the building is irrelevant in this respect.

25. In light of the above, enforcement of the decision of the District Court ordering the Russian Federation to compensate Franz J Sedelmayer for his costs through distraint of the property Lidingo Kostern 5 and of the rental payments related to that property is not barred. Thus, the decision of the Court of Appeal shall be upheld.

27

Investment arbitration awards as precedent

EXERCISE 41– SEMINAR

Review the excerpt from *AES v Argentina*, Decision on Jurisdiction, from April 26, 2005.

DISCUSSION QUESTIONS

Problem 1

Argue that consistency and predictability in investment arbitration is needed. Argue that adhering to previous awards as much as possible is the best way to achieve this goal. Use examples from investment arbitration jurisprudence.

Problem 2

From time to time you see investment arbitrators writing statements of how they perceive the law to be even if it is not strictly called for to solve the case – either in the form of *obiter dicta* or in separate dissents. Do you think this is a good approach? When is it and when is it not?

Problem 3

In a case like *AES v Argentina*, where there is a clear line of previous decisions based on similar BIT provisions and factual circumstances, what value would you assign to those decisions? Is there a difference between arbitrations under ICSID and those under other institutional rules?

Problem 4

You are the chairman of the ICSID Tribunal in a case like *AES*. The previous awards, based on similar provisions and facts, do not convince you. You decide to write the award without mentioning the previous cases at all. Explain your decision.

CASE

AES v Argentina (ICSID Case No. ARB/02/17), excerpt from Decision on Jurisdiction

[. . .]

II. Opening considerations

A. Relevance of other ICSID arbitral tribunal's decisions on jurisdiction

17. Prior to establishing its position with regard to the five objections made by the Argentine Republic to its jurisdiction, the Tribunal shall address some preliminary considerations made by both parties in their respective argumentations. All of them were raised in relation with an opinion expressed by the claimant in its counter-memorial on jurisdiction. In reaction to the objections filed by Argentina to the jurisdiction of this Tribunal, AES argued that:

> Each of Argentina's five objections are based on similar or identical arguments presented by it in other factually similar arbitrations in which Argentina is the respondent. In every instance, the same arguments have either been rejected or the corresponding ICSID Tribunal has decided to join this objection to the merits.

18. In its counter-memorial, AES further referred to several ICSID Tribunal decisions on jurisdiction, including the *Vivendi* decisions I and II, together with the *CMS* and the *Azurix* decisions on jurisdiction. Later, and in particular during the hearing, AES further referred to other decisions which, in the meantime, had become available, such as the *LG&E v Argentina*, the *ENRON v Argentina* and the *SIEMENS AG v Argentina* decisions on jurisdiction. The argument made by the claimant on the basis of these decisions, treated more or less as if they were precedents, tends to say that Argentina's objections to the jurisdiction of this Tribunal are moot if not even useless since these tribunals have already determined the answer to be given to identical or similar objections to jurisdiction.

19. In response, Argentina raises a series of issues. They deal respectively with the legal basis for the jurisdiction of the Tribunal and with the way in which, according to the respondent, the Tribunal should interpret them for determining whether it has or has not jurisdiction on this case. These arguments must indeed be considered in relation with the delimitation of the task of the Tribunal at this stage of the proceedings.

20. After having recalled that the jurisdiction of ICSID Arbitral Tribunals is based upon the ICSID Convention (Art 25), in conjunction with the bilateral treaty for the protection of investments in force between Argentina and the national State of the foreign investor, respondent insists upon the specificity of each bilateral agreement as compared to others. Argentina says in particular that: 'Each bilateral Treaty for the protection of investments has a different and defined scope of application. It is not a uniform text.'

21. Argentina further contends that: 'The consent granted by signatory States of bilateral treaties shall not be extended by means of presumptions and analogies, or by attempting to turn the *lex specialis* into *lex general* (sic).'

22. In addition, Argentina states that:

> The reading of some awards may lead to believe that the tribunal has forgotten that it is acting in a sphere ruled by a lex specialis where generalisations are not usually wrong, but, what is worst, are illegitimate. Repeating decisions taken in other cases, without making the factual and legal distinctions, may constitute an excess of power and may affect the integrity of the international system for the protection of investments.

23. For this Tribunal, Argentina is right to insist on the limits imposed on it as on any other Arbitral ICSID Tribunal. The provisions of Article 25 of the ICSID Convention together with fundamental principles of public international law dictate, among others, that the Tribunal respects:

(a) the autonomy of the will of the Parties to the ICSID Convention as well as that of the Parties to the pertinent bilateral treaty on the protection of investments;

(b) the rule according to which '*specialia generalibus derogant*', from which it derives that treaty obligations prevail over rules of customary international law under the condition that the latter are not of a peremptory character;

(c) the fact that the extent of the jurisdiction of each tribunal is determined by the combination of the pertinent provisions of two '*leges specialia*': on the one hand, the ICSID Convention and, on the other hand, the BIT in force between the two concerned States; as the case may be, the arbitration clause in contracts between the private investor and the State or its emanation may also interfere with the two previous ones for determination of the scope of the tribunal's jurisdiction;

(d) the rule according to which each decision or award delivered by an ICSID Tribunal is only binding on the parties to the dispute settled by this decision or award. There is so far no rule of precedent in general international law; nor is there any within the specific ICSID system for the settlement of disputes between one State party to the Convention and the National of another State Party. This was in particular illustrated by diverging positions respectively taken by two ICSID tribunals on issues dealing with the interpretation of arguably similar language in two different BITs. As rightly stated by the Tribunal in *SGS v Philippines*:

> . . .although different tribunals constituted under the ICSID system should in general seek to act consistently with each other, in the end it must be for each tribunal to exercise its competence in accordance with the applicable law, which will by definition be different for each BIT and each Respondent State.

The same position was echoed by the *ENRON* Tribunal on jurisdiction:

> The Tribunal agrees with the view expressed by the Argentine Republic in the hearing on jurisdiction held in respect of this dispute, to the effect that the decisions of ICSID tribunals are not binding precedents and that every case must be examined in the light of its own circumstances.

24. The present Tribunal indeed agrees with Argentina that each BIT has its own identity; its very terms should consequently be carefully analysed for determining the exact scope of consent expressed by its two parties.

25. This is in particular the case if one considers that striking similarities in the wording of many BITs often dissimulate real differences in the definition of some key concepts, as it may be the case, in particular, for the determination of 'investments' or for the precise definition of rights and obligations for each party.

26. From the above derive at least two consequences: the first is that the findings of law made by one ICSID Tribunal in one case in consideration, among others, of the terms of a determined BIT, are not necessarily relevant for other ICSID Tribunals, which were constituted for other cases; the second is that, although Argentina had already submitted similar objections to the jurisdiction of other tribunals prior to those raised in the present case before this Tribunal, Argentina has a valid and legitimate right to raise the objections it has chosen for opposing the jurisdiction of this Tribunal. According to Article 41(2) of the ICSID Convention:

> Any objection by a party to the dispute that that dispute is not within the jurisdiction of the Centre, or for other reasons is not within the competence of the Tribunal, shall be considered by the Tribunal which shall determine whether to deal with it as a preliminary question or to join it to the merits of the dispute.

27. Under the benefit of the foregoing observations, the Tribunal would nevertheless reject the excessive assertion which would consist in pretending that, due to the specificity of each case and the identity of each decision on jurisdiction or award, absolutely no consideration might be given to other decisions on jurisdiction or awards delivered by other tribunals in similar cases.

28. In particular, if the basis of jurisdiction for these other tribunals and/or the underlying legal dispute in analysis present either a high level of similarity or, even more, an identity with those met in the present case, this Tribunal does not consider that it is barred, as a matter of principle, from considering the position taken or the opinion expressed by these other tribunals.

29. In that respect, it should be noted that the US-Argentina BIT, in conjunction with the ICSID Convention, provides the very same basis for the jurisdiction in this case and in some previous ones, as, in particular, those in which Argentina faced or is still facing a dispute with *ENRON Corp, CMS, AZURIX Corp*, or *LG&E and others*; in each and every of these cases the Tribunals respectively constituted have already delivered their decisions on jurisdiction.

30. An identity of the basis of jurisdiction of these Tribunals, even when it meets with very similar if not even identical facts at the origin of the disputes, does not suffice to apply systematically to the present case positions or solutions already adopted in these cases. Each Tribunal remains sovereign and may retain, as it is confirmed by ICSID practice, a different solution for resolving the same problem; but decisions on jurisdiction dealing with the same or very similar issues may at least indicate some lines of reasoning of real interest; this Tribunal may consider them in order to compare its own position with those already adopted by its predecessors and, if it shares the views already expressed by one or more of these tribunals on a specific point of law, it is free to adopt the same solution.

28
Transparency

EXERCISE 42 – SEMINAR

DISCUSSION QUESTIONS

Problem 1

You are the counsel for a group of five NGOs in a NAFTA arbitration *(BigCo Chemicals (USA) v Canada)* with similar facts to *Methanex v United States of America*. However, BigCo has initiated its claim under the SCC Rules, in October 2012.

Argue that you should be allowed to:

(i)   file an *amicus* brief;
(ii) be present during oral hearings;
(iii) make oral submissions.

How would you frame and structure your argument?

Problem 2

How would your arguments and/or the procedure be different if the Problem 1 claim had been initiated:

(i)   under the UNCITRAL Arbitration Rules (assume the treaty is concluded after 1 April 2014)?
(ii) under the LCIA Rules?
(iii) outside the NAFTA context?

Problem 3

BigCo Chemicals initiates a new claim in 2020 against Australia, under the UNCITRAL Arbitration Rules, pursuant to a treaty between the US, New Zealand and Australia concluded on 1 April 2014. The same five NGOs (on the same basic facts) apply to make (i) an oral submission; and (ii) a written submission to the tribunal. You are the Tribunal.

(i)   How do you make your decision as to whether the NGOs should be able to make (i) oral; or (ii) written submissions? What conditions, if any, would you impose?
(ii) Does it matter that BigCo's charitable foundation (BCC Charity Fund for Environmental Issues) provides funding and trustees for two of the NGOs?
(iii) Does it matter that Australia strongly opposes *amicus* intervention on the basis that it is very late in the proceedings and the intervention, according to Australia, would add significant costs and delay to proceedings?

(iv) How much does public policy, or the public interest in the arbitration, play a role in your decision?

(v) What factors might persuade you to decide differently in relation to whether submissions may be permitted?

Problem 4

The United States wants to make a submission under Article 5 of the UNCITRAL Transparency Rules, in relation to a critical issue in dispute, namely, whether public interest regulations are carved out of the concept of expropriation. As the Tribunal, do you agree to allow this submission? What considerations do you take into account?

 CASE

Methanex Corporation v United States of America, in the matter of an arbitration under Chapter 11 of the North American Free Trade Agreement and the UNCITRAL Arbitration Rules

Decision of the Tribunal on petitions from third persons to intervene as '*amici curiae*'

I. Introduction

1. On 25 August 2000, a petition was submitted to the Tribunal by the International Institute for Sustainable Development requesting permission to submit an *amicus curiae* brief to the Tribunal (the 'Institute Petition'). On 6 September 2000, a joint petition was submitted to the Tribunal by (i) Communities for a Better Environment and (ii) the Earth Island Institute for permission to appear as *amici curiae* (the 'Communities/Earth Island Petition').

2. On 7 September 2000, the requests contained in these petitions were addressed by the claimant and the respondent at the second procedural hearing, which was attended by the legal representative from Mexico. At this point, only the claimant had filed written submissions on the issue of intervention (on 31 August 2000) and these were directed to the Institute Petition only. The Tribunal decided not to rule upon the Petitions at the Hearing. Under Item 3 of the Minutes of Order that Hearing, as modified on 10 October 2000, the Tribunal laid down it timetable for written submissions and the issue of intervention by third persons as amicus curiae, to be decided by the Tribunal as a general principle.

3. The Tribunal's timetable provided as follows:

(1) 16 October 2000: Further written submissions of Petitioners for *amicus curiae* status.

(2) 27 October 2000: Written submissions from the claimant and the respondent in respect of (1).

(3) 10 November 2000: Written submissions from Canada and Mexico as Non-Disputing State Parties as provided for by Article 1128 of NAFTA.

(4) 22 November 2000: Written submissions from the claimant and the respondent in respect of (3).

An 'Amended Petition' was duly submitted on 13th October 2000 by (i) Communities for a Better Environment, (ii) the Bluewater Network of Earth Island Institute and (iii) the Center for International Environmental Law (the 'Communities/Bluewater/Center Petition') on 16 October 2000. 'Final Submissions' were submitted by the International Institute for Sustainable Development (the 'Institute Final Petition'); on 27 October 2000, the claimant and the respondent filed their written submissions; on 10 November 2000, Canada and Mexico each filed written submissions; and on 22 November 2000, the claimant and the respondent filed their further written submissions.

4. In accordance with the procedure envisaged at the Second Procedural Meeting and agreed with the Disputing Parties, the Tribunal has been able to decide this issue on the basis of these written submissions, without the need for an oral hearing. At the outset, the Tribunal expresses its thanks to all those responsible for researching and drafting these submissions, which touch upon important general principles directly affecting the future conduct of these arbitration proceedings and the potential effect, direct and indirect, of any award on the Disputing Parties' substantive dispute.

II. Summary of the petitioners' requests

5. *The Institute*: The Institute Petition contained requests for permission (i) to file an *amicus* brief (preferably after reading the parties' written pleadings), (ii) to make oral submissions, (iii) to have observer status at oral hearings. Permission was sought on the basis of the immense public importance of the case and the critical impact that the Tribunal's decision will have on environmental and other public welfare law-making in the NAFTA region. It was also contended that the interpretation of Chapter 11 of NAFTA should reflect legal principles underlying the concept of sustainable development; and that the Institute could assist the Tribunal in this respect. A further point was made that participation of an amicus would allay public disquiet as to the

closed nature of arbitration proceedings under Chapter 11 of NAFTA. As to jurisdiction, it was argued that the Tribunal could grant the Petition under its general procedural powers contained in Article 15 of the UNCITRAL Arbitration Rules, and that there was nothing in Chapter 11 to prevent the granting of the permission requested by the Institute. Reference was also made to the practice of the WTO Appellate Body and courts in Canada and the United States.

6. These submissions were expanded in the Institute Final Petition. It was argued that there was an increased urgency in the need for amicus participation in the light of the award dated 30m August 2000 in *Metaclad Corporation v United Mexican States* and an alleged failure to consider environmental and sustainable development goals in that NAFTA arbitration. It was contended that there was no danger of the Tribunal opening – the 'floodgates' to other persons seeking to appear as amici in future NAFTA arbitrations; and that there was no overriding principle of confidentiality in arbitration that should exclude amici. Further, in this respect, the Institute would be entitled eventually to copies of the parties' written pleadings under the US Freedom of Information Act. The Institute would satisfy the special interest tests under both Canadian and US law to enable it to appear as amicus in equivalent court proceedings in those jurisdictions. Finally, it was argued that the absence of any right of appeal from the Tribunal's arbitration award made it all the more important that there should be no errors resulting from the lack of a fresh and relevant perspective which the Institute could provide to the Tribunal.

7. *Communities/Bluewater/Center*: The Communities/Earth Island Petition was in effect superseded by the Communities/Bluewater/Center Petition (as explained at paragraph I of the later submission). This petition requested permission to participate in the proceedings as amid curiae, which participation was to include the opportunity to review the parties' written pleadings, to attend hearings and to make written and oral submissions. For practical purposes, the scope of this intervention is the same sought by the Institute.

8. This petition stressed the widespread public support for the participation of amici in this arbitration. It argued that the case raised issues of constitutional importance, concerning the balance between (a) governmental authority to implement environmental regulations and (b) property rights. It contended that the outcome in this case might affect the willingness of governments at all levels in the NAFTA States (including the State of California) to implement measures to protect the environment and human health. As with the Institute Petition, it asserted that intervention was consistent with Canadian and US domestic law; and that the Tribunal

bad jurisdiction to allow the petition under Article 15 of the UNCITRAL Arbitration Rules. It was again contended that there was support for a decision by the Tribunal to allow the petition in the form of various decisions of the WTO Appellate Body. Further, the point was made that the United States had recognised the value of amicus participation in cases before the WTO Appellate Body.

III. Summary of submissions by Mexico and Canada

9. *Mexico*: Mexico stressed that Chapter 11 of NAFTA did not provide for the involvement of persons other than the Disputing Parties and NAFTA Parties on questions of the interpretation of NAFTA pursuant to Article 1128. It contended that if *amicus curiae* submissions were allowed, the amici would have greater rights than the NAFTA Parties themselves because of the limited scope of Article 1128 submissions. Such a result was clearly never intended by the NAFTA Parties; and it could lead to the abrogation of Article 1128 by NAFTA Panics submitting *amicus* briefs where they wished to make submissions on issues other than the interpretation of NAFTA. Mexico argued that the Tribunal's authority to appoint experts was limited by Article 1133 of NAFTA (i.e., subject to the disapproval of the Disputing Parties). In any event, *amici* were not to be confused with independent experts. In addition, Mexico noted that the there was no power under Mexican law for its domestic courts to receive *amicus* briefs. The Chapter 11 dispute settlement mechanism established a careful balance between the procedures of common law states, Canada (at least in part) and the United States, on the one hand and on the other a civil law state, Mexico. The existence of a specific procedure in one party's domestic state court procedure did not mean that it could be transported to a transnational NAFTA arbitration.

10. *Canada*. Canada adopted a different approach from Mexico. In its written submissions, Canada stated its support for greater openness in arbitration proceedings under Chapter 11 of NAFTA. Although mindful of the confidentiality obligations imposed by Article 25(4) of the UNCTTRAL Arbitration Rules, Canada supported public disclosure of arbitral submissions, orders and awards to the fullest extent possible. Canada contended that in this case, without prejudice to its position in other arbitrations under NAFTA Chapter 11, the Tribunal should accept the written submissions of the petitioners, notwithstanding that only NAFTA Parties have the right to make submissions on questions of the interpretation of NAFTA. Canada also stated that it would be asking its NAFTA partners to work together on the issue of *amicus curiae* participation as a matter of urgency in order to provide guidance to arbitration tribunals under Chapter 11.

IV. Summary of submissions by the disputing parties

11. The Disputing Parties responded differently to the petitioner's request for intervention. The respondent, as summarised later below, requested the Tribunal to accept part of the petitioner's request. The claimant sought the dismissal of these petitions under three principal headings: (i) confidentiality; (ii) jurisdiction; (iii) fairness of process.

(i) The claimant

12. *Confidentiality*: As to confidentiality, the claimant relied on Article 25(4) of the UNCITRAL Arbitration Rules to the effect that hearings are to be held in camera. It argued that this obligation carried with it the requirement that documents prepared for the arbitration be confidential. The authority for this proposition was to be found in the reasoning of the English Commercial Court in *Hassneh Insurance Co of Israel v Stewart J Mew* (1993] 2 Lloyd's Rep 243. Further, the Disputing Parties had come to an agreement on confidentiality by the Consent Order regarding Disclosure and Confidentiality (made by the Tribunal at the Second Procedural Meeting on 7 September 2000); and it was thereby agreed that transcripts, written submissions, witness statements, reports, etc be kept confidential. The Order did not allow for disclosure of material to non-governmental organisations or public interest groups, such as the petitioners.

13. *Jurisdiction*: As to jurisdiction, the claimant argued that the Tribunal had no jurisdiction to add a party to the proceedings without the agreement of the parties. The ability to appear in the arbitration was limited by Chapter 11 of NAFTA to the Disputing Parties and NAFTA Parties, whereas granting the petitioners the status of *amicus curiae* would be equivalent to adding them as parties. No such jurisdiction was created by Article 15 of the UNCITRAL Arbitration Rules. That rule was concerned merely with procedural matters and not the substantive issue of who were the parties to the arbitration. There was also no question of jurisdiction under Article 27 of the UNCITRAL Arbitration Rules, as that power to receive expert evidence had been specifically removed from the Tribunal. Further, after a careful search the claimant stated that it had been unable to find any precedent where a tribunal had granted *amicus curiae* status to non-parties in an arbitration under the UNCITRAL Arbitration Rules.

14. *Fairness*: As to fairness, the claimant contended that the protection of the public interest was ensured by Article 1128 of NAFTA. Private interest groups wishing to put their views before an arbitration tribunal could

convey their information to the NAFTA Parties, who had the right to intervene where there was a question of interpretation of NAFTA. Further, any of the Disputing Parties would be in a position to call upon the petitioners to offer their testimony as evidence in the proceedings, whereas if the petitioners were to appear as *amici curiae*, the Disputing Parties would have no opportunity to test by cross-examination (in particular) the factual basis of their contentions. In addition, granting to the petitioners *amici* status would substantially increase the costs of proceedings and require the claimant to respond to the submissions of others in a way not contemplated by NAFTA. An undesirable precedent would be set and other groups might be encouraged to seek to appear as amici in arbitrations under Chapter 11 of NAFTA.

15. Like Mexico, the claimant also argued that reliance on the practice relating to *amici* in the domestic courts of certain jurisdictions was inappropriate to these arbitration proceedings. Amicus briefs were not permitted in one of the NAFTA States, namely Mexico. The court processes of one NAFTA State should not be preferred over another; and the international rules governing foreign investment should not be made to give way to domestic practices. The claimant also considered that WTO practice was irrelevant and should be disregarded by the Tribunal. Further, in so far as it was aware, no WTO panel or Appellate Body had accepted for consideration an unsolicited *amicus* brief. Briefs had been filed in each case, but the WTO Panel or Appellate Body had always determined that these briefs should not be considered, and the power under Article 13 of the Dispute Settlement Understanding to seek information from outside sources had not been used in this respect. Further, in the order of 16 November 2000 in European Communities – Measures Affecting Asbestos and Asbestos Containing Products, all 17 applications for *amicus* status were rejected by the WTO.

(ii) The respondent

16. The respondent contended (i) that the procedural rules governing the arbitration permitted the acceptance of *amicus* submissions, and (ii) that *amicus* submissions were suitable when likely to assist the Tribunal and should then be allowed by the Tribunal.

17. *Power*: The respondent argued that there was an inherent flexibility in the UNCITRAL Arbitration Rules, to be applied in the context of the particular dispute. The powers under the UNCITRAL Arbitration Rules should be exercised in a manner commensurate with the public international law aspects of the case and the fact that it implicated substantial public interests. The NAFTA Parties view that the UNCITRAL Arbitration

Rules were sufficiently flexible in such instances reflected a presumption that arbitration tribunals would use the discretion granted to them in a manner appropriate to the nature of the dispute. In this respect, the current dispute was to be distinguished from a typical commercial arbitration on the basis that a State was the respondent, the issues had to be decided in accordance with a treaty and the principles of public international law and a decision on that dispute could have a significant effect extending beyond the two Disputing Parties.

18. The respondent contended that pursuant to Article 15(1) of the UNCITRAL Arbitration Rules the Tribunal had the authority to conduct the proceedings as it deemed appropriate subject to the proviso that the parties be treated with equality and given a full opportunity of presenting their cases. This rule was sufficiently broad to encompass the authority to accept amicus briefs. The respondent cited comments on the application of the UNCITRAL Arbitration Rules by the Iran-US Claims Tribunal in Baker and Davis, *The UNCITRAL Arbitration Rules in Practice*, 1992, pp. 76 and 98. The respondent also relied on the practice of the Appellate Body of the WTO in finding that it had broad authority to adopt procedural rules that did not conflict with the express rules of the WTO Dispute Settlement Understanding, therefore allowing *amicus* submissions;: see *United States Imposition of Countervailing Duties on Certain Hot-Rolled Lead and Bismuth Carbon Steel Products Originating in the United Kingdom*, paragraph 39, [WT/DS138/ABIR], adopted on 7 June 2000.

19. The respondent considered that there was nothing in the UNCITRAL Arbitration Rules that prohibited acceptance of *amicus* submissions. Article 25(4) of the Rules limited the persons who could attend a hearing, not those who could submit written briefs. In this respect, the respondent relied on the Australian case of *Esso Australia Resozuces Ltd v Plowman* (1995) 183 CLR 10 at paragraphs 30–32, in which *Hassneh Insurance Co of Israel v Steuart J Mew* was considered but not followed by the High Court of Australia. It also relied on the recent application of the *Esso* case by the Swedish Supreme Court in *Bulgarian Foreign Trade Bank Ltd v A I Trade Finance Inc* (27.x.2000); and a finding in that case that a party in an international commercial arbitration in Sweden was not bound by a duty of confidentiality unless it had agreed to that duty, and that the presence of an *in camera* rule in an arbitration agreement did not amount to such an agreement. In any event, rules of confidentiality could have no bearing on whether the Tribunal could receive written submissions from *amici*. Further, the Tribunal's discretion was not limited by Article 22 of the UNCITRAL Arbitration Rules, which did deal with written submissions.

20. Similarly, the respondent contended that there was nothing in Chapter 11 of NAFTA to prohibit the acceptance of *amicus* submissions. Article 1128 of NAFTA gave rights to Non-Disputing Parties, leaving untouched the question of how the Tribunal might exercise its discretion to permit submissions from other non-parties. There was therefore no question of *amici* being granted greater rights than the NAFTA's State Parties. In this respect, the respondent referred to the rejection of a similar argument in the WTO context: *Hot-Rolled Lead and Carbon Steel*, paragraph 41 [WTIDS 138/AB/R]. In addition, it was contended that Articles 1126(10) and 1137(4) of NAFTA recognised the public interest involved in NAFTA arbitrations in demonstrating that the NAFTA Parties expected the substance of each Chapter 11 dispute and most awards to be made publicly available. Responding to the argument raised by Mexico that the Tribunal's authority to appoint experts was limited to Article 1133 of NAFTA, the respondent maintained that *amici* did not fulfil the same function as Tribunal appointed experts; and Article 1133 was therefore irrelevant.

21. Finally, under this heading, the respondent argued that the petitioners were not seeking the status of parties so the claimant's comments in this respect were misconceived. A burden would be added if the Tribunal accepted an *amicus* submission, but this would be justified where the Tribunal had made a determination that the *amicus* submission would be helpful. The Consent Order regarding Disclosure and Confidentiality did not address the question of *amicus* briefs, and specifically envisaged that important documents generated during the course of the arbitration would be released to the public, whilst the remainder would be subject to release under the US Freedom of Information Act.

22. *Discretion.* To the second of its principal contentions, the respondent argued that a third person might have knowledge or expertise of value to the Tribunal, and that on a showing that the submission would be both relevant and helpful it should be allowed by the Tribunal. In this respect, the claimant suggested procedures by which the Tribunal could assess the value of a potential *amicus* submission before deciding to grant leave. Specific reference was made to the procedures adopted in the order of 8 November 2000 adopted in *European Communities – Measures Affecting Asbestos and Asbestos Containing Products* [WTIDS135/9]. By contrast, failure to allow any *amicus* submissions would reinforce the growing perception that Chapter 11 dispute resolution was an exclusionary and secretive process. Moreover, there was no reason to fear a deluge of petitions for *amicus* status – as was clear from what had happened both in this case as well as experience in the WTO.

23. As to the petitioners' requests that they be allowed to attend hearings and receive copies of all documents filed in the arbitration, the respondent's position was that the Tribunal's jurisdiction was effectively restricted by Article 25(4) of the UNCITRAL Arbitration Rules and the Consent Order regarding Disclosure and Confidentiality. It nonetheless was in favour of giving public access to the greatest extent possible, and therefore gave its consent to the open and public hearing of all hearings before the Tribunal, supporting disclosure consistent with the Consent Order.

V. The Tribunal's reasons and decision

24. Pursuant to Articles 1120(1)(c) and 1120(2) of NAFTA and the agreement of the Disputing Parties, this arbitration is governed by the UNCITRAL Arbitration Rules save in so far as such Rules are modified by Chapter 11, Section B, of NAFTA In the Tribunal's view, there is nothing in either the UNCITRAL Arbitration Rules or Chapter 11, Section B, that either expressly confers upon the Tribunal the power to accept *amicus* submissions or expressly provides that the Tribunal shall have no such power.

25. It follows that the Tribunal's powers in this respect might be inferred, if at all, from its more general procedural powers. In the Tribunal's view, the petitioners' requests must be considered against Article 15(1) of the UNCITRAL Arbitration Rules and it is not possible or appropriate to look elsewhere for any broader power or jurisdiction.

26. Article 15(1) of the UNCITRAL Arbitration Rules grants to the Tribunal a broad discretion as to the conduct of this arbitration, subject always to the requirements of procedural equality and fairness towards the Disputing Parties. It provides, broken down into numbered sub-paragraphs for ease of reference below, as follows:

> [1] Subject to these Rules [2] the arbitral tribunal may conduct the arbitration in such manner as it considers appropriate, [3] provided that the parties are treated with equality and that at any stage in the proceedings each party is given a full opportunity of presenting its case.

This provision constitutes one of the essential 'hallmarks' of an international arbitration under the UNCITRAL Arbitration Rules, according to the *travaux préparatoires*. Article 15 has also been described as the 'heart' of the UNCITRAL Arbitration Rules; and its terms have since been adopted in Articles 18 and 19(2) of the UNCITRAL Model Law on International

Commercial Arbitration, where these provisions were considered as the procedural '*Magna Carta*' of international commercial arbitration. Article 15(1) is plainly a very important provision.

27. Article 15(1) is intended to provide the broadest procedural flexibility within fundamental safeguards, to be applied by the arbitration tribunal to fit the particular needs of the particular arbitration. As a procedural provision, however, it cannot grant the Tribunal any power to add further disputing parties to the arbitration, nor to accord to persons who are non-parties the substantive status, rights or privileges of a Disputing Party. Likewise, the Tribunal can have no power to accord to any third person the substantive rights of NAFTA Parties under Article 1128 of NAFTA. The issue is whether Article 15(1) grants the Tribunal any lesser procedural power in regard to non-party third persons, such as the petitioners here.

28. In addressing this issue, there are four principal matters to be considered:

(i)   whether the Tribunal's acceptance of amicus submissions falls within the general scope of the subparagraph numbered [2] of Article 15(1);

(ii) if so, whether the acceptance of amicus submissions could affect the equal treatment of the Disputing Parties and the opportunity of each fully to present its case, under the sub-paragraph numbered [3] of Article 15(1);

(iii) whether there are any provisions in Chapter 1 I, Section B of NAFTA that modify the application of Article 15(1) for present purposes: and

(iv) whether other provisions of the UNCITRAL Arbitration Rules likewise modify the application of Article 15(1) in regard to this particular case, given the introductory words of the sub-paragraph numbered [1] of Article 15(1).

It is convenient to consider each matter in turn.

(i) The general scope of Article 15(1) of the UNCITRAL Arbitration Rules

29. The Tribunal is required to decide a substantive dispute between the claimant and the respondent. The Tribunal has no mandate to decide any other substantive dispute or any dispute determining the legal rights of third persons. The legal boundaries of the arbitration are set by this essential legal fact. It is thus self-evident that if the Tribunal cannot directly, without consent, add another person as a party to this dispute or treat a third person as a party to the arbitration or NAFTA, it is equally precluded from achieving

this result indirectly by exercising a power over the conduct of the arbitration. Accordingly, in the Tribunal's view, the power under Article 15(1) must be confined to procedural matters. Treating non-parties as Disputing Parties or as NAFTA Parties cannot be matters of mere procedure; and such matters cannot fall within Article 15(1) of the UNCITRAL Arbitration Rules.

30. However, in the Tribunal's view, its receipt of written submissions from a person other than the Disputing Parties is not equivalent to adding that person as a party to the arbitration. The rights of the Disputing Parties in the arbitration and the limited rights of a Non-Disputing Party under Article 1128 of NAFTA are not thereby acquired by such a third person. Their rights, both procedural and substantive, remain juridically exactly the same before and after receipt of such submissions; and the third person acquires no rights at all. The legal nature of the arbitration remains wholly unchanged.

31. The Tribunal considers that allowing a third person to make an *amicus* submission could fall within its procedural powers over the conduct of the arbitration, within the general scope of Article 15(1) of the UNCITRAL Arbitration Rules. The wording of the subparagraph numbered [2] of Article 15(1) suffices, in the Tribunal's view, to support its conclusion; but its approach is supported by the practice of the Iran-US Claims Tribunal and the World Trade Organisation.

32. *Iran-US Claims Tribunal*. Notes 5 of the Iran-US Claims Tribunal Notes to Article 15[1], of the UNCITRAL Arbitration Rules states:

> The arbitral tribunal may, having satisfied itself that the statement of one of the two Governments – or, under special circumstances, any other person – who is not an arbitrating party in a particular case is likely to assist the arbitral tribunal in carrying out its task, permit such Government or person to assist the arbitral tribunal by presenting written and [or] oral statements.

This provision was specifically drafted for the Iran-US Claims Tribunal as a supplementary guide. Although (so it appears from published commentaries) it was invoked by Iran or the US as non-arbitrating parties, it was also invoked by non-state third persons (albeit infrequently), such as the foreign banks submitting their own memorial to the Tribunal in *Iran v United States, Case A/15*: see the Award No 63-Al15- IT made by the Full Tribunal (President Böckstiegel and Judges Briner. Virally. Bahrami, Holtzmann, Mostafavi, Aldrich, Ansari and Brower) 2 Iran-US C. T.R. 40, at p.43. For present purposes, the authoritative guide to the exercise of the Iran-US Claim Tribunal's discretion under Article 15(1) and this award demonstrate that the receipt of written submissions from a non-party third person does not necessarily offend the philosophy of international arbitration involving states and non-state parties.

33. *WTO*: The distinction between parties to an arbitration and their right to make submissions and a third person having no such right was adopted by the WTO Appellate Body in *Hot-Rolled Lead and Carbon Steel*, paragraph 41:

> Individuals and organisations which are not Members of the WTO, have no legal 'right' to make submissions to be heard by the Appellate Body. The Appellate Body has no legal 'duty' to accept or consider unsolicited amicus curiae briefs submitted by individuals or organizations, not Members of the WTO. . ..

Further, the Appellate Body there found that it had power to accept *amicus* submissions under Article 17.9 of the Dispute Settlement Understanding to draw up working procedures. That procedural power is significantly less broad than the power accorded to this Tribunal under Article 15(1) to conduct the arbitration in such manner it considers appropriate. For present purposes, this WTO practice demonstrates that the scope of a procedural power can extend to the receipt of written submissions from non-party third persons, even in a juridical procedure affecting the rights and obligations of State parties; and further it also demonstrates that the receipt of such submissions confers no rights, procedural or substantive, on such persons.

34. *ICJ*: The Tribunal notes, however, that there has been a traditional reluctance on the part of the International Court of Justice to accept *amicus* submissions from non-parties, although Article 62 of the ICJ Statutes allows an interested non-party State to request intervention. As observed by Rosenne, *The Law and Practice of the International Court 1920–1996* (1997), at pp 653–4, the ICJ does not admit non-governmental organisations (which are treated as individuals); and in regard to individual petitioners, the author states:

> The practice of the Court also docs not envisage the legal representatives of an individual appearing at the bar of the Court, holding a watching brief, receiving copies of the pleadings, and being allowed – perhaps as *amicus curiae* – to present its own case.

The ICJ Registrar refused such a request in the *Namibia* Case, II Pleadings, 636, 638. Nonetheless, more recently, it appears that written submissions were received by the ICJ, unofficially, in *Case Concerning the Gabcikovo-Nagymaros Project*, lCJ Reports, 1997. In the Tribunal's view, the ICJ's practices provides little assistance to this case. Its jurisdiction in contentious cases is limited solely to disputes between States; its Statute provides for intervention by States; and it would be difficult in these circumstances to infer from its procedural powers a power to allow a non-state third person to intervene.

(ii) Safeguarding equal treatment

35. The Tribunal noted the argument raised by the claimant to the effect that a burden will be added if *amicus* submissions are presented to the Tribunal and the Disputing Parties seek to make submissions in response. That burden is indeed a potential risk. It is inherent in any adversarial procedure which admits representations by a non-party third person.

36. However, at least initially, the burden in meeting the petitioners' written submissions would be shared by both Disputing Parties; and moreover, that burden cannot be regarded as inevitably excessive for either Disputing Party. As envisaged by the Tribunal, the petitioners would make their submissions in writing, in a form and subject to limitations decided by the Tribunal. The petitioners could not adduce the evidence of any factual or expert witness; and it would not therefore be necessary for either Disputing Party to cross-examine a witness proffered by the petitioners: there could be no such witness. As to the contents of the petitioners' written submissions; it would always be for the Tribunal to decide what weight (if any) to attribute to those submissions. Even if any part of those submissions were arguably to constitute written 'evidence', the Tribunal would still retain a complete discretion under Article 25.6 of the UNCITRAL Arbitration Rules to determine its admissibility, relevance, materiality and weight. Of course, if either Disputing Party adopted a petitioner's written submissions, the other Disputing Party could not then complain at that burden: it was always required to meet its opponent's case; and that case, however supplemented, can form no extra unfair burden or unequal treatment.

37. It would always be the Tribunal's task, assisted by the Disputing Parties, to adopt procedures whereby any burden in meeting written submissions from a petitioner was mitigated or extinguished. In theory, a difficulty could remain if a point was advanced by a petitioner to which both Disputing Parties were opposed; but in practice, that risk appears small in this arbitration. In any case, it is not a risk the size or nature of which should swallow the general principle permitting written submissions from third persons. Accordingly, whilst there is a possible risk of unfair treatment as raised by the claimant, the Tribunal is aware of that risk and considers that it must be addressed as and

when it may arise. There is no immediate risk of unfair or unequal treatment for any Disputing Party or Party.

(iii) Relevant provisions of Chapter 11, Section B. of NAFTA

38. As already noted by the Tribunal, there are no provisions in Chapter 11 of NAFTA that touch directly on the question of whether a tribunal has the power to accept *amicus* submissions. Of the provisions that have been considered in the submissions received by the Tribunal, neither Article 1128 nor Article 1133 of NAFTA has any bearing on that question. The first is concerned with a right on the part of NAFTA Parties; and the second is concerned solely with a tribunal's authority to appoint experts. *Amici* are not experts; such third persons are advocates (in the non-pejorative sense) and not 'independent' in that they advance a particular case to a tribunal.

39. The respondent referred to Articles 1126(10) and 1137(4) of NAFTA. In the Tribunal's view, there is nothing relevant in these provisions for present purposes. As the Tribunal has already concluded, there is no provision in Chapter 11 that expressly prohibits the acceptance of *amicus* submissions, but likewise nothing that expressly encourages them.

(iv) Other UNCITRAL arbitration rules

40. The claimant's reliance on Article 25(4) or the UNCITRAL Arbitration Rules to the effect that hearings are to be held *in camera* is not relevant to the petitioners' request to serve written submissions to the Tribunal. In the Tribunal's view, there are no further provisions under the UNCITRAL Arbitration Rules that modify the application of its general power under Article 15 (1) to allow the petitioners to make such submissions in this arbitration.

41. However, the claimant's reliance on Article 25(4) is relevant to the petitioners' request to attend hearings and to receive copies of all submissions and materials adduced before the Tribunal. Article 25(4) provides that: '[Oral] Hearings shall be held in camera unless the parties agree otherwise. . .'. The phrase 'in camera' is clearly intended to exclude members of the public, i.e., non-party third persons such as the Petitioners. As the *travaux préparatoires* disclose, the UNCITRAL drafting committee deleted a different provision in an earlier draft which could have allowed the arbitration tribunal to admit into an oral hearing persons other than the parties. However, as discussed further below, Article 25(4) relates to the privacy of the oral hearings in the arbitration; and it does not in like terms address the confidentiality of the arbitration.

42. As to privacy, the respondent has accepted that, as a result of Article 25(4), hearings are to be *held in camera* unless both Disputing Parties consent otherwise. The respondent has given such consent. The claimant has given no such consent. The Tribunal must therefore apply Article 25(4); and it has no power (or inclination) to undermine the effect of its terms. It follows that the Tribunal must reject the petitioners' requests to attend oral hearings of the arbitration.

43. As to confidentiality, the Tribunal notes the conflicting legal materials as to whether Article 25(4) of the UNCITRAL Arbitration Rules imposes upon the Disputing Parties a further duty of confidentiality (beyond privacy) in regard to materials generated by the parties within the arbitration. The most recent decision of the Swedish Supreme Court in *Bulgarian Foreign Trade Bank Ltd v A I Trade Finance Inc* (27.x.2000) suggests that a privacy rule in an arbitration agreement does not give rise under Swedish law to a separate duty of confidentiality, at least as regards the award. That approach is strongly supported by the decision of the High Court of Australia in *Esso/ BHP v Plowman* (1993) 183 CLR 10 distinguishing between confidentiality and privacy, particularly as subsequently applied by the New South Wales Court in *Commonwealth of Australia v Cockatoo Dockyard Pty Ltd* (1995) 36 NSWLR 662 involving a public corporation.

44. The English legal materials generally point in the other direction, as invoked by the claimant., with the high-water mark being the Court of Appeal's decision in *Ali Shipping Corporation v Shipyard Trogir* [1998] 1 Lloyd's Rep 643. Even in England, however, the present position is arguably equivocal in regard to public authorities (including a state party), particularly given the absence of any statutory rule in the English Arbitration Act 1996 – for reasons explained at length in the official commentary contained in the Departmental Advisory Committee's 1996 Report on the Arbitration Bill (paragraphs 10–17). It is perhaps significant that English law on strict confidentiality is a recent innovation, dating essentially from the decision in *The Eastern Saga* [1983] 2 Lloyd's Rep 373, cited by the claimant. For example, as the DAC Report noted, the arbitration tribunal in *Lena Goldfields v USSR* (1930) decided in the public interest to publish its procedural orders and final award in the London 'Times', without any critical comment at the time (as to publication).

45. The Tribunal has also considered the position on confidentiality in the USA, in so far as it may be relevant as the law of the place of the arbitration, Washington DC. The Federal Arbitration Act is silent on the point; but like Australia and Sweden. US law maintains a distinction between privacy and

confidentiality. Indeed Professor Hans Smit's expert report on US law was adduced before the Australian Courts in *Esso/BP*. He relied on the decision of United States District Court for the District of Delaware in *USA v Panhandle Eastern Corp* 118 FRD 346, 10 Fed R Serv 3rd 686 (D Del 1988), concerning the non-confidentiality of documentation disclosed by a party in an ICC arbitration. Professor Smit also stressed the significance of a public interest, such as the petitioners suggest in this case: 'In determining to what extent arbitration is confidential, proper consideration must also be given to the public interest in knowing how disputes are settled . . . (366 [1995] *Arbitration International* 297 and 299 at 300).

46. This is however a difficult and for present purposes, the Tribunal does not have to decide the point. Confidentiality is determined by the agreement of the Disputing Parties as recorded in the Consent Order regarding Disclosure and Confidentiality, forming part of the Minutes of Order of the Second Procedural meeting of 7 September 2000. As *amici* have no rights under Chapter 11 of NAFTA to receive any materials generated within the arbitration (or indeed any rights at all) they are to be treated by the Tribunal as any other members of the public. Accordingly materials may be disclosed only as allowed in the Consent Order. Of course, pursuant to paragraph 3 of that Order, either party is at liberty to disclose the major pleadings, orders and awards of the Tribunal into the public domain (subject to redaction of Trade Secret Information). That is however a matter for the Disputing Parties and not the Tribunal.

(v) The Tribunal's conclusion

47. *Power*. The Tribunal concludes that by Article 15(1) of the UNCITRAL Arbitration Rules it has the power to accept *amicus* submissions (in writing) from each of the petitioners, to be copied simultaneously to the legal representatives of the Disputing Parties, Canada and Mexico. In coming to this conclusion, the Tribunal has not relied on the fact that *amicus* submissions feature in the domestic procedures: of the courts: in two, but not three, NAFTA Parties. The Tribunal also concludes that it has no power to accept the petitioners' requests to receive materials generated within the arbitration or to attend oral hearings of the arbitration. Such materials may however be derived from the public domain or disclosed into the public domain within the terms of the Consent Order regarding Disclosure and Confidentiality, or otherwise lawfully; but that is a quite separate matter outwith the scope of this decision.

48. *Discretion*. The next issue is whether, in the particular circumstances of this arbitration. the Tribunal should decide that it is 'appropriate' to accept

amicus submissions from the petitioners in the exercise of the discretion under Article 15(1) of the UNCITRAL Arbitration Rules. At this early stage, the Tribunal cannot decide definitively that it *would* be assisted by these submissions on the Disputing Parties' substantive dispute. The petitions set out the credentials of the petitioners, which are impressive; but for now, the Tribunal must assume that the Disputing Parties will provide all the necessary assistance and materials required by the Tribunal to decide their dispute. At the least, however, the Tribunal must also assume that the petitioners' submissions *could* assist the Tribunal. The Tribunal must look to other factors for the exercise of its discretion.

49. There is an undoubtedly public interest in this arbitration. The substantive issues extend far beyond those raised by the usual transnational arbitration between commercial parties. This is not merely because one of the Disputing Parties is a State: there are of course disputes involving States which are of no greater general public importance than a dispute between private persons. The public interest in this arbitration comes from its subject matter, as powerfully suggested in the petitions. There is also a broader argument, as suggested by the respondent and Canada: the Chapter 11 arbitral process could benefit from being perceived as more open or transparent or conversely be harmed if seen as unduly secretive. In this regard, the Tribunal's willingness to receive *amicus* submissions might support the process in general and this arbitration in particular; whereas a blanket refusal could do positive harm.

50. There are other competing factors to consider: the acceptance of *amicus* submissions might add significantly to the overall cost of the arbitration and, as considered above, there is a possible risk of imposing an extra burden on one or both the Disputing Parties. In this regard, as appears from the petitions, any *amicus* submissions from these petitioners are more likely to run counter to the claimant's position and eventually to support the respondent's case. This factor has weighed heavily with the Tribunal; and it is concerned that the claimant should receive whatever procedural protection might be necessary.

51. These are all relevant circumstances under Article 15(1) of the UNCITRAL Arbitration Rules. Less important is the factor raised by the claimant as to the danger of setting a precedent. This Tribunal can set no legal precedent, in general or at all. It has no power to determine for other arbitration tribunals how to interpret Article 15(1); and in a later arbitration, there may be other circumstances leading that tribunal to exercise its discretion differently. For each arbitration, the decision must be made by its tribunal in the particular circumstances of that arbitration only.

52. Weighing all the relevant factors, the Tribunal considers that it could be appropriate to allow *amicus* written submissions from these petitioners. Whilst the Tribunal is at present minded to allow the petitioners to make such submissions at a later stage of these arbitration proceedings, it is premature now for the Tribunal finally to decide the question at this relatively early stage. The Tribunal intends first to consider with the Disputing Parties procedural limitations as to the timing, form and conduct of the petitioners' submissions. For example, the Tribunal may wish to impose a page-limit on such submissions (including exhibits).

(vi) The Tribunal's order

53. For the reasons set out above, pursuant to Article 15(1) or the UNCITRAL Arbitration Rules the Tribunal declares that it has the power to accept *amicus* written submissions from the petitioners; whilst it is at present minded to receive such submissions subject to procedural limitations still to be determined by the Tribunal (to be considered with the Disputing Parties) it will make a final decision whether or not to receive them at a later stage of these arbitration proceedings; and accordingly the petitions are accepted by the Tribunal to this extent, but otherwise rejected Made by the Tribunal on 15 January 2001, as at Washington DC, USA.

29

The future of investment arbitration

 EXERCISE 43 – SEMINAR

Read and review the research paper *Can the Mauritius Convention serve as a model for the reform of investor-State arbitration in connection with the introduction of a permanent investment tribunal or an appeal mechanism?*, written by Gabrielle Kaufmann-Kohler and Michele Potestà, prepared for UNCITRAL and easily available online.

Also read and review the attached excerpts of Chapter Eight of the Comprehensive Economic and Trade Agreement (CETA) between Canada and the European Union (dated October 28, 2016).

? DISCUSSION QUESTIONS

Problem 1
Explain the criticisms raised against investment treaty arbitration. Are they justified?

Problem 2
What proposals have been made to change/amend the system of investment treaty arbitration? How could these proposals be implemented?

Problem 3
Discuss the *pros* and *cons* with including investor-state arbitration in larger trade and investment agreements such as the CETA.

Problem 4
Discuss how settlement of disputes concerning investment protection will/should look in 15 years.

TREATY

Section F – Resolution of investment disputes between investors and States

Article 8.18 Scope

1. Without prejudice to the rights and obligations of the parties under Chapter Twenty Nine (Dispute Settlement), an investor of a party may submit to the Tribunal constituted under this Section a claim that the other party has breached an obligation under: (a) Section C, with respect to the expansion, conduct, operation, management, maintenance, use, enjoyment and sale or disposal of its covered investment; or (b) Section D: where the investor claims to have suffered loss or damage as a result of the alleged breach.

2. Claims under subparagraph 1(a) with respect to the expansion of a covered investment may be submitted only to the extent the measure relates to the existing business operations of a covered investment and the investor has, as a result, incurred loss or damage with respect to the covered investment.

3. For greater certainty, an investor may not submit a claim under this Section if the investment has been made through fraudulent misrepresentation, concealment, corruption, or conduct amounting to an abuse of process.

4. A claim with respect to restructuring of debt issued by a party may only be submitted under this Section in accordance with Annex 8-B.

5. A Tribunal constituted under this Section shall not decide claims that fall outside of the scope of this Article.

Article 8.19 Consultations

1. A dispute should as far as possible be settled amicably. Such a settlement may be agreed at any time, including after the claim has been submitted pursuant to Article 8.23. Unless the disputing parties agree to a longer period, consultations shall be held within 60 days of the submission of the request for consultations pursuant to paragraph 4.

2. Unless the disputing parties agree otherwise, the place of consultation shall be: (a) Ottawa, if the measures challenged are measures of Canada; (b) Brussels, if the measures challenged include a measure of the European

Union; or (c) the capital of the Member State of the European Union, if the measures challenged are exclusively measures of that Member State.

3. The disputing parties may hold the consultations through videoconference or other means where appropriate, such as in the case where the investor is a small- or medium-sized enterprise.

4. The investor shall submit to the other party a request for consultations setting out: (a) the name and address of the investor and, if such request is submitted on behalf of a locally established enterprise, the name, address and place of incorporation of the locally established enterprise; (b) if there is more than one investor, the name and address of each investor and, if there is more than one locally established enterprise, the name, address and place of incorporation of each locally established enterprise; (c) the provisions of this Agreement alleged to have been breached; (d) the legal and the factual basis for the claim, including the measures at issue; and (e) the relief sought and the estimated amount of damages claimed. The request for consultations shall contain evidence establishing that the investor is an investor of the other party and that it owns or controls the investment including, if applicable, that it owns or controls the locally established enterprise on whose behalf the request is submitted.

5. The requirements of the request for consultations set out in paragraph 4 shall be met with sufficient specificity to allow the respondent to effectively engage in consultations and to prepare its defence.

6. A request for consultations must be submitted within: (a) three years after the date on which the investor or, as applicable, the locally established enterprise, first acquired or should have first acquired, knowledge of the alleged breach and knowledge that the investor or, as applicable, the locally established enterprise, has incurred loss or damage thereby; or (b) two years after an investor or, as applicable, the locally established enterprise, ceases to pursue claims or proceedings before a tribunal or court under the law of a party, or when such proceedings have otherwise ended and, in any event, no later than ten years after the date on which the investor or, as applicable, the locally established enterprise, first acquired or should have first acquired knowledge of the alleged breach and knowledge that the investor has incurred loss or damage thereby.

7. A request for consultations concerning an alleged breach by the European Union or a Member State of the European Union shall be sent to the European Union.

8. In the event that the investor has not submitted a claim pursuant to Article 8.23 within 18 months of submitting the request for consultations, the investor is deemed to have withdrawn its request for consultations and, if applicable, its notice requesting a determination of the respondent, and shall not submit a claim under this Section with respect to the same measures. This period may be extended by agreement of the disputing parties.

Article 8.20 Mediation

1. The disputing parties may at any time agree to have recourse to mediation.

2. Recourse to mediation is without prejudice to the legal position or rights of either disputing party under this Chapter and is governed by the rules agreed to by the disputing parties including, if available, the rules for mediation adopted by the Committee on Services and Investment pursuant to Article 8.44.3(c).

3. The mediator is appointed by agreement of the disputing parties. The disputing parties may also request that the Secretary-General of ICSID appoint the mediator.

4. The disputing parties shall endeavour to reach a resolution of the dispute within 60 days from the appointment of the mediator.

5. If the disputing parties agree to have recourse to mediation, Articles 8.19.6 and 8.19.8 shall not apply from the date on which the disputing parties agreed to have recourse to mediation to the date on which either disputing party decides to terminate the mediation. A decision by a disputing party to terminate the mediation shall be transmitted by way of a letter to the mediator and the other disputing party.

Article 8.21 Determination of the respondent for disputes with the European Union or its Member States

1. If the dispute cannot be settled within 90 days of the submission of the request for consultations, the request concerns an alleged breach of the Agreement by the European Union or a Member State of the European Union and the investor intends to submit a claim pursuant to Article 8.23, the investor shall deliver to the European Union a notice requesting a determination of the respondent.

2. The notice under paragraph 1 shall identify the measures in respect of which the investor intends to submit a claim.

3. The European Union shall, after having made a determination, inform the investor as to whether the European Union or a Member State of the European Union shall be the respondent.

4. In the event that the investor has not been informed of the determination within 50 days of delivering its notice requesting such determination: (a) if the measures identified in the notice are exclusively measures of a Member State of the European Union, the Member State shall be the respondent; (b) if the measures identified in the notice include measures of the European Union, the European Union shall be the respondent.

5. The investor may submit a claim pursuant to Article 8.23 on the basis of the determination made pursuant to paragraph 3, and, if no such determination has been communicated to the investor, on the basis of the application of paragraph 4.

6. If the European Union or a Member State of the European Union is the respondent, pursuant to paragraph 3 or 4, neither the European Union, nor the Member State of the European Union may assert the inadmissibility of the claim, lack of jurisdiction of the Tribunal or otherwise object to the claim or award on the ground that the respondent was not properly determined pursuant to paragraph 3 or identified on the basis of the application of paragraph 4.

7. The Tribunal shall be bound by the determination made pursuant to paragraph 3 and, if no such determination has been communicated to the investor, the application of paragraph 4.

Article 8.22 Procedural and other requirements for the submission of a claim to the Tribunal

1. An investor may only submit a claim pursuant to Article 8.23 if the investor: (a) delivers to the respondent, with the submission of a claim, its consent to the settlement of the dispute by the Tribunal in accordance with the procedures set out in this Section; (b) allows at least 180 days to elapse from the submission of the request for consultations and, if applicable, at least 90 days to elapse from the submission of the notice requesting a determination of the respondent; (c) has fulfilled the requirements of the notice requesting a determination of the respondent; (d) has fulfilled the requirements related

to the request for consultations; (e) does not identify a measure in its claim that was not identified in its request for consultations; (f) withdraws or discontinues any existing proceeding before a tribunal or court under domestic or international law with respect to a measure alleged to constitute a breach referred to in its claim; and (g) waives its right to initiate any claim or proceeding before a tribunal or court under domestic or international law with respect to a measure alleged to constitute a breach referred to in its claim.

2. If the claim submitted pursuant to Article 8.23 is for loss or damage to a locally established enterprise or to an interest in a locally established enterprise that the investor owns or controls directly or indirectly, the requirements in subparagraphs 1(f) and (g) apply both to the investor and the locally established enterprise.

3. The requirements of subparagraphs 1(f) and (g) and paragraph 2 do not apply in respect of a locally established enterprise if the respondent or the investor's host State has deprived the investor of control of the locally established enterprise, or has otherwise prevented the locally established enterprise from fulfilling those requirements.

4. Upon request of the respondent, the Tribunal shall decline jurisdiction if the investor or, as applicable, the locally established enterprise fails to fulfil any of the requirements of paragraphs 1 and 2.

5. The waiver provided pursuant to subparagraph 1(g) or paragraph 2 as applicable shall cease to apply: (a) if the Tribunal rejects the claim on the basis of a failure to meet the requirements of paragraph 1 or 2 or on any other procedural or jurisdictional grounds; (b) if the Tribunal dismisses the claim pursuant to Article 8.32 or Article 8.33; or (c) if the investor withdraws its claim, in conformity with the applicable rules under Article 8.23.2, within 12 months of the constitution of the division of the Tribunal.

Article 8.23 Submission of a claim to the Tribunal

1. If a dispute has not been resolved through consultations, a claim may be submitted under this Section by: (a) an investor of a party on its own behalf; or (b) an investor of a party, on behalf of a locally established enterprise which it owns or controls directly or indirectly.

2. A claim may be submitted under the following rules: (a) the ICSID Convention and Rules of Procedure for Arbitration Proceedings; (b) the ICSID Additional Facility Rules if the conditions for proceedings pursuant

to paragraph (a) do not apply; (c) the UNCITRAL Arbitration Rules; or (d) any other rules on agreement of the disputing parties.

3. In the event that the investor proposes rules pursuant to subparagraph 2(d), the respondent shall reply to the investor's proposal within 20 days of receipt. If the disputing parties have not agreed on such rules within 30 days of receipt, the investor may submit a claim under the rules provided for in subparagraph 2(a), (b) or (c).

4. For greater certainty, a claim submitted under subparagraph 1(b) shall satisfy the requirements of Article 25(1) of the ICSID Convention.

5. The investor may, when submitting its claim, propose that a sole Member of the Tribunal should hear the claim. The respondent shall give sympathetic consideration to that request, in particular if the investor is a small- or medium-sized enterprise or the compensation or damages claimed are relatively low.

6. The rules applicable under paragraph 2 that are in effect on the date that the claim or claims are submitted to the Tribunal under this Section, subject to the specific rules set out in this Section and supplemented by rules adopted pursuant to Article 8.44.3(b).

7. A claim is submitted for dispute settlement under this Section when: (a) the request under Article 36(1) of the ICSID Convention is received by the Secretary-General of ICSID; (b) the request under Article 2 of Schedule C of the ICSID Additional Facility Rules is received by the Secretariat of ICSID; (c) the notice under Article 3 of the UNCITRAL Arbitration Rules is received by the respondent; or (d) the request or notice initiating proceedings is received by the respondent in accordance with the rules agreed upon pursuant to subparagraph 2(d).

8. Each party shall notify the other party of the place of delivery of notices and other documents by the investors pursuant to this Section. Each party shall ensure this information is made publicly available.

Article 8.24 Proceedings under another international agreement

Where a claim is brought pursuant to this Section and another international agreement and: (a) there is a potential for overlapping compensation; or (b) the other international claim could have a significant impact on the resolution of the claim brought pursuant to this Section, the Tribunal shall, as soon as possible after hearing the disputing parties, stay its proceedings or otherwise ensure that proceedings brought pursuant to another international agreement are taken into account in its decision, order or award.

Article 8.25 Consent to the settlement of the dispute by the Tribunal

1. The respondent consents to the settlement of the dispute by the Tribunal in accordance with the procedures set out in this Section.

2. The consent under paragraph 1 and the submission of a claim to the Tribunal under this Section shall satisfy the requirements of: (a) Article 25 of the ICSID Convention and Chapter II of the ICSID Additional Facility Rules regarding written consent of the disputing parties; and, (b) Article II of the New York Convention for an agreement in writing.

Article 8.26 Third-party funding

1. Where there is third-party funding, the disputing party benefiting from it shall disclose to the other disputing party and to the Tribunal the name and address of the third-party funder.

2. The disclosure shall be made at the time of the submission of a claim, or, if the financing agreement is concluded or the donation or grant is made after the submission of a claim, without delay as soon as the agreement is concluded or the donation or grant is made.

Article 8.27 Constitution of the Tribunal

1. The Tribunal established under this Section shall decide claims submitted pursuant to Article 8.23.

2. The CETA Joint Committee shall, upon the entry into force of this Agreement, appoint 15 Members of the Tribunal. Five of the Members of the Tribunal shall be nationals of a Member State of the European Union, five shall be nationals of Canada and five shall be nationals of third countries.

3. The CETA Joint Committee may decide to increase or to decrease the number of the Members of the Tribunal by multiples of three. Additional appointments shall be made on the same basis as provided for in paragraph 2.

4. The Members of the Tribunal shall possess the qualifications required in their respective countries for appointment to judicial office, or be jurists of recognised competence. They shall have demonstrated expertise in public international law. It is desirable that they have expertise in particular, in international investment law, in international trade law and the resolution of disputes arising under international investment or international trade agreements.

5. The Members of the Tribunal appointed pursuant to this Section shall be appointed for a five-year term, renewable once. However, the terms of seven of the 15 persons appointed immediately after the entry into force of the Agreement, to be determined by lot, shall extend to six years. Vacancies shall be filled as they arise. A person appointed to replace a Member of the Tribunal whose term of office has not expired shall hold office for the remainder of the predecessor's term. In principle, a Member of the Tribunal serving on a division of the Tribunal when his or her term expires may continue to serve on the division until a final award is issued. Either party may instead propose to appoint up to five Members of the Tribunal of any nationality. In this case, such Members of the Tribunal shall be considered to be nationals of the party that proposed his or her appointment for the purposes of this Article.

6. The Tribunal shall hear cases in divisions consisting of three Members of the Tribunal, of whom one shall be a national of a Member State of the European Union, one a national of Canada and one a national of a third country. The division shall be chaired by the Member of the Tribunal who is a national of a third country.

7. Within 90 days of the submission of a claim pursuant to Article 8.23, the President of the Tribunal shall appoint the Members of the Tribunal composing the division of the Tribunal hearing the case on a rotation basis, ensuring that the composition of the divisions is random and unpredictable, while giving equal opportunity to all Members of the Tribunal to serve.

8. The President and Vice-President of the Tribunal shall be responsible for organisational issues and will be appointed for a two-year term and shall be drawn by lot from among the Members of the Tribunal who are nationals of third countries. They shall serve on the basis of a rotation drawn by lot by the Chair of the CETA Joint Committee. The Vice-President shall replace the President when the President is unavailable.

9. Notwithstanding paragraph 6, the disputing parties may agree that a case be heard by a sole Member of the Tribunal to be appointed at random from

the third country nationals. The respondent shall give sympathetic consideration to a request from the claimant to have the case heard by a sole Member of the Tribunal, in particular where the claimant is a small- or medium-sized enterprise or the compensation or damages claimed are relatively low. Such a request shall be made before the constitution of the division of the Tribunal.

10. The Tribunal may draw up its own working procedures.

11. The Members of the Tribunal shall ensure that they are available and able to perform the functions set out under this Section.

12. In order to ensure their availability, the Members of the Tribunal shall be paid a monthly retainer fee to be determined by the CETA Joint Committee.

13. The fees referred to in paragraph 12 shall be paid equally by both parties into an account managed by the ICSID Secretariat. In the event that one party fails to pay the retainer fee the other party may elect to pay. Any such arrears by a party will remain payable, with appropriate interest.

14. Unless the CETA Joint Committee adopts a decision pursuant to paragraph 15, the amount of the fees and expenses of the Members of the Tribunal on a division constituted to hear a claim, other than the fees referred to in paragraph 12, shall be those determined pursuant to Regulation 14(1) of the Administrative and Financial Regulations of the ICSID Convention in force on the date of the submission of the claim and allocated by the Tribunal among the disputing parties in accordance with Article 8.39.5.

15. The CETA Joint Committee may, by decision, transform the retainer fee and other fees and expenses into a regular salary, and decide applicable modalities and conditions.

16. The ICSID Secretariat shall act as Secretariat for the Tribunal and provide it with appropriate support.

17. If the CETA Joint Committee has not made the appointments pursuant to paragraph 2 within 90 days from the date that a claim is submitted for dispute settlement, the Secretary General of ICSID shall, at the request of either disputing party appoint a division consisting of three Members of the Tribunal, unless the disputing parties have agreed that the case is to be heard by a sole Member of the Tribunal. The Secretary General of ICSID shall make the appointment by random selection from the existing nominations. The Secretary-General of ICSID may not appoint as chair a national of either

Canada or a Member State of the European Union unless the disputing parties agree otherwise.

Article 8.28 Appellate Tribunal

1. An Appellate Tribunal is hereby established to review awards rendered under this Section.

2. The Appellate Tribunal may uphold, modify or reverse a Tribunal's award based on: (a) errors in the application or interpretation of applicable law; (b) manifest errors in the appreciation of the facts, including the appreciation of relevant domestic law; (c) the grounds set out in Article 52(1) (a)–(e) of the ICSID Convention, in so far as they are not covered by paragraphs (a) and (b).

3. The Members of the Appellate Tribunal shall be appointed by a decision of the CETA Joint Committee at the same time as the decision referred to in paragraph 7.

4. The Members of the Appellate Tribunal shall meet the requirements of Articles 8.27.4 and comply with Article 8.30.

5. The division of the Appellate Tribunal constituted to hear the appeal shall consist of three randomly appointed Members of the Appellate Tribunal.

6. Articles 8.36 and 8.38 shall apply to the proceedings before the Appellate Tribunal.

7. The CETA Joint Committee shall promptly adopt a decision setting out the following administrative and organisational matters regarding the functioning of the Appellate Tribunal: (a) administrative support; (b) procedures for the initiation and the conduct of appeals, and procedures for referring issues back to the Tribunal for adjustment of the award, as appropriate; (c) procedures for filling a vacancy on the Appellate Tribunal and on a division of the Appellate Tribunal constituted to hear a case; (d) remuneration of the Members of the Appellate Tribunal; (e) provisions related to the costs of appeals; (f) the number of Members of the Appellate Tribunal; and (g) any other elements it determines to be necessary for the effective functioning of the Appellate Tribunal.

8. The Committee on Services and Investment shall periodically review the functioning of the Appellate Tribunal and may make recommendations to the CETA Joint Committee. The CETA Joint Committee may revise the decision referred to in paragraph 7, if necessary.

9. Upon adoption of the decision referred to in paragraph 7: (a) a disputing party may appeal an award rendered pursuant to this Section to the Appellate Tribunal within 90 days after its issuance; (b) a disputing party shall not seek to review, set aside, annul, revise or initiate any other similar procedure as regards an award under this Section; (c) an award rendered pursuant to Article 8.39 shall not be considered final and no action for enforcement of an award may be brought until either: (i) 90 days from the issuance of the award by the Tribunal has elapsed and no appeal has been initiated; (ii) an initiated appeal has been rejected or withdrawn; or (iii) 90 days have elapsed from an award by the Appellate Tribunal and the Appellate Tribunal has not referred the matter back to the Tribunal; (d) a final award by the Appellate Tribunal shall be considered as a final award for the purposes of Article 8.41; and (e) Article 8.41.3 shall not apply.

Article 8.29 Establishment of a multilateral investment tribunal and appellate mechanism

The parties shall pursue with other trading partners the establishment of a multilateral investment tribunal and appellate mechanism for the resolution of investment disputes. Upon establishment of such a multilateral mechanism, the CETA Joint Committee shall adopt a decision providing that investment disputes under this Section will be decided pursuant to the multilateral mechanism and make appropriate transitional arrangements.

Article 8.30 Ethics

1. The Members of the Tribunal shall be independent. They shall not be affiliated with any government. They shall not take instructions from any organisation, or government with regard to matters related to the dispute. They shall not participate in the consideration of any disputes that would create a direct or indirect conflict of interest. They shall comply with the International Bar Association Guidelines on Conflicts of Interest in International Arbitration or any supplemental rules adopted pursuant to Article 8.44.

2. In addition, upon appointment, they shall refrain from acting as counsel or as party-appointed expert or witness in any pending or new investment dispute under this or any other international agreement. If a disputing party considers that a Member of the Tribunal has a conflict of interest, it shall send to the President of the International Court of Justice a notice of challenge to the appointment. The notice of challenge shall be sent within 15 days of the date on which the composition of the division of the Tribunal has been communicated to the disputing party, or within 15 days of the date on which the

relevant facts came to its knowledge, if they could not have reasonably been known at the time of composition of the division. The notice of challenge shall state the grounds for the challenge.

3. If, within 15 days from the date of the notice of challenge, the challenged Member of the Tribunal has elected not to resign from the division, the President of the International Court of Justice shall, after hearing the disputing parties and after providing the Member of the Tribunal an opportunity to submit any observations, issue a decision within 45 days of receipt of the notice of challenge and notify the disputing parties and the other Members of the division. A vacancy resulting from the disqualification or resignation of a Member of the Tribunal shall be filled promptly. For greater certainty, the fact that a person receives remuneration from a government does not in itself make that person ineligible.

4. Upon a reasoned recommendation from the President of the Tribunal, or on their joint initiative, the Parties, by decision of the CETA Joint Committee, may remove a Member from the Tribunal where his or her behaviour is inconsistent with the obligations set out in paragraph 1 and incompatible with his or her continued membership of the Tribunal.

Article 8.31 Applicable law and interpretation

1. When rendering its decision, the Tribunal established under this Section shall apply this Agreement as interpreted in accordance with the Vienna Convention on the Law of Treaties, and other rules and principles of international law applicable between the parties.

2. The Tribunal shall not have jurisdiction to determine the legality of a measure, alleged to constitute a breach of this Agreement, under the domestic law of the disputing party. For greater certainty, in determining the consistency of a measure with this Agreement, the Tribunal may consider, as appropriate, the domestic law of the disputing party as a matter of fact. In doing so, the Tribunal shall follow the prevailing interpretation given to the domestic law by the courts or authorities of that party and any meaning given to domestic law by the Tribunal shall not be binding upon the courts or the authorities of that party.

3. Where serious concerns arise as regards matters of interpretation that may affect investment, the Committee on Services and Investment may, pursuant to Article 8.44.3(a), recommend to the CETA Joint Committee the adoption of interpretations of this Agreement. An interpretation adopted by the CETA Joint Committee shall be binding on a Tribunal established under this

Section. The CETA Joint Committee may decide that an interpretation shall have binding effect from a specific date.

Article 8.32 Claims manifestly without legal merit

1. The respondent may, no later than 30 days after the constitution of the division of the Tribunal, and in any event before its first session, file an objection that a claim is manifestly without legal merit.

2. An objection shall not be submitted under paragraph 1 if the respondent has filed an objection pursuant to Article 8.33.

3. The respondent shall specify as precisely as possible the basis for the objection.

4. On receipt of an objection pursuant to this Article, the Tribunal shall suspend the proceedings on the merits and establish a schedule for considering such an objection consistent with its schedule for considering any other preliminary question.

5. The Tribunal, after giving the disputing parties an opportunity to present their observations, shall at its first session or promptly thereafter, issue a decision or award stating the grounds therefor. In doing so, the Tribunal shall assume the alleged facts to be true.

6. This Article shall be without prejudice to the Tribunal's authority to address other objections as a preliminary question or to the right of the respondent to object, in the course of the proceeding, that a claim lacks legal merit.

Article 8.33 Claims unfounded as a matter of law

1. Without prejudice to a Tribunal's authority to address other objections as a preliminary question or to a respondent's right to raise any such objections at an appropriate time, the Tribunal shall address and decide as a preliminary question any objection by the respondent that, as a matter of law, a claim, or any part thereof, submitted pursuant to Article 8.23 is not a claim for which an award in favour of the claimant may be made under this Section, even if the facts alleged were assumed to be true.

2. An objection under paragraph 1 shall be submitted to the Tribunal no later than the date the Tribunal fixes for the respondent to submit its counter-memorial.

3. If an objection has been submitted pursuant to Article 8.32, the Tribunal may, taking into account the circumstances of that objection, decline to address, under the procedures set out in this Article, an objection submitted pursuant to paragraph 1.

4. On receipt of an objection under paragraph 1, and, if appropriate, after rendering a decision pursuant to paragraph 3, the Tribunal shall suspend any proceedings on the merits, establish a schedule for considering the objection consistent with any schedule it has established for considering any other preliminary question, and issue a decision or award on the objection stating the grounds therefor.

Article 8.34 Interim measures of protection

A Tribunal may order an interim measure of protection to preserve the rights of a disputing party or to ensure that the Tribunal's jurisdiction is made fully effective, including an order to preserve evidence in the possession or control of a disputing party or to protect the Tribunal's jurisdiction. A Tribunal shall not order attachment or enjoin the application of the measure alleged to constitute a breach referred to in Article 8.23. For the purposes of this Article, an order includes a recommendation.

Article 8.35 Discontinuance

If, following the submission of a claim under this Section, the investor fails to take any steps in the proceeding during 180 consecutive days or such periods as the disputing parties may agree, the investor is deemed to have withdrawn its claim and to have discontinued the proceeding. The Tribunal shall, at the request of the respondent, and after notice to the disputing parties, in an order take note of the discontinuance. After the order has been rendered the authority of the Tribunal shall lapse.

Article 8.36 Transparency of proceedings

1. The UNCITRAL Transparency Rules, as modified by this Chapter, shall apply in connection with proceedings under this Section.

2. The request for consultations, the notice requesting a determination of the respondent, the notice of determination of the respondent, the agreement to mediate, the notice of intent to challenge a Member of the Tribunal, the decision on challenge to a Member of the Tribunal and the request for consolidation shall be included in the list of documents to be made

available to the public under Article 3(1) of the UNCITRAL Transparency Rules.

3. Exhibits shall be included in the list of documents to be made available to the public under Article 3(2) of the UNCITRAL Transparency Rules.

4. Notwithstanding Article 2 of the UNCITRAL Transparency Rules, prior to the constitution of the Tribunal, Canada or the European Union as the case may be shall make publicly available in a timely manner relevant documents pursuant to paragraph 2, subject to the redaction of confidential or protected information. Such documents may be made publicly available by communication to the repository.

5. Hearings shall be open to the public. The Tribunal shall determine, in consultation with the disputing parties, the appropriate logistical arrangements to facilitate public access to such hearings. If the Tribunal determines that there is a need to protect confidential or protected information, it shall make the appropriate arrangements to hold in private that part of the hearing requiring such protection.

6. Nothing in this Chapter requires a respondent to withhold from the public information required to be disclosed by its laws. The respondent should apply those laws in a manner sensitive to protecting from disclosure information that has been designated as confidential or protected information.

Article 8.37 Information sharing

1. A disputing party may disclose to other persons in connection with the proceedings, including witnesses and experts, such unredacted documents as it considers necessary in the course of proceedings under this Section. However, the disputing party shall ensure that those persons protect the confidential or protected information contained in those documents.

2. This Agreement does not prevent a respondent from disclosing to officials of, as applicable, the European Union, Member States of the European Union and subnational governments, such unredacted documents as it considers necessary in the course of proceedings under this Section. However, the respondent shall ensure that those officials protect the confidential or protected information contained in those documents.

Article 8.38 Non-disputing party

1. The respondent shall, within 30 days after receipt or promptly after any dispute concerning confidential or protected information has been resolved, deliver to the non-disputing party: (a) a request for consultations, a notice requesting a determination of the respondent, a notice of determination of the respondent, a claim submitted pursuant to Article 8.23, a request for consolidation, and any other documents that are appended to such documents; (b) on request: (i) pleadings, memorials, briefs, requests and other submissions made to the Tribunal by a disputing party; (ii) written submissions made to the Tribunal pursuant to Article 4 of the UNCITRAL Transparency Rules; (iii) minutes or transcripts of hearings of the Tribunal, if available; and (iv) orders, awards and decisions of the Tribunal; and (c) on request and at the cost of the non-disputing party, all or part of the evidence that has been tendered to the Tribunal, unless the requested evidence is publicly available.

2. The Tribunal shall accept or, after consultation with the disputing parties, may invite, oral or written submissions from the non-disputing party regarding the interpretation of the Agreement. The non-disputing party may attend a hearing held under this Section.

3. The Tribunal shall not draw any inference from the absence of a submission pursuant to paragraph 2.

4. The Tribunal shall ensure that the disputing parties are given a reasonable opportunity to present their observations on a submission by the non-disputing party to this Agreement.

Article 8.39 Final award

1. If the Tribunal makes a final award against the respondent, the Tribunal may only award, separately or in combination: (a) monetary damages and any applicable interest; (b) restitution of property, in which case the award shall provide that the respondent may pay monetary damages representing the fair market value of the property at the time immediately before the expropriation, or impending expropriation became known, whichever is earlier, and any applicable interest in lieu of restitution, determined in a manner consistent with Article 8.12.

2. Subject to paragraphs 1 and 5, if a claim is made under Article 8.23.1(b): (a) an award of monetary damages and any applicable interest shall provide that the sum be paid to the locally established enterprise; (b) an award of

restitution of property shall provide that restitution be made to the locally established enterprise; (c) an award of costs in favour of the investor shall provide that it is to be made to the investor; and (d) the award shall provide that it is made without prejudice to a right that a person, other than a person which has provided a waiver pursuant to Article 8.22, may have in monetary damages or property awarded under a party's law.

3. Monetary damages shall not be greater than the loss suffered by the investor or, as applicable, the locally established enterprise, reduced by any prior damages or compensation already provided. For the calculation of monetary damages, the Tribunal shall also reduce the damages to take into account any restitution of property or repeal or modification of the measure.

4. The Tribunal shall not award punitive damages.

5. The Tribunal shall order that the costs of the proceedings be borne by the unsuccessful disputing party. In exceptional circumstances, the Tribunal may apportion costs between the disputing parties if it determines that apportionment is appropriate in the circumstances of the claim. Other reasonable costs, including costs of legal representation and assistance, shall be borne by the unsuccessful disputing party, unless the Tribunal determines that such apportionment is unreasonable in the circumstances of the claim. If only parts of the claims have been successful the costs shall be adjusted, proportionately, to the number or extent of the successful parts of the claims.

6. The CETA Joint Committee shall consider supplemental rules aimed at reducing the financial burden on claimants who are natural persons or small- and medium-sized enterprises. Such supplemental rules may, in particular, take into account the financial resources of such claimants and the amount of compensation sought.

7. The Tribunal and the disputing parties shall make every effort to ensure the dispute settlement process is carried out in a timely manner. The Tribunal shall issue its final award within 24 months of the date the claim is submitted pursuant to Article 8.23. If the Tribunal requires additional time to issue its final award, it shall provide the disputing parties the reasons for the delay.

Article 8.40 Indemnification or other compensation

A respondent shall not assert, and a Tribunal shall not accept a defence, counterclaim, right of setoff, or similar assertion, that an investor or, as applicable, a locally established enterprise, has received or will receive indemnification or other compensation pursuant to an insurance or guarantee contract in respect of all or part of the compensation sought in a dispute initiated pursuant to this Section.

Article 8.41 Enforcement of awards

1. An award issued pursuant to this Section shall be binding between the disputing parties and in respect of that particular case.

2. Subject to paragraph 3, a disputing party shall recognise and comply with an award without delay.

3. A disputing party shall not seek enforcement of a final award until: (a) in the case of a final award issued under the ICSID Convention: (i) 120 days have elapsed from the date the award was rendered and no disputing party has requested revision or annulment of the award; or (ii) enforcement of the award has been stayed and revision or annulment proceedings have been completed; and (b) in the case of a final award under the ICSID Additional Facility Rules the UNCITRAL Arbitration Rules, or any other rules applicable pursuant to Article 8.23.2(d): (i) 90 days have elapsed from the date the award was rendered and no disputing party has commenced a proceeding to revise, set aside or annul the award; or (ii) enforcement of the award has been stayed and a court has dismissed or allowed an application to revise, set aside or annul the award and there is no further appeal.

4. Execution of the award shall be governed by the laws concerning the execution of judgments or awards in force where the execution is sought.

5. A final award issued pursuant to this Section is an arbitral award that is deemed to relate to claims arising out of a commercial relationship or transaction for the purposes of Article I of the New York Convention.

6. For greater certainty, if a claim has been submitted pursuant to Article 8.23.2(a), a final award issued pursuant to this Section shall qualify as an award under Section 6 of the ICSID Convention.

Article 8.42 Role of the parties

1. A party shall not bring an international claim, in respect of a claim submitted pursuant to Article 8.23, unless the other party has failed to abide by and comply with the award rendered in that dispute.

2. Paragraph 1 shall not exclude the possibility of dispute settlement under Chapter Twenty-Nine (Dispute Settlement) in respect of a measure of general application even if that measure is alleged to have breached this Agreement as regards a specific investment in respect of which a claim has been submitted pursuant to Article 8.23 and is without prejudice to Article 8.38.3. Paragraph 1 does not preclude informal exchanges for the sole purpose of facilitating a settlement of the dispute.

Article 8.43 Consolidation

1. When two or more claims that have been submitted separately pursuant to Article 8.23 have a question of law or fact in common and arise out of the same events or circumstances, a disputing party or the disputing parties, jointly, may seek the establishment of a separate division of the Tribunal pursuant to this Article and request that such division issue a consolidation order ('request for consolidation').

2. The disputing party seeking a consolidation order shall first deliver a notice to the disputing parties it seeks to be covered by this order.

3. If the disputing parties notified pursuant to paragraph 2 have reached an agreement on the consolidation order to be sought, they may make a joint request for the establishment of a separate division of the Tribunal and a consolidation order pursuant to this Article. If the disputing parties notified pursuant to paragraph 2 have not reached agreement on the consolidation order to be sought within 30 days of the notice, a disputing party may make a request for the establishment of a separate division of the Tribunal and a consolidation order pursuant to this Article.

4. The request shall be delivered, in writing, to the President of the Tribunal and to all the disputing parties sought to be covered by the order, and shall specify: (a) the names and addresses of the disputing parties sought to be covered by the order; (b) the claims, or parts thereof, sought to be covered by the order; and (c) the grounds for the order sought.

5. A request for consolidation involving more than one respondent shall require the agreement of all such respondents.

6. The rules applicable to the proceedings under this Article are determined as follows: (a) if all of the claims for which a consolidation order is sought have been submitted to dispute settlement under the same rules pursuant to Article 8.23, these rules shall apply; (b) if the claims for which a consolida-

tion order is sought have not been submitted to dispute settlement under the same rules: (i) the investors may collectively agree on the rules pursuant to Article 8.23.2; or (ii) if the investors cannot agree on the applicable rules within 30 days of the President of the Tribunal receiving the request for consolidation, the UNCITRAL Arbitration Rules shall apply.

7. The President of the Tribunal shall, after receipt of a consolidation request and in accordance with the requirements of Article 8.27.7 constitute a new division ('consolidating division') of the Tribunal which shall have jurisdiction over some or all of the claims, in whole or in part, which are the subject of the joint consolidation request.

8. If, after hearing the disputing parties, a consolidating division is satisfied that claims submitted pursuant to Article 8.23 have a question of law or fact in common and arise out of the same events or circumstances, and consolidation would best serve the interests of fair and efficient resolution of the claims including the interest of consistency of awards, the consolidating division of the Tribunal may, by order, assume jurisdiction over some or all of the claims, in whole or in part.

9. If a consolidating division of the Tribunal has assumed jurisdiction pursuant to paragraph 8, an investor that has submitted a claim pursuant to Article 8.23 and whose claim has not been consolidated may make a written request to the Tribunal that it be included in such order provided that the request complies with the requirements set out in paragraph 4. The consolidating division of the Tribunal shall grant such order where it is satisfied that the conditions of paragraph 8 are met and that granting such a request would not unduly burden or unfairly prejudice the disputing parties or unduly disrupt the proceedings. Before consolidating division of the Tribunal issues that order, it shall consult with the disputing parties.

10. On application of a disputing party, a consolidating division of the Tribunal established under this Article, pending its decision under paragraph 8, may order that the proceedings of a Tribunal appointed under Article 8.27.7 be stayed unless the latter Tribunal has already adjourned its proceedings.

11. A Tribunal appointed under Article 8.27.7 shall cede jurisdiction in relation to the claims, or parts thereof, over which a consolidating division of the Tribunal established under this Article has assumed jurisdiction.

12. The award of a consolidating division of the Tribunal established under this Article in relation to those claims, or parts thereof, over which it has

assumed jurisdiction is binding on a Tribunal appointed under Article 8.27.7 as regards those claims, or parts thereof.

13. An investor may withdraw a claim under this Section that is subject to consolidation and such claim shall not be resubmitted pursuant to Article 8.23. If it does so no later than 15 days after receipt of the notice of consolidation, its earlier submission of the claim shall not prevent the investor's recourse to dispute settlement other than under this Section.

14. At the request of an investor, a consolidating division of the Tribunal may take such measures as it sees fit in order to preserve the confidential or protected information of that investor in relation to other investors. Those measures may include the submission of redacted versions of documents containing confidential or protected information to the other investors or arrangements to hold parts of the hearing in private.

Article 8.44 Committee on Services and Investment

1. The Committee on Services and Investment shall provide a forum for the parties to consult on issues related to this Chapter, including: (a) difficulties which may arise in the implementation of this Chapter; (b) possible improvements of this Chapter, in particular in the light of experience and developments in other international fora and under the parties' other agreements.

2. The Committee on Services and Investment shall, on agreement of the parties, and after completion of their respective internal requirements and procedures, adopt a code of conduct for the Members of the Tribunal to be applied in disputes arising out of this Chapter, which may replace or supplement the rules in application, and may address topics including: (a) disclosure obligations; (b) the independence and impartiality of the Members of the Tribunal; and (c) confidentiality. The parties shall make best efforts to ensure that the code of conduct is adopted no later than the first day of the provisional application or entry into force of this Agreement, as the case may be, and in any event no later than two years after such date.

3. The Committee Services and Investment may, on agreement of the parties, and after completion of their respective internal requirements and procedures: (a) recommend to the CETA Joint Committee the adoption of interpretations of this Agreement pursuant to Article 8.31.3; (b) adopt and amend rules supplementing the applicable dispute settlement rules, and amend the applicable rules on transparency. These rules and amendments

are binding on a Tribunal established under this Section; (c) adopt rules for mediation for use by disputing parties as referred to in Article 8.20; (d) recommend to the CETA Joint Committee the adoption of any further elements of the fair and equitable treatment obligation pursuant to Article 8.10.4; and (e) make recommendations to the CETA Joint Committee on the functioning of the Appellate Tribunal pursuant to Article 8.28.8.

Article 8.45 Exclusion

The dispute settlement provisions of this Section and of Chapter Twenty-Nine (Dispute Settlement) do not apply to the matters referred to in Annex 8-C.

Index